Frommer's®

KU-769-416

Texas

4th Edition

by David Baird, Eric Peterson & Neil E. Schlecht

Here's what the critics say about Frommer's:

"Amazingly easy to use. Very portable, very complete."

—*Booklist*

"Detailed, accurate, and easy-to-read information for all price ranges."
—*Glamour Magazine*

"Hotel information is close to encyclopedic."

—*Des Moines Sunday Register*

"Frommer's Guides have a way of giving you a real feel for a place."
—*Knight Ridder Newspaper*

Wiley Publishing, Inc.

Published by:

Wiley Publishing, Inc.

111 River St.
Hoboken, NJ 07030-5774

Copyright © 2007 Wiley Publishing, Inc., Hoboken, New Jersey. All rights reserved. No part of this publication may be reproduced, stored in a retrieval system or transmitted in any form or by any means, electronic, mechanical, photocopying, recording, scanning or otherwise, except as permitted under Sections 107 or 108 of the 1976 United States Copyright Act, without either the prior written permission of the Publisher, or authorization through payment of the appropriate per-copy fee to the Copyright Clearance Center, 222 Rosewood Drive, Danvers, MA 01923, 978/750-8400, fax 978/646-8600. Requests to the Publisher for permission should be addressed to the Legal Department, Wiley Publishing, Inc., 10475 Crosspoint Blvd., Indianapolis, IN 46256, 317/572-3447, fax 317/572-4355, or online at http://www.wiley.com/go/permissions.

Wiley and the Wiley Publishing logo are trademarks or registered trademarks of John Wiley & Sons, Inc. and/or its affiliates. Frommer's is a trademark or registered trademark of Arthur Frommer. Used under license. All other trademarks are the property of their respective owners. Wiley Publishing, Inc. is not associated with any product or vendor mentioned in this book.

ISBN: 978-0-470-08298-0

Editor: Cate Latting
Production Editor: Heather Wilcox
Cartographer: Roberta Stockwell
Photo Editor: Richard Fox
Anniversary Logo Design: Richard Pacifico
Production by Wiley Indianapolis Composition Services

Front cover photo: Cow sitting in a field of bluebonnets
Back cover photo: Close-up of cowboys' boots and spurs

For information on our other products and services or to obtain technical support, please contact our Customer Care Department within the U.S. at 800/762-2974, outside the U.S. at 317/572-3993 or fax 317/572-4002.

Wiley also publishes its books in a variety of electronic formats. Some content that appears in print may not be available in electronic formats.

Manufactured in the United States of America

5   4   3   2   1

Contents

List of Maps   vii

What's New in Texas   1

1 The Best of Texas   7

by David Baird, Eric Peterson & Neil E. Schlecht

1 The Best Luxury & Historic Hotels 8
2 The Best Bed & Breakfasts &
    Boutique Hotels 10
3 The Best Hotel Bargains 11
4 The Best Restaurants 12
5 The Best Texan Dining 13
6 The Best Lone Star Experiences 15

7 The Best Museums 15
8 The Best Shopping 17
9 The Best Places for Boot-Scootin' ...18
10 The Best of Natural Texas 19
11 The Best Historical Attractions 20
12 The Best Family Adventures 21
13 The Best of Texas Online 22

2 Planning Your Trip to Texas   24

by Neil E. Schlecht

1 The Regions in Brief 24
2 Visitor Information 28
3 Entry Requirements & Customs 28
4 Money 30
5 When to Go 31
    Texas Calendar of Events 32
6 Travel Insurance 35
7 Health & Safety 37
8 Specialized Travel Resources 38
9 Planning Your Trip Online 42
    *Frommers.com: The Complete
Travel Resource* 43
10 The 21st-Century Traveler 43

11 Getting There 44
12 Package Deals for Independent
    Travelers 45
13 Escorted General-Interest Tours 46
14 Special-Interest Trips 46
15 Getting Around Texas 48
16 Tips on Accommodations 51
    Texas: Gateway to Mexico 52
17 Recommended Books,
    Films & Music 54
    Fast Facts: Texas 56

3 Suggested Itineraries in Texas   63

1 Texas in1 Week 63
2 Texas in 2 Weeks 65

3 Texas for Families 66
4 Exploring the Texas-Mexico Border ...68

(4) Dallas–Fort Worth   70

by Neil E. Schlecht

1 Orientation .70

2 Dallas 73

The Neighborhoods in Brief 75

Fast Facts: Dallas 80

Family-Friendly Hotels in DFW 87

Family-Friendly Restaurants in Dallas 95

Dinner & a Movie Deal 96

Picnic Places 99

Downtown Dallas's Outdoor Sculpture .103

3 Arlington .118

4 Fort Worth 119

Grapevine .120

The Neighborhoods in Brief 121

Fast Facts: Fort Worth 122

Family-Friendly Restaurants in Fort Worth 133

Christmas in the Stockyards 137

The Grapevine Vintage Railroad . . .140

(5) Houston & East Texas   151

by David Baird

1 Orientation 152

The Neighborhoods in Brief 155

2 Getting Around 161

Fast Facts: Houston 162

3 Where to Stay 163

Family-Friendly Hotels 172

4 Where to Dine 174

Fast Food a la Houston 177

Family-Friendly Restaurants 181

5 Seeing the Sights 184

6 Sports & Outdoor Activities 193

7 Shopping .194

8 Houston After Dark 196

9 Side Trips to East Texas 200

Race Relations in East Texas 202

Texas State Railroad State Park . . .204

(6) The Texas Gulf Coast   206

by David Baird

1 Galveston .206

The Storm .208

2 Brazosport 213

Birding along the Texas Coast 215

Texas's Most Deserted Beach 218

3 Corpus Christi 218

4 Rockport .225

Whooping Cranes: Back from the Brink of Extinction 226

5 Port Aransas 230

6 Padre Island National Seashore . . .233

The Race to Save the Sea Turtles . . .235

7 South Padre Island 237

Face to Face with a Sea Turtle 242

7 San Antonio 246

by David Baird

1 Orientation 247

The Neighborhoods in Brief 249

2 Getting Around 251

Fast Facts: San Antonio 252

3 Where to Stay 253

Family-Friendly Hotels 262

4 Where to Dine 266

Family-Friendly Restaurants 271

Local Favorites: Tacquerías 272

5 Seeing the Sights 273

6 Sports & Outdoor Activities 280

7 Shopping 281

8 San Antonio After Dark 283

Conjunto: An American Classic 286

9 Hill Country Side Trips
from San Antonio 288

A Taste of Alsace in Texas 289

8 Austin 292

by David Baird

1 Orientation 292

The Neighborhoods in Brief 294

2 Getting Around 296

Fast Facts: Austin 297

3 Where to Stay 298

It Pays to Stay 306

Family-Friendly Hotels 308

4 Where to Dine 309

Family-Friendly Restaurants 315

5 Seeing the Sights 318

Going Batty 319

6 Staying Active 324

7 Shopping 326

8 Austin After Dark 328

9 Hill Country Side Trips
from Austin 332

9 West Texas 338

by Eric Peterson

1 El Paso 338

Fast Facts: El Paso 343

El Paso's Alligator Art 345

The Copper Canyon 357

2 Small Towns of Central
West Texas 358

A Side Trip to Candelaria 361

Marfa's Mystery Lights 363

Gallery Hopping in the Big Bend . . .365

3 Midland-Odessa 366

Midland's Famous Son, George . . .368

4 San Angelo 371

5 Del Rio & Amistad National
Recreation Area 377

The Legend of Roy Bean 380

10 Big Bend & Guadalupe Mountains National Parks   385

by Eric Peterson

1 Big Bend National Park 385
2 Guadalupe Mountains
   National Park 398

3 A Side Trip to Carlsbad Caverns
   National Park 404

11 The Panhandle Plains   412

by Eric Peterson

1 Amarillo 412
   Unanticipated Rewards..........418
2 Canyon & Palo Duro Canyon
   State Park 424

   Old Route 66 426
3 Lubbock 429
   A Different Kind of Texas Tea 433

Appendix: Texas in Depth   439

by Neil E. Schlecht

1 History 101 439
   Dateline 440
2 Talk Like a Texan 443
3 Texan Style 444

4 Texan Music 446
5 Texan Cuisine 448
6 Larger Than Life: Famous Texans 450

Index   452

List of Maps

The Regions in Brief   26

Texas Driving Times & Distances   51

The Best of Texas in 1 Week   64

The Best of Texas in 2 Weeks   66

Texas for Families   67

Exploring the Texas-Mexico Border   69

Dallas–Fort Worth   72

Downtown & Deep Ellum Accommodations, Dining & Attractions   76

Uptown & Oak Lawn Accommodations & Dining   79

Fort Worth Stockyards National Historic District   125

Downtown Fort Worth   127

Fort Worth Cultural District   129

Houston   153

Central Houston Accommodations   156

Central Houston Dining & Attractions   158

East Texas   201

The Texas Gulf Coast   207

Galveston   209

Corpus Christi   219

South Padre Island   239

South-Central Texas   247

Greater San Antonio Accommodations, Dining & Attractions   254

Central San Antonio Accommodations, Dining & Attractions   257

Greater Austin Accommodations, Dining & Attractions   300

Central Austin Accommodations, Dining & Attractions   303

West Texas   339

El Paso   340

Big Bend National Park   387

Guadalupe Mountains National Park   399

Carlsbad Caverns National Park   405

The Panhandle Plains   413

Amarillo   415

Lubbock   431

An Invitation to the Reader

In researching this book, we discovered many wonderful places—hotels, restaurants, shops, and more. We're sure you'll find others. Please tell us about them, so we can share the information with your fellow travelers in upcoming editions. If you were disappointed with a recommendation, we'd love to know that, too. Please write to:

Frommer's Texas, 4th Edition
Wiley Publishing, Inc. • 111 River St. • Hoboken, NJ 07030-5774

An Additional Note

Please be advised that travel information is subject to change at any time—and this is especially true of prices. We therefore suggest that you write or call ahead for confirmation when making your travel plans. The authors, editors, and publisher cannot be held responsible for the experiences of readers while traveling. Your safety is important to us, however, so we encourage you to stay alert and be aware of your surroundings. Keep a close eye on cameras, purses, and wallets, all favorite targets of thieves and pickpockets.

About the Authors

David Baird is a writer, editor, and translator based in Austin, Texas. He was born and bred in Houston, though he spent part of his childhood in Morelia, Mexico. He has contributed to several works about Texas and Mexico, including *Frommer's Mexico.*

Eric Peterson, a Denver-based freelance writer, has contributed to *Frommer's Colorado* and has authored *Frommer's Yellowstone & Grand Teton National Parks.* When he's not on the road or writing about travel, Peterson covers Colorado's business scene and Denver's punk-rock underbelly.

Neil E. Schlecht was reared in North Dallas. He attended Plano Senior High School, returned for graduate school at UT–Austin, and married a Texan. Now living in northwestern Connecticut, he is the author and co-author of more than a dozen travel guides, including *Frommer's Peru, Spain For Dummies,* and *Frommer's Cuba.* His Texas heroes are Lance Armstrong, Stevie Ray Vaughan, and Jimmie Dale Gilmore.

Other Great Guides for Your Trip:

Frommer's San Antonio & Austin
Frommer's National Parks of the American West
Frommer's USA

Frommer's Star Ratings, Icons & Abbreviations

Every hotel, restaurant, and attraction listing in this guide has been ranked for quality, value, service, amenities, and special features using a **star-rating system.** In country, state, and regional guides, we also rate towns and regions to help you narrow down your choices and budget your time accordingly. Hotels and restaurants are rated on a scale of zero (recommended) to three stars (exceptional). Attractions, shopping, nightlife, towns, and regions are rated according to the following scale: zero stars (recommended), one star (highly recommended), two stars (very highly recommended), and three stars (must-see).

In addition to the star-rating system, we also use **seven feature icons** that point you to the great deals, in-the-know advice, and unique experiences that separate travelers from tourists. Throughout the book, look for:

Finds	Special finds—those places only insiders know about
Fun Fact	Fun facts—details that make travelers more informed and their trips more fun
Kids	Best bets for kids, and advice for the whole family
Moments	Special moments—those experiences that memories are made of
Overrated	Places or experiences not worth your time or money
Tips	Insider tips—great ways to save time and money
Value	Great values—where to get the best deals

The following **abbreviations** are used for credit cards:

AE	American Express	DISC	Discover	V	Visa
DC	Diners Club	MC	MasterCard		

Frommers.com

Now that you have this guidebook, to help you plan a great trip, visit our website at **www.frommers.com** for additional travel information on more than 3,500 destinations. We update features regularly, to give you instant access to the most current trip-planning information available. At Frommers.com, you'll find scoops on the best airfares, lodging rates, and car rental bargains. You can even book your travel online through our reliable travel booking partners. Other popular features include:

- Online updates to our most popular guidebooks
- Vacation sweepstakes and contest giveaways
- Newsletter highlighting the hottest travel trends
- Online travel message boards with featured travel discussions

What's New in Texas

DALLAS

GETTING THERE DFW International Airport inaugurated a new, 2-million-square-foot **International Terminal D.** The sleek new **Skylink,** the world's largest high-speed airport train, unites terminals.

EXPLORING DALLAS The **Dallas Museum of Art** (© 214/922-1200; http://dallasmuseumofart.org) bolstered its collection of modern and contemporary art in a huge way, receiving gifts totaling some 900 works by three prominent collectors—the Hoffman, Rachofsky, and Rose families of Dallas. The coordinated gift is expected to really put the Dallas Museum of Art, in the midst of an ever-expanding downtown Arts District, on the map.

WHERE TO STAY The new **W Dallas-Victory,** 2440 Victory Park Lane (© 877/WHOTELS), has quickly become the most talked-about place to stay and be seen in Big D, stealing a bit of the fashionable thunder from **Hotel Zaza,** 2332 Leonard St. (© 866/769-2894), which competed by adding new Magnificent Seven suites, over-the-top fantasy accommodations—with names such as Rock Star and Last Czar—several of which are larger than 2,000 square feet. **Belmont Hotel,** 901 Fort Worth Ave. (© 866/870-8010), a hipster boutique hotel carved out of a 1946 motor lodge on a bluff in Oak Cliff, is the new retro place for design-conscious people to stay and feel like they're not in Dallas.

WHERE TO DINE Stephan Pyles, 1807 Ross Ave., Suite 200 (© 214/580-7000), took 5 years off after hitting the big time with Routh Street Café and then Star Canyon, but he's again taken the city by storm with his eponymous eatery. Named Chef of the Year in 2006 by *Esquire* magazine, Pyles has expanded his palate and though he now thinks more globally, his West Texas roots are still very much apparent.

AFTER DARK One of the hottest new spots is **Ghostbar,** 2440 Victory Park Lane (© 214/871-1800), in the W Dallas-Victory Hotel. Everyone is so fabulous and wealthy that the hotel's name seems to refer to the good fortune of its patrons.

For additional information about Dallas, see chapter 4.

FORT WORTH

WHERE TO STAY The former Radisson Plaza Fort Worth, where JFK spent his last night in 1963, underwent a $10-million renovation and reopened as the **Hilton Fort Worth,** 815 Main St. (© 817/870-2100), in April 2006. The **Omni Fort Worth Hotel** (© 800/THE-OMNI), a massive luxury hotel that will be "sculpted in native stone and wrapped in glass," is due to break ground and open in fall 2008 on Houston Street. Among new, affordable hotels in Fort Worth are the **Residence Inn Fort Worth Cultural District,** 2500 Museum Way (© 817/885-8250), and **AmeriSuites,**

in the Fort Worth Stockyards, 132 E. Exchange Ave. (© **817/626-6000**), both good, dependable, family-friendly options.

WHERE TO DINE **Lanny's Alta Cocina Mexicana,** 3405 7th St. (© **817/ 850-9996**), is the big news in Cowtown. Though the young chef came from his family's down-home Tex-Mex restaurant, Joe T. Garcia's, he's gone thoroughly upscale with his creative, chic new Mexican-Mediterranean restaurant. Tim Love, of Lonesome Dove Bistro fame, opened a branch of that restaurant in New York City (!) and, in 2006, also inaugurated a new spot in his hometown—**Duce,** 6333 Camp Bowie Blvd., Suite 240 (© **817/377-4400**)—which Love calls a "modern European food lounge."

EXPLORING FORT WORTH The **Sid Richardson Collection of Western Art,** 309 Main St. (© **817/332-6554;** www.sidrmuseum.org), dedicated to the Old West paintings of Frederic Remington and Charles Russell, among others, reopened in November 2006 after a year-long renovation by Fort Worth's favorite architect, David Schwarz. The museum has a new facade and a new two-section gallery.

In 2005 the **Fort Worth Zoo,** 1989 Colonial Pkwy. (© **817/759-7555;** www.fortworthzoo.org), inaugurated a large permanent exhibit displaying the flora and fauna of the Australian Outback and Great Barrier Reef, including an aquatic exhibit featuring three saltwater tanks containing more than 10,000 gallons of water, fish, coral, and sharks.

The **Texas Civil War Museum,** 760 Jim Wright Fwy. N. (© **817/246-2323;** www.texascivilwarmuseum.com), which contains one of the largest private collections of Civil War artifacts in the country, opened in January 2006 in a 16,000-square-foot facility in northwestern Fort Worth.

For additional information about Ft. Worth, see chapter 4.

HOUSTON

The recent explosion in investment in the city's downtown area has given way to a period of consolidation. New construction in buildings and public works projects has slowed as everybody seems to be catching their breath at the moment. After the last few years, it's a pleasure not to have to navigate construction detours and lane closures on downtown streets. Construction still continues on some of the city's major freeways, including the mammoth expansion of the Katy Freeway (I-10 west to San Antonio).

One of the big questions for the future is "What to do with the Astrodome?" The most recent proposal, put forth by a group of developers, is to make it into a self-contained convention/conferencing site, with meeting space, lodging, food, and shops all under one roof, as it were. This might happen, but the hotel industry is resistant to the proposal because of the present surplus of hotel rooms in the city, especially in the downtown/South Main corridor.

WHERE TO STAY There couldn't be a better time for staying downtown. With all the recent hotel construction you can now find great weekend discounts at the luxury hotels. A recent favorite, the "Sam," is now the **Alden-Houston Hotel,** 1117 Prairie St. (© **877/348-8800;** www.aldenhotels.com); aside from the lobby, the new owners have changed little, which is a good thing. The same can be said for the **Hotel Icon,** 220 Main St. (© **800/323-7500;** www.hotelicon. com). This new/old hotel was recently sold, and the new owners have changed little besides the lobby and bar area.

The most recent addition to the hotel scene will be **Hotel ZaZa,** 5701 Main St. (© **800/323-7500;** www.hotelzaza houston.com), scheduled to open in early 2007. The developers acquired the old Warwick Hotel, which had the most enviable location in Houston, smack in the middle of the Museum District, in the most verdant part of the city. To judge what they did with their first property, the Hotel Zaza in Dallas, this will surely prove to be a fun place to stay.

WHERE TO DINE The small and delightful eatery **17,** 1117 Prairie St. (© 832/200-8888), in the Alden-Houston Hotel, has a new chef, Ryan Pera. He has followed the lead of the former chef, Jeff Armstrong, in cooking up inventive, but not over-the-top contemporary American cooking.

Bank Jean-Georges, 220 Main St. (© 832/667-4470), in the Hotel Icon, may soon become simply "Bank," as negotiations with überchef Jean-Georges Vongerichten may lead to his disassociation from the restaurant. This has come about because Jean-Georges's chef de cuisine, Bryan Caswell, has left to start his own restaurant.

EXPLORING HOUSTON Gone are the amusement parks **Six Flags Astro-World** and **WaterWorld,** victims of rising real estate values and cash-poor corporate owners. There are still two other amusement parks in the Houston area, both of them water parks. One is Six Flags Splashtown in far north Houston (which might change owners soon), and the other is in Galveston (see below).

For additional information about Houston, see chapter 5.

GULF COAST

GALVESTON The Texas company that operates the state's most popular water park in the German Hill Country town of New Braunfels, **Schlitterbahn** (www.schlitterbahn.com), has opened a water park in Galveston (next door to Moody Gardens), which is the only water park in the state with climate control. A retractable roof covers 70,000 square feet of the park, and allows it to open on weekends throughout the year.

For more on the Gulf Coast, see chapter 6.

SAN ANTONIO

San Antonio continues to grow as a convention and family destination. The city has plans to make a number of changes to the downtown tourist area. The city council has approved a project to revamp the city's **Main Plaza,** also called Plaza de las Islas. The plan includes closing off two streets bordering the plaza, improving pedestrian access, planting lots of trees and shrubbery, and creating a space for people to sit down and enjoy the scenery. In doing this the city hopes to lure visitors from the River Walk into the western part of downtown.

Something else being discussed is banning chain restaurants from the River Walk. This is a thorny issue, and it's unclear what, if anything, can be done, but businesses and citizens groups are afraid that the River Walk may lose its identity if filled with the same restaurants one sees everywhere else in the country.

WHERE TO STAY Hotel construction continues in downtown San Antonio and elsewhere in the city. There are now more than 11,000 rooms in the downtown area, which means that there is a huge pool of rooms dependent on large-convention traffic. This condition can lead to hotel bargains for the individual traveler with a certain degree of flexibility in travel arrangements.

An old favorite, **La Mansión del Río,** 112 College St. (© 800/830-1400), is now run by the Omni hotel chain. Since taking over the hotel, Omni has completely remodeled all the guest rooms and some of the common areas.

EXPLORING SAN ANTONIO The most important—or at least longest-heralded—entry on the attractions scene, the **Museo Americano Smithsonian,** 101 S. Santa Rosa Blvd. (© 210/458-2300), hasn't opened yet. This is the third major delay, amounting now to 3 years. The new time for opening is late spring of

2007. A cornerstone of the Centro Alameda project, devoted to exploring the city's Hispanic roots, MAS—get it?—is positioned at the entryway to Market Square.

The **Marion Koogler McNay Art Museum,** 6000 N. New Braunfels Ave. (© **210/824-5368**), that jewel-like small museum with the lovely grounds and great location has announced plans for a major expansion to enable it to exhibit more of its permanent collection, which is now being rotated from storage to the exhibition rooms. It's unclear how this will affect the present design of the museum, but there is plenty of time to get the planning down right. Work should begin in 2008.

Progress continues with the infrastructure improvements to the **San Antonio Missions National Historical Park,** 6701 San José Dr. at Mission Road (© **210/932-1001**). The new hike-and-bike path built on the banks of the San Antonio River is now completed. It extends for 12 miles, passing by each of the missions.

Learn more about all these San Antonio tourist lures in chapter 7.

AUSTIN
WHERE TO STAY   In the next couple of years, expect an increase in downtown hotel rooms. A couple of luxury hotel chains are planning to enter the market (W Hotels and Kimpton). At present, hotels in Austin aren't dependent on convention traffic to fill their rooms, which means you're less likely to find bargains rates.

WHERE TO DINE   The Oasis (© **512/266-2442**), the famous watering hole where Austinites go to enjoy the sunsets, has recovered from a fire caused by lightning that destroyed much of the property. It's located high above Lake Travis and comprises many decks that spread out across the hillside. Many of these were burned in the fire, but now things have pretty much returned to normal.

Another famous spot, **Las Manitas,** 211 Congress Ave. (© **512/472-9357**), may become yet another victim of progress, sharing the same fate as so many other places Austinites have held dear. The owners are in negotiations with the landlords to save both the restaurant and the day-care school next door from becoming a Marriott hotel. There have been discussions between all parties and the city council, but nothing has been resolved.

EXPLORING AUSTIN   Austin's major cultural event of 2006 was the opening of the new **Blanton Museum of Art,** Martin Luther King at Congress Avenue (© **512/471-7324**). It generated the kind of excitement for art that hasn't been seen here in a long time. Now, the museum plans to keep the excitement up with monthly happy hours for the art crowd, and other programs that combine art with other activities such as yoga. So far, the **B Scene** happy hours that occur on the first Friday of the month have been well attended.

SHOPPING   There is a new shopping district downtown, along a 2-block stretch of **West 2nd Street,** just off Congress Avenue. It's home to a lot of new stores for Austin, including clothing, interior furnishings, and designs.

Tesoros, 209 Congress Ave. (© **512/479-8377**; www.tesoros.com), the popular arts-and-crafts store next to Las Manitas (see above), faces the same fate as its neighbor and will probably have to move.

AFTER DARK   Clifford Antone died. He was Austin's long-time patron of the blues and owner of **Antone's,** 213 W. 5th St. (© **512/320-8424**)—the club and the record label. There have been a number of tribute concerts, as his death deeply affected many in the local music scene. It appears that the club will continue operations as a venue for great blues performers, from here and elsewhere.

A recent smoking ban in all public areas of Austin was overturned by a judge recently. The ban was narrowly passed by referendum in 2005, with many club owners arguing that it would be the death of Austin's music scene. The judge ruled the ban illegal because of vague wording and because it made the club owners responsible for policing the ordinance. The city council is appealing the ruling. Until it is settled, the de facto situation has been a lot of lip service about banning smoking but no enforcement.

For more information about Austin, see chapter 8.

WEST TEXAS

EL PASO   Downtown El Paso is looking towards redevelopment and is showing some early signs towards a revitalized center. One is the flashy **Artisan Hotel,** 325 N. Kansas St. (© © **915/225-9100**), opened in February 2007. Another is the coming of the **El Paso Museum of History,** 510 N. Santa Fe St. (© **915/858-1928**), in 2007. The old warehouse district around the convention center is seeing some new life as an arts and entertainment district.

Across the bridge in Juárez, Mexico, two local institutions became part of the history books since our 2005 edition: Lorenzo Garcia, inventor of the margarita at the Kentucky Club, passed away in August 2005, and the fabled Monumental Bullring was demolished to make way for new development.

ALPINE   The artsy college town has a slick new place to stay in the **Maverick Inn,** 1200 E. Holland Ave. (© **432/837-0628**), with woody, adobe-walled rooms (with Saltillo tile floors with cowhide rugs) and an oasis of a pool area. The former roadside motel was given new life in 2005.

SAN ANGELO   Downtown between Historic Concho and Twohig avenues is a block of fanciful off-street art: **Paint Brush**

Alley. The new mural project by multiple local artists is worth a look. Contact the **San Angelo Convention and Visitors Bureau,** 418 W. Ave. B. (© **800/375-1206**), for additional information.

For more on West Texas, see chapter 9.

BIG BEND & GUADALUPE MOUNTAINS NATIONAL PARKS

BIG BEND NATIONAL PARK Homeland Security policy continues to ban the onetime tradition of park visitors crossing the Rio Grande into the adjacent Mexican villages. Recently, there has been a push for a reopening of the historic La Linda Bridge just east of the park, but such a reality remains a long way away.

Park entrance fees went up in early 2007 from $15 to $20 for a 7-day pass. Backcountry camping permits, once free, now cost $10.

Castolon was expanded from a visitor contact station to a full-fledged visitor center, open November to March.

Since opening in late 2004, **Ten Bits Ranch,** 10 miles north of Study Butte at 6000 N. County Rd. (© **866/371-3110**), a one-of-a-kind re-creation of an old Western town, replete with boardwalks and storefronts masking the guestrooms, has emerged as one of the most charming places to bunk down in the vicinity. The ranch is sustainable and off the grid, meaning water use is limited and modern amenities few—you can really get away from it all here.

GUADALUPE MOUNTAINS NATIONAL PARK Where admission was previously $3, the park raised it to $5 per person in early 2007.

For more on Big Bend and Guadalupe national parks, see chapter 10.

PANHANDLE PLAINS

AMARILLO   Downtown Amarillo is undergoing revitalization, with several slick new bars and eateries (especially the 600–800 blocks of S. Polk St.), including

Asian fusion restaurant **Zen 721,** 614 S. Polk St. (© **806/372-1909**), and upscale wine bar **Bodega's,** 709 S. Polk St. (© **806/378-5790**).

The **Amarillo Dillas,** Amarillo's long-time minor league baseball franchise that ceased operations after the 2004 season, are back in action at the Dilla Villa.

On an abandoned rail line in city limits, the new **Rock Island Rail Trail** runs from Coulter Street on the west side to 7th and Crockett streets near downtown. It boasts 4 miles of jogging/biking/walking terrain in all.

CANYON There's a new lodging in the **Best Western Canyon Inn & Suites,** 2801 4th Ave. (© **800/937-8376** or 806/655-1818), which has an indoor pool and exercise room.

LUBBOCK We like the new **Arbor Inn & Suites,** 5310 Englewood Ave. (© **866/644-2319**), which opened in 2005. Among the perks: a great outdoor pool (with a faux beach and waterfall) and Texas-shaped waffles for breakfast. The **American Wind Power Center,** 1701 Canyon Lake Dr. (© **806/747-8734**), installed a massive Vestas wind turbine in 2005, 164 feet tall with 77-foot blades.

For more on the Panhandle Plains, see chapter 11.

1

The Best of Texas

by David Baird, Eric Peterson & Neil E. Schlecht

Texans are a unique bunch, unapologetic in their swaggering embrace of the place they call home. "It's flat and dry," you say. "Yup, parts are," they reply. "It's hot," you say. "Hotter 'n hell," they confirm. "Texans talk funny," you say. "Y'all do too," they retort. Self-confident and independent almost to a fault, Texas seems to embody all that's good, bad, and especially big about the United States. The former independent Republic of Texas—which shook off the landlord claims of Spain, Mexico, France, and even the United States—has diehards who still wish Texas would suck it up and secede.

Texans don't seem to mind too much if outsiders get caught up in the myths and clichés about Texas (that way they get to keep the truth to themselves). A 10-gallon hat doesn't hold 10 gallons of anything, nor is Texas flat, dry, and featureless, filled with cowboys on the range, oilmen watching their backyard gushers spit up black gold, and helmet-haired beauty queens. But it's hard to compete with the state's image, the canvas for 100 Western flicks. The big-sky frontier of Texas and the West is the quintessential American landscape, the mythic cowboy leading his longhorn cattle on long drives a heroic figure. The outlaws who thumbed their noses at authority (behind the barrel of a gun) and the boomtown gamblers who struck it rich are also part of the romantic tale of Texas.

The cowboy still exists, but Texas is now decidedly more urban than rural. Three of the nation's 10 largest cities are here: Houston, Dallas, and San Antonio. Texas today is as much a leader of high-tech industries as it is an agricultural and ranching state. There are world-class art museums and collections in Houston, Fort Worth, and Dallas, where local philanthropists have used their money and influence to import the world's most celebrated architects to build some of the nation's most talked-about museums. Although Texas is by and large a conservative place, Austin has for decades supported thriving hippie and renegade musician communities, and Dallas is nipping at its heels with a thriving music scene. The state is a melting pot dotted by pockets of Czech, German, and Irish communities; bilingual populations in the lower Rio Grande Valley and border towns; and more than four million people of Hispanic descent statewide.

This enormous state also has immense geographical diversity. Cross Texas and you'll see desert plains in the Texas Panhandle, the Piney Woods in East Texas, beaches in the Gulf Coast, North Texas prairies, scenic wildflowers and lakes in Central Texas Hill Country, desert canyons in Big Bend National Park, and the rugged Guadalupe Mountains.

Still, some of the clichés are true. Texas, the second-largest state in the United States in both land mass and population, is larger than any country in Europe. You can set out from Amarillo in your car and drive south for 15 hours and still not reach the Mexico border. And everything is bigger in Texas, of course: The ranches are bigger, the steaks are bigger, and the bigger and badder cars—Cadillacs with longhorns on the grille and monster pickup trucks with gun racks in back—really do exist. In Texas you can carry a concealed handgun—even in church—and the state is known as the capital punishment capital of the world. "Don't Mess with Texas" is more than an effective antilitter campaign.

Texans, though, are startlingly friendly and hospitable folks. Deals are still completed with handshakes, and adults say "yes, ma'am" and "nossir" to each other. Also, Texans love their sports, especially football. This is a place where entire towns pack the bleachers for Friday night high school games and preachers mention the game in their sermons, praying for victory in a kind of gridiron holy war.

Former Texas governor and owner of the Texas Rangers baseball team George W. Bush, who delights in using the down-home moniker "Dubya," lost the popular vote but was elected the 43rd president of the U.S. in 2000 and reelected in 2004. Bush regularly draws the national media corps to his sprawling ranch in Crawford, Texas, outside of Waco, when he takes long breaks from Washington "to get back in touch with real people." (Cindy Sheehan, the antiwar activist who lost a son in the Iraq war and camped outside the ranch, may not have been what he had in mind.) Bush usually makes the best of a photo op by strapping on his cowboy boots and homespun airs and hopping in the pickup, showing that he knows how to make the most of his transplanted Texan status.

It's hard for most people to be indifferent about Texas. It's a place to romanticize and ridicule, to dream about and dismiss. Texans can leave the state, but sooner or later they'll admit their weaknesses for Texas dance halls and Old West saloons, Tex-Mex and barbecue, cowboy boots, and country music. From the big sky and flat plains and the Hill Country highways lined by Texas bluebonnets to the larger-than-life personalities like LBJ, Anne Richards, and Willie Nelson: Texas stays with you.

—Neil E. Schlecht

1 The Best Luxury & Historic Hotels

• **The Adolphus Hotel** (Dallas; © **800/221-9083** or 214/742-8200): This landmark Beaux Arts hotel, built by beer baron Adolphus Busch, looks and feels like a European château. Luxuriate among dark-wood parlors, baroque art and antiques, and an opulent dining room, one of Big D's best restaurants. Rooms are English country style, and a three-course English tea is served in the lobby living room every afternoon. See p. 82.

• **The Mansion on Turtle Creek** (Dallas; © **800/422-3408** or 214/599-2100): Repeatedly named one of the top five hotels in the United States, the Mansion draws movie stars, princes, presidents, and luxury mavens. Formerly the grand estate of a cotton magnate in the 1920s and 1930s, the Mansion is refined and supremely elegant throughout, with service to match. The innovative Southwestern restaurant has slipped a notch, but is still among the most prized in town. See p. 85.

• **Hotel Zaza** (Dallas; © **866/769-2894** or 214/468-8399): This super-fashionable Uptown boutique hotel has a catchy name and a cachet few can match. It is luxurious but überhip, with eclectic style to burn. The numerous "concept" suites with funky themes (the "Shag-a-delic" Suite, anyone?) now pale in comparison with the new, fantasy-land "Magnificent Seven" suites. See p. 86.

- **W Dallas-Victory** (Dallas; ℂ 877/ **WHOTELS** or 214/397-4100): The most buzzed-about hotel in Big D has an unwieldy name, but panache to burn. With a striking tower design, views of the Dallas skyline, a 10,000-square-foot Bliss spa, an outpost of NYC's Craft restaurant, and Michael Kors–designed uniforms, it's got all the star power it needs to attract a healthy portion of the fabulous and beautiful. See p. 86.

- **Stockyards Hotel** (Fort Worth; ℂ 800/423-8471 or 817/625-6427): Over-the-top luxury would be gauche in the old stockyards, so this extremely comfortable and authentic slice of the Old West qualifies as a Fort Worth indulgence: cowboy luxury. Outlaws on the run, cowpokes and their madames, and the C&W elite have all propped up their boots here. Cowtown's cattle-ranching and railroad past are effortlessly evoked in the rooms, each of which is different: Tie your horse to the post (okay, park the Taurus in the lot) and bunk in the Bonnie & Clyde, Geronimo, or Victorian Parlor room. See p. 124.

- **Four Seasons Hotel Houston Center** (Houston; ℂ 800/332-3442 or 713/650-1300): Lots of space to stretch out in and lots of service so you don't have to stretch too far. This hotel surpasses all others in amenities and services. Within a few blocks are the baseball park, the new basketball arena, a shopping mall, and the convention center. A bit beyond that is the city's theater district and nightlife hub. See p. 164.

- **Hotel Derek** (Houston; ℂ 866/292-4100 or 713/961-3000): The most comfortable and most fun place to stay in Houston's highly popular Uptown/Galleria area. The Derek offers a rare combination of practicality and style, making it a perfect choice for the business traveler or the vacation shopper. Service is smooth, and the hotel's restaurant is winning raves from the local food writers. See p. 170.

- **Lancaster Hotel** (Houston; ℂ 800/231-0336 or 713/228-9500): Personal service, charming rooms, and great location are the keys to this hotel's success. If there's one hotel that makes having a car unnecessary in Houston, this is it. A block away are the symphony, the opera, three theaters, and the ballet. Also within a block or two are a multiplex cinema and several restaurants and clubs—you'll have the best part of the city at your feet. See p. 165.

- **Omni Corpus Christi Hotel** (Corpus Christi; ℂ 800/843-6664 or 361/887-1600): The two towers of the Omni overlook Corpus Christi Bay, and the floor-to-ceiling windows of the 20-story Bayfront Tower offer spectacular views of the Gulf, particularly from its upper floors. Pamper yourself with a massage from the in-house massage therapist or relax in the whirlpool. Then have dinner in their Republic of Texas Bar & Grill. See p. 223.

- **Radisson Resort South Padre Island** (South Padre Island; ℂ 800/333-3333 or 956/761-6511): From the high-ceilinged lobby to the beautiful landscaping around the swimming pools, this Radisson spells luxury. Many rooms have grand views of the ocean, and everything is at your fingertips. See p. 243.

- **Omni La Mansión del Río** (San Antonio; ℂ 800/830-1400 or 210/518-1000): Occupying what was once the local seminary, this hotel has kept the local feel of the building, with architectural features such as beamed ceilings and stone balconies.

La Mansión is not a high rise, and it enjoys a wide frontage along the River Walk. It is, in short, the best hotel for experiencing San Antonio. See p. 258.

- **Watermark Hotel & Spa** (San Antonio; © 866/605-1212 or 210/396-5800): If relaxation and pampering are what you seek, the Watermark should be your first choice in San Antonio. From the moment you step foot into the lobby, everything is taken care of effortlessly. The hotel has a great location on the River Walk, but the rooms are so attractive and comfortable, the service so personal, and the spa so easy to enjoy that you might never leave the premises. See p. 258.

- **The Driskill** (Austin; © 800/252-9367 or 512/474-5911): If you want to play cattle baron, you can't do better than stay in this opulent 1886 hotel, restored to its former glory at the end of the 20th century. See p. 299.

- **Four Seasons Austin** (Austin; © 800/332-3442 or 512/478-4500): With panoramic views of the lake, the wonderful service that this chain is known for, and a spa that consistently wins high praise, nothing is lacking here. Rooms are large and comfortable and come with all the amenities. Right outside the door is Austin's popular hike-and-bike trail, which rings the lake, and Austin's comfortable and fun downtown. See p. 302.

- **Cibolo Creek Ranch** (Shafter; © 432/229-3737): Tucked under the Chinati Mountains in some of the most wide-open country in all of Texas, this is a getaway for the most special of occasions, and accordingly priced. The idyllic setting plays host today to a first-class resort, featuring picture-perfect guest rooms with red tile floors, adobe walls, and sumptuous border decor. The recreation is as impressive as the scenery. See p. 363.

2 The Best Bed & Breakfasts & Boutique Hotels

- **Hôtel St. Germain** (Dallas; © 214/871-2516): Ever wanted to stay with your spouse at a plush bordello? This intimate boutique hotel and elegant, prix-fixe restaurant is about as close as you'll come to that fantasy. A gorgeous mix of early-20th-century France and New Orleans, the seven suites are so swank, with such pampering features as wood-burning fireplaces, draped Napoleon sleigh beds, bidets, and soaking tubs, that you may not want to leave. But your budget may force you to. See p. 84.

- **Belmont Hotel** (Dallas; © 866/870-8010 or 214/393-2000): Dallas usually goes gaga over mirrored glass and brand-spanking-new buildings, so it's a refreshing change to find this vintage 1940s motor lodge in Oak Cliff transformed into a stylish, retro-styled boutique hotel. With its cool lounge bar and mid-century modern decor, it's a dollop of Palm Springs with views of downtown Dallas. See p. 83.

- **The Ashton Hotel** (Fort Worth; © 866/327-4866 or 817/332-0100): Just off Sundance Square, this new boutique hotel—Fort Worth's only small luxury hotel—offers plush rooms and smooth service, as well as one of the best restaurants in North Texas. It's the new place to be in Cowtown. See p. 126.

- **Etta's Place** (Fort Worth; © 866/355-5760 or 817/255-5760): A cozy and relaxing small hotel that feels like a B&B is just a heartbeat from Fort Worth's charming nightlife, shops, and restaurants of Sundance Square. It bears the name of Etta Place, the handsome girlfriend of the Sundance

Kid, who no doubt would approve of the spacious, modern rooms with lots of light and Texas touches. Kick back in the clubby library and music rooms. See p. 128.

- **La Colombe d'Or** (Houston; ℂ 713/524-7999): Have a four-course French dinner served in your suite's separate dining room. With such personal service and with only five suites, there's no way you'll get lost in the shuffle. Occupying a mansion built for an oil tycoon in the 1920s, the hotel has uncommon architectural features, and is furnished with antiques. Its location in Houston's Montrose District puts it squarely in the middle of the hippest part of town. See p. 168.

- **George Blucher House Bed & Breakfast Inn** (Corpus Christi; ℂ 866/884-4884 or 361/884-4884): This wonderful B&B combines the ambience of an elegant historic home—it was built in 1904—with modern amenities. Breakfasts are served by candlelight; and you're just across the street from a prime bird-watching area. See p. 223.

- **Ogé House Inn on the River Walk** (San Antonio; ℂ 800/242-2770 or 210/223-2353): The King William area abounds with B&Bs, but the Ogé House stands out as much for its professionalism as for its gorgeous mansion and lovely rooms. You don't have to sacrifice service for warmth here. See p. 261.

- **Mansion at Judges Hill** (Austin; ℂ 800/311-1619 or 512/495-1800): A room in the original mansion evokes the feel of a more relaxed and gracious era, especially the second-floor rooms which have a large and inviting porch, tempting one to linger and enjoy the view. The service, which is friendly and helpful, does everything to reinforce such a feeling. See p. 306.

- **Villa del Rio Bed & Breakfast** (Del Rio; ℂ 800/995-1887 or 830/768-1100): A luxurious Mediterranean-style villa—actually a mix of Italian and Mexican styles—built in 1887, the Villa del Rio gets our vote for the best place to stay in this area for anyone who appreciates old-world ambience and pampering and an exciting breakfast. See p. 379.

3 The Best Hotel Bargains

- **The Bradford at Lincoln Park** (Dallas; ℂ 888/486-7829 or 214/696-1555): A new residential-style hotel that primarily targets businesspeople, it's also superb for other travelers and families. The nicely styled and spacious suites have fully equipped kitchens, and there are a pool and small spa, exercise room, and business center, as well as free continental breakfast and local calls. See p. 89.

- **The Hotel Lawrence** (Dallas; ℂ 877/396-0334 or 214/761-9090): Downtown used to be a wasteland after dark, but now it's become a cool spot where a number of upscale hotels

and restaurants are thriving. But you won't have to pay through the nose to stay near the famed grassy knoll and the original Neiman Marcus. This historic hotel has nice rooms and good services—in addition to its coveted location—for the cost of a roadside motel. See p. 84.

- **Lovett Inn** (Houston; ℂ 800/779-5224 or 713/522-5224): This B&B offers attractive, comfortable rooms with private balconies for a low price. Add a pool and a central location that is handy but quiet, and you have a winning combination. See p. 169.

- **Best Western Sunset Suites—Riverwalk** (San Antonio; © **866/560-6000** or 210/223-4400): Low room rates, lots of free perks, and a convenient location near downtown—not to mention superattractive rooms in a historic structure—make staying here a super deal. See p. 200.
- **Austin Motel** (Austin; © **512/441-1157**): Look for the Austin's classic neon sign in Austin's hip SoCo area. The rooms have been individually furnished, many in fun and funky styles, but the place retains its 1950s character and its lower-than-1990s prices. See p. 305.
- **Travelodge Hotel–La Hacienda Airport** (El Paso; © **800/772-4231** or 915/772-4231): Some roadside motels surprise you with their attention to detail—this is definitely one of them. We like the eight Jacuzzi rooms, featuring picture windows that separate the tubs from the bedrooms, and the family suites, amusingly decorated with plenty of room. See p. 351.

4 The Best Restaurants

- **The French Room** (Dallas; © **214/742-8200**): This formal but thankfully not intimidating restaurant in the historic Adolphus Hotel is dreamy, like dining at Versailles. Indulge in superb classic French cuisine and museum-quality wines surrounded by a rococo-painted ceiling, flowing drapes, and crystal chandeliers. See p. 90.
- **Stephan Pyles** (Dallas; © **214/580-7000**): The legendary West Texas chef, back after a long hiatus, has upped the ante in dramatic fashion in his new, chic but still very Texan, eponymous restaurant in the Arts District. Pyles, *Esquire* magazine's Chef of the Year in 2006, says what emanates from his massive kitchen is "new millennium Southwestern cuisine." The man behind Star Canyon has taken Big D by storm once again. See p. 91.
- **Javier's Gourmet Mexicano** (Dallas; © **214/521-4211**): The owners and devotees of this gourmet Mexico City restaurant will gently inform you that, no, this isn't Tex-Mex. Javier's serves deliciously prepared grilled fish and meat dishes and mesquite-smoked chicken in a Spanish colonial setting. Come for a top-shelf margarita at the clubby bar, but I guarantee you'll stay for dinner. See p. 94.
- **Café Ashton** (Fort Worth; © **817/332-0100**): The creative New American bistro fare at this swank restaurant, in a boutique hotel of the same description, quickly shot to the top of everyone's best-of lists in Fort Worth. Hotel dining is rarely this good or this intimate. See what all the fuss is about. See p. 132.
- **Lanny's Alta Cocina Mexicana** (Fort Worth; © **817/850-9996**): The young great-grandson of the man behind Fort Worth's longtime standard for Tex-Mex, Joe T. Garcia's, has struck out on his own with this sensational fine-dining take on Mediterranean cooking with Mexican sensibilities. Sophisticated but unfussy, it's *the* place to dine in downtown Fort Worth. See p. 134.
- **Mark's** (Houston; © **713/523-3800**): No fussy French nouvelle here, and no boring steak and potatoes either. Mark's manages to serve up dishes that can satisfy at some deep subconscious level while they fulfill our eternal quest for something new. This is New American cooking as it should be performed. See p. 178.
- **Cafe Annie** (Houston; © **713/840-1111**): No other restaurant in Houston garners quite the attention that this place does from both food critics

and the public alike. With its innovative Southwestern cooking, the best wine list in the city, and a master sommelier (the only "master" in Texas), the restaurant has its credentials. Chef/owner Robert Del Grande offers up wonderful dishes that show just how fertile the crossbreeding of Mexican and American cooking can be. See p. 183.

- **Le Rêve** (San Antonio; ☎ 210/212-2221): Regularly designated the best restaurant in Texas, Le Rêve never disappoints. Owner/chef Andrew Weissman is exacting in the practice of his craft and produces a dining experience that is close to being other-worldly. See p. 266.

- **Uchi** (Austin; ☎ 512/916-4808): Don't think of this restaurant as just a good place for sushi and Japanese cuisine. It's a great restaurant, period, with creative cooking that transcends its humble roots. The setting, in a beautifully revamped 1930s house, is transcendent, too. See p. 311.

- **Café Central** (El Paso; ☎ 915/545-2233): Well worth the splurge, Café Central is a sleek urban bistro serving sophisticated international cuisine. The menu changes daily, but always offers a wide range of standout fare—most notably creative Southwestern interpretations of traditional Continental dishes. The wine list is one of the city's best, with nearly 300 bottles, and desserts include the best *leches* (Mexican milk cakes) in all of Texas. See p. 352.

- **Ocotillo** (Lajitas; ☎ 432/424-5000): For our money, this is the best restaurant on the entire Texas-Mexico border. Ocotillo specializes in wild game with Mexican-inspired sauces; the interplay between the two is a revelation. Executive Chef Blas Gonzales brought 20 years of experience from Austin. Everything is fresh: Seafood is flown in daily from both coasts, and many ingredients are grown in a terrace garden on-site. See p. 397.

5 The Best Texan Dining

- **Sonny Bryan's Smokehouse** (Dallas; ☎ 214/357-7120): Sonny Bryan's has been turning out sweet barbecue since 1910, and the little smoke shack out on Inwood has acquired legendary status. Salesmen perch on their car hoods with their sleeves rolled up and wolf down hickory-smoked brisket, sliced-beef sandwiches, and succulent onion rings. Thinner sorts squeeze into tiny one-armed school desks and get ready to douse their brisket with superb, tangy sauce. A classic. See p. 98.

- **Bob's Steak & Chop House** (Dallas; ☎ 214/528-9446): Bob's will satisfy the steak connoisseur—the real Texan—in you. With a clubby but relaxed mahogany look and behemoth wet-aged prime beef and sirloin filets, this is a place for the J. R. crowd. Even the accompaniments—"smashed" potatoes and honey-glazed whole carrots—are terrific. And the meat-shy need not fear: The chophouse salad is a meal in itself. Cigar aficionados should keep their noses trained for Bob's cigar dinners: Every course is served with a different cigar. See p. 93.

- **Lonesome Dove Western Bistro** (Fort Worth; ☎ 817/740-8810): The work of a daring young couple, this friendly and eclectic restaurant challenges Cowtown to broaden its horizons. The Southwestern menu at this Stockyards eatery successfully stretches the popular theme in new ways, adding unique Texas touches that are both avant-garde and comforting. Pop in for the cheap Stockyards lunch special or dive into a blowout dinner. See p. 131.

- **Angelo's** (Fort Worth; © **817/ 332-0357**): Fort Worth's classic Texas barbecue joint is as unpretentious as they come: Its wood paneling, mounted deer and buffalo heads, metal ceiling fans, and Formica tables might have come from a Jaycees lodge. That's kitschy cool to some, meaningless to everyone else. What is important is the fantastic hickory-smoked barbecue. See p. 135.

- **Loma Linda** (Houston; © **713/ 924-6074**): Bursting the bubble of a perfectly puffed tortilla smothered in chile con queso is the moment where anticipation meets realization in the Tex-Mex experience. The aroma, the texture, the taste . . . words fail me. You can scour the borderlands a long time before coming up with an old-fashioned Tex-Mex joint like this one. The restaurant even has its own special tortilla maker for producing these puffed-up beauties. Also of note are the perfectly seasoned classic Tex-Mex enchiladas with chili gravy. See p. 176.

- **Gaidos** (Galveston; © **409/762-9625**): Offering traditional cooking as it is practiced on the Texas Gulf Coast, Gaidos is the keeper of the flame for lovers of seafood that steers clear of fads and trends. The family has been serving up stuffed snapper, gumbo, and fried oysters for four generations. See p. 212.

- **La Playa** (Corpus Christi; © **361/ 980-3909**): For a Tex-Mex restaurant to be considered truly great, it must, of course, do a good job with the traditional enchiladas in chili gravy, have excellent fajitas, and pay attention to the details in cooking the rice and beans. It helps if it has a signature dish or two. In this case, it's deep-fried avocadoes. No place but Texas, baby! See p. 224.

- **La Playa** (Port Aransas; © **361/ 749-0022**): This place is in no way connected to La Playa of Corpus Christi. But the cooking is just as local and does a great job with Tex-Mex style seafood dishes such as *campechana* cocktails and fish tacos. The margaritas transcend cultures, but La Playa's got that hominess and welcoming feel that is as much Texas as anything else. See p. 233.

- **Mi Tierra** (San Antonio; © **210/ 225-1262**): Some people dismiss this cafe as touristy. Not so. It is the practitioner of old San Antonio cooking traditions. Order any of the Tex-Mex specialties and sit back and enjoy the ambience—both the food and the decor are expressions of local tastes when celebrating is called for. And travelers need no excuse to celebrate once they've hit upon this gem. See p. 268.

- **Shady Grove** (Austin; © **512/ 474-9991**): This is the most quintessentially Austin restaurant in town. It offers a laid-back Texan menu, a huge outdoor patio, and an "unplugged" music series. See p. 313.

- **L&J Café** (El Paso; © **915/566-8418**): An El Paso landmark since it opened its doors in 1927, the L&J is both inexpensive and offers some of the best Tex-Mex food you'll find anywhere. The chicken enchiladas, overflowing with fluffy meat and buried under chunky green chile and Jack cheese, approach perfection. It doesn't hurt that the salsa is spicy, the beer is cold, and the service is quick and friendly, even when the place is filled to capacity—as it is most of the time. See p. 353.

- **Starlight Theatre** (Terlingua; © **432/ 371-2326**): A 1930s movie palace abandoned when the mines in Terlingua went bust in the following decade, the Starlight Theatre was reborn as an eatery and watering hole in 1991. The stage is still here, but the silver screen takes a backseat to the food (especially the trademark enchiladas, filet mignon, and sautéed chicken), drink (namely Texas beers and prickly pear margaritas), and desserts (the cobbler for two is legendary). See p. 396.

6 The Best Lone Star Experiences

- **Hopping Aboard the Grapevine Vintage Railroad:** The Old West comes alive aboard the Tarantula Railroad. A nostalgic train (when running, a restored 1896 steam locomotive called *Puffy*) rumbles along the track from Stockyards Station in Fort Worth, tracing the route of the Chisholm Trail, to the Cotton Belt Depot in historic Grapevine, Texas, a town with 75 restored turn-of-the-20th-century buildings. See p. 140.

- **Lassoing the Fort Worth Stock Show and Rodeo:** Fort Worth ain't called Cowtown for nothing. In late January and early February, the Southwestern Exposition and Livestock Show, as it's officially called, recalls the glory cowboy days with horse shows, auctions, and all sorts of livestock, from beef cattle to llamas and swine. The nightly rodeos are big draws. See "Fort Worth" in chapter 4.

- **Attending a Mariachi Mass at Mission San José:** The Alamo may be more famous, but hearing a congregation of San Antonians raise their voices in spirited prayer reminds you that the city's Spanish missions aren't just, well, history. See p. 276.

- **Tubing on the River:** In central Texas, upstream from the town of Gruene, is a stretch of the Guadalupe River that Texans love to float down "leisurely like" in tubes (one tube per person and one for the ice chest). During the late spring and early summer the air is hot, the water is cold, and the "tuber" (tube-potato?) finds life most agreeable. There is no shortage of outfitters who can set you up with a tube and put you in the water. See p. 336.

- **Explore Tejas/Cross the Border:** There are nearly 800 miles of Texas-Mexico border, and the Rio Grande from the Gulf of Mexico to El Paso is a fascinating region. We are big fans of Ciudad Acuña, across the river from Del Rio, and the amazing canyons in Big Bend National Park, but the entire "borderlands" region is more attractive and diverse than most visitors realize. See chapters 9 and 10.

- **Exploring Big Bend National Park:** Vast and wild, this rugged terrain harbors thousands of species of plants and animals—some seen practically nowhere else on earth. A visit can include a hike into the sun-baked desert, a float down a majestic river through the canyons, or a trek among high mountains where bears and mountain lions rule. See "Big Bend National Park" in chapter 10.

7 The Best Museums

- **The Nasher Sculpture Center** (Dallas): This world-class collection of modern sculpture recently debuted in the downtown Dallas Arts District. Ray Nasher and his wife Patsy spent 4 decades assembling what has been called the finest private collection in the world (it includes superlative works by Miró, David Smith, Brancusi, Moore, Giacometti, Picasso, Matisse, Calder, and many more). Designed by Renzo Piano, it has a gorgeous open-air sculpture garden with landscape design by Peter Walker. See p. 102.

- **Meadows Museum of Art** (Dallas): Now in a new building with more room to show off the greatest collection of Spanish masters outside Spain, the Meadows was built by a Dallas oilman fascinated by Spanish art. The museum proudly displays a wealth of works by Velázquez, Goya, Ribera, Murillo, Zurbarán—just about all the biggies from Spain's golden era as well as the 20th-century masters Picasso, Dalí, and Miró. See p. 106.

- **Kimbell Art Museum** (Fort Worth): Probably the country's finest small museum, this masterwork by Louis Kahn is a joyous celebration of architecture and a splendid collection of art to boot. Kahn's graceful building, a wonder of technology and natural light, is now a chapter in architectural studies worldwide. The small permanent collection ranges from prehistoric Asian and pre-Columbian pieces to European old masters, Impressionists, and modern geniuses. The Kimbell also gets some of the world's most important traveling shows. See p. 142.

- **Modern Art Museum of Fort Worth** (Fort Worth): In a spanking new modernist building designed by the Japanese architect Tadao Ando, the new Modern—actually the oldest art museum in Texas—is now the nation's second largest dedicated to contemporary and modern art. The permanent collection includes works by Picasso, Rothko, Warhol, Rauschenberg, and Pollock. See p. 142.

- **Amon Carter Museum of Western Art** (Fort Worth): The newly expanded Amon Carter Museum is one of the finest collections of Western and American art in the country, including the most complete group of works by Frederic Remington and Charles M. Russell, two behemoths of Western art. It also possesses a great photography collection and important paintings by Georgia O'Keeffe and others. See p. 140.

- **Menil Collection** (Houston): One of the great private collections of the world, it could very well have ended up in Paris or New York, but was graciously bestowed by the collectors on their adopted city. To experience the Menil is pure delight; very little comes between the viewer and the art, which includes works by many of the 20th-century masters, classical works from the ancients, and tribal art from around the world. See p. 190.

- **Museum of Fine Arts, Houston** (Houston): With the addition of the Audrey Jones Beck Building, the Fine Arts museum has doubled its exhibition space and has especially put its collection of Impressionist and baroque art in the best possible light. The museum also has several satellite facilities and attracts major touring exhibitions. See p. 188.

- **The Center for the Arts & Sciences** (Brazosport): One of those rare entities that does a lot of things exceptionally well, The Center includes a terrific natural history museum, a delightful small planetarium, an attractive art gallery, two theaters for a variety of performing arts events, and a nature trail. See p. 214.

- **San Antonio Museum of Art** (San Antonio): Almost as impressive for its architecture as for its holdings, this museum combines several castlelike buildings of the 1904 Lone Star Brewery. The $11-million Nelson A. Rockefeller Center for Latin American Art is the most comprehensive collection of its kind in the United States. See p. 275.

- **Marion Koogler McNay Art Museum** (San Antonio): A beautiful collection beautifully located and beautifully displayed. This small museum is a delight to visit for everyone, but especially for fans of modern art, who will devour its collection of works by the modern masters. See p. 275.
- **McDonald Observatory** (northwest of Fort Davis): McDonald Observatory is considered one the world's best astronomical research facilities, and twice a day visitors can glimpse sunspots, flares, and other solar activity. Additionally, nighttime "Star Parties" are held 3 evenings a week, when visitors can view celestial objects and constellations through the observatory's high-powered telescopes. See p. 359.
- **Panhandle-Plains Historical Museum** (Canyon): The largest history museum in Texas, this excellent museum is anything but a dusty collection of spurs and bits. Well thought out, engaging, and informative, it is largely hands-on—you can sit in a Ford Mustang and listen to Buddy Holly tunes or try out a sidesaddle. There are also comprehensive exhibits on the region's history in terms of petroleum, art, transportation, Western heritage, and paleontology/geology. See p. 425.

8 The Best Shopping

- **Neiman Marcus** (Dallas): Established in 1907, Neiman Marcus is intimately identified with Big D and its shopaholics. The luxury purveyor's annual holiday catalog, with his-and-her fantasies for the rich, has become an institution. The downtown store is classy and retro-cool, the best place in North Texas to drape yourself in Prada and Chanel. See p. 112.
- **NorthPark Center** (Dallas): Dallas loves to shop, and while there are more malls than most people (except Dallasites) know what to do with, NorthPark is the most traditional and elegant (even with its recent expansion that doubled its size); it also has a graceful layout that outclasses its more garish competitors. Besides top anchor stores (Neiman Marcus, Tiffany's), it enjoys rotating pieces from owner Ray Nasher's spectacular collection of modern sculpture, on display throughout the mall. See "p. 113.
- **Stockyards National Historic District** (Fort Worth): In Cowtown, looking the part is important. Pick up Western duds—suits and shirts with elegant piping and embroidered yokes that would have made you a star in the Old West, plus cowboy boots and other Western paraphernalia—just steps away from the old Stockyards livestock pens. Right on the main drag is **Maverick,** which has upscale Western wear and a bar serving up Lone Star longnecks. **M. L. Leddy's** is a longtime family-owned shop with a big boot sign out front and top-quality hats, hand-tooled belts, and custom-made boots. And just down the street, plunk down the cash for exquisite custom cowboy boots at **Ponder Boot Company.** See "Fort Worth" in chapter 4.
- **Uptown** (Houston): In this one, relatively small district of the city you can find Houston's Galleria (with over 300 retailers including Saks, Neiman Marcus, Tiffany's, and Versace) and four other malls fronting Post Oak (including such retailers as Cartier and FAO Schwarz). See "Shopping" in chapter 5.
- **Paris Hatters** (San Antonio): Pope John Paul II, Prince Charles, Jimmy Smits, and Dwight Yoakam have all had Western headgear made for them

by Paris Hatters, in business since 1917 and still owned by the same family. About half of the sales are special order, but the shelves are stocked with high-quality ready-to-wear hats, too. See p. 283.

- **Capitol Saddlery** (Austin): The custom-made boots of this classic three-level Western store near the capitol, run by the same family for 7 decades, were immortalized in a song by Jerry Jeff Walker. Come here for hand-tooled saddles, belts, tack, and altogether unyuppified cowboy gear. See p. 328.

- **Fredericksburg** (Texas Hill Country): It's hard to say how a town founded by German idealists ended up being a magnet for Texas materialists, but Fredericksburg's main street is chock-a-block with boutiques. This is the place to come for everything from natural chocolate mint–scented room deodorizer to handmade dulcimers. See p. 332.

- **El Paso Chile Company** (El Paso): We love this shop for its tongue-searing delicacies, with fiery names such as "Hellfire & Damnation," and all things spicy. See p. 350.

9 The Best Places for Boot-Scootin'

- **Adair's Saloon** (Dallas): Deep Ellum's down-'n'-dirty honky-tonk is unfazed by the new wave discos, rock clubs, and preppy SMU students in its midst. It sticks to its down-to-earth antistyle, knee-slapping country and redneck rock bands, cheap beer, and tables and walls blanketed in graffiti. See p. 116.

- **Gilley's Dallas** (Dallas): Gilley's is where John Travolta rode a bucking bronco in *Urban Cowboy,* and now Big D has a branch of the famous Houston honky-tonk. If bigger is better, this one's right up there with the best of them: It's got 90,000 square feet of dance floor, bars, and stages. See p. 116.

- **Billy Bob's Texas** (Fort Worth): Kind of like a big-tent country theme park, Billy Bob's has it all: 40 bars, a huge dance floor for two-stepping, pro bull riding, and live performances by some of the biggest names in country music. And of course dance lessons: Shuffle and two-step like a Texan after a few hours with instructor Wendell Nelson. See p. 149.

- **Blanco's** (Houston): This is one of those genuine honky-tonks where you go for the music and the dancing and not for dressing up in Western duds. It's strictly come as you are, and this place attracts 'em from all walks of life, from bankers to oil field workers. It's a small venue, but gets some of the best of Texas's country music bands. See p. 199.

- **Floore's Country Store** (San Antonio): Not much has changed since the 1940s when this honky-tonk, boasting the largest dance floor in South Texas (half an acre), opened up. Boots, hats, and antique farm equipment hang from the ceiling of this typical Texas roadhouse. There's always live music on weekends; Willie Nelson, Dwight Yoakam, Robert Earl Keen, and Lyle Lovett have all played here. See p. 285.

- **Texas Hill Country** (San Antonio and Austin): The Texas Hill Country has some of the best honky-tonks in the state. In Gruene, just outside of New Braunfels, **Gruene Hall** is the oldest country-and-western dance hall in Texas and still one of the mellowest places to listen to music. Don't miss **Arkey Blue & The Silver Dollar Bar,** a genuine spit-and-sawdust cowboy honky-tonk on the Main Street of Bandera. When there's no live music, plug a quarter in the old jukebox and play a country ballad by owner Arkey. And look for the table where Hank Williams, Sr., carved his name. See "Hill Country Side Trips" in chapters 7 and 8.

- **Broken Spoke** (Austin): This is the gen-u-ine item, a Western honky-tonk with a wood-plank floor and a cowboy-hatted, two-steppin' crowd. Still, it's in Austin, so don't be surprised if the band wears Hawaiian shirts, or if tongues are planted firmly in cheeks for some of the songs. See p. 330.

10 The Best of Natural Texas

- **Dallas Arboretum & Botanical Garden:** Who knew Dallas had more than dust, concrete, steel, and glass? This surprising oasis on the edge of White Rock Lake is a great spot to duck the Texas sun. Relax on 70 acres of groomed gardens and natural woodlands, interspersed with a handful of historic homes. The gardens are especially colorful in spring and fall. See p. 104.
- **Fort Worth Botanic & Japanese Gardens:** A rambling, spacious showcase of 2,500 native and exotic species of plants on 100-plus acres, this is the oldest botanical garden in Texas, created back in the late 1920s. The Texas Rose Garden, 3,500 roses that bloom in late April and October, and beautiful Japanese Garden are terrific places to hide out from the world. Bring a picnic, a book, and a flying disk. See p. 141.
- **Big Thicket National Preserve:** It has been called "the American Ark" for its incredibly rich variety of plants and wildlife, all packed into 100,000 acres of watery bottomland in deepest East Texas. You can explore the area on foot or in canoe, and see firsthand how the woods grow so thickly here that they all but blot out the sun, and make trailblazing almost impossible. See "Side Trips to East Texas" in chapter 5.
- **Aransas National Wildlife Refuge:** A mecca for birders, with some 300 species sighted here, the refuge is also

home to a variety of frogs and other amphibians, plus snakes, turtles, lizards, and numerous mammals. But Aransas has become famous for being the main winter home of the near-extinct whooping crane, the tallest bird in America—5 feet high with an 8-foot wingspan. See "Rockport" in chapter 6.
- **Mustang Island State Park:** This barrier island has more than 5 miles of wide, sandy beach, with fine sand, few rocks, and broken shells, and almost enough waves for surfing. The park is one of the most popular of Texas state parks, and is especially busy on summer weekends. See "Port Aransas" in chapter 6.
- **Lady Bird Johnson Wildflower Center:** Few people remember that it was Lady Bird Johnson who started a program to beautify America's highways—and that she began practicing it in her home state. This flower-powered research center is a natural outgrowth of this first lady's lifelong efforts to beautify the state. See p. 320.
- **McKittrick Canyon:** The canyon is forested with conifers and deciduous trees. In autumn, the maples, oaks, and other hardwoods burst into color, painting the world in bright colors set off by the rich variety of the evergreens. See "Guadalupe Mountains National Park" in chapter 10.
- **Palo Duro Canyon State Park:** This 60-mile canyon, sculpted by the Prairie Dog Town Fork of the Red

River over the last 90 million years, is a grand contrast to the ubiquitous, treeless plains of the Texas Panhandle. Its 800-foot cliffs, striped with orange, red, and white rock and adorned by groves of juniper and cottonwood trees, present an astoundingly stark beauty. See "Canyon & Palo Duro Canyon State Park" in chapter 11.

11 The Best Historical Attractions

- **The Sixth Floor Museum at Dealey Plaza** (Dallas): The events of November 22, 1963, shook the world. John F. Kennedy's assassination in Dallas is remembered by everyone old enough to remember, and argued over still. Visitors can tour the sixth floor of the Texas School Book Depository, from where the Warren Commission concluded that a single sniper, Lee Harvey Oswald, felled the president. The museum also examines the life, times, and legacy of the Kennedy presidency, making it a place to revisit not only the tragic episode but also an era. See p. 100.

- **The Stockyards National Historic District** (Fort Worth): Still very much looking the part, this area north of downtown was once the biggest and busiest cattle, horse, mule, hog, and sheep marketing center in the Southwest. Put on your boots and best Western shirt and tour the Livestock Exchange Building; Cowtown Coliseum (the world's first indoor rodeo arena); former hog and sheep pens now filled with Western shops and restaurants; and Billy Bob's Texas, the "world's largest honkytonk." Then grab a longneck at the White Elephant saloon—the oldest bar in Fort Worth and the site of the city's most famous gunfight in 1897—and check in at the historic Stockyards Hotel. To enhance the experience, check out the "longhorn cattle drive" that rumbles down Exchange Avenue daily—or take the Vintage Train into Grapevine. See "Fort Worth" in chapter 4.

- **San Jacinto Monument** (Houston): Here on the battlefield of San Jacinto, a small army of Texans led by General Sam Houston charged the much larger, better equipped Mexican army and dealt them a crushing blow. The victory gave Texas its independence. A monument and museum occupy the battlefield to honor and explain the history of the battle and its significance. See p. 185.

- **USS *Lexington* Museum on the Bay** (Corpus Christi): Exploring this huge World War II–era aircraft carrier offers non-naval persons the opportunity to get an idea of what it was like to live for sometimes months in the claustrophobic conditions of such a limited area. In addition to sleeping, dining, and cooking areas, the ship provided a hospital, rec room, and, of course, numerous necessary working areas. See p. 221.

- **The Alamo** (San Antonio): It's smaller than you might expect, and it sits smack in the heart of downtown San Antonio, but the graceful mission church that's come to symbolize the state is a must-see, if only to learn what the fuss is all about. See p. 273.

- **San Antonio Missions National Historical Park:** It's impossible not to remember the Alamo when you're in San Antonio; more difficult to recall is that the Alamo was originally just the first of five missions established by the Franciscans along the San Antonio River. Exploring these four missions, built uncharacteristically close to each other, will give you a glimpse of the city's early Spanish and Indian history. See p. 276.

- **State Capitol** (Austin): The country's largest state capitol, second only in size to the U.S. Capitol—but 7 feet taller—underwent a massive renovation and expansion in the 1990s, which left it more impressive than ever. See p. 319.
- **New Braunfels:** Trying to decide which of the Hill Country towns is the most representative of the area's rich German heritage is tough, but the *gemütlich* inns, history-oriented museums, and sausage-rich restaurants—not to mention the major celebration of Oktoberfest—make New Braunfels a standout. See "Hill Country Side Trips from Austin" in chapter 8.
- **El Paso Mission Trail:** Established in the 17th and 18th centuries, these three historic Spanish missions provide a link to El Paso's colonial past. They are among the oldest continually active missions in the country, and warrant a visit for their architectural and historic merit. Especially impressive is the large Presidio Chapel San Elceario, near the site of "The First Thanksgiving," said to have taken place in 1598, 23 years before the Plymouth Thanksgiving. See p. 344.

12 The Best Family Adventures

- **Old City Park** (Dallas): Dallas is determinedly modern, with gleaming skyscrapers and a love for newness, but its Western heritage lives on museum-like in this facsimile of the Old West, a 13-acre park of historic buildings. Mounted like a late-19th-century village, it has a redbrick Main Street, Victorian homes, train depot, general store, one-room church, schoolhouse, and bank, all relocated from the Dallas area. The "Living Farmstead" re-creates a 19th-century prairie with actors in period garb. See p. 106.
- **The Stockyards** (Fort Worth): Far from a dry old historic district, the Stockyards come alive with the flavor of the Old West. Kids will adore the twice-daily "cattle drive" of the Fort Worth Herd, which rumbles down the cobbled main drag, led by cowhands in 19th-century duds. They'll also love to find their way around the **Cowtown Cattlepen Maze,** a human maze made to look like old cattle pens. See "Fort Worth" in chapter 4.
- **Fort Worth's Children's Museums** (Fort Worth): The **Fort Worth Museum of Science and History** is large and multifaceted, with a domed IMAX theater, planetarium, and a bunch of great hands-on science displays, including life-size Lone Star dinosaurs. The **National Cowgirl Museum and Hall of Fame** teaches little cowgirls and cowboys about pioneering women of the American West, but in a way that really brings the culture to life: Jukeboxes pump out country tunes, and kids can ride a simulated bucking bronco, see the film of their adventure on the museum's website, and get their pictures superimposed on Old West film posters. And don't forget the **Fort Worth Zoo,** one of the best in the country. See "Fort Worth" in chapter 4.
- **Arlington:** Sandwiched between Dallas and Fort Worth is a kids' suburban dream world, where youngins can stumble from the roller coasters at Six Flags Over Texas to the water slides at Hurricane Harbor, followed by a visit to Ripley's Believe It or Not and The Palace of Wax, topped off by paying their respects to baseball's greats at the Legends of the Game Baseball Museum at The Ballpark in Arlington. See "Arlington" in chapter 4.

- **Space Center Houston** (Houston): Always the most popular attraction in the city, NASA's Space Center Houston is a joint effort powered by NASA technology and Disney know-how. It is the epitome of interactive display and simulation that manages to fascinate both kids and parents. During your visit, you can check out what's going on at the Johnson Space Center through a tram ride and video feeds. See p. 187.

- **The Gulf Side of South Padre Island:** Fine white sand and warm water lapping at your toes—what more do you want? Although the shore is lined with hotels and condos, the beaches are public and open to everyone. See "Padre Island National Seashore" in chapter 6.

- **Six Flags Fiesta Texas** (San Antonio): Major thrill rides, a huge swimming pool shaped like Texas, and entertainment/food areas with Texas history themes—there's something for every family member at this theme park, and it's even slightly educational. See p. 277.

- **The Austin Bats:** The majority of adults and kids alike tend to finds bats a bit creepy—until they learn more about them, that is. From March to November, you can watch thousands of bats emerge in smoky clouds from under the Congress Avenue Bridge, and find out why Austinites adore the little critters. See "Seeing the Sights" in chapter 8.

- **Balmorhea State Park:** This is one of the crown jewels of the Texas state parks and also one of the smallest, at 45 acres. The main attraction is the massive, 1¾-acre swimming pool— 3.5 million gallons of water at a fairly constant 74°F (23°C). Not your usual swimming pool, it's teeming with small fish and laden with rocks. But swimming, snorkeling, and scuba diving are all popular. There's also a reconstructed *cienega* (desert wetland) where you might spot native wildlife such as a Texas spiny softshell turtle, a blotched water snake, or a green heron. See "Small Towns of Central West Texas" in chapter 9.

13 The Best of Texas Online

- **The Handbook of Texas Online** (www.tsha.utexas.edu/handbook/online): The Handbook is an encyclopedia offering concise entries that explain who's who, what's what, and where's where in Texas. It's easy to use and has information on just about everything, from the locations of towns and counties to explanations of some of the state's legends, to biographical data on the many characters who left their mark on Texas history.

- **Texas Department of Transportation** (www.traveltex.com): The state's official tourism website is practically the only site you'll need to type in— everything else will be a link. We especially like the section that offers easily printable discount coupons, primarily for lodging and attractions.

- **Texas Outside** (www.texasoutside.com): This is a great resource for planning outdoor activities for just about anywhere in the state. It breaks Texas down into different regions and has separate pages for Texas's largest cities. You'll find maps and information on all sorts of outdoor sports, such as hiking, hunting, fishing, biking, and canoeing.

- **Dallas–Fort Worth Area Official Visitors' Website** (www.visitdallas-fortworth.com): For purely practical matters, this frighteningly bureaucratic-sounding address gives you the lowdown on area events and even allows you to download coupons good for saving a few bucks at museums, theme parks, and other local attractions.

- **Guidelive.com:** The entertainment Web page of the *Dallas Morning News,* North Texas's major newspaper, contains the most current events listings, as well as restaurant, movie, music, and show reviews for both Dallas and Fort Worth. It even has a shopping blog that promises the inside guide to the best local finds and deals.
- **MySanAntonio.com:** The website of the city's only mainstream newspaper, the *San Antonio Express-News,* not only provides the daily news, but also links to local businesses such as dry cleaners and florists (via its Power Pages) and to movie, nightlife, and dining listings and reviews.

- **Austin 360** (www.austin360.com): Movie times, traffic reports, restaurant picks, homes, jobs, cars. . . . This site, sponsored in part by the *Austin-American Statesman,* the city's main newspaper, is a one-stop clicking center for a variety of essentials. It's easy to navigate, too.
- **Texas fun:** We all know the Internet's best for purely personal and marginal interests, so check out these sites once you're done with your trip planning. Visit **www.texascooking.com** for authentic Texas cooking, including recipes and discussions of mysteries such as the Texas fruitcake subculture conspiracy. Then there's **www.texascooking.com/notable.htm**: Which is the best three in a row? Morgan Fairchild, Farrah Fawcett, and Freddy Fender, or George "Spanky" McFarland of "Our Gang," Larry McMurtry, and Meat Loaf?

2

Planning Your Trip to Texas

by Neil E. Schlecht

As everyone knows, Texas is big—really big. For travelers there isn't just a lot of ground to cover, but a vast number of things to do and places to see, as well as varieties of climate, terrain, and even cultures. Depending on where you choose to go, you can experience an Old West adventure, a relaxing (or rowdy) trip to the beach, some of America's finest museums, first-class shopping and dining, a rugged and remote national park, or home-grown live music. This chapter gives you the information you need to get started.

1 The Regions in Brief

You can plan your trip to Texas in a couple of ways. If you're interested in a particular activity, such as birding, you might choose two or three locations and divide your time among them. Conversely, you could first select a destination, such as one of the state's major cities or national parks, and then decide what to do while you're there.

This book is organized geographically, and because this is such a large state many visitors will limit their Texas vacation to one or two regions. We've summarized our coverage of the state to help you decide what kind of Texas experience you want to have.

For other suggestions on ways to spend your time, please see the chapter "Suggested Texas Itineraries in Texas," which begins on p. 63.

THE DALLAS–FORT WORTH METROPLEX Made famous by a TV show about a Texas oil family and a football team, and infamous by the assassination of JFK, Dallas is a center of commerce, home to headquarters for numerous banking, insurance, and other businesses. Big D, as it's known to locals, is one of the most sophisticated cities in Texas, with excellent restaurants, glitzy shopping, swank hotels, and a continually expanding arts scene. Dallas's unpretentious sister, Fort Worth, is equal parts Old West and "Museum Capital of the Southwest." Longhorns still rumble through the Stockyards National Historic District, while the city attracts art lovers to its top-notch museums. Both cities make good bases for outdoor recreation, children's activities, and professional sports outings; the city of Arlington, sandwiched between Dallas and Fort Worth, is home to several theme parks and the Texas Rangers baseball team.

HOUSTON & EAST TEXAS The state's largest city (and the fourth most populous city in the United States), Houston is the heart of the nation's oil and gas industry. Although not considered a primary tourist destination, Houston offers an abundance of attractions, including several excellent museums, performing arts such as the city's outstanding symphony orchestra, and a variety of outdoor activities. NASA's Johnson Space Center made Houston famous and is the city's most popular attraction. Nearby Galveston combines small-town easiness with a good mix of museums and children's activities, plus beaches that draw hordes of springbreakers and families throughout the warm months. East Texas, along the Louisiana border, is a prime destination for anglers, boaters, and other outdoor recreationists.

THE TEXAS GULF COAST A world removed from the rest of the state, the coastal areas fronting the Gulf of Mexico feature beach activities as well as good boating and even some surfing (okay, it's no Hawaii, but you *can* surf here). The Texas Gulf Coast is among the nation's top bird-watching regions, and also offers superb fishing. You'll also find a handful of good museums and an active art scene.

SAN ANTONIO The most popular destination for vacationers, the delightful, Latin-inflected city of San Antonio hosts the most famous historic site in Texas: the Alamo, where in 1836 Davy Crockett and about 187 other Texas freedom fighters died at the hands of the much larger Mexican army. San Antonio also offers numerous other historic sites, a delightful River Walk, fine cultural attractions, and a madcap schedule of festivals that make it a popular party spot. West and north of the city, the Texas Hill Country is one of the prettiest areas of Texas, dotted with hills (of course!), lakes, rivers, wildflowers, and picturesque small towns with authentic Texas flavor. There are numerous historic inns, antiques stores, small museums, and opportunities for watersports and other outdoor activities.

AUSTIN The state capital, Austin is a laid-back but sophisticated and suddenly bustling, large city with a distinct personality—a little unusual, a bit intellectual, and a lot different from other Texas cities of its size. It's a place where you'll see bumper stickers that read "Keep Austin Weird," even though it's experienced a technology-based boom and a huge influx of money and new residents from California and elsewhere across the nation. In addition to museums, historic sites, and a wide range of outdoor activities, you'll find the best nightlife in the state, with live music practically everywhere, any night of the week—from country to blues to rock to swing. To the west, the Hill Country is easily accessible via day trips.

WEST TEXAS Though Texas is largely an urban state, those of us who grew up watching TV and movie Westerns, would be more likely to believe the plains of West Texas are the real Texas, a land of dusty roads, weathered cowboys, and huge cattle ranches. Although the shootouts are now staged and the cattle drives are by truck and rail, this region retains much of the small-town Old West flavor, and even the region's biggest city, El Paso, is in many ways just an overgrown cow town. The area's history comes alive at numerous museums and historic sites, such as the combination courtroom and saloon used in the late 1800s by Judge Roy Bean, the self-styled "Law West of the Pecos." West Texas also offers some surprises, such as 67,000-acre Lake Amistad, a national recreation area along the U.S.–Mexico border.

BIG BEND & GUADALUPE MOUNTAINS NATIONAL PARKS Among America's lesser-visited national parks, Big Bend and Guadalupe Mountains contain rugged mountain scenery the likes of which is found nowhere else in Texas, or even in surrounding states. There are spectacular and inspiring views from dizzying peaks, as well as hiking,

The Regions in Brief

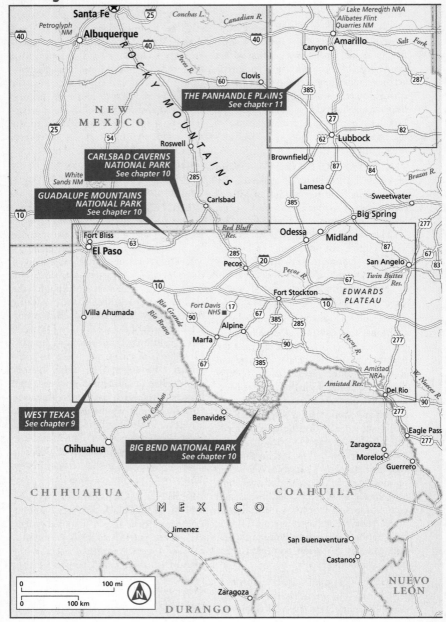

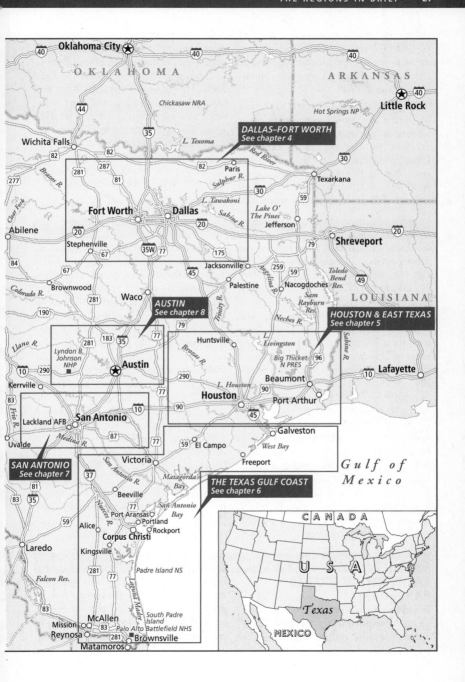

rafting, and other outdoor activities. We also include in this section a discussion of Carlsbad Caverns National Park, just over the state line in New Mexico, an easy side trip for those visiting Guadalupe Mountains National Park.

THE PANHANDLE PLAINS A mix of terrain and varied experiences await visitors to this vast, rugged region that occupies the northern reaches of Texas. Close to an entire day's drive from the coast, here you'll find small-town charm, good museums, fascinating historic sites, and one of the most outrageous steakhouses in Texas. The main cities—just big towns, actually—are Amarillo and Lubbock, and each provides comfortable lodging and good eats. The region also offers plenty to do and see, with watersports on Lake Meredith National Recreation Area, and hiking, horseback riding, and some of the area's most spectacular scenery at Palo Duro Canyon State Park. This is also home to a monument to rock-'n'-roll pioneer Buddy Holly and a display of old Cadillacs, noses buried in the ground with their unmistakable fins pointed skyward.

2 Visitor Information

Contact the **Texas Department of Transportation,** Travel Division, P. O. Box 141009, Austin, TX 78714-1009 (© **800/888-8TEX;** www.traveltex.com), for a free copy of the official state vacation guide, which includes a state map and describes attractions, activities, and lodgings throughout Texas. The Texas Department of Transportation also publishes the *Texas Accommodations Guide,* which is usually sent along with the official state vacation guide, or can be ordered separately by calling © **800/452-9292.**

The nonprofit **Historic Accommodations of Texas** (© **800/428-0368;** www.hat.org) offers a free directory describing well over 100 member bed-and-breakfasts, country inns, unique hotels, and guesthouses. You can also get lodging information from the **Texas Hotel & Motel Association** (© **512/474-2996;** www.texaslodging.com).

The Texas Department of Transportation maintains a dozen excellent **Texas Travel Information Centers** around the state, offering free maps, brochures, and one-on-one travel counseling. Locations are as follows: **Amarillo,** I-40 East; **Anthony,** I-10 at the New Mexico state line; **Austin,** 112 E. 11th St., at the Capitol complex; **Denison,** U.S. 75 at the Oklahoma state line; **Gainesville,** I-35 at the Oklahoma state line; **Harlingen,** U.S. 77 at U.S. 83; **Langtry,** off U.S. 90 on Tex. Loop 25; **Laredo,** I-35 North at U.S. 83; **Orange,** I-10 at the Louisiana state line; **Texarkana,** I-30 at the Arkansas state line; **Waskom,** I-20 at the Louisiana state line; and **Wichita Falls,** I-44 at U.S. 277/281. The centers are open daily from 8am to 5pm except on January 1, Easter Sunday, Thanksgiving Day, and December 24 and 25. For information, call © **800/452-9292.**

3 Entry Requirements & Customs

ENTRY REQUIREMENTS
PASSPORTS
For information on how to get a passport, go to **"Passports"** in the **"Fast Facts"** section of this chapter—the websites listed provide downloadable passport applications as well as the current fees for processing passport applications. For an up-to-date, country-by-country listing of passport requirements around the world,

go to the "Foreign Entry Requirement" Web page of the U.S. Department of State at **http://travel.state.gov**. International visitors can obtain a visa application at the same website.

VISAS

For information on how to get a visa, go to **"Visas"** in the **"Fast Facts"** section of this chapter.

The U.S. Department of State has a **Visa Waiver Program** allowing citizens of the following countries (at press time) to enter the United States without a visa for stays of up to 90 days: Andorra, Australia, Austria, Belgium, Brunei, Denmark, Finland, France, Germany, Iceland, Ireland, Italy, Japan, Liechtenstein, Luxembourg, Monaco, the Netherlands, New Zealand, Norway, Portugal, San Marino, Singapore, Slovenia, Spain, Sweden, Switzerland, and the United Kingdom. Citizens of these nations need only a valid passport and a round-trip air or cruise ticket upon arrival. If they first enter the United States, they may also visit Mexico, Canada, Bermuda, and/or the Caribbean islands and return to the United States without a visa, though visitors will need to show passports. Further information is available from any U.S. embassy or consulate. Canadian citizens may enter the United States without visas, but as of January 2007, they will need a passport.

Citizens of all other countries must have (1) a valid passport that expires at least 6 months later than the scheduled end of their visit to the United States, and (2) a tourist visa, which may be obtained without charge from any U.S. consulate.

MEDICAL REQUIREMENTS

Unless you're arriving from an area known to be suffering from an epidemic (particularly cholera or yellow fever), inoculations or vaccinations are not required for entry into the United States.

If you have a medical condition that requires **syringe-administered medications,** carry a valid signed prescription from your physician—the Federal Aviation Administration (FAA) no longer allows airline passengers to pack syringes in their carry-on baggage without documented proof of medical need. If you have a disease that requires treatment with **narcotics,** you should also carry documented proof with you—smuggling narcotics aboard a plane is a serious offense that carries severe penalties in the U.S.

For **HIV-positive visitors,** requirements for entering the United States are somewhat vague and change frequently. For up-to-the-minute information, contact **AIDSinfo** (© **800/448-0440** or 301/519-6616 outside the U.S.; www.aidsinfo.nih.gov) or the **Gay Men's Health Crisis** (© **212/367-1000;** www.gmhc.org).

CUSTOMS
WHAT YOU CAN BRING INTO TEXAS

Every visitor more than 21 years of age may bring in, free of duty, the following: (1) 1 liter of wine or hard liquor; (2) 200 cigarettes, 100 cigars (but not made in Cuba), or 3 pounds of smoking tobacco; and (3) $100 worth of gifts. These exemptions are offered to travelers who spend at least 72 hours in the United States and who have not claimed them within the preceding 6 months. It is altogether forbidden to bring into the country foodstuffs (particularly fruit, cooked meats, and canned goods) and plants (vegetables, seeds, tropical plants, and the like). Foreign tourists may carry in or out up to $10,000 in U.S. or foreign currency with no formalities; larger sums must be declared to U.S. Customs on entering or leaving, which includes filing form CM 4790. For details regarding U.S. Customs and Border Protection, consult your nearest U.S. embassy or consulate, or **U.S. Customs** (© 202/927-1770; www.customs.ustreas.gov).

WHAT YOU CAN TAKE HOME FROM TEXAS
Canadian Citizens

For a clear summary of Canadian rules, write for the booklet *I Declare,* issued by the **Canada Border Services Agency** (© 800/461-9999 in Canada, or 204/983-3500; **www.cbsa-asfc.gc.ca**).

U.K. Citizens

For information, contact **HM Customs & Excise** at © 0845/010-9000 (from outside the U.K., 020/8929-0152), or consult their website at **www.hmce.gov.uk**.

Australian Citizens

A helpful brochure available from Australian consulates or Customs offices is *Know Before You Go.* For more information, call the **Australian Customs Service** at © 1300/363-263, or log on to **www.customs.gov.au**.

New Zealand Citizens

Most questions are answered in a free pamphlet available at New Zealand consulates and Customs offices: *New Zealand Customs Guide for Travellers, Notice no. 4.* For more information, contact **New Zealand Customs,** The Customhouse, 17–21 Whitmore St., Box 2218, Wellington (© 04/473-6099 or 0800/428-786; **www.customs.govt.nz**).

4 Money

In general, Texas is not particularly expensive, especially compared to destinations on the East and West coasts. You'll find a wide range of prices for lodging and dining, and admission to most attractions is less than $10 (it's sometimes free, especially in the smaller towns). Prices in Dallas, Houston, and Austin now place them firmly in line with large Southern cities such as Atlanta and Miami. Smaller cities and rural areas are much less expensive, while resort areas such as Corpus Christi can be a bit more expensive, especially during winter holidays. Traveler's checks and credit cards are accepted at almost all hotels, restaurants, shops, and attractions, plus many grocery stores; and ATMs are practically everywhere.

ATMs

Nationwide, the easiest and best way to get cash away from home is from an ATM (automated teller machine), sometimes referred to as a "cash machine" or "cashpoint." The **Cirrus** (© 800/424-7787; www.mastercard.com) and **PLUS** (© 800/843-7587; www.visa.com) networks span the country; you can find them even in remote regions. Look at the back of your bank card to see which network you're on, then call or check online for ATM locations at your destination. Be sure you know your personal identification number (PIN) and daily withdrawal limit before you depart. *Note:* Remember that many banks impose a fee every time you use a card at another bank's ATM, and that fee can be higher for international transactions (up to $5 or more) than for domestic ones (where they're rarely more than $2). In addition, the bank from which you withdraw cash may charge its own fee. To compare banks' ATM fees within the U.S., use **www.bankrate.com**. For international withdrawal fees, ask your bank.

CREDIT CARDS & DEBIT CARDS

Credit cards are the most widely used form of payment in the United States: **Visa** (Barclaycard in Britain), **MasterCard** (EuroCard in Europe, Access in Britain, Chargex in Canada), **American Express, Diners Club,** and **Discover.**

They also provide a convenient record of all your expenses, and they generally offer relatively good exchange rates. You can withdraw cash advances from your credit cards at banks or ATMs, provided you know your PIN.

Visitors from outside the U.S. should inquire whether their bank assesses a 1% to 3% fee on charges incurred abroad.

It's highly recommended that you travel with at least one major credit card. You must have one to rent a car, and hotels and airlines usually require a credit card imprint as a deposit against expenses.

ATM cards with major credit card backing, known as **"debit cards,"** are now a commonly acceptable form of payment in most stores and restaurants. Debit cards draw money directly from your checking account. Some stores enable you to receive "cash back" on your debit-card purchases as well. The same is true at most U.S. post offices.

TRAVELER'S CHECKS

Traveler's checks are widely accepted in the U.S., but foreign visitors should make sure that they're denominated in U.S. dollars; foreign-currency checks are often difficult to exchange.

You can buy traveler's checks at most banks. Most are offered in denominations of $20, $50, $100, $500, and sometimes $1,000. Generally, you'll pay a service charge ranging from 1% to 4%.

The most popular traveler's checks are offered by **American Express** (© **800/807-6233;** © 800/221-7282 for card holders—this number accepts collect calls, offers service in several foreign languages, and exempts Amex gold and platinum cardholders from the 1% fee); **Visa** (© **800/732-1322**)—AAA members can obtain Visa checks for a $9.95 fee (for checks up to $1,500) at most AAA offices or by calling © **866/339-3378**—and **MasterCard** (© **800/223-9920**).

If you do choose to carry traveler's checks, keep a record of their serial numbers separate from your checks in the event that they are stolen or lost. You'll get a refund faster if you know the numbers.

5 When to Go

As would be expected in a state as big as Texas, climate varies, sometimes dramatically, by location; it can be snowing in one area of the state, such as Amarillo, while people are swimming at South Padre Island. High temperatures in the summer average in the 90s (30s Celsius) in most of the state, while average winter temperatures drop—sometimes much lower than you might expect—as you travel north. Southern Texas is known for its muggy summers, which make it feel hotter than it really is, and contrasts with the dryness of the West Texas deserts. The state's few mountainous areas have more extremes of temperatures, hitting the 80s and 90s (upper 20s and 30s Celsius) during the day, only to plummet into the 30s and 40s (single digits Celsius) at night. All areas of Texas get more sunshine than most other parts of the United States.

The beaches along the Gulf Coast are busiest in winter, although they're seldom really crowded. But unless you're a college kid looking for some rowdy spring-break action, you should avoid all resort areas, including the beaches and national parks, during March and early April.

Average Monthly High/Low Temperatures & Precipitation

	Jan	Feb	Mar	Apr	May	June	July	Aug	Sept	Oct	Nov	Dec
Dallas												
Temp. (°F)	54/33	59/37	68/46	76/55	83/63	92/70	97/74	96/74	88/67	79/56	67/45	58/36
Temp. (°C)	12/1	15/3	20/8	24/13	28/17	33/21	36/23	36/23	31/19	26/13	19/7	14/2
Precip. (in.)	1.6	1.9	2.4	3.1	4.3	2.4	1.7	1.8	2.9	2.8	2.0	1.5
Houston												
Temp. (°F)	62/43	65/45	75/53	79/61	85/67	90/73	92/75	92/75	88/71	81/61	72/53	65/45
Temp. (°C)	17/6	18/7	24/12	26/16	29/19	32/23	33/24	33/24	31/22	27/16	22/12	18/7
Precip. (in.)	3.2	2.8	2.4	2.5	4.4	5.3	3.9	3.8	4.9	3.4	3.6	3.0
San Antonio												
Temp. (°F)	61/38	66/41	74/50	80/58	85/66	92/73	95/75	95/74	89/69	82/59	72/49	63/41
Temp. (°C)	16/3	19/5	23/10	27/14	29/19	33/23	35/24	35/23	32/21	28/15	22/9	17/5
Precip. (in.)	1.2	1.5	1.2	2.0	3.5	3.0	1.2	1.8	2.6	2.6	2.3	1.0
Corpus Christi												
Temp. (°F)	65/45	69/48	76/55	82/63	86/69	90/73	93/75	93/75	90/72	84/64	76/56	68/48
Temp. (°C)	18/7	21/9	24/13	28/17	30/21	32/23	34/24	34/24	32/22	29/18	24/13	20/9
Precip. (in.)	1.7	2.0	0.9	1.7	3.3	3.4	2.4	3.3	5.5	3.0	1.6	1.3
Amarillo												
Temp. (°F)	49/21	53/26	62/33	72/43	79/52	88/61	92/66	89/64	82/56	73/45	60/32	50/24
Temp. (°C)	9/–6	12/–3	17/1	22/6	26/11	31/16	33/19	32/18	28/13	23/7	16/0	10/–4
Precip. (in.)	0.3	0.5	0.7	0.8	2.2	3.2	2.3	2.9	1.7	1.2	0.5	0.3

TEXAS CALENDAR OF EVENTS

January

AT&T Cotton Bowl Classic (& Parade), Dallas. The annual college football bowl game, somewhat less prestigious than it once was, but still important in pigskin circles. Call ℭ **214/634-7525.** January 1.

River Walk Mud Festival, San Antonio. Each year, the horseshoe bend of the San Antonio River Walk is drained for maintenance, and San Antonians cheer up by electing a king and queen to reign over such events as Mud Stunts Day and the Mud Pie Ball. Call ℭ **210/227-4262.** Mid-January.

Super Bull, Amarillo. Don't come expecting football—this is a bull-riding event at the Amarillo Civic Center. Call ℭ **800/692-1338** or 806/376-7767. Mid-January.

Southwestern Exposition and Livestock Show and Rodeo, Fort Worth. Fort Worth's famous rodeo and livestock show is the nation's oldest, drawing nearly a million people to Will Rogers Memorial Center for 30 rodeo performances. It's kicked off by the All-Western Parade, the biggest horse-drawn parade in the world. Call ℭ **817/877-2400.** Mid-January to early February.

February

Stock Show and Rodeo, San Antonio. San Antonio hosts more than 2 weeks of rodeo events, livestock judging, country-and-western bands, and carnivals at the SBC Center. Call ℭ **210/225-5851.** Early February.

Mardi Gras, Galveston. The city's biggest party of the year, with parades, masked balls, and a live-entertainment district around the Strand. Call ℭ **888/425-4753.** Late February to early March.

March

Houston Livestock Show and Rodeo, Houston. Billed as the largest event of its kind, the rodeo includes all the usual events like bull riding and calf roping, plus performances by famous country-and-western artists. A parade downtown kicks off the celebration. Call Ⓒ **713/791-9000.** March 1 to 20.

South by Southwest, Austin. The Austin Music Awards kick off this huge conference, with hundreds of concerts at more than two dozen city venues. Keynote speakers have included Johnny Cash. Call Ⓒ **512/467-7979.** Mid-March (during spring break at the University of Texas).

Dyeing o' the River Green and Pub Crawl, San Antonio. Are leprechauns responsible for turning the San Antonio River into the green River Shannon? Irish dance and music fill the Arneson River Theatre from the afternoon on. Call Ⓒ **210/227-4262.** March 17.

April

Texas Hill Country Wine and Food Festival, Austin. Book a month in advance for the cooking demonstrations; beer, wine, and food tastings; and celebrity chef dinners. For the food fair, just turn up hungry. Call Ⓒ **512/329-0770.** First weekend after Easter.

International Festival, Houston. This festival highlights the culture, food, music, and heritage of a different country every year. Call Ⓒ **713/926-6368.** Last 2 weekends in April.

San Jacinto Festival and Texas History Day, West Columbia. Highlights include a parade, talent show, arts and crafts show, and barbecue cook-off. The talent show, where you never know what's going to happen next, is the fun part. Call Ⓒ **800/938-4853** or 979/265-2508 or visit www.west columbiachamber.org. Mid-April.

Fiesta San Antonio, San Antonio. What started as a modest marking of Texas's independence more than 100 years ago is now a huge event, with an elaborately costumed royal court presiding over 10 days of revelry: parades, balls, food fests, sporting events, concerts, and art shows all over town. Call Ⓒ **877/SA-FIESTA** or 210/227-5191. Mid- to late April.

May

Art Car Parade and Ball, Houston. The parade of decorated cars is marvelous and hilarious and attracts participants from around the country. The ball—held in a large downtown parking garage—is guaranteed to be a spirited event. Call Ⓒ **713/926-6368.** Second weekend in May.

Tejano Conjunto Festival, San Antonio. This festival celebrates the lively and unique blend of Mexican and German music born in South Texas. The best conjunto musicians perform at the largest event of its kind in the world. Call Ⓒ **210/271-3151.** Mid-May.

Return of the Chili Queens, San Antonio. An annual tribute to chili, said to have originated in San Antonio, with music, dancing, crafts demonstrations, and, of course, chili aplenty. Bring the Tums. Call Ⓒ **210/207-8600.** Memorial Day weekend.

June

American Institute of Architects Sandcastle Competition, Galveston. More than 80 architectural and engineering firms from around the state build sand castles and sand sculptures, taking this pastime to new heights. Call Ⓒ **713/520-0155.** Early June.

Juneteenth Festival, statewide. News of the Emancipation Proclamation didn't reach Texas until June 19, 1865—nearly 3 years after Lincoln signed it. This day is celebrated with blues, jazz, and gospel music, family reunions, and a variety of events. Houston has a major celebration; call ℰ **713/284-8352** for more information. Weekend nearest June 19.

July

Gran Fiesta de Fort Worth, Fort Worth. An outdoor festival celebrating Texas's Hispanic culture with Latin music, art, food, and parades. Call ℰ **214/855-1881.** Third week in July.

Great Texas Mosquito Festival, Clute. A joyous celebration to divert everyone from the annoying pest. Call ℰ **800/938-4853** or 979/265-2508. Late July.

Miss Texas USA Pageant, Lubbock. This annual beauty contest takes place at Lubbock Municipal Coliseum and area hotels. Call ℰ **800/692-4035** or 806/747-5232. Last week in July.

August

***Austin Chronicle* Hot Sauce Festival,** Austin. The largest hot sauce contest in the world features more than 300 salsa entries, judged by celebrity chefs and food editors. The music at this super party is hot, too. Call ℰ **512/454-5766.** Last Sunday in August.

September

Marfa Lights Festival, Marfa. Celebration of the lights that inexplicably appear on the horizon just east of town. Expect street dances, live music, parades, and lots of food. Call ℰ **800/650-9696** or 915/729-4942. Labor Day weekend.

Grapefest, Fort Worth. Yes, Texas makes wine—some of it quite good. It flows freely at this, one of the country's biggest wine festivals. There's also live music and other entertainment. Call ℰ **817/410-3185.** Early September.

Fiestas Patrias, Houston. One of the largest community-sponsored parades in the Southwest celebrating Mexico's independence from Spain. Houston's several *ballet folklórico* troupes twirl their way through downtown streets in a pageant of color and traditional Mexican music. Call ℰ **713/926-2636.** Mid-September (around the 16th).

Pioneer Days, Fort Worth. A festival commemorating Fort Worth's early pioneer and cattle rancher heritage with country music, rodeos, and Wild West shows. Call ℰ **817/336-8791** or 817/625-7005. Mid-September.

Bayfest!, Corpus Christi. This huge festival fills Shoreline Drive from I-37 down to Bayfront Park with music, games, food, arts and crafts, and fireworks over the bay. Call ℰ **800/678-6232** or 361/881-1888. Late September.

State Fair of Texas, Dallas. The nation's biggest state fair, held at the fairgrounds built in 1936 in grand Art Deco style. Call ℰ **214/565-9931.** Late September to third week of October.

October

Commemorative Air Force Annual AIRSHO, Midland. Come see vintage aircraft on display and strutting their stuff in flight. Call ℰ **800/624-6435** or 915/683-3381. First weekend in October.

Wings over Houston Airshow, Houston. This thrilling event usually features displays of current military aircraft and performances of aerial acrobatics. Call ℰ **281/531-9461.** Mid-October.

Texas Jazz Festival, Corpus Christi. This free and popular festival attracts hundreds of big-name musicians from across the United States. Call ℰ **800/678-6232** or 361/881-1888. Mid- to late October.

Halloween, Austin. One hundred-thousand costumed revelers take over

7 blocks of historic 6th Street. Call ✆ **800/926-2282.** October 31.

November
South Padre Island Kite Festival, South Padre Island. What could be more fun than flying a kite above blue waters? Or prettier to watch? For all those still young at heart. Call ✆ **800/678-6232** or 361/881-1888. Early November.

Lighting Ceremony and River Walk Holiday Parade, San Antonio. Trees and bridges along the river are illuminated by some 80,000 lights, and Santa Claus arrives on a boat during this floating river parade. Call ✆ **210/227-4262.** Friday after Thanksgiving.

December
Christmas in the Stockyards, Fort Worth. Cowtown's classic Old West corner is lit up even more than usual for holiday shopping and caroling with a Texas accent. Call ✆ **817/626-7921.** Throughout December.

Fiestas Navideñas, San Antonio. The Mexican market hosts piñata parties, a blessing of the animals, and surprise visits from Pancho Claus. Call ✆ **210/207-8600.** Weekends in December.

Zilker Park Tree Lighting, Austin. The lighting of a magnificent 165-foot tree is followed by the Trail of Lights, a mile-long display of life-size holiday scenes. Call ✆ **512/499-6700.** Sundays through December 24.

Harbor Lights Celebration, Corpus Christi. The harbor is decked out for the holidays. There's an illuminated boat parade, fireworks, entertainment, and a visit from Santa Claus. Call ✆ **800/678-6232** or 361/881-1888. First weekend in December.

Dickens on the Strand, Galveston. This street party in the historic district of the city features revelers dressed up in Victorian costume. There are parades, performers, street vendors, and lots of entertainment. Call ✆ **409/765-7834.** First weekend in December.

Las Posadas, San Antonio. Children carrying candles lead a procession along the river, reenacting the search for lodging in a moving multifaith rendition of the Christmas story. Call ✆ **210/224-6163.** Second Sunday in December.

6 Travel Insurance

TRAVEL INSURANCE AT A GLANCE
Texas may have a rough-and-tumble reputation, but unless you're planning an extended stay at a dude ranch, where you'll learn to ride a bucking bronco, or be doing extreme sports, there's no particular reason why you'd need specific insurance for traveling to Texas.

The cost of travel insurance varies widely, depending on the cost and length of your trip, your age and health, and the type of trip you're taking, but expect to pay between 5% and 8% of the vacation itself. You can get estimates from various providers through **InsureMyTrip.com.** Enter your trip cost and dates, your age, and other information, for prices from more than a dozen companies.

TRIP-CANCELLATION INSURANCE
Trip-cancellation insurance will help retrieve your money if you have to back out of a trip or depart early, or if your travel supplier goes bankrupt. Permissible reasons for trip cancellation can range from sickness to natural disasters to the Department of State declaring a destination unsafe for travel.

For more information, contact one of the following recommended insurers: **Access America** (© 866/807-3982; www.accessamerica.com); **Travel Guard International** (© 800/826-4919; www.travelguard.com); **Travel Insured International** (© 800/243-3174; www.travelinsured.com); or **Travelex Insurance Services** (© 888/457-4602; www.travelexinsurance.com).

MEDICAL INSURANCE

Although it's not required of travelers, health insurance is highly recommended. Most health insurance policies cover you if you get sick away from home—but verify that you're covered before you depart, particularly if you're insured by an HMO.

International visitors should note that unlike many European countries, the United States does not usually offer free or low-cost medical care to its citizens or visitors. Doctors and hospitals are expensive, and in most cases will require advance payment or proof of coverage before they render their services. Good policies will cover the costs of an accident, repatriation, or death. Packages such as **Europ Assistance's "Worldwide Healthcare Plan"** are sold by European automobile clubs and travel agencies at attractive rates. **Worldwide Assistance Services, Inc.** (© 800/777-8710; www.worldwideassistance.com) is the agent for Europ Assistance in the United States.

Though lack of health insurance may prevent you from being admitted to a hospital in nonemergencies, don't worry about being left on a street corner to die: The American way is to fix you now and bill the living daylights out of you later.

INSURANCE FOR BRITISH TRAVELERS Most big travel agents offer their own insurance and will probably try to sell you their package when you book a holiday. Think before you sign. **Britain's Consumers' Association** recommends that you insist on seeing the policy and reading the fine print before buying travel insurance. **The Association of British Insurers** (© 020/7600-3333; www.abi.org.uk) gives advice by phone and publishes *Holiday Insurance*, a free guide to policy provisions and prices. You might also shop around for better deals: Try **Columbus Direct** (© 0870/033-9988; www.columbusdirect.net).

INSURANCE FOR CANADIAN TRAVELERS Canadians should check with their provincial health plan offices or call **Health Canada** (© 866/225-0709; www.hc-sc.gc.ca) to find out the extent of their coverage and what documentation and receipts they must take home in case they are treated in the United States.

LOST-LUGGAGE INSURANCE

On flights within the U.S., checked baggage is covered up to $2,500 per ticketed passenger. On flights outside the U.S. (and on U.S. portions of international trips), baggage coverage is limited to approximately $9.07 per pound, up to approximately $635 per checked bag. If you plan to check items more valuable than what's covered by the standard liability, see if your homeowner's policy covers your valuables, get baggage insurance as part of your comprehensive travel-insurance package, or buy Travel Guard's "BagTrak" product.

If your luggage is lost, immediately file a lost-luggage claim at the airport, detailing the luggage contents. Most airlines require that you report delayed, damaged, or lost baggage within 4 hours of arrival. The airlines are required to deliver luggage, once found, directly to your house or destination free of charge.

7 Health & Safety

STAYING HEALTHY

Vacationers in Texas generally need take no extra health precautions than they would at home. It is worth noting, however, that those hiking in the drier parts of the state, such as in the deserts of West Texas or the mountains of Big Bend and Guadalupe Mountains national parks, should carry more water than they think they will need, and drink it.

When heading into the great outdoors, keep in mind that Texas has a large number of poisonous snakes and insects, and you should be very careful where you put your hands and feet. If you're hiking, stick to designated hiking areas, stay on established trails, and carry rain gear. When boating, be sure to wear a life jacket.

COMMON AILMENTS

DIETARY RED FLAGS While Tex-Mex cuisine is generally milder than Mexican cooking, travelers who are unfamiliar with hot chiles and jalapeños or who have weak stomachs or ulcers should proceed with caution when eating Mexican food. Tap water is potable throughout the state, but not to everyone's liking. Texans are big meat eaters in general, but in larger cities, vegetarian-friendly restaurants are widely available, especially in more progressive cities like Austin.

BUGS, BITES & OTHER WILDLIFE CONCERNS If you venture into the West Texas desert, snakes, spiders, and scorpions could be an issue, so it would be wise to carry appropriate medicines, especially if camping.

SUN/ELEMENTS/EXTREME WEATHER EXPOSURE Perhaps the biggest health concern in Texas, with its big sky and blistering heat, is sun exposure. Travelers should make every attempt to protect themselves, including headgear, sunscreen, and sufficient hydration.

GENERAL AVAILABILITY OF HEALTH CARE

Unless you're camping out in remote Big Bend and other areas, OTC medicines are widely available, as are generic equivalents of common prescription drugs.

Contact the **International Association for Medical Assistance to Travelers (IAMAT; © 716/754-4883,** or 416/652-0137 in Canada; www.iamat.org) for tips on travel and health concerns and for lists of doctors. The United States **Centers for Disease Control and Prevention (© 800/311-3435;** www.cdc.gov) provides up-to-date information on health hazards by region or country and offers tips on food safety. The website **www.tripprep.com**, sponsored by a consortium of travel medicine practitioners, may also offer helpful advice on traveling abroad. You can find listings of reliable clinics overseas at the **International Society of Travel Medicine** (www.istm.org).

WHAT TO DO IF YOU GET SICK AWAY FROM HOME

Most reliable health-care plans provide coverage if you get sick away from home. If you get sick in Texas, consider asking your hotel concierge to recommend a local doctor—even his or her own. You can also try the emergency room at a local hospital; many have walk-in clinics for emergency cases that are not life-threatening.

We list **hospitals** and **emergency numbers** under "Fast Facts," p. 56.

If you suffer from a chronic illness, consult your doctor before your departure. Pack **prescription medications** in your carry-on luggage, and carry them in their original containers, with pharmacy labels—otherwise they won't make it through airport security. Visitors from outside the U.S. should carry generic names of prescription drugs. For U.S. travelers, most reliable health-care plans provide coverage if you get sick away from home. Foreign visitors may have to pay all medical costs upfront and be reimbursed later. See "Medical Insurance," under "Travel Insurance," above.

STAYING SAFE

Most areas of Texas are as safe as any other part of the U.S. However, large cities such as Houston, Dallas, and San Antonio have their share of big-city crime (a few years back downtown Houston had a particularly dangerous reputation), as do border towns such as El Paso. Drug smuggling is common along the U.S.–Mexico border. To protect yourself from stumbling into a drug transaction or police raid, avoid hiking alone in isolated areas along the border and stay in the major tourist areas in border towns.

If you're in doubt about which neighborhoods are safe, don't hesitate to make inquiries with the hotel front desk staff or the local tourist office.

DEALING WITH DISCRIMINATION

Texas has a lamentable history of race-related incidents (like the 1998 murder of

James Byrd, Jr., in Jasper), and bigoted and racist opinions are still found in some small towns and among some less cosmopolitan Texans. Regrettably, discrimination is still occasionally directed toward African-Americans and Hispanics (and more recently, people of Middle Eastern descent or appearance), as well as openly gay travelers. However, most travelers of color and ethnicity, and gays and lesbians, will likely encounter few (if any) problems on a trip to Texas. African-American travelers might want to be cautious, however, when traveling through the small towns of East Texas; see "Race Relations in East Texas" on p. 202. Also, around border towns, travelers of Hispanic descent or appearance may find that they are stopped by the border patrol more frequently than non-Hispanics, so be sure to carry a current, government-issued picture ID. See also "Gay & Lesbian Travelers," below.

8 Specialized Travel Resources

TRAVELERS WITH DISABILITIES

Most disabilities shouldn't stop anyone from traveling. There are more options and resources out there than ever before. Travelers with physical disabilities should find Texas relatively easy to explore. Although some older hotels and restaurants might not be wheelchair-accessible, newer properties, plus most major parks and historical monuments, are. To be on the safe side, call ahead to make sure facilities are suitable.

The **Golden Access Passport** gives visually impaired or permanently disabled persons (regardless of age) free lifetime entrance to all properties administered by the National Park Service, the U.S. Fish and Wildlife Service, the U.S. Forest Service, the U.S. Army Corps of Engineers,

the Bureau of Land Management, and the Tennessee Valley Authority. This may include national parks, monuments, historic sites, recreation areas, and national wildlife refuges.

You may pick up a Golden Access Passport at any NPS entrance fee area by showing proof of medically determined disability and eligibility for benefits under federal law. Besides free entry, the Golden Access Passport also offers a 50% discount on federal-use fees charged for such facilities as camping, swimming, parking, boat launching, and tours. For more information, go to www.nps.gov/fees_passes.htm or call © **888/467-2757.**

Many travel agencies offer customized tours and itineraries for travelers with disabilities. Among them are **Flying Wheels**

Travel (© 507/451-5005; www.flying wheelstravel.com); **Access-Able Travel Source** (© 303/232-2979; www.access-able.com); and **Accessible Journeys** (© 800/846-4537 or 610/521-0339; www.disabilitytravel.com). **Avis Rent a Car** has an "Avis Access" program that offers such services as a dedicated 24-hour toll-free number (© **888/879-4273**) for customers with special travel needs; special car features such as swivel seats, spinner knobs, and hand controls; and accessible bus service.

Organizations that offer assistance to disabled travelers include **MossRehab** (www.mossresourcenet.org); the **American Foundation for the Blind (AFB;** © **800/232-5463;** www.afb.org); and **SATH** (Society for Accessible Travel & Hospitality; © **212/447-7284;** www.sath.org). **AirAmbulanceCard.com** is now partnered with SATH and allows you to preselect top-notch hospitals in case of an emergency.

Check out the quarterly magazine *Emerging Horizons* (www.emerging horizons.com) and *Open World* magazine, published by SATH.

GAY & LESBIAN TRAVELERS

Texas is one of only four states (the others are Missouri, Kansas, and Oklahoma) that criminalize homosexual activity, with an antisodomy law that dates to the late 1800s. That law is occasionally enforced (two Houston men were arrested in 1998, spent a day in jail, and paid fines), but a gay-rights group is working to have the law overturned.

Despite the official policy, most gay and lesbian travelers will find they are treated just like any other visitors to Texas, as Texans generally have a "live and let live" attitude. There are vibrant gay and lesbian communities in all of the larger cities, particularly Austin, Dallas, and Houston. A gay-and lesbian-oriented weekly newspaper, *Texas Triangle* (© 877/903-8407 or

512/476-0576; www.txtnewsmagazine. com) is available at newsstands with state and national news, features, nightlife listings, a calendar of events, and classified ads. Information is also available from the **Lesbian/Gay Rights Lobby of Texas,** P.O. Box 2340, Austin, TX 78768 (© 512/474-5475; www.lgrl.org).

The **International Gay and Lesbian Travel Association (IGLTA;** © 800/448-8550 or 954/776-2626; www.iglta. org) is the trade association for the gay and lesbian travel industry, and offers an online directory of gay- and lesbian-friendly travel businesses; go to their website and click on "Members."

Many agencies offer tours and travel itineraries specifically for gay and lesbian travelers. Among them are **Above and Beyond Tours** (© 800/397-2681; www.abovebeyondtours.com); **Now, Voyager** (© **800/255-6951;** www.nowvoyager. com); and Olivia **Cruises & Resorts** (© **800/631-6277;** www.olivia.com).

Gay.com Travel (© 800/929-2268 or 415/644-8044; www.gay.com/travel or www.outandabout.com) is an excellent online successor to the popular *Out & About* print magazine. It provides regularly updated information about gay-owned, gay-oriented, and gay-friendly lodging, dining, sightseeing, nightlife, and shopping establishments in every important destination worldwide.

SENIOR TRAVEL

Many Texas hotels and motels offer discounts to seniors (especially if you're carrying an AARP card; see below), and an increasing number of restaurants, attractions, and public transportation systems do so as well.

Members of **AARP** (formerly known as the American Association of Retired Persons), 601 E St. NW, Washington, DC 20049 (© **888/687-2277;** www. aarp.org), often get discounts on hotels, airfares, and car rentals. AARP offers members a wide range of benefits, including *AARP: The Magazine* and a monthly newsletter. Anyone over 50 can join.

The **U.S. National Park Service** offers a **Golden Age Passport** that gives seniors 62 years or older lifetime entrance to properties managed by the National Park Service for a one-time processing fee of $10, which must be paid in person at any NPS facility that charges an entrance fee. Besides free entry, a Golden Age Passport also offers a 50% discount on federal use fees charged for such facilities as camping, swimming, parking, boat launching, and tours. For more information, click onto www.nps.gov/fees_passes.htm or call ℂ **888/467-2757.**

Many reliable agencies and organizations target the 50-plus market. **Elderhostel** (ℂ **877/426-8056;** www.elderhostel. org) arranges study programs for those ages 55 and older. Recommended publications offering travel resources and discounts for seniors include the quarterly magazine *Travel 50 & Beyond* (www. travel50andbeyond.com); *Travel Unlimited: Uncommon Adventures for the Mature Traveler* (Avalon); *101 Tips for Mature Travelers,* available from Grand Circle Travel (ℂ **800/221-2610** or 617/ 350-7500; www.gct.com); and *Unbelievably Good Deals and Great Adventures That You Absolutely Can't Get Unless You're Over 50* (McGraw-Hill), by Joann Rattner Heilman.

FAMILY TRAVEL

Texas is a family-friendly state, with lots of things for all ages to enjoy. Throughout this book you'll find numerous attractions, lodgings, and even restaurants that are especially well suited to kids. These include places such as the Fort Worth Zoo, Six Flags Over Texas in Arlington, the Children's Museum of Houston, and the Zilker Zephyr Miniature Trail in Austin. See "Best Of" selections in chapter 1, as well as "Just for Kids" sightseeing sections in destination chapters.

To locate accommodations, restaurants, and attractions that are particularly kid-friendly, refer to the "Kids" icon throughout this guide.

Recommended family travel websites include **Family Travel Forum** (www. familytravelforum.com), a comprehensive site that offers customized trip planning; **Family Travel Network** (www. familytravelnetwork.com), an award-winning site that offers travel features, deals, and tips; and **Family Travel Files** (www. thefamilytravelfiles.com), which offers an online magazine and a directory of off-the-beaten-path tours and tour operators for families.

STUDENT TRAVEL

The top spots for college students heading to Texas for spring break are **South Padre Island** for sun and fun and, to a lesser extent, **Big Bend National Park** for serious hiking, but any of the beach areas and parks are popular.

A valid student ID will often qualify students for discounts on airfare, accommodations, entry to museums, cultural events, movies, and more. **STA Travel** (ℂ **800/781-4040** in North America; www.sta.com or www.statravel.com). If you're no longer a student but are still younger than 26, you can get an **International Youth Travel Card (IYTC)** from **STA Travel** (see above), which entitles you to some discounts (but not on museum admissions). **Travel CUTS** (ℂ **800/667-2887** or 416/614-2887; www.travelcuts.com) offers similar services for both Canadians and U.S. residents. Irish students may prefer to turn to **USIT** (ℂ **01/602-1600;** www.usitnow. ie), an Ireland-based specialist in student, youth, and independent travel.

ECO-TOURISM

Much of Texas's eco-tourism activities are still confined to do-it-yourself trips to state and national parks (with Big Bend the number-one attraction). However, birding is of growing interest, particularly along the Gulf Coast and in other parts of South Texas, and some travel operators now offer birding trips.

Texas Parks and Wildlife devotes part of its literature and website to **"Great Texas Wildlife Trails"** (www.tpwd.state. tx.us/huntwild/wild/wildlife_trails) that include birding trails. Additionally, the **World Birding Center** (www.world birdingcenter.org) is located in the lower Rio Grande Valley, and it offers a wealth of information on birding events, tours, and sites, such as the 50-acre **South Padre Island Birding and Nature Center** (✆ **956/761-3005**). Another resource is www.traveltex.com, where you can search under "Activities" for a mixed bag of "nature & outdoors" events, tours, and activities across the state.

You can find other eco-friendly travel tips, statistics, and touring companies and associations—listed by destination under "Travel Choice"—at the TIES website, **www.ecotourism.org**. Ecotravel.com is part online magazine and part eco-directory that lets you search for touring companies in several categories (water-based, land-based, spiritually oriented, and so on). Also check out **Conservation International** (www.conservation.org)—which, with *National Geographic Traveler,* annually presents **World Legacy Awards** to those travel tour operators, businesses, organizations, and places that have made a significant contribution to sustainable tourism.

VEGETARIAN TRAVEL

While carnivorous Texans are famous for their cattle raising, vegetarian options, while perhaps not as prevalent as in the most progressive states, are available in all large cities. It is particularly conspicuous in Austin, the largest college town in Texas and the state's most progressive-leaning city (ranked by GoVeg.com as America's eighth most vegetarian-friendly large city, it is home to the ever-growing chain Whole Foods). Some helpful websites include **www.vegetarianusa.com/city/ Texas.html**, which includes a list of health-food stores and vegetarian restaurants; **www.ecomall.com/vegi/tex.htm**, which contains a smattering of restaurants across the state; and the general sites **VegDining.com** and **VegCooking.com**.

TRAVELING WITH PETS

If you're considering traveling to Texas with your pet, websites worth consulting include **www.petswelcome.com, www. pettravel.com,** and **www.travelpets. com.** Note that all Motel 6 motels accept pets. Throughout this book, we've noted the lodgings that have an explicit policy of accepting pets. Some properties require you to pay a fee or damage deposit in advance, and most insist they be notified at check-in that you have a pet.

Be aware, however, that national parks and monuments and other federal lands administered by the National Park Service are not pet-friendly. Dogs are generally prohibited on hiking trails, must always be leashed, and in some cases cannot be taken more than 100 feet from established roads. On the other hand, U.S. Forest Service and Bureau of Land Management (BLM) areas, as well as many state parks, are pro-pet, allowing dogs on trails and just about everywhere except inside buildings. State parks require that dogs be leashed; regulations in national forests and BLM lands are generally looser.

Just as people need extra water in the desert, so do pets. We especially like those clever little no-spill pet water bowls available in pet stores (or online at www.vet vax.com). Also keep in mind that many trails are rough, and jagged rocks can cut the pads on your dog's feet. One final note: Never leave a dog or cat inside a closed car parked in the sun, which can literally be a killer in Texas. The car heats up more quickly than you'd think—so don't do it, even for a minute.

9 Planning Your Trip Online

SURFING FOR AIRFARE

The most popular online travel agencies are **Travelocity** (www.travelocity.com, or www.travelocity.co.uk), **Expedia.com** (www.expedia.com, www.expedia.co.uk, or www.expedia.ca), and **Orbitz** (www.orbitz.com).

In addition, most airlines now offer online-only fares that even their phone agents know nothing about. Other helpful websites for booking airline tickets online include

- www.biddingfortravel.com
- www.cheapflights.com
- www.hotwire.com
- www.kayak.com
- www.lastminutetravel.com
- www.opodo.co.uk
- www.priceline.com
- www.sidestep.com
- www.site59.com
- www.smartertravel.com

SURFING FOR HOTELS

In addition to **Travelocity, Expedia.com, Orbitz, Priceline,** and **Hotwire** (see above), the following websites will help you with booking hotel rooms online.

- www.hotels.com
- www.quickbook.com
- www.travelaxe.net
- www.travelweb.com
- www.tripadvisor.com

It's a good idea to **get a confirmation number** and **make a printout** of any online booking transaction.

SURFING FOR RENTAL CARS

For booking rental cars online, the best deals are usually found at rental-car company websites, although all the major online travel agencies also offer rental-car reservations services. Priceline and Hotwire work well for rental cars, too; the only "mystery" is which major rental company you get, and for most travelers the difference between Hertz, Avis, and Budget is negligible.

TRAVEL BLOGS & TRAVELOGUES

The ever-expanding blogosphere is filled with blogs on things great and public as well as obscure and personal, and weblogs originating in Texas are no exception. To read a few blogs about Texas, have a look at the directory of Texas-related blogs found at www.technorati.com/blogs/ Texas and http://dir.blogflux.com/state/ texas.html. Unsurprisingly, you'll find several blogs dedicated to Texas football and real estate, but you'll also find one dedicated to the "musings of a real Texas cowgirl" (http://realtexascowgirl.blogspot. com) and another, "Grits for Breakfast" (http://gritsforbreakfast.blogspot.com), that investigates the murky world of Texas justice. Proudly Texan, with the Stetson and the rifle to prove it, is "Big White Hat: (http://bigwhitehat.com). A guide to political blogs in Texas can be found at: www.dallasblog.com/guest-commentary/2006/5/7/a-guide-to-texas-blogs-left-and-right-by-vince-leibowitz. html.

OTHER TRAVEL-RELATED BLOGS

- www.gridskipper.com
- www.salon.com/wanderlust
- www.travelblog.com
- www.travelblog.org
- www.worldhum.com
- www.writtenroad.com

Frommers.com: The Complete Travel Resource

For an excellent travel-planning resource, we highly recommend **Frommers.com** (www.frommers.com), voted Best Travel Site by *PC Magazine*. We're a little biased, of course, but we guarantee that you'll find the travel tips, reviews, monthly vacation giveaways, bookstore, and online-booking capabilities thoroughly indispensable. Among the special features are our popular **Destinations** section, where you'll get expert travel tips, hotel and dining recommendations, and advice on the sights to see for more than 3,500 destinations around the globe; the **Frommers.com Newsletter,** with the latest deals, travel trends, and money-saving secrets; our **Community** area featuring **Message Boards,** where Frommer's readers post queries and share advice (sometimes even our authors show up to answer questions); and our **Photo Center,** where you can post and share vacation tips. When your research is done, the **Online Reservations System** (www.frommers.com/book_a_trip) takes you to Frommer's preferred online partners for booking your vacation at affordable prices.

10 The 21st-Century Traveler

INTERNET ACCESS AWAY FROM HOME
WITHOUT YOUR OWN COMPUTER

To find cybercafes in your destination, check **www.cybercaptive.com** and **www.cybercafe.com**.

Aside from formal cybercafes, most **youth hostels** and **public libraries** offer Internet access. Avoid **hotel business centers** unless you're willing to pay exorbitant rates.

Most major airports now have **Internet kiosks** scattered throughout their gates. These give you basic Web access for a per-minute fee that's usually higher than cybercafe prices.

WITH YOUR OWN COMPUTER

More and more hotels, cafes, and retailers are signing on as Wi-Fi (wireless fidelity) "hotspots." Mac owners have their own networking technology, Apple AirPort. **T-Mobile Hotspot** (www.t-mobile.com/hotspot) serves up wireless connections at

more than 1,000 Starbucks coffee shops nationwide. **Boingo** (www.boingo.com) and **Wayport** (www.wayport.com) have set up networks in airports and high-class hotel lobbies. iPass providers (see below) also give you access to a few hundred wireless hotel lobby setups. To locate other hotspots that provide **free wireless networks** in cities around the world, go to **www.personaltelco.net/index.cgi/WirelessCommunities**.

For dial-up access, most business-class hotels in the U.S. offer dataports for laptop modems, and a few thousand hotels in the U.S. and Europe now offer free high-speed Internet access. Wherever you go, bring a **connection kit** of the right power and phone adapters, a spare phone cord, and a spare Ethernet network cable—or find out whether your hotel supplies them to guests.

For information on electrical currency conversions, see "Electricity," in the "Fast Facts" section at the end of this chapter.

CELLPHONE USE IN THE U.S.

Just because your cellphone works at home doesn't mean it'll work everywhere in the U.S. (thanks to our nation's fragmented cellphone system). It's a good bet that your phone will work in major cities, but take a look at your wireless company's coverage map on its website before heading out; T-Mobile, Sprint, and Nextel are particularly weak in rural areas. If you need to stay in touch at a destination where you know your phone won't work, **rent** a phone that does from **InTouch USA** (© **800/872-7626;** www.intouch global.com) or a rental car location, but beware: You'll pay $1 a minute or more for airtime.

If you're venturing deep into national parks, you may want to consider renting a **satellite phone** ("satphones"). It's different from a cellphone in that it connects to satellites rather than ground-based towers.

Unfortunately, you'll pay at least $2 per minute to use the phone, and it only works where you can see the horizon (that is, usually not indoors). In North America, you can rent Iridium satellite phones from **RoadPost** (www.roadpost.com; © **888/290-1606** or 905/272-5665). InTouch USA (see above) offers a wider range of satphones but at higher rates.

If you're not from the U.S., you'll be appalled at the poor reach of our **GSM (Global System for Mobiles) wireless network,** which is used by much of the rest of the world. Your phone will probably work in most major U.S. cities; it definitely won't work in many rural areas (to see where GSM phones work in the U.S., check out www.t-mobile.com/coverage/national_popup.asp). And you may or may not be able to send SMS (text messaging) home.

11 Getting There

BY PLANE

Several airports accommodate commercial service in Texas, and choosing which one to fly to will depend on which particular airline you want to use and the part of Texas you plan to visit. The state's major airports are **Dallas/Fort Worth International (DFW), El Paso International (ELP), George Bush Intercontinental (IAH),** and **William P. Hobby (HOU)** in Houston, and **San Antonio International (SAT).** Major airlines include **Air Canada** (© 888/247-2262; www.aircanada.ca), **American** (© 800/433-7300; www.aa.com; hub is DFW), **America West** (© 800/235-9292; www.americawest.com), **British Airways** (© 800/247-9297; www.britishairways.com), **Continental** (© 800/525-0280; www.continental.com), **Delta** (© 800/221-1212; www.delta.com), **Frontier** (© 800/432-1359; www.frontierairlines.com), **Midwest Airlines** (© 800/452-2022; www.midwestairlines.com),

Northwest (© 800/225-2525; www.nwa.com), **Southwest** (© 800/435-9792; www.southwest.com), **United** (© 800/864-8331; www.united.com), and **US Airways** (© 800/428-4322; www.usairways.com).

IMMIGRATION & CUSTOMS CLEARANCE Foreign visitors arriving by air, no matter what the port of entry, should cultivate patience and resignation before setting foot on U.S. soil. Clearing immigration control can take as long as 2 hours. People traveling by air from Canada, Bermuda, and certain Caribbean countries can sometimes clear Customs and Immigration at the point of departure, which is much faster.

BY CAR

If you're planning a road trip, it's a good idea to join the **American Automobile Association** (© **800/336-4357;** www.aaa.com). In Texas, AAA regional headquarters is at 6555 N. State Hwy. 161,

(Tips) Prepare to Be Fingerprinted

As of January 2004, many international visitors traveling on visas to the United States will be photographed and fingerprinted at Customs in a new program created by the Department of Homeland Security called **US-VISIT**. Non-U.S. citizens arriving at airports and on cruise ships must undergo an instant background check as part of the government's efforts to deter terrorism by verifying the identity of incoming and outgoing visitors. Exempt from the extra scrutiny are visitors entering by land or those (mostly in Europe; see p. 29) that don't require a visa for short-term visits. For more information, go to the Homeland Security website at **www.dhs.gov/dhspublic**.

Irving (© **469/221-6006**); there are also offices in many other cities, including Amarillo, Austin, Dallas, Houston, and El Paso. Members can get excellent maps, tour guides, and emergency road service; they'll also help you plan an exact itinerary. Members can get free emergency road service by calling **AAA's emergency number** (© **800/AAA-HELP**).

More than 3,000 miles of interstate highways crisscross this huge state, connecting four major urban areas to each other and to cities in nearby states. Some relevant mileages: Houston to New Orleans, 350 miles; Houston to Phoenix, 1,180 miles; Dallas to Little Rock, 320 miles; Dallas to Kansas City, 550 miles; and Dallas to Denver, 880 miles.

BY TRAIN

Amtrak (© **800/USA-RAIL;** www. amtrak.com) has several routes through Texas. The **Sunset Limited** has stops at Beaumont/Port Arthur, Houston, San Antonio, Del Rio, Sanderson, Alpine, and El Paso on its New Orleans–to–Los Angeles run; the **Heartland Flyer** travels from Oklahoma City to Fort Worth (where it connects with the Texas Eagle); and the **Texas Eagle,** which runs from Los Angeles to San Antonio (where you can connect with the Sunset Limited) and on to Chicago, with stops at El Paso, Austin, Dallas, and Fort Worth, among others.

12 Package Deals for Independent Travelers

Package tours are simply a way to buy the airfare, accommodations, and other elements of your trip (such as car rentals, airport transfers, and sometimes even activities) at the same time and often at discounted prices.

One good source of package deals is the airlines themselves. Most major airlines offer air/land packages, including **American Airlines Vacations** (© 800/ 321-2121; www.aavacations.com), **Delta Vacations** (© 800/221-6666; www.delta vacations.com), **Continental Airlines**

Vacations (© 800/301-3800; www.co vacations.com), and **United Vacations** (© 888/854-3899; www.unitedvacations. com). Several big **online travel agencies**—Expedia.com, Travelocity, Orbitz, Site59, and Lastminute.com— also do a brisk business in packages.

Travel packages are also listed in the travel section of your local Sunday newspaper. Or check ads in the national travel magazines such as *Arthur Frommer's Budget Travel Magazine, Travel & Leisure, National Geographic Traveler,* and *Condé Nast Traveler.*

13 Escorted General-Interest Tours

Escorted tours are structured group tours, with a group leader. The price usually includes everything from airfare to hotels, meals, tours, admission costs, and local transportation.

Gray Line Tours (© 800/803-5073; www.grayline.com), one of the largest tour operators in the world, organizes a number of escorted bus trips, package tours, and day trips in Dallas, Fort Worth, Austin, Houston/Galveston, San Antonio, and South Padre Island—though it's most active in Dallas and Fort Worth.

Sí Texas Tours, in Bandera, Texas (© 888/748-3927 or 830/460-4565; www.sitexastours.com), offers escorted tours to San Antonio, the Texas Hill Country, and South Texas.

Texas Wine Tours (© 877/839-9463; http://txwines.com) takes trips to 14 Hill Country wineries, including stops in Fredericksburg and occasional events in places such as Luckenbach. Wine tours in white stretch-limos are the focus of **TexasWine tours.com** (© 800/940-7007 or 512/329-7007; www.texaswinetours.com).

For adventure travel to Texas, check out **GORPtravel** (© 877/440-GORP; http://gorptravel.away.com), which offers Big Bend hiking, Rio Grande canoeing, and Hill Country and ranch horseback riding tours. See also the following section, "Special-Interest Trips."

At www.infohub.com/TRAVEL/SIT/sit_pages/Texas.html, you'll find links to a number of other themed trips (such as cycling the Hill Country).

Despite the fact that escorted tours require big deposits and predetermine hotels, restaurants, and itineraries, many people derive security and peace of mind from the structure they offer. Escorted tours—whether they're navigated by bus, motorcoach, train, or boat—let travelers sit back and enjoy the trip without having to drive or worry about details. They take you to the maximum number of sights in the minimum amount of time with the least amount of hassle. They're particularly convenient for people with limited mobility and they can be a great way to make new friends.

On the downside, you'll have little opportunity for serendipitous interactions with locals. The tours can be jam-packed with activities, leaving little room for individual sightseeing, whim, or adventure—plus they often focus on the heavily touristed sites, so you miss out on many a lesser-known gem.

14 Special-Interest Trips

Texas is dotted with lakes and has numerous rivers, almost 700 miles of Gulf Coast, plenty of forest lands, and several mountain ranges. Its two national parks offer plentiful hiking opportunities, and there are also scenic canyons, spectacular caves, and vast areas of rugged desert.

The **official state vacation guide** (see "Visitor Information," earlier in this chapter) is a good source of information for those planning outdoor recreation in the state. Information on fishing, hunting, and the numerous state parks in Texas is available from the **Texas Parks and Wildlife Department** (© 800/792-1112 or 512/389-8950; www.tpwd.state.tx.us). Reservations for camping at state parks can be made through the department's website or by calling © 512/389-8900. General outdoor recreation information is also online at **www.texas outside.com**.

Both RV and tent **campers** will find plenty of campsites throughout Texas, although tent campers will have fewer choices, especially along the Gulf Coast where numerous RV parks cater to "Winter Texans"—usually retired residents of northern states and Canada who spend winters in the sunny warmth of Texas and often arrive in plush motor homes or large trailers. The **Texas Association of Campground Owners** (© 800/657-6555 or 512/459-8226; www.texascampgrounds.com) offers a free booklet describing commercial campgrounds and RV parks in Texas and New Mexico. It's a generally good guide, with fairly complete information and directions, but, unfortunately, it does not include rates. However, it does include a "Texas Saver Card," for discounts of 10% or 15% at many facilities.

OUTFITTERS & OPERATORS

With a state as huge as Texas, you'd expect lots of outdoor adventures, and although there are lots of opportunities for outdoor activities in Texas, the state hasn't quite caught on with most of the major national adventure travel companies. However, we do recommend **GORP-travel** (© 877/440-GORP or 303/516-1153; http://gorptravel.away.com), which offers several Texas trips, ranging from rafting or canoeing the Rio Grande to Old West dude ranch vacations, where you get to play cowboy when you're not busy fishing, swimming, or just loafing. Another good national company that offers bicycling tours, walking tours, and multisport adventures in Texas is **Planet Earth Adventures** (© 800/923-4453; www.planetearthadventures.com). Multi-activity adventures in Texas are also available from **Tauck World Discovery** (© 800/788-7885 or 203/221-6891; www.tauck.com), which features a working-ranch trip. The **Audubon Society** (© 800/967-7425; www.audubon.org) occasionally offers what it calls "nature odysseys" in Texas, with birding destinations such as Big Bend National Park.

You can obtain information on the state's outfitters, including numerous hunting and fishing guides, from the **Texas Outfitters and Guides Association,** P.O. Box 33141, Kerrville, TX 78029-3141 (© 830/238-4207; www.texasoutfittersguide.com).

ACTIVITIES A TO Z

Texas offers a wide variety of outdoor activities, and moderate year-round temperatures in most of the state give you more time to do them.

BIRD-WATCHING & WILDLIFE VIEWING Texas has some of the best bird-watching opportunities in the United States, especially along the Gulf Coast, where you often see colorful Neotropical species found nowhere else in the United States. Check out the numerous national wildlife refuges, or stop practically anywhere along the coast—we like the Rockport. You can get bird checklists from most visitor centers and wildlife refuges, and online from the **Northern Prairie Wildlife Research Center** (www.npwrc.usgs.gov/resource/othrdata/chekbird/r2/48.htm). Also, check with the **Audubon Society** (© 800/967-7425; www.audubon.org) to see what the national organization and its various Texas chapters are offering in the way of birding tours. Wildlife viewing is especially good at Big Bend National Park (see chapter 10).

BOATING Opportunities for boating are abundant along the Gulf Coast—there are boat ramps practically everywhere—but the state's many lakes are also ideal for boating. Especially good is Amistad National Recreation Area, a huge lake along the U.S.–Mexico border in West Texas; see "Del Rio & Amistad National Recreation Area" in chapter 9.

DUDE RANCHING As one would expect in a major cattle-ranching state like Texas, there are ample opportunities for visitors to saddle up and hit the trail with genuine bow-legged cowboys (spitting chewing tobacco is optional). Close to 100 working ranches welcome guests.

There are a number of ranches in the San Antonio area, and of course the West Texas plains have more than its share. A complete list of ranches, with contact information and other details, is available on the Texas Tourism website at **www. traveltex.com**.

FISHING & HUNTING   Texans love fishing and hunting, and you'd be hard pressed to find an area of the state without a popular fishing hole or nearby hunting location. The lakes of East Texas are especially good fishing spots, and the San Angelo area offers excellent fishing and hunting opportunities (see chapters 5 and 9, respectively). Gulf Coast towns such as Rockport, Corpus Christi, and South Padre Island have dozens of fishing boats available for bay and deep-sea fishing (see chapter 6). Hunting for birds, white-tailed deer, and even javelina is popular in many areas, including West Texas. For current license information, check with the Texas Parks and Wildlife Department (see above).

FOUR-WHEELING   Visitors to Texas who brought along a street legal 4×4 will find miles of beach to explore at Padre Island National Seashore (see chapter 6).

GOLF   Texas is one of the better golfing destinations in the U.S., with more than 900 golf courses that offer plenty of challenges and a wide variety of terrain. The best courses are near major cities such as Dallas, San Antonio, Houston, and Austin, but even out in the plains you're likely to stumble across an oasis of well-manicured green with a row of golf carts awaiting your tee time. Among top golfing destinations in Texas is the **Four Seasons Resort and Club at Las Colinas** (p. 89), in the Dallas–Forth Worth area, with two challenging courses, more trees

than you can count, and a beautiful lake. In Houston (and with another course in the Dallas–Fort Worth area), **Tour 18** does a splendid job of capturing the feel and even look of some of the greatest and best-known golf holes in the country (see chapters 4 and 5).

HIKING   There are plenty of hiking trails in Texas, including those at the numerous state parks. Perhaps the most scenic trails are in the Big Bend and Guadalupe Mountains national parks—it's especially hard to beat the spectacular beauty of a fall hike in McKittrick Canyon at Guadalupe Mountains National Park (see chapter 10). Also very attractive are the hiking trails at Palo Duro Canyon State Park in the Panhandle Plains (see chapter 11). Hikers need to be prepared though; take plenty of water when hiking in the desert, watch for poisonous snakes and insects most everywhere, and use mosquito repellent in the Gulf Coast area.

WATERSPORTS   Swimming and water-skiing are practically year-round activities along the Gulf Coast and at Amistad National Recreation Area in West Texas (see chapters 6 and 9). The many lakes around the state—especially in East Texas and the Hill Country around San Antonio—also offer ample opportunity for a variety of watersports, especially canoeing and power boating. In Austin, a highlight is swimming at the natural springs pool called Barton Springs, a revered local favorite. Rafters usually head to the Rio Grande near Big Bend National Park, where they can float downstream on their own or go with one of the local rafting companies (see chapter 10). For beachcombing, try Padre Island National Seashore (see chapter 6).

15 Getting Around Texas

Texas is huge, so it's highly unlikely you'll want to try to see it all in one visit. Most

visitors will be exploring either one or two cities or a relatively small section of

Fun Fact
Texas maintains 77,000 miles of roadways, including interstates, U.S. highways, state highways, and farm-to-market (designated FM on signs) roads. Furthermore, it has some 48,000 bridges on public roads—the most in the nation.

the state. For those visiting major cities it's easy to fly in, use public transportation, and then fly or take the train to the next city (see the individual city chapters for airline and rail information). However, those who plan to see a variety of Texas locales—within reasonable distance—will find that the most practical way to see Texas is by car.

BY PLANE
A number of airlines offer flights between Texas's major cities; see the "Essentials" sections in individual destinations for airline information.

Overseas visitors can take advantage of the APEX (Advance Purchase Excursion) reductions offered by all major U.S. and European carriers. In addition, some large airlines offer transatlantic or transpacific passengers special discount tickets under the name **Visit USA,** which allows mostly one-way travel from one U.S. destination to another at very low prices. Unavailable in the U.S., these discount tickets must be purchased abroad in conjunction with your international fare. This system is the easiest, fastest, cheapest way to see the country.

BY CAR
Driving is an excellent way to see Texas in small chunks—roads are well maintained and well marked, and a car is often the most economical and convenient way to get somewhere; in fact, if you plan to explore beyond the cities—which we highly recommend—it's practically the only way to get to some places.

Once you leave the interstates, there is a veritable spider web of roads that will take you just about anywhere you want to go, at least until you venture into the vast emptiness of the southwest plains. This seemingly uncharted area contains two of the gems of the state, however: Big Bend and Guadalupe Mountains national parks. These two places make it worth the effort of finding a way to get there.

Traffic in major cities, such as Houston, Dallas, and Austin, can be very congested and frustrating, especially at rush hour, and distances are often great. Be sure to leave extra time to get places. Away from the cities, you'll often find the roads to be practically deserted.

Because much of Texas has a relatively mild climate, snow and ice are not usually a problem. However, those traveling to or through Amarillo and other northern sections of the state in winter should check weather reports frequently—we were once stranded in the Panhandle for several days by an ice storm that left the highways a sheet of glass.

If you're visiting from abroad and plan to rent a car in the United States, you probably won't need the services of an additional automobile organization. If you're planning to buy or borrow a car, automobile-association membership is recommended. **AAA (℃ 800/222-4357;** http://travel.aaa.com) is the country's largest auto club and supplies its members with maps, insurance, and, most important, emergency road service. *Note:* Foreign driver's licenses are usually recognized in the U.S., but you should get an international one if your home license is not in English.

CAR & RV RENTALS   National rental agencies readily available in Texas include **Advantage** (℃ 800/777-5500; www. arac.com), **Alamo** (℃ 800/462-5266;

www.alamo.com), **Avis** (© 800/230-4898; www.avis.com), **Budget** (© 800/527-0700; www.budget.com), **Dollar** (© 800/800-3665; www.dollar.com), **Enterprise** (© 800/736-8222; www.enterprise.com), **Hertz** (© 800/654-3131; www.hertz.com), **National** (© 800/227-7368; www.nationalcar.com), **Payless** (© 800/729-5377; www.paylesscar.com), and **Thrifty** (© 800/847-4389; www.thrifty.com). Motor homes and campers are available from **Cruise America** (© 800/327-7799; www.cruiseamerica.com), which has outlets in Austin, Beaumont, Dallas, Fort Worth, Houston, and San Antonio.

INSURANCE   If you hold a private auto insurance policy, you probably are covered for loss or damage to the rental car, and liability in case a passenger is injured. The credit card you used to rent the car also may provide some coverage.

Car-rental insurance probably does not cover liability if you caused the accident. Check your own auto insurance policy, the rental company policy, and your credit card coverage for the extent of coverage: Is your destination covered? Are other drivers covered? How much liability is covered if a passenger is injured? (If you rely on your credit card for coverage, you may want to bring a second credit card with you, as damages may be charged to your card and you may find yourself stranded with no money.)

DRIVING RULES   Texas law requires all drivers to carry proof of insurance, as well as a valid driver's license. Safety belts must be worn by all front seat occupants of cars and light trucks; children under 17 must wear safety belts regardless of where they are in the vehicle; and children younger than age 4 or under 36 inches tall, regardless of where they're sitting, must be in approved child seats. The maximum speed limit on interstate highways is 70 mph; and the maximum on numbered noninterstates is 70 mph during daylight and 65 mph at night, unless otherwise posted. Motorcyclists are required to wear helmets, and radar detectors are legal.

MAPS   A good state highway map is available free at any state information center or by mail (see "Visitor Information," earlier in this chapter). Maps can also be purchased at bookstores, gas stations, and most supermarkets and discount stores.

ROAD CONDITIONS   Texas roads are among the best in the western United States, and the state's generally moderate weather keeps snow closures to a minimum. However, icy roads are fairly common in the northern sections of the state

---

Tips The "Drive Friendly" State

For years the Texas Department of Transportation has been urging motorists to "drive friendly," and apparently many of them, especially in rural areas, have taken that message to heart. When you approach a vehicle from behind on a two-lane road, more often than not that vehicle will pull onto the shoulder, while maintaining speed, to let you pass without having to go into the oncoming lane. Fortunately, most Texas state highways have good, wide shoulders so there's little danger. We're not sure if this is technically legal or not, but everybody in rural Texas does it, including state troopers. However, road rage is not uncommon in Texas, and I usually think twice before sending an obscene gesture the way of a driver who has just cut me off—especially if that driver's in a pickup toting a gun rack on the back.

Texas Driving Times & Distances

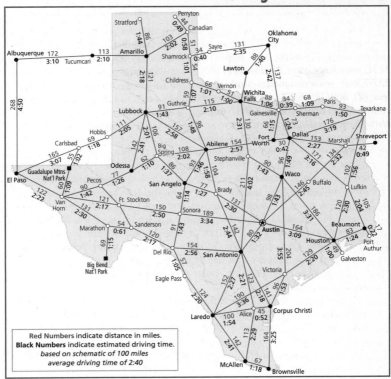

Red Numbers indicate distance in miles.
Black Numbers indicate estimated driving time.
*based on schematic of 100 miles
average driving time of 2:40*

during the winter, and hurricanes can cause flooding in late summer and early fall along the Gulf Coast. A recorded **24-hour hot line** (C 800/452-9292) provides information on road conditions statewide, and information is also available online at www.dot.state.tx.us/travel/road_conditions.htm.

BY TRAIN

More than a dozen towns and cities in Texas are linked by rail, with mostly daily service from Amtrak. See "Getting There," earlier in this chapter, and individual destinations for more information.

16 Tips on Accommodations

Texas offers a variety of lodging options, from typical American chain motels to luxury hotels, historic hotels and bed-and-breakfast inns, and some pleasant and inexpensive mom-and-pop independent motels, cabins, and ranch-style

resorts. To make your lodging an integral part of your Texas experience, we recommend choosing a historic property where available. There are quite a few historic bed-and-breakfast inns discussed in the following pages, and especially when you

Texas: Gateway to Mexico

Many travelers believe that a vacation in western or southern Texas would not be complete without an excursion across the border into Mexico, to visit the picturesque shops, dicker for colorful pottery and inexpensive jewelry, and sample genuine Mexican food. In our experience, the shopping is especially enjoyable—you really can get some bargains—and the food is great, though we generally stay away from street vendors and patronize only the well-established restaurants. Mexican border towns welcome tourists and almost universally accept U.S. currency—in fact, for many of these communities, tourism is their primary source of income.

However, remember that a trip across the border, even if you just walk across for the afternoon, is in fact a trip to a foreign country, and the laws of Mexico, not the United States, apply. In addition, these border towns are often hotbeds of drug smuggling, so stick to the main tourist areas, and don't let anyone try to convince you to carry anything across the border for them.

U.S. and Canadian citizens must carry a passport (as of Jan 2007) if they plan on crossing back into the U.S. A Mexican tourist card (available from Mexican officials at the border) is required for those going beyond the border towns into Mexico's interior, or those planning to stay in the border towns for more than 72 hours. Other foreign nationals will need a passport and the appropriate visas.

Travelers driving cars beyond the border towns will need vehicle permits, available from Mexican officials at the border, and those driving cars across the border for any distance at all should first buy insurance from a Mexican insurance company (short-term insurance is available at the border and at travel clubs such as AAA). If you're only planning to cross the border, visit a

---

take into consideration the wonderful breakfasts prepared at most of them, the rates are fairly reasonable. Why spend $80 for a boring motel room and then another $10 to $15 for breakfast when for just a bit more you can instead sleep in a handsome inn, decorated with antiques, and be served a delightful home-cooked breakfast?

SAVING ON YOUR HOTEL ROOM

The **rack rate** is the maximum rate that a hotel charges for a room. Hardly anybody pays this price, however, except in high season or on holidays. Here are a few tips to lower the cost of your room.

- **Ask about special rates or other discounts.** You may qualify for corporate, student, military, senior, frequent flier, trade union, or other discounts.
- **Dial direct.** When booking a room in a chain hotel, you'll often get a better deal by calling the individual hotel's reservation desk rather than the chain's main number.
- **Book online.** Many hotels offer Internet-only discounts or supply rooms to Priceline, Hotwire, or Expedia.com at rates much lower than the ones you can get through the hotel itself.
- **Remember the law of supply and demand.** Resort hotels are most crowded and therefore most expensive

few shops, maybe sample the Mexican food, and then cross back into Texas, consider leaving your car on U.S. soil and walking. This will save the hassles of getting Mexican car insurance and the red tape if you are involved in an accident; of course, then you'll end up having to carry any purchases you make.

Warning: It is a felony to take any type of firearm or ammunition into Mexico (you could easily end up in jail and have your car confiscated). In addition, there are a number of regulations regarding taking pets across the border, plus fees, so it is usually best to board pets on the U.S. side.

When reentering the United States from Mexico, you will be stopped and questioned by U.S. Customs officials, and your car may be searched. U.S. citizens may bring back up to $800 in purchases duty-free every 30 days, including 1 liter of liquor, 100 cigars (except Cuban cigars, which are prohibited), and one carton of cigarettes. Duty fees are charged above those amounts, and Texas charges a tax of about $1 per liter on all alcoholic beverages. Items that may not be brought into the United States, or which require special permits, include most fruits and vegetables, plants, animals, and meat.

The above is just a brief summary of the somewhat complex laws on traveling between the United States and Mexico. There are more details in the official state vacation guide available from the Texas Department of Transportation (see "Visitor Information," earlier in this chapter), and for complete information contact **U.S. Customs** (© 202/354-1000; www.customs.gov) and the **Mexican Government Tourism Office** (© 800/446-3942 or 713/722-2581; mgtotx@ix.netcom.com). A good online source of information is **www.mexonline.com**.

on weekends, so discounts are usually available for midweek stays. Business hotels in downtown locations are busiest during the week, so you can expect big discounts over the weekend. Many hotels have high-season and low-season prices, and booking even 1 day after high season ends can mean big discounts.

- **Look into group or long-stay discounts.** If you come as part of a large group, you should be able to negotiate a bargain rate. Likewise, if you're planning a long stay (at least 5 days), you might qualify for a discount. As a general rule, expect 1 night free after a 7-night stay.

- **Avoid excess charges and hidden costs.** When you book a room, ask whether the hotel charges for parking. Use your own cellphone, pay phones, or prepaid phone cards instead of dialing direct from hotel phones, which usually have exorbitant rates. And don't be tempted by the room's minibar offerings: Most hotels charge through the nose for water, soda, and snacks. Finally, ask about local taxes and service charges, which can increase the cost of a room by 15% or more.

- **Book an efficiency.** A room with a kitchenette allows you to shop for groceries and cook your own meals.

This is a big money saver, especially for families on long stays.

- **Consider enrolling in hotel "frequent-stay" programs,** which are upping the ante lately to win the loyalty of repeat customers. Frequent guests can now accumulate points or credits to earn free hotel nights, airline miles, in-room amenities, merchandise, tickets to concerts and events, discounts on sporting facilities—and even credit toward stock in the participating hotel, in the case of the Jameson Inn hotel group. Perks are awarded not only by many chain hotels and motels (Hilton HHonors, Marriott Rewards, and Wyndham ByRequest, to name a few), but individual inns and B&Bs as well. Many chain hotels partner with other hotel chains, car-rental firms, airlines, and credit card companies to give consumers additional incentive to do repeat business.

17 Recommended Books, Films & Music

Of the seemingly infinite number of books concerning the Lone Star State, there are a few novels this book's authors especially like, primarily for the view they provide into the soul of Texas (both the real and the mythical). Fans of James Michener will appreciate his historical novel *Texas.* Although a bit too wordy and tedious for some of us, Michener is an excellent storyteller as well as historian, and he (exhaustively) brings the state and its people to life. (It's a big state, but couldn't he have done it in less than 1,344 pages?) The superb novels of Cormac McCarthy also bring Texas to life, especially its raw, violent ways. Especially recommended are *All the Pretty Horses,* a sort of coming-of-age story known for its magnificent prose (and part of *The Border Trilogy*), and his tense *Blood Meridian: Or the Evening Redness in the West.* His latest, which has again garnered rave reviews, is *The Road.* You might also pick up a copy of Annie Proulx's *That Old Ace in the Hole,* which is set in the Panhandle. For powerful, critically acclaimed short stories, try *Woman Hollering Creek* by Texas author Sandra Cisneros. *The Gates of the Alamo* by Stephen Harrigan is a gripping, fictionalized version of Texas's most famous battle.

On the much lighter side, *Baja Oklahoma,* by Dan Jenkins, offers a funny, poignant, and somewhat raunchy look at what we might call classic modern Texans, at least the Fort Worth trailer-trash variety. The book was made into an equally good movie by the same name, starring Leslie Ann Warren and Peter Coyote, with a bit part played by a young Julia Roberts. William Sidney Porter, better known as O. Henry, published a satirical newspaper in Austin and also worked in San Antonio in the late 19th century. A number of his short stories are set in the state, and can be found in *O. Henry's Texas Stories.*

Among nonfiction titles, serious history buffs may want to dip into Robert A. Caro's excellent multivolume biography of Lyndon B. Johnson, the consummate Texas politician whose career led him to the White House. For a quick and easy look at what Texas is all about, try *All Hat & No Cattle,* a collection of somewhat irreverent observations on Texas fashions, cuisine, music, animals, and the like by humorist Anne Dingus. *Friday Night Lights,* by H. G. Bissinger, is a sports classic, a memorable dissection of small-town Texas and its obsession and quasi religion: high school football. Focusing on Odessa Permian High, my high school's (Plano) perennial rival, the book went on to become a motion picture starring Billy Bob Thornton in 2004 (the soundtrack featured the expansive sounds of the Austin-based alternative instrumental band Explosions in the Sky). The book and movie have now been adapted for a television series on NBC.

Even readers who don't cook will enjoy *The Only Texas Cookbook* by Linda West Eckhardt. Interspersed among its 300 recipes—including classics such as Fuzzy's Fantastic South Texas Road Meat Chili and Bad Hombre Eggs—are numerous humorous anecdotes on food-related subjects. Those who savor biting political humor—and don't mind seeing every Texas Republican mercilessly skewered—will thoroughly enjoy any book of essays by the late newspaper columnist Molly Ivins, who is credited with bestowing the nickname "Dubya" on George W. Bush.

As a larger-than-life state with a character and spirit that both attract and repel but always seem to fascinate, it's no surprise that Texas has been the setting for epic films. Foremost among them, of course, were Westerns starring John Wayne, many of which were placed in Texas, including *The Alamo, Red River,* and *Three Texas Steers.* John Ford's 1956 *The Searchers*—also starring Wayne—is generally considered one of the greatest Westerns ever filmed. *Giant* (also from 1956) is expansive like Texas itself, set on a massive ranch location under a huge sky with Rock Hudson as a ranch baron who wins over Elizabeth Taylor. In 1969's *Easy Rider,* Peter Fonda and Dennis Hopper take a motorcycle road trip through Texas and meet up with Jack Nicholson. *The Last Picture Show,* based on the novel by Larry McMurtry and directed by Peter Bogdanovich, is a tribute both to classic Hollywood filmmaking and small-town Texas. *Tender Mercies,* which won Robert Duvall an Oscar, is a stunning portrait of a has-been Texas country singer named Mac Sledge. In the cheesy *Urban Cowboy,* John Travolta lit up a honky-tonk called Gilley's and did for country dancing what he'd earlier done for disco in *Saturday Night Fever.*

Texas has also given birth to eccentric independent movies, such as the B-movie classic *The Texas Chainsaw Massacre;* Wim Wenders's idiosyncratic *Paris, Texas;* the Coen brothers' *Raising Arizona* and *Blood Simple;* and Richard Linklater's *Slacker* and *Dazed and Confused,* dead-on portraits of laid-back Austin.

Films are increasingly being filmed in Texas. Austin has emerged as the "Third Coast" alternative to Los Angeles and New York City as a filmmaker's haven. Texas filmmakers include legendary director Terence Malick *(The Thin Red Line, Days of Heaven, Badlands, The New World)* and young moviemakers creating an Austin school of sorts: Linklater *(Before Sunrise, School of Rock, Fast Food Nation)* and Robert Rodriguez *(El Mariachi, Spy Kids).* Several well-known actors make their homes in Austin, too, including Matthew McConnaughey and Sandra Bullock.

On the tube, there was *Dallas,* of course, the entertainingly over-the-top series about the Ewing oil clan, and the classic miniseries adaptation of Larry McMurtry's novel *Lonesome Dove,* which starred Robert Duvall and Tommy Lee Jones as former Texas Rangers a little long in the tooth who organize an epic cattle drive. PBS's *Austin City Limits* is a legendary, long-running live-music program featuring diverse artists from all over the country and globe.

The role that Texas musicians have played in creating a particularly American idiom of popular music, from country to blues, jazz, and rock, is impossible to overestimate. It's a topic sufficiently vast to be treated in greater detail; see "Texan Music" in the appendix. For rock and alternative music lovers, two of the biggest music festivals in the country are held annually in Austin: South by Southwest (S×SW), in March, and the outdoors Austin City Limits Festival (cruelly held in Sept, at the tail end of the brutal Central Texas summer).

FAST FACTS: Texas

American Express There are branches throughout Texas; see "Fast Facts" in individual chapters for locations. To report a lost card, call ℂ **800/528-4800**. To report lost traveler's checks, call ℂ **800/221-7282**.

Area Codes Area codes for Dallas are 214 and 972; Fort Worth, 817; Houston, 713 and 281; San Antonio, 210; and Austin, 512.

ATM Networks See "Money," p. 30.

Automobile Organizations Auto clubs will supply maps, suggested routes, guidebooks, accident and bail-bond insurance, and emergency road service. The **American Automobile Association (AAA)** is the major auto club in the United States. If you belong to an auto club in your home country, inquire about AAA reciprocity before you leave. You may be able to join AAA even if you're not a member of a reciprocal club; to inquire, call AAA (ℂ **800/222-4357**). AAA is actually an organization of regional auto clubs; so look under "AAA Automobile Club" in the White Pages of the telephone directory. AAA has a nationwide emergency road service telephone number (ℂ **800/AAA-HELP**).

Business Hours Offices are usually open weekdays from 9am to 5pm. Banks are open weekdays from 9am to 3pm or later and sometimes Saturday mornings. Stores typically open between 9 and 10am and close between 5 and 6pm Monday through Saturday. Stores in shopping complexes or malls tend to stay open late, until about 9pm on weekdays and weekends, and many malls and larger department stores are open on Sundays. A growing number of discount stores (such as Wal-Mart) and grocery stores are open 24 hours a day.

Car Rentals See "Getting Around Texas," p. 48.

Currency See "Money," earlier in this chapter.

Drinking Laws The legal drinking age is 21, although minors can legally drink as long as they are within sight of their 21-or-older parents, guardians, or spouses. Where you can or cannot buy a drink and what kind of drink is determined in Texas by local option election, so the state is essentially a patchwork of regulations. In most parts of the state you can buy liquor, beer, and wine by the drink. However, there are a few areas where you can buy only beer (which Texas defines as having no more than 4% alcohol; anything higher is "ale"), and others where you can purchase beer or wine by the glass but not liquor. There are also some areas that are completely dry—mostly in the Panhandle Plains and near the state's eastern border—and other confusing areas where one county will be dry (meaning you have to join private clubs—membership is normally free and immediately granted—to drink in restaurants, and liquor stores will stock beer and wine only) and the county right next to it will be wet.

Driving Rules See "Getting Around Texas," p. 48.

Electricity Like Canada, the United States uses 110 to 120 volts AC (60 cycles), compared to 220 to 240 volts AC (50 cycles) in most of Europe, Australia, and New Zealand. If your small appliances use 220 to 240 volts, you'll need a 110-volt transformer and a plug adapter with two flat parallel pins to operate them here. Downward converters that change 220 to 240 volts into 110 to 120 volts are difficult to find in the United States, so bring one with you.

Embassies & Consulates All embassies are located in the nation's capital, Washington, D.C. Some consulates are located in major U.S. cities, and most nations have a mission to the United Nations in New York City. If your country isn't listed below, call for directory information in Washington, D.C. (© 202/555-1212), or log on to www.embassy.org/embassies.

The embassy of **Australia** is at 1601 Massachusetts Ave. NW, Washington, DC 20036 (© 202/797-3000; www.austemb.org). There are consulates in New York, Honolulu, Houston, Los Angeles, and San Francisco.

The embassy of **Canada** is at 501 Pennsylvania Ave. NW, Washington, DC 20001 (© 202/682-1740; www.canadianembassy.org). Other Canadian consulates are in Buffalo, N.Y.; Detroit; Los Angeles; New York; and Seattle.

The embassy of **Ireland** is at 2234 Massachusetts Ave. NW, Washington, DC 20008 (© 202/462-3939; www.irelandemb.org). Irish consulates are in Boston, Chicago, New York, and San Francisco.

The embassy of **Japan** is at 2520 Massachusetts Ave. NW, Washington, DC 20008 (© 202/238-6700; www.embjapan.org). Japanese consulates are located in many cities including Atlanta, Boston, Detroit, New York, San Francisco, and Seattle.

The embassy of **New Zealand** is at 37 Observatory Circle NW, Washington, DC 20008 (© 202/328-4800; www.nzemb.org). New Zealand consulates are in Los Angeles, Salt Lake City, San Francisco, and Seattle.

The embassy of the **United Kingdom** is at 3100 Massachusetts Ave. NW, Washington, DC 20008 (© 202/588-6500; www.britainusa.com). Other British consulates are in Atlanta, Boston, Chicago, Cleveland, Houston, Los Angeles, New York, San Francisco, and Seattle.

Emergencies Call © 911 to report a fire, call the police, or get an ambulance anywhere in the United States. This is a toll-free call. (No coins are required at public telephones.)

If you encounter serious problems, contact the **Traveler's Aid Society International** (© 202/546-1127; www.travelersaid.org). The Texas office is at the Dallas/Fort Worth International Airport (© 972/574-4420). This nationwide, nonprofit, social-service organization geared to helping travelers in difficult straits offers services that might include reuniting families separated while traveling, providing food and/or shelter to people stranded without cash, or even emotional counseling. If you're in trouble, seek them out.

Gasoline (Petrol) Petrol is known as gasoline (or simply "gas") in the United States, and petrol stations are known as both "gas stations" and "service stations." Texas often has some of the lowest gasoline prices in the United States; although prices fluctuate, at press time regular unleaded gas ranged from $1.90 to $2.40 per gallon, with the lowest prices in the Gulf Coast area (for current prices, check out www.texasgasprices.com). Taxes are already included in the printed price. One U.S. gallon equals 3.8 liters or .85 imperial gallons.

Holidays Banks, government offices, post offices, and many stores, restaurants, and museums are closed on the following legal national holidays: January 1

(New Year's Day), the third Monday in January (Martin Luther King, Jr., Day), the third Monday in February (Presidents' Day, Washington's Birthday), the last Monday in May (Memorial Day), July 4 (Independence Day), the first Monday in September (Labor Day), the second Monday in October (Columbus Day), November 11 (Veterans Day/Armistice Day), the fourth Thursday in November (Thanksgiving Day), and December 25 (Christmas). Also, the Tuesday following the first Monday in November is Election Day and is a federal government holiday in presidential-election years (held every 4 years, and next in 2008). Also, see "Texas Calendar of Events," earlier in this chapter.

Internet Access You'll have trouble finding convenient Internet access in the smaller towns, where you might have the best luck at the local library. Before you go, check for an Internet cafe in your destination at **www.cybercafes.com** or **www.netcafeguide.com/mapindex.htm**.

Legal Aid If you are "pulled over" for a minor infraction (such as speeding), never attempt to pay the fine directly to a police officer; this could be construed as attempted bribery, a much more serious crime. Pay fines by mail, or directly into the hands of the clerk of the court. If accused of a more serious offense, say and do nothing before consulting a lawyer. Here the burden is on the state to prove a person's guilt beyond a reasonable doubt, and everyone has the right to remain silent, whether he or she is suspected of a crime or actually arrested. Once arrested, a person can make one telephone call to a party of his or her choice. Call your embassy or consulate.

Lost & Found Be sure to contact all of your credit card companies the minute you discover your wallet has been lost or stolen and file a report at the nearest police precinct. Your credit card company or insurer may require a police report number or record of the loss. Most credit card companies have an emergency toll-free number to call if your card is lost or stolen; they may be able to wire you a cash advance immediately or deliver an emergency credit card in a day or two. Visa's U.S. emergency number is ⓒ **800/847-2911** or 410/581-9994. American Express cardholders and traveler's check holders should call ⓒ **800/ 221-7282**. MasterCard holders should call ⓒ **800/622-7747**. If you need emergency cash over the weekend when all banks and American Express offices are closed, you can have money wired to you via **Western Union** (ⓒ **800/325-6000**; www.westernunion.com).

Mail At press time, domestic postage rates were 26¢ for a postcard and 41¢ for a letter. For international mail, a first-class letter of up to 1 ounce costs 90¢ (69¢ to Canada and Mexico); a first-class postcard costs the same as a letter. For more information go to **www.usps.com** and click on "Calculate Postage."

If you aren't sure what your address will be in the United States, mail can be sent to you, in your name, c/o General Delivery at the main post office of the city or region where you expect to be. (Call ⓒ **800/275-8777** for information on the nearest post office.) The addressee must pick up mail in person and must produce proof of identity (driver's license, passport, and so forth). Most post offices will hold your mail for up to 1 month, and are open Monday to Friday from 8am to 6pm, and Saturday from 9am to 3pm.

Always include zip codes when mailing items in the U.S. If you don't know your zip code, visit www.usps.com/zip4.

Maps See "Getting Around Texas," earlier in this chapter.

Newspapers & Magazines The state's largest daily newspapers include the *Dallas Morning News, Houston Chronicle, Fort Worth Star-Telegram,* and the *San Antonio Express-News.* Other cities and large towns, especially regional hubs, have daily newspapers, and many smaller towns publish weeklies. Free arts-heavy weeklies include the *Dallas Observer* and the *Austin Chronicle.* National newspapers such as *USA Today* and the *Wall Street Journal* can be purchased at newsstands in cities and major hotels; and you can also purchase two good monthly magazines, *Texas Highways* and *Texas Monthly,* throughout the state.

Passports **For Residents of Australia:** You can pick up an application from your local post office or any branch of Passports Australia, but you must schedule an interview at the passport office to present your application materials. Call the **Australian Passport Information Service** at ✆ **131-232,** or visit the government website at **www.passports.gov.au.**

For Residents of Canada: Passport applications are available at travel agencies throughout Canada or from the central **Passport Office,** Department of Foreign Affairs and International Trade, Ottawa, ON K1A 0G3 (✆ **800/567-6868;** www.ppt.gc.ca). *Note:* Canadian children who travel must have their own passport. However, if you hold a valid Canadian passport issued before December 11, 2001, that bears the name of your child, the passport remains valid for you and your child until it expires.

For Residents of Ireland: You can apply for a 10-year passport at the **Passport Office,** Setanta Centre, Molesworth Street, Dublin 2 (✆ **01/671-1633;** www.irlgov.ie/iveagh). Those under age 18 and over 65 must apply for a 3-year passport. You can also apply at 1A South Mall, Cork (✆ **021/272-525**), or at most main post offices.

For Residents of New Zealand: You can pick up a passport application at any New Zealand Passports Office or download it from their website. Contact the **Passports Office** at ✆ **0800/225-050** in New Zealand or 04/474-8100, or log on to **www.passports.govt.nz.**

For Residents of the United Kingdom: To pick up an application for a standard 10-year passport (5-year passport for children younger than 16), visit your nearest passport office, major post office, or travel agency or contact the **United Kingdom Passport Service** at ✆ **0870/521-0410** or search its website at **www.ukpa.gov.uk.**

Police Dial ✆ **911** for a police or medical emergency.

Safety See "Health & Safety," earlier in this chapter.

Taxes The United States has no value-added tax (VAT) or other indirect tax at the national level. Every state, county, and city may levy its own local tax on all purchases, including hotel and restaurant checks and airline tickets. These taxes will not appear on price tags. Texans like to brag that the state is a great place to live because there is no state income tax. However, money for government services has to come from somewhere, and one of those sources is you, the traveler. Texas lodging taxes are among the highest in the region, ranging from the basic hotel rate of 6% to 17%, with the steepest rate in Houston. Sales taxes in Texas vary by county, but usually total from the basic state sales tax of 6.25% to 8.25%, slightly higher than most surrounding states.

Telephone, Telegraph, Telex & Fax Generally, hotel surcharges on long-distance and local calls are astronomical, so you're better off using your **cellphone** or a **public pay telephone.** Many convenience groceries and packaging services sell **prepaid calling cards** in denominations up to $50; for international visitors these can be the least expensive way to call home. Many public phones at airports now accept American Express, MasterCard, and Visa credit cards. **Local calls** made from public pay phones in most locales cost either 25¢ or 35¢. Pay phones do not accept pennies, and few will take anything larger than a quarter.

Most long-distance and international calls can be dialed directly from any phone. **For calls within the United States and to Canada,** dial 1 followed by the area code and the seven-digit number. **For other international calls,** dial 011 followed by the country code, city code, and the number you are calling.

Calls to area codes **800, 888, 877,** and **866** are toll-free. However, calls to area codes **700** and **900** (chat lines, bulletin boards, "dating" services, and so on) can be very expensive—usually a charge of 95¢ to $3 or more per minute, and they sometimes have minimum charges that can run as high as $15 or more.

For **reversed-charge or collect calls,** and for person-to-person calls, dial the number 0 then the area code and number; an operator will come on the line, and you should specify whether you are calling collect, person-to-person, or both. If your operator-assisted call is international, ask for the overseas operator.

For **local directory assistance** ("information"), dial 411; for long-distance information, dial 1, then the appropriate area code and 555-1212.

Telegraph and telex services are provided primarily by Western Union. You can telegraph money, or have it telegraphed to you, very quickly over the Western Union system, but this service can cost as much as 15% to 20% of the amount sent.

Most hotels have **fax machines** available for guest use (be sure to ask about the charge to use it). Many hotel rooms are even wired for guests' fax machines. A less expensive way to send and receive faxes may be at stores such as **The UPS Store** (formerly Mail Boxes Etc.).

Time Almost all of Texas is in the Central Standard Time zone (CST); the only exception is the state's far western tip, which observes Mountain Standard Time (MST). The continental United States is divided into **four time zones:** Eastern Standard Time (EST), Central Standard Time (CST), which includes all of Texas except its far western tip, Mountain Standard Time (MST), and Pacific Standard Time (PST). Alaska and Hawaii have their own zones. For example, noon in New York City (EST) is 11am in Dallas (CST), 10am in Denver (MST), 9am in Los Angeles (PST), 8am in Anchorage (AST), and 7am in Honolulu (HST).

Daylight saving time is in effect from 1am on the second Sunday in March to 1am on the first Sunday in November, except in Arizona, Hawaii, the U.S. Virgin Islands, and Puerto Rico. Daylight saving time moves the clock 1 hour ahead of standard time.

Tipping   Tips are a very important part of certain workers' income, and gratuities are the standard way of showing appreciation for services provided. (Tipping is certainly not compulsory if the service is poor!) In hotels, tip **bellhops** at least $1 per bag ($2–$3 if you have a lot of luggage) and tip the **chamber staff** $1 to $2 per day (more if you've left a disaster area for him or her to clean up). Tip the **doorman** or **concierge** only if he or she has provided you with some specific service (for example, calling a cab for you or obtaining difficult-to-get theater tickets). Tip the **valet-parking attendant** $1 every time you get your car.

In restaurants, bars, and nightclubs, tip **service staff** 15% to 20% of the check, tip **bartenders** 10% to 15%, tip **checkroom attendants** $1 per garment, and tip **valet-parking attendants** $1 per vehicle.

As for other service personnel, tip **cab drivers** 15% of the fare; tip **skycaps** at airports at least $1 per bag ($2–$3 if you have a lot of luggage); and tip **hairdressers** and **barbers** 15% to 20%.

Toilets   You won't find public toilets or "restrooms" on the streets in most U.S. cities, but they can be found in hotel lobbies, bars, restaurants, museums, department stores, railway and bus stations, and service stations. Large hotels and fast-food restaurants are probably the best bet for good, clean facilities. If possible, avoid the toilets at parks and beaches, which tend to be dirty; some may be unsafe. Restaurants and bars in resorts or heavily visited areas may reserve their restrooms for patrons. Some establishments display a notice indicating this. You can ignore this sign or, better yet, avoid arguments by paying for a cup of coffee or a soft drink, which will qualify you as a patron.

Useful Phone Numbers

Texas Parks & Wildlife Park Information ✆ **800/792-1112**
Hunting information ✆ **512/389-4505**
Fishing information ✆ **512/389-4505**
Poison Center ✆ **800/POISON-1**
Road conditions hot line ✆ **800/452-9292**
Weather hot line ✆ **512/232-4265**
U.S. Department of State 24-hour Travel Advisory ✆ **202/647-5225**
U.S. Passport Agency ✆ **202/647-0518**
U.S. Centers for Disease Control international traveler's hot line ✆ **404/332-4559**

Visas   For information about U.S. visas go to **http://travel.state.gov** and click on "Visas." Or go to one of the following:

Australian citizens can obtain up-to-date visa information from the **U.S. Embassy Canberra,** Moonah Place, Yarralumla, ACT 2600 (✆ **02/6214-5600**) or by checking the U.S. Diplomatic Mission's website at **http://usembassy-australia.state.gov/consular**.

British subjects can obtain up-to-date visa information by calling the **U.S. Embassy Visa Information Line** (✆ **0891/200-290**) or by visiting the "Visas to the U.S." section of the American Embassy London's website at **www.us embassy.org.uk**.

Irish citizens can obtain up-to-date visa information through the **Embassy of the USA Dublin**, 42 Elgin Rd., Dublin 4, Ireland (© **353/1-668-8777**), or by checking the "Consular Services" section of the website at **http://dublin.us embassy.gov**.

Citizens of **New Zealand** can obtain up-to-date visa information by contacting the **U.S. Embassy New Zealand**, 29 Fitzherbert Terrace, Thorndon, Wellington (© **644/472-2068**), or get the information directly from the "For New Zealanders" section of the website at **http://usembassy.org.nz**.

3

Suggested Itineraries in Texas

When Texas became a state in 1845, the relevant legislation included a clause allowing it to split into up to five distinct states if the state legislature approved it. Likewise, planning a Texas road trip can be something like planning a road trip across five states. El Paso is closer to Tucson, Arizona (319 miles away), than it is to Dallas (634 miles away). There is a lot of ground to cover: big cities; beautiful, wide-open spaces; and miles and miles of highway in between. With all of the acreage, it's important to not stretch yourself too thin. It's easy to spend too much time behind the wheel in Texas. As always, tailor your itinerary to your interests. If you like cowboy culture, Fort Worth and Amarillo might be focal points; hikers and paddlers will want to beeline to Big Bend National Park; city-slickers might head to Dallas and Houston; and music lovers should flock to Austin. During your time on the Texas road, take the opportunity to explore places off the beaten path, and get out and gander at those wide-open spaces. This big state has a lot to offer, so take advantage of as much as you can.

1 Texas in 1 Week

This route brings you to the four major metro areas in Texas—Dallas–Fort Worth, Austin, San Antonio, and Houston—while diverting for a Gulf Coast getaway on Padre Island National Seashore.

Day ❶: Arrive in Dallas–Fort Worth

The Dallas–Fort Worth area is a good starting point for any Texas trip, and there are plenty of transportation options for getting here by plane, train, or automobile. Rent a car if you don't already have one, and pick lodging accessible to the attractions you want to see in either city and get your bearings. Visit the **John F. Kennedy Memorial** (p. 99) and the **Sixth Floor Museum at Dealey Plaza** ✹✹ (p. 100), and, if you have time, make an excursion to **Fair Park** ✹ (p. 104). After dinner at **Sonny Bryan's Smokehouse** ✹ (p. 98) or another Dallas dining staple, check out **Lower Greenville**'s nightlife (p. 115).

Day ❷: Explore Dallas–Fort Worth

Split your time between the artistic highlights of Dallas and Fort Worth, hitting the Arts District in Dallas (be sure to visit the **Nasher Sculpture Center** ✹✹✹, p. 102), but leave plenty of time to roam in Fort Worth's incomparable Cultural **District** (p. 130), where the **Modern Art Museum of Fort Worth** ✹✹✹ (p. 142) and **Kimbell Art Museum** ✹✹✹ (p. 142) are must-sees. In the evening, have dinner in the **Stockyards National Historic District** ✹✹ before paying a visit to **Billy Bob's Texas** ✹✹✹ (p. 149), a mega–country club, or taking in live music at another one of the city's many honky-tonks. See p. 149.

The Best of Texas in 1 Week

TEXAS IN 1 WEEK ———→
1. Arrive in Dallas-Fort Worth
2. Dallas-Fort Worth
3. Austin
4. San Antonio
5-6. Padre Island National Seashore
7. Galveston & Houston

Day ❸: Explore Austin

Get going early for the 200-mile drive to Austin. If it's hot, head immediately to **Barton Springs Pool** ✪✪ (p. 320), for a dip to cool off. Visit the new **Blanton Museum of Art** ✪ (p. 318) in the afternoon, then make it to the **Congress Avenue Bridge** for the sundown bat exodus (p. 319). Have dinner downtown and explore the famed **Austin music scene** in the Warehouse District, on 6th Street, on Red River, or in South Austin. Stay either downtown or on South Congress at the **Austin Motel** ✪ (p. 305) or the **Hotel San José** ✪ (p. 305).

Day ❹: Explore San Antonio

It's an 80-mile drive south from Austin to San Antonio. Park downtown and visit the **Alamo** ✪✪ (p. 273), naturally, then walk around in one of the city's historic neighborhoods, or alternately spend the afternoon visiting the five lesser known missions that comprise the **San Antonio Missions Historical Park** ✪✪ (p. 276). Return downtown for some time on the **River Walk** ✪✪✪ (p. 274), culminating in dinner at one of the many restaurants in the vicinity.

Days ❺–❻: Explore Padre Island National Seashore

From San Antonio, head down to Padre Island Seashore, a 180-mile drive, and take your time unwinding from the hectic urban pace of the first 4 days of the trip. Explore **Padre Island National Seashore** ✪ (p. 233). Take time to wander the beach, surf, fish, swim, or simply read a book and nap in the sun. Stay in **Corpus Christi** (p. 218), or—if you are up for more driving—head further down the Gulf Coast to **South Padre Island** (p. 237). But, as it's a 410-mile drive to Galveston, you might want to start heading north sometime in the afternoon of Day 6. See p. 206.

Day ❼: Explore Galveston & Houston

From Corpus Christi, it's about 150 miles to **Galveston** (p. 206), where you can spend more time on the beach or delve into the city's fascinating history. Drive back east into Houston for the afternoon for a visit to **Space Center Houston** ✸✸✸ (p. 187) before toasting your trip over dinner at one of Houston's many terrific eateries. See p. 174.

2 Texas in 2 Weeks

Start with the first 3 days of the preceding 1-week itinerary, then divert to West Texas and Big Bend Country for a week before working your way back to San Antonio for Day 11, and then continue with the final 3 days of the preceding 1-week itinerary before heading back home.

Day ❹: Drive to Del Rio & explore

From San Antonio, it is only 154 miles to **Del Rio** ✸✸ (p. 377), so you'll have time to get a late start and spend more time in the former. Or you can get going early, take the scenic drive from Junction to Rocksprings on U.S. 377 to Del Rio, and visit **Amistad National Recreation Area** ✸, the **Whitehead Memorial Museum** ✸ (p. 379), or **Seminole Canyon State Park** (p. 383) in the area before checking in at the **Villa Del Rio Bed & Breakfast** ✸✸ (p. 379) or another lodging. For dinner, head across the Rio Grande into Mexico for dinner in **Ciudad Acuña** (p. 378), one of our favorite border towns.

Days ❺–❼: Explore Big Bend National Park & vicinity

From Del Rio, drive west towards **Big Bend National Park** ✸✸ (p. 385). There is plenty to see along the way: You can stop at the Pecos River for a dramatic view, or visit Langtry and learn a bit about Judge Roy Bean, and the aforementioned **Seminole Canyon** (p. 383) is also a worthwhile diversion. Do some hiking and exploring before stopping at the **Gage Hotel** ✸✸ in Marathon (p. 396) for the night of Day 5. You can also drive to Terlingua,

Studya Butte, or Lajitas as a base for your Big Bend excursions. Another option is camping in Big Bend National Park or staying in park limits at **Chisos Mountains Lodge** ✸ (p. 395). Make plans to go on day hikes or do a rafting trip on the Rio Grande, a 2-day trip if possible. There are also interesting sights, stores, and restaurants in **Terlingua** (p. 395) and plenty of cultural history along the river in and outside of the park.

Days ❽–❾: Explore Big Bend Ranch State Park & Marfa

From Big Bend, drive the Wild and Scenic River portion of FM 170 to Presidio, taking time to get out on a few hikes in Big Bend Ranch State Park. From Presidio, take U.S. 67 to **Marfa** (p. 361). Stay and eat in Marfa (or south of town at **Cibolo Creek Ranch** ✸✸✸, p. 363) or **Alpine** (p. 364). On Day 9, check out the **Chinati Foundation**'s ✸✸ (p. 362) avant-garde installations (it requires your time from 10am–4pm to go on a guided tour) and downtown Marfa while the sun is up. Once it goes down, take U.S. 90 9 miles east to see the **Marfa Mystery Lights** (p. 363), or else head north to the **McDonald Observatory** ✸, p. 359, if there's a Star

The Best of Texas in 2 Weeks

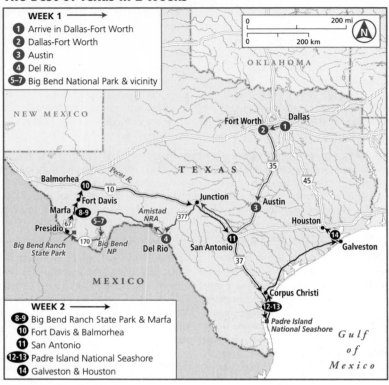

WEEK 1 ➞
1. Arrive in Dallas-Fort Worth
2. Dallas-Fort Worth
3. Austin
4. Del Rio
5-7. Big Bend National Park & vicinity

WEEK 2 ➞
8-9. Big Bend Ranch State Park & Marfa
10. Fort Davis & Balmorhea
11. San Antonio
12-13. Padre Island National Seashore
14. Galveston & Houston

Party that night. If Marfa accommodations are booked, Alpine is a great alternative, as it has some noteworthy galleries and the **Museum of the Big Bend** ⚜ (p. 365).

Day ⑩: Explore Fort Davis & Balmorhea

Spend your final day in West Texas before heading east for the Gulf Coast exploring **Fort Davis National Historic Site** ⚜ (p. 358) or **Davis Mountains**

State Park (p. 359). You can stay in Fort Davis, or continue—stopping at the oasis of a swimming pool at **Balmorhea State Park** ⚜⚜ (p. 360) if it's hot—and cut down on the drive to the Gulf Coast. After bunking in Balmorhea or somewhere off I-10 for the night, continue with Day 5 from the 1-week itinerary for the last 3 days of your trip.

3 Texas for Families

Texas is a good choice for a family vacation, but because of its sheer size, it's best to pare back the car time from the above itinerary. The major cities all have plenty of kid-friendly attractions and pursuits, so feel free to adjust your time in each place accordingly; families with budding astronauts will want to dedicate a whole day to Space Center Houston, other families might want to spend more time in the attraction-packed suburb of Arlington.

0   200 mi

0   200 km

OKLAHOMA

NEW MEXICO

Fort Worth ← **1** Dallas
2 •
Arlington

T E X A S   35

45

Austin **7**

Houston **3-4**

7
San Antonio ↕

Galveston

37   **5-6**
Corpus Christi

Padre Island
National Seashore   *Gulf*

MEXICO   *of*

Mexico

1 Arrive in Dallas-Fort Worth
2 Arlington & Fort Worth
3-4 Houston
5-6 Gulf Coast & Padre Island National Seashore
7 Austin or San Antonio

Day **1**: Arrive in Dallas

As we mentioned above in the 1-week itinerary, Dallas is a good starting point for any Texas trip. Rent a car if you don't already have one and pick lodging accessible to the attractions you want to see in either city and get your bearings. In Dallas, visit the **Old City Park** ⚘ (p. 106) and make an excursion to **Fair Park** ⚘ (p. 104). Eat at **Fireside Pies** ⚘ (p. 97) or **Sonny Bryan's Smokehouse** ⚘ (p. 98), both family-friendly mainstays in Big D.

Day **2**: Explore Arlington & Fort Worth

Arlington (p. 118) is a top Texas family destination, located roughly midway between Dallas and Fort Worth. The suburb is home to such attractions as **Six**

Flags Over Texas (p. 119) and the **Legends of the Game Baseball Museum** ⚘ at the home stadium of the Texas Rangers (p. 118). You can combine the day with some time in Fort Worth, or bypass Arlington altogether if your kids are old enough to appreciate the fantastic art museums in Fort Worth. The **Cowtown Cattlepen Maze** (p. 137) and the **Fort Worth Zoo** ⚘⚘⚘ are good bets for kids of all ages. That night, stay in Fort Worth after dinner at **Joe T. Garcia's Mexican Dishes** (p. 132).

Days **3**–**4**: Explore Houston

Get a good start on your drive to Houston, because there is plenty to see and do in the 2 days you'll spend there: **Space Center Houston** ⚘⚘⚘ (p. 187), the

Children's Museum of Houston 𝒢𝒢 (p. 187), the **Orange Show** 𝒢𝒢 (p. 186), the **Downtown Aquarium** (p. 184), the **Kemah Boardwalk** (p. 186), and the **Museum of Health & Medical Science** 𝒢𝒢𝒢 (p. 189) are all worthy destinations. **Lupe Tortilla** (p. 181) is a reliable kid-friendly restaurant in town.

Days ❺–❻: Explore the Gulf Coast & Padre Island National Seashore

Make your way down the Gulf Coast from Houston to Corpus Christi and spend some time at **Padre Island National Seashore** 𝒢 (p. 233). This is a great time to get out of the car for a couple of days and burn off some steam swimming, fishing, flying kites, and otherwise playing in the surf and sun. See p. 206.

Day ❼: Explore Austin or San Antonio

To cap off your Texas family vacation, take your pick of the **Alamo** 𝒢𝒢 (p. 273) and **HemisFair Park** (p. 278) in San Antonio or **Zilker Park** 𝒢 (p. 323), the **Texas State Capitol** 𝒢𝒢 (p. 319), and the **Austin Children's Museum** 𝒢𝒢 (p. 324) in Austin. If you can extend your trip by a few days, you can do both cities better justice.

4 Exploring the Texas-Mexico Border

A political boundary and one of the most recognizable lines on a Texas map—the dual curves of the Rio Grande (known in Mexico as the Rio Bravo)—makes for a fascinating route through two countries and cultures. You'll finish out the itinerary in San Antonio, a city which embodies and embraces the diversity and coexistence of the cultures.

Day ❶: Arrive in El Paso

The largest metro area on not only the U.S.-Mexico border but any border in the world, this booming community of nearly 4 million people on both sides of the river wears its many layers of history on its sleeves: There are 17th-century Spanish missions, Victorian downtown storefronts, skyscrapers, suburban strip malls, factories, and poor Mexican neighborhoods. Base yourself in downtown El Paso, if you want easy access to cross into **Juárez** by foot, or by the airport, where you'll find more numerous accommodations options. The **L&J Café** 𝒢𝒢 (p. 353) is a great choice for dinner. See p. 338.

Day ❷: Explore El Paso & Ciudad Juárez

In El Paso, I recommend the **El Paso Museum of Art** 𝒢𝒢 (p. 345), **San Jacinto Plaza** (p. 345), and the **El Paso Mission Trail** 𝒢 (p. 344). Cross into **Juárez** (p. 354) on foot in the afternoon and shop the city markets, and then check out the historic plaza and 1668 mission, before retreating to the **Kentucky Club** (p. 356)—the alleged birthplace of the margarita—and **Nuevo Martino** 𝒢 (p. 356) for dinner.

Day ❸: Explore Candelaria en route to Big Bend National Park

Start the day with breakfast at the **H&H Car Wash and Coffee Shop** 𝒢 (p. 352). From El Paso, take I-10 and U.S. 90 back east to Marfa, then U.S. 67 to Presidio before diverting back northeast along the border on FM 170. The drive to **Candelaria** (p. 361) is scenic and has little traffic. Backtrack through Presidio en route to stay for the night in the Big Bend area. Grab dinner at the **Starlight Theatre** 𝒢𝒢 (p. 396).

Days ❹–❺: Big Bend National Park

Make a point of exploring the river canyons in Big Bend, and take a few hikes in the park. Camp or stay at **Chisos Mountains Lodge** 𝒢 (p. 395) at

Exploring the Texas-Mexico Border

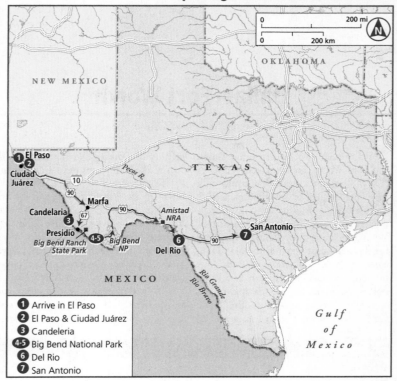

1 Arrive in El Paso
2 El Paso & Ciudad Juárez
3 Candeleria
4-5 Big Bend National Park
6 Del Rio
7 San Antonio

night or stay in one of the gateway towns. (Unfortunately, there are no official crossings into Mexico in the vicinity and once-traditional unofficial crossings for dinner are now prosecuted.) If time permits, explore the adjacent Big Bend Ranch State Park. If you have more time for this trip, this is a great place to spend several days, perhaps taking a multiday rafting or canoeing trip on the river border itself. See p. 394.

Day **6**: Del Rio

From Big Bend, get back on U.S. 90 and continue east to **Del Rio** (p. 377). En route, visit **Amistad National Recreation Area** ✲ (a joint U.S.–Mexico reservoir on the Rio Grande; p. 381) and the Pecos River before checking in at the **Villa Del Rio Bed & Breakfast** ✲✲ (p. 379) or another lodging. Have dinner in **Ciudad Acuña** (p. 378), a colorful Mexican border town. See p. 377.

Day **7**: San Antonio

From Del Rio head east on U.S. 90 about 150 miles for San Antonio. Spend the day ambling the **River Walk** ✲✲✲ (p. 274), enjoying some Mexican food, shopping the import stalls at **Market Square** ✲ (p. 274), or taking a tour of one of the famous local attractions such as the **Alamo** ✲✲ (p. 273) or the **San Antonio Missions Historical Park** ✲✲ (p. 276).

4

Dallas–Fort Worth

by Neil E. Schlecht

North Texas's two biggest cities, Dallas and Fort Worth, are often referred to as "DFW"—or, in a term that could only have been devised by so-called marketing geniuses, the "Metroplex"—as though they were closely intertwined twin cities. While unrelenting development has filled the flat land gaps between them and created a greater population of some four million, the fact is that the two cities remain 30 miles and worlds apart. Slick and glitzy Dallas, home of the NFL's Cowboys, "America's Team," thrives on an identity of banking and big business; it's "where the East peters out," in the words of Will Rogers. Fort Worth, the "Cowtown" of the legendary cattle drives and now the cultural capital of North Texas, has long identified itself quite differently: as the spot where the West begins. Much more laid-back than Dallas, Fort Worth might even be considered a bit pokey, were it not for its surprising roster of world-class museums, progressive civic-mindedness, good-natured downtown nightlife, and thriving Western character.

1 Orientation

ARRIVING
BY PLANE
DALLAS/FORT WORTH INTERNATIONAL AIRPORT   Most visitors will arrive via **DFW Airport** (© 972/574-6000; www.dfwairport.com), located midway between the two cities and one of the largest in the nation. The airport, the world's third busiest and larger than the island of Manhattan (take that, New York!), has four terminals connected by a "people mover." **DFW Airport Visitor Information** (© 972/574-3694) provides hotel, sightseeing, and transportation information, and the **Airport Assistance Center** (© 972/574-4420) offers crisis counseling, foreign language assistance, and car-seat rental. You'll also find currency exchange booths and ATMs in terminals A, B, D (International, the newest terminal), and E. All the major car-rental companies have representatives here (though note that if you're returning a car here, the rental terminal is a good 5 miles away, so allow a little extra time before your departure). Transportation between terminals is quick and easy on Skylink, the world's largest airport train.

Ground transportation to Dallas, Fort Worth, or the surrounding area is by **Dallas Area Rapid Transit (DART)** bus, airport shuttle, private car, charter limo, courtesy car, or taxi. Many hotels offer courtesy transportation to and from the airport; check to see if yours does. Transport by bus is the cheapest option, but the best value is taking the airport shuttle. For additional information on ground transportation, call © 972/574-5878.

DART (© 214/979-1111; www.dart.org) offers two means of travel between DFW Airport and downtown Dallas: the **Trinity Railway Express (TRE)** and **DART**

Express Route 202. Passenger terminals at DFW Airport are served by two DART shuttles serving terminals A and C, and serving terminals B and E; both operate from CentrePort/DFW Airport Station. Express Bus 202 departs from the DFW Airport ground transportation level in terminals A and E and travels directly to the West Transfer Center in downtown Dallas. The TRE operates Monday through Saturday (*note:* not on Sun); the 202 Express Bus runs hourly, 7 days a week, from 6am to 11pm. Single-ride fares on either are $2.25. An Express 1-day pass is available for $4.50 and is good for unlimited rides on DART and The T (including your return trip) until 3am the next day. For more information, call ℭ **214/979-1111** or 877/657-0146 or visit www.trinityrailwayexpress.org.

Another convenient mode of transportation to and from the airport is **Super Shuttle DFW** (ℭ **800/BLUE-VAN,** 817/329-2000, or 972/615-3005; www.supershuttle. com/htm/cities/dfw.htm), which can be reached 24 hours a day. A typical fare to downtown Dallas is $17 to $24, to Fort Worth $16 to $29. **The Airporter Bus Service** (ℭ **817/267-5150;** www.the-T.com/airporter.html) runs between DFW Airport (upper level) and downtown Fort Worth (making 33 round-trips daily). It departs from the Airporter Park and Ride Lot, at 1000 E. Weatherford St. in Fort Worth, and Fort Worth's Ramada Plaza every half-hour between 6am and 10pm daily, and will even pick up at certain hotels ($12 per adult from the airport [or $15 by advance reservation from scheduled hotels to the airport], $7 for children 12 and younger).

Taxis are also on hand at airport arrival gates. You can also make airport transportation reservations by calling **Yellow Checker** (ℭ **214/426-6262** or 817/426-6262) or **Cowboy Cab** (ℭ **214/428-0202**). If you prefer limousine service, try **ExecuCar** (ℭ **800/410-4444**), **Agency Limousine** (ℭ **800/277-LIMO** or 817/284-7575) or **DFW Towncars** (ℭ **214/956-1880**). The taxi fare to downtown Dallas is about $40, downtown Fort Worth, $43; limo service is about $55 and $60 respectively.

Driving from DFW Airport   International Parkway connects directly to major freeways serving both Dallas and Fort Worth (Hwy. 114 and 635 north, and 183 and 360 south). Signs clearly indicate the route; each city is 18 miles from the airport. Despite that seemingly short distance, the drive to downtown Dallas or Fort Worth in peak hours takes up to an hour.

LOVE FIELD   Love Field (ℭ **214/670-6073;** www.dallas-lovefield.com) is just 7 miles from downtown Dallas. After DFW Airport was built, Love Field became primarily a private plane and cargo airport for DHL and Federal Express. Southwest Airlines has continued to operate out of it, and recently it has been resurrected as a commercial airport, with Delta and Continental Express building or revamping terminals. While you're hanging around in the Southwest terminal, drop in on the **Frontiers of Flight Museum** (ℭ **214/350-3600**), open Monday through Saturday from 10am to 5pm, and Sunday from 1 to 5pm. Admission costs $2 for adults, $1 for children younger than 12.

All the major car-rental companies are represented here. The same ground transportation services for DFW Airport also travel to Love Field. A taxi downtown costs about $13; the Super Shuttle is $15, $6 for each additional passenger.

BY CAR

You'll almost surely need a car to get around Dallas–Fort Worth (unless you stick to the downtown areas), so it's not a bad idea to arrive in one. The major roads into Dallas are **I-635** (better known as LBJ Fwy.), which goes from DFW Airport east to

Dallas–Fort Worth

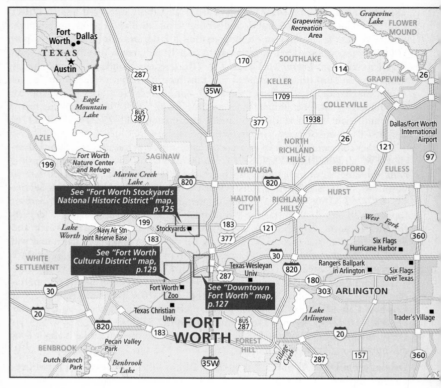

Dallas; **I-20,** which joins I-635 and heads west to Fort Worth; **I-35,** north–south from the border towns in South Texas, through San Antonio, Austin, and Dallas, and all the way to Oklahoma; and **U.S. 75** (better known as Central Expwy.), which runs north–south from downtown Dallas to the northern suburbs. From Houston, the drive to Dallas (or Fort Worth) is about 5 hours; from Austin, 4 hours. Dallas is about an hour from Fort Worth.

BY TRAIN
Amtrak's Texas Eagle serves Dallas's **Union Station,** 400 S. Houston St. (© **214/ 653-1101**), and Fort Worth's **Intermodal Transportation Center (ITC)** in the southeast corner of the city at 1001 Jones St. and 9th Street (© **817/332-2931**). Trains arrive from Chicago, St. Louis, Little Rock, San Antonio, and Los Angeles; Heartland Flyer trains serve Oklahoma City and Fort Worth. For more information and reservations, contact Amtrak at © **800/USA-RAIL** or visit www.amtrak.com or www.texaseagle.com.

The **Trinity Railway Express (TRE)** travels back and forth between Dallas and Fort Worth (day pass, $4.50); for more information, call © **214/979-1111** or 817/215-8600 (www.trinityrailwayexpress.org).

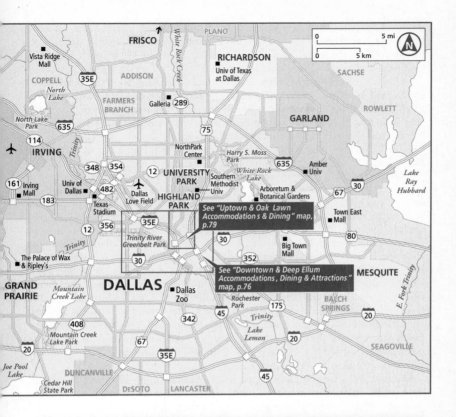

2 Dallas ⭑

Known to locals as simply "Big D," this North Texas upstart certainly doesn't lack for confidence. The indoctrination starts early. I grew up in North Dallas, and the refrain that all school kids had to parrot was from a little ditty that went "Big D, little a, double-l, a-s." Dallasites, like most Texans who are given to hyperbole when talking about their state, are proud to declare that their city is nicknamed "Big D" because, well, everything's bigger and better in Dallas.

Americans and people around the world have grown up with images of Dallas—some big, some not necessarily better. A sniper gunned down President John F. Kennedy as his motorcade snaked through downtown Dallas in 1963; while the nation mourned, a local nightclub owner murdered the presumed assassin, Lee Harvey Oswald, right under the noses of local police. The Dallas Cowboys, a football club whose supporters had the audacity to call it "America's Team," won five Super Bowls and made scantily clad cheerleaders with big hair and big boobs a required accessory in professional sports. Bonnie and Clyde began their wanton spree of lawlessness in Dallas. J. R. Ewing presided over an oil empire in the TV soap opera *Dallas,* and propagated an image of tough-talking businessmen who wore cowboy boots with their pinstriped suits and had oil rigs pumping in the backyard. The irascible H. Ross Perot—remember him?—made a fortune in technology and thought he deserved to run the country. His pop-culture place has now been taken by Mark Cuban, high-tech billionaire and owner of the Dallas Mavericks.

Dallas has come to symbolize the kind of place where such larger-than-life characters live out the American dream, even if their versions are slightly skewed. Big D is about dreaming big, so the city, not much more than 400 square miles of flat prairie land broken up by shiny skyscrapers and soaring suburban homes, adopts all things big. Big cars. Big hair. Big belt buckles. Big attitude.

With 1.2 million inhabitants, Dallas ranks as the ninth-largest city in the United States, but, flat and featureless, it has little in the way of natural gifts or historical precedents that might have predicted its growth. Yet the city grew from a little Republic of Texas pioneer outpost in the mid–19th century into a major center for banking, finance, and oil. It is a staunchly conservative city, and its residents' biggest passions seem to be making money and spending it, often ostentatiously. In the city that spawned Neiman Marcus, shopping is a religion, and megamalls fan out in every direction, part of an endless commercial sprawl. Dallasites are also fiercely passionate about big-time sports, and not just the Cowboys. Just about every professional sports league has a franchise in Dallas, and there's also rodeo and the Texas Motor Speedway. This is a place where the top high school football teams routinely sell out playing fields that seat 20,000 and schedule their playoff games in Texas Stadium, home of the Cowboys, to accommodate a fan base that reaches far beyond parents and teachers. Dallas is also a place where Southern Baptist churches pack in nearly as many for Sunday services, and for the most part conservative politics reign supreme (the future presidential library of No. 43, George W. Bush, will be located at Dallas's top university, SMU, the alma mater of Laura Bush).

Dallas ranks as the top business and leisure destination in Texas (and the second most popular convention site in the country). The city has grown much more cosmopolitan in recent years, even though it's always been amazing to me how quickly newcomers from all over assimilate and begin to think Texan. Dallas is trying hard to establish a cultural life on a par with business opportunities, and a recent burst of arts philanthropy is finally allowing it to play catch-up. Slick and newly sophisticated Dallas has plenty to entertain visitors, many of whom come on business and stay around to play a bit: great hotels, eclectic restaurants, thriving nightlife, and even a pretty robust alternative music scene. And, lest we forget, the enduring appeal of nonstop shopping.

ESSENTIALS

VISITOR INFORMATION

Besides the DFW Airport Visitor Information (see above), there is a visitor information outlet at the **Old Red Courthouse** in downtown Dallas (at junction of Houston, Main, and Commerce sts.; © **214/571-1301**, 24-hr. hot line; Mon–Fri 8am–5pm, Sat–Sun 9am–5pm). It has Internet terminals and touch-screen computer information kiosks. Before your travels, you might want to visit the website of the **Dallas Convention & Visitors Bureau** at www.dallascvb.com or www.visitdallas.com.

To get an immediate handle on what's happening in Dallas, check out the *Dallas Morning News* "Weekend Guide" (www.guidelive.com) or *Dallas Observer* (www.dallas observer.com), a free weekly paper with arts, entertainment, and dining information.

CITY LAYOUT

Dallas is extremely spread out, covering nearly 400 square miles. Traditionally, most people have worked in the downtown central business district and commuted to their homes in residential districts primarily north and east (but also south and west) of the city. New business attracted to the city has resulted in many more offices in outlying areas, particularly the corridor from Richardson to Plano, north of Dallas along U.S. 75 (Central Expwy.) and west of the city in Carrollton and Irving/Las Colinas.

The West End Historic District, financial center, and Arts District are all downtown, just west of Central Expressway (though Deep Ellum, also part of downtown, is on the east side of U.S. 75). Central, in fact, divides east and west Dallas. LBJ Freeway, or I-635, runs through far north Dallas. It connects to I-20, which runs a loop south of the city. Irving, Grand Prairie, and Arlington are all due west, between Dallas and Fort Worth. I-30 leads directly west to Fort Worth.

THE NEIGHBORHOODS IN BRIEF

In addition to the six major neighborhoods discussed below, the city is surrounded by concentric rings of ever-expanding suburbs. (I grew up in one, Richardson, and went to high school in another, Plano, which was one of the fastest-growing small cities in the United States until displaced by new juggernauts farther north, such as Frisco.) In addition to ever-bigger homes, these areas, especially north of the city, are marked by scores of megamalls, minimalls, and strip malls of chain stores and restaurants that make the new developments very difficult to distinguish from one another. However, new stadiums and shopping and entertainment facilities are drawing more and more people to Plano, McKinney, and Frisco.

Downtown Dallas This area encompasses the **Dallas Arts District,** the small nexus of downtown Dallas's fine and performing arts, including the Dallas Museum of Art, Nasher Sculpture Center, Meyerson Symphony Center, Crow Collection of Asian Art, and former warehouse district and one of the oldest parts of the city transformed into a popular hotel, restaurant, nightlife, and shopping scene; and the core of downtown offices that extend east from **Reunion Arena** and **Dealey Plaza,** where the flagship Neiman Marcus store is the sole remaining department store. Though some urban-minded professionals are finally beginning to renovate residential loft spaces, downtown Dallas remains pretty much a ghost town after 6pm (except for West End). Still, it has a number of major hotels and makes a good place to drop anchor, especially for visiting businesspeople.

Deep Ellum Located east of downtown and bounded by Elm, Main, Commerce, and Canton streets, is Deep Ellum. Until recently, this area was Big D's best impersonation of Austin, the live music capital of the Southwest. Unfortunately, Deep Ellum has experienced a recent eruption of violence, gang-related and otherwise, so the nightlife scene here is not what it once was, though there are still a number of nightclubs and bars. Simultaneously ragged and chic, the former industrial district is home to alternative, blues, rock, and other music clubs interspersed with discos, honky-tonks, art galleries, furniture and secondhand shops, and upscale restaurants. During the day the area is dead, but at night and on weekends it gets pretty rowdy. The name is said to be a southern drawl pronunciation of the main street, Elm.

Uptown & Oak Lawn Located northeast of downtown and promoted as "Uptown," **McKinney Avenue** and

Downtown & Deep Ellum Accommodations, Dining & Attractions

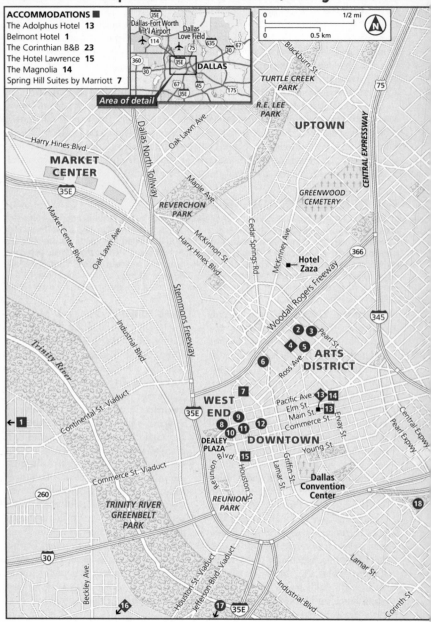

ACCOMMODATIONS ■
The Adolphus Hotel **13**
Belmont Hotel **1**
The Corinthian B&B **23**
The Hotel Lawrence **15**
The Magnolia **14**
Spring Hill Suites by Marriott **7**

Dallas-Fort Worth
Int'l Airport
Dallas
Love Field
DALLAS

Area of detail

0   1/2 mi
0   0.5 km

TURTLE CREEK
PARK

R.E. LEE
PARK

UPTOWN

Harry Hines Blvd.

**MARKET
CENTER**

Oak Lawn Ave.

Maple Ave.

GREENWOOD
CEMETERY

CENTRAL EXPRESSWAY

REVERCHON
PARK

McKinnon St.

Cedar Springs Rd.

McKinney Ave.

Hotel
Zaza

Woodall Rogers Freeway

Market Center Blvd.

Oak Lawn Ave.

Harry Hines Blvd.

Stemmons Freeway

Industrial Blvd.

Trinity River

Continental St. Viaduct

Pearl St.

ARTS
DISTRICT

Ross Ave.

WEST
END

Pacific Ave.
Elm St.
Main St.
Commerce St.

Evay St.

DOWNTOWN

Young St.

DEALEY
PLAZA

Reunion Blvd.

Houston St.

Lamar St.

Griffin St.

Dallas
Convention
Center

Central Expwy.

Pearl Expwy.

Commerce St. Viaduct

TRINITY RIVER
GREENBELT
PARK

REUNION
PARK

Beckley Ave.

Houston St. Viaduct

Jefferson Blvd. Viaduct

Industrial Blvd.

Lamar St.

Corinth St.

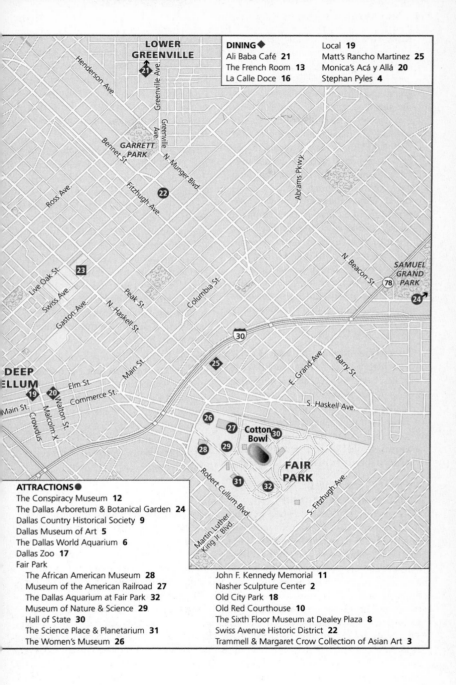

LOWER
GREENVILLE

GARRETT
PARK

DEEP
ELLUM

SAMUEL
GRAND
PARK

Cotton
Bowl

FAIR
PARK

DINING ◆
Ali Baba Café **21**
The French Room **13**
La Calle Doce **16**
Local **19**
Matt's Rancho Martinez **25**
Monica's Acá y Allá **20**
Stephan Pyles **4**

ATTRACTIONS ●
The Conspiracy Museum **12**
The Dallas Arboretum & Botanical Garden **24**
Dallas Country Historical Society **9**
Dallas Museum of Art **5**
The Dallas World Aquarium **6**
Dallas Zoo **17**
Fair Park
   The African American Museum **28**
   Museum of the American Railroad **27**
   The Dallas Aquarium at Fair Park **32**
   Museum of Nature & Science **29**
   Hall of State **30**
   The Science Place & Planetarium **31**
   The Women's Museum **26**
John F. Kennedy Memorial **11**
Nasher Sculpture Center **2**
Old City Park **18**
Old Red Courthouse **10**
The Sixth Floor Museum at Dealey Plaza **8**
Swiss Avenue Historic District **22**
Trammell & Margaret Crow Collection of Asian Art **3**

Knox-Henderson are chic restaurant rows and shopping meccas, one of the *in* places to live (chic, modern condos defy housing slowdowns and just keep going up). McKinney Avenue, once the site of elegant old homes, is now the center of the Dallas art gallery scene, while Knox-Henderson is split right down the middle between trendy restaurants and upscale furnishings stores. Some of the hottest shopping and nightlife options are in the so-called **West Village** in Uptown. Also poised to take off as an entertainment enclave is the new **Victory Park** area around American Airlines Center, where a host of hip, upscale hotels is going in. **Oak Lawn, Cedar Springs,** and **Turtle Creek,** the heart of artsy gay Dallas, are also home to some of its finest hotels, restaurants, shopping, and the Dallas Theater Center, built by Frank Lloyd Wright.

Greenville Avenue & East Dallas The high point of Dallas nightlife, as it has been for decades, is this long strip located northeast of downtown Dallas, from LBJ Freeway south to Ross Avenue. Upper Greenville draws a slightly older and sophisticated crowd, while Lower Greenville (below Mockingbird) swims with nightclubs, bars both shabby and snooty, bohemian restaurants, vintage clothing stores, and resale furniture shops. East Dallas is home to the party district Deep Ellum, the Lakewood residential neighborhood, and old Dallas sites like the Cotton Bowl and Texas fairgrounds.

Park Cities The traditional haunt of the Dallas elite, Park Cities encompasses one of America's wealthiest residential districts, **Highland Park,** as well as the none-too-shabby **University Park** and the city's major university, preppy Southern Methodist University (SMU), where the presidential library of George W. Bush will be located in the near future. Park Cities is located north of downtown and west of Central Expressway. Plenty of Dallasites tend to refer to the entire zone as Highland Park, if only to use the best-known district as shorthand.

North Dallas The northern edge of the city and southern edge of the suburbs is where the hard-core shopping begins (in places such as the Galleria, Valley View, and Prestonwood malls in Addison). It is also home to an ever-growing contingent of hotels and restaurants away from the downtown business scene.

GETTING AROUND
By Public Transportation

Until recently, Dallas used to be a typical Southern city covering a huge area but where there wasn't a lick of public transportation. Things have really improved with the addition of **Dallas Area Rapid Transit (DART) buses and light rail,** whose coverage is constantly expanding out from the downtown area. Pick up a map at any visitor information center as well as most hotels and major attractions. Single ride fare (no transfers) is $1.25 (50¢ for seniors, students, and children). Day passes are available for $2.50 ($1 for seniors, students, and children). Of particular interest to visitors in the downtown area is the free **McKinney Avenue Streetcar Service** ✦ (also called the **M-Line Trolley**), which travels from the Dallas Arts District to Cityplace Station and the West Village (it goes along McKinney Ave. from Uptown's Allen St. to downtown's Ross Ave. and St. Paul Ave., next to the Dallas Museum of Art). The vintage trolleys are from 1906, 1913, and 1920. It operates 7 days a week (365 days a year) between 7am and 10pm weekdays, 10am and 10pm weekends (every 15 min. during peak and

Uptown & Oak Lawn Accommodations & Dining

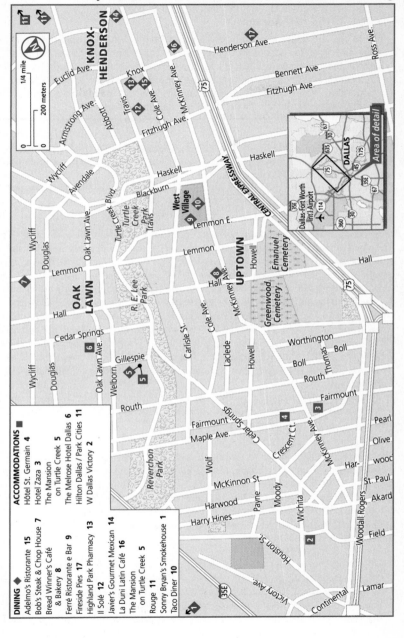

ACCOMMODATIONS ■
Hôtel St. Germain **4**
Hotel Zaza **3**
The Mansion
  on Turtle Creek **5**
The Melrose Hotel Dallas **6**
Hilton Dallas / Park Cities **11**
W Dallas Victory **2**

DINING ◆
Adelmo's Ristorante **15**
Bob's Steak & Chop House **7**
Bread Winner's Café
  & Bakery **8**
Ferré Ristorante e Bar **9**
Fireside Pies **17**
Highland Park Pharmacy **13**
Il Solé **12**
Javier's Gourmet Mexican **14**
La Duni Latin Café **16**
The Mansion
  on Turtle Creek **5**
Rouge **11**
Sonny Bryan's Smokehouse **1**
Taco Diner **10**

Tips **DART Rail Passes**

If you plan on doing a lot of hop-on, hop-off sightseeing and shopping, consider getting a day pass, good for all DART bus and light-rail travel. For local service, the 1-day pass is $2.50 ($1 for travelers with disabilities, students, and seniors); for premium routes (serving the suburbs), the 1-day pass is $4.50 ($2 discounted). You can purchase single tickets and day passes from the new Ticket Vending Machines (TVMs) on all rail station platforms.

---

lunch hours, every half-hour off-peak hours and weekends). The trolley is perfect for bar, gallery, and restaurant-shopping in Uptown, and it's a great way to get from hotels in the area to the Arts District downtown.

For additional route and fare information for all of DART, call ℂ **214/979-1111,** or log on to www.dart.org.

By Car

Believe it or not, you can now actually get around Dallas without a car, if you stick to the major downtown sights, hotels, and restaurants. However, if you want to visit shopping centers in North Dallas or outlying areas, like Arlington and Fort Worth, most people will be better off with an automobile. Be advised, though, that if your hotel doesn't have parking, street parking can be an expensive hassle in the downtown area.

The major car-rental agencies, which have outlets at DFW and Love Field airports and at several addresses throughout the Metroplex, include **Alamo** (ℂ 800/462-5266; www.alamo.com), **Avis** (ℂ 800/230-4898; www.avis.com), **Budget** (ℂ 800/527-0700; www.budget.com), **Dollar** (ℂ 800/800-3665; www.dollar.com), **Enterprise** (ℂ 800/736-8222; www.enterprise.com), **Hertz** (ℂ 800/654-3131; www.hertz.com), **National** (ℂ 800/227-7368; www.nationalcar.com), and **Thrifty** (ℂ 800/847-4389; www.thrifty.com).

Note: Yellow lights do little to slow down drivers in Dallas; even the running of red lights seems to have become epidemic in recent years, so be very careful before proceeding when the light turns green.

By Taxi

Don't expect to hail a cab as you would in midtown Manhattan, though you will find taxis parked in front of the bigger, upscale hotels and at the airports. Mostly, though, you'll need to call a cab. There are more than a dozen taxi companies, including **Cowboy Cab Company** (ℂ 214/428-0202) and **Yellow Checker** (ℂ 214/426-6262).

Fares are $2.25 (initial drop) and 45¢ each additional quarter-mile. Extras might include a $2 extra passenger charge, a $3.60 airport exit fee, and a 52¢ airport drop-off fee.

FAST FACTS: **Dallas**

American Express There are offices at 8317 Preston Center Plaza (ℂ **800/826-8759;** Mon–Fri 9am–6pm), and at **Landmark Travel Services,** Two Turtle Creek Village Tower, 3838 Oak Lawn, no. 230 (ℂ **214/520-9998;** Mon–Fri 8:30am–5pm).

Babysitters If your hotel doesn't offer babysitting services, contact **Guardian Angel Sitting Services** (© 214/521-3185; www.guardianangelsittingservice.com) for child (and pet) care.

Dentists To find a local dentist, call © **800/DENTIST.**

Doctors The **Doctor Directory** at St. Paul Medical Center (© 214/879-3099) is a physician's referral service that can direct you to an appropriate health professional or specialist.

Drugstores There are 24-hour **Eckerd** drugstores located at 10455 N. Central Expwy. at Meadow (© 214/369-3872), and 703 Preston Forest Center (© 214/363-1571). There's also **Kroger,** 17194 Preston Rd. at Campbell Road (© 972/931-9371), and **Albertsons,** 7007 Arapaho Rd. (© 972/387-8977).

Hospitals Major hospitals include the **Baylor University Medical Center,** 3500 Gaston Ave. (© 214/820-0111; for 24-hr. emergency, 214/820-2501); the **Children's Medical Center of Dallas,** 1935 Motor St. (© 214/456-7000); and **Presbyterian Hospital of Dallas,** 8200 Walnut Hill Lane at Greenville Avenue (© 214/345-6789).

Internet Access The **Visitor Information Office** at the Old Red Courthouse (Houston, Main, and Commerce sts.) has computers with Internet access for an hourly fee. Decidedly hipper is **Main Street Internet,** 2656 Main St. (© **214/237-1121**); it's got a full bar, overstuffed couches, and occasional live music.

Maps The Visitor Information Offices at DFW Airport and the Old Red Courthouse (at Houston, Main, and Commerce sts.) have several maps of varying detail of Dallas and the surrounding area. If that's not enough, contact **MAP Dallas/Fort Worth** (© 817/949-2225), which provides free street maps and visitor's guides.

Newspapers & Magazines Both the *Dallas Morning News* "Weekend Guide" (which comes out on Fri) and *Dallas Observer,* a free weekly, have plenty of current arts, entertainment, and dining information. *D Magazine,* a local monthly, has similar listings, as well as restaurant reviews. *Dallas Voice* is a free weekly serving the Dallas gay and lesbian communities, with listings of upcoming events.

Police For a police emergency, dial © **911;** for nonemergencies, call © **214/742-1519** or 972/574-4454. The main precinct headquarters is located at 334 S. Hall, in the central business district (© **214/670-5840**).

Post Office The central post office, 400 N. Ervay St. (© **800/275-8777** or 214/760-4700), is open Monday through Saturday from 8:30am to 5pm.

Safety In most areas during the day, Dallas is as safe as any big American city. You should exercise particular care, though, around Fair Park and after 7pm in downtown. Gay and lesbian travelers should exercise caution in the Oak Lawn section; even though it is the area of greatest concentration of gay residents and establishments, harassment has historically been a problem.

Taxes The general sales tax is 8.25%, hotel tax is 15%, and restaurant tax is 7%.

Transit Information For public transportation questions, call © **214/979-1111.**

Weather For weather information, call © **214/787-1111;** for current time and temperature, call © **214/844-6611.**

Tips Real Highway Names

To get around Dallas, you'll need to know and adopt the colloquial names of the major local thoroughfares. As a general rule, numbers give way to proper names.

Official Name	Real Folks Name
U.S. 75	Central Expressway ("Central")
I-635	LBJ Freeway ("LBJ")
Northwest Highway	Loop 12
I-35E	Stemmons
I-35/U.S. 77/I-635/I-30	R. L. Thornton

WHERE TO STAY

If you're in Dallas for a business trip or just a brief vacation, or you simply abhor the thought of driving everywhere, you'd do well to choose your hotel according to neighborhood. Some of the city's best hotels are downtown near the central business and Dallas Arts District, and in the fashionable area called Uptown, but many more hotels (especially more affordable chains) are nestled in North Dallas and near Irving. For most people, the latter locations will involve considerably more highway time, because Dallas is so spread out.

Dallas has a bundle of excellent choices at the top end, a number of them surprisingly old-world in feel. The majority of hotel offerings in the city are large and luxurious, well-run hotels aimed squarely at business travelers, though some very appealing boutique hotels have also taken root. The high-end luxury market is really taking off, with new Mandarin and Ritz five-star hotels coming soon to compete with the most ballyhooed properties. The best of the cheaper options are all-suites hotels. **Note:** Reservations in Dallas are toughest to come by when conventions take over the city. Check as early as possible with the **Dallas Convention & Visitors Bureau** (www.dallascvb.com) or www.visitdallas.com to see if your visit coincides with major business traffic to the city.

The rates cited below are high-season rack rates—few people pay list price, and you shouldn't either. At a minimum, request the lower, corporate rate and ask about special deals. Virtually all hotels offer some deals, especially on weekends when their business clientele dries up. Check the individual hotels' websites for special online offers. The hotel occupancy tax in Dallas is 15% (the rates quoted below do not include tax). Breakfast, either continental or buffet, is offered free at several hotels, as noted below. Do not assume that breakfast is included; if it is not, it can really add to your bill.

DOWNTOWN & DEEP ELLUM
Expensive

The Adolphus Hotel ★★★   Built in 1912 by the Missouri beer baron Adolphus Busch, this hotel is the grande dame of Dallas hotels. In the midst of the financial district, just a couple of blocks from another, more contemporary landmark—Neiman Marcus—this Beaux Arts hotel exudes luxury and refinement. Behind its historic facade guests enter a world of baroque splendor and deep pampering: dark-wood parlors, beautiful art and antiques such as 17th-century Flemish tapestries and crystal chandeliers, a grand ballroom, and an opulent dining room. Rooms are very large and tastefully appointed in English country-house style, with marble bathrooms and separate sitting and dining areas. The suites are about as large as Texas. The graceful, old-world style of the Adolphus is epitomized by the three-course English tea served in the lobby living room every afternoon from 3 to 5pm. The French Room (p. 90), serving classic French cuisine, is one of Dallas's finest restaurants; it is about as baroque a dining room as you'll find in town.

1321 Commerce St. (at Akard), Dallas, TX 75202. © 800/221-9083 or 214/742-8200. Fax 214/651-3563. www.hotel adolphus.com. 428 units. $219–$285 double; $425–$455 suite. Special packages are sometimes as low as $159 double; see website for details. AE, DC, DISC, MC, V. Valet parking $15. DART Light Rail: Akard station. **Amenities:** Restaurant; bar; fitness room and athletic club; 24-hr. concierge; free airport shuttle; salon; 24-hr. room service; babysitting; same-day laundry service/dry cleaning. *In room:* A/C, TV w/pay movies, dataport, Wi-Fi, hair dryer.

The Magnolia ★★   This 7-year-old hotel, in the city's most famous building, the landmark 1922 headquarters of Magnolia (later Mobil) Oil—known by its illuminated rooftop sign sculpture of Pegasus, the winged horse—is now one of the most prized properties in the heart of downtown. Many of the building's original architectural details have been lovingly preserved. The hotel is refined and state-of-the-art, with a terrific fitness center and business facilities. Rooms are quite a bit larger than most and handsomely designed in contemporary style, with leather club chairs and sleek desks, and many are two-bedroom suites with full kitchens, perfect for families or longer business stays. The Magnolia Room, which occupies the entire second floor, is a great place to unwind: It's got a stocked library, billiards, TV, bar, and Wi-Fi, and a complimentary continental breakfast, and evening milk and cookies are served there. Shoppers will be happy to discover that the original Neiman Marcus is just down the block.

1401 Commerce St., Dallas, TX 75201. © 888/915-1110 or 214/915-6500. Fax 214/253-0053. www.magnoliahotel dallas.com. 320 units. $199–$279 double; $319–$500 suite. Weekend rates as low as $119 double; romance, restaurant, and other packages available; check website for details. AE, DC, DISC, MC, V. Valet parking $15. DART Light Rail: Akard station. **Amenities:** Restaurant; bar; full fitness center; sauna; concierge; 24-hr. room service; in-room massage; babysitting; same-day laundry service/dry cleaning. *In room:* A/C, TV w/pay movies, dataport, Wi-Fi, minibar, hair dryer, safe.

Moderate

Belmont Hotel ★ *Finds*   Though retro chic is all the rage in Dallas, nobody does it more authentically than this 1-year-old hipster boutique hotel at the edge of Oak Cliff (a 5-min. drive from downtown). Rising from the ashes of a 1946 motor lodge, and from a bluff with panoramic views of downtown Dallas, it's a great spot for arts, architecture, and design-conscious sorts to stay—and feel like they're not in Dallas. It does mid-century modern without the heavy dose of glamour other new hotels insist on. It's cozy and comfortable, and a variety of rooms spread out over four distinctly flavored buildings, including garden rooms, two-story loft suites, and bungalow rooms. Accommodations echo the spare aesthetic of the period, but add nice doses of warmth and color. Bonuses include flat-panel TVs, plush robes, and Kiehl's products, making this nifty little place an excellent value. An outdoor terrace and lounge area frame the Big D skyline at sunset, and the lounge bar, BarBelmont, has become the watering hole of choice for the cognoscenti fleeing the slick Uptown scene.

901 Fort Worth Ave. (Oak Cliff, 1 block north of the I-30/Sylvan Rd. exit), Dallas, TX 75208. © 866/870-8010 or 214/393-2000. http://belmontdallas.com. 40 units. $179–$199 double; $238–$475 suite. AE, DC, DISC, MC, V. Free parking. **Amenities:** Diner restaurant; bar; fitness room; spa services; outdoor heated pool; room service (from neighborhood restaurants); same-day laundry service/dry cleaning. *In room:* A/C, TV w/pay movies, free Wi-Fi, minibar, hair dryer, safe.

The Corinthian Bed and Breakfast ☆ *Finds*   B&B's aren't much of a Dallas thing—in fact there are just a handful of them—but the Corinthian is closer to a boutique hotel than a traditional B&B. As such, it's a great alternative in Big D. On the east side of Central Expressway, north of Deep Ellum and near Swiss Avenue, the house is an elegant 1905 structure—which once served as a boardinghouse for young ladies and was converted to a B&B in 2001—with a formal dining room, a handsome parlor (complete with the original fireplace and antique grand piano), a grand staircase, and a modern carriage house out back. The rooms are cozy and nicely decorated with a smattering of antiques, homey without trying too hard. Gourmet breakfasts are a source of pride.

4125 Junius St., Dallas, TX 75246. ✆ **866/598-9988** or 214/818-0400. Fax 214/818-0401. www.corinthianbandb. com. 5 units. $95–$245 double. AE, DC, DISC, MC, V. Free parking. **Amenities:** Concierge services; small business center; media and game room. *In room:* A/C, TV/DVD, Wi-Fi, hair dryer.

The Hotel Lawrence *Value*   Staying (as well as eating, partying, and even living) in downtown Dallas has suddenly become fashionable, but most of the hotels grabbing all the attention will take plenty from your wallet as well. The Lawrence, a historic hotel in a 1925 building near the Sixth Floor Kennedy Museum, is more about value than flash. Accommodations are straightforward and small but nicely outfitted for the price, with good beds and all the amenities most guests need, including continental breakfast and (!) evening cookies and milk. For the cost of a cheapo chain motel, you get a prime downtown location, a bit of history, and style. Check online for Internet specials as low as $117.

302 S. Houston St., Dallas, TX 75202. ✆ **877/396-0334** or 214/761-9090. Fax 214/761-0740. www.hotellawrence dallas.com. 118 units. $149–$249 double. AE, DC, DISC, MC, V. Valet parking $12. **Amenities:** Restaurant; bar; fitness room; room service; same-day laundry service/dry cleaning. *In room:* A/C, TV w/pay movies, dataport, minibar, hair dryer, safe, dial-up Internet service.

Spring Hill Suites by Marriott   If you want to be right in the thick of it—within walking distance of the restaurants and rowdy bars of the West End, the Sixth Floor Museum and Dealey Plaza, the Arts District, and downtown's business district—but don't want to burn through your savings or the company per diem, this Marriott property (formerly an AmeriSuites hotel) is a good, safe, and convenient choice. All the rooms are good-size, comfortable suites with basic kitchenettes and sleeper sofas—nothing fancy, but solid accommodations. Visiting businesspeople should find the business center to their liking, while more leisure-oriented visitors should take to the second-floor outdoor pool, which, though small, has privileged views of the Big D skyline.

1907 N. Lamar St. (at Corbin), Dallas, TX 75202. ✆ **888/287-9400** or 214/999-0500. Fax 214/999-0501. http:// marriott.com/DALWE. 168 units. $169 double. Rates include breakfast buffet. AE, DC, DISC, MC, V. Valet parking $12. **Amenities:** Outdoor pool; fitness center; high-speed Internet access; laundry service. *In room:* A/C, TV, dataport, kitchenette, fridge, coffeemaker, hair dryer, iron, safe.

UPTOWN & OAK LAWN
Very Expensive
Hôtel St. Germain ☆☆☆   The St. Germain is blissfully out of place in Dallas. The tiny, intimate boutique hotel and restaurant envelops guests in old-world luxury, with a library, parlors, and sumptuous style that borders on bordello. Equal parts late-19th-century France and New Orleans, each of the seven suites is individually decorated, with pampering features such as wood-burning fireplaces, tapestries, draped Napoleon

> **Tips** **Hotel & Motel Chains**
>
> The following national chains have several hotels in the Dallas area and can serve as dependable, affordable places to stay, especially if many of those reviewed in this chapter are full: **La Quinta** (© 800/642-4271; www.lq.com; "Texas Specials" starting at $49); **Comfort Inn** (© 877/424-6423; www.comfortinn.com; 10% discount for booking online); **Courtyard by Marriott** (© 800/321-2211; www.courtyard.com); **Holiday Inn Select** (© 800/315-2621; www.hiselect.com); **Days Inn** (© 800/329-7466; www.daysinn.com); **Hampton Inn** (© 800/HAMPTON; www.hamptoninn.com); and **Super 8** (© 800/800-8000; www.super8.com).

sleigh beds, bidets, and Jacuzzis and soaking tubs. Indulgence is rarely cheap, and of course it isn't here (though the two largest and most expensive suites really skew the price range), but you get an awful lot of refined white-glove treatment for the price of admission. Continental breakfast is included. The romantic restaurant, which overlooks an ivy-covered garden courtyard and serves a seven-course, prix-fixe gourmet dinner (Tues–Sat, on antique Limoges china and by candlelight for $85 per person), is ideal for a very special occasion (jackets required) or merely a superior meal. The candlelit, parlorlike Champagne Bar is capable of making Dallas feel like Paris, and that's saying something!

2516 Maple Ave. (at Mahon St.), Dallas, TX 75201. © **214/871-2516.** Fax 214/871-0740. www.hotelstgermain.com. 7 units. $290–$650 suite. AE, DC, DISC, MC, V. Free parking. DART Light Rail: Pearl station. **Amenities:** Restaurant; fitness center; concierge; 24-hr. room service; in-room massage; same-day laundry service/dry cleaning. *In room:* A/C, TV w/pay movies, dataport, minibar, hair dryer, safe.

The Mansion on Turtle Creek ✸✸✸   Where movie stars, princes, and presidents stay, and most of the rest of us paupers merely dream about, the hilltop Mansion, usually lauded as the most desirable hotel in the city, is luxury personified. Whereas the Adolphus (see above) has an old-world moneyed feel, the Mansion has a brasher new-money atmosphere. It is perhaps the top place in the state for a blowout splurge; it consistently lands among the very top hotels in polls in national glossy travel magazines. If it feels like a home—albeit a very grand and showy one—that's because it once was the spectacular residence of a Texas cotton magnate in the 1920s and 1930s. The Mansion, a Rosewood hotel, is all marble floors, inlaid wood ceilings, and stained-glass windows. Regular rooms are gargantuan, as are the beds and bathrooms, and the suites ridiculously so. All have top-quality linens and bath products (Lady Primrose), but some visitors report that the rooms routinely dispensed for weekend rates suffer in comparison with the top-flight ones. Service, though, is faultless across the board. The Mansion's restaurant (p. 93), which serves sumptuous Southwestern fare, continues to be one of Dallas's finest hotel dining experiences.

2821 Turtle Creek Blvd. (off Cedar Springs Rd.), Dallas, TX 75219. © **800/422-3408** or 214/599-2100. Fax 214/528-4187. www.mansiononturtlecreek.com. 141 units. $495–$550 double; from $800 suite. Weekend rates and other packages available. AE, DC, DISC, MC, V. Valet parking $18. Small pets allowed with surcharge. **Amenities:** Restaurant; bar; outdoor heated pool; fitness center; sauna; concierge; 24-hr. room service; high-speed Internet access; in-room massage; babysitting; same-day laundry service/dry cleaning. *In room:* A/C, TV w/pay movies, dataport, minibar, hair dryer, safe.

W Dallas-Victory ✦ This splashy property, one of the most talked-about new hotels in Dallas, is part of the ever-expanding W chain. It rises with transparent, glass-happy hubris, facing the Big D skyline, and it's received oodles of attention from local scenesters who dash to the new big thing; in this case it's the trendy Ghostbar and local incarnation of Craft, a NYC restaurant that's taken up residence in the W. The hotel, near downtown and the chic shopping and restaurant destinations of Uptown, is a striking 15-story tower (along with pricey residential condos) with a 16th-floor infinity pool. Inside it's stylishly minimalist, if noticeably self-conscious; attractive hotel staff wear Michael Kors uniforms and, in the lounges, dispense drinks as well as attitude. Rooms have plenty of rich, spare style, with colored tile bathrooms, swank furnishings and fabrics, and large windows overlooking the city. Accommodations aren't merely doubles or deluxes; they're called "spectacular rooms," "wonderful rooms," "fabulous rooms," "mega rooms," and, not to be outdone by adjectives, "wow suites" and "extreme wow suites." That strikes me as just a little too precious; for much less dough, I'd haul my bags over to the Palomar (p. 88) or Lumen (p. 89) if it's contemporary stylings you want. But if you're Paris Hilton, with a toy dog in tow (yes, pets are welcome), you'll undoubtedly be happy here; trendy Ghostbar even comes with its own helipad, and there's a 10,000-square-foot Bliss Spa for all the required pampering. The rest of us, who presumably aren't fleeing the traffic and/or paparazzi, can hit Ghostbar for people-watching (enjoy the neck bobbing as the crowd tries to spot someone more famous or beautiful than their own companions!).

2440 Victory Park Lane (next to the American Airlines Center), Dallas, TX 75219. ✆ 877/WHOTELS or 214/397-4100. Fax 214/397-4105. www.whotels.com/dallas. 252 units. $309–$599 double. AE, DC, DISC, MC, V. Valet parking $15. **Amenities:** 2 restaurants; bar; outdoor heated infinity pool; fitness center; full-service Bliss spa; 24-hr. room service; 24-hr. business center; 24-hr. laundry service. *In room:* A/C, TV, DVD/CD player, free Wi-Fi, minibar, coffeemaker, hair dryer, iron, safe.

Expensive

Hotel Zaza ✦✦✦ Dallas's former "it" hotel now has a host of competitors, including the new W Hotel, as the place to be seen, but it's still full of confident, brash style and populated by the young and fabulous, fashionable, and merely wealthy. The Zaza is pretty much a cocktail of SoHo, San Francisco, and Los Angeles as served up in Dallas, but with the friendliness common in Texas. A business hotel for many in the arts-and-entertainment world, this swank four-story boutique lodging at the southern end of McKinney Avenue, the main axis of chic Uptown, is a pleasure-fest of exclusive style. Stylishly decorated standard rooms have plush fabrics and good taste, but the real stars are the array of fabulous, spacious suites with themed decor (ranging from "Out of Africa" and "Erotica" to the expected "Texas" and, no lie, the "Shag-a-delic" Suite) and balconies. Zaza has gone even more gaga with its massive new suites, which are more like apartments (named, with the kind of humility Dallas is famous for, "The Magnificent Seven"). The eyepoppingly gorgeous—if typically over-the-top—Dragonfly restaurant and cocktail lounge have quickly become fixtures in the Big D nightlife firmament.

2332 Leonard St. (at McKinney), Dallas, TX 75201. ✆ 866/769-2894 or 214/468-8399. Fax 214/468-8397. www.hotelzaza.com. 145 units. $245–$349 double; $350–$525 suite. Special rates are available for some Sun and holidays; call for details. AE, DC, DISC, MC, V. Valet parking $18. DART Light Rail: Pearl station. **Amenities:** Restaurant; bar; outdoor pool; fitness room and full-service spa; 24-hr. concierge; 24-hr. room service; Wi-Fi in public areas; babysitting; same-day laundry service/dry cleaning. *In room:* A/C, TV w/pay movies, hair dryer.

Kids   Family-Friendly Hotels in DFW

Embassy Suites Park Central (p. 89)   Large and airy, with glass elevators that stream up the interior of a huge central atrium, this hotel welcomes the whole family—even pets. Distractions include a nice pool, full free breakfasts, and racquetball courts. The kids will actually think they're on vacation. For the parents, there are free cocktails every evening.

Four Seasons Resort and Club at Las Colinas (p. 89)   Your kids don't have to be golfers, but if they're into any sports at all, this resort should seem like an amusement park to them, with tennis courts, three outdoor pools, and one indoor pool, as well as a host of complimentary children's programs.

Residence Inn Fort Worth (p. 131)   Perfect for families, this friendly hotel has rooms that are more like apartments, with fully equipped kitchens and comfortable sitting areas. When you tell the kids they can walk to the acclaimed Fort Worth Zoo, they're sure to think you've made the right choice.

Residence Inn Forth Worth Cultural District (p. 130)   The spacious rooms, full kitchens, outdoor pool, and foldout couches are just a few of the amenities that make this hotel, on the edge of the Cultural District, a welcome spot for families.

The Melrose Hotel Dallas 🍸   This is another one of Dallas's upscale hotels with an old-world, rather than an Old West, atmosphere. In the heart of the Oak Lawn neighborhood, near the nightlife of Cedar Springs and Turtle Creek, the midsize Melrose feels like a gracious old neighbor. Built in 1924, the eight-floor hotel was completely renovated in 1999. Once a favorite of artists and entertainers such as Arthur Miller, Elizabeth Taylor, and Luciano Pavarotti, today the newly revamped hotel caters mostly to execs and couples on weekend getaways. No two rooms are alike, though they are uniformly luxurious and inviting, with 10-foot ceilings, crown molding, antiques, and marble-tiled bathrooms. The renovated Landmark restaurant consistently wins accolades in the local and national press, and the stately Library Bar is a terrific spot for a nightcap.

3015 Oak Lawn Ave. (at Cedar Springs Rd.), Dallas, TX 75219. ℂ 800/MELROSE or 214/521-5151. Fax 214/521-2470. www.melrosehoteldallas.com. 184 units. $249 double; $349 suite. Weekend and Internet-only rates available. AE, DC, DISC, MC, V. Free parking. **Amenities:** Restaurant; piano bar; 24-hr. fitness center; concierge; complimentary local shuttle service; 24-hr. room service; high-speed Internet access; 24-hr. dry cleaning. *In room:* A/C, TV w/pay movies, dataport, minibar, hair dryer, safe.

NORTH & EAST DALLAS
Expensive
The Guest Lodge at Cooper Aerobic Center 🍸 *Finds*   Worried that every time you go on vacation you seem to put on a few pounds? Then I've got the place for you. This isn't one of those hard-core boot-camp spas, but an inviting retreat at one of the nation's foremost health facilities, the Cooper Clinic. Set on 30 acres of trees, trails, and duck ponds in North Dallas, the Guest Lodge is a place to relax, if not necessarily a place to relax your gut. The small hotel—called the "second healthiest hotel in the

country" by *USA Today*—remains a bit of a well-kept secret, a place to unwind and work off stress and pounds. The spacious, comfortable rooms have French doors that open onto private balconies. Guests have complimentary access to the Cooper Fitness Center, which is connected to the famous sports clinic named for Dr. Kenneth Cooper, the author of a dozen fitness books and one of the most influential figures in American fitness training and diagnostics. The facilities include a 40,000-square-foot health club, tennis courts, pools, and running track as well as a Mediterranean-style spa for all manner of relaxing body treatments. You can't very well stay at a place like this without eating healthfully, so most guests take full advantage of the complimentary full continental breakfast and "heart-healthy" fare at the Colonnade Room restaurant.

12230 Preston Rd. (at Churchill), Dallas, TX 75230. ⓒ 800/444-5187 or 972/386-0306. Fax 972/386-2942. www.cooperaerobics.com. 62 units. $199–$289 double; $315–$355 suite. All-inclusive spa packages available. AE, DC, DISC, MC, V. Free parking. **Amenities:** Restaurant; outdoor pool; tennis courts; fitness center; spa; Wi-Fi; laundry service. *In room:* A/C, TV, dataport, minibar, hair dryer, safe.

Hilton Dallas/Park Cities ⚑   Although it's a large chain hotel, this Hilton is a quiet, discreet retreat; it feels like a neighborhood boutique hotel. Tucked into a small street in the heart of Highland Park, it's a favorite with business travelers looking for excellent service and accommodations but no fuss and hassle. It's perfectly located for access either to the arts-and-business district of downtown, Uptown restaurants, Northpark shopping, and the outer reaches of North Dallas, and attractively priced relative to other top-notch hotels. Rooms are large and nicely equipped, if unsurprising. The buffet breakfast is especially good, and is included in executive-level rooms.

5954 Luther Lane (off Douglas), Dallas, TX 75225. ⓒ **800/HILTONS** or 214/368-0400. Fax 214/619-3157. www.dallas parkcities.hilton.com. 224 units. $239–$304 double. AE, DC, DISC, MC, V. Parking $16. DART Light Rail: Park Lane station. **Amenities:** Restaurant; bar; rooftop pool; fitness center; sauna; concierge; 24-hr. room service; in-room massage; babysitting; same-day laundry service/dry cleaning. *In room:* A/C, TV w/pay movies, dataport, minibar, hair dryer, safe.

Palomar Dallas ⚑⚑⚑   A marvelous renovation of a '60s-era Hilton (which had become a run-down eyesore on Central Expwy.) has created one of Dallas's newest and most fashionable hotels. Respecting just enough of the 1960s bones, the Palomar—which opened in September 2006—now struts its stuff with chic, retro glamour. It not only competes but even upstages some of the big boys on the scene, such as the new, self-consciously cool W Hotel. Public areas and rooms exude mid-century-modern cool, with brick walls in the hallways, and brightly colored accents in the rooms. Elegant furnishings and bedding are enlivened by geometric patterns. Executive king rooms, usually occupying corner locations, are especially spacious and comfortable. Unusual for a hotel of this level of luxury, pets are welcome. Excellent amenities include a chic outdoor infinity pool, a plush Exhale Spa with yoga classes, and a restaurant and bar, Central 214, which looks like an update of a swank Palm Springs hangout and has quickly become an urban hipster's destination. Taking the retro flavor a step further, the hotel is set to open a Trader Vic's, an early '70s Polynesian restaurant and local fixture my mom waxes nostalgically about. Service at this new hotel is impeccable, and special needs are more than taken care of: "Tall Rooms" can accommodate visiting basketball players, and the "Bone Appetite" package welcomes four-legged guests.

5300 E. Mockingbird Lane (at Central Expwy.), Dallas, TX 75206. ⓒ **214/520-7969.** Fax 214/520-8025. www.hotel palomar-dallas.com. 198 units. $189–$309 double. AE, DC, DISC, MC, V. Free parking. **Amenities:** 2 restaurants; bar; outdoor heated pool; fitness center; full-service spa; 24-hr. room service; 24-hr. business center. *In room:* A/C, TV/DVD/CD player, free Wi-Fi, minibar, coffeemaker, hair dryer, iron, safe.

Moderate

The Bradford at Lincoln Park 𝒦 (Value)   This residential-style hotel—the most upscale member of this small chain that operates in Texas and Colorado—is a very good value (though it faces stiff competition from newer, cooler places like Hotel Lumen). Popular with business visitors who stay for a week or more, the stylish and spacious suites are coolly decorated in muted tones, with fully equipped kitchens. (There are three different floor plans to choose from, but for most visitors the "Executive," the cheapest room, will be more than sufficient.) Conveniently located just off Central Expressway and near NorthPark Center and Northwest Highway, it's just 10 minutes from downtown (unless you catch rush hour, when it could take forever) and even nearer to the nightlife options of Greenville and McKinney avenues.

8221 N. Central Expwy. (U.S. 75 at Northwest Hwy.), Dallas, TX 75225. © **888/486-7829** or 214/696-1555. Fax 214/696-1550. www.bradfordsuites.com. 161 units. $159–$179 double. Weekend rates available; rate reductions for stays of more than 6 nights. AE, DISC, MC, V. Free parking. **Amenities:** Outdoor pool; fitness center; business center; Wi-Fi; laundry service. *In room:* A/C, TV, dataport, kitchen, minibar, hair dryer, iron, safe.

Embassy Suites Park Central (Value) (Kids)   In far North Dallas, on the edge of the bedroom community Richardson, this hotel is equally comfortable for families and business travelers (especially those with Texas Instruments and the telecom businesses along the corridor just north on Central Expwy.). Rooms are all suites; they're comfortable and simply outfitted with separate living areas and sleeper sofas, and are built around a large central, airy atrium.

13131 N. Central Expwy. (just north of LBJ Fwy.), Dallas, TX 75243. © **888/254-0637** or 972/234-3300. Fax 972/437-9863. www.embassy-suites.com. 279 units. $125–$169 double. Special offers frequently available. AE, DC, DISC, MC, V. Free parking. Pets 25 lb. or less allowed with $25 surcharge. **Amenities:** Restaurant; bar; indoor pool; fitness center; sauna; laundry service. *In room:* A/C, TV, dataport, minibar, coffeemaker, hair dryer, iron, safe.

Hotel Lumen 𝒦𝒦 (Finds)   An unexpected delight in the Park Cities area, right next to the SMU campus, this terrifically stylish, discreet boutique hotel opened in the spring of 2006. It oozes contemporary panache and confidence, with luxurious mid-century-modern-inspired rooms and a dark, swanky bar and restaurant, Social, that has become a destination among those in the know. Though it clearly targets a hip crowd of upscale business, media, and arts patrons, it's also a bargain, and it's even pet-friendly (pet packages are available, with complimentary "pawdicures"). Accommodations, done in rich chocolates and crèmes, feature angular desks, plasma TVs, plush linens, and cool tiled bathrooms. The most enticing rooms, the Spectra studios, are very spacious and have large picture windows with LED lighting facing Hillcrest Avenue and SMU. Though the Lumen's sister hotel, the excellent and similarly hip Palomar (see above), has captured most of the media buzz, this small hotel is the one for anyone looking for a quiet stay in chic surroundings.

6101 Hillcrest Ave. (just north of Mockingbird Lane), Dallas, TX 75205. © **214/219-2400.** Fax 214/219-2402. www.hotellumen.com. 52 units. $99–$169 double; $249 suite. AE, DC, DISC, MC, V. Free parking. **Amenities:** Restaurant; bar; fitness center; limited room service; 24-hr. laundry service. *In room:* A/C, TV/DVD/CD player, free Wi-Fi, minibar, coffeemaker, hair dryer, iron, safe.

NEAR THE AIRPORT
Very Expensive

Four Seasons Resort and Club at Las Colinas 𝒦𝒦 (Kids)   Plenty of visitors come to Dallas to work, but at the Four Seasons they also come to play, and seriously. With one of the top golf courses in the area (off-limits to nonguests), this is the place to stay if you've got to play golf and any old course won't do. The pros show up to play the PGA Byron Nelson Classic here every May, and the course consistently wins accolades as one of the best in the nation. Other sports enthusiasts will also be happy: The property was a top-of-the-line sports club before it became a resort hotel, and there are tennis courts, pools, tracks, and a full-service European spa on the 400-acre grounds. Guest rooms are large, airy, and very elegant; golf villa rooms have terraces overlooking the 18th green or the handsomely landscaped pool garden. The hotel is only about 15 minutes from DFW Airport.

4150 N. MacArthur Blvd. (at Mills Lane), Irving, TX 75038. ℰ 800/819-5053 or 972/717-0700. Fax 972/717-2550. www.fourseasons.com. 357 units. $360 double; from $650 suite (rates include use of sports club and spa; greens fees are extra). Weekend rates, sports and other packages available. AE, DC, DISC, MC, V. Valet parking $10. **Amenities:** Restaurant; bar; 3 outdoor pools and an indoor lap pool; golf course; 8 lit outdoor and 4 indoor tennis courts; fitness center; children's programs; concierge; 24-hr. business center; 24-hr. room service; Wi-Fi; babysitting; same-day laundry service/dry cleaning. *In room:* A/C, TV, dataport, hair dryer, iron, safe.

Inexpensive
Quality Suites DFW North *Value*   As its name makes clear, this new addition to the Quality Suites chain offers convenience to travelers on their way in or out of Dallas. What you'll find are good, standard-size rooms (with surprisingly bold bed covers and curtains) and a range of services and amenities designed to make your short stay hassle-free. One-bedroom suites feature extra sofa sleepers in the living room and large work desks, while executive rooms sport cathedral ceilings and skylights, and some come equipped with whirlpool tubs. And if you're not inclined to stay in your room and work, you can take advantage of the free full continental breakfast.

4100 W. John Carpenter Fwy. (just south of I-114, between Esters and International Pkwy.), Irving, TX 75063. ℰ 877/424-6423 or 972/929-4008. Fax 972/929-4224. www.choicehotels.com. 108 units. $69–$89 double. Weekend rates available. Rates include continental breakfast. AE, DC, DISC, MC, V. Free parking. **Amenities:** Outdoor pool; exercise room; Jacuzzi; car-rental desk; free airport shuttle; business center; laundry service. *In room:* A/C, TV, dataport, fridge, coffeemaker, hair dryer, iron, safe.

WHERE TO DINE
It wasn't all that long ago that the Dallas dining scene was pretty unexciting: It was mostly run-of-the-mill Mexican and Tex-Mex, undistinguished steakhouses, and half-hearted Southwestern themes. That has changed drastically, and today the Dallas restaurant scene has exploded. While you can still get home cooking, Tex-Mex, and barbecue in abundance, Dallas has suddenly become resolutely cosmopolitan, with chic and sophisticated Pan-Asian, Italian, and Southwestern newcomers injecting life into the local dining scene, a vigor that has even jolted the old stalwarts. Some of the hippest new spots are in fashionable hotels, including the excellent restaurants **Central 214** at Palomar Dallas; Hotel Lumen's **Social;** and **Craft** at W Dallas-Victory (see hotel reviews above). The Dallas Visitors Bureau once claimed four times more restaurants per capita in Dallas than New York City; since I'm from the former and spend much of my time in the latter, I'm more than a bit dubious about such a claim, but it's certain that you won't suffer from lack of choice.

DOWNTOWN & DEEP ELLUM
Very Expensive
The French Room ✦✦✦ FRENCH/CONTINENTAL   Dinner here is the closest thing in Dallas to a state dinner at Versailles. This is the restaurant that will make the biggest impression on your dining companions (and perhaps, though not necessarily, on your credit card statement). The grand French Room—under an elaborate vaulted

ceiling and crystal chandeliers in the historic Adolphus Hotel (p. 82)—with a new chef at the helm and named the top hotel restaurant in the country by Zagat, is a standout in every way. Formal but not stuffy, with impeccable service, it's a place to feel like king and queen for a day. The three-course prix fixe at $69 and the six-course Chef's Selection tasting menu at $85 ($135 with wine) represent excellent values for such a setting and all-around elegance and quality. From beef tenderloin with a black truffle-potato terrine to miso-marinated Alaskan halibut with baby shiitake and sweet potatoes in carrot-ginger sauce, the menu is superb throughout. Dessert might be a crème brûlée trio or, even better, the soufflé of the day (flavors change daily). As you might expect, the wine list is museum-quality, but there are also accessible options. Coat and tie are required for men.

In the Adolphus Hotel, 1321 Commerce St. (at Akard). (C) **214/742-8200**. www.hoteladolphus.com. Reservations required. Prix-fixe dinners $69–$85. AE, DC, DISC, MC, V. Tues–Sat 6–10pm. DART Light Rail: Akard station.

Stephan Pyles ☆☆☆ NEW SOUTHWESTERN   The local celebrity chef Stephan Pyles, a fifth-generation Texan, made his name with Southwestern cooking at Routh Street Café and then, most famously, Star Canyon, before taking a long hiatus. He has returned to Dallas with a heap of fanfare and critical raves, establishing his eponymous restaurant downtown in the Arts District. Large, but not overwhelming in size, and flashy, but not ridiculously so, the new restaurant is more refined and cosmopolitan— a little like Dallas itself—than Pyles's earlier efforts. It features exposed brick and Texas stone, an O'Keefe-like stick chandelier, copper-covered bar and dividing curtain, and comfortably spaced tables and semi-circular, leather-clad booths. The main attraction of the dining room, though, is the huge, glass-enclosed kitchen. From it spills forth a delectable roster of Southwestern, Latin, and international dishes, opening with eight types of ceviche (available individually or in tasting groups), iced gazpacho shooters, and spit-roasted sucking pig and apple-pecan empanadas. Main courses boast similarly interesting twists but don't try too hard to be cutting edge. The boneless barbecued beef short rib, served with a tamal-criollo-and-chipotle salsa, is perfection, and a Star Canyon favorite, the bone-in cowboy rib-eye with red-chile onion rings and mushroom ragout, will also satisfy traditionalists. The wine list is about as good as it gets in Dallas, with an emphasis on lesser known finds from around the world as well as bigspender California cabs and Bordeaux. Value diners should check out lunch, which local businesspeople know to be a real bargain, with main courses under $15.

1807 Ross Ave., Suite 200 (at St. Paul St.). (C) **214/580-7000**. www.stephanpyles.com. Reservations required. Main courses $28–$36. AE, DC, DISC, MC, V. Mon–Fri 11:30am–2pm and Mon–Wed 6–10:30pm; Thurs–Sat 6–11pm. DART Light Rail: Akard station.

Expensive

Local ☆☆ NEW AMERICAN   With an arty, intimate, minimalist design that would be perfectly at home in Manhattan or San Francisco, tiny Local chicly inhabits Deep Ellum's Boyd Hotel, built in 1908 and the oldest standing hotel in Dallas. Original walls (one with painted period outdoor advertising that reads "Take Cardui the Woman's Tonic") and hardwood floors have been preserved, adding a warm feel to the Eames chairs and black leatherette booths. With just 50 seats, the restaurant caters to the cognoscenti among Dallas diners, though the food has a decidedly homespun and laid-back angle. The well-executed menu is composed of "tall order" and "short order" dishes, with items such as skillet-fried buttermilk chicken and hazelnut-mustard-crusted halibut among the former, and tuna tartare and Nantucket bay scallops among the latter. Wine and beer only are served (the wine list has some hard-to-find selections from boutique producers), though a terrific idea for getting the evening underway is the aperitif of champagne with scoops of homemade grapefruit rosemary sorbet.

2936a Elm St. (at Malcolm X Blvd.). © 214/752-7500. Reservations required. Main courses $12–$35. AE, DC, DISC, MC, V. Tues–Sat 6–10pm.

Moderate

La Calle Doce ★ *Value* *Kids* MEXICAN/SEAFOOD   This cozy Mexican joint, in a modest old blue house in Oak Cliff, south of Dallas, has been one of the best home-style Mexican restaurants in the area for 25 years. A cult favorite, it deserves to be much better known. The extensive menu focuses on nouvelle Mexican fish dishes, such as superb ceviche (fish and shrimp marinated with lime), Mexican seafood (such as octopus) cocktails, mahimahi tacos, and other main courses such as *chile relleno de mariscos* (poblano pepper stuffed with shrimp, scallops, octopus, and fish). They even do respectable Spanish paella, or you can opt for the more standard Tex-Mex plates. The soups, such as *sopa de pescado* (fish soup) and *caldo Xochitl* (Oaxacan-style chicken soup) make wonderful appetizers. The margaritas are also some of the best in town, and they've got stiff competition. If your kids like Mexican and Tex-Mex, they should feel like they're eating at Grandma's house—that is, if they called Grandma Abuela.

If you can't make it to Calle Doce's south-of-downtown Oak Cliff location, try the branch in Lakewood at 1925 Skillman Dr. (© 214/824-9900); it's much less atmospheric but serves the same menu.

415 W. 12th St. (between Zang and Tyler, west of I-35E; best to call for directions). © 214/941-4304. Reservations recommended. Main courses $6–$18. AE, DC, DISC, MC, V. Mon–Fri 11am–9:30pm; Sat 11am–10:30pm; Sun 11am–9pm.

Monica's Acá y Allá ★ *Value* TEX-MEX   Tex-Mex in a funky Deep Ellum setting—part restaurant, part bar, part dance floor—is the ticket at "Monica's Here and There," now in its second decade of consistent popularity. The inviting space is big on atmosphere, with deep-red bordello walls, a long pale-yellow banquet, and funky sconces, the perfect venue for high-volume salsa music and dressed-up margaritas (which are excellent, by the way). The creative menu offers new twists on Tex-Mex such as Mexican lasagna, snapper *verde* (in a green tomatillo sauce), and sirloin noir. If the food makes you want to get up and dance, feel free; Friday and Saturday nights, the place heats up like a loud nightclub, but Sunday afternoons and early evenings are quieter, and there are free Latin dance lessons. Sunday brunch is popular, and weeknight specials include half-price entrees on Tuesday and 50¢ margaritas on Wednesday. But one of the best bargains in the city is the daily lunch special for just $5. If you like Monica's, you'd be wise to check its sister restaurant, the more refined and upscale **Ciudad,** 3888 Oak Lawn Ave. in Turtle Creek Village (© 214/219-3141); locals have been quick to proclaim it the finest Mexican in town.

2914 Main St. © 214/748-7140. Reservations recommended. Main courses $7–$18. AE, DISC, MC, V. Tues–Fri 11am–2pm; Tues–Thurs 5–10pm; Fri–Sat 5pm–midnight; Sat 11am–3pm; Sun 9am–3pm and 6–11pm.

GREENVILLE AVENUE & EAST DALLAS

Inexpensive

Ali Baba Café ★ *Value* MIDDLE EASTERN   Family-owned (two brothers and their mom, by way of Syria), Ali Baba draws crowds for its good, cheap Middle Eastern fare during limited dining hours. Don't be surprised to find a line of customers clamoring to get in. This plain, tiny place, tucked in among the vintage shops, bars, and furniture stores of Lower Greenville, packs them in for great rich hummus, marinated beef, grilled chicken, falafel, and Syrian and Lebanese dishes like stuffed kibbe. The tab-bouleh and signature rice dish, made with vermicelli and sautéed in seasoned olive oil, are standouts. If you find yourself in North Dallas rather than downtown, check out **Ali Baba Café & Market,** 19009 Preston Rd. (© **972/248-8855**), a larger and better lighted branch that contains a small market selling pastries and other foodstuffs.

1905 Greenville Ave. (at Alta). © 214/823-8235. Main courses $6–$14. Tues–Sat 11:30am–2pm and 5:30–9pm.

Matt's Rancho Martinez *Value Kids* TEX-MEX   In the gently bohemian Lakewood neighborhood east of downtown, Matt's is a Tex-Mex favorite—the real deal. Simple and relaxed, with a nice patio dining area, it's Texan to the core, and laid-back as all get out (though it can get pretty noisy when the margarita-drinking hordes descend). Start with great chips and salsa, of course (or the renowned Bob Armstrong queso dip—stir the ingredients), and move on to the chile rellenos topped with green sauce, raisins, and pecans. If you're not big into Tex-Mex, try the chicken-fried steak: Matt's version of the classic Texas dish even found its way into the pages of *Gourmet* maga-zine. Matt's has 10 different types of fajitas, grilled specials such as quail, and 14 daily lunch specials, bargains at $6.25 (Mon–Sat and all day Tues). Next door is **Matt's No Place** (© **214/823-9077**), a country cousin that skips the Mex and goes full throttle with funky Texas prairie fare such as wild boar.

Lakewood Theater Plaza, 6312 La Vista Dr. (at Gaston). © 214/823-5517. Reservations recommended on weekends. Main courses $8–$17. AE, DISC, MC, V. Mon–Thurs 11am–10pm; Fri–Sat 11am–11pm.

UPTOWN & OAK LAWN
Very Expensive
Bob's Steak & Chop House *★★* STEAK   Consistently ranked one of the top steakhouses in the country, Bob's—back up and running after a recent fire—has the requisite masculine look down: dark and clubby with mahogany booths and crisp white table linens. But its steaks set it apart. Bob Sambol serves monster portions of wet-aged (a difference that steak connoisseurs will recognize), corn-fed Midwestern prime beef and sirloin filets. And they come accompanied by "smashed" potatoes, heavy on butter, bits of chopped onion, and a honey-glazed whole carrot. That adds up to a ton of food. The porterhouse weighs in at 28 ounces; the signature, though, is a 20-ounce, bone-in prime rib broiled like a steak. Other entrees worth considering include a perfect rack of lamb, veal chop, and lobster. And the chophouse salad—mixed greens with cucumber, tomato, bell pepper, onion, bacon, and hearts of palm—is splendid. Bob's is a bit homier than other big-time steakhouses; even though it gets plenty of businessmen in suits and boots, if you're not wearing a jacket, you won't feel out of place—especially in the back room, where diners don denim. Serious cigar smokers are in luck, especially if they catch one of Bob's cigar dinners in which every course is served with a different cigar. A popular outpost of Bob's is now located in Plano (North Dallas).

4300 Lemmon (at Wycliff). © 214/528-9446. Reservations required. Main courses $20–$49. AE, DISC, MC, V. Mon–Thurs 5–10pm; Fri–Sat 5–11pm.

The Mansion on Turtle Creek *★★★* NEW AMERICAN   The Mansion remains one of Dallas's biggest splurges, though it must now compete with Stephan Pyles's new restaurant for the attentions of the glitterati. The big news at the Mansion is that Southwestern cuisine, which had run its high-end course, is no longer king; a new executive chef, John Tesar—a Yankee, born and bred in New York—has replaced all but the signature lobster tacos and tortilla soup. The restaurant is still high glam all the way, but it's gone more cosmopolitan. Fresh seafood flown in daily is a focus, as are fresh local ingredients and East Coast items Tesar surely can't live without, such as Hudson Valley foie gras, and poached Maine lobster on a bed of sweet corn pudding with corn-and-white-truffle foam. Meat lovers will be happy to find braised short ribs served with chipotle mac and cheese and chanterelles. This represents a big change in Big D, but one that people appear to be ready for. One thing that hasn't changed is that guests are still expected to be attired for a mansion: A jacket is required for men and a tie is recommended. Brunch remains a good-value and a low-key way to sample the restaurant.

2821 Turtle Creek Blvd. (off Cedar Springs Rd.). © **800/422-3408** in Texas, or 214/599-2100. Reservations (and jackets for men) required. Main courses $26–$55. AE, DC, DISC, MC, V. Mon–Sat 11:30am–2pm; Sun 11:30am–2:30pm; daily 6–10pm.

Expensive

Il Solé ★★ *Value* MEDITERRANEAN   Il Solé calls itself both a restaurant and wine bar, which suits its fashionable, affluent clientele perfectly. The place's restrained look might not bowl you over, but the menu and wine list should. Its wine cellar will satisfy the most demanding oenophiles, while the Mediterranean menu, though it steers clear of showy inventiveness, is consistently appealing, with such items as tamarind-glazed Chilean sea bass in a sweet and spicy portobello sauce or espresso-cured venison. The succulent, thick pork chop with balsamic-vinegar glaze, served with fava-bean whipped potatoes, is also a winner. A splendid appetizer is the Frico salad, greens served in an edible bowl of *montasio* (a hard Italian cheese). Il Solé, in a difficult second-story walk-up location in one of Dallas's hottest spots for restaurants, is a kitchen spin-off from the family that runs Mi Piaci, another very successful Italian eatery in North Dallas. Under the guidance of Chef Matt Bodnar, Il Solé is solid, and the four-course chef's special for $55 with wine ($35 without) is an outstanding bargain (made even sweeter on Tues nights, when it's the lower price with wine). Even sweeter is the executive menu, served Monday through Friday at lunch: just $13 for a three-course meal. Whether you come for a simple weeknight plate of puttanesca pasta or a blowout meal on a weekend, though, Il Solé's worth the walk up.

4514 Travis St., Suite 201 (Travis Walk, at Armstrong). © **214/559-3888.** Reservations recommended. Main courses $12–$32. AE, DC, DISC, MC, V. Mon–Fri 11am–2:30pm; Sun–Thurs 5–10pm; Fri–Sat 5pm–midnight.

Javier's Gourmet Mexicano ★ GOURMET MEXICAN   For a quarter of a century, Javier's has been the top spot in Dallas for authentic, gourmet Mexico City cuisine. The valet parking out front might be your first clue that you can't expect cheapo fajitas or enchilada plates here. Javier's serves exquisitely prepared grilled fish and meat dishes, and it's justly famous for its black-bean soup. Also well done is the *barra de Navidado,* shrimp in diablo sauce flavored with coffee and orange juice, and *pollo ahumado,* mesquite-smoked chicken. The handsome, clubby setting (Spanish colonial in feel) is all dark wood, leafy plants, copper-zinc bar tops, and stuffed animal heads. There's even a full-size stuffed bear. That may sound like a mess, but it's very inviting, with separate dining rooms and three bars, one of which is a fancy cigar bar where the young, fashionable, and affluent sip yummy top-shelf margaritas and primo tequilas and choke on big stogies.

4912 Cole Ave. (between Monticello and Harvard; it's difficult to find, so call for directions). © **214/521-4211.** www.javiers.net. Reservations required. Main courses $17–$32. AE, DISC, MC, V. Mon–Thurs 5:30–10:30pm; Fri–Sat 5:30–11pm; Sun 5:30–10pm.

Family-Friendly Restaurants in Dallas

Fireside Pies (p. 97) This is no '50s pizza parlor. In a funky, energetic atmosphere, parents and kids can enjoy pecan wood-fired pies made from a creative list of fixin's and cheeses.

Highland Park Pharmacy (p. 98) This old-time soda fountain and lunch counter serves the kind of food a kid and nostalgic parent should love: grilled cheese sandwiches and chicken salad, followed by a milkshake or root-beer float.

La Calle Doce (p. 92) This cheery, brightly painted Mexican home is sure to delight the kids. The parents can sample affordable but well-prepared seafood dishes, while the kids pig out on enchiladas and other familiar Tex-Mex.

La Duni Latin Cafe (p. 96) Latin American tortas and more are offered at this eclectic spot. Save room for dessert—their sweets are excellent.

Matt's Rancho Martinez (p. 93) Tex-Mex the way it was meant to be—simple and relaxed. The kids can start with the chips and salsa while Mom and Dad sip a margarita on the patio.

Peggy Sue BBQ (p. 98) An inexpensive, down-home, 1950s-style barbecue joint in a stylish neighborhood, Park Cities (near SMU). It has a more varied menu than most barbecue places, with a terrific salad bar and veggies.

Sonny Bryan's Smokehouse (p. 98) Kids may wonder if they're really on vacation when they sit down to eat at a one-armed school desk at this atmospheric little shack, but the beef sandwich with barbecue sauce, a heckuva sloppy joe, should keep them from squirming.

Taco Diner (p. 97) Though it's a hipster location for good, authentic Mexico City tacos, this is also a clean, family-friendly place to dabble in Mex rather than Tex-Mex, and service is almost as fast as fast food.

Moderate
Adelmo's Ristorante ★★ *Value* TUSCAN A charming, traditional Italian eatery occupying a cute two-story house tucked into a nexus of high-end design and furnishings shops, as well as a bevy of upscale bars and restaurants, Adelmo's is a refreshing and unexpected find in the Knox-Henderson corridor, which is obsessed with being chic. Adelmo's may not be fashionable, but it is as low key, cozy and friendly as it looks, with excellent, personal service, and a good value to boot. It's one of the few restaurants where entrees still come with a dinner salad. Classic dishes include homemade pastas, of course, and *osso buco*. I recently took my mom here for dinner, and we enjoyed stuffed mushrooms and gnocchi, pork loin medallions Florentine, and a gorgonzola-crusted buffalo rib-eye. The wine list has some delightful finds and good deals. Dallas has plenty of restaurants hoping to be the next big thing, but Adelmo's is content to be good in its own skin.

4537 Cole (at Knox). © **214/559-0325.** Reservations recommended. Main courses $16–$29. AE, DC, DISC, MC, V. Mon–Fri 11:30am–2pm; Mon–Sat 6–10pm.

Dinner & a Movie Deal

Ferré Ristorante e Bar, a slick Italian eatery serving Tuscan favorites in the oh-so-chic West Village district of Uptown, is a more-than-dependable, upscale spot for dinner, but it offers one of the best night-on-the-town deals I've come across: a three-course meal and admission to a movie at the Magnolia Theater next door for just $25. Given that your entree may normally run $21, that qualifies as a steal. The only catch is that you have to eat before 6:30pm, any weekday, but that gives you plenty of time to see the film. The Magnolia is one of Dallas's coolest cinemas, showing artier Hollywood and foreign releases. (If you're not up for a movie, check out the bargain-priced three-course lunch for $14.) Ferré is at 3699 McKinney Ave., in West Village (© **214/522-3888**).

Bread Winners Café & Bakery *(Value* AMERICAN/BAKERY   With tables outside under trees on a relaxed patio fronting McKinney Avenue, and a display case full of scrumptious desserts just inside the door—not to mention a name promising exactly little else—it would be easy to think of this charming spot as a place for a quick lunch or dessert and coffee. But step back into the gardenlike series of dining rooms and you'll find a more serious restaurant, one specializing in well-executed American dishes with very fresh ingredients. In the warrenlike house that was once the legendary Andrew's (where I had a memorable first date with my wife many eons ago), built around an enclosed courtyard, the restaurant is transformed into a romantic, easygoing dinner affair—still a great spot for a date after all these years. Pork loin Briand is excellent, and vegetarians will be pleased by a veggie menu (on request) as well as a long roster of pastas and salads. Of course, if all you want is a burger (okay, smoked-apple-bacon-Gorgonzola burger) or any of the couple dozen sandwiches for lunch, or one of those diet-busting desserts, Bread Winners is a winner at that, too.

3301 McKinney Ave. (at Hall). © **214/754-4940.** Reservations recommended weekend nights. Main courses $18–$24. AE, DC, DISC, MC, V. Mon–Sat 7am–4pm; Wed–Sat 5–10pm; Sun 9am–3pm and 5–10pm.

La Duni Latin Cafe 🌟🌟 *(Kids* LATIN AMERICAN/BAKERY   How cool is a restaurant that has its own "artisan" car wash next door? Pretty cool, I'd say. One of my favorite spots to hang out in Dallas, this extremely popular place trots out extremely fresh, carefully prepared, and tasty versions of favorites from across the Americas. Although it may be best known among sweet tooths for its sinful desserts and pastries, it's also a terrific spot for lunch and dinner (and brunch on weekends). Good appetizers include the stuffed *arepa* (corn masa patty) and *empanadas criollas* (stuffed turnover pastries). Great for lunch are the array of yummy *tortas* (Latin sandwiches). And classic entrees include *pollo al aljibe,* quite a bit fancier than I've had in Cuba, and grilled *asado* (chimichurri-marinated beef). Desserts are not to be missed; the sweet and moist *cuatro leches* cake is nearly famous, but I'm just as fond of the cupcakes and triple-chocolate truffle cake. Slickly attractive, La Duni's fantastic cocktails, such as the famed margarinha and the mojito, also draw aficionados and give it a bit of a bar scene in the evening. Children will feel at home in the relaxed atmosphere, and they'll surely enjoy some of the simpler items on the menu, such as chicken-and-cheese enchiladas and quesadillas. But their eyes will really light up when they see the dessert counter. Brunch is a deservedly popular affair.

4620 McKinney Ave. (just north of Knox). © 214/520-7300. Reservations recommended. Main courses $6.95–$20. AE, DC, DISC, MC, V. Tues–Fri 11am–5pm; Sun–Thurs 5–9:30pm; Fri–Sat 5–10:30pm; Sat–Sun brunch 9am–3pm; Tues–Sun tea 3–5pm.

Rouge ✿ *Value* SPANISH   Off the beaten track and, with its giant tufted red-velvet headboards along one wall and curtain-enclosed private room, looking something like a Moroccan opium den, this authentic Spanish restaurant is a welcome if surprising addition to the Dallas dining scene. Though the original chef and owner sold the place and packed his bags for Arizona, Rouge remains a good spot for Spanish dining. Start with a selection of classic tapas, such as *pimientos de piquillo* (shrimp-stuffed red peppers) or garlic-braised clams in dry sherry; several can be shared as a group appetizer. Excellent entrees include sea scallops en brochette with Serrano ham, a rich *rabo de vaca* (roasted oxtail), and of course, classic paella Valenciana (seafood, chicken, and sausage baked in saffron rice). The newly expanded wine list is mostly a very good roster of Spanish selections from Ribera del Duero, Rioja, and newer buzz regions, with a handful of prized wines and vintages.

5027 W. Lovers Lane (just west of Inwood). © 214/350-6600. Reservations recommended. Main courses $14–$21. AE, MC, V. Tues–Thurs and Sun 5–10pm; Fri–Sat 5–11pm.

Taco Diner *Value* *Kids* MEXICAN/TACOS   Squeaky clean and cleanly modern, with cool leather booths and colorful chairs, this new spot is a hybrid of an upscale Mexico City *taquería* and American fast-food pit stop. Sure, the service is fast and the food is simple and good, but the place is too fresh and too popular with Dallas's community of hip young professionals to be the kind of fast-food joint the prosaic name would imply. The house specialty is, of course, tacos—of the gourmet, soft variety. The spicy fish tacos, as well as those made with beef and marinated grilled pork, are all excellent. Although tacos are the way to go, there are also enchiladas and less-expected numbers such as Oaxacan *sopes*, corn patties fried with *frijoles* (beans), and salad and meat.

In West Village shopping center, 3699 McKinney Ave., Suite 307. © 214/521-3669. No reservations accepted. Main courses $8.25–$17. AE, DISC, MC, V. Sun–Thurs 11am–10pm; Fri–Sat 11am–11pm.

Inexpensive
Fireside Pies ✿ *Kids* PIZZA   While Fireside serves up the best New York–style pizza in Dallas, locals talk about this funky, casual, and energetic place in the revered tones usually used for fine dining—which means it's packed every night. They don't take reservations, so that often means you're in for a wait. But hang in there and have a beer, because the wait is worth it. The hand-stretched, pecan-wood-fired pies are spectacularly fresh and scrumptious, as well as monstrous in size. They use a "heavy-handed" cheese blend of mozzarella, fontina, fontinella, and Parmegiano Reggiano. Picking faves from the creative list is hugely difficult, though the Peta Pie (goat cheese, portobello mushrooms, arugula, roasted red peppers, and roasted pinyon nuts) has my name all over it. There are also great fresh salads (also huge) and grinders, and beer by the pitcher, a compact wine list, and a full range of cocktails and soda floats. Whether you're inside the plant-filled main room or out on the patio, you'll be in good company, with a crowd of cheerful regulars.

2820 N. Henderson Ave. (east of Central Expwy.). © 214/370-3916. www.firesidepies.com. Reservations not accepted. Main courses $9–$13. AE, DISC, MC, V. Daily 5pm–midnight.

Highland Park Pharmacy *Finds* *Kids* LUNCHEONETTE/SODA FOUNTAIN   It's sad that most places like this have disappeared across the country. Amazingly, this one, in Dallas since 1912, is still here, blissfully out of place with all the home-goods and high-end restaurants that surround it. An authentic slice of Americana, this old-time soda fountain and lunch counter (and yes, pharmacy) has stood its ground, even as everything in its midst has become an ultrachic bar, restaurant, or home-furnishings store. If you've got a hankering for a grilled pimento cheese sandwich, homemade chicken salad, or a limeade, chocolate milkshake, or root-beer float, this is the place; just grab a bar stool. It's a good spot for breakfast, too. Just don't ask the soda jerk for a latte or other fancy fixin's.

3229 Knox St. (at Travis). ☎ 214/521-2126. Reservations not accepted. Dishes $3–$8. AE, MC, V. Mon–Fri 7am–6pm; Sat 9am–5:30pm.

Peggy Sue BBQ *Value* *Kids* BARBECUE   Though this comfy, casual, cheery place looks like it's been around forever, it only opened in 1989 (albeit on the spot where a local barbecue haunt did exist since the 1940s). If it looks and feels like a neighbor-hood spot—though somewhat incongruous in fancy Park Cities—stuck in mid-cen-tury mode, well, that's exactly the way the owners would have it. With meats smoked on the premises, and a salad bar and a full roster of delicious fresh vegetables (choose three for a meal), it's a perfect place to bring hungry carnivores, the kids, and even veg-etarians. Parents will appreciate the inexpensive kids' menu, which comes with a veg-gie the kids may even eat. Brisket quesadillas and onion rings are great starters for the table; adventurous sorts can try the Texas Torpedoes (cream-cheese filled, batter-fried jalapeños). Terrific sandwiches include the chopped brisket and Piggy Soo (pulled pork), while full-meal standards (served with two veggies) worth a bet are the smoky baby back ribs and Polish kielbasa sausage. If you can make it to dessert, '50s-style heaven awaits: fried pies, peach cobbler, and root-beer floats.

6600 Snider Plaza (at Hillcrest). ☎ 214/987-9188. Reservations recommended. Main courses $6–$14. AE, DC, DISC, MC, V. Sun–Thurs 11am–9pm; Fri–Sat 11am–10pm.

Sonny Bryan's Smokehouse *Finds* *Kids* BARBECUE   Barbecue is serious busi-ness down here. Everybody's got a favorite, whose merits they'll defend like it was the Alamo, but just about all Dallasites agree that legendary Sonny Bryan's is the original, the one barbecue spot you've gotta visit before you leave Dallas. Dating from Febru-ary 1910 (when it was in Oak Cliff), the ramshackle little building in a humble sec-tion of Oak Lawn is so popular that even on 100°F (38°C) days, you'll see businesspeople with their sleeves rolled up, leaning against their cars, trying in vain not to get barbe-cue sauce all over themselves. Inside the smoke shack, there are just two rows of tiny one-armed school desks, under signs that read "Reserved, Phyllis" or "Little Jerrie." Place your order for hickory-smoked brisket, meaty ribs, sliced beef sandwiches, and juicy "handmade" onion rings at the counter. Then grab a bottle of sauce in a mini-Mexican beer bottle and a fistful of napkins, and squeeze into a desk—or grab a spot at one of the picnic tables in the parking lot (or, heck, jump on the hood of your car). Come early though; Sonny's is open only until the food runs out, which is apt to happen before the stated closing time. There are now new, more consumer-friendly branches of Sonny Bryan's serving up the same great and sloppy barbecue across Dallas and the suburbs, and while they're great for fast barbecue, they don't have any-where near the authentic appeal of the original.

2202 Inwood Rd. (near Harry Hines Blvd.). ☎ 214/357-7120. Reservations not accepted. Dishes $4–$9. AE, DISC, MC, V. Mon–Fri 10am–4pm; Sat 10am–3pm.

Tips Picnic Places

Dallas isn't really the kind of place with great public spaces ideal for mount-
ing a picnic lunch. Mostly it's either too hot or too cold, and people stick to
their offices and cars. However, picking up some foodstuffs on your way
over to the **Dallas Arboretum** and **White Rock Lake** is a fine idea. One of the
best places to pick up some healthful eats is **Whole Foods Market,** 2218
Greenville Ave. at Belmont (© 214/824-1744). The market, which started in
Austin, has a great selection of fruits, vegetables, cheeses, and breads, as
well as a cafe serving prepared foods and sandwiches. A superb gourmet
takeout market is **Eatzi's,** 3403 Oak Lawn Ave. (© 214/526-1515), which has
made inroads into New York City and stocks literally thousands of items,
including dozens of prepared entrees and enough cheeses to make a
Frenchman weep. The time to go is after 9pm, when the day's prepared
foods that have to go get marked down to half-price.

EXPLORING DALLAS

Dallas has long been better known for its business and banking instincts than its cultural treasures and must-see attractions—in fact, Fort Worth gallops fast ahead of it
on the cultural radar (though the 2003 opening of the world-class Nasher Sculpture
Center may finally put Dallas on the art map). Plenty of visitors simply come to Dallas and go native: Shop during the day, eat, drink, and attend big-time sporting events
at night and on weekends. But Big D, a young city, can certainly entertain visitors for
a few days or more: It has its infamous Kennedy legacy (which it has reluctantly
decided to embrace), revitalized state fairgrounds, a growing arts scene, and a handful
of parks and enjoyable places for the kids.

THE TOP ATTRACTIONS
Historic Downtown Dallas
Dallas County Historical Plaza   Just a couple of blocks from the spot where JFK's
motorcade slowly rolled by the Texas School Book Depository is the heart of historic
downtown Dallas—though nothing of permanence was built here until the 1890s. In
the middle of the plaza is a reminder of Dallas's recent origins as a Western outpost:
John Neely Bryan Cabin, a replica of the one-room log structure built by the Ten-
nessee-born attorney credited with founding the city in 1841. The original cabin
stood on the banks of the Trinity River.

Across Main Street is the **John F. Kennedy Memorial,** funded by private donations
and designed by the famed architect Philip Johnson in 1970. The open-roofed square
room, made of limestone, is a "cenotaph" (an empty tomb), according to Johnson.
Unfortunately, the memorial is also empty of emotion—not the moving testament to
a president and event that so marked the American national psyche. Inside the four
solemn walls is a black marble slab, which looks like a low coffee table, engraved with
the words "John Fitzgerald Kennedy." Johnson's intent was for the open roof to symbolize the "freedom of spirit of JFK," but I doubt that many visitors will feel their own
spirits soar here.

Just west of the Kennedy Memorial, across Record Street, is the **Old Red Courthouse,** built in self-important Romanesque Revival style in 1890 on the site of the original log courthouse (property donated by city founder John Neely Bryan). The blue granite and red sandstone building today houses the **Dallas Visitors Center** (which has Internet access and plenty of sightseeing and hotel and restaurant information).

For years, true nonbelievers used to swarm around the Texas School Book Depository trumpeting far-fetched, wacky, and occasionally plausible tales about the JFK assassination. Their presence was made redundant by **The Conspiracy Museum** (© **214/741-3040**), an essential Dallas stop for anyone who doubts that Lee Harvey Oswald acted alone. Although in late 2006 the museum was displaced from its brazen location—across the street from the Kennedy Memorial—organizers expect to reopen it sometime in early 2007 (the new location is still, at press time, to be determined). Rejecting the conclusions of the Warren Commission Report and claiming "The Truth Shall Set You Free," the small, private collection of artifacts, photos, videos, and minutiae addresses the wealth of conspiracy theories, unsubstantiated but never let go of by a large segment of the population, that have swirled around the JFK assassination and other alleged cover-ups. A huge poster hanging from the ceiling proclaims that all the Kennedy brothers were the victims of conspiracy. This is the kind of off-beat place where the staff, who call themselves "assassinologists," place an "Out to Lunch" sign on the door that says: "We look forward to seeing you (and that guy following you!)." The Conspiracy Museum is open daily from 10am to 6pm; admission is $9 for adults, $8 for seniors and students, and $3 for children. Allow a little less than an hour to visit the museum, unless you get caught up rehashing the assassination and reading all the supporting minutiae.

Junction of Main, Market, Elm, and Record sts. No admission fees for memorial. Memorial open year-round daily 24 hr. DART Light Rail: West End station.

The Sixth Floor Museum at Dealey Plaza ★★ *Kids*   November 22, 1963, is a day Dallas can't live down and the world can't forget. A sniper's bullets assassinated the nation's 35th president, John Fitzgerald Kennedy, in Dallas as his motorcade traveled west on Elm Street. Whether or not there was a single shooter or more camped out on the grassy knoll below, and whether or not the Cubans or the Russians or the CIA were involved, the Warren Commission concluded that 24-year-old Lee Harvey Oswald fired his rifle at least three times from a window perch on the sixth floor of the Texas School Book Depository, killing JFK and critically injuring the Texas governor, John Connally. (Oswald had only days earlier secured a menial job at the School Book offices.)

The redbrick building overlooks Dealey Plaza, an otherwise unremarkable spot that is ingrained in the memory of most Americans and people across the globe. The museum, the top draw in North Texas, preserves the spot where Oswald crouched and

---

Tips **A Dollar Saved . . .**

Look for $1 and $2 coupons for museums and other attractions in the *Dallas/ Fort Worth Area Visitors Guide* and other tourism board publications (available free at the CVB office in the Old Red Courthouse as well as at some hotels and restaurants in Dallas).

Moments **At the Top of the Tower**

Dominating the Big D skyline is sphere-topped **Reunion Tower** (© **214/651-1234;** DART Rail: Union station), the top of which is lit up like a giant pincushion at night. The tower, located in Reunion Park at Reunion Boulevard, rises 50 stories, and the dome rotates very slowly (completing a single rotation in just under an hour), though imperceptibly to the naked eye. Take an exterior elevator to an observation deck for panoramic views of the city and surrounding plains, or have a drink at the Top of the Dome cocktail lounge, where you can blame your spinning head on something other than the libations in front of you.

fired his rifle (now encased in Plexiglas), but it also examines the life, times, and legacy of the Kennedy presidency. The exhibit provides a moment-by-moment account of the day of the assassination and a day-by-day recollection of that harrowing November week. The display, which includes documentary film footage and more than 400 photos, summons the "Camelot" White House before getting to the event that put Dallas on the quivering lips of people across the globe. On view are images from the famous Zapruder film, whose frames have been isolated and examined more than any footage in history. However, there is no original evidence on display; everything examined by the Warren Commission forms part of the National Archives in Washington, D.C. The JFK assassination has been so hashed over and occupies such a place in pop culture that few visitors are likely to discover much in the way of new information. It is, however, a place to revisit the tragic episode, as children's drawings from the period and visitor remarks inscribed in "Memory Books" at the museum's exit attest. Unless the information here is new to you or you want to relive the episode in great detail, spending no more than a couple of hours here should be plenty.

Dealey Plaza, which draws two million curious visitors annually, remains a stark public square at the junction of a triple underpass, virtually unchanged from 4 decades ago. A red X marks the spot on the asphalt of Elm Street where Kennedy was struck; incredibly, many visitors to Dallas feel compelled to dodge traffic and have their pictures taken while standing on the X as cars hurtle by. Unless you really want to follow in the footsteps of JFK, however, I strongly advise against such reckless participation in our nation's history.

411 Elm St. at Houston (entrance on Houston St.). © **214/747-6660.** www.jfk.org. Admission $10 adults, $9 seniors, students, and children ages 7–18, free for children 6 and younger. Audio tours $3.50 extra (in 7 languages). Daily 9am–6pm. Closed Thanksgiving and Dec 25. DART Light Rail: West End station.

The Arts District

Art lovers will want to spend the better part of a morning or afternoon in the Arts District, though you could do a drive-by through a couple of the museums in a little over an hour. To get there via public transport, take DART Light Rail to Pearl or St. Paul station.

Dallas Museum of Art 🌟   Though always considered a notch below a world-class institution, the Dallas Museum of Art significantly improved its standing within the art world in 2005 when it received the undeniably world-class modern and contemporary art collections of three prominent local collectors (the Hoffmans, the Rachofskys, and the Roses); the collections, which were gifted together in an unprecedented deal, total more than 800 works as well as future acquisitions. Beyond that exciting news, the I. M. Pei–designed museum contains impressive collections of international art, especially from the Americas, Africa, and Asia and the Pacific. The Arts of the Americas section is the largest and most impressive, with valuable contributions from pre-Columbian lost civilizations of the Aztec, Maya, and Nazca peoples and Spanish colonial arts. The more limited Art of Europe gallery exhibits a handful of works by the biggies—van Gogh, Monet, Cézanne, Gauguin, and Degas—while the small 20th-century collection includes Picasso, Mondrian, and Giacometti, among others. The contemporary collection includes works by Mark Rothko, Jackson Pollock, the Texan Robert Rauschenberg, and Jasper Johns. In the Wendy & Emery Reves Collection is a curious re-creation of Coco Chanel's French summer home, complete with her collection of furnishings and paintings by such French Impressionists as Monet, Toulouse-Lautrec, and Degas. The DMA mounts interesting occasional shows, including "Van Gogh's Sheaves of Wheat" and the blockbuster "Splendors of China's Forbidden City" exhibit. In the atrium, where jazz combos play for free on Thursday evenings, hangs a gorgeous, monumental blown-glass sculpture by Dale Chihuly. A couple of hours should be sufficient, unless you're a dedicated art hound.

1717 N. Harwood (at Ross St.). ℂ 214/922-1200. http://dallasmuseumofart.org. Admission $10 adults, $7 seniors, $5 students, free for children younger than 12, free to all Thurs evenings after 5pm and 1st Tues of every month. Special exhibits $16 adults, $14 seniors, $12 students, $8 children 6–11. Joint admission tickets to the Dallas Museum of Art and the Nasher Sculpture Center $16 adults, $12 seniors, $8 students. Tues–Wed and Fri–Sun 11am–5pm; Thurs 11am–9pm. Open until midnight on 3rd Fri of the month. Guided tours Sat–Sun at 2pm; "gallery talks" Wed at 12:15pm and "art talks" Thurs at 7pm.

Nasher Sculpture Center ★★★ *Kids*   Despite its status as the principal art museum in a city of considerable wealth, the rather modest permanent collection of the Dallas Museum of Art is proof that either North Texans don't collect much great art or they don't donate it on a grand scale to local institutions. One notable exception to that rule is Raymond Nasher, one of the world's foremost collectors of contemporary sculpture. A local businessman, by way of New York, who made his banking and real estate fortune in Dallas (with the shopping mall NorthPark Center, among other properties), Nasher decided, after years of being wooed by the Dallas Museum of Art as well as such major institutions as the Guggenheim Museum in New York and the National Gallery of Art in Washington, D.C., to establish a public sculpture garden in his adopted city. The $50-million project was entirely funded by the private Nasher Foundation.

The **Nasher Sculpture Center** opened in 2003 on a 2½-acre site adjacent to the Dallas Museum of Art, in a glass-and-marble structure infused with natural light, designed by the renowned architect Renzo Piano. The center should change the way art aficionados think about Dallas and make it an art destination. The collection, which includes high-quality pieces by virtually all of the great modern masters and was amassed over 4 decades by Ray and his wife Patsy, is considered by some art experts to be the finest private sculpture collection in the world. The tasteful 54,000-square-foot center, a place of quiet refuge in downtown Dallas, features an outdoor sculpture garden landscaped by Peter Walker, with pieces from Nasher's immense collection exhibited both indoors and out. The collection includes some of the finest individual works from the likes of Pablo Picasso, Auguste Rodin, Joan Miró, David Smith, Constantin Brancusi, Henry Moore, Alberto Giacometti, Henri Matisse, Alexander Calder, Isamu Noguchi, Richard Serra, Mark di Suvero, Magdalena Abakanowicz,

Downtown Dallas's Outdoor Sculpture

Fans of monumental contemporary sculpture should, after visiting the Nasher Center and the outdoor sculpture garden at the Dallas Museum of Art, pick up the **"Walking Sculpture"** brochure (available at the Visitors Center), which details 33 outdoor public sculptures in the downtown area. Along the way you'll find works by Richard Serra, Ellsworth Kelly, Mark di Suvero, and Henry Moore. On the first Saturday of each month, a guided walking tour is offered, departing from the Crow Collection of Asian Art (see above) at 10:30am. Call ℂ **214/953-1977** for required reservations and more information.

Joseph Beuys, Roy Lichtenstein, and many others. Among the monumental pieces in the open-air museum, there are too many highlights to mention, though James Turrell's "skyspace" *Tending (Blue)* perhaps deserves special recognition as a site-specific piece commissioned for the museum. At the back of the garden, near the bathrooms, it is a walk-in box open to the sky, with optical effects and an unexpected perspective. One of the newest acquisitions, in the Sculpture Garden, is Jonathan Borofsky's 2004 *Walking to the Sky*, which depicts seven life-size figures defying gravity and climbing a 100-foot pole that reaches toward the clouds. Although the Nasher Sculpture Center—which has some of the biggest names in art and architecture attached to it—opened with big publicity and truly ought to be one of Dallas's most highly prized treasures, it has had some difficulty attracting visitors, especially locals. In an attempt to draw a wider range of potential art-goers, the museum is now free on the third Thursday night of the month (6–11pm), when it stages "salons" on topics of popular culture and urban living and opens up the N Bar, with cocktails and DJs spinning tunes. Among a smart, cultured set, it's becoming a hip downtown thing to do on Thursday nights. If you're at all a fan of modern art, or even of contemporary architecture, don't miss the opportunity to see this spectacular museum.

2001 Flora St. (between Harwood and Olive sts.). ℂ **214/242-5100.** www.nashersculpturecenter.org. Admission (which includes audio tour) $10 adults, $7 seniors, $5 students, free for children younger than 12. Joint admission tickets to the Nasher Sculpture Center and the Dallas Museum of Art $16 adults, $12 seniors, $8 students; free 3rd Thurs of every month, 6–11pm. Tues–Wed and Fri–Sun 11am–5pm; Thurs 11am–9pm.

Trammell & Margaret Crow Collection of Asian Art ℛ   This exceptionally displayed collection is the product of one of Dallas's best-known real estate developer's fascination with the arts of Japan, China, and India. The 500 pieces on display (taken from a collection of more than 7,000 objects) range from 1000 B.C. to the 20th century. The first floor is dedicated to the arts of Japan; its galleries hold Japanese scrolls and screens, as well as ceramics and bronzes. The Chinese galleries focus mostly on painting, sculpture, and decorative arts from the last Chinese empire, the Qing dynasty (1644–1911). Across a sky bridge is the third gallery, dedicated to Indian culture, with Hindu sculptures and features of Indian architecture, including a large residence facade in elaborately carved red limestone. There are also a number of sculptures from Cambodia—a standout is the pre-Khmer 7th-century figure of Vishnu—and Nepalese and Tibetan objets d'art. Allow an hour or two to see it all.

Crow's non-Asian sculpture collection is on display at the **Trammell Crow Center,** located at 2001 Ross Ave. at Harwood. It includes 19th- and 20th-century French bronzes (by Rodin and Maillol) throughout the office building and in the garden.

2010 Flora St. (between Harwood and Olive sts.). Ⓒ **214/979-6430.** www.crowcollection.com. Free admission. Tues–Sun 10am–5pm (Thurs until 9pm). Free guided public tours Sat–Sun 1pm. Audio tours ($5) also available and gallery talks ($10) regularly scheduled.

The Outskirts of Downtown: Historic Parks, Fairgrounds & Museums

The Dallas Arboretum & Botanical Garden Ⓕ   Dallas may not be celebrated for its cool green beauty, but the area around White Rock Lake, and more specifically the Arboretum and Botanical Garden, is a welcome oasis. Just 15 minutes from the gleaming skyscrapers of downtown Dallas are nearly 70 acres of carefully planted and groomed gardens and natural woodlands, interspersed with a handful of historic residences, that meander along the banks of the lake. The Jonsson Color Garden features one of the nation's largest collections of azaleas, which bloom spectacularly in spring, and nearly 6 acres of chrysanthemums in the fall. And while North Texas is not exactly New England, October and November are as ablaze in color as anything you'll see in this neck of the woods. If you find yourself in Dallas during the torrid summer (or spring and fall) months, the Palmer Fern Deli is a secluded, shady spot where mist-sprayers drop the temperature at least 10° to 15°—reason enough for a visit here. An hour is probably enough time to see most of the gardens, though it's a fine place to linger, read, and relax.

8617 Garland Rd. (Tex. 78). Ⓒ **214/327-8263,** or 214/327-4901 information hot line. www.dallasarboretum.org. Admission $8 adults, $7 seniors, $5 children ages 3–12, free for children younger than 3. Daily 9am–5pm. Closed Thanksgiving, Christmas, and New Year's Day. Parking $5.

Fair Park Ⓕ Ⓚⁱᵈˢ   Fair Park, a classic conglomeration of Art Deco buildings and spacious grounds built for the 1936 Texas Centennial Exposition, is undergoing a renaissance. Built to commemorate the Republic of Texas's independence from Mexico, it is the only intact and unaltered, pre-1950s world's fair site in the United States. Recognized as a National Historic Landmark for its architecture (the only such landmark in Dallas), Fair Park is an attraction year-round, but especially so during the annual State Fair of Texas (last weekend of Sept and first 3 weeks of Oct).

The 277-acre grounds include several museums and performance and sporting facilities like the State Fair Coliseum, Cotton Bowl, Fair Park Bandshell, and Starplex Amphitheater, one of the city's top concert venues. The two major areas are the Esplanade and the Lagoon. There's much to see and do at Fair Park, so depending on your time, you may have to pick and choose. Plan on 2 or 3 hours minimum, and a full day during the State Fair of Texas. Below are the highlights:

Fair Park Passport

Get in to all eight Fair Park Museums for a single price, a savings of 40% over retail admission prices, with the newly inaugurated **Fair Park Passport,** available by calling Ⓒ **214/428-5555** or logging on to www.fairpark.org. Tickets are $24 for adults and $14 for children ages 3 to 12. Participating museums are: the African American Museum, the Hall of State, the Museum of the American Railroad, the Science Place, the Dallas Aquarium at Fair Park, Texas Discovery Gardens, the Museum of Nature and Science, and the Women's Museum.

The **Women's Museum** ✿, 3800 Parry Ave. (© **214/915-0860**; www.thewomens museum.org), is a huge coup for Dallas. The pet project of a trio of Texas women and designed by Wendy Joseph, the chief designer behind the Holocaust Museum in Washington, D.C., this exciting $25-million museum is an ambitious, high-tech architectural feast, audacious enough to encompass the accomplishments of women over the past century.

The museum presents two dozen mostly interactive exhibits, with a clear predilection for engaging the visitor with technological wizardry. Audio guides (handheld cellphones) feature the voices of "mentors" Connie Chung, Gladys Knight, and the late Texas governor Ann Richards. "It's Amazing" is a glass labyrinth of female stereotypes, behind which are revealed several women who defied convention; "Mothers of Invention" showcases popular inventions by women (such as Liquid Paper, conceived by a Dallas secretary, and the brown paper bag). The museum is open Tuesday through Sunday from noon to 5pm. Admission is $5 for adults, $4 for seniors and students ages 13 to 18, and $3 for children ages 5 to 12.

The **Hall of State,** 3939 Grand Ave. (© **214/421-4500;** www.hallofstate.com; Tues–Sat 9am–5pm, Sun 1–5pm; free admission), is the centerpiece and principal Art Deco legacy at Fair Park. Inside is a Texan's dream, the Hall of Heroes, with larger-than-life (as any Texan will tell you they were in real life) stalwarts of the Republic of Texas, including Sam Houston and Stephen F. Austin. Venture into the four-story-high Great Hall, yet more proof that bigger is always better in Texas.

Trains evoke nostalgic feelings of travel and exploration in just about everyone; the collection at the **Museum of the American Railroad,** 1105 Washington St. (© **214/ 428-0101;** www.dallasrailwaymuseum.com), including 28 locomotives, steam-era Pullman passenger cars, and Dallas's oldest surviving train depot, is sure to feed such impulses in visitors of all ages. The entry in the "Bigger in Texas" sweepstakes? Big Boy, the world's largest steam locomotive. The museum is open Wednesday through Sunday from 10am to 5pm; admission is $5 for adults, $2.50 for children; guided tours are $7.

The **African American Museum,** 3536 Grand Ave. (© **214/565-9026;** www.aam dallas.org), is the only museum in the Southwest (and one of eight in the country) that focuses on the African-American experience and culture. The standout exhibit is the fine collection of African-American folk art, supplemented by a survey of African art objects and contemporary African-American art. Admission is free; it's open Tuesday through Friday from noon to 5pm, Saturday from 10am to 5pm, and Sunday from 1 to 5pm.

The small but diverse collection of marine life at the **Dallas Aquarium at Fair Park,** 1300 Cullum Blvd. (© **214/670-8443;** www.dallaszoo.com), highlights some of the weirder aquatic specimens in the marine and freshwater world, including walking fish, four-eyed fish, upside-down jellyfish, and desert fish. And who can resist watching the piranhas and sharks being fed? The newest and largest addition is the Amazon Flooded Forest, a 10,000-gallon tank with 30 species from the Amazon River. The aquarium is open daily from 9am to 4:30pm; admission is $4 for adults, $3 for children ages 3 to 11.

The **Museum of Nature and Science,** 3535 Grand Ave. (© **214/428-5555;** www.natureandscience.org), is the former Dallas Museum of Natural History now merged with The Science Place and IMAX theater. Families can view the kind of wildlife that roamed Texas before steers and longhorns, namely, dinosaurs, and explore permanent exhibits like "Paleontology Lab" and "Prehistoric Texas." You can also entertain the kids with more than 300 hands-on science exhibits—where they can amaze themselves by lifting a half-ton with one hand and playing with electricity—and the massive, domed IMAX theater. The Planetarium features stargazing shows Monday through Saturday.

The museum is open Tuesday through Saturday from 10am to 5pm, Sunday from noon to 5pm; admission is $8.50 for adults, $7.50 for seniors, $5 for children ages 3 to 12. Admission to the planetarium shows is $4 for all, while IMAX screenings are $7 for adults, $6 for seniors and children ages 3 to 12. Combo-pack tickets for all exhibits, including one IMAX screening, are $15 for adults, $13 for seniors, and $10 for children ages 3 to 12. Parking is free.

3809 Grand Ave. (bordered by S. Fitzhugh, Washington, and Parry aves., and Cullum Blvd.). © **214/670-8400**, or 214/421-9600 for museum and event information. www.fairpark.org.

Meadows Museum of Art ★★ *Finds*   On the campus of Southern Methodist University is one of the city's best-kept secrets: the finest collection of Spanish art outside Spain (so significant, in fact, that it spent much of 2000 on display at the top-tier Thyssen-Bornemisza museums in Madrid and Barcelona). A Dallas oil magnate, Algur Meadows, went to Spain to search for oil, entertaining himself at the Prado Museum. He came up dry, but his sojourn into Spanish art history bore fruit: Meadows began to assemble a splendid collection of works from the 15th to 20th centuries, including pieces by Spanish masters from the Golden Age of Spanish painting (such as Velázquez, Goya, Ribera, Murillo, Zurbarán—just about the only big name missing is El Greco). Having moved into a new building six times larger than the old site, Meadows Museum is one of the best small museums with a singular focus in the U.S. Of special note among the nearly 700 items on display are Ribera's *Retrato de un Caballero de Santiago* and Goya's *El Corral de los Locos* (by many accounts the finest Goya found in the United States), as well as a series of 200 works on paper by Goya. The 20th-century Spanish masters Picasso, Dalí, Miró, and Tàpies are also represented.

Owens Fine Arts Center, SMU Campus, 5900 Bishop Blvd. (1 block north of Mockingbird Lane, west of I-75). © **214/768-2516**. www.meadowsmuseumdallas.org. Admission $8 adults and students, free for children younger than 12; $4 after 5pm and free Thurs after 5pm. Tues–Wed and Fri–Sat 10am–5pm; Thurs 10am–5pm; Sun noon–5pm. Free public tours Sept–May Sun 2pm and occasional Sun in summer.

Old City Park ★ *Kids*   Dallas's Old West heritage is on self-conscious display in this downtown 13-acre park of three dozen historic buildings. The complex re-creates a late-19th-century village, complete with a redbrick Main Street, Victorian homes, a log cabin dating from 1847, and Old West standards such as a train depot, general store, one-room church, schoolhouse, bank (said to have been robbed by Bonnie and Clyde in the 1930s), and law offices. All have been transported from their original locations in and around Dallas, immaculately restored and reconstructed on the attractive grounds, which have the glittering city skyline as a backdrop. Guided tours escort visitors inside several of the buildings, including a "Living Farmstead," a re-creation of a North Texas farm (ca. 1860). On selected dates during the first 2 weeks of December, the village celebrates Candlelight at Old City Park, a popular "Victorian Holiday Celebration." (Candlelight admission tickets are $3 more than regular prices.)

A pretty good restaurant, Brent Place, occupies an 1876 "architecture catalogue" farmhouse (ordered by mail and shipped by rail to rural areas) and serves lunch Tuesday through Saturday from 11am to 3pm; call © **212/421-3057** for reservations. Visitors are also allowed to picnic on the grounds. Plan to spend 1½ hours or so here.

1717 Gano St. (between Harwood and Ervay sts., south of I-30). ℂ 214/421-5141. www.oldcitypark.org. Admission $7 adults, $5 seniors, $4 children ages 3–12. Tues–Sat 10am–4pm; Sun noon–4pm (buildings closed Mon, but grounds remain open).

Swiss Avenue Historic District   Toward the turn of the 20th century, the Dallas elite began to abandon the area that now comprises the Arts District and move east (near the modestly funky Lakewood neighborhood). Sprawling, grand homes from the early 1900s—English Tudor, Georgian, Spanish, you name it—line a broad avenue, about 4 blocks of which are listed in the National Register of Historic Places. The Wilson Blocks (2800 and 2900), named for Frederick Wilson, who built a number of the homes there, are especially attractive. Around the holidays, Swiss Avenue is a favorite for Christmas lights cruisers. A drive-by can be done in 15 minutes; allow a half-hour if you want to stroll.

Northeast of downtown, along Swiss Ave. between La Vista Dr. and Fitzhugh Ave. (take Fitzhugh east from I-75).

MORE TO SEE & DO

The Dallas World Aquarium *Kids*   Housed in a former warehouse in the West End district, the Dallas aquarium *not* at Fair Park is a good place to hide out from the sun downtown. My niece and nephew enjoy communing with the stingrays, sea turtles, sharks, and reef fish. Their favorite, though, is "Orinoco—Secrets of the River," an immersion into the tropical rainforest of Venezuela, a cool area teeming with Peruvian squirrel monkeys, endangered Orinoco crocs, jaguars, and soft-billed toucans. The newest exhibit is "Mundo Maya," with a 400,000-gallon shark tank. Plan on about an hour's visit. A restaurant and a cafe are on the premises.

1801 N. Griffin (West End District). ℂ 214/720-2224. www.dwazoo.com. Admission $16 adults, $13 seniors, $8.95 children ages 3–12, free for children under 3. Daily 10am–5pm. DART Light Rail: West End station.

Dallas Zoo *Kids*   If you're headed west to Fort Worth and one zoo trip will do, you'd be better off waiting (the Fort Worth Zoo, along with the one in San Antonio, are the two best in Texas and two of the best in the country). Otherwise, if the kids are clamoring for some wild animals, the recently renovated Dallas Zoo—the oldest zoo in Texas, founded in 1888—isn't likely to disappoint (indeed, one exhibit, "Wilds of Africa," was named the top African zoo exhibit in the country by *The Zoobook: A Guide to America's Best*). The sprawling 95-acre park also features a habitat for rare Sumatran tigers, a chimpanzee forest, and a monorail safari ride. A couple of hours spent here should suffice for the kids.

650 S. R. L. Thornton Fwy. (in Oak Cliff, 3 miles south of downtown Dallas). ℂ 214/670-5656. www.dallas-zoo.org. Admission $8 adults, $4 seniors, $5 children ages 3–11, free for children younger than 3. Daily 9am–4pm. Parking $5. DART Light Rail: Dallas Zoo station.

ESPECIALLY FOR KIDS

Older children who have studied the 1960s and Kennedy should appreciate the **Sixth Floor Museum.** Younger kids are likely to have a better time at the **Dallas Zoo** or either **The Dallas Aquarium at Fair Park** or **The Dallas World Aquarium.**

Fair Park has plenty to offer families, especially if you happen to be in Dallas during the State Fair of Texas (Oct). Even if you miss the fair, Fair Park's **The Science Place/Planetarium** (with its Robot Zoo) and **IMAX Theater** are great places to hide from the Texas sun. Girls of all ages (and open-minded boys) may find interactive inspiration at the new **Women's Museum.** Kids tend to like trains, so a whistle stop at the **Age of Steam Railroad Museum** should be diverting, as should a visit to the **Dallas Museum of Natural History** (with its life-size dinosaur models).

The staging of life on the prairie at **Old City Park,** with actors re-creating the late 19th and early 20th centuries, is plenty of fun for both kids and adults. Check out family theater productions at the **Dallas Children's Theater,** Crescent Theater, 2215 Cedar Springs at Maple (*©* 214/978-0110). The Dallas Museum of Art's **Gateway Gallery** has cool interactive art displays for kids. Children into movies may want to check out Hollywood sets and memorabilia at **The Studios at Las Colinas.**

The **Plano Balloon Festival,** a 3-day event held in mid-September in Oak Point Park, 2801 E. Spring Creek Pkwy., is one of the country's largest. More than 100 hot-air balloons, many of them curious shapes and recognizable figures, launch each day at 7am and 6pm. It's worth the drive (and early rise), unless it's too windy to launch; call *©* 972/867-7566 or visit www.planoballoonfest.org for more information. **Sporting events,** such as games of the Cowboys, Rangers, Sidekicks, and Stars, draw huge family crowds. Finally, just getting around parts of Dallas can be fun for children; take the **DART Light Rail system** around downtown (especially direct to the Dallas Zoo) and be sure to hop aboard the historic **trolleys** that patrol McKinney Avenue.

Arlington, midway between Dallas and Fort Worth, is the big draw for families, with **Six Flags Over Texas** amusement park, **Texas Rangers baseball** (including the excellent Legends of the Game Baseball Museum), **Hurricane Harbor** water park, **The Palace of Wax & Ripley's Believe It or Not,** and more. And if you're looking to combine shopping with entertainment for the kids, Texas malls are in themselves theme parks (with skating rinks and much more). See "Arlington," later in this chapter.

ORGANIZED TOURS

Gray Line/Coach USA (*©* 214/988-3000; www.grayline.com) is the big daddy of bus tours. It offers at least six themed sightseeing tours in the Dallas–Fort Worth area. Choose from JFK Historical Tour, Rodeo Roundup, or a Western-themed daylong tour of Fort Worth that includes horseback riding and a hayride. Prices range from $30 per person for a 3-hour tour to $45 per person for a 9-hour Dallas and Fort Worth trip (half-price for children). For simple, standard, dependable tours, these are an okay deal. Other sightseeing tours of Dallas and Fort Worth are handled by **All In One Tour Services** (*©* 214/698-0332; www.allinonetourservices.com).

Dallas Surrey Services, 381 E. Greenbriar Lane (*©* 214/946-9911), offers horse-drawn carriage tours of historic Dallas 7 nights a week, weather permitting. Standard tours originate in the West End and visit Dealey Plaza and the Texas School Book Depository, Pioneer Plaza, and the Arts District, lasting about 20 minutes ($30 for up to four people). Longer, custom tours can last up to an hour ($100, four people). **Belle Starr Carriages** (*©* 972/734-3100) also offers horse-drawn tours of downtown Dallas, including Christmas Light Tours through Highland Park during the month of December.

DFW Heli-Tours (*©* 972/723-5364; www.dfwhelitours.com) takes up to six passengers out over Dallas for a bird's-eye view in a red Bell 'copter, starting from $25 per person for a short 5-minute ride.

Hour-long, free **Walking Arts District Strolls** covering the zone's art and architecture are conducted the first Saturday of every month at 10:30am, leaving from in front of the Trammell & Margaret Crow Collection of Asian Art, 2010 Flora St. Call *©* 214/953-1977 for additional information and reservations.

OUTDOOR ACTIVITIES

BIKING, IN-LINE SKATING & JOGGING   White Rock Lake, 5 miles east of downtown Dallas (off Loop 12), is the most popular area for cycling, skating, and running (and, of course, walking). A 12-mile loop traces the banks of the lake. The park is open from 6am to midnight, though I wouldn't advise hanging about too long after dark falls. Nearby bike and skate shops offer rentals.

GOLF   North Texas, where such golf legends as Byron Nelson, Ben Hogan, and Lee Trevino hail from, has a huge number of golf courses, from challenging championship courses to comfortable courses suited to players of all stripes. **TPC at the Four Seasons Resort and Club** (© 972/717-2400; greens fees $150), home of the PGA Byron Nelson Classic, is the best and most spectacular course in the area—but you'll have to stay at the Four Seasons to play (see p. 89 for a full review). Another hotel golf course, rated among the top 50 resorts in the United States, is **Bear Creek Golf Club,** 3500 Bear Creek Court/DFW Airport (© 972/456-3200; www.bearcreek-golf.com; greens fees and cart $78–$88, with twilight reduced rates available), featuring two nicely designed championship 18-hole courses on 355 acres of rolling hills.

The City of Dallas operates several courses open to the public. The newest addition is **Keeton Park Golf Course,** 2323 Jim Miller Rd. southeast of downtown Dallas off I-30 (© 214/670-8784), which has pecan tree–lined fairways and numerous ponds. Greens fees are $17. **Tenison Golf Course,** 3501 Samuell Blvd. (© 214/670-1402), just 5 miles east of downtown, has two 18-hole courses divided by White Rock Creek. Greens fees are $14 to $34, on weekends $17 to $39.

Local duffers (as well as football fans) rave about the **Cowboys Golf Club,** 1600 Fairway Dr., in Grapevine (© 817/481-7277; www.cowboysgolfclub.com; greens fees all-inclusive VIP package $140, twilight play $75), which is certainly unique: Not only does it boast huge changes in elevation, it claims to be the "world's first NFL-themed golf course." The clubhouse is packed with Dallas Cowboys memorabilia and Super Bowl trophies, and markers along the course pay tribute to key moments in Cowboys lore. Also a healthy drive from Dallas, named among the "Best Places to Play" by *Golf Digest* (and rated one of the top five public courses in Texas) is **Buffalo Creek Golf Club,** 624 Country Club Dr., Rockwall (© 972/771-4003), near Lake Ray Hubbard. Greens fees, including cart and range balls, are $69 Monday through Friday, $89 Saturday and Sunday. One of the most difficult courses is **Sleepy Hollow Country Club,** 4747 S. Loop 12 (© 214/371-3433), just 10 minutes south of downtown, which is private but allows the public to play as guests. Greens fees Monday through Friday are $22 before noon and $27 after noon; Saturday through Sunday, $32 before noon, $42 after noon. All rates include a cart; if you're walking, fees are $13 less.

Golf fanatics who like to imagine themselves winning the Masters or British Open may want to venture north of Dallas and Fort Worth, to Flower Mound, Texas, where the **Tour 18 Dallas** course reproduces 18 of the best-known holes in golf (from courses such as Winged Foot and Augusta National). The course, 8718 Amen Corner, Flower Mound (© 800/946-5310; www.tour18golf.com), is west of I-35E and 121. Greens fees are $65 to $140.

TENNIS   Even though tennis in Dallas is mostly confined to swank (and off-limits) private tennis clubs, there are several public courts where visitors can play a few sets. The following are city-owned but have privately run pro shops: **Fair Oaks,** 7501 Merriman Pkwy. (© 214/670-1495), near White Rock Creek (4 miles north of White Rock Lake), has 16 lighted courts; **Fretz Park,** 14700 Hillcrest (© 214/670-6622), where I took lessons as a kid, has 15 lighted courts.

Packin' Heat, Texas-Style

The right to own, use, and brag about firearms is a protected birthright in Texas. I'm not necessarily advocating this—I mean, personally I think it's a little odd that the local concealed gun law allows Texans to take their pistols to church on Sunday, and museums have to post signs that warn "No Firearms"— but heaven knows I wouldn't dare offend gun owners. If you want to play Texan while in Big D, what better way than to fire off a few rounds? If that's your idea of R&R, get yourself over to the **DFW Gun Club & Training Center,** 1607 Mockingbird Lane (✆ 214/630-4866; www.dfwgun.com), which operates the DFW Gun Range for a little indoor shooting. Featured hilariously in the film about Borat, the fictional reporter from Kazakhstan, the club offers shooting instruction and even concealed handgun license classes.

SPECTATOR SPORTS

Dallas is sports-mad, one of the only cities in the U.S. to support teams in six professional sports. Tickets to pro sporting events are available from **Central Tickets** (✆ 817/335-9000), **Star Tickets** (✆ 972/660-8300), and **Ticketmaster** (✆ 214/373-8000).

AUTO RACING   For information on the Texas Motor Speedway, see the "Auto Racing" entry in the Fort Worth section of this chapter (p. 145).

BASEBALL   The **Texas Rangers** (formerly owned by the current president of the U.S., George W. Bush) play from April to October at one of the finest stadiums in the country, **Rangers Stadium in Arlington,** I-30 at Highway 157 (✆ 817/273-5100; www.texasrangers.com), a home field that recalls the glory days of baseball. Of special interest is the fascinating **Legends of the Game Baseball Museum,** with rare pieces on loan from the Cooperstown Baseball Museum (the only stadium so fortunate). See p. 118 for additional information.

The **Frisco Rough Riders** (✆ 972/334-1909; www.ridersbaseball.com), the Texas Rangers feeder team, play minor league at the new stadium at Highway S. 12 between Dallas North Tollway and Parkwood Boulevard.

BASKETBALL   The **Dallas Mavericks** (✆ 214/747-MAVS or 214/665-4797; www.nba.com/mavericks), one of the top teams in the NBA, call the American Airlines Center home. The excellent arena, built by the same architect who created the critically acclaimed Rangers Stadium in Arlington for the Texas Rangers, opened in July 2001. Single-game tickets (available at Ticketmaster, ✆ 214/373-8000) are $10 to $225 and can be a bit hard to come by, as popular as the Mavs are at home. Tours of the arena are available on nonevent days at 10:30am.

FOOTBALL   The **Dallas Cowboys,** five-time Super Bowl Champions and (at least formerly) "America's Team," play from August to December at **Texas Stadium,** 2401 E. Airport Fwy., Irving (✆ 972/785-4800; www.dallascowboys.com), the arena with the famous hole in the roof. Individual game tickets, which cost $36 to $68, aren't easy to come by, so plan ahead if you want to avoid paying high broker's fees. The **Dallas Cowboy Cheerleaders,** who started a professional trend of scantily clad females bouncing around on the sidelines, still shimmy and cheer them on, big hairdos, cleavage, and all. Tours of Texas Stadium are available on a daily basis. The **Dallas Desperados**

play arena football (AFL) in the spring at American Airlines Stadium in Irving; call ℂ **972/785-4900** or visit www.dallasdesperados.com for information.

GOLF   The PGA **Byron Nelson Classic,** named for a local legend, has been held in Dallas for the past 3 decades every May. Check out some of the top names in professional golf at the **Four Seasons Resort and Club** (call ℂ **972/717-1200** for tickets).

HOCKEY   Dallas may not seem like the most logical place for a professional ice hockey team, but Big D has one of the best, the **Dallas Stars** (the 2000 Western Conference Champions), and Dallasites are wild about them. The Stars play at the American Airlines Center; the season is September through April. The Stars sell out all of their home games, so plan ahead if you want to see a game (ℂ **214/GO-STARS;** www.dallasstars.com). Tickets (available at Ticketmaster, ℂ **214/373-8000**) range from $25 to $300, and family packs (tickets and food) are available.

RODEO   One of the top rodeos in Texas, and a huge draw for out-of-towners and travelers from abroad, is the **Mesquite Championship Rodeo,** about 20 miles northeast of downtown at Resistol Arena, 1818 Rodeo Dr. (ℂ **800/833-9339** or 972/285-8777; www.mesquiterodeo.com). You can check out some authentic professional rodeo action—bull riding, saddle and bareback riding, calf roping, and chuckwagon races—on Friday and Saturday nights at 8pm (reserved grandstand seating $14; general admission $10 adults, $7 seniors, $4 children younger than 12). Animal-rights sympathizers might feel a bit squeamish watching some of the roping exercises, which violently snap calves' heads back. There's a petting zoo for kids and a gift shop for Western duds just like the ones the cowboys and their fans will be sporting. Rodeo season is April through October.

SOCCER   The newest professional team in the area, **FC Dallas,** plays outdoor soccer (MLS). Conference champions in 2006, FC Dallas moved from the Cotton Bowl to Pizza Hut Park in Frisco, 30 miles north of Dallas, and drew 1.5 million fans to the 20,000-capacity stadium in its first full year there. The season lasts from April to October. Tickets cost $9 to $60. Call ℂ **888/FCD-GOAL** or visit http://fc.dallas.mlsnet.com for more information.

The **Dallas Sidekicks** of the Major Indoor Soccer League used to play at the American Airlines Center, but the team has been inactive during the last couple seasons. The league still hopes that the team will make its return to Dallas in the near future; visit www.dallassidekicks.com for updates.

SHOPPING

In Big D, shopping isn't merely a mundane chore necessary to outfit yourself, your kids, and your home. Shopping is a sport and a pastime, a social activity and entertainment. Dallasites don't pull on sweats and go incognito to the mall; they get dolled up and strut their stuff. Having grown up in North Dallas, I know all too well that locals are world-class shoppers. Every time I return home, I initially have a hard time even finding my way around—retail outlets, mostly national chain stores, seem to continually reproduce like a computer virus, blanketing all four corners of every intersection in the bedroom communities that envelop Big D. The Dallas Convention and Visitors Bureau likes to tout that there are more shopping opportunities per capita in Dallas than any other city in the United States. So if you're a shopper, and come from a place less rich in retail mania, you've got your work cut out for you.

If you need to focus your shopping attention, incline it toward Western duds (especially Texas-made cowboy boots) and upscale clothing and accessories (this is the home of world-famous Neiman Marcus, after all). Texans aren't fond of taxes (there's no state income tax, still), but there is a state sales tax, and it's one of the highest in the country: 8.25%.

GREAT SHOPPING AREAS

Downtown Dallas largely has been eviscerated of shopping outlets as inhabitants flocked to the suburbs. Only Neiman Marcus, the mother of all Dallas purveyors of luxury goods, has stayed put. The **West End MarketPlace** (www.westendmarket placedallas.com) was carved out of an old candy and cracker warehouse to draw hungry tourists and get things going downtown. The real high-volume shopping is done north of downtown, in **Uptown** as well as **Highland Park, North Dallas** (north of LBJ Fwy.), and **suburbs** such as Plano and Frisco. The best spot in Plano is the chic **Shops at Legacy (Legacy at the Toll Road).**

In the area real-estate agents have designated **Uptown,** a vintage trolley line travels along McKinney Avenue, allowing shoppers to jump off to duck into its many antiques shops, art galleries, furniture stores, restaurants, and specialty shops. **West Village** is an outdoor, European-style mall full of chic shops, restaurants, bars, and a movie theater at the north end of McKinney Avenue. The streets Knox and Henderson, bisected by Central Expressway, are lined with home-furnishing stores and antiques dealers, with an eclectic decoration shop or two mixed in. Routh and Fairmount streets have a large number of art galleries and antiques shops. **Greenville Avenue** is home to a dizzying array of funky shops, including antiques dealers and vintage clothing stores. The avenue gets a little funkier the farther south you travel, with Lower Greenville in particular home to plenty of bars and restaurants that make great pit stops. **Deep Ellum,** which rules the alternative night, is loaded by day with offbeat furnishings stores, art galleries, folk-art shops, and vintage resale shops. Of course, locals head straight for the malls, and if you're in Dallas doing some big-volume shopping, you might do the same; the best are listed below.

NATIVE TO BIG D

Neiman Marcus ★★★ (which my father-in-law never tires of calling "Needless Markups"), established in 1907, is a local institution; its annual holiday catalog has become part of pop culture (a once-a-year opportunity to order "His & Her Mummies" or perhaps your own personal $20-million submarine). Beyond those attention-grabbing stunts, Neiman Marcus remains one of the classiest high-end retail stores around, and its downtown flagship store has a chic retro look that is suddenly very hip today. It's not to be missed, even if you can't fritter away your rent money on a pair of Manolo Blahniks. The downtown store, a beauty of retro 1960s style at 1618 Main at Ervay Street (© **214/741-6911;** www.neimanmarcus.com), is open Monday through Saturday from 10am to 5:30pm; stores in the NorthPark and Prestonwood malls are open on Sunday. Another department store where customers are dripping in diamonds and their drivers wait outside to gather the bags is **Stanley Korshak,** in the Crescent Court hotel (suite 500) on McKinney Avenue between Maple and Pearl (© **214/871-3600**).

Dallas is an especially good place to pick up Western wear—boots, hats, shirts, and belts—whether you want to look the part of a real cowboy or prefer the more adorned "drugstore cowboy" look. Boots of all leathers and exotic skins, both machine- and handmade, from Texas boot companies (Justin, Tony Lama, Nocona) are good deals in Dallas. You can even order custom-made boots if you've got a grand or so to burn. Compare pricing at any of the following, all of which have excellent selections, and be sure to ask about proper boot fit: **Boot Town,** 5909 Belt Line Rd. at Preston (© 972/385-3052; www.boottown.com), or 2821 LBJ Fwy. at Josey Lane (© 972/243-1151); **Wild Bill's,** West End MarketPlace, 3rd floor (© 214/954-1050); **Cavender's Boot City,** 5539 LBJ Fwy. (© 972/239-1375); and **Western Warehouse,** 2475 Stemmons Fwy. (© 214/634-2668), or 10838 N. Central Expwy. at Meadows (© 214/891-0888). Very fancy Western wear can be found at **Cowboy Cool,** in the West Village at 3699 McKinney Ave. (© 214/521-4500); it's the place to go if you want to drop $500 on a Western shirt or a grand on a pair of boots. Vintage Western clothing can be a bit hard to come by. **Ahab Bowen,** 2614 Boll St. (© 214/720-1874), occasionally stocks vintage Western shirts, along with one of Dallas's best selection of other carefully chosen items for both men and women. Another cool vintage shop is **Artfunkles Vintage Boutique,** in the West Village at 3699 McKinney Ave., Suite C311 (© 214/526-5195). **Ragwear,** 200 Greenville (© 214/827-4163), is a laid-back vintage store that stocks collectible Western shirts at $100 and up, as well as more pedestrian models. (If you're headed to Fort Worth, there are several excellent Western wear stores clustered around the Stock-yards; see "Shopping" in Fort Worth, later in this chapter.) Fancy gift items for the upscale cowboy—sterling silver money clips, Michel Jordi wristwatches and belt buckles with longhorns and state-of-Texas and cowboy insignias, and the like—can be had for a price at **Bohlin,** 5440 Harvest Hill, Suite 172 (© 972/960-0335; www.bohlinmade.com).

Dallas Farmers' Market, 1010 S. Pearl Expwy. (© **214/939-2808**), spread over 12 acres just south of downtown Dallas, is one of the nation's largest open-air produce markets. First opened in 1941, it looks across at the glittering Dallas skyline. Farmers from around the area sell directly to the consumer. The market is open daily from 7am to 6pm.

DEPARTMENT STORES & MALLS

It would be impossible to cover Dallas's dozens of major shopping malls here—and more difficult still to hit them all on your visit to Dallas. A few of the best follow, both for the number and quality of stores and their general ambience.

NorthPark Center 🌟🌟, Northwest Highway/Loop 12 at I-75 (© **214/363-7441**), is the most traditional mall and, to my mind, the most elegant. NorthPark has 160 shops and major anchor stores (including Neiman Marcus, Tiffany's, and Nordstrom), as well as natural lighting and, best of all, a rotating display of owner Ray Nasher's fabu-lous sculpture collection of modern masters throughout the mall (the majority of his collection can be seen at Nasher Sculpture Center). NorthPark recently underwent a makeover that doubled its size, making it the largest mall in the Metroplex, but respected the good taste of the original 1960s structure. Not a mall, but not far from NorthPark, is one of my favorite shopping stops in Dallas: the sprawling flagship store **Half Price Books Records & Magazines** 🌟🌟 at 5915 E. Northwest Hwy., just east of Central Expressway (© **214/363-8374**). The massive selection of books—includ-ing art and architecture books, coffee-table books, books on tape, and language books—blows away almost any new bookstore, and everything at half-price or less. It's a place to load up.

The Galleria, LBJ Freeway and Dallas Parkway North (© **972/702-7100;** www.dallasgalleria.com), is a huge mall with a light-filled atrium (said to mimic the original Galleria in Milan, Italy). It attracts some of Dallas's most sophisticated shoppers to Macy's, Nordstrom, Saks Fifth Avenue, Versace, Cartier, and Hugo Boss. You'll also find an ice-skating rink, a Westin Hotel, and a host of restaurants—but many people seem to come just to stroll.

Highland Park Village ★★, Mockingbird Lane at Preston Road (© 214/559-2740), is as close as you'll get to Beverly Hills' Rodeo Drive in Dallas. This ultrachic corner of high-end shopping in the midst of Dallas's most exclusive neighborhood was built in the 1930s—it was reportedly the first shopping mall in the U.S.—and sports an eclectic mix of today's most fashionable boutiques (such as Calvin Klein, Prada, Chanel, Bottega Veneta, and Hermès). Shops aren't enclosed like a traditional suburban American mall; rather, they face inward for a more enjoyable (or shall we say, European) shopping experience.

BIG D AFTER DARK

Dallas has a lively nightlife scene, with enough in the way of performing arts and theater to entertain highbrows and more than enough bars and clubs to satisfy the young and the restless. If you've come to North Texas to wrangle a mechanical bull, you may have to drop in on Fort Worth, but there are a couple of sturdy honky-tonks in Big D where you can strap on your boots and your best Stetson and do some two-steppin' and Western swing dancing.

THE PERFORMING ARTS

The **Morton H. Meyerson Symphony Center** ★★, 2301 Flora St. at North Pearl (© 214/670-3600; www.dallassymphony.com), is home to the Dallas Symphony Orchestra, a very respectable outfit led by maestro Andrew Litton. The I. M. Pei–designed auditorium is equipped with excellent acoustics and a spectacular pipe organ. Tickets to events are as little as $8, and free concerts are occasionally held. (Free tours are available on selected days at 1pm; call in advance for schedule.) The **Dallas Opera** performs at Campbell Center #1, 8350 N. Central Expwy. (© 214/443-1043; www.dallasopera.org). The **Dallas Theater Center** ★, Kalita Humphreys Theater, 3636 Turtle Creek Blvd. (© 214/526-8210; www.dallastheatercenter.org), is a little gem, the only professional working theater built by the famed American architect Frank Lloyd Wright, and the best place for theater in the Dallas area. Local and touring productions, some fairly adventurous by Dallas standards (like *Angels in America*), are on the card here. The ornate, nicely restored **Majestic Theater,** 1925 Elm St. (© 214/880-0137), built in 1920, is the last of the vaudeville theaters in Dallas. It plays host to dance, comedy, and theater, including the Dallas Summer Musicals' Majestic Series. Less traditional theater is performed by the acclaimed **Kitchen Dog Theater Company,** 3120 McKinney Ave. (© 214/953-1055). Of interest to families may be the shows put on by the **Dallas Children's Theater,** 2215 Cedar Springs (© 214/978-0110; www.dct.org).

LIVE MUSIC

The biggest news in live music, dance clubs, and bars is the decline—indeed, near death—of **Deep Ellum,** the rowdy district east of downtown, after 25 years as the epicenter of live music and late-night dance clubs. Once a nightlife destination, it fell victim to a sustained spate of unsettling gang violence, bar fights, robberies, occasional shootings, and mismanaged clubs. Venerable stalwarts of the Dallas scene, including Trees, Club Clearview, and Deep Ellum Blues all went under in the past year. For those young daredevils who still wish to live on the edge in Deep Ellum, a free

Tips Ticket Central

For tickets to sporting events and performances, try **Central Tickets**
(© 800/462-7979 or 817/335-9000; www.centralticketoffice.com), **Star Tickets**
(© 888/597-STAR; www.startickets.com), or **Front Gate Tickets** (© 888/512-
7469; www.frontgatetickets.com). For many events, there's little need to secure
tickets in advance of your trip, but that's not the case with big sporting and
musical performances.

shuttle service for barhoppers runs throughout Deep Ellum on Fridays and Saturdays
from 6:30pm to 2:30am. **Gypsy Tea Room** ✸, 2548 Elm St. (© 214/74-GYPSY;
www.gypsytearoom.com), long Dallas's standard-bearer for live performance, including
national touring acts of alternative and roots-based rock and country (Wilco, Steve Earle),
is still going, but it is now a shadow of its former self. Still competing for some of the
same acts as the Gypsy Tea Room is the more spacious **Sons of Hermann Hall** ✸, 3414
Elm St. (© 214/747-4422), a classic Texas dance hall that's equal parts pickup bar,
live music venue, and honky-tonk, hosting rock, country, and occasional rockabilly
acts (and swing dance classes on Wed). **The Bone,** 2724 Elm St. (© 214/
744-2663), is ostensibly a blues club, but, much more than that, it is a crowded,
sweaty drinking spot for young and rowdies. **Double Wide,** 3510 Commerce
(© 214/887-6510), is the place to go if you want to get your trailer park on; it's got
Lone Star beer, gimme caps, and live, loud rock music.

Christian music and culture is picking up some of the Deep Ellum void. For live,
all-ages (really all-ages—if you're younger than 10, you get in free!) rock and pop gigs,
including emo (short for emotional) punk rock and Christian acts (sometimes a whole
slew of bands in a single night), check out **The Door,** 3202 Elm St. (© 214/742-
DOOR). It has a large concert space as well as a lounge and theater.

Lower Greenville Avenue has been around forever, but is newly hot again for bars
and clubs in the wake of Deep Ellum's demise. **Greenville Bar & Grill,** 2821 Lower
Greenville Ave. (© 214/823-6691), has been cool since I used to sneak in there as a
high school senior. The crowd, mostly folks intent on defying the big 4-0, come for
rock, country, and blues nightly. The **Granada Theater** ✸✸, 3524 Greenville Ave.
(© 214/824-9933), is a converted old movie theater that now books such popular
acts as Bob Dylan and Sigur Rós that also appeal to a somewhat older but still hip
crowd. **The Cavern** ✸, 1914 Lower Greenville Ave. (© 214/828-1914), is a tiny but
cool spot that books good alternative acts (such as Devendra Banhart) and has upstairs
DJs for those who find the live space too claustrophobic.

Once a dark and ambience-heavy jazz cafe, **Sambuca** has gone thoroughly uptown
now that it's in Uptown, at 2120 McKinney Ave. (© 214/744-0820). A spacious,
upscale supper club, it draws a trendy crowd for cocktails, dinner, and live jazz (much
of it jazz fusion you can dance to) 7 nights a week. It has another North Dallas branch,
also a Mediterranean restaurant, at 15207 Addison Rd. at Belt Line, in Addison
(© 972/385-8455). Perhaps Dallas's best club for live jazz is **Brooklyn** ✸✸, 1701 S.
Lamar (© 214/428-0025), which has moved to a new location and a big space with
an outdoor patio. **Balcony Club,** 1825 Abrams at La Vista (© 214/826-8104),
upstairs from the Landmark (movie) Theater, is a cool, dark spot with intimate
booths, perfect for some relaxing beats and a drink. It has live jazz nightly. **Poor**

David's Pub ✮ ((C) **214/821-9891**), a venerable old club whose stage has been graced by many great Texas singer-songwriters, recently moved into new, decidedly not poor digs at 1313 S. Lamar, near Gilley's (see below). It aims to retain some of the old ambience, as well as provide a platform for live jazz and blues, albeit with slightly greater capacity.

   Dallas Alley, in the West End, Munger Avenue at Marker Street ((C) **214/720-0170**), is a touristy mix of bars and restaurants primarily aimed at businessmen entertaining clients and visitors staying in downtown hotels. From karaoke to country and oldies clubs, it's one-stop shopping for most groups looking for a night out on the town with a view of the skyline. Don't count on heaps of local flavor and authenticity, but the drinking and carousing seem contagious for most. The newest and best spot for big-ticket touring rock and pop acts is **Nokia Live Center** ✮, 1001 NextStage Dr., Grand Prairie ((C) **972/854-5050**).

DANCE CLUBS

Lizard Lounge ✮, 2424 Swiss Ave. ((C) **214/826-4768**), is the city's best dance club; trendy and slightly seedy, but resolutely sexy, it trades in percolating dance beats and a hot crowd, with occasional live bands. Sunday night is Goth Night. For something out of the ordinary—dancing to Tejano and ranchero music, along with what seems like half of Dallas's Latino population—check out massive **Escapade 2001** ✮✮, 10707 Finnell St. ((C) **214/654-9950**). About 5,000 people get their Latin groove on here nightly.

HONKY-TONK HEAVEN

Top Rail Ballroom ✮✮, 2110 W. Northwest Hwy. ((C) **972/556-9099**), with wagon-wheel chandeliers and a neon covered wagon, is a classic Texas C&W dance hall, a place where you'll find more authentic cowboys than transplanted wannabes. Open daily, it's the best boot-scootin' this side of Fort Worth. **Gilley's Dallas,** a Big D branch of Houston's famous honky-tonk (which shot to fame with John Travolta on a bucking bronco in *Urban Cowboy*), finally opened at 1135 S. Lamar ((C) **888/ GILLEYS**). It is absolutely Texan in size, with more than 90,000 square feet to accommodate all those boots, hats, and hair. **Cowboys Red River Dancehall** ✮✮, 10310 Technology Blvd. ((C) **214/352-1796**), has live country music nightly, mechanical bull riding, a huge dance floor, and dance lessons. Worth the drive if you're a boot-scooter or country music fan is the must-see **Billy Bob's Texas** in Fort Worth (p. 149).

   For a more intimate, down-and-dirty take on the honky-tonk scene, check out **Adair's Saloon** ✮, 2624 Commerce St., in Deep Ellum ((C) **214/939-9900**), which the regulars call "Aayy-dares." It gets its share of clean-scrubbed SMU students, but mostly you'll find down-to-earth patrons and infectious country and redneck rock bands that go down well with the cheap beer, shuffleboard, and tables and walls blanketed in graffiti. The perfectly greasy burgers with a whole jalapeño on top are surprisingly tasty; some say they're the best in Dallas. The only rule here is in plain English on the sign behind the bar: NO DANCIN' ON TABLES WITH SPURS.

THE BAR SCENE

Many of the hottest spots in Dallas are in Uptown. **Nikita** ✮, 3699 McKinney Ave., A306 ((C) **214/520-6454**), is a sexy, dark two-level lounge bar, with a sleek long bar downstairs, low-slung couches, good cocktails (including 60 vodkas), and a very trendy crowd. Nearby, **Cru,** 3699 McKinney Ave., A306 ((C) **214/526-9463**), is a restaurant that features an excellent wine list, but many, if not most, of its patrons treat it primarily as a wine bar to sample vintages from the many different wine flights on offer. But the must-see-and-be-seen spot for wealthy Dallasites and visiting celebs (you'll know immediately if you fit in here) is the much-talked about **Ghostbar** 𝕬𝕬, a paragon of chic in the new W Hotel, 2440 Victory Park (© **214/871-1800**). It's got a helipad tailor-made for scene-stealing arrivals. Before Ghostbar, the "it" nightlife spot was another hotel bar, **Dragonfly** 𝕬, 2332 Leonard St. (© **800/597-8399**), at the restaurant of trendy Hotel Zaza. On weekend nights it is still stuffed to the rafters with guys and gals both busting out of their shirts, but otherwise it's a luxurious spot for a cocktail, such as predinner drinks poolside. **Samba Room,** 4514 Travis St., at Knox Street (© **214/522-4137**), is another trendy, high-decibel, Latin-chic hangout for Big D's beautiful people. On one side is a surprisingly good restaurant, the other a packed watering hole with a cool serpentine bar. It's a good place to sip a mojito, the Cuban rum, lime, and mint favorite. If you're looking for a quieter, but still fashionable spot, venture inside Hotel Lumen, 6101 Hillcrest Ave. (© **214/219-8282**), to **Social,** a swank lounge and restaurant that's a haunt of trendsetting nightlife types.

   The Old Monk 𝕬, 2847 N. Henderson (© **214/821-1880**), is a dark, handsome bar 1 block east of Central Expressway with an excellent selection of Belgian beers, single malts, and great pub grub—go with the Belgian mussels with fries and spicy mayo. In Uptown, just off McKinney Avenue, **The Ginger Man,** 2718 Boll St. (© **214/754-8771**), has a great beer garden and a beer selection to die for: about 200 beers from around the world, including 70 on tap.

   Downtown, if you want to heighten the effect an expensive cocktail has on you, check out **The Dome,** 50 stories above ground in the revolving Reunion Tower ball, 300 Reunion Blvd. (© **214/712-7145**). A great new option is the rooftop garden terrace, with a view of the skyline, at **Luqa and Petrus Lounge** 𝕬, 1217 Main St. (© **214/760-9000**). Spearheading the new downtown scene, it features a massive wine tower and 1,500 wines from around the world. Also, check out the third Thursday of every month at **Nasher Sculpture Center,** 2100 Flora St. (© **214/242-5100**), where free admission, DJs, and cocktails transform the chic museum into the N Bar lounge until 11pm.

   A step up from karaoke is **Pete's Dueling Piano Bar,** 4980 Belt Line Rd. #200, Addison (© **972/726-7383**), a piano bar where four accomplished players tickle the ivories on two baby grands and everybody sings along (loudly, enthusiastically) to tunes by the Stones, Beatles, and other boomer faves.

THE GAY & LESBIAN SCENE

The Crew's Inn, 3215 N. Fitzhugh Ave. (© **214/526-9510**), caters to the widest, rather than the wildest, common denominator of the gay community. Another longtime favorite, with a consistently good vibe and a wall of video monitors, is **J. R.'s Bar and Grill,** 3923 Cedar Springs Rd. (© **214/528-1004**). **Village Station,** 3911 Cedar Springs Rd. (© **214/559-0650**), is a gay dance club that features nightly drag shows in the Rose Room and Trash Disco every Sunday. **Sue Ellen's,** 3903 Cedar Springs Rd. (© **214/559-0650**), is a friendly gay and lesbian bar with live rock, a dance floor, and an outdoor patio. **Buddies II,** 4025 Maple Ave. (© **214/526-0887**), is tops for lesbians: hot music and SGWF looking for same. Gay country swing and line dancers should check out the **Texas Twisters** (www.texastwisters.org), a group that organizes two-stepping and the like for gays and lesbians around the Dallas area, frequently at the **Round-Up Saloon,** 3912 Cedar Springs Rd. (© **214/522-9611**), a gay country bar that features a Monday karaoke night.

3 Arlington

Sandwiched between Dallas and Fort Worth, the medium-size city of Arlington has become known as a pro-sports center and the family playground of the Metroplex. If you're a sports fan, or have kids in tow (or are a kid at heart), it makes a good day trip. If none of those applies, you're probably better off in Arlington's bigger and more important cousins. To get to Arlington, take I-30 from either Dallas or Fort Worth. If traffic's heavy, plan on it taking you about an hour from either city. Having your own car is pretty much required to get around to any of the places below.

Arlington's **Visitor Information Center** is located at 1905 E. Randol Mill Rd. (© **800/342-4305** or 817/461-3888; www.arlington.org).

THE TOP ATTRACTIONS

Louis Tussaud's Palace of Wax & Ripley's Believe It or Not *Kids*   Merged under one roof are these two oddballs of family fun. The Palace of Wax features wax dummies of movie stars and historical figures such as Mother Teresa, Tom Hanks as Forrest Gump, Jesus Christ, and Dorothy and her *Wizard of Oz* pals. Ripley's is a collection of the hard-to-swallow and bizarre, such as the giraffe-necked woman of Burma and the double-eyed man of China. Really small kids may get freaked, but most children older than 5 are likely to find the exhibits pretty cool.

601 E. Safari Pkwy./I-30 at Belt Line, Grand Prairie. © **972/263-2391**. Admission to either attraction $16 adults, $9 children ages 4–12, free for children younger than 4. Combination visit to both $19 adults, $10 children ages 4–12, free for children younger than 4. Visit website for discount coupon. Mon–Fri 10am–5pm; Sat–Sun 10am–6pm. Parking $6.

Rangers Stadium in Arlington/Legends of the Game Baseball Museum *★* *Kids*   The home of the Texas Rangers professional baseball team is one of the finest ballparks in the country. The graceful, redbrick-and-granite 50,000-seat stadium was designed (by the architect David Schwarz) to echo classic American baseball parks. The flat, painted billboards in the outfield with retro graphics and the absence of glaring neon lend a yesteryear feel to the park. It's a terrific place to see a game, even for folks (like me) who aren't huge baseball fans.

Even if you can't see a Rangers game (Apr–Sept), you can take a 50-minute tour of the park, which visits the dugout, press box, clubhouse, batting cages, and owner's suite, and visit the **Legends of the Game Baseball Museum.** The museum traces the history of baseball in this country, with uniforms and artifacts on loan from Cooperstown, the Hall of Fame Museum. See Joe DiMaggio's glove; the jerseys of Babe Ruth, Mickey Mantle, Ted Williams, Hank Aaron, and Walter Johnson; and cool antique baseball cards. Upstairs is a neat little Learning Center of hands-on baseball exhibits for Little Leaguers.

1000 Ballpark Way, Arlington. © **817/273-5220**, 817/273-5100 ticket office, or 817/273-5600 museum. www.texasrangers.com. Guided ballpark tour admission $5 adults, $4 seniors and students, $3 children ages 4–18. Museum admission $5 adults, $4 seniors, $3 children ages 6–13. Ballpark tours Mon–Sat hourly 9am–4pm and 9am–1pm on game days. Museum Apr–Oct Mon–Sat 9am–5:30pm, Sun 11am–4pm (game days open until 7:30pm); Nov–Mar Tues–Sat 10am–4pm. To get there, take I-30 from either Dallas or Fort Worth and exit at Nolan Ryan Expwy./Ballpark Way.

Six Flags Hurricane Harbor *Kids*   The biggest water park in North Texas is 3 million gallons of water and 50 acres of relief from the Texas sun. The kids will go nuts at such feature attractions as Hook's Lagoon (pirate ships and 12 levels of interactive features), Black Hole (a tentacle-like thrill ride that plunges through dark wet tubes), and the Bubba Tub (an inner-tube ride that begins at the top of a 70-ft. tower). There

THE TRAVELOCITY GUARANTEE

...THAT SAYS EVERYTHING YOU BOOK WILL BE RIGHT, OR WE'LL WORK WITH OUR TRAVEL PARTNERS TO MAKE IT RIGHT, RIGHT AWAY.

*To drive home the point,
we're going to use the word "right" in every single sentence.*

Let's get right to it. Right to the meat! Only Travelocity guarantees everything about your booking will be right, or we'll work with our travel partners to make it right, right away. Right on!

Here's a picture taken smack dab right in the middle of Antigua, where the Guarantee also covers you.

The Guarantee covers all but one of the items pictured to the right.

For example, what if the ocean view you booked actually looks out at a downright ugly parking lot? You'd be right to call – we're there for you. And no one in their right mind would be pleased to learn the rental car place has closed and left them stranded. Call Travelocity and we'll help get you back on the right track.

Now, you may be thinking, "Yeah, right, I'm so sure." That's OK; you have the right to remain skeptical. That is until we mention help is always right around the corner. Call us right off the bat, knowing our customer service reps are there for you 24/7. Righting wrongs. Left and right.

Now if you're guessing there are some things we can't control, like the weather, well you're right. But we can help you with most things – to get all the details in righting,* visit travelocity.com/guarantee.

*Sorry, spelling things right is one of the few things not covered under the Guarantee.

I'd give my right arm for a guarantee like this, although I'm glad I don't have to.

travelocity
You'll never roam alone.

© 2006 Travelocity.com LP. CST # 2056372-50.

> **Tips** **Coupon Discounts**
>
> In addition to the coupons available in the *Dallas/Fort Worth Area Visitors Guide* (available from tourist information offices), look for the brochure "The Dallas Metroplex: One Exciting Savings Place," which contains coupons worth $10 at Six Flags.

are a couple of dozen more rides, slides, and pools, including a 1-million-gallon wave pool, to entertain and douse you and your families. Professional lifeguards are on duty.

1800 E. Lamar Blvd., Arlington. ℂ 817/265-3356. www.sixflags.com. $30 adults, $23 children less than 4 ft. tall, seniors, and visitors with disabilities, free for children 2 and younger (adult tickets occasionally available online for $25). Mid-May to Aug 22 daily; check website for hours. Parking $7.

Six Flags Over Texas *(Kids)*   Now 40 years old, Six Flags is the place I used to dream about going as a kid. The 200-acre amusement park, one of the biggest and best in the country, is the top draw in Texas (and it can be a little crowded on summer weekends). It has Texas-size roller coasters, including the Texas Giant (the world's tallest wooden coaster that hits speeds of more than 60 mph), Batman the Ride (a suspended looping coaster with six inversions and corkscrew spirals), and Mr. Freeze (the fastest and tallest roller coaster in the Southwest). There are also tons of shows, eateries, and nostalgic rides such as the Parachute Drop and the Log Ride, with its peculiar green water that thrilled my little girlfriends and me back in the '70s.

I-30 at Hwy. 360, Arlington. ℂ 817/530-6000. www.sixflags.com. $45 adults, $35 children less than 4 ft. tall and seniors, free for children 2 and younger (adult tickets occasionally available online for $40). Mid-May to late Aug daily; Mar to mid-May and Sept–Oct weekends only; check website for hours. Parking $9.

Trader's Village   A rollicking and locally famous flea market (spread out over 100 acres), Trader's Village has been trading everything under the sun since the early 1970s. It attracts a couple of thousand dealers each weekend and tens of thousands of shoppers searching through the junk for the occasional find. There are also rides and games for the kids.

2602 Mayfield Rd., off Hwy. 360 in Grand Prairie, south of Arlington. ℂ 972/647-2331. www.tradersvillage.com. Free admission. Sat–Sun 8am–dusk. Parking $2.

4 Fort Worth ★★★

In recent years, easygoing Fort Worth has lived in the shadow of Dallas, its brash cousin to the east. Yet one gets the feeling that others' perceptions of their city as second-class don't matter much to Fort Worth natives. The city exudes a quiet confidence, reserve, and sense of comfort that are often missing in Big D.

Fort Worth, nicknamed "Cowtown," revels in its role as the gateway to the West; the mythic qualities of the American West—wide-open spaces and even grander dreams—are still palpable here. In the mid–19th century, on the heels of the war between Texas and Mexico, Fort Worth began as a frontier army town in the Republic of Texas, assigned with protecting settlers from Native American attacks. The outpost grew into the last major stop along the Chisholm Trail, the major thoroughfare of the great Texas cattle drives that took ranchers and their livestock 500 miles north to the railheads and more lucrative markets of Dodge City and Abilene, Kansas. The

Grapevine

One of the oldest settlements in North Texas, Grapevine—north of DFW Airport and wedged between Dallas and Fort Worth—is known for its handsomely restored historic Main Street, the Grapevine Opry, several Texas wineries, and a number of art galleries housed in turn-of-the-20th-century buildings. Downtown there are some 75 historic buildings, including the **Torian Log Cabin,** Liberty Park, 201 S. Main St., and the **1901 Cotton Belt Train Depot.** The **Grapevine Opry,** which inhabits the 1940 Palace Theatre at 308 S. Main St. (© 817/481-8733), holds foot-stomping hootenannies on Saturday nights and features concerts by top-name country stars throughout the year.

The **Grapevine Visitor Information Center** is located at 701 S. Main St. (© 800/457-6338 or 817/410-8136; www.ci.grapevine.tx.us). You can pick up information about **wine tours** and tastings at La Buena Vida Vineyards, La Bodega Winery, and North Star Winery.

The best way to visit old Grapevine is by train. The Tarantula Steam Train travels from Stockyards Station in Fort Worth to historic Grapevine; see p. 140 for additional information on this nostalgic locomotive. Otherwise, take Highway 114 northwest from Dallas or Highway 121 northeast from Fort Worth.

trail's importance transformed little Fort Worth into a busy trading post. By 1881, more than five million head of cattle had been driven through town on their way to market. Saloons, bordellos, and gambling houses staked out the rough-hewn area of town called "Hell's Half Acre."

With the arrival of the railroad, the stampede of cattle north grew exponentially, and strategically positioned Fort Worth became a place for ranchers to keep their herds before moving them for sale. The Fort Worth Stockyards opened in 1890, followed by the arrival of major meat-packing plants, transforming Fort Worth into a major cattle shipping center and one of the country's top livestock markets. Fort Worth had become a wealthy city, a cow town to be reckoned with. The rise of the oil business in West Texas bolstered Fort Worth's commercial prospects, and oil fortunes replaced the cattle-ranching riches of the early 20th century.

If in frontier days Fort Worth was where the East fizzled out and the West began; today the city is a place where cowboy culture meets high culture. It is probably the most authentically Texan city in the state. The city of nearly half a million is home not only to a tenacious pride in its Old West past, and plenty of modern-day cowboys and Western flavor, but also to one of the country's most celebrated cultural scenes. Cultural cognoscenti call it the Museum Capital of the Southwest. Local oil-rich philanthropists have endowed the city with superlative collections of art and hired some of the world's most prestigious architects—Philip Johnson, Louis Kahn, and Tadao Ando—to build the esteemed Kimbell, newly expanded Amon Carter, and spectacular new Museum of Modern Art. Fort Worth is also home to a symphony orchestra, an impressive botanic garden, several theater companies, and the Van Cliburn International Piano Competition. It turns out that this cowboy town with a rough-and-tumble past has a remarkably sophisticated and arts-minded soul. Even if you come to the Dallas area with little time to spare, enjoyable Fort Worth is absolutely worth a visit. For me, it is the highlight of North Texas.

As if by well-devised plan, Fort Worth's downtown, a charming and dignified center of business and entertainment, is almost perfectly equidistant between the Stockyards National Historic District and the Cultural District. Fort Worth natives may like to keep the essential elements of their city separate, but they seem to recognize that they add up to a cohesive whole.

ESSENTIALS
VISITOR INFORMATION
Besides the DFW Airport Visitor Information (see section 1, earlier in this chapter), the **Fort Worth Convention & Visitors Bureau** (© **800/433-5747** or 817/336-8791; www.fortworth.com) maintains tourist information centers downtown on Sundance Square at 415 Throckmorton St. (© **817/336-8791**); in the Stockyards National Historic District at 130 E. Exchange Ave. (© **817/624-4741**); and in the Cultural District at 3401 Lancaster Ave., in the Will Rogers Memorial Center (© **817/882-8588**). Of the three, only the one in the Stockyards is open Sundays (noon–5pm).

The city's events hot line is © **817/332-2000.**

CITY LAYOUT
Fort Worth lies just west of I-35, which runs north-south. Fort Worth for most visitors means three distinct districts, which the city calls the "Western Triangle": the Stockyards National Historic District, 2 miles north of downtown; historic downtown, which includes Sundance Square, just north of I-30, running east–west; and the Cultural District, 2 miles west of downtown. See "Dallas–Fort Worth" map on p. 72 to help orient yourself.

THE NEIGHBORHOODS IN BRIEF

Stockyards National Historic District This area was the focus of the old cattle-raising and livestock business of Fort Worth. Today the district retains its Old West feel and is where rodeos and Wild West shows take place, as well as daily cattle drives down Exchange Avenue. A handful of hotels and restaurants aimed at visitors are located here, though it's not overly touristy.

Downtown Downtown is the center of the Fort Worth business community and includes **Sundance Square,** where much of the city's restaurant, bar, and theater nightlife and most business-oriented hotels are located. Staying in this area is best if you want to get around easily between the Cultural District, the Stockyards District, and downtown's attractions.

Cultural District Fort Worth's outstanding museums, including the Kimbell, Modern, and Amon Carter, are clustered in the Cultural District. Just south are parks and gardens, including the Fort Worth Zoo and Botanic Garden. Art lovers will want to base themselves here, but the Stockyards District and downtown are better for families.

Medical District Immediately south of downtown, this is the site of major hospitals and several residential areas, and Fort Worth's major university, Texas Christian University (TCU). Many hotels and restaurants are located south of I-30 as well. There's no major benefit to basing yourself here, but it's where you'll find some of the cheaper hotel options.

GETTING AROUND
By Public Transportation

For information on getting to Fort Worth from DFW Airport, see section 1, earlier in this chapter.

Within the city, the only public transportation most visitors will need are city buses (the T) that run every 20 minutes among the three major districts, from the Fort Worth Zoo all the way to the Stockyards, making stops downtown on the way. Buses run daily from 6:15am to 10:15pm. The regular one-way fare is $1.25 for adults; 50¢ for seniors, travelers with disabilities, and students ages 6 to 16; and $2.50 ($1 students and seniors) for a Day Pass. Within the downtown area, service is free. Route 1 (brown) travels from North Main Street to the Stockyards; Route 2 (blue) from Camp Bowie to the Cultural District; and Route 7 (green) from University/Montgomery to the Cultural District. Trolley Route 15 travels Saturday only to the Stockyards from downtown hotels and the ITC rail station. A trolley also runs on Saturdays from the ITC rail station to the Fort Worth Zoo with stops in the Cultural District. Pick up a schedule at any of the visitor information centers or obtain information on schedules by calling © 817/215-8600 or 817/334-0092, or by visiting the website at www.the-t.com.

Red, white, and blue **T buses** traveling downtown routes are also free of charge.

The **Trinity Railway Express (TRE)** is the most convenient and hassle-free way to travel to Dallas without having to worry about traffic. It's an express commuter train connecting the two cities, traveling to DFW Airport, Irving, Dallas's American Airlines Center (for Mavericks and Stars games), and Dallas Union Station ($4.50 round-trip). Pickup and drop-off points are the Texas & Pacific Station and the Intermodal Transportation Center downtown. Call © 877/215-8600 or 817/215-8600 or visit www.the-t.com for route and schedule information.

By Car

With the city's efficient bus and trolley services, you can quite easily manage to get around Fort Worth without a car. However, if you want to spend time in Dallas or Arlington, you will be better off with an automobile. Car-rental agencies in Fort Worth include **Avis,** 801 W. Weatherford (© 800/230-4898; www.avis.com); **Budget,** 1001 Henderson (© 800/527-0700; www.budget.com); **Enterprise,** 2832 W. 7th St. (© 800/RENT A CAR; www.enterprise.com); and **Hertz,** 917 Taylor St. (© 817/654-3131; www.hertz.com).

By Taxi

You'll have to call a cab unless you're lucky enough to catch one outside a hotel. The major companies operating in Fort Worth are **Yellow Checker Taxi** (© 817/426-6262) and **Cowboy Cab** (© 817/428-0202). Fares are $2.25 (initial drop) and 45¢ for each additional ¼ mile. Extras include $2 extra passenger charge, $3.60 airport exit fee, and 52¢ airport drop-off fee.

FAST FACTS: Fort Worth

Babysitters If your hotel does not offer babysitting services, **Sitters Unlimited** (© 817/535-4449) arranges babysitting at hotels throughout Fort Worth.

Dentists Call © 800/577-7320 for a dentist referral service.

Doctors Call the **Tarrant County Medical Society** (📞 817/732-3997) for a doctor referral.

Drugstores Area locations for **Eckerd Drugs** include 3208 N. Main St., near the Stockyards (📞 817/625-6179), and 611 Houston St. at Sundance Square (📞 817/336-7105). The Eckerd store at 6389 Camp Bowie Blvd. in the Cultural District (📞 817/737-3125) is open 24 hours.

Hospitals Two large, full-service hospitals located in the Medical District, south of downtown, are **Columbia Plaza Medical Center,** 900 8th Ave. (📞 817/336-2100), and **All Saints Episcopal Hospital–Fort Worth,** 1400 8th Ave. (📞 817/926-2544).

Internet Access One centrally located cybercafe is **Cyber Rodeo,** 1309 Calhoun St., within the Rodeo Steakhouse (📞 817/332-1288). Free wireless hotspots include **8.0 Restaurant and Bar,** 111 E. 3rd St. (📞 817/336-0880) and **Flying Saucer Drought Emporium,** 111. E. 4th St. (📞 817/336-7468).

Maps Any of the Fort Worth tourist information centers can provide you with free maps of all of Fort Worth or of individual districts.

Newspapers & Magazines Both the *Fort Worth Star-Telegram* and the *Dallas Morning News* "Weekend Guide" have plenty of arts, entertainment, and dining information for Fort Worth and the Metroplex.

Police For an emergency, dial 📞 911. For nonemergencies, call 📞 817/871-6458. The main police station in downtown Fort Worth is located at 350 W. Belknap (at Taylor).

Post Office The main downtown post office, 251 W. Lancaster (📞 817/348-0565), is open Monday through Friday from 7:30am to 7pm.

Safety For a city of nearly 500,000, Fort Worth is a relaxed and, from most appearances, a safe city. Still, as in any large city, visitors should exercise caution and keep an eye on their handbags, especially at night, in major tourist destinations such as the Stockyards and Cultural District, and downtown around Sundance Square. Beyond Sundance Square, which is very lively at night, much of downtown Fort Worth is virtually deserted after 9pm. Drive or take a taxi late at night.

Taxes The general sales tax is 8.25%, hotel tax is 15%, and restaurant tax is 7%.

Transit Info For general public transportation questions, call the **Fort Worth Transportation Authority** at 📞 817/871-6200. For "the T" bus schedule information, call 📞 817/215-8600 or 817/334-0092 or visit the website, www.the-t.com.

Weather For the latest weather information, call 📞 817/787-1111.

WHERE TO STAY

Fort Worth may not be loaded with superdeluxe places with all the amenities, but it does have a nice mix of affordable hotels, including an attractive roster of Western-flavored small hotels and bed-and-breakfasts. Accommodations are spread fairly evenly among the major districts of interest, so you can stay on the main drag of the Stockyards, downtown on Sundance Square, or south of town near the Cultural District. Everything in Fort Worth is pretty close and easily accessible, though, so you needn't choose your hotel strictly according to your primary sightseeing interests.

At Stockyards District hotels, unlike in most places, weekends are higher than weekday rates. The rates quoted below do not include 15% hotel occupancy tax. Breakfast, either continental or buffet, is offered free at several hotels, as noted below. Do not assume that breakfast is included; if it is not, it can really add to your bill.

The rates cited below, it bears repeating, are high-season rack rates. At a minimum, request the lower corporate rate, and ask about special deals. Virtually all hotels offer some deals, especially on weekends when their business clientele dries up. This is not the case in the Stockyards, however, where prices rise on weekends. Check individual hotels' websites for special online offers.

STOCKYARDS NATIONAL HISTORIC DISTRICT
Expensive
Stockyards Hotel ✦✦   A true taste of the Old West, the Stockyards Hotel has, since 1907, been the heart of Fort Worth's illustrious cowboy and railroad past (the original hotel was destroyed by fire in 1915). Bonnie and Clyde hid out here, Wild West poker games and gunslinging fights went down here, and country music stars have come to perform at nearby Billy Bob's. Behind the historic brick facade, each of the rooms works a different aspect of an Old West theme. You can stay in the Davy Crockett, Geronimo, or Victorian Parlor room, or sleep where Bonnie and Clyde did in the early '30s (that's cool enough to make it my favorite). The Stockyards Hotel gets the look and feel right: It's not a stretch to imagine cowboys riding up in a cloud of dust and tying their horses up to the posts out front, making it the ideal place to stay in Fort Worth for a real Western experience. The connected restaurant is the H3 Ranch Steakhouse, just a notch below the Cattlemen's Steakhouse (see "Where to Dine," below) around the corner, but a good place for wood-fired steaks, ribs, and spit-roasted pork and chicken. The bar, with horse-saddle barstools, is called Booger Red's Saloon (where you can down a cold Buffalo Butt beer).

109 W. Exchange Ave., Fort Worth, TX 76106. © **800/423-8471** or 817/625-6427. Fax 817/624-2571. www.stockyardshotel.com. 52 units. $159–$189 double; $225–$425 suite. Weekend and other packages available. AE, DC, DISC, MC, V. Valet parking $8. **Amenities:** Restaurant; bar; concierge; 24-hr. room service; laundry service. *In room:* A/C, TV, dataport, minibar, hair dryer, safe.

Moderate
Azalea Plantation B&B (Value   Near the Stockyards, but secluded on a couple of acres of oaks, magnolias, and azaleas, this 1948 plantation-style home is a peaceful place that invites relaxation: It has a gazebo and wooden yard swing, a fireplace in the parlor, crystal and china, and a Victorian dining room. There are two upstairs rooms and two cottages, all with comfortable beds. The Lily of the Valley Room has a whirlpool tub, king-size poster-bed, and veranda; the Bluebonnet Bungalow is a cottage with a cow-town theme; and the Rose of Sharon room has a king-size canopy bed, marble-floored bathroom, and opens onto a veranda. The Magnolia cottage features a private parlor and giant Jacuzzi. Some guests might find the furnishings and decor to be a bit frilly for their tastes, though others will eat it up. Early-morning coffee and a "hearty plantation" breakfast will start you out on the right foot.

1400 Robinwood Dr., Fort Worth, TX 76111. © **800/687-3529** or 817/838-5882. www.azaleaplantation.com. 4 units. $149 double; $179 cottage suite. Rates include full breakfast. AE, DC, DISC, MC, V. Free parking. *In room:* A/C, TV, Wi-Fi, complimentary minibar, CD player.

Hyatt Park Place ✦ (Value (Kids   Although it looks a bit out of place in the historic Stockyards district, this new hotel, recently purchased and converted from an

Fort Worth Stockyards National Historic District

ACCOMMODATIONS ■
Azalea Plantation B&B **16**
Hotel Texas **1**
Hyatt Park Place **15**
Miss Molly's Bed & Breakfast Hotel **2**
Stockyards Hotel **6**

DINING ◆
Cattlemen's Steakhouse **5**
Lonesome Dove Western Bistro **4**
Joe T. Garcia's Mexican Dishes **3**

ATTRACTIONS ●
Billy Bob's Texas **7**
Cowtown Cattlepen Maze **10**
Cowtown Coliseum **8**
Grapevine Vintage Railroad **13**
Livestock Exchange Building/
    Stockyard Museum **9**
Stockyards Station **14**
Texas Cowboy Hall of Fame **12**
White Elephant Saloon **11**

AmeriSuites property, is a welcome addition to this part of Cowtown. Thankfully, it's set back from the main drag, so its rather generic large facade doesn't disparage too greatly the look of the old cobblestone street that's lined with former stables and historic buildings. Its excellent location and good-value accommodations, which are clean and modern, if unexciting, are what recommend this hotel (prices below are those given when the hotel was still an AmeriSuites; they may rise after the sale is completed). It's not as Fort Worth cool as the Stockyards Hotel up the street, but if you get a nice low rate here, it will be worth it, especially if you've got kids in tow—they'll appreciate the pool and the location across the street from the Cattle Pen maze.

132 E. Exchange Ave., Fort Worth, TX 76106. ℂ **800/833-1516** or 817/626-6000. Fax 817/626-6018. www. amerisuites.com. 102 units. $159–$199 double. AE, DC, DISC, MC, V. Free parking. **Amenities:** Bar; outdoor pool; fitness center; concierge; 24-hr. room service; laundry service. *In room:* A/C, TV, Wi-Fi, minibar, microwave, hair dryer, safe.

Miss Molly's Bed & Breakfast Hotel (*Overrated*   Above a raucous bar, Miss Molly's is a slightly bawdy little place (it was a former bordello, after all) that's seen all manner of folks come through: cattle barons, outlaws, railroaders, and cowboys. Today, it's much more likely to host couples looking to indulge in a little Old West romanticism. The landmark 1910 Victorian building, a second story wedged in among the saloons and Western shops on the main drag of the Stockyards, is decorated with Western quilts, handsome period pieces, and Victorian lamps. The seven rooms are arranged around the lobby/living room, at the top of a staircase. Rooms are named for their decorative theme; for example, the Cattlemen's room has a carved oak bed beneath mounted longhorns, and Miss Amelia's has lace curtains, a white iron bed, and handmade linens. Miss Josie's, the Victorian bedroom of the former madam and the closest thing to a den of iniquity, is twice as large as the other rooms. Be forewarned, though, that guests share three bathrooms (albeit with claw-foot tubs), and the Star Café saloon downstairs can be very noisy, often until 3am on weekends. But worst of all, some travelers report that off-site management has let the place get run down, is apt not to provide the breakfast in "bed and breakfast," and isn't terribly responsive to entreaties.

109½ W. Exchange Ave., Fort Worth, TX 76106. © 817/626-1522. Fax 817/625-2723. www.missmollyshotel.com. 7 units. $125–$200 double. Online booking 20% discount. Rates include breakfast. AE, MC, V. Free parking. *In room:* A/C.

Inexpensive

Hotel Texas   A very simple, even spartan, cowboy-themed small hotel right on the main drag of the Stockyards, this 1939 hotel has a convenient location and is easy on the wallet. Don't expect much in the way of service or amenities, however; it's strictly for those on a budget. The former Exchange Hotel, reopened in 1995, retains the airs of a place where cattlemen might have stayed when venturing into the big city for auction. The 21 rooms, including a couple of spacious suites, are modest, though the Honeymoon Room has a Jacuzzi and the second-story, family-size but very pricey Bob Wills Suite comprises four separate guest rooms and has good views of the Stockyards. Within easy walking distance of all the major attractions, restaurants, and nightlife in the Stockyards district, Hotel Texas is a serviceable place to camp out in Cowtown, as long as your expectations aren't too high. Though I'm usually one to champion a small independent hotel over a chain, it's probably worth comparing prices at the Hyatt Park Place down the street.

2415 Ellis Ave. (at W. Exchange Ave.), Fort Worth, TX 76106. © 800/866-6660 or 817/624-2224. Fax 817/624-7177. 21 units. Fri–Sat $79–$149 double, $149 honeymoon suite, $400 suite; Mon–Fri $49–$99 double, $300 suite. Rates include continental breakfast. AE, DC, DISC, MC, V. Free parking Thurs–Sat (other days free street parking available). *In room:* A/C, TV.

DOWNTOWN
Expensive

The Ashton Hotel ★★★   Incorporating meticulously restored historic buildings on Main Street, the 1890 Winfree Building and the 1915 Fort Worth Club Building, the city's only small luxury hotel—a member of Small Luxury Hotels of the World—fills a niche in Fort Worth. Just a few slow paces from Bass Performance Hall and Sundance Square, it features richly appointed, elegant rooms with custom-designed mahogany furnishings, invitingly plush king-size beds and Italian linens, and very attentive service. Some rooms have romantic two-person claw-foot Jacuzzi tubs. The hotel is decorated with a collection of paintings from the Fort Worth Circle, a group of local artists active from the 1930s to the 1960s. The elegant restaurant, Café Ashton, one of the most notable new eateries to open in the Dallas–Fort Worth area in recent years, serves breakfast, lunch, and dinner, as well as an elegant afternoon tea (p. 132).

610 Main St. (between 5th and 6th sts.), Fort Worth, TX 76102. © 866/327-4866 or 817/332-0100. Fax 817/477-8274. www.theashtonhotel.com. 39 units. $280–$370 double. Weekend, executive, and special promotional packages available; see website. AE, DC, DISC, MC, V. Valet parking $12, self-parking $8 per day. Small pets welcome. **Amenities:** Restaurant; piano bar; gym; concierge; 24-hr. room service; same-day laundry service/dry cleaning. *In room:* A/C, TV, dataport, minibar, hair dryer, iron.

Downtown Fort Worth

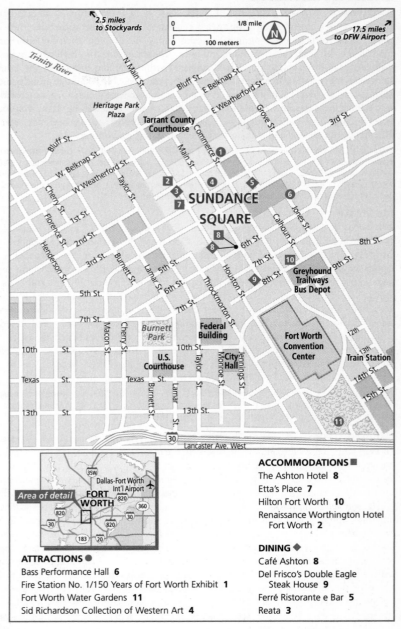

2.5 miles
to Stockyards

0 | 1/8 mile

0 | 100 meters

17.5 miles
to DFW Airport

Trinity River

Heritage Park
Plaza

Tarrant County
Courthouse

N Main St.

Bluff St.

E Belknap St.

E Weatherford St.

Grove St.

3rd St.

Commerce St.

Main St.

Bluff St.

W. Belknap St.

W Weatherford St.

Cherry St.

1st St.

Florence St.

2nd St.

Henderson St.

3rd St.

Taylor St.

Burnett St.

Lamar St.

5th St.

6th St.

7th St.

SUNDANCE

SQUARE

Jones St.

Calhoun St.

8th St.

6th St.

7th St.

8th St.

Houston St.

Throckmorton St.

9th St.

Greyhound
Trailways
Bus Depot

5th St.

7th St.

Burnett
Park

Federal
Building

U.S.
Courthouse

10th St.

Texas St.

13th

St.

Macon St.

Cherry St.

Burnett St.

Lamar St.

Texas St.

13th St.

Taylor St.

Monroe St.

City
Hall

Jennings St.

Fort Worth
Convention
Center

12th

13th

Train Station

14th St.

15th St.

30

Lancaster Ave. West

35W

Dallas-Fort Worth
Int'l Airport

**FORT
WORTH**

820

Area of detail

820

30

360

30

820

183

20

ATTRACTIONS ●

Bass Performance Hall **6**

Fire Station No. 1/150 Years of Fort Worth Exhibit **1**

Fort Worth Water Gardens **11**

Sid Richardson Collection of Western Art **4**

ACCOMMODATIONS ■

The Ashton Hotel **8**

Etta's Place **7**

Hilton Fort Worth **10**

Renaissance Worthington Hotel
Fort Worth **2**

DINING ◆

Café Ashton **8**

Del Frisco's Double Eagle
Steak House **9**

Ferré Ristorante e Bar **5**

Reata **3**

Renaissance Worthington Hotel Fort Worth 🔑   Downtown's largest and swankiest hotel, the monolithic but newly renovated Worthington is the place where modern-day cattle barons—oilmen and other execs—like to cool their heels in Fort Worth. A block from the courthouse and only steps away from Bass Performance Hall and the array of restaurants and bars clustered around Sundance Square, the hotel dominates one part of downtown like a huge, docked cruise ship. The large and elegant, surprisingly understated lobby is a hint of the spacious rooms, which are warm, sedate and handsomely appointed, with very comfortable beds, large writing desks, colorful accents, and large bathrooms. The Kalamatas Restaurant and Martini Bar serves Mediterranean cuisine and is open for breakfast, lunch, and dinner.

200 Main St., Fort Worth, TX 76102. ℂ 800/433-5677 or 817/870-1000. Fax 817/338-9176. http://marriott.com/ property/propertypage/dfwdt. 504 units. $239–$269 double; $339–$1,000 suite. Moonlight and weekend packages available. AE, DC, DISC, MC, V. Valet parking $16, self-parking $12 per day. **Amenities:** 2 restaurants; bar; indoor pool; fitness center; tennis courts; sauna; concierge; business center; 24-hr. room service; babysitting; same-day laundry service/dry cleaning. *In room:* A/C, TV, dataport, minibar, coffeemaker, hair dryer, iron.

Moderate

Etta's Place 🔑🔑 *(Value)*   In the heart of historic downtown, Etta's is much more a cozy boutique hotel than a mom-and-pop B&B. Occupying the second floor of a landmark building, which once housed Fort Worth's venerable jazz club, Caravan of Dreams, on Sundance Square, the inn is within easy walking distance of all the downtown shops and restaurants, and just a short drive or trolley ride from the Cultural District and Stockyards. Named for Etta Place, the girlfriend of the Sundance Kid (and said to be the most comely of Wild West women), the 6-year-old inn has spacious rooms with lots of light and well-chosen Texas touches, including antique chairs, horseshoe lamps, and Americana quilts. The handsome library and music rooms, with clubby leather chairs, are great places to relax with a book or chat with other guests. There are six good-size rooms, three roomy luxury suites with king-size beds and kitchenettes, and Etta's Attic, a penthouse suite with a kitchenette. A full home-cooked breakfast is included.

200 W. 3rd St., Fort Worth, TX 76102. ℂ 866/355-5760 or 817/255-5760. Fax 817/878-2560. www.ettas-place.com. 11 units. $125–$160 double; $170–$240 suite. Rates include full breakfast. AE, DC, DISC, MC, V. **Amenities:** Restaurant; game room; laundry service. *In room:* A/C, TV, fax, dataport, kitchenette in suites.

Hilton Fort Worth 🔑🔑 *(Value)*   This large, historic, and centrally located hotel—opened in 1921 as the Texas Hotel and where JFK spent the night before and was memorably photographed on the morning of his assassination in Dallas—was recently renovated and incorporated into the Hilton family. The badly needed, $9-million makeover, which jettisoned an adjacent annex, has transformed this hotel from a dowdy also-ran to one of the top large hotels in downtown Fort Worth. Behind a beautiful old brick facade is a soaring, impressive lobby; guest rooms are now swank and serene, with handsome (even masculine) color schemes, elegant furnishings, and plush bedding. Bathrooms have also been overhauled. Though the hotel has long been popular with groups, conventioneers, and other visiting businesspeople, it is now a superb place to stay for virtually anyone visiting Fort Worth (and children stay free when occupying their parents' room), and it's a good value for this level of sophistication, style, and convenience to Sundance Square's lively restaurants and bars. Look for a new restaurant soon to complement the casual Texas Café.

815 Main St., Fort Worth, TX 76102. ℂ 800/HILTONS or 817/870-2100. Fax 817/335-3408. www.hilton.com. 294 units. $149–$229 double. Weekend rates available. AE, DC, DISC, MC, V. Valet parking $10, self-parking $7. **Amenities:** 2 restaurants; fitness center; spa; concierge; business center; 24-hr. room service; laundry service. *In room:* A/C, TV, dataport, coffeemaker, hair dryer, iron.

Fort Worth Cultural District

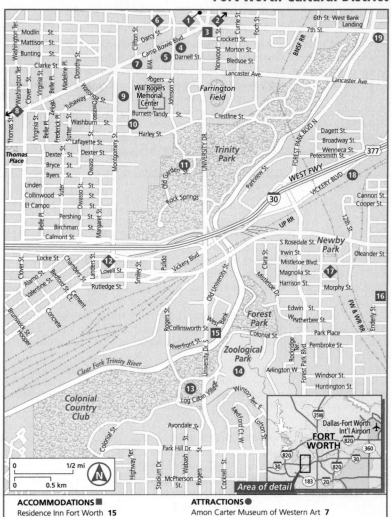

ACCOMMODATIONS ■
Residence Inn Fort Worth **15**
The Texas White House Bed & Breakfast **16**

DINING ◆
Angelo's BBQ **2**
Duce **8**
Kinkaid's **8**
Lanny's Alta Cocina Mexicana **6**
Paris Coffee Shop **17**
Railhead Smokehouse **12**
Sardines Ristorante Italiano **1**

ATTRACTIONS ●
Amon Carter Museum of Western Art **7**
Cattle Raisers Museum **19**
Fort Worth Botanic & Japanese Gardens **11**
Fort Worth Museum of Science and History **9**
Fort Worth Zoo **14**
Kimbell Art Museum **5**
Log Cabin Village **13**
Modern Art Museum of Fort Worth **4**
National Cowgirl Museum and Hall of Fame **10**
Thistle Hill House Museum **18**

Tips **Hotel Chains in a Pinch**

If you can't get a room in any of the suites hotels reviewed in this section, four additional, good-value chain hotels especially worth looking into in Fort Worth are **La Quinta Inn**, 4900 Bryant Irvin Rd. (© **800/531-5900**; www.lq.com), which has attractive two-room suites with kitchenettes, a pool, and a gazebo; **Courtyard by Marriott/University**, 3150 Riverfront Dr. (© **817/335-1300**; http://marriott.com/property/propertypage/dfwms); the recently renovated **Courtyard by Marriott Downtown/Blackstone**, 601 Main St. (© **817/885-8700**; http://marriott.com/property/propertypage/dfwch); and, near the Stockyards, **Country Inn & Suites by Carlson**, 2200 Mercado Dr. (© **817/831-9200**; www.countryinns.com/fortworthtx).

CULTURAL DISTRICT
Expensive
Residence Inn Fort Worth Cultural District *★ Value Kids*   A new extended-stay hotel at the edge of the Cultural District (perfectly convenient as well to downtown, which is less than a mile away), this large and very comfortable hotel is great for families and anyone staying a while in Fort Worth. With an elegant stone exterior, large outdoor pool, and nicely decorated rooms, it's a big step up from the standard Residence Inn. The spacious rooms, which include studios, one-bedroom and two-bedroom suites, are essentially apartments, with full kitchens and large bathrooms. They're larger than just about any hotel room in town (save big-bucks presidential suites). Most have additional fold-out sleeping couches and can easily accommodate a family of four.

2500 Museum Way, Fort Worth, TX 76107. © **800/331-3131** or 817/885-8250. Fax 817/885-8252. 150 units. www.marriott.com/residence-inn/travel.mi. $169–$179. Rates include full breakfast buffet and daily cocktail hour. AE, DC, DISC, MC, V. Free parking. Pets welcome. **Amenities:** Outdoor pool; fitness center and paddle-ball court; Jacuzzi; laundry facilities/same-day dry cleaning. *In room:* A/C, TV, dataport, kitchens, hair dryer.

Moderate
The Texas White House Bed & Breakfast *★ Value*   A big, handsome, and yes, white house with a wraparound porch and backyard with gazebo, this elegant, immaculate country home is a fine place to kick up your boots. In the Medical District, near All Saints Episcopal Hospital, the house has hardwood floors, a spacious parlor, a living room with fireplace, formal dining room, and well-maintained, warm accommodations with plush beds. There's no Lincoln Bedroom, but The Lone Star Room has nice antiques like a triple armoire, and a parson's bench sitting area and claw-foot tub. The Land of Contrast Room is done in black and white and has a large bathroom and queen-size brass bed; it may be a little frilly for some cowboys. And the Tejas Room has light oak furniture, his-and-hers rocking chairs, and a large platform tub. The Mustang and Longhorn suites have special amenities such as a balcony porch and fireplace (the Mustang even has a two-person, in-room sauna). The friendly owners serve a full gourmet breakfast and are happy to dispense all sorts of dining and activities recommendations.

1417 8th Ave., Fort Worth, TX 76104. © **800/279-6491** or 817/923-3597. Fax 817/923-0410. www.texaswhitehouse.com. 5 units. $125 double; $235 suite. Rates include full breakfast. Reduced rates for more than 1-night stays; special packages for honeymoons and anniversaries. AE, DC, DISC, MC, V. *In room:* A/C, TV, dataport, hair dryer, iron.

Inexpensive

Residence Inn Fort Worth (Value (Kids)   A former apartment complex, Residence Inn still feels much more like a residence than a chain motel. The spacious layouts, on two floors, have fully equipped kitchens and sitting areas. Most suites even have fireplaces. The penthouse suites are lofts. Many visitors are relocating businesspeople and families, and the inn does its best to foster a community; every evening there's a happy hour with free beer and wine and enough snacks to amount to a light evening meal. This place is great for families, as it's within walking distance of the Fort Worth Zoo and near the Cultural District.

1701 S. University Dr., Fort Worth, TX 76107. **(C)** **800/331-3131** or 817/870-1011. Fax 817/732-2114. www. marriott.com/hotels/travel/dfwrp. 120 units. $175 double; $199 suite. Rates include full breakfast buffet. AE, DC, DISC, MC, V. Free parking. Pets welcome. **Amenities:** Outdoor pool; fitness center privileges; Jacuzzi; limited room service; laundry facilities/same-day dry cleaning. *In room:* A/C, TV, dataport, kitchenette.

WHERE TO DINE

STOCKYARDS NATIONAL HISTORIC DISTRICT

Expensive

Cattlemen's Steakhouse (Kids STEAK   Cattlemen's has been serving the good people of Fort Worth for 60 years now. It's a relaxed (if frequently boisterous), affordable, and nicely worn place for a thick steak in the heart of cattle country, just around the corner from the Stockyards' main drag. It's great for families: There are separate rooms, like pens, and the server will bring place mats with barnyard animal stickers, a good kiddie menu, and a lollipop at the end of the meal. The thick, juicy, charcoal-broiled cuts of beef include a 13-ounce Kansas City sirloin, three cuts of rib-eye, a 16-ounce Texas T-bone, and a pretty good and juicy version of chicken-fried steak. The service is friendly and low key, and the crowd is a mix of families and, as my nephew observed, "lotsa men drinkin' wine and tellin' jokes." Those are the same guys who know that Cattlemen's is a good place to bust your aorta without breaking the bank.

2458 N. Main St. **(C)** **817/624-3945.** www.cattlemenssteakhouse.com. Reservations recommended. Main courses $7.95–$14 lunch, $11–$40 dinner. AE, DC, DISC, MC, V. Mon–Thurs 11am–10:30pm; Fri–Sat 11am–11pm; Sun 1–9pm.

Lonesome Dove Western Bistro GOURMET WESTERN   A wildly successful little restaurant, this cozy venture riding a wave of cowboy cool, is decorated in the style of an old saloon, with a long bar, high-backed Mexican iron barstools, copper-toned tin ceiling, bold paintings with Western themes, and a kitchen staff donning cowboy hats. The eclectic menu is a bit of a shock, though a thoroughly welcome one, in the Old West neighborhood of the Stockyards. Appetizers include chile-rubbed foie gras brûlée (on Texas toast) and seared sweet lobster cakes with corn/black-bean salsa and cilantro-orange butter sauce. The offbeat main courses opt for unique touches, such as the pancetta-wrapped Texas red fish or the grilled New Zealand deer chops with truffled mac and cheese and morels. Straight-up meat-eaters will delight in the hand-cut prime steaks, priced by the ounce. For lunch, check out the fresh buffalo burger or quail quesadillas. For dessert, the cappuccino flan is creamy and delicious. Chef Tim Love has ridden his newfound celebrity with aplomb, even opening an outpost of the restaurant in the hostile restaurant terrain of New York City.

2406 N. Main St. **(C)** **817/740-8810.** www.lonesomedovebistro.com. Reservations required. Main courses lunch $5–$14, dinner $19–$34. AE, MC, V. Tues–Sat 11am–2:30pm; Sun–Thurs 5–10pm; Fri–Sat 5–11pm.

Inexpensive

Joe T. Garcia's Mexican Dishes *Value* *Kids* TEX-MEX   At this enduringly popular Cowtown Tex-Mex institution just south of the Stockyards, almost everyone already knows that they don't have menus, only do two dinner dishes, and only take cash (or check). That's because they've been here many times before and will be back again and again. This 65-year-old restaurant, in a rambling home that looks like a pretty Mexican hacienda, has a lush outdoor patio sitting area (incredibly, large enough to seat 1,000 hungry eaters, though it never feels massified) set around a pool. Indoors is comfortably relaxed, but outdoors is the place to be—unless the Texas heat is suffocating. Ordering couldn't be simpler: Choose between a heaping plate of succulently grilled chicken or beef fajitas, a big family-style dinner with tacos and enchiladas, or chiles rellenos, tamales, and chicken flautas at lunch. Joe T.'s is a margarita factory, spitting out thousands of margaritas on the rocks and frozen (pitchers are a good deal, at $15). Service can be a little erratic, though it's frequently lightning fast. A Mexican-style brunch is served on Saturdays and Sundays from 11am to 2pm.

2201 N. Commerce St. © 817/626-4356. Reservations not accepted. Main courses $9.25–$13. No credit cards. Mon–Thurs 11am–2:30pm and 5–10pm; Fri–Sat 11am–11pm; Sun 11am–10pm.

DOWNTOWN
Expensive

Café Ashton ★★ NEW AMERICAN   Fort Worth natives aren't usually too impressed by anything too slick or haute, but this fine new addition to the dining scene, in the elegant Ashton Hotel (p. 126), may change the way diners think about this cow town. The New American menu, with Asian and Latin accents, at Café Ashton, a sleek restaurant quietly decorated in soothing colors, is stellar. Dine on such creative dishes as beef stroganoff with morels in brandy-laced cream sauce or Chilean sea bass with a fresh crab and potato purée, tomato, and mandarin-orange chutney. The deceptively simple-looking roasted harissa chicken, served on a bed of Swiss chard and with a base of black-truffle potato rosti, is scrumptious. For an appetizer, the seared diver scallops and warm shrimp beignets, served on greens with mango salsa and crème fraîche, are not to be missed. The small but select wine list is, refreshingly, reasonably priced. Even if you're not staying at this fine hotel, make an effort to eat here, even if it's only for a rewarding breakfast.

610 Main St. © 817/332-0100. Reservations required. Main courses $14–$32. AE, MC, V. Daily 6:30–10am and 11am–2pm; Sun–Thurs 5–9pm; Fri–Sat 5–10pm.

Del Frisco's Double Eagle Steak House ★★ STEAK   Fort Worth's top steakhouse is a clubby two-level place for cattle barons, power brokers, jet-setters, and mere steak lovers. In a redbrick corner building (ca. 1890s), huge top-notch steaks are the story. The filet mignon (in 8- and 12-oz. versions) is butter-soft; other cuts of prime beef include a marbled rib-eye, prime porterhouse, and Santa Fe peppercorn steak. Pinstripe and new economy types will love the cigar lounge, which has a nice selection of Robustos, and the deep wine cellar. Desserts, if you make it to them, are every bit as artery-clogging and overwhelming as the main courses. For some Fort Worth natives, though, this bit of Big D swagger and priceyness is a bit much for their laid-back downtown. Cattlemen's Steakhouse is a little more low-key, though a step down in quality for beef lovers.

812 Main St. at 8th St. © 817/877-3999. Reservations recommended. Main courses $18–$38. AE, DC, DISC, MC, V. Mon–Thurs 5–10pm; Fri–Sat 5–11pm.

(Kids) Family-Friendly Restaurants in Fort Worth

Cattlemen's Steakhouse (p. 131)   No slick banker's steakhouse, this homey, well-worn place in the heart of the Stockyards has several separate rooms, and kids get place mats adorned with barnyard animal stickers, a kiddie menu, and a lollipop treat. And parents get what they come for: a good-value steak.

Ferré Ristorante e Bar (see below)   Kids will love the views of the Bass Hall angels. Parents will love the attractive and spacious dining area as well as the good Tuscan fare.

Joe T. Garcia's Mexican Dishes (p. 132)   No menus? No problem. This Tex-Mex institution serves up two dishes daily, so you can spend less time deciding what to order and more time sipping margaritas. Parents and kids will both enjoy the delightful outdoor patio.

Kinkaid's Grocery Market (p. 135)   Burger heaven in Fort Worth is an old-time 1940s grocery store that makes just about the best burgers in Texas. Kids are sure to be entertained by the protocol: You place your order at the open kitchen in back, get a white paper bag with your name scrawled on it, pay at the register, and then pick out a spot at a communal table beneath a jungle of inflatable toys hanging from the ceiling.

Railhead Smokehouse (p. 136)   A Fort Worth barbecue fave that draws families every night of the week for its tasty barbecue and relaxed atmosphere. The place is noisy without rising to the levels of a Chuck E. Cheese's, and excellent-value children's plates will keep the kids happy.

Sardines Ristorante Italiano (p. 135)   The good vibes and generous helpings keep folks coming back. The pasta dishes, inexpensive wines, and nightly jazz make this a destination for the whole family.

Ferré Ristorante e Bar (Kids) TUSCAN   Occupying the coveted spot across the street from Bass Hall, where the defunct Angeluna used to be, this new outpost of the very popular restaurant of the same name in Dallas's yuppie Uptown district, should be equally successful in Fort Worth. I ate here on only its second night open, and though it had some obvious kinks to work out, it has all the makings of a place sure to please local business folk, couples on dates, concert-goers, and families. It's a smart-looking, spacious restaurant that's not overwhelming in size, with lots of windows that show off the huge angels of Bass Hall's illuminated facade. The menu isn't overly adventurous, though it offers good Italian and Tuscan standards, including homemade pastas, such as tortellini stuffed with braised beef, and pizzas. Main courses for now are more hit or miss; my sister's veal scaloppine was unforgivably tough, but my brother-in-law's sea bass was delicious.

215 E. 4th St. (C) 817/332-0033. Reservations required. Main courses $12–$27. AE, MC, V. Mon–Fri 11:30am–3:30pm and Sat noon–4pm; Sun–Wed 4–10pm and Thurs–Sat 4–11pm.

Reata SOUTHWESTERN   Still proudly spearheading the Southwestern cuisine movement, which may have run its course elsewhere but is perfectly at home in

Cowtown, Reata moved to a new location after the great Fort Worth tornado of 2000 condemned its former home, the Bank One tower. Named for the ranch in the movie *Giant*, Reata, in the space formerly inhabited by Fort Worth's once-loved and sadly gone jazz club, Caravan of Dreams, sports a great rooftop Grotto Bar and dining area inside the glass dome on the roof. The restaurant has basic fare, such as chicken-fried steak, chicken chile rellenos, and marbled rib-eye, as well as more creative interpretations, such as carne asada with cacciota cheese enchiladas, which are consistently well prepared enough to keep more adventurous diners interested. Portions are still huge, and some dishes suffer from cheese, cream, and sauce overkill. The waitstaff are appropriately outfitted in jeans and cowboy vests; they efficiently herd the crowds of casual and big-night-out diners through this mainstay of Texas urban chic.

310 Houston St. ℂ **817/336-1009.** Reservations recommended. Main courses $15–$41. AE, MC, V. Daily 11am–2:30pm and 5–10:30pm.

CULTURAL DISTRICT
Very Expensive
Lanny's Alta Cocina Mexicana ✦✦✦ NOUVEAU MEXICAN   You'd never know by dining at this upscale, refined, small restaurant that the chef and owner is the great-grandson of the gentleman who opened the Stockyards' Joe T. Garcia's, a legendary slinger of crowd-pleasing fajitas, enchiladas, and margaritas. Lanny Lancarte takes an entirely different approach to Mexican dining, infusing it with Mediterranean flair (or perhaps it's the other way around, Mediterranean fare with Mexican accents). Whatever it is, it is stylishly presented, elegant, and delicious. It's also pricey. These are New York tariffs and then some, but if you're willing to foot the bill, you can be assured of a creative meal, tantalizing new tastes, and a superb international wine list. Kobe beef ceviche and tapas such as *mole*-braised pork tamales get one's taste buds in gear for prime carne asada with macaroni gratin or black sea bass in a poblano and asparagus sauce. The small house is warmly contemporary, with chocolate-brown leather chairs, terra-cotta colored curtains, and modern track lighting. The five-course tasting menu ($60) is the best way to get a handle on Lancarte's cooking, and also a relatively good deal (with wine pairing, $90). *Fort Worth* magazine named Lanny's (the full name of the restaurant means "Mexican haute cuisine," a perfect description of its high aims) Best New Restaurant 2005.

3405 W. 7th St. ℂ **817/850-9996.** www.lannyskitchen.com. Reservations required. Main courses $30–$42. AE, DISC, MC, V. Tues–Fri 11:30am–2pm; Tues–Thurs 5:30–10pm; Fri–Sat 5:30–10:30pm.

Expensive
Duce ✦✦ MODERN STEAKHOUSE   The newest project of local celebrity chef Tim Love (of Lonesome Dove fame; see p. 131) is this appealingly clean and chic contemporary restaurant in an upscale strip mall west of the Cultural District. Though it opened in 2006 serving tapas and "modern European cuisine," it has since switched gears and become a steakhouse, which apparently Fort Worth has more of a stomach for. The restaurant still sports the same pretentious slogan, however: "eat.drink.live." I'm sorry to see creative curiosities (such as wild boar empanadas) go, but fans of *Lonesome Dove* will cotton to six cuts of prime beef, a Kobe beef, and shrimp K-bob, as well as lobster and sushi. With a roster of creative specialty cocktails and an interesting international wine list, as well as a swank outdoor patio with a waterfall, fireplaces, and a retractable roof, Duce is also a great spot for happy hour (daily 4–7pm, with wine tastings Wed from 6–8pm) and late-night drinking; a DJ takes over the patio

every Saturday night. The West Side special at lunch, always just $8, or the three-course lunch for $20, are both excellent deals.

6333 Camp Bowie Blvd. (west of I-30). ℭ 817/377-4400. Reservations recommended. Main courses $19–$42. AE, DISC, MC, V. Tues–Sat 11:30am–2:30pm and 4pm–midnight.

Moderate

Sardines Ristorante Italiano *(Value)* *(Kids)* ITALIAN   After a protracted, heated battle, this Fort Worth landmark, which had seemingly forever welcomed locals from a spot just across from the museums, finally succumbed to the big bad development monster (the old digs were flattened and transformed into a parking lot). The popular, quirky Italian restaurant moved to West Fort Worth and, amazingly, succeeded in transplanting its unique look and ambience—a cross between a smoky jazz dive and a neighborhood Italian joint in Brooklyn—to the new spot. All the antique pieces, metal signs, and photographs have been relocated, and the dark and intimate feel closely replicated. Sardines is perfect for dependable, generous helpings of Italian grub, inexpensive wine, and an abundance of good vibes and good nightly jazz starting at 7pm. Some veal dishes can be mediocre; your best bet is to stick to the list of good pastas such as *linguine alla rosa* (with artichokes, capers, and olive oil) and seafood. The weekday lunch specials ($5.95) are bargain basement, and there's a popular happy hour Monday through Friday from 2 to 5pm.

509 N. University Dr. (at Rockwood Park Dr. N). ℭ 817/332-9937. www.sardinesristorante.com. Reservations recommended. Main courses $11–$25. AE, DISC, MC, V. Mon–Thurs 11am–11:30pm; Fri 11am–12:30am; Sat 5pm–12:30am.

Inexpensive

Angelo's ⭐ *(Value)* BARBECUE   Fort Worth's classic Texas barbecue joint, in this spot since 1958, is the real deal, a Cowtown legend. A few blocks north of the Cultural District and west of downtown, it looks kind of like a large Texas Jaycees convention hall, with wood paneling, mounted deer and buffalo heads, metal ceiling fans, and Formica tables. It's nearly as full of flavor as the hickory-smoked barbecue. The sliced beef sandwich and beef brisket plates are the standard, though you can also detour toward salami, ham, turkey, and Polish sausage. The side dishes, such as coleslaw, pinto beans, and potato salad, are all excellent. Chicken and pork ribs are served all day "while they last," though hickory-smoked beef ribs don't make an appearance until after 3:30pm. Cold Bud comes in frosted steins. This place is so low-key that there's not even "waitress service" until 3pm.

2533 White Settlement Rd. ℭ 817/332-0357. Reservations not accepted. Main courses $3.35–$11. No credit cards. Mon–Sat 11am–10pm.

Kinkaid's Grocery Market *(Value)* *(Kids)* BURGERS   As down home and folksy as could be, Kinkaid's, a 1940s grocery store that one day started making burgers, is now a beloved institution in Fort Worth and the perennial winner of "Best Burger in Texas" polls. The standard order is a thick, juicy burger and fries or onion rings. There are a few other items, such as grilled chicken, hot dogs, and grilled cheese sandwiches, but few people move beyond the time-tested basics. The large space, with pistachio-ice-cream-colored green cinder-block walls, has a few communal picnic tables in front, long rows of stand-up counters, and an open kitchen in back. Place your order at the kitchen, pick up a white paper bag with your name scrawled on it, pay at the register, and find a spot under the inflatable toys hanging from the ceiling.

4901 Camp Bowie Blvd. (at Eldridge). ℭ 817/732-2881. Reservations not accepted. Main courses $3.50–$7. No credit cards. Mon–Sat 11am–6pm.

Paris Coffee Shop *(Value* DINER/BREAKFAST AND LUNCH   Around since the Great Depression, this big, wood-paneled dining room heaving with hungry Texans for breakfast and lunch is a longtime down-home favorite. There's not an ounce of Paris in it save the name. (Or maybe it's referring to Paris, Texas.) Service is classic Southern hospitality. Breakfast is the star: Choose from awesome pancakes, omelets, grits, and biscuits and gravy (on weekdays you can get "red-eye gravy," made with coffee, cinnamon, and bacon grease). Lunch is such standard fare as sandwiches, plate lunches (with a choice of meats and vegetables for $7), and chili, though there are lunch specials such as enchiladas and ham steak—and that famous red-eye gravy. Try the pies; in a place like this, you know they're good.

700 W. Magnolia Ave. (at Hemphill). (C) 817/335-2041. Reservations not accepted. Main courses $6–$9. AE, DISC, MC, V. Mon–Fri 6am–2:30pm; Sat 6–11am.

Railhead Smokehouse *(★ Kids* BARBECUE   No Old West town can sit on its barbecue laurels, and Fort Worth has several new Texas barbecue joints to go along with the old-time favorites. Neither the newest nor the oldest, Railhead is one of the best. It's certainly slicker than Angelo's, but it still attracts the hats-and-boots crowd in their pickups, as well as soccer moms and families pulling up in Lexus SUVs for takeout. The smoky barbecue with tangy sauce gets rave reviews; the plates are heaping; and the ribs, sliced beef, fries, and cheddar peppers (cheese-stuffed jalapeños) are excellent; the chicken, though, gets universally panned. Come for absurdly cheap weekday plate specials and have a beer or margarita out on the patio, which is something of a happy-hour hot spot, or hang out at the lively bar, which often features live music. Cheap and filling children's plates are served, and you can also load up on barbecue by the pound, though I can't vouch for how well the stuff travels.

2900 Montgomery St. (at Vickery). (C) 817/738-9808. Reservations not accepted. Main courses $6.75–$11. AE, DISC, MC, V. Mon–Thurs 11am–9pm; Fri–Sat 11am–10pm.

EXPLORING FORT WORTH

Despite its laid-back image and small size, Fort Worth abounds with sights, sounds, and things to do. Whether you're a cowboy, aesthete, or historian—or just plain folk—Fort Worth, an enjoyable and relaxed city that's also remarkably well organized for visitors, should prove entertaining. There are three distinct parts, each a couple of miles from one another: the Stockyards National Historic District, the focus of the city's cattle-raising and livestock auction legacy as the cow town of the cattle drives north in the 19th century; newly revitalized historic downtown Fort Worth, a beautifully laid-out, clean, and renovated core; and the Cultural District, a world-class museum, arts, and architecture center with the superlative Kimbell Museum (perhaps Texas's finest art museum), the Amon Carter Museum of Western Art, and the fantastic new Modern

---

Tips **Coupon Discounts**

Visit the Fort Worth Convention & Visitors Bureau website for money-saving coupons at major attractions, including the Stockyards, Museum of Science and History, Cowgirl Museum, and Billy Bob's Texas, as well as the airport shuttle. Go to www.fortworth.com/16coupons/16coupons.shtml and print out any of more than a dozen coupons.

Christmas in the Stockyards

A fairly new tradition in the Stockyards, **Christmas in the Stockyards,** is held the first Saturday in December. Perfect for families, it features games, crafts, roping lessons, a parade, and Cowboy Ride for Toys, all of which is followed by the lighting of a 45-foot tree and Christmas carols. For more information, call ℭ **817/625-9715** or visit www.fortworthstockyards.org.

Art Museum. We'll take them in that order, though where you start should be in accord with your interests in either art or a living museum of the Old West.

Plenty of attractions in Fort Worth are free; pick up the flyer "Everything Free to Do in Fort Worth" at the visitor center if you want to see how much you can do for no money.

THE TOP ATTRACTIONS
The Stockyards National Historic District ☆☆
Two miles north of downtown Fort Worth, off North Main Street, is the still-beating heart of Fort Worth's Old West heritage. The Stockyards National Historic District—where women police officers patrol on horseback, and a cattle drive takes place daily on the cobblestones of Exchange Avenue—is part Western theme park and part living history museum. The livestock industry's 1880s roots are here, and it became the biggest and busiest cattle, horse, mule, hog, and sheep marketing center in the Southwest (and quite a pocket of wealth). The 125-acre district encompasses the **Livestock Exchange Building,** the focus of old livestock business; **Cowtown Coliseum,** the world's first indoor rodeo arena; **Stockyards Station,** the former hog and sheep pens, now overrun with Western shops and restaurants; **Billy Bob's Texas,** known as the world's largest honky-tonk; Western shops and authentic saloons, such as the **White Elephant;** and the historic **Stockyards Hotel,** where bar stools are topped by saddles and Bonnie and Clyde once camped out while on the lam. Such Western heroes as Gene Autry, Dale Evans, Roy Rogers, and Bob Wills are honored in bronze along Exchange Avenue's **Trail of Fame.**

The **Fort Worth Stock Show & Rodeo** is held the last 2 weeks of January and first week of February. It's hands-down the time in Fort Worth to see a surfeit of rodeo performances, as well as the nation's oldest continuous livestock show. For information, call ℭ **817/877-2420** or get tickets at Ticketmaster outlets or online at www.fwssr.com.

Cowtown Cattlepen Maze *(Kids* A "Texas-size human maze," constructed to resemble the cattle pens of the Old West, is a fun diversion for kids (and older folks eager to test their skills against the labyrinth). Parents can watch from the observation deck to track how the kids are doing.

E. Exchange Ave. (across from Stockyards Station). ℭ 817/624-6666. www.cowtowncattlepenmaze.com. $5 adults, $4 children ages 5–12 (additional trips to score a faster time, $3). Special group rates and unlimited 45-min. runs for birthday parties available. Daily 10am–dusk (5pm in winter, 8–9pm in summer). Closed Thanksgiving, Dec 25, and Jan 1.

Stockyards Museum This small museum, part of the North Fort Worth Historical Society, is located inside the historic Livestock Exchange building that dates from 1893. It displays artifacts—guns, barbed wire, furniture, and clothing—from Fort

Tips **Longhorn Express: Fort Worth Herd**

Amazingly, the Fort Worth Stockyards still look the part of the Old West. To enhance the atmosphere even more, a twice-daily "cattle drive," the **Fort Worth Herd,** takes place on the main drag, Exchange Avenue (at N. Main St.), at 11:30am and again at 4pm. About 15 head of 1-ton longhorn steers, led by cowhands dressed the part in 19th-century duds, rumble down the redbrick street past the Stockyards, on their way to grazing near the West Fork of the Trinity River and back again to the Stockyards. Claimed to be the world's only daily longhorn cattle drive, it's perfect for photo ops. The best places to view the longhorns are the front lawn of the Livestock Exchange building and from the catwalk above the cattle pens. For more information, call ✆ **817/336-HERD.**

Worth's glory days. Have a look in the section on women at the exhibit of the 1920s Fort Worth Stock Show Queen's coronation and the 19th-century "bad luck" wedding dress, which "brought personal misery or disaster to everyone who wore it or planned to wear it." There's a livestock auction center inside the building, where you can see a few cowboys checking out the animals on the monitors.

131 E. Exchange Ave. ✆ **817/625-5082.** Free admission (donation requested). Mon–Sat 10am–5pm.

Texas Cowboy Hall of Fame Fans of rodeo and the cowboy life will appreciate this small museum, in restored horse and mule barns, honoring the stalwarts of Texas rodeo, including such (Texas) household names as Larry Mahan and Ty Murray. On display are the honorees' saddles, chaps, belt buckles, and trophies collected over the course of their careers. Also of interest are the fully restored 60 Sterquell Wagons dating from the 18th and 19th centuries. About an hour should be sufficient to take in the cowboys, though some visitors could do a run-through in half that time.

For those who want to broaden their knowledge of the Old West, the **National Cowboys of Color Museum & Hall of Fame,** east of the Stockyards at 3400 Mount Vernon Ave. (✆ **817/534-8801;** www.cowboysofcolor.org), pays much-needed tribute to a group of cowboys whose contributions were critical to opening the American West and are sadly often overlooked. The museum is open Wednesday through Saturday from 11am to 6pm; admission is $6 adults, $4 seniors, $3 students, free for children 5 and younger.

128 E. Exchange Ave., Barn A. ✆ **817/626-7131.** www.texascowboyhalloffame.com. Admission $5 adults, $4 seniors, $3 children 3–12, $15 families. Discounts available online. Mon–Thurs 10am–6pm; Fri–Sat 10am–7pm; Sun noon–6pm.

Historic Downtown & Sundance Square ★

Charming, unassuming, and remarkably unhurried, downtown's centerpiece, Sundance Square (named for the Sundance Kid, who hid out here with the Hole-in-the-Wall Gang and a prime stop along the Chisholm Trail during the cattle drives of the 1800s), is 14 blocks of redbrick streets, late-19th-century buildings, and attractions that include the Bass Performance Hall, a couple of museums, and a pair of Art Deco movie theaters. It's a model of urban planning, and a real rarity in Texas: a place with sidewalks that invites nonmotored strolling. Downtown Fort Worth is lit up like a Christmas tree at night, and Sundance Square's bars and restaurants are the heart of downtown nightlife.

Bass Performance Hall ⚑ Fort Worth's magnificent music hall, inaugurated in 1998 and funded entirely by private donations, is a spectacular addition to the city's already thriving cultural life. Touted as one of the top ten opera houses in the world, Bass Hall is a handsome showpiece, constructed in a tiered horseshoe shape with excellent acoustics and great sight lines. The work of the architect David Schwarz (who built The Ballpark at Arlington and the American Airlines arena), Bass Hall is a 10-story, 2,000-seat jewel. Gracing the exterior are two huge limestone angels, trumpets to lips, heralding patrons to the evening's performance. Inside, the entrance hall is paved with cut Italian marble and the dome is painted with a Texas noonday sky, ringed by silvery laurel leaves. The bathrooms are charmingly decorated with notes from Dvorak's "Going Home." Guided tours—best for those with a keen interest in architecture—last about 45 minutes. Bass Hall hosts the Fort Worth opera, symphony, theater, and dance companies; see "Fort Worth After Dark," later in this chapter, for more details.

4th and Calhoun sts. ✆ **877/212-4280,** or 817/212-4325 information hot line. www.basshall.com. Free guided public tours given Sat 10:30am (performance schedule permitting); meet in East Portal at the corner of Calhoun and Commerce.

Fire Station No. 1/150 Years of Fort Worth Exhibit Tucked away in historic Fire Station No. 1 (which dates from 1907), this annex of the Fort Worth Museum of Science and History tells the history of Cowtown from its frontier days and the Chisholm Trail cattle drives to present day. Good for a quick and painless overview of Old West history.

Corner of 2nd and Commerce sts. ✆ **817/255-9300.** Free admission. Daily 9am–8pm.

Sid Richardson Collection of Western Art Admirers of art depicting the Old West should tack a visit to the Sid Richardson, now reopened after a year-long renovation by noted architect David Schwarz, onto a visit at the more important Amon Carter Museum (p. 140). This small but focused collection, which belonged to a Fort Worth oilman, comprises 60 paintings by Frederic Remington and Charles M. Russell, two late-19th- and early-20th-century biggies of Western art. The museum now has a new facade and galleries. If you're not a fan of colorful renderings of wagon trails and Native Americans on horseback, this may not be your glass of whiskey, but the museum does have a couple of great saddles with silver ornamentation. Allow about a half-hour.

309 Main St. ✆ **817/332-6554.** www.sidrmuseum.org. Free admission. Mon–Thurs 9am–5pm; Fri–Sat 9am–8pm; Sun noon–5pm. Free tours Sat 11am.

The Cultural District ⚑⚑⚑
Fort Worth is the cultural capital of the Southwest, with the finest art museums in Texas and the most impressive small art museum in the country. The city ropes off the Cultural District, making it an elite island by placing it safely apart from downtown business interests, a couple of miles west. Arts philanthropy has thrived in Fort Worth to a degree unmatched in Texas and many parts of the United States. Wealthy patrons

---

Tips **A Water Break**

Take a breather at the refreshing **Fort Worth Water Gardens,** designed by the famed architect Philip Johnson—4 acres of water (19,000 gal. per minute) cascading over cement and into five pools. At Commerce and 15th streets, downtown, call ✆ **817/871-7699** for more information.

(Kids) The Grapevine Vintage Railroad

To jump into the turn-of-the-20th-century Old West character of the Stock-yards, don your best Western duds and hop aboard the **Grapevine Vintage Railroad.** The 100-year-old steam train of the Tarantula Railroad (purchased from Walt Disney and affectionately called "Puffy" by locals)—and its diesel brethren—make the Trinity River Run, a 1-hour trip from Stockyards Station to 8th Avenue in Fort Worth, and another travels along the Chisholm Trail to the Cotton Belt Depot in historic Grapevine, Texas. The 1896 steam train runs on Saturday and Sunday, the 1953 vintage diesel on Friday. April through August, the trains run from Thursday to Sunday only; other months they run Friday to Sunday (but there is no service in Jan). The train trip to Grapevine is more involved and interesting (as well as more expensive) than the one that ends in Forth Worth. The name Tarantula stems from a tale in the late 19th century, when a local newspaperman's plans for rail lines were derided as looking like "the legs of a hairy tarantula."

Call ② **817/410-3123** or visit www.grapevinesteamrailroad.com for exact schedules and the running status of the steam train. To 8th Avenue, the train leaves the Stockyards on Saturdays at noon and Sundays at 3pm (round-trip $10 adults, $9 seniors, $6 children ages 3–12). To Grapevine, the train leaves the Stockyards Saturdays at 2pm and Sundays at 4:45pm, arriving in Grapevine an hour and 15 minutes later (round-trip $20 adults, $18 seniors, and $10 children ages 3–12).

and an enthusiastic city have welcomed some of the world's most celebrated architects, including Louis Kahn, Philip Johnson, and Tadao Ando, to create museums that make much larger and more cosmopolitan cities salivate with envy. The presence of the glorious new Modern Art Museum across the street from the Kimbell and down the block from Philip Johnson's expanded Amon Carter has entrenched Fort Worth as perhaps the top art and architecture city between the two coasts. South of downtown is an area of parks, gardens, historic homes, and the Fort Worth Zoo, considered one of the top five in the country.

Amon Carter Museum of Western Art ⭐⭐   Reopened in 2001 after a 2-year, $39-million expansion by the original architect, Philip Johnson, which tripled the size of its galleries, the Amon Carter is now an even more splendid showcase for its wide-ranging collection of American art. The museum possesses the finest and most complete collection of works by Frederic Remington and Charles M. Russell, two giants of Western art, as well as a major photography collection (works by Ansel Adams, Man Ray, Elliot Porter, Robert Frank, Alfred Stieglitz, Walker Evans, and many others); early scenes of the West by John Mix Stanley and Albert Bierstadt; and important contemporary paintings by Marsden Hartley, Georgia O'Keeffe, Arthur Dove, and Stuart Davis. Amon G. Carter was the creator and publisher of the *Fort Worth Star-Telegram.* His original collection of 400 paintings, drawings, and works of sculpture by Remington and Russell has grown to over 300,000 works. I'd suggest allowing about 2 hours here, though fans of Americana may need even more time.

3501 Camp Bowie Blvd. (at Montgomery and W. Lancaster). ℂ 817/738-1933. www.cartermuseum.org. Free admission (admission fee for special exhibits). Tues–Wed and Fri–Sat 10am–5pm; Thurs 10am–8pm; Sun noon–5pm. Free public tours 3:30pm Fri–Sun.

Cattle Raisers Museum (Kids)

A minor museum dedicated to the history of cattle ranching as a lifestyle, this small collection makes good use of talking dummies—ranchers and longhorn cattle—to give you a picture of life on the range. There's a theater presentation on rustlers, ropers, and mavericks, and lots of cowboy artifacts, including what is reputed to be the world's largest documented collection of branding irons, including some of those owned by famous Texans (LBJ, Stephen F. Austin, Nolan Ryan). A half-hour or so should be sufficient here, unless the kids are entranced by the talking cowboys.

1301 W. 7th St. ℂ 817/332-8551. www.cattleraisersmuseum.org. $3 adults, $2 seniors and students ages 13–18, $1 children ages 4–12. Mon–Fri 10am–5pm. (also open Sat during the Fort Worth Stock Show & Rodeo).

Fort Worth Botanic & Japanese Gardens 👁

Created during the Great Depression, this spacious showcase of more than 2,500 native and exotic species of plants in 109 acres of attractive gardens and natural settings is the oldest botanical garden in Texas. Its highlights include the Texas Rose Garden, 3,500 roses that bloom in late April and October; a serene, 7-acre Japanese Garden, which features waterfalls, a tea house and meditation space, and colorful koi-stocked ponds; and a 10,000-square-foot conservatory of exotic plants and tropical trees from around the world. You can drive through roads in the gardens and park at several of the individual sites. You should allow a couple of hours here, though it would be all too easy to while away an entire afternoon.

3220 Botanic Dr. ℂ 817/871-7686. www.fwbg.org. Free admission to gardens. Enclosed conservatory $1 adults, 50¢ seniors and children ages 4–12, free for children younger than 4. Japanese Garden $3 adults ($3.50 weekends and holidays), $3 seniors, $2 children ages 4–12, free for children younger than 4. Botanic garden daily 10am–5pm. Conservatory Mon–Fri 10am–4pm; Sat 10am–6pm; Sun 1–6pm.

Fort Worth Museum of Science and History (Kids)

One of the largest of its kind in the country, with a domed Omni (IMAX) theater, planetarium, eight exhibition galleries, and hands-on science displays, this museum offers tons of fun and adventure for families. Kids should eat up the life-size Lone Star dinosaurs (at "Dinodig" they can even hunt for fossils and dig for dinosaur bones), while younger ones can hang out at Kidspace, which has a puppet theater and materials for building a house. When the tots and parents get hungry, a courtyard cafe on the premises makes for a good stop. Allow a couple of hours here unless the kids get cranky.

1501 Montgomery St. ℂ 888/255-9300 or 817/255-9540. www.fortworthmuseum.org. Exhibit admission $8 adults, $7 seniors and children ages 3–12. Omni admission $7 adults, $6 seniors and children ages 3–12. Planetarium admission $3.50. Combination admission $14 adults, $12 seniors and children ages 3–12. Admission includes admittances to National Cowgirl Museum and Hall of Fame. Mon–Thurs 9am–5:30pm; Fri–Sat 9am–8pm; Sun 11:30am–5:30pm.

Fort Worth Zoo ★★★ (Kids)

One of the top zoos in the country, the award-winning Fort Worth Zoo has a great layout of natural habitats and fantastic animals from around the world. I took my nephew here for his fifth birthday, and we had a total blast. The zoo has an African Savannah with endangered rhinos and giraffes; a Koala Outback with kangaroos, wallabies, and lazy koalas; and Komodo dragons, lots of apes, orangutans and rainforest monkeys, and white tigers. The newest exhibit has a local theme: "Texas Wild!," an 8-acre expansion showcasing native Texas animals and a late-19th-century town. Allow 2 or 3 hours here, though your kids are unlikely to want to leave.

1989 Colonial Pkwy. ℂ 817/759-7555. www.fortworthzoo.org. Admission $11 adults, $7 seniors, $8 children ages 3–12, free for children younger than 2; half-price tickets Wed. Mar–Sept daily 10am–5pm; Oct–Feb daily 10am–4pm. Parking $5.

Kimbell Art Museum 🎭🎭🎭   One of the country's (if not the world's) top small museums is this remarkable and gracious place, the jewel in Cowtown's crown. In 1972, the great American architect Louis Kahn created perhaps his finest building to house the art collection of local philanthropist Kay Kimbell. His modern, natural concrete structure, a masterpiece of light, symmetry, and geometry, is a reference work in worldwide architectural studies. Its cycloid-shaped vaults are suffused with natural light entering discreetly through slatted skylights. The building is essentially a shell; it has no real interior walls, which allows curators total creativity to use movable walls to design exhibits. The TV art evangelist, Sister Wendy Beckett, calls the Kimbell "probably the nearest such an institution can come to perfection . . . one of the greatest achievements in the world." It is widely held to be the greatest museum building of the late 20th century.

The permanent collection matches the grace and drama of the building. Though small, it contains several superlative works, ranging from prehistoric Asian and pre-Columbian pieces to European old masters (Velázquez, El Greco, Rubens, Rembrandt) and the Impressionist and modern masters (van Gogh, Monet, Cézanne, and Picasso). Outdoors is a Zen-like, sunken sculpture garden by Isamu Noguchi. With its reputation as such an outstanding place to display and view art, the Kimbell receives some of the finest national and international shows that virtually every top-notch museum vies for. Recent major exhibits have included "Mondrian: The Path to Abstraction" and "Gauguin and Impressionism." Depending upon your interest in and the popularity of the current itinerant special exhibit, you might plan to spend a good 3 to 4 hours here.

3333 Camp Bowie Blvd. ℂ 817/332-8451. www.kimbellart.org. Free admission to general collection; special exhibitions $12 adults, $10 seniors and students, $8 children ages 6–11, Tues half price for all. Tues–Thurs and Sat 10am–5pm; Fri noon–8pm; Sun noon–5pm. Tours of the collection Wed 2pm and Sun 3pm.

Log Cabin Village *Kids*   Six mid-19th-century log cabins, presented as a living history museum, were transplanted to Forest Park southwest of downtown in the 1950s. The village includes a gristmill and actors decked out in pioneer costumes, who recreate the Old West of early Cowtown posing as spinners, candle makers, and blacksmiths. Pay a visit primarily if you need an inexpensive way to entertain your kids.

2100 Log Cabin Village Lane. ℂ 817/926-5881. www.logcabinvillage.org. Admission $3.50 adults, $3 seniors and children ages 4–17, free for children younger than 4. Tues–Fri 9am–4pm; Sat–Sun 1–5pm (gates close at 4:30pm). Closed Dec 25–Jan 1, Jan 29–Feb 11, Aug 20–Sept 2.

Modern Art Museum of Fort Worth 🎭🎭🎭   The most noteworthy recent development in Fort Worth—and one of the most important on the national culture scene—is the Modern, a landmark design by the celebrated modernist Japanese architect Tadao Ando and a true notch on the city's belt. It is my favorite new museum—or work of architecture, period—since Frank Gehry's Guggenheim Bilbao in Spain. Opened in 2002, the museum, quickly hailed as a masterpiece, contains over 50,000 square feet of gallery space, making it second in size only to the Museum of Modern Art in New York among museums dedicated to contemporary and modern art. The galleries, of warmly textured poured concrete with 20-foot-high ceilings and suffused with spectacular natural light, are housed in three rectangular, flat-roofed pavilions built around a large pond. In fact the oldest art museum in Texas (chartered in 1892), the Modern possesses an impressive permanent collection of modern and contemporary paintings, sculpture, and works on paper by Picasso, Mark Rothko, Andy Warhol,

Frank Stella, Robert Rauschenberg, David Smith, Gerhard Richter, Francis Bacon, and Jackson Pollock, as well as an impressive contemporary photography collection. A sculpture by Martin Puryear, *Ladder for Booker T. Washington,* proves very popular with kids; it's a two-story wooden ladder reaching to the ceiling, ever-so narrow at the top. Another piece not to miss is Ron Mueck's stunningly lifelike and creepy *Seated Woman.* The outdoor sculpture collection includes large-scale works by Tony Cragg, George Segal, and Antony Gormley and a massive piece outside by Richard Serra. Plan to spend at least a couple of hours here. The restaurant overlooking the reflection pool, Café Modern, is a very good spot for lunch.

3200 Darnell St. (across the street from the Kimbell Museum). © 866/824-5566 or 817/738-9215. www.themodern. org. $8 adults, $4 students and seniors, free for children 12 and younger, free admission on Wed and 1st Sun of each month. Tues–Thurs and Sat 10am–5pm; Fri 10am–8pm; Sun 11am–5pm. Feb–April and Sept–Nov, open Tues 10–7. Free public tours daily 2pm (no prior arrangement necessary). Call for information about artist-led tours (3rd Sun of the month) and lectures.

National Cowgirl Museum and Hall of Fame ★ *(Kids*   Opened in 2002 in a beautiful, Texas-style Art Deco building, the newest addition to Fort Worth's Cultural District recognizes not just cowgirls but the importance of an array of plucky women who shaped the American West. It's the only museum in the world honoring their pioneering spirit. A fun and educational visit for the entire family, the museum's interactive exhibits in three gallery spaces and a state-of-the-art theater depict cowgirls working their ranches, their role in the media and fashion (with displays of cowboy couture), and cutting horse and barrel-racing displays. A rotunda with 12 cool glass murals that slowly change as you walk through the hall honors more than 150 notable Western women (from Dale Evans and the first woman to cross the Rockies to Annie Oakley and the artist Georgia O'Keeffe). The interactive exhibits are terrific for little cowpokes of both sexes; kids can hop on a (simulated) bucking bronco and get filmed (which can later be viewed on the Internet), have their pictures superimposed on old Western film posters, and listen to jukeboxes playing country tunes. Don't miss the gift shop, a great place to score such things as vintage suitcases, antique Western goodies, and rhinestone duds. Allow an hour or two.

1720 Gendy St. (west of intersection of Montgomery and Burnett-Tandy, next to Will Rogers Memorial Center). © 800/476-FAME or 817/336-4475. www.cowgirl.net. $8 adults, $7 seniors, $7 children ages 6–18, free for children younger than 6. Admission includes admittances to Fort Worth Museum of Science and History. Discount coupon available online. Mon–Thurs 9am–5:30pm; Fri–Sat 9am–8pm; Sun 11:30am–5:30pm.

Moments **Fort Worth Stock Show & Rodeo**

If you're in Fort Worth at the end of January and first few days of February, you can't miss attending the Fort Worth Stock Show (officially known as the Southwestern Exposition and Livestock Show), which harkens back to its earliest days at the end of the 19th century. At the Will Rogers Memorial Center near the art museums (on Amon Carter Sq.), you'll see horse shows and auctions, and be able to check out all sorts of livestock, from beef cattle to llamas and swine. There's plenty of entertainment during the show and also an all-Western parade on the first Saturday. The rodeo is especially lively during the Stock Show; tickets are $16 to $18. For more information and an exact schedule of events, call © 817/877-2400 or visit www.fwstockshowrodeo.com.

Thistle Hill House Museum   This historic 1903 Georgian Revival mansion, the former residence of two prominent Fort Worth families, has been lovingly restored with period furnishings. The residence, rumored to be ghost-ridden, has an elegant oak grand staircase and a wealth of interesting details, including eight fireplaces, five full bathrooms, and, unusual for the period, electric and gas lighting and built-in closets. The 45-minute guided tour, which has recently really jumped in price, relates the curious anecdotes of the mansion's history. The cattle baron W. T. Waggoner built the home for his eccentric daughter Electra (who took milk baths and is said to have been the first to spend $20,000 in a single day at Neiman Marcus); it then passed to Winfield Scott, who made many changes in the home, adding its limestone columns; and it finally became a girl's school, later abandoned.

1509 Pennsylvania Ave. ⓒ 817/336-1212. www.thistlehill.org. Admission $10 adults, $7 seniors, $5 children ages 7–12. Tours on the hour Mon–Fri 11am–3pm; Sun 1–3pm.

ESPECIALLY FOR KIDS

Fort Worth is loaded with activities for children. The top choice among the options is the **Fort Worth Zoo,** one of the very finest in the country and a splendid array of exotic animals in natural habitats. Kids can play and learn at the **Fort Worth Museum of Science and History,** which has an Omni (IMAX) theater and hands-on science displays, including Dinodig, where they can play amateur paleontologist. If the kids are restless and just need to get outside, take them to the **Fort Worth Botanic Garden,** with acres and acres of gardens, exotic plants, and tropical trees.

The **Stockyards National Historic District** should entertain little cowboys and cowgirls. Twice a day, a herd of longhorn cattle rumbles down brick-paved Exchange Avenue. **Texas Town** in Stockyards Station is a theme park of sorts: an Old West hotel, bar, outhouse, and jail, as well as a vintage ride park, with an antique merry-go-round. Actors in chaps and vests enact *High Noon* gun duels. Nearby, kids can try to find their way through the **Cowtown Cattlepen Maze,** designed to resemble the cattle pens of the Old West. An enjoyable excursion for families is the **Grapevine Vintage Train,** a steam locomotive (or its diesel substitute) that travels from Stockyards Station to 8th Avenue in Fort Worth and to historic Grapevine. Young cowboys and cowgirls will enjoy **horseback trail rides** at the Stockyard Station Livery (chuck-wagon dinners available for groups of 10 or more; call ⓒ 817/624-3446 for more information), and, if you're here in January, the **Fort Worth Stock Show & Rodeo.** The gals may feel empowered by a visit to the **National Cowgirl Museum and Hall of Fame,** which has cool interactive exhibits (such as filming yourself on a bucking bronco). If the kids are hungry for more Old West adventures, trot them over to the **Cattle Raisers Museum,** which depicts life on the range shown through talking ranchers and cattle and a theater presentation.

See additional family activities, such as Six Flags Amusement Park, in the "Arlington" section earlier in this chapter.

ORGANIZED TOURS

Hourly guided **Walking Tours of the Stockyards,** with visits to the major sights, leave from the Visitor Information Center at 130 E. Exchange Ave. (ⓒ 817/624-4741). Tours cost $6 for adults, $5 for seniors, and $4 for children ages 6 to 12, and they are given every 2 hours, Monday through Saturday from 10am to 4pm and Sunday from noon to 4pm. The **Wrangler Tour** takes in the Livestock Exchange, cattle pens on the Cattleman's Catwalk, Mule Alley, Cowtown Coliseum, Exchange Avenue, and the old Hog and Sheep Barns (Stockyards Station). The **Cowboy Tour** adds a visit to Billy Bob's and a buck to the price.

See additional Fort Worth and Dallas tours in "Organized Tours" in the "Dallas" section of this chapter.

OUTDOOR ACTIVITIES

BIKING, IN-LINE SKATING & JOGGING   Excellent for all outdoor activities are **Trinity Park** (near the Cultural District just north of I-30) and **Forest Park** (south of I-30). Depression-era Trinity Park encompasses the Botanic Garden and 8 miles of cycling and jogging trails. Forest Park is the site of another well-known Fort Worth landmark, the Fort Worth Zoo. The scenic **Trinity River Trails,** which run 35 miles along the Trinity River, are my pick for biking, hiking, and in-line skating. Pick up a map at a tourist information center.

Serious runners may want to come prepared to participate in (or watch) the **Cowtown Marathon** (including a half-marathon, 10K, 5K, and a three-person marathon relay), which for 27 years has drawn runners from around the world to the Stockyards National Historic District in late February. Call © **817/735-2033** for specific dates and other information. You can also obtain a monthly runners' calendar at © **800/433-5747.**

GOLF   Fort Worth has five public courses. **Meadowbrooks Golf Course,** 1815 Jenson Rd. (© **817/457-4616**), just east of downtown, is one of the top 25 municipal golf courses in Texas. The popular par-71 course is set amid rolling terrain. Also at the top of the list is **Pecan Valley Golf Course,** 6400 Pecan Dr. (© **817/249-1845**); it has two 18-hole golf courses: the "River" and the "Hills." **Rockwood Golf Course,** 1851 Jacksboro Hwy. (© **817/624-1771**), has a short 18-hole course and an additional, fairly difficult 9 holes called the Blue Nine. **Sycamore Creek Golf Course,** Martin Luther King, Jr., Freeway (© **817/535-7241**), is a 9-hole layout with narrow tree-lined fairways. And **Z. Boaz Golf Course,** 3200 Lackland Rd. (© **817/738-6287**), west of downtown, is a pretty straightforward 18-hole course. Greens fees for all five public courses range from $4 to $20, depending on the day and time. For general information, visit www.fortworthgolf.org.

HORSEBACK RIDING   **Stockyards Station Livery,** 130 E. Exchange Ave. (© **817/624-3446**), offers horseback trail riding for riders of all skill levels (as well as wagon rides and chuck-wagon dinners). Trail riding costs $22 for the first hour and $15 for each additional hour.

TENNIS   The swank **Renaissance Worthington Hotel** (p. 128) has two rooftop courts available for $10 per day to nonguests; call © **817/882-1000** to reserve. The public can get on an indoor or outdoor court at the **Don McLeland Tennis Center,** 1600 W. Seminary (© **817/921-3134**), or the **TCU Tennis Center,** 3609 Bellaire N. on the campus south of downtown (© **817/921-7960**), which has two dozen lit outdoor courts and five indoor courts. There are **public clay courts** at 7100 S. Hulen (© **817/292-9787**).

SPECTATOR SPORTS

See "Spectator Sports" in the "Dallas" section of this chapter for professional football, baseball, soccer, basketball, and more hockey and golf.

AUTO RACING   The **Texas Motor Speedway,** I-35W at Highway 114, north of Fort Worth (© **817/215-8500;** www.texasmotorspeedway.com), is said to be the third-largest sporting complex in the world. It's the place to see NASCAR, Indy, and motorcycle racing. Plan on joining a crowd; more than 150,000 people can attend the races here.

GOLF   Fort Worth's stop on the PGA tour is the **MasterCard Colonial Golf Tournament,** which takes place every May at Fort Worth's prestigious Colonial Country Club (© **817/927-4278** or 817/927-4280).

HOCKEY   The **Fort Worth Brahmas** of the CHL play from January to March at the Fort Worth Convention Center, though this past season was cancelled; the organization hopes to get things together for the 2007–08 season. Call © **817/336-3342** or visit www.brahmas.com for news and, perhaps, ticket information.

RODEO/LIVESTOCK SHOWS   Fort Worth's famous **Cowtown Coliseum,** 121 E. Exchange Ave. (© **817/625-1025**), is the top place to see professional rodeo. Rodeos are usually every Friday and Saturday night (tickets $7.50–$13). Popping up frequently on the Coliseum schedule is **Pawnee Bill's Wild West Show,** a reenactment of the original, which was once the largest Wild West show anywhere. Events range from trick roping to trick shooting and are accompanied by Western music and an arena full of buffalo, longhorns, and horses. For information and tickets, call © **888/COWTOWN** or 817/625-1025 or visit www.stockyardsrodeo.com. Look for $2 coupons in the *Fort Worth Key Magazine,* available at tourist information offices.

The **Kowbell Rodeo,** about 15 minutes from downtown, has rodeos year-round on Saturday and Sunday nights, as well as bull riding Monday, Wednesday, and Friday evenings. Call © **817/477-3092** for more information.

The big event in Fort Worth is the annual **Southwestern Exposition and Livestock Show & Rodeo,** which is staged from the end of January to early February. The nation's oldest livestock show features a Western parade, auctions, and cowboys and cowgirls at the nightly rodeo at **Will Rogers Memorial Center,** located in the Cultural District at 3301 W. Lancaster (© **817/877-2400**).

SHOPPING
Great Shopping Areas
Fort Worth can't compare to Dallas as a shopping mecca (and nor, I suspect, would it want to), but, especially if you're looking for Western clothing and souvenirs of the city's cow-town history, you're in luck. The top tourist area, the **Stockyards National Historic District** (and particularly **Stockyards Station,** a mall of pure Texan shops converted from the old sheep and hog pens), has plenty of authentic Western fashions, antiques, art, and souvenirs, many found in shops inhabiting historic quarters. **Sundance Square** in the downtown historic district is gushing with art galleries, museum gift shops, and fashionable clothing and furnishing stores, most in turn-of-the-20th-century buildings. Along Camp Bowie Boulevard in the **Cultural District,** there are a number of art galleries and design-oriented shops. The **Downtown Fort Worth Rail Market,** a European-style market that bills itself as "Texas's First True Public Market," is located in the historic Santa Fe Warehouse, 1401 Jones St. (© **817/335-6758**). It has a good farmers' market and a couple dozen permanent merchants.

If you're in town at the end of November through mid-December, don't miss the **Western Mercantile** show (© **817/244-6188;** www.nchacutting.com) in the Amon G. Carter Exhibit Hall in the Cultural District. Besides demonstrations of cutting horses, there are booths selling custom saddles, boots, and every kind of Western paraphernalia you can imagine (as well as luxe custom horse trailers).

Western Gear
Two of the best Western shops, for real ropers, urban cowboys, and rodeo queens, are on the Stockyards' classic Exchange Avenue. Family-owned **M. L. Leddy's** ⚑, 2455

N. Main at Exchange (© **817/624-3149**), with the big neon boot sign out front, is one of the city's oldest Western wear shops. Originally a bootmaker and saddlery, it has fine cowboy duds such as handmade belts, formalwear, custom-made boots, saddles, and the best-selling top-of-the-line cowboy hat, the pure Beaver. It has another, slightly slicker and "uptown" shop, called **Leddy's Ranch at Sundance,** 410 Houston St. (© **817/336-0800**), with a full range of boots and Western clothing. Across the street from the Stockyards Hotel, **Maverick** ✦✦, 100 E. Exchange Ave. (© **817/ 626-1129;** www.maverickwesternwear.com), has such high-end Western wear as hand-embroidered shirts, saloon-ready 19th-century-style suits, and other swank cowboy duds. It even has a long bar inside, so you can grab a longneck while shopping and look the part of the cowboy or cowgirl you are (or hope to become).

Also in the Stockyards, **Ponder Boot Company** ✦✦, 2358 N. Main St. (© **817/ 626-3523;** www.ponderboot.com), is the place to go for custom boots. Step inside and choose your leather and get your own brand or initial on a boot that will last you a lifetime, for not all that much more than a top-of-the-line factory-made boot (most will run $600–$850). Georgia, the owner, will demonstrate the superior quality of one of her handmade, custom boots using a pair of dissected boots (if you ask nicely).

Peters Brothers Hats ✦, 909 Houston St., at 9th Street (© **800/TXS-HATS;** www.petersbros.com), has been around since 1911, stocking Stetsons and hats of all kinds, including Western fedoras and custom-made cowboy hats. Also check out **Retro Cowboy,** 406 Houston St., on Sundance Square (© **817/338-1194**), for women's Western apparel, sterling silver jewelry, and men's vintage shirts. If the duds at these rather upscale Western stores are a bit too dear for your cowboy wallet, check out **Western Wear Exchange,** 2809 Alta Mere, 183S at I-30 (© **817/738-4048**), a rare resale shop dealing exclusively in Western wear. If it's already broken in, you'll be closer to looking and feeling the part of a real roper.

Once you've got the duds, you need the tunes. **Ernest Tubb's Record Shop,** 140 E. Exchange Ave., in Stockyards Station (© **800/229-4288** or 817/624-8449), has a great stock of honky-tonk, cowboy, and country-and-western recordings, including old vinyl and hard-to-find stuff.

Antiques & Furnishings

Bum Steer, 2400 N. Main St. (© **817/626-4565**), just a block from the Stockyards' main drag, sells Western antiques, vintage clothing, chaps and saddles, mounts and hides, and those loveable antler chandeliers. Just up the street is **Cross-Eyed Moose,** 2340 N. Main St. (© **817/624-4311**), run by the same folks and stocking slightly more affordable Western goods, some used clothing and antiques, as well as custom furnishings, game mounts, and Western decorative stuff. I picked up a great pair of $10 boots here for my nephew. **The Antique Colony,** 7200 Camp Bowie Blvd. (© **817/731-7252**), has some 120 dealers of antiques and collectibles.

Department Stores & Malls

Stockyards Station, 140 E. Exchange Ave. (© **817/625-9715**), once the Southwest's largest hog and sheep marketing center, has been converted into a cute center of nearly several dozen restaurants and shops featuring Western apparel, Lone Star wines, country-and-western music, leather goods, Texas products, and arts and crafts. There's even a **Stockyards Wedding Chapel** (© **817/624-1570**) for cowboys and girls dying for a true Old West ceremony.

University Park Village, located 2 blocks south of I-30 on S. University Drive near Texas Christian University (© **817/654-0521**), is an upscale shopping center with Talbot's, Williams-Sonoma, Ann Taylor, Voyagers—The Travel Store, and Wolf Camera.

FORT WORTH AFTER DARK

Despite its decent size, Fort Worth still feels like a small town, and plenty of young people looking for a bigger scene split for Big D on weekends. Still, Cowtown has a few good nightlife options, especially at the two extremes of the scale: high culture and cowboy culture. Whether you're inclined toward opera, symphony, and theater, or up for some boot-scootin', Fort Worth has some fine venues. **Exchange Avenue** in the Stockyards is where you want to be on weekends for some hot Western swing, Texas shuffle, and honky-tonk tunes. The street becomes a cruising strip of souped-up trucks, guys and dolls in cowboy and cowgirl finery strutting their stuff, and dancers ducking into honky-tonks and cowboy discos. Meanwhile, **Sundance Square** is full of bars, restaurants, cafes, and movie theaters, and is mobbed on weekend nights (luckily, there's plenty of free parking after 5pm and on weekends right in and around the square). **City Streets,** 425 Commerce St. (© **817/335-5400**), is a one-stop-shopping entertainment complex, generic and mild-mannered but popular with visitors for its range of bars, lounges, and pool halls—and, of course, happy hours.

For listings, check out the "Entertainment" section of the *Fort Worth Star-Telegram* or check the weekly listings posted on its website, www.dfw.com. For tickets, try Arts Line at **Ticketmaster** (© **817/467-ARTS** or 214/631-ARTS; www.ticketmaster.com) or **Texas Tickets** (© **817/277-3333**).

THE PERFORMING ARTS

Bass Performance Hall 😀😀 (© **877/212-4280** or 817/212-4280; www.basshall.com) is one of the top places in the country to see a musical or theater performance. Home to the distinguished Fort Worth Symphony Orchestra, its stage has welcomed an eclectic range of productions including *The Nutcracker* and Handel's *Messiah, Madame Butterfly,* Broadway shows (such as *Bring in 'Da Noise, Bring in 'Da Funk*), and pop, jazz, and country concerts by the likes of Tony Bennett, the Oak Ridge Boys, Nanci Griffith, and Pink Martini.

Casa Mañana Theater, 3101 W. Lancaster, at University Drive (© **817/332-2272;** www.casamanana.org), the country's first permanent theater designed for the musicals-in-the-round, is an aluminum geodesic dome with an oval stage. It recently underwent a $3-million renovation. Casa, as it's known locally, puts on a wide range of dramas, comedies, and musicals, and is home to one of the top children's theater operations in the United States, mounting productions such as *Aladdin.*

The **Jubilee Theatre,** 506 Main St. (© **817/338-4411;** www.jubileetheatre.org), is home to intimate African-American theater, staging such dramas as *Brother Mac* (adapted from Shakespeare's *Macbeth*) and *A Raisin in the Sun* as well as musicals such as *Lysistrata Please* (a rock version of the Aristophanes classic) and *Road Show,* an original production.

The **Rose Marine Theater,** 1440 Main St. (© **817/624-8333;** www.rosemarine theater.com), an 85-year-old movie theater just south of the Stockyards, has been restored and converted by the Latin Arts Association; here you'll find plays in Spanish, Latin films, and other arts targeting the Latino population.

THE BAR SCENE

The oldest bar in Fort Worth and the site of the city's most famous gunfight in 1897, **White Elephant Saloon** 😀, 106 E. Exchange Ave. (© **817/624-1887**), is an authentic Cowtown saloon, a great place to knock back a Lone Star longneck in the afternoon or check out some live Western music nightly on the small stage. The atmospheric bar is decorated with donated hats (from the likes of Ray Wylie Hubbard and Jimmie Dale Gilmore) and cases of porcelain and ceramic white elephants. There's also a nice beer garden, with live bands under the trees.

Flying Saucer Draught Emporium, 111 E. 4th St. (© **817/336-7470**), is a beer snob's dream, boasting 75 beers on tap and 125 bottles, including a slew of American microbrews and exotics such as Belgian *guerze* and German seasonals. For the novice or anyone looking for something new, there are "flights," sampler trays from around the world. The place can get rowdy on weekends with cigar-smoking types and TCU students, but it's still one of the best places in Fort Worth to wet your whistle. Food tends toward such beer-complementary items as bratwurst and beer cheese soup (yes, you read that right). It also features an eclectic roster of live music on weekends. A swank bar with an outdoor patio and live music in warm months, frequented by Fort Worth's young and beautiful, is **8.0** (© **817/336-0880**), just off Sundance Square. The outdoor rooftop bar **Grotto,** complete with waterfall, at Reata (p. 133) is another great place for a drink before or after dinner.

A great spot for a glass of wine before dinner or a show at Bass Performance Hall is **The Grape Escape,** 500 Commerce St. (© **817/336-9463**). The agreeable little spot specializes in wines from around the world, served by the glass, half-glass, and in sampling flights. Lots of snack foods, including minipizzas and fries, are also served.

HONKY-TONK HEAVEN

The one place that's practically a required stop in Fort Worth is **Billy Bob's Texas** ★★★, 2520 Rodeo Plaza (© **817/624-7117;** www.billybobstexas.com). A cavernous barn for prize cattle in a former life, this absurdly large honky-tonk, a symbol of Texas for many people, has it all. With 40 bar stations, a monster dance floor for hard-core boot-scootin', a rodeo arena, video games, pool tables, mechanical bulls, and pro bull riding, it's 125,000 square feet (er, 7 acres) of country-and-western heaven. Open for over 20 years, Billy Bob's continues to draw the biggest names in country music, including George Jones, LeAnn Rimes, Willie Nelson, and Jerry Jeff Walker. Its fame is such that you'll see real ropers in their best hats and tight jeans, drugstore cowboys, and a swell of German and Japanese tourists, all soakin' up the flavor. Located in the heart of the Stockyards, Billy Bob's does business Monday through Saturday from 11am to 2am, and Sunday from noon to 2am. The cover charge varies according to the musical act; day visits cost $1. Don't miss the pro live bull riding on Friday and Saturday at 9 and 10pm; admission is $2.

Another "Texas-size" honky-tonk is the family-owned and -operated **Stagecoach Ballroom** ★, 2516 E. Belknap at the corner of Sylvania, off Airport Freeway (© **817/831-2261;** www.stagecoachballroom.com), a real contender for most authentic old-time ballroom in Texas. It sports traditional country music and dance, and is a good spot to pick up some moves if you're not exactly a smooth-footed kicker. Wednesday is Ladies Night, and cover for live music guests is usually $15. (There is live music on Wed and Fri–Sun, beginning at 7pm. Thurs nights are newly dedicated to "smoke-free" C&W, Big Band, and Back to the '50s dancing, from 6–10pm; $5 cover. Also, look for Lone Star Talent Night contests on Tues.)

Sadly, **Big Balls of Cowtown,** one of my very favorite dancehalls, where classic Western swing was practiced with a fervor, is no longer around. In the same space is **Pearl's Dancehall & Saloon** ★, 302 W. Exchange Ave. (© **817/624-2800;** www.pearlsdancehallandsaloon.com), which now features live traditional, Western

> **Tips   Everybody, Get in Line**
> If you want to learn to line dance, shuffle, and two-step like a Texan, why not
> do it in one of the most famous honky-tonks in the world, Billy Bob's Texas?
> Wendell Nelson is the dance man who will lead you—and even the whole
> family—through the basics. Free classes are Thursdays at 7pm for the family.
> Call © **817/923-9215** for additional information.

swing and honky-tonk music on Tuesday, Thursday, Friday, and Saturday. Although
it's a bit spiffier in its new incarnation, it's still the best spot in the Stockyards for non-
touristy C&W music (featuring name acts such as Dale Watson) and dancing.

Also in the Stockyards District, there's often live country music at **Rodeo Exchange,**
221 W. Exchange Ave. (© **817/626-0181**), and **Ernest Tubb's Record Shop,** 140 E.
Exchange Ave. (© **817/624-8449**), the latter only on Saturday afternoons.

OTHER LIVE MUSIC

Sadly, Fort Worth's premier jazz venue, **Caravan of Dreams,** bit the dust several years
ago. And while nothing has sprung up to fill its big shoes, there are a handful of other
live music venues in town that don't go the country route. **Ridglea and Vine Wineroom,** 6100 Camp Bowie Blvd. (© **817/731-7700**), is a spot to enjoy live jazz and
kick back with a glass from a large wine selection. **Sardines Ristorante Italiano**
(p. 135) features the live jazz of Johnny Case. **The Black Dog Tavern,** 903 Throckmorton St. (© **817/332-8190**), a friendly neighborhood-styled pub, has nightly jazz,
rockabilly, and blues jams, as well as open-mic comedy sessions on Sunday evenings
and occasional poetry open-mic nights. The top rock venue in town is the **Ridglea
Theater** ⚛, 6025 Camp Bowie Blvd. (© **817/738-9500;** www.ridgleatheater.com), a
hip, restored 1940s Art Deco theater that plays host to touring rock bands, including
alternative flavors of the month. **Aardvark** ⚛, 2905 W. Berry St. (© **817/926-7814;**
www.the-aardvark.com), is a cool small space that hosts a wide-ranging roster of pop,
alternative rock, and neo-folk acts with small cover charges Tuesday through Saturday.
Wreck Room, 3208 W. 7th St. (© **817/348-8303**), is a cool club in the cultural district with slacker style. It schedules an array of loud rock bands on weekends.

The top blues joint in town is **J&J Blues Bar** ⚛, 937 Woodward St. (© **817/
870-2337;** www.jjbluesbar.com), just north of the Cultural District. A little rough
around the edges—how else would you want your blues bar?—it hosts both national
and local acts Wednesday through Sunday nights. The crowd is a mix of blues traditionalists and college kids from TCU.

For traditional live C&W, also check out the bands scheduled at two of the most
famous spots in Fort Worth, **Billy Bob's Texas** and **White Elephant Saloon,** as well
as **Pearl's Dancehall and Saloon** and **Stagecoach Ballroom** (see "Honky-Tonk
Heaven," above).

RODEO

The Stockyards Championship Rodeo is held most weekends on Friday and Saturday nights at Cowtown Coliseum in the Stockyards, 121 E. Exchange Ave. (© **817/
888-COWTOWN;** www.stockyardsrodeo.com). Tickets range from $4.50 for chil-
dren to $13 for reserved box seats. **Pawnee Bill's Wild West Show** (p. 146) runs dur-
ing summer months and holiday weekends.

5

Houston & East Texas

by David Baird

Situated on a flat, near featureless Gulf Coast plain, Houston sprawls from its center in vast tracts of subdivisions, freeways, office parks, and shopping malls. In undisturbed areas you'll find marshy grasslands in the south and woods in the north. Meandering across this plain are several bayous on whose banks cypress and southern magnolia trees chance to grow. Many visitors, imagining the Texas landscape as it is usually drawn—barren and treeless—are surprised by such green surroundings, but, in fact, the city is at the tail end of a large belt of natural forest coming down through East Texas, and the climate is much the same as coastal Louisiana and Mississippi—warm and humid with ample rainfall.

Houston is the fourth most populated city in the United States. If we compare the populations of greater metro areas rather than cities, then it ranks only 10th. Yet in geographical expanse Houston ranks second. The city is more than half as large as the state of Rhode Island and continues to expand outward. But in the past few years there has been a shift in residential construction toward downtown and the inner city. Town houses in the central part of the city are going up at a furious rate, and lofts, condos, and apartments are now a major part of downtown construction.

Houston is not usually considered a tourist destination; most visitors come for business or family reasons and are lured into playing tourists only after getting here. It's a business town, and the oil and gas industry remains the big enchilada, but other sectors have added so much to the local economy that oil and gas's contribution is only about 50%. The Texas Medical Center is the largest concentration of medical institutions in the world. It's virtually a city within a city, with 14 hospitals and many clinics, medical schools, and research facilities. Construction and engineering companies also contribute much to the economy, and the newest big player is the high-tech industry.

Houston's society is socially and economically wide open. Houstonians inherently dislike being told what to do, and this dislike cuts across the political spectrum: Opinion surveys show that gun control is highly unpopular but so is government control over reproductive rights. Among urban planners, Houston is famous (or infamous) as the only major U.S. city that doesn't have zoning, allowing the market to determine land-use instead. On the plus side, this love for individual freedoms gives Houston a dynamism that is palpable and has brought a flood of newcomers from around the world, who have found here a welcoming city. Houston seems to be growing more cosmopolitan every day, as ethnic restaurants and specialty shops spring up throughout the city along with exotic temples and churches—Taoist, Buddhist, Hindu, Islamic, Russian Orthodox—built much like they would be back in the mother country.

On the minus side, this is the land of Enron, the go-go company that preached to state and federal governments to deregulate the energy markets and then profited illegally from it. Though it's the worst offender, Enron is not alone. And now, a political storm is set to blow when Houston's electric utility market completes the final stage of deregulation, allowing rates to float according to market forces. Some experts are predicting that rates will go up even though they are currently among the highest in the state. Also, Houston is struggling with an air pollution problem that has the local government painfully considering unpopular regulations to keep the city in compliance with the Clean Air Act.

The arts give proof to the city's dynamism. In the performing arts, Houston excels, with an excellent symphony orchestra, highly respected ballet and opera companies, and a dynamic theater scene that few cities can equal in quantity or quality. There are some excellent museums, too, and, if art isn't your bag, there's the world-famous NASA Space Center, which is like nothing else on this planet. While you're enjoying the attractions, keep your eyes open and you can appreciate another thing Houston is known for, its architecture, which stands out for its bold, even brash character. This is, after all, home to the first dome stadium—the Astrodome—which was billed at the time as "the eighth wonder of the world." Several buildings are striking not only for their dramatic appearance but for their irreverence—one skyscraper is crowned with a Mayan pyramid, another wryly uses the architectural features of Gothic churches for a bank building, and a pair of towers in the Medical Center unmistakably represents two giant syringes. There is little that is staid about this city, and the more time one spends here, the more this is appreciated.

1 Orientation

ARRIVING

BY PLANE

Houston has two major airports: the George Bush Intercontinental Airport (IAH), 22 miles north of downtown, and the smaller William P. Hobby Airport, 9 miles southeast of downtown. Express Shuttle USA offers shuttle service between the airports for $20 (see below).

GEORGE BUSH INTERCONTINENTAL AIRPORT   Houston's primary airport (www.fly2houston.com/iahhome) functions as a hub for Continental Airlines, though it's serviced by all of the major national and international carriers. The airport has all the facilities of major international airports, including ATMs and currency exchange desks.

Getting to & from the Airport   Taxi service from IAH to downtown costs $45 to $55 and the ride takes 30 to 45 minutes; getting to the Galleria area costs a few dollars more. **Professional Airport Shuttle** (© 713/988-5126; www.houstonproshuttle.com), **Super Shuttle** (© 713/523-8888 or 800/BLUE VAN; www.supershuttle.com), and **Airport Shuttle America** (© 281/530-4000) all ferry passengers to and from this airport to almost all hotels. Prices vary according to the hotel's location. To or from downtown costs $22 to $26. Shuttle ticket counters are at all airport terminals. Professional Airport Shuttle is a good option for cruise-ship customers traveling to the port of Galveston. Another option is the **city's bus service** (© 713/635-4000; www.ridemetro.org), which operates bus route 102 (http://ridemetro.org/pdf/routes/102-iah.pdf). The fare is $1.50. Exact change is required, but dollar bills are accepted. Buses run about every 30 minutes, and travel time to downtown is an hour, a little longer for rush hour.

Houston

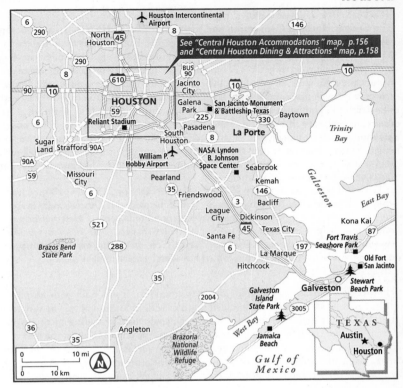

The major car-rental companies have counters at each of the terminals. John F. Kennedy Boulevard is the main artery into and out of the airport. When leaving the airport, you'll see signs pointing the way either toward the North Freeway (I-45) or the Eastex Freeway (Tex. 59). Both take you downtown, but the Eastex is shorter and usually quicker.

WILLIAM P. HOBBY AIRPORT   Hobby Airport (www.fly2houston.com/hobby home) is used mostly by Southwest Airlines. All the major car-rental agencies have counters here with either staff or a service phone. Taxis from Hobby to the downtown area cost about $30, and to the Galleria area $40. For airport shuttle service, see companies listed above. The fair runs about $17.

BY CAR

Houston is connected to Dallas and Fort Worth by I-45, and to San Antonio, New Orleans, and Beaumont by I-10. From Austin, you can take either Tex. 71 through Bastrop to Columbus, where it joins I-10, or you can take Tex. 290 east through Brenham.

BY TRAIN

Amtrak (© **800/872-7245;** www.amtrak.com) trains from New Orleans, Chicago, and Los Angeles (and points in between) arrive and depart from the **Southern Pacific Station** at 902 Washington Ave. (© **713/224-1577**), close to downtown.

VISITOR INFORMATION

The **Greater Houston Convention and Visitors Bureau (GHCVB)** has an elaborate visitor center located in the city hall building at 901 Bagby St. between Walker and McKinney (© **713/437-5556;** www.visithoustontexas.com). Enter through the door on Walker. Here you can get lots of brochures, a range of city maps, architectural and historical guides, and answers from the center's staff. Pick up a copy of the *Official Guide to Houston* magazine; it has a helpful calendar of events. You can also play with the interactive computer stations and see a short introductory film of the city. The center is open daily from 9am to 4pm. If you're driving, park your car at the underground lot that is 1 block north of city hall. To get there, turn onto Walker, drive past city hall, and immediately turn right on Bagby, then right again on Rusk; you'll see a sign that says THEATER DISTRICT PARKING 2. It's free for visitors; just get your parking ticket stamped at the visitor center.

For advance information, try © **800/4-HOUSTON** or 713/227-3100, or www.visithoustontexas.com. You can request a copy of the magazine *Official Guide to Houston* or visit the magazine's Web page (www.houton-guide.com). Other websites you might find helpful are operated by the local newspapers. The *Houston Chronicle* (**www.chron.com**) is the daily newspaper, and the *Houston Press* (**www.houstonpress.com**) is the weekly tabloid freebie, which has a large entertainment section.

CITY LAYOUT

Houston is a difficult city to find your way around in; it was built with no master plan, and most of its streets are jumbled together with little continuity. The suburban areas look alike and have indistinctive street names, usually ending in things like "crest," "wood," and "dale." To make matters worse, the terrain is so flat the only visible points of reference are tall buildings. But for the visitor, things aren't so bad. Most of the main attractions are not far off the freeways or other main arteries. With a basic knowledge of these, you can keep your bearings and get from one place to another.

To understand the layout of Houston's freeways, it's best to picture a spider web with several lines radiating out from the center, which are connected to each other by two concentric circles. The lines that radiate outwards are in the following clockwise order: At 1 o'clock is the Eastex Freeway (Tex. 59 north), which usually has signs saying CLEVELAND, a town in East Texas; at 3 o'clock is the East Freeway (I-10 east to Beaumont and New Orleans); between 4 and 5 o'clock is the Gulf Freeway (I-45 south to Galveston); at 6 o'clock is the South Freeway (Tex. 228 to Lake Jackson, Freeport, and Surfside); between 7 and 8 o'clock is the Southwest Freeway (Tex. 59 to Laredo, look for signs that read VICTORIA); at 9 o'clock is the Katy Freeway (I-10 west to San Antonio); at 10 o'clock is the Northwest Freeway (Tex. 290 to Austin); and at 11 o'clock is the North Freeway (I-45 north to Dallas). The first circular freeway is Loop 610 (known as "the Loop"), which has a 4- to 5-mile radius from downtown. The second is known alternately as Sam Houston Parkway or Beltway 8. It has a 10- to 15-mile radius and is mostly a toll road except for the section near the Bush Intercontinental Airport.

In addition to the freeways, there are certain arteries that most newcomers would do well to know. Here are brief descriptions of each.

Main Street bisects downtown and then heads south–southwest, changing its name to South Main. It passes through the Museum District, then along Hermann Park and Rice University before reaching the Texas Medical Center. This stretch of South Main has lots of green space and is lined with oak trees. Beyond the Medical Center, the street passes by the new Reliant Park football stadium, a new exhibition center, and the old Astrodome.

In the middle of the Museum District is a traffic circle called **Mecom Fountain,** where South Main intersects **Montrose Boulevard.** Montrose runs due north from the Mecom Fountain crossing Westheimer Road and Buffalo Bayou. It gives its name to the Montrose area and is lined by several bistros around the Museum District. After it crosses the bayou, Montrose becomes Studemont and then Studewood when it enters a historic neighborhood known as the Heights.

Westheimer Road is the east–west axis around which most of western Houston turns. It begins in the Montrose area and continues for many miles through various urban and suburban landscapes without ever seeming to come to an end. Past the Montrose area, Westheimer crosses Kirby Drive and then passes by River Oaks, a neighborhood where Houston's rich folk live. Farther along is Highland Village Shopping Center, then Loop 610, where it enters the popular commercial district known as the Galleria area or Uptown. Farther west, Westheimer passes through an endless series of fast-food restaurants, strip malls, and chain retail stores as it runs through suburbia.

Kirby Drive is an important north–south artery. It intersects Westheimer Road by River Oaks and runs due south skirting the Greenway Plaza and passing under the Southwest Freeway. Once south of the freeway, Kirby enters University Place, a neighborhood that curls around the western borders of the Rice University campus and is the favorite residential area for Houston's doctors, lawyers, and other professionals. Kirby eventually intersects South Main Street in the vicinity of Reliant Stadium.

THE NEIGHBORHOODS IN BRIEF

Downtown Once a ghost town in the evenings and on weekends, downtown Houston is now the place to be. Restaurants and bars are opening (and in some cases closing) in quick succession. Hotels have multiplied, too. Much of the revitalization is taking place on the northwest side of downtown, in and around Old Market Square and the theater district, where Houston's symphony orchestra, ballet, opera, and its principal theater company all reside. To the east, within walking distance, are the George Brown Convention Center; the baseball park, Minute Maid Field (formerly Enron Field); and the Toyota Center basketball arena. Also fueling downtown's revitalization is a new light rail that runs up and down Main Street and connects to the Museum District and the Medical Center. Beneath downtown is a network of pedestrian tunnels

lined by shops and restaurants, forming an underground city. As is typical of Houston, almost all of these tunnels are private, not public, developments.

South of downtown is **Midtown,** an area in transition, with town houses and shops gradually replacing vacant lots and small office buildings. Vietnamese shopkeepers and restaurateurs have settled into the western side, especially along Milam Street, where you can find an array of excellent Vietnamese restaurants with reasonable prices.

East End Before Houston was established on the banks of Buffalo Bayou, the town of Harrisburg already existed 2 miles downstream. As Houston grew eastward, it incorporated Harrisburg, leaving behind little of the old town. A small commercial Chinatown lies a couple of blocks east of the convention

Central Houston Accommodations

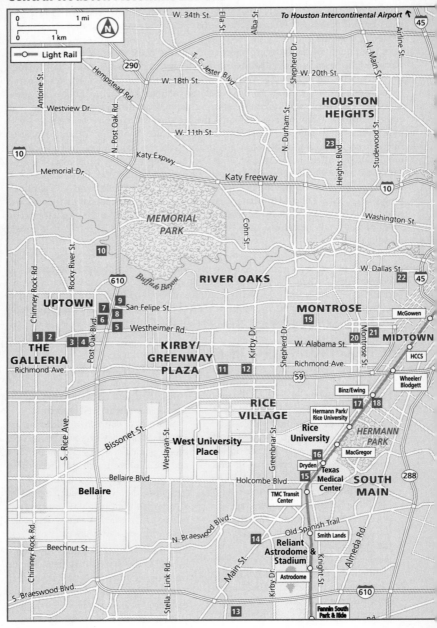

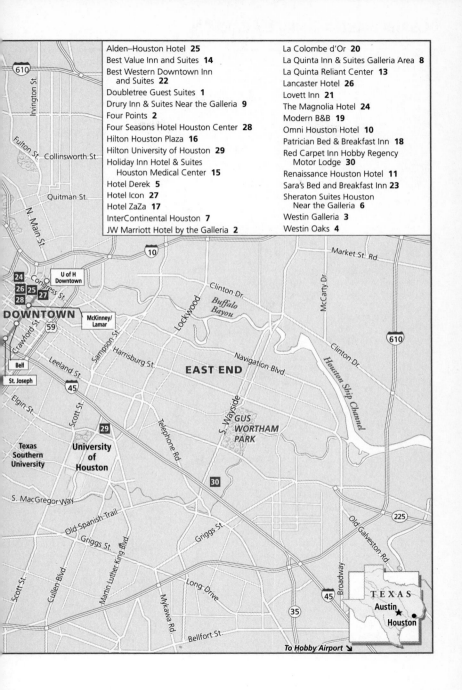

Alden–Houston Hotel **25**
Best Value Inn and Suites **14**
Best Western Downtown Inn
    and Suites **22**
Doubletree Guest Suites **1**
Drury Inn & Suites Near the Galleria **9**
Four Points **2**
Four Seasons Hotel Houston Center **28**
Hilton Houston Plaza **16**
Hilton University of Houston **29**
Holiday Inn Hotel & Suites
    Houston Medical Center **15**
Hotel Derek **5**
Hotel Icon **27**
Hotel ZaZa **17**
InterContinental Houston **7**
JW Marriott Hotel by the Galleria **2**

La Colombe d'Or **20**
La Quinta Inn & Suites Galleria Area **8**
La Quinta Reliant Center **13**
Lancaster Hotel **26**
Lovett Inn **21**
The Magnolia Hotel **24**
Modern B&B **19**
Omni Houston Hotel **10**
Patrician Bed & Breakfast Inn **18**
Red Carpet Inn Hobby Regency
    Motor Lodge **30**
Renaissance Houston Hotel **11**
Sara's Bed and Breakfast Inn **23**
Sheraton Suites Houston
    Near the Galleria **6**
Westin Galleria **3**
Westin Oaks **4**

Central Houston Dining & Attractions

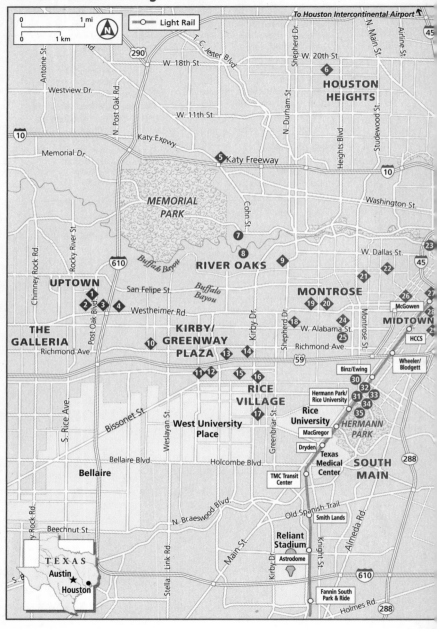

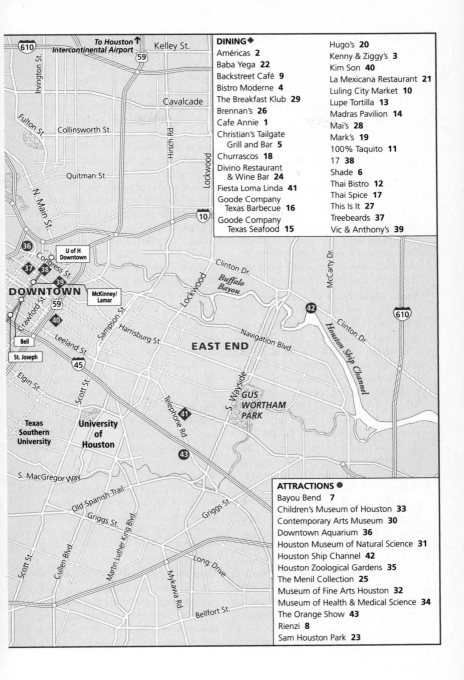

DINING ◆

Américas **2**
Baba Yega **22**
Backstreet Café **9**
Bistro Moderne **4**
The Breakfast Klub **29**
Brennan's **26**
Cafe Annie **1**
Christian's Tailgate
　Grill and Bar **5**
Churrascos **18**
Divino Restaurant
　& Wine Bar **24**
Fiesta Loma Linda **41**
Goode Company
　Texas Barbecue **16**
Goode Company
　Texas Seafood **15**

Hugo's **20**
Kenny & Ziggy's **3**
Kim Son **40**
La Mexicana Restaurant **21**
Luling City Market **10**
Lupe Tortilla **13**
Madras Pavilion **14**
Mai's **28**
Mark's **19**
100% Taquito **11**
17 **38**
Shade **6**
Thai Bistro **12**
Thai Spice **17**
This Is It **27**
Treebeards **37**
Vic & Anthony's **39**

ATTRACTIONS ●

Bayou Bend **7**
Children's Museum of Houston **33**
Contemporary Arts Museum **30**
Downtown Aquarium **36**
Houston Museum of Natural Science **31**
Houston Ship Channel **42**
Houston Zoological Gardens **35**
The Menil Collection **25**
Museum of Fine Arts Houston **32**
Museum of Health & Medical Science **34**
The Orange Show **43**
Rienzi **8**
Sam Houston Park **23**

center; beyond that, the area becomes residential. The inner East End is an up-and-coming neighborhood of mixed ethnicity. As you move farther east, the residences mix with small-scale manufacturing, auto mechanic and body shops, and service industries for the ship channel. In the far southern part is NASA's Space Center Houston; Kemah, which is Houston's version of Fisherman's Wharf; and Galveston Island. Most of the hotels located in this area are along the Gulf Freeway. The main reason for staying here is that the hotel rates, for the most part, are economical, and the location between downtown, Hobby Airport, and the above-mentioned attractions makes the East End convenient.

South Main South of downtown and midtown is the **Museum District** and Hermann Park. This is a lovely part of town with lots of green space. Most of the museums are within a few blocks of one another. Here also are the Houston Zoological Gardens and the Rice University campus. On the south side of the park begins the Texas Medical Center. A bit farther south is a complex of buildings holding Reliant Stadium and the old Astrodome. This part of town has many hotels to suit all budgets. The location is quite convenient, and the city's new light rail connects this area with downtown.

Montrose & the Heights Directly west of downtown is the Montrose area, a hip, artsy, and colorful part of town known for its clubs, galleries, and shops. The Museum District extends into this neighborhood to include the famous Menil Collection and its satellite galleries, a must-see for any visitor interested in the arts. Upscale in certain sections, downscale in others, the Montrose contains a broad cross-section of Houston society. It's also the

de facto center of Houston's large and active gay community.

North of the Montrose area, across Buffalo Bayou, is the Heights. It was conceived and built as an independent, planned residential community in the 1890s and remained so until 1918, when it was annexed by Houston. Several of the houses in the area are lovely Texas Victorians. One curious fact about the Heights is that the original articles of incorporation required it to be "dry" (no sale of alcohol)—and this has stood in place for the last hundred years. Consequently, only a few good restaurants are found here. But some great shopping can be had, especially for antiques and folk art. With downtown to the east, the Museum District to the south, and Kirby to the west, the Montrose area and the Heights are well located.

Kirby District & Greenway Plaza The area bordering Kirby Drive from River Oaks to University Place offers the most restaurants of any district in Houston. Near Kirby Drive's midway point, where it crosses the Southwest Freeway, is the Greenway Plaza, an integrated development of office buildings, movie theaters, shops, and a sports arena, which has been made over into a well-known mega church called Lakewood. Farther south is the Rice Village, a retail development consisting of 16 square blocks of smart shops and restaurants. It is phenomenally popular with Houstonians and visitors and attracts all kinds of shoppers and diners.

Uptown Farther west, all the way to Loop 610, is where Uptown begins. It is still informally called the **Galleria area,** after the large indoor shopping mall, entertainment, and hotel complex. But the district's business owners had to devise another name for it because the developer of the Galleria protected its name so jealously that it became problematic to use the word in any commercial context. Thus, we have "Uptown."

Shops, restaurants, and other businesses front Westheimer and Post Oak Boulevard.

North Houston All the neighborhoods described above, except for the Heights, are south of I-10, which bisects Houston into northern and southern halves. North Houston is largely a mix of working- and middle-class neighborhoods and commercial centers and, with the exception of the Heights, has little to offer visitors.

Over the years, developers tried to establish upscale communities here, but an inherent quality of suburbanism is that you can always build farther out, and, with each successive subdivision, the inner suburbs lose a little more of their luster. Ultimately, the developers took this to its logical extreme, skipping over vast tracts of land to build so far north that the city will never touch them. Thus we have the Woodlands and Kingwood, two upscale residential developments that are so far out, one can't consider them part of Houston.

2 Getting Around

BY CAR

Houston is organized around the automobile. Having a car is almost a necessity unless you confine your explorations to the downtown area and the South Main corridor (including the Museum District), which are connected by the new light rail. This makes it possible to stay in a downtown or South Main hotel and go up and down this corridor with ease. For trips to other parts of the city, you can use the hotel's shuttle, if available, or the occasional taxi.

Houston's freeways are no place for the meek: Many drivers don't obey speed limits, bob and weave through the lanes, and make their turnoffs at the last possible moment. You should have a clear idea of where you're headed and what exit you need to take before you get on a freeway. All this said, I actually enjoy driving Houston's freeways. It's a good way to grasp what it's like to be a Houstonian. My own practice is not to bother looking down at the speedometer; for all practical purposes it's irrelevant. It's more important to stay in the flow of traffic at the same speed as most of the cars around you. As freeway systems go, Houston's is logical and has good directional signs. Traffic can be slow during rush hour or anywhere there's construction. You can use the **Texas Department of Transportation Info Hot Line** (© 713/802-5074) to check for lane closures on local freeways. The *Houston Chronicle* provides this information, too, as well as info on street closures. Don't be surprised to encounter construction during your visit.

RENTALS The prices for rental cars in Houston are lower than those for many tourist destinations, but tacked on to the final cost are several taxes that raise the price by as much as 27%. Keep this in mind when the salesperson tries to bump you up to a higher-priced model. As is the case when renting cars anywhere, you probably don't

Freeway Delays

One thing you can count on: Expect delays on the Katy Freeway (I-10 west of Loop 610). The state has begun a multiyear construction project for widening the freeway to 20 lanes. It is scheduled for completion by the spring of 2009.

need to buy extra insurance if you're already covered by your personal auto insurance. The major car-rental companies with locations around the city include: **Alamo** (© 800/462-5266; www.alamo.com), **Avis** (© 800/230-4898; www.avis.com), **Budget** (© 800/527-7000; www.budget.com), **Dollar** (© 800/800-3665; www.dollar.com), **Enterprise** (© 800/736-8222; www.enterprise.com), **Hertz** (© 800/654-3131; www.hertz.com), **National** (© 800/227-7368; www.nationalcar.com), and **Thrifty** (© 800/847-4389; www.thrifty.com).

BY PUBLIC TRANSPORTATION

LIGHT RAIL   The **Metropolitan Transportation Authority (Metro;** © 713/635-4000; www.ridemetro.org) inaugurated its first light rail line in 2004. So far it's been a big success with locals and is quite helpful for visitors, as it ties together some of the main areas of interest—downtown, the Museum District, the Medical Center, and Reliant Park. Train tickets cost a dollar, are good for 3 hours, and are valid as bus transfers if not traveling in the return direction. A day pass costs $2 and is good for all train and bus travel for 24 hours. Train tickets can be purchased at each station from vending machines that accept cash, debit cards, and credit cards. The trains run as frequently as every 6 minutes and in slow times are not more than 18 minutes apart.

Note: In the last few years, there have been numerous collisions involving the light rail train and private vehicles. The train usually wins. Almost all of these accidents occurred because the drivers of the cars were distracted. Pay attention to directional signs and signals when crossing the rail line. There are a few confusing intersections: at the end of the line, where Main Street reaches Buffalo Bayou, in the Medical Center, and where the tracks shift from Main Street to San Jacinto. Otherwise, it's all straight forward.

BUS SERVICE   The citywide bus service operated by Metro can get you to most places in the city. To find out what bus to catch and where and when to catch it, your best option is to call the customer service number listed above. The staff can tell you over the phone how to get from point A to point B. If you're planning in advance, you can use the website and click on "Trip Planner." It takes 3 days to get a response. Once you know the bus routes you're going to use, you can download schedules from the same website. The standard bus fare is $1 (seniors pay 40¢ and children younger than 4 ride free); exact change is required, and the machines accept dollar bills. If needed, ask for a transfer, which will be good for 3 hours for other buses or the train. Metro no longer operates downtown trolleys.

BY TAXI

Taxis are plentiful in the city, but trying to hail one on the street can be an exercise in frustration. Call ahead or use hotel taxi stands. The principal companies are **Yellow Cab** (© 713/236-1111), **Fiesta Cab** (© 713/225-2666), **Liberty Cab** (© 800/TAXICAB), and **United Cab** (© 713/699-0000). Rates are set by the city: $4 for the first mile; $1.85 for each additional mile.

FAST FACTS: **Houston**

American Express   There is an office at 5085 Westheimer, Suite 4600, on the third floor of the Galleria Mall II (© **713/626-5740**). It's open Monday through Friday from 9am to 6pm and Saturday from 10am to 5pm.

Area Codes Houston has 10-digit dialing for local calls. Local numbers begin with one of three area codes: 713, 281, or 832.

Dentists For a referral, call ⓒ **800/922-6588.**

Doctors For minor emergencies or to see a doctor without an appointment, call **Texas Urgent Care** at ⓒ **800/417-2347.**

Drugstores **Walgreens,** 3317 Montrose Blvd., at Hawthorne Street (ⓒ **713/520-7777**), is open 24 hours a day. In the vicinity of the Medical Center, there is a 24-hour **Eckerd Drug Store** at 7900 S. Main St. (ⓒ **713/660-8934**).

Hospitals The **Ben Taub General Hospital,** 1502 Taub Loop, at the Texas Medical Center (ⓒ **713/873-2600**), has a fully equipped emergency room.

Internet Access **Copy.com,** 1201-F Westheimer, in the Montrose area (ⓒ **713/528-1201**), has several computers and is open from 7am to midnight on weekdays, 11am to 7pm on Saturdays, and noon to 9pm Sundays.

Maps Salespeople, repairmen, and others who must travel about rely on something called a "Key Map," a binder of detailed maps that divides Houston into a grid system. This homegrown Houston creation became so popular here that it has been copied by map companies in other cities. It may offer more information than most visitors want. You can buy standard street maps at any drugstore and at many convenience stores, and you'll find some helpful maps of downtown, the Museum District, and other parts of the city at the visitor center in city hall.

Newspapers & Magazines The local daily is the *Houston Chronicle.* The *Houston Press,* a weekly freebie that covers local politics and culture, can be found around town at restaurants, stores, and just about anywhere people congregate.

Police Dial ⓒ **911** in an emergency; for nonemergencies, dial ⓒ **311.**

Post Office The downtown branch, 401 Franklin St. (ⓒ **713/226-3066**), is open Monday through Friday from 9am to 7pm and Saturday from 9am to noon.

Safety Houston is a safe town for visitors. Exercise caution at night in the downtown areas that lie outside the theater district.

Taxes The local hotel tax is 17%, the local sales tax 8.25%.

Transit Information Call ⓒ **713/802-5074.**

Weather Call ⓒ **713/228-8703.**

3 Where to Stay

Downtown and the Uptown/Galleria area have most of the city's luxury hotels. Both are great locations for getting to know the city, but don't make them your automatic choice without first giving some thought to where you'll be spending your time in Houston. See the "Neighborhoods in Brief" section above for more suggestions about where to stay.

The hotel listings that follow include "rack rates" (the base retail price for a room with no discount) for double occupancy. You should use this as a basis for comparison and not think of these prices as etched in stone. Always ask about promotional rates. Houston is a business town; you'll find deep discounts for weekend stays, especially at the luxury hotels, which often offer prices that are competitive with some moderate hotels. There is a 17% hotel tax, which is not included in the rates shown here and is rarely included in hotel price quotes.

DOWNTOWN
VERY EXPENSIVE

Alden-Houston Hotel ✦✦✦   This hotel, originally called the Sam Houston, was taken over by Alden Hotels in 2005. A couple of years earlier it had been completely remodeled in modern decor. This remains the case now, and I use "modern" in the best of senses—sleek, uncluttered interiors that seek simplicity but avoid the "lab" look, which always leaves me with a chill. The guest rooms exert a comforting, quieting influence—a respite from bustling downtown Houston. They also rack up lots of style points with unexpected touches, such as nicely chosen fixtures and sharply dressed beds. The standard rooms are medium size and have ample, very attractive bathrooms. The two kinds of suites are larger and come with extras such as plasma TVs. But the electronics in all the rooms are quite good, and there's a DVD library free for the use of guests. The original Sam Houston Hotel was opened in the '20s and closed in the '70s. At that time, its location wasn't in the best part of downtown; now the location is great, just 2 blocks from the ballpark and Main Street. For more on the hotel's highly acclaimed restaurant, **17,** see "Where to Dine," below.

1117 Prairie St., Houston, TX 77002. ✆ **877/348-8800** or 832/200-8800. Fax 832/200-8811. www.aldenhotels.com. 97 units. $255–$355 standard; $355–$420 suite one; $375–$450 suite two. Special weekend and Internet rates available. AE, DC, DISC, MC, V. Valet parking $25. Pets under 25 lbs. allowed with a $150 deposit. **Amenities:** Restaurant; bar; state-of-the-art fitness center; concierge; car-rental; courtesy car; 24-hr. room service; same-day laundry service/dry cleaning. *In room:* A/C, TV/DVD, Wi-Fi and high-speed Internet access, minibar, hair dryer, iron, safe.

Four Seasons Hotel Houston Center ✦✦✦   This member of the luxury hotel chain does everything right. It stands out especially in the areas of service (reliable concierge, attentive staff, and a luxury spa) and spaciousness (everything about the hotel is large—guest rooms, suites, and all common areas). Rooms are decorated traditionally: draperies with valances, furniture with neoclassic lines, upholstery with brocades and other rich fabrics. What impresses me the most about this hotel is the ease with which services are provided. Need a fridge, a fax machine, or a VCR delivered to your room? No problem. Need your suit dry-cleaned at 2 in the morning for use later that day? No problem. The hotel can do this because it employs a large staff. The location is convenient, by the city's convention center, baseball park, and basketball arena. Connected to the hotel are a small shopping center and the Houston Center Athletic Club, whose facilities are available to guests free of charge. (The hotel has a large, well-equipped health club of its own and offers guests access to a nearby racquet club, too.) The hotel's restaurant, Quattro, is an Italian grill. It has won much praise from food critics.

1300 Lamar St., Houston, TX 77010. ✆ **800/332-3442** or 713/650-1300. Fax 713/276-4787. www.fourseasons.com. 404 units. $335–$395 double; $445–$495 executive suite; $575 and up 1-bedroom suites. Weekend rates and packages available. AE, DC, DISC, MC, V. Valet parking $26. Pets allowed. **Amenities:** Restaurant; 2 bars; large outdoor heated pool; health club; spa; Jacuzzi; sauna; concierge; courtesy car; business center; 24-hr. room service; in-room massage; babysitting; 24-hr. laundry service/dry cleaning. *In room:* A/C, TV w/pay movies, Wi-Fi, minibar, hair dryer, iron, safe.

Hotel Icon ✦✦✦   I like a hotel that's not afraid of a bit of fringe, a splash of gold damask, a touch of refined decadence. So many hotels I see opt for the zero-risk approach to traditionalism: conservative furniture with American Colonial or neoclassical elements—what I call the George-Washington-slept-here look. Hotel Icon goes more for the Lola-Montez-slept-here look: lots of texture, ornament, and a "boudoir" feel to the rooms, all of which makes this hotel a fun place to stay. In renovating the old Union National Bank Building (built in 1912), the designers sought to capture something of the feel of that golden age of refinement and exuberance. The most fun is to be had in the suites on the top floor, each named after a glorious old hotel. These rooms are extra large and extra plush and touched by a bit of idiosyncrasy. The standard rooms also offer atmosphere and amenities. The higher rate is for rooms with extra-large bathrooms equipped with a pass-through above the bathtub that opens up to the bedroom. There is talk that the hotel's restaurant, Bank, might change hands and cease to be a Jean-Georges restaurant.

220 Main St., Houston, TX 77002. ⓒ 800/323-7500 or 713/224-4266. Fax 713/223-3223. www.hotelicon.com. 135 units. $295–$350 double; $450 and up suite. Weekend rates sometimes available. AE, DC, DISC, MC, V. Valet parking $25. **Amenities:** Restaurant; bar; fitness center; spa; concierge; courtesy limo; business center; 24-hr. room service; in-room massage; same-day laundry service/dry cleaning. *In room:* A/C, TV, high-speed Internet access, minibar, coffeemaker, hair dryer, iron.

Lancaster Hotel 🏨🏨🏨   For those who enjoy the performing arts and nightlife, there is no better place to stay in Houston. Within 1 block of the Lancaster are the symphony, the ballet, the opera, and the Alley Theatre (see "Houston After Dark," later in this chapter), and when reserving a room you can have the concierge buy tickets for performances at any of these venues as well as others in the Theater District. Also a block away is Bayou Place, where you can catch a movie or a live blues or rock act, and within a few blocks are many restaurants and clubs. The hotel occupies a small 12-story building that dates from the 1920s and looks all the smaller for being near the Chase Tower (the tallest skyscraper west of the Mississippi). Rooms are a little smaller than their counterparts at the Four Seasons, but furnished with more of the character of an old hotel. Bathrooms are ample and have lots of counter space. Service is excellent and includes many personal touches. In 2006 the hotel was purchased by the Valencia group, which owns the Valencia hotel in San Antonio.

701 Texas Ave., Houston, TX 77002. ⓒ 800/231-0336 or 713/228-9500. Fax 713/223-4528. www.thelancasterhouston. com. 93 units. $189–$319 standard; $315–$550 suite. Children younger than 18 stay free in parent's room. Weekend packages available. AE, DC, DISC, MC, V. Valet parking $21. **Amenities:** Restaurant; bar; fitness room; concierge; courtesy car; 24-hr. room service; in-room massage; babysitting; overnight laundry service/dry cleaning. *In room:* A/C, TV/VCR w/pay movies, fax, Wi-Fi and high-speed Internet access, minibar, hair dryer, iron, safe, CD player.

EXPENSIVE

The Magnolia Hotel 🏨🏨   Opened in 2003 in what was the Houston Post Dispatch Building (1920s), the Magnolia goes for an anachronistic blend of new and old. The guest rooms mix gold scalloped trim and traditional patterned fabrics with the clean lines of modern furniture. The overall effect is charming and comfortable and can hardly go out of date. Rooms are large. The bathrooms have quality amenities and fixtures. Suites are very large and come with a full kitchen and dining area. The studio suites are especially attractive and come with a kitchenette. The mezzanine club offers a free continental breakfast in the morning, and cocktails and snacks in the afternoon and evening (the hotel doesn't have a restaurant but does have a kitchen for room service). This club is designed to be a comfortable place where guests can relax outside the four walls of their hotel room, socialize, perhaps play a little billiards in the game room, read the paper in the library, or surf the Web over a drink (the club is set up for high-speed wireless access). The lower rates listed below are for weekends.

1100 Texas Ave., Houston, TX 77002. ⓒ 888/915-1110 or 713/221-0011. Fax 713/221-0022. www.magnoliahotels.com. 314 units. $129–$199 standard; $199–$269 studio suite; $399 1-bedroom suite. Rates include continental breakfast and evening cocktails. AE, DC, DISC, MC, V. Valet parking $22. **Amenities:** Bar; heated rooftop pool; fitness center; Jacuzzi; game room; concierge; courtesy car; secretarial services; limited 24-hr. room service; overnight laundry service/dry cleaning; executive level rooms. *In room:* A/C, TV w/pay movies, minibar, coffeemaker, hair dryer, iron, safe.

MODERATE

Best Western Downtown Inn and Suites   Located in the shadow of downtown's skyline, this hotel offers convenient location and extra large rooms with one king-size or two queen-size beds. On the down side, style takes a back seat to comfort and convenience, and there's no restaurant or room service. The greatest savings are had during the week; for a weekend, I would pay a bit extra to stay at one of the fancy hotels, which give better discounts.

915 W. Dallas St., Houston, TX 77019. ✆ **800/528-1234** or 713/571-7733. Fax 713/571-6680. www.bestwestern.com. 77 units. $139 double; $149 suite. Rates include continental breakfast. AE, DC, DISC, MC, V. Free guarded parking. **Amenities:** Covered outdoor pool; fitness room; Jacuzzi; courtesy shuttle; overnight laundry service; coin-op laundry. *In room:* A/C, TV, high-speed Internet access, fridge, coffeemaker, hair dryer, iron, safe, microwave.

EAST END
MODERATE

Drury Inn & Suites Houston Hobby *Value*   This hotel, in the vicinity of the Hobby Airport, is virtually identical (except in price) to the Drury Inn & Suites Near the Galleria (p. 173). It's worth your while to check prices here because the rooms and amenities are competitively priced and often discounted, and the property is well managed. Suites are large and come with a fridge and microwave. Complimentary cocktails are served in the afternoon from Monday to Thursday. Guests also receive an hour of free long-distance calls within the U.S.

7902 Mosely Rd., Houston, TX 77061. ✆ **800/378-7946** or ✆/fax 713/941-4300. www.druryhotels.com. 134 units. $110 double; $120 king; $130 suite. Rates include breakfast buffet. Weekend and Internet specials available. AE, DC, DISC, MC, V. Free parking. Pets accepted with restrictions. **Amenities:** Heated indoor/outdoor pool; exercise room; Jacuzzi; coin-op laundry; same-day laundry service/dry cleaning. *In room:* A/C, TV, Wi-Fi, coffeemaker, hair dryer, iron.

Hilton University of Houston *⊕*   This is unlike any other Hilton Hotel in that it is part of the Conrad Hilton College of Hotel and Restaurant Management and is staffed not only by professional full-timers, but also students performing their lab work. It deserves consideration because of its rates, which often drop significantly when there are no academic conferences or parents' weekends; its location on the University campus between downtown and the attractions in Houston's southeast side; and its service, which is often excellent. Rooms throughout the hotel's eight floors are large L-shaped layouts with modern furnishings that include a sleeper sofa. Eric's, the hotel's restaurant, is far better than most hotel restaurants and offers a menu with a Latin flair. The University Center next door has a health club, a large pool, game room, and beauty salon, all of which the guests have access to. Note that the parking garage has a low ceiling and cannot accommodate vehicles such as large SUVs and pick-up trucks.

4800 Calhoun Rd., Houston, TX 77004. ✆ **800/HOTELUH** or 713/741-2447. Fax 713/743-2472. www.hilton.com. 86 units. $99–$150 double. AE, DC, DISC, MC, V. Parking $6. **Amenities:** Restaurant; bar; limited room service; same-day dry cleaning. *In room:* A/C, TV w/pay movies, dataport, coffeemaker, hair dryer, iron.

INEXPENSIVE

Red Carpet Inn Hobby Regency Motor Lodge   This place is cheap and offers an adventure into working class, urban-cowboy Houston. The rooms aren't much to look at—midsize with '70s furniture and imitation wood paneling. The real character of the place comes from the restaurant and the lounge. The former is a roadside Tex-Mex

joint; the latter is a good example of the typical Houston blue-collar bar with red carpet that smells of stale beer, a pool table, dartboards, and a TV always tuned to sports.
The location is a bonus.

6161 Gulf Fwy., Houston, TX 77023. (✆ 800/928-2871 or 713/928-2871. Fax 713/928-3050. www.redcarpetinn
houston.com. 150 units. $37–$50 double. Weekly rates available. AE, DC, DISC, MC, V. Free off-street parking. **Amenities:** Restaurant; bar; outdoor pool (open in season); coin-op laundry. *In room:* A/C, TV.

SOUTH MAIN
VERY EXPENSIVE
Hotel ZaZa   What we have here may be the perfect marriage of old property and new
owners. It's too early to tell for certain because, as of press time, the hotel is still closed
for renovation. Before the purchase, this was the Warwick Hotel, which, in the '60s, was
the hotel in Houston. The hotel was owned by John Mecom, an oilman who was exceed-
ingly fond of the color powder blue, which became known in Houston as "Mecom
blue." This was the predominant color of the hotel and, combined with a strange mix
of '60s modern and traditional French furniture, made for an accidental funkiness that
was amusing and would have been even more so had it not been altered by later renovations. Enter the new owners, who made their first property, Hotel ZaZa in Dallas, not
only luxurious, but a fun hotel to stay in by being playful with colors and textures and
going for a chic campy look. The Houston property, in the middle of the Museum District in the greenest part of the city, is scheduled to open in the spring of 2007. I only
hope that they find a way to incorporate Mecom blue into the color scheme.

5701 Main St., Houston, TX 77005. (✆ 800/298-6199 or 713/526-1991. Fax 713/526-0359. www.hotelzazahouston.
com. 315 units. $250–$300 double; $350 and up suite. AE, DC, DISC, MC, V. Valet parking $15; self-parking $8.
Amenities: Restaurant; bar; heated outdoor pool; fitness center; spa; concierge; courtesy shuttle; business center;
room service; in-room massage; laundry service/dry cleaning. *In room:* A/C, TV w/pay movies, high-speed Internet
access, minibar, hair dryer.

EXPENSIVE
Hilton Houston Plaza 🏨🏨   In terms of amenities, service, and location, this is the
best of the hotels around the Medical Center. Consequently, it enjoys a high occupancy rate, especially with people attending medical conferences. As the occupancy
rate increases, so do the prices. Try to book early, and, if you have any flexibility, get
rates for different dates. Most of the rooms are suites, which, for the money, are a better value than their standard king room.

The hotel's facilities set this hotel apart from neighboring hotels. The large rooms
are comfortable and well furnished. The building is 19 stories tall. Ask for a room facing out over Rice University. The hotel's location on the rim of the Medical Center
can actually be an advantage over its principal Medical Center rivals (a Marriott and
a Crowne Plaza) because it makes getting to and from the hotel easier, avoiding the
Medical Center traffic jams and the tight parking garages.

6833 Travis St., Houston, TX 77030. (✆ 800/HILTONS or 713/313-4000. Fax 713/313-4660. www.houstonplaza.hilton.com.
181 units. $219 double; $229 suite. Weekend rates available. AE, DC, DISC, MC, V. Valet parking $17; self-parking $10.
Amenities: Restaurant; bar; large outdoor heated pool; health club; Jacuzzi; sauna; courtesy shuttle; business center; limited room service; same-day laundry service/dry cleaning. *In room:* A/C, TV w/pay movies, Wi-Fi, minibar, fridge, coffeemaker,
hair dryer, iron.

MODERATE
Holiday Inn Hotel and Suites Houston Medical Center   This hotel has an excellent location across from the Medical Center, at the intersection with Holcombe Boulevard. The hotel often offers big discounts on weekend rates. Rooms are comfortable but

furnished with little effort to hide their institutional feel. (Extensive remodeling to all rooms in 2007 will greatly improve matters.) Some suites have full kitchens. What's not to like is the shortage of staff at the front desk and guest services, which makes getting attended to an exercise in patience. The same is true for the hotel restaurant.

6800 S. Main St., Houston, TX 77035. © **800/HOLIDAY** or 713/528-7744. Fax 713/528-6983. www.holiday-inn.com. 285 units. $155 double; $165–$175 suite; $319 apartment. Medical rates for hospital outpatients available. AE, DC, DISC, MC, V. Free parking. **Amenities:** Restaurant; bar; small pool; fitness room; courtesy shuttle; salon; limited room service; overnight laundry service/dry cleaning. *In room:* A/C, TV, high-speed Internet access, coffeemaker, hair dryer, iron.

Patrician Bed & Breakfast Inn   This is a smart choice for those who want a location near the Museum District that's a straight shot into downtown on the light rail line. The decor has a marked feminine feel, with wood floors, lots of area rugs, a few period pieces, and old-fashioned wallpaper. Rooms are small to medium size and come with queen-size beds, cable TV, and terry-cloth robes. Two smaller rooms on the third floor have the use of a kitchen off the hallway. With its proximity to downtown and convenient parking, this B&B gets a number of businesspeople on the weekdays. For the weekenders there are rooms sporting two-person whirlpool tubs. Prices vary according to room size and location. Guests have use of a video and CD library, a microwave, and a fridge stocked with complimentary bottled water and soft drinks.

1200 Southmore Blvd., Houston, TX 77004. © **800/553-5797** or 713/523-1114. Fax 713/523-0790. www.texasbnb. com. 7 units. $115–$165 double. Rates include full breakfast. Internet specials sometimes available. AE, DC, DISC, MC, V. Free parking. *In room:* A/C, TV (VCR in some units), Wi-Fi, hair dryer, iron, CD player.

INEXPENSIVE

Best Value Inn and Suites   This is a simple motel with two stories of rooms lining a large parking lot. The quietest rooms are the ones at the back of the property; the front ones can be noisy. All rooms have simple painted-wood furniture and two full-size beds or a king size; suites come with a small fridge and a microwave, which makes them a value for people wanting to save money on dining. Suites are twice the size of the standard rooms and come with kitchenettes, dining table and chairs, and a sleeper sofa. Bathrooms are clean but a little small.

9000 S. Main St., Houston, TX 77025. ©/fax **713/666-4151**. www.bestvalueinn.com. 98 units. $49–$59 double; $59–$79 suite. Rates include continental breakfast. AE, DC, DISC, MC, V. Free parking. **Amenities:** Outdoor pool; coin-op laundry. *In room:* A/C, TV.

La Quinta Inn Reliant Center *(Value*   This two-story motel is just down the road from the Astrodome and Reliant Stadium. The rooms include extras such as free local calls and large TVs. Bathrooms are spacious and well lit. The furniture and decoration are the result of a renovation that succeeded in making the rooms comfortable and attractive, albeit unmistakably motel-like. More important is the fact that they shield out the noise from the freeway.

9911 Buffalo Speedway (at Loop 610), Houston, TX 77054. © **800/531-5900** or 713/668-8082. Fax 713/668-0821. www.laquinta.com. 115 units. $79–$99 double. Rates include continental breakfast. Children younger than 18 stay free in parent's room. AE, DC, DISC, MC, V. Free parking. **Amenities:** Outdoor pool (open in season). *In room:* A/C, TV, coffeemaker, hair dryer, iron.

MONTROSE/THE HEIGHTS
EXPENSIVE

La Colombe d'Or ★★★   If you enjoy the smallness of scale of a B&B and the fact that the rooms don't look like hotel rooms, but you want more space, in-room dining, and more privacy, this is the hotel for you. The five suites are extremely large, with hardwood floors, area rugs, antiques, king-size beds, and large bathrooms. Some suites come with separate dining rooms, and the in-room service, from either the bar or the restaurant, is one of the things this hotel is known for. The mansion that the hotel occupies was built in the 1920s for oilman Walter Fondren. The interior has some beautiful architectural features, and its location puts you close to museums, restaurants, and the downtown area. The top floor of the original house is now an art gallery.

3410 Montrose Blvd., Houston, TX 77006. ⓒ 713/524-7999. Fax 713/524-8923. www.lacolombedor.com. 6 units. $199–$275 suite. AE, DC, DISC, MC, V. Free valet parking. Pets allowed with $150 deposit. **Amenities:** Restaurant; bar; room service; limited laundry service. *In room:* A/C, TV, hair dryer and iron available upon request.

MODERATE

Lovett Inn ⓐ *Value*   Located a block off Westheimer and 3 blocks from Montrose Boulevard, this B&B is on a quiet street right in the middle of the busy restaurant and club district of the Montrose area. The house dates from the early 1900s and was built by one of Houston's mayors. Most rooms are large (well above the usual size for B&Bs). The four rooms in the main house and two in the carriage house are attractive and well furnished with period pieces, wood floors, and area rugs, yet eschew the cuteness that so many B&Bs feel obliged to deliver. Almost all have private balconies. There are also four town-house units around the corner (two per house), which have separate entrances and greater privacy. These are comfortable but modern. One town house has a full kitchen for the use of guests if they rent both rooms.

501 Lovett Blvd., Houston, TX 77006. ⓒ 800/779-5224 or 713/522-5224. Fax 713/528-6708. www.lovettinn.com. 12 units. $110–$150 traditional doubles; $95–$125 town-house doubles. Rates include continental breakfast. AE, DC, DISC, MC, V. Free parking. **Amenities:** Outdoor pool, Wi-Fi in public areas. *In room:* A/C, TV, fridge (in most units), hair dryer, iron.

Modern B&B ⓐ   There is no law that says a bed-and-breakfast must be in a period house. This one actually occupies two recently built townhouses in the heart of the Montrose, and it exists because the original project fell through when Enron tanked. It's great for those who like modern architecture (exposed beams, airy spaces). It's also good for those who like baked goods and an honor bar. Rooms vary but are grouped in three categories: "mod," which is on the ground floor (with the bathroom up a flight of stairs), standard (one of which comes with a Jacuzzi), and top floor, which are much larger than the others and have the use of a large porch. The owners, Lisa and Rodney Collins, live on the premises, are gracious hosts, and keep lots of information on things to do in town. All of these factors make this place a great alternative to staying in a hotel.

4003 Hazard, Houston, TX 77098. ⓒ 800/462-4014 or 832/279-6367. www.modernbb.com. 8 units. $100 mod; $145–$165 standard; $200 top shelf. Rates include full breakfast. 3-night minimum stay for holidays. AE, DC, DISC, MC, V. Kids accepted when renting an entire house. Pets accepted with a $30/day fee. **Amenities:** Outdoor pool. *In room:* A/C, TV (DVD upon request), Wi-Fi, hair dryer, iron.

Sara's Bed and Breakfast Inn ⓐ   For the traditional B&B experience—period decor, themed rooms, beautifully furnished common rooms—this is the place to stay. Sara's occupies a large Texas Victorian house in the Heights. From here it's easy to get to all of central Houston. The house is immaculately kept and brightly decorated. Most rooms come with a queen-size or king-size bed. Several are inspired by other cities of Texas, including Fort Worth, San Antonio, and Galveston. The carriage house suite is extra large and has a king-size and a double bed. The hosts serve a full breakfast except on Mondays.

941 Heights Blvd., Houston, TX 77008. ⓒ 800/593-1130 or 713/868-1130. Fax 713/868-3284. www.saras.com. 12 units. $70–$130 double; $150–$200 suite. AE, DC, DISC, MC, V. Free parking. No children younger than age 12. *In room:* A/C, TV/VCR, Wi-Fi, hair dryer, iron.

KIRBY DISTRICT
VERY EXPENSIVE

Renaissance Houston Hotel 🏵🏵 The only hotel in the Greenway Plaza (though there are a few nearby), this 20-story hotel enjoys access to Greenway's office buildings through its concourse level of shops, food court, a post office, and a movie theater. It's also connected to the Houston City Club by another walkway, and hotel guests can enjoy the use of its facilities including indoor tennis courts, racquetball, and jogging track. The hotel's location off the Southwest Freeway means quick access to either downtown or Uptown.

All standard rooms are spacious and decorated in an eclectic style that makes them a bit more interesting than your standard hotel room. Bathrooms are roomy as well and a cut above most of what you see in this price range.

6 Greenway Plaza East, Houston, TX 77046. © 800/HOTELS-1 or 713/629-1200. www.renaissancehotels.com. 388 units. $239–$299 double; $350–$1,200 suite. Weekend rates available. AE, DC, DISC, MC, V. Valet parking $14; self-parking $8. **Amenities:** 2 restaurants; bar; outdoor heated pool; health club; sauna; concierge; complimentary shuttle; business center; salon; 24-hr. room service; same-day laundry service/dry cleaning; nonsmoking rooms; concierge level. *In room:* A/C, TV, dataport, coffeemaker, hair dryer, iron.

MODERATE

Four Points This is a businessperson's hotel that's comfortable and well situated. It has easy access to the freeway, and you can get in and out quickly without having to negotiate a parking garage. The location is convenient—between downtown, the Rice University/Village area, and the Galleria. Rooms are being thoroughly remodeled and have plenty of light. The furnishings are modern and functional without looking cheap; some rooms have sofa sleepers. Improvements include plush new mattresses—one king-size or two doubles—and well-finished bathrooms (medium size).

2828 Southwest Fwy., Houston, TX 77098. © 800/368-7764 or 713/942-2111. Fax 713/526-8709. www.fourpoints.com. 216 units. $100 double. Weekend rates available. AE, DC, DISC, MC, V. Free parking. **Amenities:** Restaurant; bar; outdoor pool (open in season); fitness room; car-rental desk; courtesy car; business center; limited room service; same-day laundry service. *In room:* A/C, TV/VCR, Wi-Fi, coffeemaker, hair dryer, iron.

UPTOWN
VERY EXPENSIVE

Hotel Derek 🏵🏵🏵 The creators of this hotel have gone to great lengths to separate it from the pack. They've even given it a persona—its namesake, Derek, a fictitious aging rock star/hotel owner. Given the premise, it would have been easy to lapse into cliché, but not so. Yes, there are some nods to the 1960s, but these are cleverly mixed with unexpected touches and the playful use of materials new and old to express a light-hearted vision of the counterculture. With the guest rooms, the designers have succeeded in creating a space that is functional for the business traveler while having the feel of a "pad" with all the accompanying informality. The decor is modern: The desk, side tables, and bathroom counter are thick glass with metal supports; the mattresses are mostly king size. The sitting area is a wonderful mohair velvet built-in stretching the width of the room. Details throughout show thoughtfulness: Instead of drawers, there are baskets (which make a lot more sense in a hotel room) and safes that are big enough to accommodate a briefcase. On weekends this hotel gets mainly couples. The restaurant, Bistro Moderne, is reviewed on p. 183.

2525 W. Loop South, Houston, TX 77027. © 866/292-4100 or 713/961-3000. Fax 713/297-4393. www.hotelderek.com. 314 units. $350 standard; $380 studio; $800 and up suite. Weekend and promotional rates sometimes available. AE, DC, DISC, MC, V. Valet parking $16. Pets up to 50 lbs. accepted with $50 fee. **Amenities:** Restaurant; bar; fitness center with spa treatments; concierge; courtesy car; business center; 24-hr. room service; in-room massage; same-day laundry service/dry cleaning. *In room:* A/C, TV w/pay movies, dataport, minibar, hair dryer, iron, safe.

InterContinental Houston ★★★   Walking into the busy lobby of this new hotel, I was astonished at how quickly people were being attended to. I was most impressed by the number of staff on duty, their efficiency, the concierge's abilities, and with the attention I received before anyone knew my business there. The rooms also impress, and space-age insulated windows make them remarkably quiet. Room design inserts high-tech amenities into warm, comforting surroundings that steer clear of trendiness. Rooms are informal but make use of expensive materials, including marble, granite, and leather. Highlights include an oversize safe with outlets for recharging cellphones or computers, comfortable pillow-top beds, and well-thought-out desks with lots of workspace and multiple connection options.

2222 W. Loop South, Houston, TX 77027. © 800/327-0200 or 713/627-7600. Fax 713/961-3327. www.ichouston intro.com. 485 units. $299 standard; $349 deluxe; $499 and up suite. Promotional rates and packages available. AE, DC, DISC, MC, V. Valet parking $25. **Amenities:** Restaurant; bar; heated outdoor pool; 24-hr. state-of-the-art health club; spa treatments; outdoor Jacuzzi; concierge; courtesy car; business center with 24-hr. secretarial services; 24-hr. room service; in-room massage; same-day laundry service/dry cleaning; club level rooms. *In room:* A/C, TV w/pay movies, high-speed Internet access, minibar, coffeemaker, hair dryer, iron, safe, CD player.

JW Marriott Hotel by the Galleria   On Westheimer, facing the Galleria, this high-rise hotel offers lots of amenities and a central location. Rooms are smaller than at the Westin hotels but are more attractive. The service and the amenities are better, too. Bathrooms are well lit and come with make-up mirrors and terry-cloth robes. All guest rooms were remodeled in 2005. The decor is a good-looking mix of modern and traditional. The remodeling project placed a lot of emphasis on the beds, and it shows. They are plush and comfortable; you have a choice of two doubles or one king size with a pull-out sofa. Avoid reserving a room on the fifth floor, where the health club is located. The hotel is completely nonsmoking.

5150 Westheimer Rd., Houston, TX 77056. © 800/228-9290 or 713/961-1500. Fax 713/961-5045. www.jwmarriott houston.com. 514 units. $279–$339 double; $600 and up suite. AE, DC, DISC, MC, V. Valet parking $25; self-parking $15 in garage; limited free parking in open lot. **Amenities:** Restaurant; bar; heated indoor/outdoor pool; health club; Jacuzzi; sauna; concierge; business center; salon; 24-hr. room service; massage; babysitting; laundry service/dry cleaning; concierge level. *In room:* A/C, TV w/pay movies, high-speed Internet access, coffeemaker, hair dryer, iron.

Omni Houston Hotel ★ *Kids*   This hotel is an island of tranquillity in Uptown's sea of commotion. Flanking it on one side is a broad expanse of lawn with a decorative pool fed by cascading water and adorned with a small troop of black swans; on the other side is the heavily wooded Memorial Park. You'd think that you're miles from the busy Uptown malls, but you're not. In contrast to the modern exterior of this 11-story building— angular lines, bold colors, stark surfaces—the guest rooms are pictures of traditionalism, with 18th-century-style furniture and bedspreads with flounces in neoclassical patterns. The rooms are large and come with a view either of Memorial Park with downtown in the background or of the pools, the lawn, and the black swans. The Omni Kids Program, with special games and goodies for children, makes this a great choice for families.

4 Riverway, Houston, TX 77056. © 800/THE-OMNI or 713/871-8181. Fax 713/871-8116. www.omnihouston.com. 373 units. $269–$299 double; $369 and up suite. Promotional rates available. AE, DC, DISC, MC, V. Valet parking $20; free outdoor self-parking. Pets accepted for $50 fee. **Amenities:** Restaurant; 2 bars; 2 large outdoor pools (1 heated); 4 lit tennis courts; health club; Jacuzzi; sauna; children's programs; game room; concierge; courtesy limo; 24-hr. room service; massage; babysitting; same-day laundry service/dry cleaning. *In room:* A/C, TV/VCR w/pay movies, Wi-Fi, minibar, coffeemaker, hair dryer, iron, CD player.

Kids Family-Friendly Hotels

Doubletree Guest Suites (p. 173)   The two-bedroom suites here are a good value, and the full kitchens and dining areas give guests flexibility with such things as breakfast and snacks and buying take-out.

Omni Houston Hotel (p. 171)   With its Omni Kids Program, this hotel makes a special effort to keep smaller children amused. Kids receive a packet of goodies at check in, and parents can even request a small, pretend suitcase that holds more games and such. As part of the program, the concierge can organize activities and trips for children to such places as the zoo.

Sheraton Suites Houston Near the Galleria   The rooms at this all-suite hotel are attractive, with more character than most hotel rooms in the Galleria area. The headboards and accents are postmodern, and the granite countertops are snazzy. These suites aren't as big as those at the Doubletree Guest Suites, but they are, in some ways, more comfortable and attractive. An easy-to-use retractable door makes the living room and bedroom usable as one large space or as two separate rooms, with the ample bathroom accessible from either. Bed options include two doubles or a king. Some rooms have sleeper sofas. On weekends, the hotel gets mainly families. The best rooms face westward away from Loop 610. There are 18 business suites that include features such as fax machines and copiers. The service here is attentive. This hotel is 2 blocks from the Galleria.

2400 W. Loop South, Houston, TX 77027. (C) **800/325-3535** or 713/586-2444. Fax 713/586-2445. www.sheraton suiteshouston.com. 281 suites. $309–$329 suite. AE, DC, DISC, MC, V. Valet parking $20; self-parking $11. Pets up to 80 pounds accepted with no fee. **Amenities:** Restaurant; bar; small, heated outdoor pool; state-of-the-art fitness center; Jacuzzi; concierge; courtesy shuttle; business center; room service until midnight; babysitting; same-day laundry service/dry cleaning. *In room:* A/C, TV w/pay movies, Wi-Fi, fridge, coffeemaker, hair dryer, iron, safe.

Westin Galleria and Westin Oaks   Similar in size, name, and appearance, these two hotels are often confused by travelers who arrive believing the destination has been reached only to find that they must yet again negotiate the mall parking lot. The Westin Oaks is on the east side of the Galleria mall (the side closest to Loop 610) and faces Westheimer Road. It's a family hotel, with no alcohol in the minibars. The Westin Galleria is attached to the west side of the Galleria and faces West Alabama Street. It targets business travelers, offering a business center and more formal dining than the Westin Oaks.

In other aspects the hotels are much alike. I find them a mix of good and bad. On the good side, they have the great location that allows you to walk from your hotel room into the shopping mall without ever having to leave the great indoors. The rooms are extra large, the beds are comfortable, and the balconies—an uncommon feature in urban hotels—offer the best way to enjoy the view of perpetual motion below and the serene skyline above (get a north-facing room at the Westin Oaks, a south-facing room at the Westin Galleria). On the bad side, the rooms are awkwardly designed and plainly furnished. Another problem is the service: There wasn't enough staff present on my visits, and the concierge, once located, didn't inspire confidence. Having said that, I must add that all of this would be perfectly fine for a hotel in a lower price range, and that might be just what we're looking at here. I found the discounting of rates so common that I don't believe anyone pays the published rate here.

5060 W. Alabama St. and 5011 Westheimer Rd. Houston, TX 77056. (C) **800/WESTIN-1** or 713/960-8100. Fax 713/960-6553 (Westin Galleria) or 713/960-6554 (Westin Oaks). www.westin.com. 487 units in Westin Galleria, 406 units in Westin Oaks. $299 double; $519 suite. AE, DC, DISC, MC, V. Valet parking $22; free self-parking. **Amenities:** 1 restaurant in each hotel; 1 bar in each hotel; heated outdoor swimming pool; health club access ($11/day fee); children's program; concierge; car-rental desk; business center; 24-hr. room service; babysitting; same-day laundry service/dry cleaning. *In room:* A/C, TV w/pay movies, dataport, minibar, coffeemaker, hair dryer, iron, safe.

EXPENSIVE

Doubletree Guest Suites (★) (Kids)   This 26-story hotel, located a block west of the Galleria shopping complex, offers extra-large, plainly furnished suites, each with a fully equipped kitchen (including microwave and dishwasher) and a dining area for four people. (A grocery store is 4 blocks away, and Kenny & Ziggy's, a deli with takeout [see "Where to Dine," below], is even closer.) The bedroom includes two full-size beds or a king size; the sitting room has a sofa or two, armchairs, and a large TV. The furniture and decor are plain but comfortable and ideal for families with small children. Bathrooms are large with plenty of counter space. The hotel is well priced, gets a lot of repeat business, and is a favorite for extended stays. The service is good.

5353 Westheimer Rd., Houston, TX 77056. (C) **800/222-TREE** or 713/961-9000. Fax 713/877-8835. www.doubletree hotels.com. 335 suites. $199 1-bedroom suite; $289 2-bedroom suite. AE, DC, DISC, MC, V. Valet parking $20; self-parking $11. Pets allowed for $25 deposit and $25 fee. **Amenities:** Restaurant; bar; outdoor pool; fitness room; Jacuzzi; concierge; courtesy shuttle; business center; 24-hr. room service (limited menu after 11pm); in-room massage; babysitting; coin-op laundry; same-day laundry service/dry cleaning. *In room:* A/C, TV w/pay movies, dataport, coffeemaker, hair dryer, iron, safe.

MODERATE

Drury Inn & Suites Near the Galleria (Value)   One of the best lodging values in this area is the Drury Inn. Rooms are midsize and comfortable, with extra-long double beds for tall folk. Instead of the usual easy chair and ottoman, there's a recliner; the TV is larger than normal. King rooms are slightly larger and come with microwave and fridge. While the bathrooms are of okay size, they offer limited counter space. The hotel doesn't have a restaurant, but it offers free evening cocktails Monday through Thursday and a breakfast buffet every morning. Guests also receive an hour of free long-distance calls within the U.S.

Post Oak Park at W. Loop South, Houston, TX 77027. (C) **800/378-7946** or (C)/fax 713/963-0700. www.druryhotels. com. 134 units. $140 standard; $150 king room; $160 suite. Rates include breakfast buffet. Promotional and weekend rates available. AE, DC, DISC, MC, V. Free parking. Pets accepted with restrictions. **Amenities:** Indoor/outdoor heated pool; fitness room; Jacuzzi; coin-op laundry; same-day laundry service/dry cleaning. *In room:* A/C, TV, high-speed Internet access, coffeemaker, hair dryer, iron.

La Quinta Inn & Suites Galleria   You can tell at first glance that this inn, constructed in 1998, is a new breed of La Quinta, with a gurgling fountain in the lobby, a fitness room, and a fairly large outdoor heated pool with separate hot tub. Proximity to the shopping along Post Oak and in the Galleria seals the deal. Standard rooms are medium to large and come with two double beds; the "King Plus" room comes with king-size bed and a recliner.

1625 W. Loop South, Houston, TX 77027. (C) **800/687-6667** or 713/355-3440. Fax 713/355-2990. www.laquinta. com. 173 units. $150 double; $160 king plus; $199 suite. Weekend rates available. Rates include breakfast. AE, DC, DISC, MC, V. Free parking. **Amenities:** Outdoor heated pool; Jacuzzi; coin-op laundry; same-day dry cleaning. *In room:* A/C, TV w/pay movies, high-speed Internet access, coffeemaker, hair dryer, iron.

NEAR BUSH INTERCONTINENTAL AIRPORT
EXPENSIVE

Houston Airport Marriott ✮   Don't let the address fool you—this hotel is not on "Hotel Row." It's located smack-dab in the middle of the airport itself between terminals B and C, and it's on the airport tram line, which means no messing with taxis, shuttle buses, or rental cars. With this enviable location, the hotel gets a lot of business conferences. The revolving rooftop restaurant adds to the hotel's popularity—you'll see planes landing and taking off with a view that is pretty much the same as that of the airport's control tower. Guest rooms at the hotel are large and attractively furnished. The bathrooms are not particularly big, but the beds are comfortable, and everything else about the rooms is great. The revolving rooftop restaurant is a lovely place for dinner, which is served from 5:30 to 10pm (open for lunch to groups only).

18700 JFK Blvd., Houston, TX 77032. ✆ **800/228-9290** or 281/443-2310. Fax 281/443-5294. www.marriott.com. 566 units. $229–$259 double; $450 suite. Weekend discounts. AE, DC, DISC, MC, V. Free self-parking. **Amenities:** 2 restaurants; 2 bars; heated outdoor pool; large exercise room; Jacuzzi; limited room service (includes Pizza Hut pizzas); same-day laundry service; nonsmoking rooms. *In room:* A/C, TV w/pay movies, dataport, coffeemaker, hair dryer, iron.

MODERATE

Airport Inn *(Value)*   As far as airport hotels go, this one has the most extras for the buck. Rooms are large, comfortable, and well equipped, including two phone lines (including a cordless phone) with free local calls, microwave, and in-room safe. Most come with two full beds. Services include free airport shuttle and continental breakfast (even though there's no restaurant).

15615 JFK Blvd., Houston, TX 77032. ✆ **281/987-8777.** Fax 281/987-9317. 101 units. $89 double. Weekend rates available. Rates include continental breakfast. Children younger than 18 stay free in parent's room. AE, DC, DISC, MC, V. Free parking. **Amenities:** Small outdoor pool; exercise room; Jacuzzi; complimentary shuttle; same-day laundry service. *In room:* A/C, TV, high-speed Internet access, fridge, coffeemaker, hair dryer, iron, safe.

4 Where to Dine

The Houston restaurant scene, like the city itself, is cosmopolitan. The primary influences come from Louisiana, Mexico, and Southeast Asia, but you can find restaurants serving just about any cuisine you can think of. What constitutes Houston's native cooking would be steaks, chili, barbecue, soul food, and Tex-Mex. For locals, the proper accompaniment for any of these would be beer or iced tea. The extra-large glass of iced tea is a cultural fixture in this town, as it is in the rest of the state. It is the perfect palate cleanser after a bite of something dense and spicy such as enchiladas in chili gravy.

DOWNTOWN/MIDTOWN
VERY EXPENSIVE

Brennan's ✮✮ SOUTHERN/CREOLE   Fine dining a la New Orleans: Brennan's opened in 1967 as a sister restaurant to the famous New Orleans original, and it's a perennial favorite on most local "Top Restaurant" lists. It's now independent and offers some great dishes that the original doesn't. The various dining rooms are strikingly elegant. (I don't think you'll find a lovelier table in all of Houston.) The service is superb, and the menu will be new territory to all but those coming from Louisiana. The selection of dishes varies daily but usually has a few classic Creole specialties such as roux-less seafood gumbo and turtle soup. Brennan's is also known for its chef's table, which is located in the restaurant's kitchen. The table must be reserved far in advance and can accommodate between 4 and 10 people at $75 per person. For that price, guests are treated to several of the chef's special creations right as they come off the stove.

3300 Smith (at Stuart). ℂ **713/522-9711.** Reservations recommended. Main courses $27–$32. AE, DC, DISC, MC, V. Mon–Fri 11:30am–2pm and 5:45–10pm; Sat 11am–2pm and 5:45–10pm; Sun 10am–2pm and 5:45–10pm. Take Smith St. (one-way headed south from downtown); when it crosses Elgin/Westheimer, look for the restaurant on your right. Be careful not to pass it, or you will get fed onto the Southwest Fwy.

17 ✿✿✿ NEW AMERICAN   Chef Jeff Armstrong is gone, but not the wonderful cooking. The new chef, Ryan Pera, who has worked in New York under Jonathan Waxman and at Le Cirque, has kept the direction and the concept of the original menu intact, and has even provided a bit more brio to the contrasting tastes that made the original menu such a hit. Among the starters, the crab salad with avocado and bits of grapefruit is a case in point. It's a holdover that has been kept simple, but with the addition of a little ponzu sauce to balance the sweetness of the grapefruit. The main courses present some difficult decisions. Deciding which to order is a matter of what you're most in the mood for—comfort food, such as the pan-roasted chicken or the steak, or something new such as the ahi tuna with oxtail. Located in the Alden–Houston Hotel, the restaurant's dining room is small, the furniture is comfortable, and the service is attentive.

1117 Prairie St. (In the Alden–Houston Hotel). ℂ **832/200-8888.** Reservations recommended. Main courses $21–$34. AE, DC, DISC, MC, V. Daily 6:30am–4pm and 5:30–10pm.

Vic & Anthony's ✿ STEAKS   This is a steakhouse of the posh sort, with lots of wood, stone, and leather. These kinds of places are supposed to look substantial, and Vic & Anthony's doesn't disappoint. The rooms are establishment with a touch of drama. Once you're seated, you'll be tempted by the long list of appetizers, but, before ordering, first ask yourself why you've come here. If your answer is "to eat steak," you should ignore these distractions (and perhaps the protestations of your dining companion) and go right for the 40-ounce USDA Prime porterhouse steak for two (your fellow diner will thank you later). This and the individual steaks are what this place is all about. In the words of Sancho Panza: "Hunger is the best condiment." And steak is always enjoyed best when you're ravenous. It's one of those deep Paleolithic pleasures.

1510 Texas Ave. ℂ **713/228-1111.** Reservations recommended. Main courses $19–$40. AE, DISC, MC, V. Sun–Thurs 5–10pm; Fri 11am–11pm; Sat 5–11pm.

MODERATE

Mai's ✿ VIETNAMESE   Occupying a two-story brick building with green awnings on Milam Street in the midtown area, Mai's is the last of a half-dozen Vietnamese restaurants you'll pass in the preceding 6 blocks. In several ways it's the best choice, but it should not be thought of as having a lock on good Vietnamese food. I do appreciate, however, its dependability and the long hours it keeps because you never know when you might get a yen for a bowl of Vietnamese noodles (and they're all good). This would be a good place to try *pho,* the national dish, a soup to which you add vegetables and aromatic herbs and lime juice. Sample the ever-popular spring and summer rolls served with *nam pla* and/or peanut sauce, and try a chicken stir-fry with chile and lemon grass. Favorites include the *nam noung* (ground pork and shrimp with thin vermicelli) and the Mekong sweet-and-sour soup (try the catfish version).

3403 Milam St. ℂ **713/520-7684.** Reservations recommended on weekends. Main courses $6–$16. AE, DC, DISC, MC, V. Mon–Thurs 10am–3am; Fri–Sat 10am–4am.

INEXPENSIVE

The Breakfast Klub *(Finds)* BREAKFAST/LUNCH   In midtown, this is the hip place for a late breakfast or casual lunch. On the menu are such down-home offerings as biscuits and gravy; pork chops and eggs; and catfish and grits. Standard breakfasts are available, too. You place the order at the counter and then take a seat. On Saturday mornings the line goes out the door. The choice of coffees is good. The surroundings are simple, with the works of local artists on the walls and a mix of soft jazz and gospel on the stereo. For lunch, the Klub offers sandwiches and salads and an occasional special, such as crawfish fettuccine.

3711 Travis St. ℂ **713/528-8561.** Breakfast $6–$8.50; sandwiches $3.50–$7. AE, DISC, MC, V. Mon–Fri 7am–2pm; Sat 8am–2pm.

This Is It SOUL FOOD   If you yearn for soul food plain and simple, make your way over to this little place just southwest of downtown. Chitlins, clove-scented yams, meatloaf, braised oxtails, and lots of greens are served cafeteria-style to all comers. Owner Craig Joseph's wall of fame, photos of celebrities who have visited the restaurant, and the work of African-American artists adorn the walls of this popular establishment. This neighborhood is part of the Fourth Ward, which includes Freedmen's town, where the newly liberated slaves built their houses shortly after the Civil War. According to local historians, it was one of the most prosperous black communities in the South.

207 W. Gray. ℂ **713/659-1608.** Reservations not accepted. Main courses $7–$9. AE, DISC, MC, V. Mon–Sat 11am–8pm; Sun 11am–6pm; breakfast daily 6:30–10am. West Gray is a continuation of Gray, which crosses Main St. 1 block south of the freeway overpass. The restaurant is near the intersection with Bagby.

Treebeards *(★) (Value)* CREOLE   This place gets my vote for best food for your money. Others see it the same way, and this is why Treebeards restaurant on Old Market Square gets such a crowd of office workers for lunch. Beat the crowd by going late or early and you won't have to wait in line. The chicken and shrimp gumbo, the étouffée, and the jambalaya are all good, but I somehow always return for the red beans and rice. Food is served cafeteria-style. Look for three more downtown locations: 1117 Texas Ave. (next to Christ Church Cathedral), 1100 Louisiana (in the tunnel), and at 700 Rusk, at the corner of Louisiana Street.

315 Travis St. (between Preston and Congress). ℂ **713/228-2622.** www.treebeards.com. Reservations not accepted. Main courses $6–$9. AE, DC, MC, V. Mon–Fri 11am–2pm; Fri 5–9pm.

EAST END
MODERATE

Kim Son VIETNAMESE/CHINESE   The menu is the most imposing part of this casual, highly regarded Vietnamese restaurant. Don't worry, though, because there are no poor choices among the 100 or so options. Enjoy finely prepared delicacies as well as the expected fare, such as terrific spring rolls and lovely noodle dishes. (The pan-seared shrimp with jalapeños and onions proves a delightful combination.) The menu includes several vegetarian dishes. Look for the exotic fish pool at the entrance.

2001 Jefferson. ℂ **713/222-2461.** Reservations accepted for parties of 8 or more. Main courses $8–$19. AE, DC, DISC, MC, V. Daily 11am–midnight. Located in the small Chinese commercial center 1 block east of the Brown Convention Center and the elevated Tex. 59 Fwy.

INEXPENSIVE

Loma Linda *(★★)* TEX-MEX   I like my Tex-Mex restaurants to be homey, unpretentious places where you're not likely to run into the see-and-be-seen crowd. Of course,

Fast Food a la Houston

When you need to find a meal that can be had quickly and cheaply, you don't have to suffer at the hands of the national fast-food chains, where the fare tastes the same whether you're in Houston or Honolulu. A number of local chains do a good job of cooking up fast food with character. Here are four worth considering:

James Coney Island Hot Dogs started up in Houston in the 1930s. It's famous for its Texas-style chili dogs. (Most Houstonians consider hot dogs without chili as either unfulfilled potential or foreign novelty.) You can also order the chili with or without beans or as a chili pie. For hot dogs, I recommend the Texas chili dog. There are 24 locations around Houston, including downtown (815 Dallas St.), in the Kirby District (3607 Shepherd at the corner of Richmond), in the Galleria area (1600 S. Post Oak), and out along the Gulf Freeway (6955 Gulf Fwy. and 10600 Gulf Fwy.).

In 1962, the Antone family, originally from Lebanon, opened an exotic import grocery store on Taft Street near Allen Parkway called **Antone's.** There they introduced Houston to their now famous po' boy (sub) sandwiches, which caught on in a big way. For lunch, you can't go wrong with one of these, which come already prepared. Get the original green label or the super red label, both of which are a combination of ham, salami, cheese, pickles, and special chowchow on fresh baked bread. Antone's locations include 2424 Dunstan (in the Village), 8110 Kirby (near Reliant Stadium), and 3823 Bellaire (at Stella Link, just west of the Medical Center). You can also find these po' boys for sale at some of the small grocery stores in town.

Beck's Prime is a local chain of upscale burger joints that are known for big juicy burgers and great shakes. Locations include 2902 Kirby Dr. (near Westheimer), 1001 E. Memorial Loop (in Memorial Park by the golf course), and at 910 Travis (in the downtown tunnel system below Bank One Center).

Café Express operates under the guiding principle that fast food can be nutritious, fresh, and cooked with at least some artistry. The owner of the chain is the chef at Cafe Annie's. Specialties at Café Express include a variety of salads, lively pasta dishes, juicy roast chicken, and various sandwiches. There are several items for children, including small burgers, which are sure to please. One location is in the basement of the Fine Arts Museum (the new building); other locations include 3200 Kirby Dr. (near the Village), 1422 W. Gray (in the River Oaks Shopping Center), 650 Main St. (downtown), and 1101 Uptown Park (just off Post Oak in the Galleria area).

that was true of all Tex-Mex restaurants before the rise of the fajita, which eventually pulled Tex-Mex into the orbit of the truly trendy. Loma Linda brings to mind those simpler times with its unselfconscious decoration and furniture and its utter lack of anything approaching trendiness. It also has an old-time 1930s tortilla maker specially designed to make the old-fashioned puffy tortillas that you always used to get when ordering chile con queso. The things to order here are, of course, the puffy chile con queso for an appetizer and the puffy beef tacos, the Texas-style enchiladas with chile gravy, and the combination dinners.

2111 Telephone Rd. ℂ 713/924-6074. Reservations not accepted. Main courses $6–$10; lunch specials $5.50–$6.50. AE, DC, DISC, MC, V. Daily 10am–10pm (until 11pm on weekends). Located 6 blocks off the Gulf Fwy. (I-45). Exit Telephone Rd. and turn north; it will be on your right.

MONTROSE/THE HEIGHTS
VERY EXPENSIVE
Mark's ✫✫✫ NEW AMERICAN   Mark Cox, a former chef at Tony's, has a good idea of the direction in which American cooking should be headed—fresh ingredients prepared in a manner that's new and creative while being hearty and satisfying. Mark's has a set menu that changes seasonally and a menu of daily specials. A representative sampling of dishes might include grilled shrimp on a bed of fennel, basil, and tomato with a crab risotto; bourbon-glazed pork with yams and an apple compote; roasted breast of chicken with Mississippi-style grits scented with white truffles; or lamb in a basil sauce with white-cheddar potatoes. The restaurant occupies an abandoned church on Westheimer; the main dining room is in the nave and the choir loft. Alongside the nave, the owners have built an eye-catching smaller dining room with Gothic rib vaulting.

1658 Westheimer. ℂ 713/523-3800. www.marks1658.com. Reservations recommended. Main courses $19–$40. AE, DC, DISC, MC, V. Mon–Fri 11am–2pm; Mon–Thurs 6–11pm; Fri–Sat 5:30pm–midnight; Sun 5–10pm.

EXPENSIVE
Backstreet Café ✫✫ NEW AMERICAN   Wonderful cooking, a good selection of wines, and excellent service make this place perennially popular, especially in good weather when diners flock to the tree-shaded patio. The starters are delicious creations, especially the lobster pot pie and the smoked corn crab cakes. Among the main courses, the meatloaf tower with mushroom gravy and garlic mashed potatoes warms my heart like nothing else and is a work of architectural splendor. A delicious lighter option would be the pecan-crusted chicken. Side dishes can be anything from corn pudding to fried green tomatoes. Dining areas include two upstairs rooms, one downstairs, and the patio. For dessert try the bread pudding, with macadamia nut brittle and vanilla ice cream (if you dare). Don't even try to park your car; let the valet do it.

1103 S. Shepherd. ℂ 713/521-2239. Reservations recommended. Main courses $15–$28. AE, DC, DISC, MC, V. Sun–Thurs 11am–10pm; Fri–Sat 11am–11pm. Despite the address, the restaurant is located 1 block east of Shepherd and 2 blocks north of W. Gray and the River Oaks Shopping Center, off McDuffie St.

Divino Restaurant & Wine Bar ✫✫ NORTHERN ITALIAN   Ten years ago such a place couldn't have existed in Houston—a neighborhood restaurant serving northern Italian and showcasing an elaborate wine list. That it has thrived is a testament not only to the cooking but to the changing palates of Houstonians. Divino's owner is a native who has lived in Italy for years and is passionate about the cooking. The menu mixes letter-perfect traditional renditions with dishes that blend tradition with personal inspiration. It includes some southern Italian as well. Wine is a big deal here; the restaurant has its own wine newsletter and even sells by the case at good prices. (*Tip:* If, after your meal, you feel like having something sweet and fattening, walk across the street to the Chocolate Bar and get some ice cream. This sweet shop makes some of the best ice cream I've had—several varieties of chocolate and a lemon that is irresistible.)

1830 W. Alabama St. ℂ 713/807-1123. Reservations recommended. Main courses $12–$25. AE, DISC, MC, V. Mon–Thurs 5:30–10pm; Fri–Sat 5:30–10:30pm.

Hugo's ★★★ MEXICAN   Chef Hugo Ortega offers up excellent interior Mexican food, often with a wonderful contemporary twist. For an appetizer try the tostadas or the *sopecitos* (small, thick handmade tortillas with toppings) or the lobster tacos. Main courses include duck in a *mole poblano* (the classic dark red, bittersweet sauce of the Mexican highlands) and a chile relleno with roasted chicken smothered in a *pipián* (a spicy sauce in a base of ground roasted pumpkin seeds). In addition, there's a seasonal menu. Chef Ortega has local sources for hard-to-get fresh ingredients, which, when available, become part of the offerings. For dessert, the specialty is the homemade Mexican hot chocolate, accompanied by small *churros* (the Spanish equivalent of donuts). These were delicious, but so were the margaritas, which, for me, also make an excellent dessert. The dining room is large and airy with comfortable furniture. There is a high ceiling made of pressed tin, part of the original building (1935), which was once a drugstore. Sometimes the noise reverberates a bit.

1602 Westheimer Rd. (at Mandell St.). © 713/524-7744. Reservations recommended. Main courses $13–$25. AE, DC, DISC, MC, V. Sun–Thurs 11am–10pm; Fri–Sat 11am–midnight.

Shade ★★ NEW AMERICAN   A strong current of thought in cooking these days believes that everything from everywhere should be in play. Critics of this position hold that in mixing techniques and ingredients from around the globe, you lose the moorings and character of place. I'm not so sure. Unlike that found in the long-established cuisines of the world, America has less tradition to follow and has always been about innovation and borrowing from others. What I find to be more alarming is the mindless use of disparate ingredients for the sake of notoriety or simply because our modern distribution network now makes it possible. Local celebrity chef Claire Smith is immune to these criticisms. Her cooking is purposeful and shows a distinctly American sensibility, and not some bowdlerized version of foreign cooking for local tastes. It is often new and inventive. And when it's not inventive, it's just plain good. The salads are fresh and well dressed, the soups are soul-satisfying, and the main courses show flash. The restaurant's decor also shows some flash—unabashedly modern, simple, and with a couple of playful references to 1960s Dada. Shade is in the Heights and is a pioneer of another sort in being the first to circumvent the neighborhood's 100-year-old code prohibiting the sale of drinks. Cheers!

250 W. 19th St. © 713/863-7500. Reservations recommended. Main courses $12–$26. AE, DISC, MC, V. Mon–Fri 11am–2:30pm and 5–10pm; Sat 9am–3pm and 5–10:30pm; Sun 9am–3pm and 5–9pm.

MODERATE

Baba Yega *(Finds* SANDWICHES/PASTA/VEGETARIAN   Set in a small bungalow on a side street off Westheimer, Baba Yega is one of the hippest places in the Montrose. The restaurant offers several small dining areas, all of which are agreeable, particularly the garden veranda in back. Next door is an herb shop that belongs to the owner, and, whenever possible, he cooks with his own herbs. The most popular lunch items are the sandwiches, of which there are several vegetarian choices. For dinner, the daily specials are what most people order, and these usually include at least one chicken and one fish dish. Tuesday is the Italian Special, a plate of pasta and a glass of wine.

2607 Grant St. © 713/522-0042. Reservations not accepted. Main courses $10–$16; sandwiches $7–$9. AE, DC, DISC, MC, V. Sun–Thurs 11am–10pm; Fri–Sat 11am–11pm.

INEXPENSIVE

Christian's Tailgate Grill and Bar *(Finds* BURGERS   I include this place not only because the burgers are really good, but also because it's a very Texas sort of place—a combination neighborhood bar and burger joint. Just west of the Heights, at the northeast corner of the intersection of Washington and I-10, Christian's is set in a large shack with a cement floor and cheap furniture. Catfish po' boys and Cajun fried chicken are also on the board. Happy hour runs all day Saturday, 5 to 8pm weekdays. It has a pool table and a couple of electronic games.

7340 Washington. © 713/864-9744. Burgers $4.50–$7. AE, DISC, MC, V. Mon–Fri 10am–9pm; Sat 11am–9pm.

La Mexicana Restaurant ★★ MEXICAN   Once a little Mexican grocery store, La Mexicana started serving tacos and gradually turned exclusively to the restaurant business. It's well known for delicious Mexican breakfasts such as *huevos a la mexicana* (eggs scrambled with onions, tomatoes, and serrano chiles) or *migas* (eggs cooked with fried tortilla strips)—both particularly good, as are their frijoles and the green *salsa de mesa*—and classic enchilada plates (red and green are good choices). Some dishes are *muy auténtico,* such as the *nopalitos en salsa chipotle* (cactus leaves cooked in chipotle chile sauce) or the tacos *de guisado de puerco* (pork stewed in dried chile sauce) or *de chicharrón en salsa verde* (pork cracklings in tomatillo sauce; one of my favorites, but not for everyone). Other dishes are Tex-Mex standbys, such as the fajitas and the combination plates. There's a choice of dining outside or inside.

1018 Fairview St. © 713/521-0963. www.lamexicanarestaurant.com. Reservations not accepted. Main courses $7–$14. AE, DC, DISC, MC, V. Daily 7am–11pm.

KIRBY DISTRICT
EXPENSIVE

Churrascos ★★ SOUTH AMERICAN/STEAKS   When this restaurant opened about 12 years ago, it caught on like a house afire. The owners have since opened another restaurant, Américas (p. 183). This has thinned the crowds somewhat, and fans of this place couldn't be happier. Churrascos is simpler than Américas. The main draw is the beef tenderloin butterflied, grilled, and served with chimichurri sauce, the garlicky Argentine condiment that always accompanies steak. Also very different for the Houston dining scene are the fried plantain chips served at every table, the Argentinean empanadas, the Cuban-style black-bean soup, and the Peruvian-style ceviche. Grilled vegetables come "family style" with every entree. For dessert, the restaurant is justifiably famous for its *tres leches* cake.

2055 Westheimer Rd. © 713/527-8300. www.cordua.com. Reservations recommended. Main courses $15–$28; lunch $8–$10. AE, DC, DISC, MC, V. Mon–Thurs 11am–10pm; Fri 11am–11pm; Sat 5–11pm.

Goode Company Texas Seafood SEAFOOD   Jim Goode, a local restaurateur, operates a few places on or just off Kirby Drive. He does a great job with local cooking, which is why I like to steer visitors here. This restaurant is my favorite place to get catfish fried in cornmeal, executed here to a Texas T. Lighter choices include the mesquite-grilled flounder or red snapper. Texas-style seafood is a lot like Southern seafood, but with some Mexican and Southwestern influences, such as grilling with mesquite wood, and using fresh chiles, such as in the Mexican seafood cocktail known as a *campechana.* Here it's usually made with shrimp and crawfish tails (depending on what's fresh). A *campechana* sauce is tomato based, like the American version of cocktail sauce, but gently spiked with green chile instead of horseradish, providing a nice, fresh piquancy, to which a little chopped avocado and some cilantro and onion are added. Gumbo and oyster po' boys are also on the menu.

2621 Westpark Dr. © 713/523-7154. www.goodecompany.com. Reservations not accepted. Main courses $12–$23. AE, DC, DISC, MC, V. Sun–Thurs 10am–10pm; Fri–Sat 10am–11pm.

Kids Family-Friendly Restaurants

Café Express (see "Fast Food a la Houston")   These restaurants offer miniature burgers that kids just love, while the parents can enjoy salads, roast
chicken, or a pasta.

James Coney Island Hot Dogs (see "Fast Food a la Houston")   What hot
dog place isn't popular with kids? But most of these restaurants are decorated in bright colors that make them especially attractive to the young,
and they offer kid specials.

Lupe Tortilla (see below)   This is a great place to go when the kids don't
feel like sitting still, and the parents want something more in the way of
real food than what kiddy places can offer. The fajitas are excellent. When
the weather is cooperating, the patio is perfect for a relaxing meal.

MODERATE

Lupe Tortilla *Kids* TEX-MEX   Don't let the silly name draw your attention away
from the important fact that this kid-friendly establishment offers the family a perfect
respite from shopping or sightseeing. While the kids burn off some excess energy on
the restaurant's playscape, the parents can relax at a table sipping one of the restaurant's excellent margaritas and choose from the menu's Tex-Mex offerings. Featured
are superb fajitas and other grilled specialties, such as the Three-Pepper Cheese Steak
or the milder Steak Lupe. There are nachos and chalupas and the like for kids, and,
for the adults . . . uh, did I mention the margaritas?

2414 Southwest Fwy. *©* 713/522-4420. Reservations not accepted. Main courses $8–$15. AE, MC, V. Sun–Thurs
11am–9pm; Fri–Sat 11am–10pm.

Madras Pavilion *☆☆* INDIAN VEGETARIAN   The way I see it, no one does vegetarian as well as the Indians, especially those of the south. They've had centuries of
practice and know what they're doing. As evidence, I would offer this restaurant—an
unassuming establishment tucked into a strip center on Kirby. It's a good choice as a
respite from steaks, fajitas, barbecue, and other Texas specialties. The food is mouthwatering, and there's plenty to choose from: curries, different flavored rices, delicacies
such as *masala dosai* (rice flour crepes filled with a deliciously spiced mixture of potatoes and onion) with or without chutney, *paneer* (cottage cheese curds usually cooked
in spinach), a full range of Indian bread, including the puffy *channa batura*, served
with chickpea curry, and a spicy pizzalike dish, *uthappam*. Most of these are spicy, but
there is also much to choose from that is mild. With such variety, you would do well
to go midday, when you can try a bit of everything from the lunch buffet ($8 on week-
days, $10 on weekends). Service can be slow.

3910 Kirby (1 block north of the Southwest Fwy., facing a parking lot on the north side of the building). *©* 713/
521-2617. Reservations not accepted. Main courses $6–$15. MC, V. Mon–Thurs 11:30am–3pm and 5:30–9:30pm;
Fri 11:30am–3pm and 5:30–10pm; Sat–Sun 11:30am–10pm.

Thai Bistro *☆☆* THAI   Houston is particularly rich in Thai restaurants, having
more than 70. This one is in a strip center along the Southwest Freeway, practically
next door to a taco joint, 100% Taquito, that I recommend below. You, the reader,

might suspect that I'm being lazy for listing two restaurants practically next door to each other, but if you go and taste the food, you'll see that I only have your best interests at heart. If you have an appetite, do yourself a favor and order the assorted appetizer platter. From there you can go in any number of directions: healthy (barbecued lemon grass tofu or lettuce wraps), spicy (blazing noodles), classic (pad Thai), or curry (Panang). These are all favorites. Also on the menu are some Vietnamese-style vermicelli dishes, which are there through historical accident. The restaurant used to be Vietnamese, and when the present owner bought the place, the neighborhood regulars wouldn't allow him to drop these dishes from the menu.

3241 Southwest Fwy. ⓒ 713/669-9375. Main courses $10–$16; lunch $7–$10. AE, DC, DISC, MC, V. Mon–Fri 11am–3pm and 5–10pm; Sat 11am–10:30pm; Sun 11am–9pm.

Thai Spice ⓡ ⓥⓐⓛⓤⓔ THAI   In the Rice Village there are three commendable Thai restaurants, each with its own loyal following. Of these, Thai Spice gets the nod, mostly because the service is friendlier and the dining area is roomier, more attractive, and better furnished, but also because the food is a particularly appealing interpretation of Thai that doesn't burn out your taste buds. The lunch buffet is worthy of special note for being more complete than in most other places. The dinner menu is well laid out and doesn't try to confuse you with options by listing the same basic dish four times. The spicy shrimp soup is good, and the Summer Palace is a great spicy option for a stir-fry. There are also several mild dishes, including a wonderfully simple grilled lemon grass chicken breast. All of the curries are worth ordering, and the pad Thai is excellent.

5117 Kelvin (at Dunstan). ⓒ 713/522-5100. www.thaispice.com. Main courses $8.50–$11; lunch buffet $7.95. AE, DC, DISC, MC, V. Mon–Sat 11am–2:30pm (lunch buffet) and 5–10pm; Sun 11:30am–3pm and 5–9pm.

INEXPENSIVE

Goode Company Texas Barbecue BARBECUE   Mr. Goode cooks up some great barbecue at this rickety joint on Kirby, 4 blocks south of the Southwest Freeway. To get great smoked flavor, he cooks with the greenest wood he can find. Especially tasty are the pork ribs and the brisket, but you can also get duck, chicken, and links. Order by the pound, the plate, or the sandwich. For dessert, the pecan pie is a must. Beer signs and country music on the jukebox set the scene.

5109 Kirby Dr. ⓒ 713/522-2530. Barbecue plates $7–$10. AE, DC, DISC, MC, V. Daily 11am–10pm.

Luling City Market BARBECUE   This is great barbecue served in a traditional setting, which for Texas barbecue joints means that any effort spent decorating appears, at least, as purely an afterthought and, at most, as the owner's misguided attempt to find a place for all the objets d'art that have been cluttering up his attic. This place follows the minimalist approach. Service is lunch counter style. I recommend the ribs and the sausage. At night, the quiet little bar fills up with regulars with whom you can chew the fat, mostly about sports.

4726 Richmond Ave. ⓒ 713/871-1903. Reservations not accepted. Barbecue plates $7.50–$9. AE, DC, DISC, MC, V. Mon–Sat 11am–9pm; Sun noon–7pm.

100% Taquito MEXICAN   The owner hails from Mexico City, where, more than anywhere else in Mexico, good *taquerías* (taco joints) are enshrined right up there with all that Mexicans hold dear. I count myself among the faithful, and I have tried to get Frommer's to send me off to write the definitive guide to *taquerías,* but no such luck. Tacos in Mexico are usually served on small, soft tortillas and sprinkled with a little fresh cilantro and onion. The traditional fillings might be prepared on a grill, a griddle, or in a stew pot. To explain a few terms: *al pastor* is pork that has been marinated in ancho chile, guajillo chile, annatto, and sour orange and served with a little grilled pineapple; *tinga* is pork or beef stewed in a chipotle sauce; and *barbacoa* is a simple style of Mexican barbecue. All are delicious, as are the *banderillas*: fried *taquitos* done up like the Mexican flag. Tacos are served in small orders of three. One order would be enough if you're just feeling peckish, two if you're hungry.

3245 Southwest Fwy. (℃) 713/665-2900. Orders of 3 tacos $3.25–$5. AE, DISC, MC, V. Daily 11am–10pm.

UPTOWN
VERY EXPENSIVE

Américas 🎔🎔 PAN-AMERICAN   This is a different sort of place to dine. From the over-the-top decor to the menu of dishes loosely inspired by the national cuisines of the New World, there is nothing ho-hum about dining here. On my first visit, I was a bit overwhelmed by it all, but on subsequent visits I've gotten quite comfortable with the place. When crowded, it's noisy, but the furniture is comfortable, and there are several large round booths that are fun. As with its sister restaurant, Churrasco's, one of the favorites here is the grilled tenderloin—always a good choice. But for something more inventive, try the *relleno,* a boneless pork loin stuffed with the masa of a tamal, topped with a grilled shrimp, and bathed in a butter sauce with a *hint* of habanero chile. Or perhaps the *chileno,* a broiled Chilean sea bass with sweet corn and *poblano* spoon bread.

1800 Post Oak Blvd. (℃) 713/961-1492. www.cordua.com. Reservations recommended. Main courses $18–$45. AE, DC, DISC, MC, V. Mon–Thurs 11am–10pm; Fri 11am–11pm; Sat 5–11pm.

Bistro Moderne 🎔🎔🎔 FRENCH   If I'm going to eat French food in Houston, I'm going to eat it here. Luxury hotels are vying with each other to lure talented chefs to Houston, making for great dining choices. In this case, the Hotel Derek persuaded a top French chef, Philippe Schmit, to come and employ his energies to create wonderful dishes and present them in surroundings that are sleek, modern, understated, and comfortable. The main dining area is in a long gallery just beyond an inviting bar. Perhaps the best-known dish is the delicious "crab bomb" made much the same way as the dessert *bombe,* with a rounded dome but made with an avocado purée instead of ice cream. Except for the bits of cilantro on the plate, it had all the appearance of a dessert with a glossy finish and a wonderful green color, more like mint than avocado. The main courses include both original and standards. The shrimp with saffron risotto with squid ink sauce was delicious. There's a lovely pork stuffed with apricots. If some of your party are conservative eaters, this place is a good choice, with sirloin, filet mignon, and roast chicken on the menu. The dessert menu would also please just about anyone, with its mix of retro and nouveau choices.

2525 W. Loop South. (℃) 713/297-4383. www.bistromoderne.com. Reservations recommended. Main courses $19–$36. AE, DC, MC, V. Mon–Thurs 11:30am–2:30pm and 5–10:30pm; Fri 11:30am–2:30pm and 5–11pm; Sat 5–11pm.

Cafe Annie 🎔🎔🎔 SOUTHWESTERN   Singing the praises of this restaurant makes me feel like nothing more than a member of the choir. Over the last 20 years, no restaurant in Houston has received more coverage, more acclaim, and more awards than Cafe Annie. If you're looking for *the* restaurant in Houston, and especially if you're on a fat expense account, this should be your choice. Those of us who aren't so fortunate can save money by going for lunch or ordering from the bar menu. One of the restaurant's signature dishes is the crabmeat tostadas, available on the dinner, lunch, and bar menus. These are wonderful compositions of fresh lump crabmeat, avocado, a little finely shredded cabbage, and a touch of piquancy. Delicious main courses include the cinnamon-roasted pheasant, the beef with *chile pasilla* sauce, or the red fish with pumpkinseed sauce. The tortilla soup is one of the perennial favorites on the menu. Everything I sampled has been delicious and different. The dining room is perfectly in character with the restaurant—nice and quiet, softly lit, with lots of dark woodwork.

1728 Post Oak Blvd. (just south of San Felipe). © **713/840-1111.** www.cafe-annie.com. Reservations recommended. Main courses $28–$45. AE, DC, DISC, MC, V. Mon 6:30–10pm; Tues–Fri 11:30am–2pm and 6:30–10pm; Sat 6:30–10:30pm.

MODERATE
Kenny & Ziggy's *Kids* DELI This is a good place to know if you're staying in the Uptown/Galleria area. Delis aren't common in Houston, and good ones are especially rare. This one is the real deal. It's smack dab in the middle of Uptown (in a strip center on the northeast corner of the intersection of Westheimer and Post Oak), and it offers the convenience of take-out that you can call in, and a full service restaurant. So, if you have an urge for an honest pastrami on rye, you won't be disappointed. There are many sandwiches to choose from and a variety of dinners, from corned beef and cabbage to Hungarian goulash to grilled snapper. Bulk deli items (meets, cheeses, lox) are sold by the pound.

2327 Post Oak Blvd. © **713/871-8883.** www.kennyandziggys.com. Sandwiches (served with 2 sides) $9–$16. Dinners $15–$18. MC, V. Mon–Fri 7am–9pm; Sat–Sun 9am–9pm.

5 Seeing the Sights

Because Houston isn't a major tourist destination, there isn't much in the way of tourism infrastructure except for the downtown visitor center. Most of the available resources are geared toward conventions and large groups, not independent travelers. From the visitor center, there is often a visitors' tour of downtown that looks at architecture, public sculpture, the tunnel system, and the view from the observation deck from the J.P. Morgan Tower, the tallest building in Houston.

THE TOP ATTRACTIONS
DOWNTOWN
Downtown Aquarium *Kids* In the northwest corner of downtown, a few blocks from the visitor center, is this aquarium/restaurant/amusement park complex. The major exhibit consists of several tanks in the main building displaying different aquatic ecosystems. These are nicely done, and lots of little tanks hold highly specialized species from places like the Amazon. There are also touch tanks and an exhibit of rare white tigers. Upstairs is a seafood restaurant where you can enjoy another large aquarium while you have a bite to eat. Outside the building, the main attraction is a large shark tank, which you view from a glass tunnel while seated in a miniature train. Among the rides are a Ferris wheel and a carousel. You can buy a 1-day pass or buy separate tickets for each attraction. The main exhibit takes about an hour; the train ride takes 10 minutes, with 2 to 3 minutes inside the glass tunnel.

410 Bagby St. © **713/223-3474.** www.downtownaquarium.com. Day pass $16. Daily 10am–10pm.

Downtown tunnel system There are 6 miles of tunnels below Houston's downtown; most of the system is private property. Along those corridors are restaurants, shops, and businesses of all varieties. You can get a map of the tunnels from the city's visitor center or you can take a guided tour if you schedule it in advance.

Accessible from the visitor center in city hall and all neighboring buildings, as well as most downtown hotels. Free admission. Mon–Fri 7am–6pm.

Heritage Society at Sam Houston Park A couple of blocks from Houston's visitor center is this park, which serves as a repository for eight of Houston's oldest houses and buildings, moved here from their original locations. The oldest dates from before Texas's independence; it's a small, simple cabin originally built close to where NASA is today. Another house was built by a freed slave in 1870. There's a church dating from 1892. The Heritage Society restored them to their original state and furnished them with pieces from the appropriate eras. The only way to see these buildings is by guided tour, which leaves every hour on the hour from the tour office at 1100 Bagby; it takes about 45 minutes. The guides are well informed and add a lot to a visit here. The Heritage Museum can be visited without taking the tour. It's free and features permanent exhibits on Texas history.

1100 Bagby. © 713/655-1912. www.heritagesociety.org. Tours $6 adults, $4 seniors and children ages 13–17, $2 children 6–12. Tues–Sat 10am–3pm; Sun 1–3pm.

EAST END & BEYOND

Battleship _Texas_ and San Jacinto Monument & Museum 🎃 _Kids_ On the San Jacinto Battleground in 1836, Texas won its independence from Mexico with a crushing surprise attack by the Texan forces, whose battle cry was "Remember the Alamo!" To commemorate that victory, civic leaders in 1936 built a towering obelisk as tall as the Washington Monument but topped with a Texas Lone Star. In the base of the monument is a small museum of Texas history with some interesting exhibits, such as one about the relatively unsung Texas hero, "Deaf" Smith, and a collection of watercolors of the Mexican War painted by Sam Chamberlain. There is also a small auditorium where you can watch a 35-minute documentary of the battle. If you would like to view some of the Port of Houston as well as the rest of the land for miles around, you can take the elevator up to the observation room in the top floor of the tower, which is more than 500 feet above the ground.

Across from the monument, in roughly the same place where the Texans began their advance, is the USS _Texas_. Built in 1914, before improvements in warplane technology made these large dreadnought battleships vulnerable, she is the last of her kind. Between the wars, the navy modernized the ship with antiaircraft and torpedo defenses, but it's still surprising that it survived World War II, having fought in both the Atlantic and the Pacific theaters. When you visit, you can clamber up to its small-caliber guns or onto the navigation bridge, inspect the crew's quarters and check out the engine room. Life on board was no picnic—the quarters were cramped and facilities were minimal—so it's interesting to learn that this ship was considered a lucky assignment. Plan on at least an hour to see the _Texas,_ and as much again for the monument.

3523 Battleground Rd. © 281/479-2431. www.tpwd.state.tx.us/park/sanjac. Battleship admission $5 adults, $4 seniors, $3 children ages 6–18; free admission to the monument and museum; observation room $3 adults, $2 children; movie $3.50 adults, $2.50 children. Daily 10am–5pm. Take the La Porte Fwy. (Tex. 225) east from Loop 610 east. For 15 miles you will pass large refineries and tank farms. (If tears well up in your eyes and your throat muscles begin to constrict involuntarily, you'll know you're headed in the right direction.) Exit Battleground Rd. (Tex.134) and turn left.

Houston Ship Channel 🎃 For those fortunate enough not to live among the industrial areas of the Texas Gulf Coast, the landscape of refineries and their intricate tangle of pipes, their forests of cooling towers and stacks, and their fields of tanks are as exotic as the Zanzibar coast. If you find this sort of thing intriguing, you can take a free boat ride on the M/V *Sam Houston,* which tours the upper 7 miles of the deep water channel. The boat dates from the 1950s and has a lovely cabin trimmed in mahogany as well as fore and aft observation decks. I hail from Houston but rarely have the opportunity to see the ship channel up close, and I enjoyed this trip. You should probably make reservations well in advance during the summer months when it is quite popular, though I'm told that the ship channel is best seen in cooler weather, when there is no risk of bad smells. The trip takes a total of 90 minutes, during which you will most likely see large container ships, tall grain elevators, tugs, and barges. If, after the trip, you want to see more of the channel, you can drive to the San Jacinto Battlefield, where the Battleship *Texas* is on display (see review above).

7300 Clinton Dr. at Gate 8. ② 713/670-2416. www.portofhouston.com. Free admission. Tues–Sun 10am and 2:30pm; no morning trips Sun or Thurs. Call for reservations. Closed Sept and holidays. Take the Gulf Fwy. south; get on Loop 610 east, which takes you over the ship channel; exit Clinton Dr. Turn right on Clinton (look for small green signs pointing the way); after a mile, you'll come to a traffic light and a sign reading PORT GATE 8. Turn left.

Kemah Boardwalk *(Kids*   Many visitors to Space Center Houston (see review below) will afterward go out for seafood at nearby Kemah, which is as touristy as the Houston area gets. It used to be a rustic shrimping port on Galveston Bay where you could buy some shrimp and a beer and sit by the dock on an afternoon to watch the shrimp boats come in. Most of the pier was washed away in 1984 by a hurricane, and in the 1990s it was bought by a developer who built the boardwalk, several restaurants, a hotel, and some touristy stores and attractions. The restaurants overlook the water; if you stroll down the boardwalk you'll pass every one. Pick the one that most appeals to you. Among the attractions is a 50,000-gallon, floor-to-ceiling aquarium housing more than 100 species of tropical fish in the Aquarium Restaurant.

Tex. 146, Kemah. ② 877/285-3624. www.kemahboardwalk.com.

The Orange Show *(★★ (Finds (Kids*   This may not be the "greatest show on earth," but it must be the quirkiest. In truth, it's not a show at all, at least not as we commonly understand the word. Rather, it's the life work of one man, former postman Jeff McKissack, who spent his last 25 years assembling a collection of found objects and building materials into an architectural collage that students of folk art call a "folk art environment." It stands in a quiet working-class neighborhood just off the Gulf Freeway, where it dares to be different. With the many flagpoles, spindles, wagon wheels, and wrought-iron birds rising up from behind its walls, it seems like an outpost for spontaneity in a wilderness of cookie-cutter ranch-style houses.

Inside, the viewer is presented with all kinds of curiosities: two small arenas, observation decks, a small museum, and lots of cheerful wrought-iron decoration and tile work. Inscriptions adorn the walls; many of these honor that best of all fruits, "The orange: a great gift to mankind." Seeing the whole thing takes less than an hour. Upon the death of Mr. McKissack, The Orange Show fell into decay until it was rescued by the Orange Show Foundation, located in the house across the street and a center for Houston's folk art world. It is the organizer of the Art Car Parade and the Art Car Ball (see "Texas Calendar of Events," in chapter 2). It is also the organizer of Eyeopener Tours (see "Organized Tours," later in this section). If you like folk art, consider purchasing their driving tour audiocassette of Houston's other folk art treasures. (The tape comes with a map.)

2401 Munger St. © 713/926-6368. www.orangeshow.org. Admission $1 adults, free for children younger than 12. Summer Wed–Fri 9am–1pm, Sat–Sun noon–5pm; spring and fall Sat–Sun noon–5pm. From downtown, take Gulf Fwy. Exit Telephone Rd. and make the 3rd right off the feeder road onto Munger (before you get to the Telephone Rd. intersection).

Space Center Houston ★★★ *Kids*   Space Center Houston is the visitor center for NASA's Johnson Space Center. It's the product of the joint efforts of NASA and Disney Imagineering. Easily the most popular attraction in the Houston area, there's nothing like it anywhere else in the world. You'll find plenty of exhibits and activities to interest both adults and children, and they do a great job of introducing the visitor to different aspects of space exploration. The center banks heavily on interactive displays and simulations on the one hand and actual access to the real thing on the other. For instance, the Feel of Space gallery simulates working in the frictionless environment of space by using an air-bearing floor (something like a giant air hockey table). Another simulator shows what it's like to land the lunar orbiter. For a direct experience of NASA, you can take the 1½-hour tram tour that takes you to, among other places, the International Space Station Assembly Building and NASA control center. You get to see things as they happen, especially interesting if there's a shuttle mission in progress. You might also see astronauts in training. And, on top of all this, Space Center Houston has the largest IMAX in Texas. Plan on staying here 3 to 4 hours.

1601 NASA Rd. 1, Clear Lake. © 281/244-2100. www.spacecenter.org. Admission (including tours and IMAX theater) $19 adults, $18 seniors, $15 children ages 4–11. June–July daily 10am–7pm; Aug–May Mon–Fri 10am–5pm, Sat–Sun 10am–6pm. Parking $5. The Space Center is about 25 miles from downtown Houston. Take the Gulf Fwy. to NASA Rd. 1, turn left, and go 3 miles.

SOUTH MAIN/MUSEUM DISTRICT

Children's Museum of Houston ★★ *Kids*   The goal behind the Children's Museum was to create a place where children can engage the world around them on their own terms, a place that will spark their imaginations, and where they will learn the joy of discovery. It is for children up to 12 years old, but even if you're without kids in tow, you might like to take a glance at the museum's fun exterior designed by Robert Venturi in association with Jackson & Ryan Architects of Houston. It's a playful send-up of the classical museum facade and is apt clothing for this institution that blurs the distinction between museum and playhouse.

The museum's staff seems to be very much in touch with the inner child. They have developed such fun interactive exhibits as Bubble Lab and Kid-TV, which gives kids the opportunity to imitate what they see on the tube while giving them a behind-the-scenes understanding of television production. Another exhibit re-creates the Mexican Indian village of Yalalag; another, called Tot Spot, focuses on the 6-month- to 3-year-old crowd, helping build motor skills through ingenious forms of play. The museum managers bring in many visitors and special shows; inquire about what they might be planning to do during your visit. The best time to go is in the afternoons when there is less probability of school trip crowds.

1500 Binz. © 713/522-1138. www.cmhouston.org. Admission $5 per person, free for children younger than 2, free family night Thurs 5–8pm. Tues–Sat 9am–5pm; Sun noon–5pm; Mon 9am–5pm summer only. The Children's Museum is on the same street as the Museum of Fine Arts, Houston (the street name changes from Bissonnet to Binz), 4 blocks to the east.

Contemporary Arts Museum   This silver-aluminum parallelogram, located on the corner of Montrose and Bissonnet cater-cornered to the Fine Arts Museum, presents temporary exhibitions of modern art and design. It has no permanent collection; what you might find here is purely the luck of the draw. When I go to the Museum of Fine Arts (see below), I always stick my head into the CAM to see what's going on because it's right across the street and it's free.

5216 Montrose Blvd. © **713/284-8250.** www.camh.org. Free admission. Tues–Sat 10am–5pm (Thurs until 9pm); Sun noon–5pm.

Hermann Park   This park has 545 acres of land and lies just beyond the Museum District, on the west side of South Main Street. The parkland is well wooded and has an 18-hole public golf course, picnic areas, and playscapes. Near the Houston Museum of Natural Science, which borders the park, is a garden center with beautiful rose gardens and a garden of aromatic herbs. Also in that vicinity is a Japanese garden and the Miller Outdoor Theater, which often holds free plays and musical performances.

Fannin St. at Hermann Park Dr.

Houston Museum of Natural Science 🌟🌟 *Kids*   This is quite a lot more than your average natural history museum. Yes, it has everything you expect (and some you might not): dinosaur skeletons, displays of Texas wildlife, a stunning gem and mineral collection, a Foucault pendulum, and exhibits on early cultures of the Americas, climatology, chemistry, and oil and gas exploration. But what gets most of the buzz is the miniature rainforest environment created in the Butterfly Center. You can walk among hundreds of living butterflies as they dance about in the steamy air amidst a small waterfall. As you enter, you pass through the insect zoo, which holds some fascinating and bizarre living specimens of beetles, spiders, and other bugs that you wouldn't necessarily want running around freely with you.

Also in the museum are an IMAX theater and a planetarium. The museum recently reequipped the planetarium with new computer animation projectors that enhance the quality of its programs about stars, galaxies, nebulas, and other astral bodies. In years past, the directors have assembled some great temporary exhibits, so ask about any that might be open during your visit. The museum occupies a corner of the Hermann Park about 3 blocks from the Museum of Fine Arts next to the equestrian statue of Sam Houston.

1 Hermann Circle Dr. © **713/639-4629.** www.hmns.org. Museum $9 adults, $7 seniors and children ages 3–11; Butterfly Center $8 adults, $6 seniors and children; IMAX tickets $8 adults, $7 seniors and children. Multivenue ticket packages available. General hours Mon–Sat 9am–5pm, Sun 11am–5pm; hours are more extended during summer; hours for Butterfly Center and IMAX can differ. Parking $5 (garage entrance on Caroline St.).

Houston Zoological Gardens *Kids*   Located within Hermann Park is this 50-acre zoo featuring a gorilla habitat, rare albino reptiles, a cat facility, a large aquarium, and vampire bats. Every few years the zoo builds a new facility for a portion of its residents. The Brown Education Center, open daily from 10am to 6pm, allows visitors to interact with the animals.

1513 N. MacGregor. © **713/533-6500.** www.houstonzoo.org. Admission $8.50 adults, $5 seniors, $4 children ages 2–11. Daily 9am–5pm (Apr–Oct until 6pm).

Museum of Fine Arts, Houston (MFAH) 🌟🌟🌟   This is by far the best and biggest public art museum in Texas. It's a wonderful testament to what a lot of oil money can do, and the manner in which it evolved tells something about the development of the city's sense of aesthetics. The original museum, built in the 1920s, was pure neoclassical—the attitude was that if Houston was to have a museum, it was to look like a museum. In the '50s, the MFAH directors hired Mies van der Rohe, the grand architect of the

---

Tips . . . But It's a Wet Heat

Hot and humid, Houston has earned the unofficial title of "Air-Conditioning Capital of the World." If you're unaccustomed to high humidity and its consequences (profuse sweating, bad-hair days), you might want to take it easy at first and work on acquiring some degree of philosophical acceptance. (I like to envision the Buddha.) One more thing—bopping around Houston in summertime means jumping from the frying pan into the freezer (to mangle yet another saying). You'll be repeatedly going from steamy outdoors into super-chilled shops, restaurants, and so on. The natives are used to it, but many visitors complain, to deaf ears, I might add.

International Style to build an addition. In the '70s, that addition received an addition, also designed by Mies. Both of these were bold statements of modern architecture—lots of glass and steel forming a light and airy space—but, unfortunately, not the kind of space that lends itself well for much of the museum's collection.

In the '90s, the museum's directors hired Spanish architect Rafael Moneo to design a building that would be a return to traditional galleries. It, the Audrey Jones Beck Building, is across South Main Street from the main building. (A tunnel connects the two; make a point of visiting it.) The new building aims at reconciling the boldness of modernism with the staid character of traditional design. Constructed with rich materials and designed on grand proportions, the building feels monumental. All the galleries on the second floor take advantage of interesting "roof lanterns," which allow Houston's plentiful natural light to enter in regulated amounts. The Beck building doubles MFAH's gallery space and allows the directors to attract first-rate traveling exhibitions. The museum's collection of more than 40,000 pieces is varied, but it is perhaps strongest in the area of Impressionist and post-Impressionist works, baroque and Renaissance art, and 19th- and 20th-century American art. There is also a fine collection of African tribal art, as well as ancient artwork from several civilizations.

Aside from the two gallery buildings, there is a large sculpture garden designed by Isamu Noguchi located across Bissonnet from the main building, and the Glassell School of Art, which can be seen just to the north of the sculpture garden. Look for a building made of a strangely reflective glass brick (another architectural pun). The museum also owns two collections of the decorative arts that are displayed in two mansions in the River Oaks area; see Bayou Bend (p. 191) and Rienzi (p. 191).

1001 Bissonnet St. ℂ 713/639-7300. www.mfah.org. Admission $7 adults, $3.50 seniors and children ages 6–18; free general admission every Thurs. Tues–Wed 10am–5pm; Thurs 10am–9pm; Fri–Sat 10am–7pm; Sun 12:15–7pm.

Museum of Health & Medical Science ★★★ *Kids*   We've all heard about what an amazing thing the human body is, but just how much do most of us know about its workings? This family museum will surprise most visitors with its extensive use of audio, video, holograms, and medical technology to provide a graphic view of human physiology.

Because of the Texas Medical Center, Houston has a large medical community, which has been the driving force behind the creation of this museum. With additional contributions from corporations and individual doctors, it has constructed an eye-catching interactive exhibition called the **Amazing Body Pavilion.** The exhibit is itself a metaphor for the body. Visitors enter through the mouth and proceed down the digestive tract learning about all the organs that process our food. (Children seem to think this is pretty cool.) The exhibit covers all the major organs in ways that provide lots of interaction for children, and explanatory text and monologues by little holographic figures are well written and manage to provide info that most adults will find interesting. Of course, with so many doctors involved, you can be sure that there will be some preaching about the need for a good diet and to avoid smoking, and don't expect the museum's snack bar to offer any junk food. But do check out the gift shop; it has an assortment of curious and intriguing items that you won't easily find elsewhere.

Seeing the exhibit takes a little more than an hour. *One other note:* You might want to ask at the front desk about the next scheduled organ dissection. When I was there, the organ of the month was the sheep brain; I opted to forego the performance.

1515 Hermann Dr. ⓒ 713/521-1515. www.mhms.org. Admission $6 adults, $4 seniors, $4 children ages 4–17; free admission Thurs 2–5pm. Tues–Sat 9am–5pm (Mon in summer); Sun noon–5pm. The museum is 1 block south of the Children's Museum.

MONTROSE
Menil Collection 🌟🌟🌟 *Value*   Here, on display in an unremarkable neighborhood near the University of St. Thomas, is one of the world's great private collections. Jean and Dominique de Menil arrived in Houston in the 1940s, fleeing the war in Europe. For more than 4 decades, they purchased and commissioned works of art; brought artists, architects, and academics to the city; organized groundbreaking exhibitions; and did much for Houston's art museums and for the art departments of Rice University and St. Thomas University. Their collection, especially the modern art, is vast, so much so that only a fifth of it can be exhibited in the museum at one time. The structure housing the collection was designed by Renzo Piano, who worked closely with Mrs. de Menil. It's graceful and personable and doesn't seek to impress the visitor or impose itself on the collection. In these qualities, it's the physical embodiment of Mrs. de Menil's ideas about experiencing art. When you walk into the museum, there is nothing between you and the art—no grand lobby with marble stairway, no large banners or gift shop vying for attention, no tickets to buy, no tape-recorded tours. Viewing the art becomes a direct and personal experience.

The Menil Collection is concentrated in four areas: antiquity, Byzantine and medieval, tribal art, and 20th century. This may seem an incongruous mix, but, strangely enough, it holds together. The collectors never intended to gather up the most representative of a period; they simply followed their own tastes, which were modern. And one interesting consequence of this fact (intended or not) is that, in walking through these galleries one right after another, the viewer gradually discerns a universality in some modern art that connects it all the way back to antiquity and across the boundaries of Western culture to the tribal peoples of other continents.

In addition to the main museum, four satellite buildings form a museum campus. One of these satellite buildings is the much-talked-about **Rothko Chapel,** with its 14 brooding paintings by Mark Rothko, created specifically for this installation and the last works before the artist's death. In front of the chapel stands Barnett Newman's *Broken Obelisk.* A block south of the Rothko Chapel is the **Byzantine Fresco Chapel Museum,** which is worth seeing as much for the building that houses them (designed by François de Menil, son of Jean and Dominique) as for the frescoes themselves, which were ransomed from international art thieves. Across the street from the main museum, in a building also designed by Renzo Piano, is a permanent exhibition of the works of Cy Twombly, which, though perhaps difficult to approach, are easy to view because of the gallery's exquisite light. It lends a luminous quality to the large artworks, and just being in the place somehow livens one's spirits. Finally, **Richmond Hall,** 2 blocks south of the campus, holds an installation by neon light artist Don Flavin.

1515 Sul Ross St. ℂ **713/525-9400.** www.menil.org. Free admission. Wed–Sun 11am–7pm.

KIRBY DISTRICT

Bayou Bend ✮✮ Ima Hogg was the daughter of Gov. Jim Hogg, a man who obviously had a cruel sense of humor. Miss Hogg, however, did not grow up shy and self-effacing. Long after the governor was dead, she was a power to be reckoned with in local affairs and did much to keep the chicanery in city hall to a minimum. Her mansion, Bayou Bend, was built in the 1920s by Houston's most prominent architect, John F. Staub. It holds in its 28 rooms a treasure trove of American furniture, paintings, and decorative objects dating from Colonial times to about 1870, and is set amid 14 acres of beautifully tended gardens in a variety of styles. This is a must-see for antiques collectors and gardeners.

Part of the Museum of Fine Arts, the collection can be seen by self-guided audio tour or by guided tour, for which you must make reservations. I prefer the guided tour, mostly because I like to ask questions. It takes 90 minutes and costs the same as the audio tour. Guided tours leave every 15 minutes. You can see the gardens on your own. Bayou Bend is on the backside of River Oaks, but is unapproachable from the main entrance to the neighborhood. The only way to get there is to go down Memorial Drive, which follows the north shore of Buffalo Bayou, and then turn left onto Westcott to enter the grounds.

1 Westcott St. ℂ **713/639-7750.** www.mfah.org/bayoubend. Admission (includes audio tour) $10 adults, $8.50 seniors, $5 youths ages 11–18. Tues–Fri 10am–5pm; Sat–Sun 1–5pm. Reservations required for guided tour.

Rienzi In a 1950s River Oaks mansion designed by John F. Staub, the Museum of Fine Arts displays its collection of European decorative arts. Most of the collection predates 1800. Both the house and the collection were donated by the family that lived here. This museum will be of most interest to collectors of English porcelain and of no interest to children. Call for a tour. On Sundays you can take a self-guided tour, from 1 to 4pm.

1406 Kirby Dr. ℂ **713/639-7800.** www.mfah.org/rienzi. Admission $6 adults, $4 seniors. Mon and Thurs–Sat 10am–4pm; Sun 1–4pm. Reservations required.

FARTHER AFIELD

George Ranch Historical Park *Kids* Experience the life of four generations of a Texas family on this 400-acre outdoor museum, a working cattle ranch. Wander through a restored 1820s pioneer farm, an 1880s Victorian mansion, an 1890s cowboy encampment, and a 1930s ranch house. Savor Victorian-style tea on the porch of an 1890s mansion, or sit around the campfire with cowboys during a roundup and watch crafts demonstrations such as rope twisting. Picnic areas are provided. Plan to spend a half-day here.

10215 FM 762, Richmond. ℂ **281/343-0218.** www.georgeranch.org. Admission $9 adults, $8 seniors 62 and older, $5 children ages 5–15. Daily 9am–5pm. Take the Southwest Fwy. (Tex. 59 south); before getting to the town of Richmond, exit FM Hwy. 762 and go 6 miles south.

National Museum of Funeral History Do you give much thought to how you would like to be remembered once you've shuffled off this mortal coil? Or perhaps your thoughts just naturally drift toward things funereal? If so, then this private museum is the thing for you. Its owner, Service Corporation International, is the largest funeral company in the United States, and it has obviously been at pains to assemble the nation's largest collection of funeral memorabilia. The exhibits include a restored horse-drawn hearse, antique automobile hearses, and a 1916 Packard funeral bus. You can see memorabilia and trivia from the funerals of many famous people, including Martin Luther King, Jr., John Wayne, Elvis, Abraham Lincoln, JFK, Nixon, and many more. Other attractions include a full-size replica of King Tut's sarcophagus.

415 Barren Springs (north Houston, near airport). © 281/876-3063. www.nmfh.org. Admission $6 adults, $5 seniors and veterans, $3 children younger than 12, free for children younger than 3. Mon–Fri 10am–4pm; Sat–Sun noon–4pm.

Six Flags SplashTown *(Kids)* A 45-minute drive from downtown, SplashTown holds special events and live entertainment throughout the season. It gets really crowded here, mainly with kids from northern Houston suburbs and The Woodlands.

Northbound I-45 at Louetts Rd., Spring. © 281/355-3300. www.sixflags.com. $33 admission, $26 children less than 48 in. Daily 11am–9pm during summer months. Hours vary; call or check website. Follow I-45 north toward Dallas; take Exit 69-A.

ESPECIALLY FOR KIDS

As a parent can quickly grasp, Houston is kid-friendly. Easily half of the above-mentioned attractions are geared for kids or have a large component especially suitable for them.

A tour of southeast Houston will take you to **The Orange Show,** with which young kids display an almost instinctual connection; the boat trip on the **Ship Channel;** a visit to the **Battleship *Texas;*** and the wonders of **Space Center Houston.** After that there's a visit to the boardwalk in **Kemah** or a trip to the **beach** or to **Moody Gardens** in Galveston (see "Galveston" in chapter 6).

South of downtown you have the Museum District, which includes the **Children's Museum,** the **Houston Museum of Natural Science,** and the **Museum of Health & Medical Science.** And, of course, there's **Houston Zoological Gardens,** which has a special children's zoo that explores the different ecological zones of Texas. To the north is **SplashTown,** a water park, and to the southwest is the **George Ranch Historical Park** for kids interested in cowboys and the Old West.

ORGANIZED TOURS

If you'd like a bus tour of the city to help you get your bearings, you're out of luck. Companies such as Gray Line offer tours only to conventions and visiting groups, not the general public. There is, however, a different kind of tour that can introduce you to what makes Houston unique. If you're planning to be in Houston during the second weekend of the month, you might be able to sign up for one of the offbeat tours offered by **Eyeopener Tours.** Part of the Orange Show Foundation, in some months they put together a tour that focuses on a particularly interesting aspect of the city. Transportation by charter bus, snacks, and drinks are included in the price (usually around $40). Past tours have included folk art sites of the city, places of worship, architectural highlights, architectural lowlights, blues centers, and ethnic markets. Most of those who participate are resident Houstonians who want to learn about an unknown part of the city. Eyeopener Tours also sells an audiocassette and map for a self-guided tour of Houston's folk art environments. This is a good offering if you're pretty good at following directions and working with a map. For information, call © 713/926-6368 or check www.orangeshow.org/eyeopener.

The other option is to hire a guide. You can find one through the Web page of Houston's **tour guide association** (www.ptgah.org). One of the founding members, Sandra Lord, operates a tour agency called **Discover Houston Tours** (© 713/222-9255; www.discoverhoustontours.com). In addition to individual guide services, it offers some regularly scheduled walking tours of downtown and other places and the occasional special-interest tour that people can sign up for.

6 Sports & Outdoor Activities

OUTDOOR FUN

BIKING, JOGGING & WALKING   By far the most popular jogging and walking track is in **Memorial Park.** This is a large and beautiful park clothed in pine trees along Buffalo Bayou west of downtown. It's easy to reach; take Memorial Drive, which follows the north bank of Buffalo Bayou, from downtown to the park. It can be very crowded. There is a lovely hike and bike trail along the banks of **Buffalo Bayou** from North Shepherd to downtown. It runs along both banks of the bayou for 1.5 miles, so you can run a 3-mile loop. It offers lovely vistas of the downtown skyline and is decorated with numerous sculptures that can be both fun and interesting (and it takes you right into the Theater District). During the day it's fine, but I wouldn't advise venturing along the bayou at night. To rent a bike in this area, see **West End Bicycles** at 5427 Blossom (© 713/861-2271). They can set you up and give you information about good rides.

A 10-mile hike and bike trail runs along the banks of **Brays Bayou** from Hermann Park through the Medical Center, where it goes under South Main Street then heads southwest almost all the way to Beltway 8.

GOLF   The easiest way to make it out onto the links is to contact **Golf Guys** (© 800/470-9634; www.golfguys.net) before you come to town. These people will consult with you about the local courses, help you choose one, and reserve a tee time for no more than it would cost you to do it yourself.

Houston proper has public golf courses at most of the city's biggest parks, but with the exception of the Memorial Park Golf Course, the best public courses are outside the city. Probably the best public course (and one of the most difficult) in the area is the **Tournament Players Course at the Woodlands,** located 25 miles north of Houston in The Woodlands (© 281/364-6440). Greens fees range from $95 to $125; tee times must be made at least 3 days in advance. One of the loveliest and best-regarded courses in the area is the **Longwood Golf Club** (© 281/373-4100; www.longwood gc.com), 13300 Longwood Trace in Cypress, at the northwest edge of Houston; to get there, take Tex. 290 (45 min. from downtown). Fees are $29 to $69 and include cart; tee times should be reserved 7 days in advance. Another course that a lot of people talk about is **Tour 18 Houston** (© 281/540-1818), which copies 18 of the greatest holes in golf. The course is at 3102 FM 1960 East in Humble, about 12 miles north of Houston and about 35 minutes from downtown. Greens fees are $40 to $80; reservations can be made 30 days in advance.

In town are some municipal courses that are cheap, but somewhat tricky to get tee times for. The **Memorial Park Golf Course** (© 713/862-4033 or www.memorial parkgolf.com to reserve a tee time) is the most enjoyable. Greens fees are $37 to $48. **Hermann Park's golf course** (© 713/526-0077) is centrally located, with greens fees ranging from $37 to $48. At both the Memorial Park and Hermann Park courses, there is an extra $10 to $15 fee for reservations more than 3 days in advance.

TENNIS   Of course, the best strategy to get some tennis in is to stay at a hotel with courts. **Memorial Park** has some of the best of the public courses; make reservations well in advance by calling ℂ **713/867-0440.**

SPECTATOR SPORTS

If you're in Houston and decide on the spur of the moment to try to get tickets to a game, you can call **Ticket Stop,** 5925 Kirby Dr. #D (ℂ **713/526-8889**), a private ticket agency. They charge extra for the tickets, so it's best to buy direct or in advance if possible.

BASEBALL   **Houston Astros** fans enjoy the indoor/outdoor downtown stadium, Minute Maid Field. Its retractable roof is open mostly in the early part of the season before the weather gets too hot. With a little planning, tickets aren't hard to come by; call ℂ **877/9-ASTROS,** or visit www.astros.com.

BASKETBALL   The **Houston Rockets** (www.nba.com/rockets) and **Comets** (www.wnba.com/comets) play at the new Toyota Center. It's downtown at 1510 Polk St., just south of the convention center and baseball park. Both the men's and the women's teams are popular, and tickets must be purchased well in advance (ℂ **713/ 627-3865** or 713/627-9622).

FOOTBALL   The **Houston Texans** play host to opponents at high-tech Reliant Stadium. It's located off South Main, not far from the Medical Center. For information and/or tickets, call ℂ **832/667-2000,** or check out www.houstontexans.com.

GOLF TOURNAMENTS   The **Shell Houston Open** is held in late March or early April. For information and tickets, call ℂ **281/454-7000** or go to www.shellhouston open.com.

RODEO   Houstonians go all out "Western" for a couple of weeks in early March, when the **Houston Livestock Show and Rodeo** is held. Billed as the largest of all rodeos, it includes the usual events such as bull riding and calf roping as well as performances by famous country artists. It is now held in Reliant Stadium. Call ℂ **832/ 667-1000,** or go to www.hlsr.com for more information. For tickets, call **Ticketmaster** at ℂ **713/629-3700.**

7 Shopping

If you're anywhere in Houston, you probably aren't far from a mall, of which there are many more than can be mentioned here. They're usually located at or near an intersection of a freeway with the Loop or Beltway 8 or other major artery. These are good for general shopping, but hold little of interest for most visitors. A different story is the outlet malls, the principal one being **Katy Mills** out at the far western boundary of Houston, in the town of Katy. Take the Katy Freeway (I-10 west) until you spot the signs; the drive is about 25 miles. This mall is a mammoth collection of about 200 factory outlet stores that offer a large selection of merchandise at discount prices. The size of the discounts varies; some are good deals. There are also restaurants and a large movie theater present.

GREAT SHOPPING AREAS

Whether you're a purposeful shopper or a last-minute accidental one, you'll need to know something about the shopping terrain of Houston. Of course, the main shopping area in Houston is Uptown, but other areas have a diversity of offerings that might prove to be just what you're looking for.

DOWNTOWN

Foley's, the oldest of Houston's department stores, is now a **Macy's.** The original store on Main Street at Lamar is still a popular shopping destination ((C) **713/405-7035**). It's a large five-story building that occupies an entire block. It carries several lines of expensive clothing and perfumes as well as some moderately priced ones. The other happy shopping ground downtown is **The Park Shops,** 1200 McKinney, across the street from the Four Seasons Hotel ((C) **713/759-1442**). It's a group of about 40 small stores, mostly boutiques and specialty shops.

EAST END

Just the other side of the freeway from the George Brown Convention Center is a commercial **Chinatown,** where you can find all kinds of goods imported from across Asia. Furniture, foods, curios—you can browse your way through a number of little import stores, all within a 4-block area, between Dowling on the east, Chartreuse on the west, Rusk on the north, and Dallas on the south.

MONTROSE/THE HEIGHTS

Along Westheimer from Woodhead to Mandell you'll find several antiques and junk shops that are perfect for the leisurely shopper who's out to find a diamond in the rough. If after browsing through these you haven't had your fill, a grouping of similar stores can be found on 19th Street in the Heights. In these dozen or so stores, merchandise is set down just about anywhere the owners can find a place for it, and dusting is a once-in-a-while practice. This is for bargain hunters. One Latin American folk art shop called **Casa Ramírez,** 239 W. 19th St. ((C) **713/880-2420**), displays a panoramic collection of Mexican folk art from across the country. (For the more discriminating antiques stores, go to the Kirby District.) Don't ever accept the first price you're offered at these places—they almost always will lower the price.

Also along Westheimer are a number of vintage clothing stores that offer some entertaining shopping. North of Westheimer, on West Gray where it intersects with Shepherd, a whole different sort of shopping awaits at the **River Oaks Shopping Center.** This is Houston's oldest shopping center. It's 2 blocks long and extends down both sides of West Gray in white-and-black Art Deco. It's a chic collection of galleries, boutiques, antiques shops, and specialty stores as well as some fine restaurants and an art cinema.

KIRBY DISTRICT

Kirby is more uniformly upscale than the Montrose. Where it begins by Westheimer there are a couple of strip malls, the largest of which is **Highland Village,** 4000 Westheimer ((C) **713/850-3100**). Highland Village, like so much of the retail business in this part of town, is aimed at the upper-middle-class shopper with such stores as Williams-Sonoma and Pottery Barn and a few one-of-a-kind boutiques. From this part of Kirby Drive to where it passes the Rice Village is a section known informally as Gallery Row, with a mix of galleries, designer showrooms, and shops of antiques and special furnishings. Finally there's the **Village,** a 16-block neighborhood of small shops now mixed with outlets from high-dollar national retailers. A few of the small shops are survivors from simpler times that are now a bit at odds with their new environment of day spas, expensive shoe stores, and famous designer boutiques. There is also a wide variety of restaurants to choose from in the Village when it's time to take a break from browsing.

UPTOWN

The **Galleria,** 5075 Westheimer (© **713/622-0663**), occupies a long stretch of land along Westheimer and Post Oak. It has 320 stores that include big department stores such as Saks Fifth Avenue, Lord & Taylor, Neiman Marcus, and Nordstrom and small designer retailers such as Gucci, Emporio Armani, and Dolce & Gabbana. Across Westheimer from the Galleria is another shopping center called **Centre at Post Oak.** If you're looking for the finest in Western wear, go to **Pinto Ranch,** 1717 Post Oak Blvd. (© **713/333-7900;** www.pintoranch.com). This store sells the best in clothing, boots, belt buckles, hats, and saddles.

SOUTHWEST

In southwest Houston just beyond the Loop is where the Asian bazaar meets American suburb. I find the area fascinating. This is simultaneously adventure shopping and an exploration into the brave new world of postmodern America. First, drive down **Harwin Drive** between Fondren and Gessner. You will see store after store and strip mall after strip mall selling jewelry, designer clothes, sunglasses, perfumes, furniture, luggage, and handbags. Most of the stores are run by Indian, Pakistani, Chinese, and Thai shopkeepers, but other cultures are represented, too. Occasionally one will get raided for selling designer knock-offs. Everything is said to be at bargain-basement rates, but buyer beware. What I like the best are the import stores where you're never sure what you'll find. Farther out, on **Bellaire Boulevard** in the middle of a large commercial Chinatown, is an all-Chinese mall, where you can get just about anything Chinese, including tapes and CDs, books, food and cooking items, of course, and wonderful knickknacks.

8 Houston After Dark

THE PERFORMING ARTS

For fans of the performing arts, Houston is fertile ground. Few cities in the country can equal it in the quality of its resident orchestra, opera, ballet, and theater companies. In addition, there are several organizations that bring talented artists and companies here from around the country and the world, presenting everything from Broadway shows to Argentine tango groups to string quartets. Tickets aren't usually discounted for the opera, ballet, or symphony, but you should ask anyway. For information about performances, visit **www.houston-guide.com** or the websites of the various organizations listed below.

The symphony, the ballet, the opera, and the Alley Theatre (the city's largest and oldest theater company), all hold their performances in the theater district downtown. The opera and the ballet share the **Wortham Center,** 500 Texas Ave. (© **713/237-1439**); the symphony plays a block away at **Jones Hall,** 615 Louisiana St. (© **713/227-3974**); and the **Alley Theatre** is one of those rare companies that actually owns its own theater, located at 615 Texas Ave. (© **713/228-8421**), cater-cornered from the symphony. Also in the theater district is **Hobby Center for the Performing Arts,** 800 Bagby (© **713/315-2400**), which is shared by the Society for Performing Arts and Theater Under the Stars.

The **Society for the Performing Arts (SPA),** 615 Louisiana St. (box office © **713/227-4772;** www.spahouston.org), is a nonprofit organization that brings to Houston distinguished dance companies, jazz bands, theater productions, and soloists. Within SPA, there's a program called the Broadway Series, which brings popular productions from Broadway and London's West End. The organization uses Jones Hall, the Wortham Center, and the Hobby Center.

Following are brief descriptions of the principal organizations; there are many more, especially independent theater companies that present several plays a year.

CLASSICAL MUSIC, OPERA & BALLET

The **Houston Symphony** (© 713/224-7575; www.houstonsymphony.org) is the city's oldest performing arts organization. Its season is from September to May, during which it holds about 100 concerts in Jones Hall. The classical series usually contains a number of newer compositions with visits by several guest conductors and soloists from around the world. There is also a pops series and a chamber music series, which often holds its performances at Rice University.

Da Camera of Houston (© 713/524-5050; www.dacamera.com) brings classical and jazz chamber music orchestras to the city and holds concerts either at the Wortham or in the lobby of the Menil Collection. You can buy tickets from the box office at 1427 Branard St. in the Montrose area.

The nationally acclaimed **Houston Grand Opera** is the fifth-largest opera company in the United States. Known for being innovative and premiering new operas such as *Nixon in China,* its productions of classical works are brilliant visual affairs. The opera season is from October to May. For tickets and information go to the Wortham Center box office at 550 Prairie St. during regular business hours, or buy online at www.houstongrandopera.org.

The **Houston Ballet** (© 713/227-2787; www.houstonballet.org) has garnered enormous critical acclaim from across the country. A lot of the credit belongs to director Ben Stevenson, who came to Houston more than 25 years ago under the condition that the company create its own school to teach dance as Stevenson believed it should be taught. This school, the Houston Ballet Academy, now supplies the company with 90% of its dancers, and its graduates dance in many other top ballet companies. The company tours a great deal but manages around 80 performances a year at the Wortham Center in Houston. You can buy tickets over the phone or at their website.

THEATER

The **Alley Theatre,** 615 Texas Ave. (© 713/228-8421; www.alleytheatre.org), has won many awards for its productions. Its home holds a large theater and an arena theater, and during the year the company uses both to stage about 10 different productions, ranging from Shakespeare to Stoppard and even a musical or two. Ask about half-price tickets for sale the day of the show for weekday and Sunday performances. Pay-what-you-can-days are sometimes offered, but you have to show up in person to buy the tickets. Box office hours are Monday through Saturday from 10am to 6:30pm and Sunday from noon to 6:30pm.

Theatre Under The Stars, 800 Bagby (© 713/558-8887; www.tuts.org), specializes in musicals that it either brings to town or produces itself, averaging 200 performances annually. The organization got its name from having first worked at Miller Outdoor Theater in Hermann Park. It uses the new Hobby Center for the Performing Arts.

The **Ensemble Theatre,** 3335 Main St. (© 713/520-0055; www.ensemblehouston.com), is the city's largest black theater company. Founded in 1976, the Ensemble has grown from a band of strolling players into a resident professional company of 40 actors and eight directors. Their specialty is African-American and experimental theater.

THE CLUB & MUSIC SCENE

Having a night on the town in Houston doesn't require a lot of planning, but pick up a copy of the *Houston Press,* the free weekly that you can find at many restaurants and shops. It provides a good rundown of what musical and comedy acts are in town, and it includes a lot of advertising from the clubs. There's also the daily paper, the *Chronicle,* which has a well-organized entertainment section, and a pullout published on Thursdays. If you want to know what's going on in the clubs before you get to Houston, try their websites, **www.houstonpress.com** and **www.houstonchronicle.com**.

In general, the most popular locations for nightspots are the following: downtown, around the theater district and Old Market Square; in the Montrose area; and south of the Galleria along Richmond Avenue (called the Richmond Strip). There are enough clubs in these places that you can move from one to another quickly and easily until you find something you like.

MEGACLUBS

In the theater district in downtown Houston, a developer has converted the old convention center into a complex of restaurants, clubs, bars, and a movie theater. It's called **Bayou Place** (© 713/227-0957) and is located at 500 Texas Ave. It houses the **Verizon Wireless Theater,** which usually has live rock or jazz acts or comedy (© 713/230-1666; www.verizonwirelesstheater.com); the **Hard Rock Cafe** (© 713/227-1392), with some live acts on the weekends; and **Slick Willie's** (© 713/225-1277), a billiards club. Also, there are a few video and dance bars with canned music that are very popular with a younger crowd. The movie theater is called **Angelika Film Center and Café** (© 713/225-5232), which is a popular place to hang out in the evening before going clubbing or to a concert.

ROCK

One of the best venues for catching live rock acts is the old Houston institution known as **Fitzgerald's,** 2706 White Oak (© **713/862-3838**). It occupies an old Polish dance hall near the Heights neighborhood and gets talented local and touring bands. Look for their advertisement in the *Houston Press* to see who's playing while you're in town and to check ticket prices.

For alternative rock acts in a suitably grungy place, go to the **Engine Room** (© **713/654-7846**). It's in the southeast part of downtown at 1515 Pease near the intersection with La Branch. This club gets a mostly 20-something clientele, which comes to hear bands that are as far away from pop as they can get.

JAZZ

To hear some jazz, your best bet is one of two club/restaurants downtown that are fairly similar and close by each other. If you're not wild about the band at one, you can walk over to the other. The more formal and expensive one is in the old Rice Hotel and is called **Sambuca Jazz Café,** 909 Texas Ave. (© **713/224-5299**). It gets a dressed-up crowd and lines up some talented bands. The **Red Cat Jazz Café** is at 924 Congress (© **713/226-7870**), 3 blocks away. I heard a great band here playing interesting arrangements of bebop standards. Both cafes require a minimum consumption depending on the night of the week and what band is playing.

Another option is to check out some swing band music at **Scott Gertner's Skybar** (© **713/520-9688**) in the Montrose area. It's on the top floor of a 10-story building at the corner of Montrose and Hawthorne at 3400 Montrose Blvd. There are often guest bands playing other varieties of jazz. The club has a dance floor and a rooftop terrace with a great view.

BLUES

Try the **Big Easy Social and Pleasure Club,** 5731 Kirby Dr. (© 713/523-9999), in the Rice Village. This club lines up a lot of local blues talent that is uncommonly good, as well as touring zydeco acts. The clientele is a real mix of everything from yuppies to bikers. Admission can be anywhere between $5 and $15, depending upon the act.

FOLK & ACOUSTIC

Anderson Fair, 2007 Grant (© 713/528-8576), is the place to play if you're a folk singer. The club is a survivor from the 1960s, and looks every bit the product of its age. In its many years it has nurtured several folk artists who went on to become big names in folk, including Nancy Griffith. That it opens only Fridays and Saturdays only adds to its aura of counterculture. People of all ages hang out here, though there are a lot of former hippies. It's located a block off Montrose, behind the Montrose Art Supply building.

Another folk and bluegrass institution in Houston is **McGonigel's Mucky Duck** (© 713/528-5999). It offers pub grub and burgers, wine and beer, and live music every night (except Sun, when it's closed). Wednesday Irish jam sessions are free, as are Mondays. The club is at 2425 Norfolk, near Kirby Drive where it intersects the Southwest Freeway.

COUNTRY & WESTERN

Blanco's (© 713/439-0072) is a Texas-style honky-tonk that packs 'em in Mondays through Fridays, attracting all sorts, from River Oaks types to tool pushers. Lots of good Texas bands like to play here, so it's a good opportunity to see a well-known band in a small venue. There's a midsize dance floor. Monday through Wednesday is open-mic night, usually with one or another local band. Thursday and Friday offer live music, and the club is closed on Saturdays for private parties. It's located at 3406 W. Alabama, between Kirby Drive and Buffalo Speedway. When there's live music, the cover ranges from $5 to $15.

THE BAR SCENE

La Carafe, 813 Congress (© 713/229-9399), has been around for ages, and the small two-story brick building it occupies even longer. In fact, it is the oldest commercial building in the city and sits slightly askew on a tiny lot facing Old Market Square. Its jukebox is something of a relic, too, with the most eclectic mix possible and some obscure choices. The clientele is mostly older downtowners who were here before the resurgence, office types, in-line skaters, and reporters from the *Chronicle*. For sheer character, no place can beat it.

Another bar with a unique flavor is **Marfreless,** 2006 Peden (© 713/528-0083). This is the darkest bar I've ever been in. The background music is always classical, and the ambience is understated. Little alcoves here and there are considered romantic. The only trouble is finding the bar itself. It's in the River Oaks Shopping Center on West Gray. If you stand facing the River Oaks Theater, walk left then make a right into the parking lot. Look for an unmarked door under a metal stairway.

GAY & LESBIAN NIGHTLIFE

Most of Houston's gay nightlife centers on the Montrose area, where you'll find more than a dozen gay bars and clubs mostly along lower Westheimer Road and Pacific Street. For current news, pick up a copy of *Houston Voice*.

For a large and popular dance club, go to **Rich's,** 2401 San Jacinto (© **713/759-9606**), in the downtown area. Rich's gets a mixed crowd that's mostly gay men and women. It's noted for its lights and decorations and a large dance floor with a mezzanine level. It's very popular on Saturdays. For something more low-key, try **EJ's,** 2517 Ralph (© **713/527-9071**), in the Montrose area. It's just north of the 2500 block of Westheimer. Gay men of all ages come for drinks and perhaps a game of pool. There's also a dance floor, and a small stage for the occasional drag show.

9 Side Trips to East Texas

PINEY WOODS & BIG THICKET NATIONAL PRESERVE

If from Beaumont (to get to Beaumont from Houston take I-10 east towards New Orleans, you'll arrive in **Beaumont** in 1½ hr.) you drive north on Tex. 69, you immediately enter the forestland known in Texas as the **Piney Woods.** This is a lovely part of the state that stretches all the way north to Arkansas. Tex. 69 runs through the heart of it and is one of the most enjoyable drives in the state, especially in the fall or the early spring, which are my favorite times for visiting East Texas. Several of the following attractions can be reached by this road. The first of these is the **Big Thicket National Preserve.** The information station for the preserve (© **409/246-2337;** www.nps.gov/bith) is 30 miles from Beaumont, 8 miles past the town of Kountze. It will be on the right, just off the highway at the intersection of Highway 69 and Farm Road 420. The station is open daily from 9am to 5pm, except for Christmas and New Year's Day.

The Big Thicket is a lowland forest that occupies a land of swamps, bayous, and creeks. It is dotted with the occasional meadow, but for the most part grows so dense as to become impassable. In earlier times, it extended over 3 million acres and was an impenetrable and hostile place for early settlers. Stories abound of people getting lost in these woods and of outlaws using the place for their hideouts. With lumbering, oil exploration, roads, and settlement, the Big Thicket has been reduced to a tenth of its original size. Of what's left, almost 100,000 acres have been preserved by acts of Congress. The preserved area is not one large expanse of land but 12 separate units, most of which follow the courses of rivers, creeks, and bayous.

The most remarkable thing about the Big Thicket is its diversity of life: The land is checkered with different ecological niches that bring together species coexisting nowhere else. It has been called the American Ark. Hickory trees and bluebirds from the Eastern forests dwell close by cacti and roadrunners from the American Southwest and southern cypress trees and alligators from the Southern coastal marshes. The variety is astonishing. Of the five species of North American insect-eating plants, four live inside the Big Thicket.

For the visitor, the area offers opportunities for hiking, canoeing, and primitive camping. Some of the units are closed during hunting season (mid-Sept to mid-Jan) and some might be closed by flooding. You can get maps and detailed information on the hiking trails, free permits for primitive camping, and books about this fascinating area at the information station. The choice of trails here offers walks anywhere from a half-mile to 20 miles. Although leaving the designated hiking trails is permitted, you must be careful not to get lost; trailblazing in this dense brush can be slow going and painful. Canoeing in some ways has an advantage over hiking, though it limits your travel to those waterways with easy access for dropping off and picking up the canoes.

East Texas

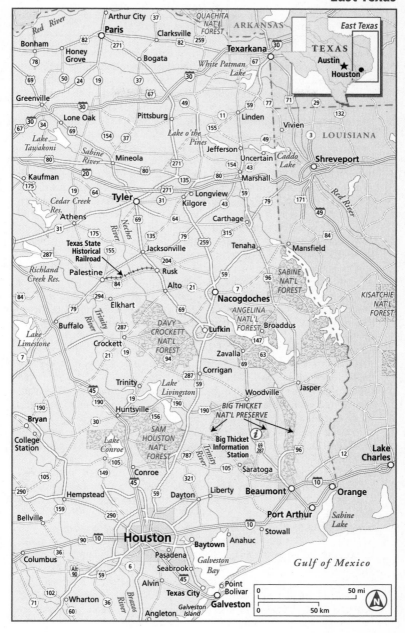

East Texas

TEXAS
Austin ★
● Houston

Red River
Arthur City 37
Paris
Bonham
82
Honey
78 Grove
271
Clarksville 259
Bogata
OUACHITA
NAT'L
FOREST
ARKANSAS
30
Texarkana 30
White Patman
Lake
67

69
50 24 19
37
30

Greenville
30
Lone Oak
Pittsburg
49
11
Linden
59 77
71
29
132

67 34
69
154 37
Lake o' the
Pines
155
Vivien
3
LOUISIANA

Lake
Tawakoni
Sabine
River
Mineola
Jefferson
Uncertain
Caddo
Lake
49
Shreveport

80
271
154 43
Marshall

Kaufman
175
20
135
80

19 64
271
Longview 59
79
171

Cedar Creek
Res.
Tyler
31
Kilgore 43
49

Athens
69
64
Carthage

31
Neches River
135
79
315

Texas State
Historical
Railroad
155
Jacksonville
259
Tenaha

204
Mansfield
SABINE
NAT'L
FOREST
KISATCHIE
NAT'L
FOREST

287
Palestine
84
Rusk
59
96

Richland
Creek Res.
Alto 21
Nacogdoches
7

84
79
Elkhart
69
ANGELINA
NAT'L
FOREST
Broaddus

Buffalo
287
DAVY
CROCKETT
NAT'L
FOREST
Lufkin
147

Lake
Limestone
Trinity River
Crockett
21 19
94
Zavalla
63

7
287
Corrigan
69

Trinity
45
Lake
Livingston
59
Woodville
Jasper

190
190
19
156
190
BIG THICKET
NAT'L PRESERVE

Bryan
Huntsville
SAM
HOUSTON
NAT'L
FOREST
Big Thicket
Information
Station
69
287
96
12
Lake
Charles

College
Station
105
30
Lake
Conroe
149 105
787
Trinity River
105
Saratoga

290
Conroe
45
321
Liberty
Beaumont
10
Orange

Hempstead
159
59
Dayton

Bellville
290

Port Arthur
Sabine
Lake

90 10
Houston
10
Stowall

Columbus
36
Baytown
Anahuc

Alt
90
59
6
Pasadena
Seabrook
Galveston
Bay
Gulf of Mexico

Alvin
45
Point
Bolivar

71
102
Wharton
36
Brazos River
Texas City
Galveston Island
Galveston

60
Angleton

0   50 mi
0   50 km
N

201

Race Relations in East Texas

Travelers to East Texas might well wonder about visiting here. In the last 10 years there have been several news stories about racially motivated hate crimes. These stories provoke—but leave unanswered—questions like "Will visitors feel safe here? Will they feel welcome?" And because the news coverage focuses on the crime first and the community second, it can invoke in the reader's mind the prevailing image of the old Southern town—closed, repressive, and ready to explode, where outsiders are viewed as either meddlers or provocateurs. This isn't the case, but one can't deny that racial prejudice exists in East Texas, that there are groups of the Klan here, and that hate crimes have occurred. Given these facts, you might be surprised by what I say next—that race relations in East Texas, as they play out day to day, are far from seething; that they are actually open, respectful, and even cordial. I've spent time in these places and I've looked into this issue. The Klansmen may be out there, but they are isolated and marginalized. Their rallies are usually better attended by the press than by their own members. In short, civil society in East Texas is not broken and divided.

A case in point is the town of Jasper (pop. 9,000), where James Byrd, an African-American man, was brutally murdered by three whites in 1998. I was there some years ago on an assignment to interview people from all sectors of society. I went expecting to find a polarized community, but what I heard and saw convinced me that Jasper was no powder keg. Roughly half of the town's population is black, and blacks occupy several of the most powerful positions in the community, including the office of mayor. Their personal safety was a nonissue for them. Yes, some people were thought to be prejudiced, but they didn't consider these people dangerous, even though one of the killers did, in fact, come from the community. The black and white communities in Jasper do tend to congregate amongst themselves, but they also interact and share a sense of community.

In other East Texas towns, I've encountered a greater or lesser degree of separation, but always with an easy interaction. The exception to this is the all-white town of Vidor (pop. 11,000), which lies about 10 miles east of Beaumont. Vidor is infamous as a stronghold of the Klan. It has been labeled by *Texas Monthly* magazine as the most hate-filled town in Texas. In 1994, the Department of Housing and Urban Development persuaded four black families to integrate Vidor's public housing, but after being harassed, snubbed, and threatened, these families chose to move.

Integration still hasn't made it to Vidor, but it has to the rest of East Texas. Its progress, to be sure, has been uneven. Vestiges of segregation remain, especially with housing: A recent study found Beaumont and Port Arthur to have the most segregated neighborhoods of any large city in Texas. Progress has been quicker in fields such as education, employment opportunities, and access to services. Nowadays racial discrimination has retreated to more subtle manifestations (the same sort of thing you'll find elsewhere) and the infrequent but chilling acts of a small throwback group filled with hate.

At the station, you can get information about canoe outfitters who operate from the towns of Kountze and Silsbee, mostly just from late spring to early fall. For lodging and food, you'll have to rely on the establishments in one of the nearby towns; there are no such facilities in the preserve. If you're in Kountze during lunchtime on any weekday, the most interesting place to eat is at the county courthouse, where most of the locals like to show up.

NATIONAL FORESTS

North and west of the Big Thicket, the ecological complexity gives way to pine forest habitat. Inside this large belt of pine forest are four national forests that provide opportunities for hiking, camping, boating, and fishing. These areas are a nice get-away, especially in the nonsummer months when the weather is more agreeable. They are much less visited than national parks and forests elsewhere. You can easily get to them from either Beaumont or Houston. Highway 69 leads directly into **Angelina National Forest,** about 50 miles north of Kountze. And the **Sam Houston National Forest** is only 55 miles north of Houston (take I-45). The other two are **Davy Crockett National Forest,** north of Sam Houston National Forest, and the **Sabine National Forest,** east of Angelina National Forest, on the Louisiana border. Each of these forests is roughly 150,000 acres, and each offers more or less the same activities: hiking, camping, boating, and fishing with such facilities as boat ramps, camping grounds, and hiking trails. For canoeing, there are a few interesting places in these forests, but it's mostly large expanses of open water, which aren't as fun as what you'll find in the Big Thicket or Caddo Lake (described below).

When the weather is agreeable, the forests are lovely places for hiking, especially in Sam Houston National Forest or Davy Crockett, which have the majority of trails. One hiking trail in Sam Houston is 126 miles long and crosses private property in three or four places; this is a real standout for Texas, which despite its image isn't such a wide-open state. Landowners here are firm believers in barbed-wire fences and the rights of private property, but this trail makes use of the goodwill of local landowners. Fishing draws many visitors, and a lot of places rent boats and equipment and can sell a temporary fishing license ($20) in the towns that lie in or next to these national forests. Your best bet for fishing is the Angelina or Sabine forests.

For general information about a specific national forest, visit **www.southernregion. fs.fed.us/texas** or call one of the following numbers. The Sam Houston National Forest ranger offices are in the town of New Waverly (© 936/344-6205); Davy Crockett National Forest ranger offices are in Crockett (© 936/655-2299); Angelina National Forest ranger offices are in Zavalla (© 936/897-1068); and the Sabine National Forest ranger offices are in Hemphill (© 409/787-3870).

CADDO LAKE & JEFFERSON

Caddo Lake and the town of **Jefferson** (pop. 2,600) share a curious history. The former owes its origin, and the latter its glory days to an immense, naturally occurring log-jam on the Red River, which was known as the "Great Raft." This logjam existed for centuries and stretched from 80 to 150 miles along the river, raising the water level upstream enough to form Caddo Lake and to make Big Cypress Bayou navigable by steamboat as far as Jefferson. The town became the biggest river port in Texas and the sixth-largest city. In fact, commerce was so good in Jefferson during the mid–19th century that of the Texas ports, only Galveston shipped more tonnage. But this prosperity

Kids Texas State Railroad State Park

After passing through the Angelina National Forest, Highway 69 continues through Lufkin before reaching the town of Rusk, a drive of about 60 miles. Here, you can ride an old steam locomotive train 25 miles through pine forest to the town of Palestine and back again. Many railroad enthusiasts consider this to be one of the best steam train rides in the country. On the days when the railroad is in operation, trains leave each terminus at the same time and pass each other at the midpoint. Passengers travel in vintage railway cars, either in first class (which has air-conditioning in summer only) or regular. The tracks and right of way and the land surrounding both terminuses belong to Texas's state parks. The train runs on a limited schedule (usually weekends) from March to May and August, and Thursday to Sunday from June to July. The round-trip journey through pine forest takes 4 hours and costs $17 regular and $24 first class for an adult, $11 and $16 for children 3 to 12 years old. For general information and reservations, call © 903/683-2561 (or 800/442-8951 toll-free in Texas). *Note:* At press time, there were rumors that the railroad may not be running after August 2007, so be sure to call ahead for information if this is important to you.

came to an abrupt end when the Army Corps of Engineers dynamited the raft in 1873, shrinking the lake and isolating the town. The lake is back, owing to an earthen damn built by the Corps in 1914.

The town is back, too, but now its livelihood depends in large part on B&Bs and antiques stores. The return of good times to Jefferson dates from about 1961 with the restoration of the old Excelsior Hotel (now called Excelsior House) by the town's garden club. This sparked a restoration frenzy that has made Jefferson the best-restored town in East Texas. The entire central part of town is listed in the National Register of Historic Places, with a number of antebellum houses (several turned into B&Bs), churches, and commercial buildings listed. It is a pleasant place to visit and stroll about. Weekends are when the town is most lively, with several tours offered; weekdays are when you get the best lodging rates. One of the best attractions is robber baron Jay Gould's personal railroad car, the **Atalanta** ($2 guided tour): It is in great condition, has a fascinating history, and gives the visitor a wonderful idea of luxury travel in the late 19th century.

Jefferson offers better lodging than what you'll find at Caddo Lake, and when in Jefferson, the place to stay for me is the **Excelsior House** (© 903/665-2513; http:// theexcelsiorhouse.com), which has been in continuous operation, more or less, since 1850. The 15 rooms are all furnished with antiques, many of which were here before the hotel was purchased by the garden club. Guests are invited to take a fun little tour of the hotel (nonguests $4). Room rates run from $119 to $149. You can also stay at one of the many B&Bs in town. For a list of these as well as information on tours, contact the **Marion County Chamber of Commerce** at © 888/GO-RELAX or 903/665-2672, or visit www.jefferson-texas.com. There are several dining options, including **Matt's,** 109 N. Polk St. (© 903/665-9237), a Tex-Mex joint, and the **Bakery**

Restaurant, 201 W. Austin St. (© **903/665-2253**), for home cooking, both of which I recommend.

Jefferson is situated between two lakes. To the west is Lake O' the Pines, which is good for swimming and general recreation, but the real point of interest is Caddo Lake, some 10 miles to the east. It is a large lake of 26,800 acres, half of which is in Louisiana; the more interesting half is in Texas, where the lake breaks up into smaller channels removed from most of the boat traffic. The small town of **Uncertain** (pop. 300) is on the western shore of the lake. Here you can get a tour and find lodging. Near Uncertain is **Caddo Lake State Park** (© **903/679-3351**). Like several state parks, it has cabins for rent, which are popular and must be reserved well in advance by calling the central reservation number at © **512/389-8900.** It also has campsites, which you can reserve by calling the park.

Caddo Lake is for boating or canoeing, not swimming. Instead of being an open expanse of water, it's more like a watery forest broken up into several smaller areas. Cypress trees draped in Spanish moss crowd the lake's broken shore, their roots rising from the murky water in deformed shapes. The lake also harbors abundant wildlife, including alligators, otters, water snakes, and many types of waterfowl.

For a tour, you have several options. You can get a seat on an old-fashioned steamboat that runs from spring to fall. **Caddo Lake Steamboat Co.** (© **903/789-3978**) offers a 1-hour trip along the main water channels that costs $15 per person. It's fun, especially for kids, but for a closer look at the lake and its wildlife, try a tour on a pontoon boat (1½ hr.) that takes you beyond the main channel of the lake; contact **Caddo Grocery** in Uncertain (© **903/789-3495;** www.caddogrocery.com). An even closer look can be had by contacting **Mystique Tours** (© **903/679-3690**), run by David J. Applebaum, a highly recommended guide. The tour takes 2 to 3 hours on a smaller boat. Your final option is to rent a canoe and paddle into the quiet parts of the lake that see few motorboats because they're too shallow and have too many roots below the surface. Try a couple of places called Carter's Lake and Clinton Lake. Talk to the rangers at the state park. They can point out on a map the canoe routes and put you in touch with the concessionaire.

6

The Texas Gulf Coast

by David Baird

Texas's coast stretches for more than 350 miles between Louisiana and Mexico. It's predominantly flat and sandy, with large bays and skinny barrier islands tripling the actual amount of shoreline. The sand varies in color from white to light brown, and the water is warm and calm and usually a dull green. It can be cloudy on some days and quite clear on others, especially the farther south you go.

Though the natural features along this coast are fairly uniform, there is one notable difference: rainfall. The eastern and central parts of Texas are much wetter than South Texas. Rivers, bayous, and creeks pour into estuaries and marshy wetlands, creating a fertile habitat that supports a broad range of wildlife. Along this coast are several national wildlife refuges, the most famous being the one at Aransas, which is the winter home of the endangered whooping crane. South of Corpus Christi the land is arid, which makes the water clearer, especially on the protected side of the barrier islands. South Padre Island has more sand dunes than the barrier islands to the north, and water on its sheltered side is extra salty because evaporation removes water faster than what is added.

There are many things for visitors to do on the Texas Gulf Coast, including all manner of watersports. Birding and eco-tourism also attract many visitors. And, thanks to its short and mild winters, the Gulf Coast attracts a lot of "winter Texans" who come fleeing the cold in their native states.

The largest cities on this coast are Corpus Christi and Galveston. Both offer the visitor a choice of recreation, lodging, and dining options. Farther south, at the very tip of the state, is the town of South Padre Island, the best known purely tourist resort in the state. This chapter covers everything from Galveston to South Padre Island, but not the bit of coast between Galveston and Port Arthur, at the Louisiana border (and believe me, nobody considers the Port Arthur coast for its recreational activities).

1 Galveston

50 miles E of Houston

Galveston is a port city on a barrier island opposite the mainland coast from Houston. Its main attractions are the downtown historic district with its Victorian commercial buildings and houses. Parts of the town are beautifully restored and ideal for just strolling around. The beaches are another attraction. They draw crowds of Houstonians and other Texans during the summer. The city is only an hour's drive from Houston and is a good destination for families; it's a quiet town with many points of interest, including Moody Gardens and the tall ship *Elissa*, and it's not far from NASA

The Texas Gulf Coast

and Kemah. Galveston is not a boomtown like Houston. Its population of 60,000 remains fairly stable.

ESSENTIALS

GETTING THERE Take the Gulf Freeway (I-45 south) from Houston. After crossing over to Galveston Island, the highway becomes a wide boulevard called Broadway.

ORIENTATION Broadway, Galveston's main street, doesn't cut directly across the island to the seashore; instead, it slants eastward and arrives at the seashore on the east end of the island, in front of Stewart Beach. Streets crossing Broadway are numbered; those parallel to Broadway have letters or names.

The East End Historic District and the old **Strand District** are north of Broadway. The Historic District is the old silk-stocking neighborhood that runs from 9th to 19th streets between Broadway and Church Street. It has many lovely houses that have been completely restored. Three large mansions-turned-museums have regular tours (see "What to See & Do," later in this chapter), and the city's historical preservation society holds tours of several private houses in May (inquire at the visitor center). The Strand District is the restored commercial district that runs between 19th and 25th

The Storm

At the end of the 19th century, Galveston was a thriving port and a fast-growing city with a bright future. In fact, it was the largest city in Texas and had the third busiest port in the country. Of course, being on the Gulf meant the risk of a hurricane, but the prevailing thought held that the shallow bottom on the western shore of the Gulf of Mexico would prevent the formation of large waves and blunt the force of any approaching storm. This assumption held sway even though a storm in 1886 completely wiped out the Texas port town of Indianola. But more evidence to the contrary came in the form of a massive storm that hit Galveston in September 1900.

It came ashore at night with a 20-foot surge that washed completely over the island. Houses were smashed into matchwood and their dwellers spilled out into the dark waters. By morning more than 6,000 islanders—one out of every six—were drowned. The city's population dropped even further when many of the survivors moved elsewhere to rebuild their lives on safer shores. Those who remained went to work to prevent a reoccurrence of the disaster. Galveston erected a stout seawall that now stretches out along 10 miles of shoreline with several jetties of large granite blocks projecting out into the sea. It also filled in land under the entire city, raising it 17 feet in some places and jacking up all the surviving houses to the new level. Despite all the effort, Galveston would never regain its momentum. The memory of "the storm" proved too compelling for many of Galveston's merchants, who preferred the safety of an inland port and provided impetus for the dredging of the Houston Ship Channel, which was completed in 1914. Houston then became a boomtown, taking Galveston's place as the commercial center for the area.

streets between Church Street and the harbor piers. When cotton was king, Galveston was a booming port and commercial center, and the Strand was dubbed the "Wall Street of the Southwest." What you see now are three- and four-story buildings along 6 blocks of the Strand and along some of the side streets; many of these are Victorian iron-fronts, so called because the facades included structural and decorative ironwork. This was a common building practice before the turn of the 20th century, but you won't find a better-preserved collection of these buildings anywhere else in the United States. Nowadays the Strand is a shopping and dining area that offers a wide variety of stores.

VISITOR INFORMATION   If you're planning a trip, check the **Galveston Convention & Visitors Bureau**'s website at www.galvestoncvb.com or call © **888/GAL-ISLE.** If you're in town already, visit their information center at 2428 Seawall Blvd., close to 25th Street (© **409/763-4311**). It's open daily from 9am to 5pm.

GETTING AROUND   Most of Galveston's hotels, motels, and restaurants are located along the seawall from where Broadway meets the shore all the way west past 60th Street. If you're on the seawall around 25th Street (near the visitor center), you

Galveston

ACCOMMODATIONS ■
Harbor House **7**
Hotel Galvez **10**
La Quinta Galveston **11**

DINING ◆
Gaidos **6**
Saltwater Grill **8**
Shrimp 'n' Stuff **4**
The Steakhouse in the
    San Luis Resort **5**

ATTRACTIONS ●
The Elissa **7**
Moody Gardens **1**
Ocean Star **9**
Pier 21 Theater **7**
Schlitterbahn Water Park **3**
Texas Aviation Hall of Fame and
    the Lone Star Flight Museum **2**
Texas Seaport Museum **7**

can take the **Galveston Island Rail Trolley** (℗ **409/797-3900**) to the Strand District. The fare is $1 (in either coins or bills) from the seawall to the Strand.

WHAT TO SEE & DO

The beaches are the most popular attraction for Houstonians and other Texans who come for a day or a weekend. They are not quite as nice as those at more popular beach resorts; the sand is closer to brown than white and the water isn't transparent. But, on the other hand, they are pure sand without rocks, and the water has the nice, warm temperature of the Gulf of Mexico. **East Beach** and **Stewart Beach,** operated by the city, have pavilions with dressing rooms, showers, and restrooms, ideal for daytrippers. Stewart Beach is located at the end of Broadway, and East Beach is about a mile east of Stewart Beach. There's a $5 per vehicle entrance fee. Most other beaches are free; many of the nicest are on the west side of the island. Another activity popular with visitors and locals alike is to walk, skate, or ride a bike atop the seawall, which extends 10 miles along the shoreline.

There are several tours offered in Galveston, but you need to call for availability: **Galveston Harbour Tours** (℗ 409/765-1700) is part of the Texas Seaport Museum, located on pier 21. It offers tours three to four times per day, depending on the season. **Duck Tours** (℗ 409/621-4771) offers its trademark amphibious bus tour. And

Ghost Tours of Galveston (© 409/949-2027) offers a walking tour of the Strand District. On Broadway, a few massive 19th-century mansions offer tours: **Ashton Villa,** 2328 Broadway (© 409/762-3933); **Moody Mansion,** 2618 Broadway (© 409/762-7668); and the **Bishop's Palace,** 1402 Broadway (© 409/762-2475), the most interesting of the bunch because there's more to see. Call for rates and additional information.

MUSEUMS

Except for Moody Gardens and its neighbor, the Lone Star Flight Museum (see below), all of Galveston's museums are in and around the Strand, the old commercial center. I enjoy the museums here; they offer variety and they aren't stuffy in the way you might think of museums. Highlights include **Pier 21 Theater** (© **409/763-8808**), which shows a short documentary about the 1900 storm that devastated the town, and another about a one-time Galveston resident, the pirate Jean Laffite. On the same pier is the **Texas Seaport Museum** (© **409/763-1877**; www.tsm-elissa.org) and the *Elissa,* a restored tall ship. Admission for both is $8 for adults, $6 for children 7 to 18, free for children 6 and younger, and a family rate of $23 for up to two adults and three children. The museum also offers a boat tour of the harbor; see above.

Next door, at Pier 19, is a one-of-a-kind museum about offshore drilling rigs. You may have already noticed in the harbor the massive rigs that are often parked on the opposite shore. These rigs are tremendous feats of engineering and are some of the largest freestanding constructions ever built. They are often in the Port of Galveston being reconditioned. Most visitors have never seen one up close, but here you have an opportunity to scamper around on one: the **Ocean Star** (© **409/766-STAR;** www.oceanstaroec.com), which is an old rig that's been converted into a museum. Through a short film, scale models, actual drilling equipment, and interactive displays, every aspect of the drilling process is explored, including the many rather daunting engineering challenges. I found the film, the exhibits, and the rig itself fascinating. I imagine that those with a grasp of technical and engineering issues will enjoy this museum more than others, but anyone will appreciate the broader aspects and the sheer size of these constructions. Admission is $6 for adults, $5 for seniors, $4 for students 7 to 18, and free for kids 6 and younger. Hours for this and the other museums around the Strand are roughly the same, daily from 10am to 4pm (until 5pm in summer).

Moody Gardens (Kids   Moody Gardens, an education/entertainment museum, is easily recognizable for its three large glass pyramids. The first one built was the rainforest pyramid, which holds trees, plants, birds, fish, and butterflies from several different rainforest habitats. A stroll through the building will fascinate anyone who has never been in a rainforest environment. The unusual species of Amazonian fish, birds, and butterflies are not often seen in zoos. The aquarium pyramid displays life from four of the world's oceans: penguins from Antarctica, harbor seals from the northern Pacific, and reef dwellers from the Caribbean and South Pacific. There is also a petting aquarium for those who feel compelled to touch the little darlings. The discovery pyramid displays space exploration but doesn't come close to the nearby Space Center Houston. Also of note are the two IMAX theaters: One is 3-D and the other is a Ridefilm. On top of all this, there is a pool and white-sand beach for children and parents and an old paddlewheel boat that journeys out into the bay. A large hotel and spa are also on the grounds.

Just down the road at 2002 Terminal Dr. is the **Texas Aviation Hall of Fame and the Lone Star Flight Museum** (© **409/740-7106;** www.lsfm.org). It has two hangars filled with aircraft in varying states of reconstruction. Many of the planes are from World War II. Admission is $6 for adults, $5 for students 13 to 17, and $4 for children ages 4 to 12.

1 Hope Blvd. ℭ 800/582-4673. www.moodygardens.org. Admission prices vary depending upon the season. You can buy a ticket to just 1 exhibit or IMAX theater, or buy a full-day pass for all exhibits and theaters that costs $40 but is sometimes cheaper during the off season. See the website for details. Daily 10am–9pm in summer; Sun–Thurs 10am–6pm, Fri–Sat 10am–8pm rest of year.

Schlitterbahn Galveston Water Park 🐸 *(Kids)* This recent addition to Galveston's attractions comes from the central Texas town of New Braunfels, where, for the last 25 years, the Schlitterbahn water amusement park has pioneered different water rides and has been voted best water park by the Travel Channel. It has now established sister parks here in Galveston and in South Padre Island, the two biggest family destinations on the coast. This one is close by Moody Gardens. It offers a wealth of tube chutes, wave tanks, and other rides. And, unlike the other two parks, this one has a large section that can be enclosed and heated for the winter season, keeping the park open throughout the year.

2026 Lockheed. ℭ 409/770-9283. www.schlitterbahn.com. Summer rates $34 adults (12 and older), $28 children 3–11 and seniors. Daily 10am–8pm in summer, open on weekends and holidays during the rest of the year. Check website for calendar.

FESTIVALS

The three most popular festivals on the island are **Mardi Gras** (Feb or Mar), the **American Institute of Architects (AIA) Sandcastle Competition** (June), and **Dickens on the Strand** (first weekend in Dec). For Mardi Gras, book a hotel room well in advance; it is a tremendously popular celebration with parades, masked balls, and a live-entertainment district around the Strand. Mardi Gras here has some advantages over New Orleans—there are fewer tourists, and it's very lively without all the public displays of drunkenness. For info, call ℭ 888/425-4753 or visit www.mardigrasgalveston.com.

The most unusual event is the annual AIA Sandcastle Competition. More than 70 architectural and engineering firms from around the state show up on East Beach and get serious about the building of sand castles and sand sculptures and take this pastime to new heights, literally. It all happens in 1 day, and the results are phenomenal. Call ℭ 713/520-0155 or check their website at **www.aiasandcastle.com** for more information.

For its Christmas celebration Galveston hosts Dickens on the Strand, a street party for which revelers dress up in Victorian costume. The entire affair is a testament to just how much we associate traditional Christmas with the Victorian era (perhaps largely due to Dickens himself). The Strand—with its Victorian architecture and the association with its namesake—is a natural venue for such a celebration. The party includes performers, street vendors, readings of Dickens, and music. In 2006 admission was $10 in advance and $12 same-day for adults; $4 in advance for children ages 7 to 12, $6 same-day; free for children 6 and younger. Those dressed in full Victorian costume are admitted free. Though Houstonians often come down for it, I'm not convinced it's worth traveling for. It's one of those things you might go to if you're already in the area. Call ℭ 409/765-7834 for more information.

WHERE TO STAY

All the economical hotel/motel chains have properties in Galveston, with higher prices for lodgings along the seawall. Of the big chains, **La Quinta Galveston,** 1402 Seawall

Blvd. (© **800/531-5900**), ranks highly. Galveston also has a dozen B&Bs, most of which are in Victorian-era houses. You can inquire into most of these through the association website: www.galvestonbedandbreakfast.com.

Harbor House 🏨 *Finds*   A very different kind of hotel for Galveston, the Harbor House is built on a pier overlooking the harbor instead of a beach. It's an excellent location, near the Strand District and next to a few restaurants and museums that have taken over the neighboring piers. The architecture and exterior design are different as well. Rooms are large and well appointed in a contemporary style without a lot of clutter. Bleached wood floors, Berber carpets, and exposed wood and steel superstructure give it a feel unlike other hotels. There are nine marina slips but no restaurant; however, with so many restaurants within 2 blocks, it isn't missed.

No. 28, Pier 21, Galveston, TX 77550. © **800/874-3721** or 409/763-3321. Fax 409/765-6421. www.harborhouse pier21.com. 42 units. Weekdays $115–$135 double; weekends $135–$195. Rates include continental breakfast. AE, DC, DISC, MC, V. Parking $10. **Amenities:** Overnight laundry service/dry cleaning. *In room:* A/C, TV, dataport, coffeemaker, hair dryer, iron.

Hotel Galvez 🏨   Galveston's historic grand hotel, the Galvez has been thoroughly renovated to make the guest rooms more comfortable and to correct the mistakes of previous renovations. Rooms are spacious, well furnished (most with two double beds), and conservatively decorated. The hotel overlooks the seawall and one of the municipal beaches. It is also on the trolley line leading to the Strand district. Rates often run less than what is listed below.

2024 Seawall Blvd., Galveston, TX 77550. © **800/WYNDHAM** or 409/765-7721. Fax 409/765-5780. www.wyndham. com. 231 units. $115–$245 double. Extra person $20. Packages available. AE, DC, DISC, MC, V. Valet parking $9; free selfparking. **Amenities:** Restaurant; bar; large outdoor pool; fitness center; Jacuzzi; limited concierge; business center; limited room service; same-day laundry service/dry cleaning. *In room:* A/C, TV, dataport, coffeemaker, hair dryer, iron.

WHERE TO DINE

Seafood is what people come to Galveston for, and with all the variety offered they won't be disappointed. There are local representatives of chain restaurants such as Landry's and Joe's Crab Shack, but for the best of Galveston's seafood try one of the places listed below. If you're craving steak, the best in town is **The Steakhouse in the San Luis Resort,** 5222 Seawall Blvd. (© **409/744-1500**).

Gaidos 🏨🏨 SEAFOOD   Owned and operated by the Gaido family for four generations, this restaurant is a Galveston tradition. The Gaidos have maintained quality by staying personally involved in all the aspects of the restaurant—thus the seafood is fresh and the service attentive. The soups and side dishes are mostly traditional Southern and Gulf Coast recipes that are comfort food for the longtime customers. Main dishes include a few chicken, pork, and beef items but are mainly seafood. The stuffed snapper is the best I've had. If pompano is on the menu, it's worth considering. The steaks and pork chops are high quality and done justice in the kitchen. The menu varies seasonally. The large dining room is inviting, and a sizeable bar area makes for a nice place to wait for a table.

3800 Seawall Blvd. © **409/762-9625.** Reservations not accepted. Main courses $15–$33; complete dinners $19–$29. AE, DISC, MC, V. Daily 11:45am–10:30pm. Closes an hour or 2 earlier during low season.

Saltwater Grill 🏨🏨 SEAFOOD   This restaurant prints up a menu daily that usually includes some inventive seafood pasta dishes. You might try the Gulf red snapper pan sautéed and topped with lump crabmeat, a fish dish with an Asian bent, or gumbo and/or bouillabaisse. A few nonseafood options are available as well. The preparation shows a light touch. The starters are excellent. I had asparagus spears fried in a tempura-style batter so thin as to be translucent—and they were cooked perfectly. Situated in an old building near the Strand, the dining room has a pleasant mix of past and present, formal and informal.

2017 Post Office St. (℃) **409/762-FISH.** Reservations recommended. Main courses $14–$29. AE, MC, V. Mon–Fri 11am–2pm and 5–10pm; Sat 5–11pm; Sun 5–9pm. Free parking in rear.

Shrimp 'n' Stuff *Value* SEAFOOD This small, unassuming restaurant where you order at the counter is thought by many locals to serve the best seafood for the money. The seafood is mostly fried Southern-style and served with hush puppies. I love the fried fish and the oysters most of all. Especially popular are the oyster and the shrimp po' boys, the fried shrimp, and the seafood platter.

3901 Ave. O. (℃) **409/763-2805.** Reservations not accepted. Main courses $7–$14. AE, DC, MC, V. Sun–Thurs 10:30am–8pm; Fri–Sat 10:30am–9pm.

2 Brazosport

65 miles SE of Galveston; 50 miles S of Houston; 185 miles NW of Corpus Christi

There's really no town or city called Brazosport. It's a term that loosely describes southern Brazoria County and its communities. These towns, which have a combined population of about 90,000, include Clute, Freeport, Surfside Beach, Lake Jackson, Angleton, Quintana Beach, and Brazoria. They are directly south of Houston, about a 1½-hour drive from downtown. This is where the Brazos River flows into the Gulf. The area is a contrasting mix of disparate elements. The towns that aren't on the beach have a pleasant small-town atmosphere. In the fishing towns, you'll find shrimp and fishing boats docked by the water. The beach towns (like Surfside) are vacation communities with lots of vacation houses owned by Houstonians. In other parts, giant petrochemical plants dominate the landscape (an especially large Dow Chemical plant lies between Surfside and Freeport). But the area also has large areas of protected wetlands and a rich variety of bird species—the annual Christmas bird count in the town of Freeport often reports more species of birds seen in a single day than at any other location in the United States.

ESSENTIALS
GETTING THERE
BY PLANE The nearest commercial airports are in Houston (see chapter 5).

BY CAR From Houston take Tex. 288 south about 45 miles to Angleton, the Brazoria County seat. Lake Jackson is another 10 miles south on Tex. 288, and Bus. 288 leads from Angleton to Clute (10 miles south). Texas highways 332 and 288 intersect in Lake Jackson, heading southeast around it and Clute and then divide, 332 continuing southeast to Surfside Beach and 288 heading south to Freeport and Quintana. Brazoria is just west of Lake Jackson on Tex. 332.

GETTING AROUND
The only practical way to explore this area is by car; the attractions discussed below are all within a 45-minute drive. Traffic and parking are seldom an issue. The major roads are Texas highways 288, 332, 35, and 36. Tex. 288/332 wraps around the west and south sides of Lake Jackson and Clute, where many motels are located.

VISITOR INFORMATION

Although most of the towns in the Brazosport area have their own chambers of commerce, and some have visitor centers, you can get area-wide information from the **Southern Brazoria County Visitors Convention Bureau,** 1239 W. Tex. 332, Clute, TX 77531 (© **800/938-4853** or 979/265-2508; www.brazosport.cc.tx.us/~sbcvcb); and the **Brazosport Convention & Visitors Council,** 420 Tex. 332 W., Brazosport (Clute), TX 77531 (© **888/477-2505** or 979/265-2505; www.tourtexas.com/brazosport). Both organizations operate visitor centers.

FAST FACTS   The **Brazosport Memorial Hospital,** 100 Medical Dr. (just off Tex. 288), Lake Jackson (© 979/297-4411), has a 24-hour emergency room. **Clute's post office,** located at 530 E. Main St., is open Monday through Friday from 8:30am to 4:30pm, Saturday from 10am to noon. The **Lake Jackson post office,** located at 210 Oak Dr. S., is open Monday through Friday from 8:30am to 5pm, Saturday from 10am to 2pm.

WHAT TO SEE & DO
THE TOP ATTRACTIONS

Brazoria County Historical Museum   This museum, located in the 1897 Brazoria County Courthouse, will be of most interest to those curious about Texas history. A major part of the museum is dedicated to the first Anglo colony established in Texas, under the supervision of Stephen F. Austin. In the 1820s he brought 297 families into the area by way of the Brazos River and established the colony's center upstream. These original settlers became known as "the old three hundred." The large exhibit, which contains 68 panels, replicas of the era's weapons and tools, and a variety of artifacts and documents, is located in the historic courtroom on the second floor (access for visitors with disabilities is available). Most of the rest of the museum is devoted to changing exhibits that include historic subjects such as the courthouses of Texas and the Civil War's impact on the area. Allow at least 1 hour.

100 E. Cedar St., just off Bus. 288, Angleton. © 979/864-1208. www.bchm.org. Free admission (donations welcome). Mon–Fri 9am–5pm; Sat 9am–3pm. Closed major holidays.

The Center for the Arts & Sciences ⊀ *Finds*   One of those rare entities that does a whole lot of things very well, The Center for the Arts & Sciences includes a fine natural history museum, a small planetarium, an attractive art gallery, two theaters for a variety of performing arts events, and a nature trail. You'll need at least 2 hours to see it. The **Museum of Natural Science** has a collection of more than 14,000 seashells, and is credited with instigating the movement to make the lightning whelk the official state shell of Texas. Also in its 12,000 square feet of floor space are exhibits on archaeology, fossils, dinosaurs, rocks, and minerals (including a fluorescent mineral room), and a collection of jade and ivory carvings. The **planetarium** has a 30-foot dome and lots of high-tech projection equipment to produce a variety of night sky experiences. A ¾-mile self-guided **nature trail** meanders through bottomland along Oyster Creek adjacent to the center. The center's **art gallery** presents nine exhibits each year, ranging from local artists to national shows.

400 College Dr., Clute. © 979/265-7661. www.bcfas.org. Free admission to the museum, art gallery, and nature trail; planetarium $3 adults, $2 students. Museum and art gallery Tues–Sat 10am–5pm; Sun 2–5pm; closed major holidays. Planetarium shows Tues 7pm. Nature trail open daily dawn–dusk. From the intersection of Texas highways 332 and 288 in Lake Jackson head east on Oyster Creek Dr., through Lake Jackson and into Clute; Oyster Creek Dr. becomes College Dr. after it crosses the railroad tracks in Clute. The center is just ahead on the left, adjoining the campus of Brazosport College.

Birding along the Texas Coast

The coastal plains of Texas are a haven for birds. The area is rich in resident species and is the winter home to many more. It offers a variety of habitats—freshwater and saltwater marshes, tidal zones, prairies, and woodlands—and abundant food sources. It's also smack in the middle of the great flyway for birds migrating from the northern parts of the U.S. and Canada to Central and South America. On their southward journey this is the last chance for R&R before they have to hop the Gulf of Mexico, and on the return it's the first landfall.

All of this is why the Texas Gulf Coast attracts lots of birders and sponsors several birding events. The reader can take for granted that throughout this chapter there are plenty of birding opportunities, even when none are specifically mentioned. The best times to visit are during the migration seasons and in winter. Most of the annual events are held in the Brazosport and the Corpus Christi areas. Here are a few highlights: The towns of Lake Jackson and Rockport hold festivals for viewing hummingbirds (lots of them) when they pass through here in September. Also in late September or early October local birders in Corpus hold the annual hawk count at Hazel Bazemore County Park where tens of thousands of raptors of various species fly through here following the Nueces River. And in April Brazosport holds its annual Migration Celebration when local birders serve as guides on birding walks. For specific information you can contact local visitor centers listed in this chapter. The state publishes three helpful maps called **"The Great Texas Coastal Birding Trail,"** one for each section of the Texas coast. These list 300 viewing sites and give driving directions and descriptions for each. Call ℂ **888/900-2577** or check the maps out at the following website: www.tpwd.state.tx.us/huntwild/wild/wildlife_trails/coastal.

Sea Center Texas   Sea Center Texas has a 50,000-gallon aquarium where you'll see marine life of the Texas Gulf Coast, including Gordon, a 250-pound grouper, and sharks up to 12 feet long. There are also tanks with exhibits on other types of marine environments, including salt marshes, reefs, and a coastal bay. A shallow touch pool contains blue crabs, hermit crabs, snails, urchins, and other marine creatures that can be handled, and just outside the visitor center is a 5-acre wetland with elevated boardwalks and signs discussing the numerous birds and other wildlife you might encounter. The facility also operates a fish hatchery producing red drum (also known as red fish—a popular sport fish). The Sea Center is a joint project of Dow Chemical and Texas Parks and Wildlife. Allow 1 hour.

300 Medical Dr., Lake Jackson. ℂ **979/299-1808.** Free admission (donations welcome). Tues–Fri 9am–4pm; Sat 10am–5pm; Sun 1–4pm. Closed major holidays. From Tex. 332/288 turn west onto Plantation Dr. to Medical Dr. and turn north (right), then follow the signs.

OUTDOOR ACTIVITIES
Birding, fishing, and hanging out on the beach are the top outdoor pursuits here.

BIRDING/WILDLIFE VIEWING The Brazosport area has three national wildlife refuges and many more publicly and privately held nature preserves. Of the national refuges, the most developed is the **Brazoria National Wildlife Refuge,** which covers 43,388 acres and was established to protect coastal wetlands for migratory birds and other wildlife. The Information Center, located near the entrance to the refuge, has interpretive panels on what you want to watch for, and a boardwalk outside the Information Center leads across wetlands, where you may spot an alligator. The boardwalk provides access to the .6-mile Big Slough Birding Trail. The refuge also has a 2-mile hiking and biking trail that follows an abandoned railway line and provides views across a terrain of prairie, where you might see more than a dozen species of sparrows, white-tailed hawks, and white-tailed kites. In addition, there's a 7-mile driving tour with access to several observation decks. The refuge, which also allows fishing and hunting, is open September through May daily from 8am to 4pm, and during the summer it's open the same hours the first weekend of each month and intermittently during the week. Admission is free. To get to the refuge, take FM 523 north from Freeport or south from Angleton to CR 227, which you follow 1¾ miles northeast to the refuge entrance. For additional information, contact the refuge at © **409/849-7771** or visit http://southwest.fws.gov.

In the community of Quintana Beach the **Neo-Tropical Bird Sanctuary** is located on Lamar Street across from the Quintana Beach Town Hall (© **979/233-0848**), where you can get a bird checklist and other information. This small wooded preserve is open 24 hours a day with free admission. It's a hot spot for viewing migrant birds that follow the Brazos River to the coast.

FISHING This area offers excellent fishing for grouper, ling, amberjack, and red snapper—the state record 36.1-pound red snapper was caught in 1995 off the Freeport coast. Anglers can choose from among about a dozen charter fishing boats, most based in Freeport Harbor, such as **Captain Elliott's Party Boats** (© **979/233-1811;** www. deep-sea-fishing.com), which offers 12-hour deep-sea fishing trips at $75 per adult weekends, $70 weekdays, and $45 for children 12 and younger. There are numerous places for shore, beach, pier, and jetty fishing, including Quintana and Surfside beaches, and a number of public boat ramps—check with one of the visitor bureaus (see "Visitor Information," above) for locations.

FUN ON THE BEACH Although the beaches here are far from pristine—they tend to be rocky and the sand is more brown than white—it's still fun to dig your toes into the cool sand, walk along the shore, build a sand castle, watch the freighters and shorebirds, and look for seashells among the stones. Driving is permitted on most beaches here, except for the pedestrian-only beach at **Quintana Beach County Park,** 5th Street, in the community of Quintana (© **800/872-7578** or 979/233-1461), which has a campground (see "Camping," below), good bird-watching, a playground, horseshoe pits, and a picnic area, and charges a $4 per vehicle day-use fee.

WHERE TO STAY

Among the national chain motels in the Brazosport area, our favorite is **La Quinta Inn,** 1126 Tex. 332 W., Clute (© 800/531-5900 or 979/265-7461), with spacious, very attractive rooms. Other reliable chains include the **Days Inn,** 805 Tex. 332 W., Clute (© 800/329-7466 or 979/265-3301); **Ramada Inn,** 925 Tex. 332, Lake Jackson (© 800/272-6232 or 979/297-1161); and **Super 8,** 915 Tex. 332, Lake Jackson (© 800/800-8000 or 979/297-3031). Also see the section on **Quintana Beach**

County Park under "Camping," below. Tax adds about 13% to lodging bills unless otherwise noted.

Roses & the River   A Texas farmhouse–style home in an idyllic setting is what you'll find at Roses & the River. Sitting on almost 3½ acres along the San Bernard River, this B&B has an abundance of beautiful rose bushes. Because of the warm Gulf Coast climate, the roses bloom year-round, although they're usually best in October and November. There are sitting areas along the river plus a long veranda offering a peaceful and protected sitting area. Inside, the lobby/living room has a fireplace with comfortable seating, and a separate dining room where the homemade breakfasts are served. There are three guest rooms, all on the second floor (no elevator), that are rose themed— somewhat elegant yet cheerful and inviting. Each of the spacious rooms has a full private bathroom (one with a fantastic claw-foot spa tub), and one queen-size bed. Guest rooms contain a few antiques, but furnishings are mostly contemporary. Two rooms have views of the river; the third overlooks the rose garden. Smoking is not permitted.

2434 C.R. 506, Brazoria, TX 77422. © **800/610-1070** or 979/798-1070. Fax 979/798-1070. www.roses-and-the-river. com. 3 units. $150 double (tax included). Rates include full breakfast. AE, DISC, MC, V. Children 12 and older allowed. From Brazoria, go southwest on Tex. 521, cross the San Bernard River and take the first right turn, onto C.R. 506. After about 1½ miles, you'll find Roses & the River on the right. *In room:* A/C, TV/DVD/VCR (free movies available), hair dryer, coffeemaker, iron, no phone.

CAMPING

Quintana Beach County Park (on 5th St., in Quintana) is practically on the water. The campsites are fairly close together, but it's a short walk to the beach. There are 56 sites (including 19 pull-through RV sites) and a small group of grassy "tent-only" sites. The campground has paved roads, showers, a self-serve laundry, an RV dump station, picnic tables, grills, a playground, and horseshoe pits. Boardwalks lead from the campground to the beach. Camping rates from May to September are $18 to $20 for full hook-ups. From October to April, rates are $17 to $18 for full hook-ups. Day use costs $4 per vehicle. There are also several cabins with sleeping areas, bathrooms, and kitchens (but no linens or kitchen utensils), which rent for $70 to $100 from May to September and $55 to $85 from October to April. Information is available by calling © **800/872-7578** or 979/233-1461. From Tex. 36/288 in Freeport, turn right onto FM 1495, and after crossing the Intercoastal Waterway on a swing bridge, turn left onto Quintana Road, which becomes Lamar Street in Quintana. Turn right on 8th Street, then left on Burnett Street to 5th Street.

WHERE TO DINE

Café Annice ✿ INTERNATIONAL   This casual modern restaurant has a decidedly uptown feel and is a favorite of local businesspeople. Lunch choices include a variety of sandwiches, such as the Caesar wrap—chicken breast, romaine lettuce, carrots, red onions, plum tomatoes, and a homemade Caesar spread, wrapped in a roasted garlic–and-herb tortilla. Dinner entrees feature tempting selections of seafood, Angus beef, and chicken, including the excellent chicken Annice—breaded chicken topped with mushrooms, artichokes, tomatoes, and capers, sautéed with Marsala wine and served with grilled vegetable ragout and garlic mashed potatoes.

24 Circle Way, Lake Jackson. © **979/292-0060.** Reservations accepted for large parties only. Main courses lunch $6–$10, dinner $6–$23. AE, DISC, MC, V. Mon–Fri 11am–2pm; Sat 11am–2:30pm; Mon–Thurs 5–9pm; Fri–Sat 5–10pm. Closed major holidays. From Tex. 332/288, turn northeast onto This Way; take the first left onto Circle Way and follow it around to downtown.

Finds Texas's Most Deserted Beach

Heading down the coast towards Corpus Christi, you come to Matagorda Bay. This is one of the least developed areas of the coast, with lots of small fishing towns and farming communities. This region has its charm, and life here is really laid-back. Protecting the coast is Matagorda Island, a 38-mile-long strip of land covering almost 44,000 acres. It's mostly federal and state land set aside as a wildlife refuge. Aside from a small state park with camping areas and a historic lighthouse, there is little development. But there are plenty of beaches, pristine and deserted, on which you will see no motorized vehicles; they are prohibited. You can swim, hike, ride your bike, if you brought one, do some bird-watching (over 300 species of birds have been spotted here, including the whooping crane), or look for shells. Fishing is another popular activity. Many locals come here to fish in the surf.

But if you decide to visit the island, you'll have to bring your own water and food; none can be purchased on the island. Primitive campsites at the state park cost $6 per night (up to four people). An outdoor cold-water rinse is available near the boat docks. The state used to operate a passenger ferry (© 361/983-2215) to the island from the town of Port O'Connor, but for the past couple of years, it's been inoperative. You might want to call and see if it's running again. Another option is to hire a boat at Port O'Connor. For more information contact **Matagorda Island State Park and Wildlife Management Area** (© 979/244-6804; www.tpwd.state.tx.us/park/matagisl/matagisl.htm).

Red Snapper Inn SEAFOOD   Although the menu is primarily classic seafood such as shrimp sautéed with garlic and mushrooms, or grilled boneless flounder stuffed with crabmeat dressing, you'll also find some Greek touches such as baked shrimp with feta cheese and fresh tomatoes, and the sautéed filet of snapper in a sauce of pulverized onions, oregano, lemon juice, and olive oil. Also a good bet are the oysters en brochette, grilled bacon-wrapped oysters (not breaded) with meunière butter and served on rice pilaf. Nonseafood items include a charbroiled choice 14-ounce rib-eye steak, the very popular charbroiled Greek meatballs with spaghetti, and that Texas standard, chicken-fried steak with cream gravy.

402 Bluewater Hwy., Surfside Beach. © 979/239-3226. Reservations accepted for large parties only. Main courses $10–$17. No credit cards. Mon–Fri 11am–2pm and 5–9pm; Sat–Sun 11am–9pm. As you enter Surfside Beach on Tex. 332, you come to a traffic light; turn northeast (left) onto Bluewater Hwy. The restaurant will be on your right a few blocks down.

3 Corpus Christi

207 miles SW of Houston; 377 miles S of Dallas; 143 miles S of San Antonio; 691 miles SE of El Paso

The bay area around Corpus Christi offers visitors the greatest variety of activities of any place along the Texas Gulf Coast. This and the following three sections cover the major destinations in the bay area. These destinations are only about 45 minutes from one another at most, so you can hop around pretty easily. And, whether you stay in

Corpus Christi

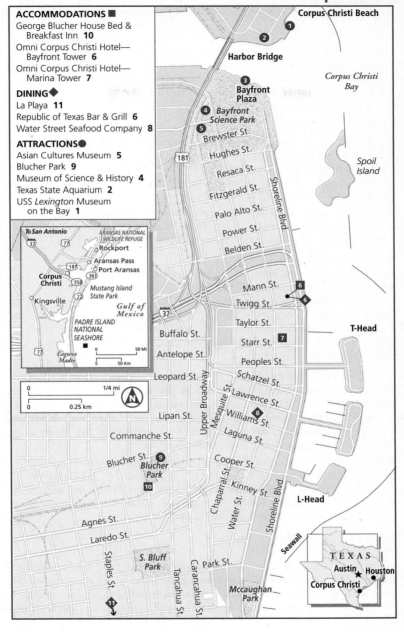

ACCOMMODATIONS ■
George Blucher House Bed &
  Breakfast Inn **10**
Omni Corpus Christi Hotel—
  Bayfront Tower **6**
Omni Corpus Christi Hotel—
  Marina Tower **7**

DINING ◆
La Playa **11**
Republic of Texas Bar & Grill **6**
Water Street Seafood Company **8**

ATTRACTIONS ●
Asian Cultures Museum **5**
Blucher Park **9**
Museum of Science & History **4**
Texas State Aquarium **2**
USS *Lexington* Museum
  on the Bay **1**

Corpus Christi Beach

Harbor Bridge

Corpus Christi Bay

Bayfront Plaza

Bayfront Science Park

Brewster St.

Spoil Island

Hughes St.

181

Resaca St.

Fitzgerald St.

Palo Alto St.

Power St.

Belden St.

Shoreline Blvd.

Mann St.

Twigg St.

T-Head

Taylor St.

Starr St.

Buffalo St.

Antelope St.

Peoples St.

Leopard St.

Schatzel St.

Lawrence St.

Upper Broadway

Mesquite St.

Lipan St.

Williams St.

Laguna St.

Commanche St.

Blucher St.

Blucher Park

Cooper St.

Kinney St.

L-Head

Chaparral St.

Water St.

Shoreline Blvd.

Agnes St.

Laredo St.

Seawall

Staples St.

S. Bluff Park

Park St.

Carancahua St.

Tancahua St.

Mccaughan Park

To San Antonio
37 77
ARANSAS NATIONAL WILDLIFE REFUGE
Rockport
181 Aransas Pass
361 Port Aransas
Corpus Christi 359
22 *Mustang Island State Park*
Kingsville
Gulf of Mexico
77 *PADRE ISLAND NATIONAL SEASHORE*
Laguna Madre
0   50 Mi
0   50 Km

0   1/4 mi
0   0.25 km

TEXAS
Austin Houston
Corpus Christi

Corpus, Port Aransas, or Rockport, you'll find great lodging, fantastic food, and lots to do.

Corpus Christi is a major deepwater seaport, with a population of just under 300,000, but it has the feel of a much smaller place. The downtown is easy to enjoy, and everything is pretty close together. The two biggest attractions are the State Aquarium and the USS *Lexington* aircraft carrier, which are right next to each other on the bay just north of downtown, across Harbor Bridge.

ESSENTIALS
GETTING THERE
BY PLANE   The **Corpus Christi International Airport,** located within the city limits on the south side of Tex. 44, west of Padre Island Drive/Tex. 358 (© 361/289-0171), is served by **American Eagle** (© 800/433-7300); **Atlantic Southeast/Delta** (© 800/221-1212); **Continental/Continental Express** (© 800/523-3273); and **Southwest** (© 800/435-9792). All the major car-rental agencies can be found here.

BY CAR   Tex. 35 follows the Gulf Coast—albeit slightly inland—from the Houston and Galveston area to Corpus Christi. From San Antonio, follow I-37 southeast to Corpus Christi. Before you see the town you'll pass the city's oil refining complex.

GETTING AROUND
Most visitors to Corpus Christi will use a car to get around. This is an easy city to navigate. Traffic isn't bad except during rush hour.

In the downtown area, highways I-37 and Tex. 286 (known as the Crosstown Expwy.) intersect. Connected to both is Corpus Christi's busiest freeway, known as South Padre Island Drive or S.P.I.D., as it appears on signs. It does in fact lead to Padre Island. For a nice drive around the bay from the downtown area, take Ocean Drive, which skirts the south shore.

VISITOR INFORMATION
Contact the **Corpus Christi Convention & Visitors Bureau,** 1201 N. Shoreline Blvd. (© **800/766-2322;** www.corpuschristicvb.com). If you're already in Corpus, go to one of the visitor centers located at 1823 N. Chaparral (© **361/561-2000**), 1433 I-37 (© **361/241-1461**), and 14252 S.P.I.D. (© **361/949-8743**). Hours at these centers are from 9am to 5pm Monday through Friday.

FAST FACTS   The **Corpus Christi Medical Center** (www.ccmedicalcenter.com) has three locations: Doctors Regional, 3315 S. Alameda (© **361/761-1400**); Bay Area, 7101 S. Padre Island Dr. (© **361/761-1200**); and The Heart Hospital, 7002 Williams Dr. (© **361/761-6800**). The main **post office,** 809 Nueces Bay Blvd., is open Monday through Friday from 8am to 5pm.

WHAT TO SEE & DO
THE TOP ATTRACTIONS
Texas State Aquarium *Kids*   Several tanks display a variety of ecosystems found in the Gulf of Mexico and coastal Texas, from coral reefs with sharks and barracuda swimming about to jetty systems populated by crabs and flounders to East Texas swamps and their alligators. Specialty tanks are dedicated to some of the most curious forms of sea life, such as octopuses, turtles, and sea horses. And in the touch pools you can touch a stingray or bamboo shark if that's what you really want to do. The latest addition to the aquarium is Dolphin Bay, a protected environment for Atlantic bottle-nosed dolphins

that are unable to survive in the wild. Children enjoy the Kids' Port Playground, and there's also a gift shop and food court. Allow 1 to 2 hours.

2710 N. Shoreline Blvd. ℂ 800/477-4853 or 361/881-1200. www.texasstateaquarium.org. Admission $14 adults, $12 seniors 60 and older, $9 ages 3–12, free for children younger than 3. Daily 9am–5pm; open until 6pm Memorial Day to Labor Day. Closed Thanksgiving and Dec 25. Parking $3.

USS _Lexington_ Museum on the Bay ★★   This World War II–era aircraft carrier is a floating naval museum. During the war, the _Lexington_ was in almost every major operation in the Pacific theater, and planes from her decks destroyed 372 enemy aircraft in flight and an additional 475 on the ground. She was dubbed "The Blue Ghost" because of the ship's blue-gray color, and because Japanese propaganda radio broadcaster Tokyo Rose repeatedly and mistakenly announced that the _Lexington_ had been sunk. The _Lexington_ was modernized in the 1950s and served in the U.S. 7th Fleet, including duty during the Vietnam War.

Tours of the "Lady Lex" are self-guided. A big-screen theater shows IMAX movies, and a video details the history of the ship with historic film footage. There are a number of exhibits, such as a Navy Seal submarine and interpretive displays of ship engines, plus a flight simulator that, for $3.75 per person, provides a wild 5-minute ride simulating the experience of flying. But being on the actual boat, climbing up and down ladders between decks, seeing the ship's hospital and mess hall, and exploring its narrow passages give the visitor a more concrete sense of what life was like on this carrier than any film. Not many museums can do this sort of thing. On the flight deck are more than a dozen aircraft from the 1930s to the 1960s, including an F-14A Tomcat and a Cobra helicopter. You can also get a close-up look at the ship's 40-millimeter anti-aircraft guns. The _Lexington_ has a large gift shop and a snack bar. Allow at least 2 hours.

Note: Although some parts of the USS _Lexington_ are easily accessible by anyone, seeing many of the best parts, such as the flight deck, bridge, and engine room involves climbing a lot of steep, old metal stairs and ladders, stepping over metal barricades, and maneuvering through tight passageways. Those with mobility problems will most likely not be able to get to everything.

2914 N. Shoreline Blvd., in Corpus Christi Bay. ℂ 800/523-9539 or 361/888-4873. www.usslexington.com. Admission $12 adults, $7 children ages 4–12, $10 seniors 60 and older and active military. Free admission to the Hanger Deck for those with disabilities. Daily 9am–5pm; open until 6pm Memorial Day to Labor Day. Last entry half-hour before closing. Parking $3.

OTHER ATTRACTIONS

Just north of downtown is the city's striking convention center. Nearby are a visitor center at 1823 N. Chaparral St. and a handful of small museums including the **South Texas Art Museum,** the **Asian Cultures Museum,** and the **Museum of Science and History.** Before going to any of these, first step into the visitor center to see if any coupons are available. Visiting these museums, which are small to medium size, is nice way to spend a rainy afternoon.

Adding to Corpus Christi's small-town charm will be a new minor league baseball team in the Texas league called the **Corpus Christi Hooks** (ℂ 361/866-TEAM). It will be hosting games at the new Whataburger Field, which is in the same part of town as the above-mentioned museums. (Whataburger is the name of a large burger joint chain with restaurants all across the South and Southwest. It began in Corpus in 1950 with one burger stand. During your stay here you'll see lots of these restaurants with their trademark orange-and-white roofs.) Another popular spectator sport is greyhound racing at the **Corpus Christi Racetrack** at 5302 Leopard St. (✆ **361/884-1693**). It holds evening and matinee races and charges $1 general admission.

OUTDOOR ACTIVITIES

Watersports, birding, and fishing are the most popular activities. Certain parts of this area lend themselves to different kinds of watersports. Birding is good throughout; it just depends on what species you're looking for. Here is a rundown of activities and where best to do them.

DOLPHIN TOURS   Dolphins are plentiful in these waters. These tours are offered in both Rockport and Port Aransas (see those respective sections).

FISHING/BOATING   For deep-sea fishing, you're better off going to Port Aransas, which is on Mustang Island facing the open water. You'll save fuel costs that way. For bay fishing, you can find guides and charter boats in Corpus, Rockport, or Port Aransas. Shoreline fishing is popular in these parts, with numerous piers, jetties, and beaches, depending on your tastes. In Corpus a charter boat usually costs from $300 to $400 for a full-day trip for one or two people. Available guides include **Don Hand** (✆ 361/993-2024), **Salty Aggie Guide Service** (✆ 800/322-3346 or 361/991-6045), and **Ingram's Guide Service** (✆ 800/619-0702; www.fishcorpuschristi.com). For party boats and general boat trips, contact **Captain Clark's Flagship** (✆ 361/884-1693), in downtown Corpus on People's Street. Regular cruises are seasonal.

SAILING   Corpus has a wonderful large bay for sailing, and every Wednesday afternoon there's a friendly sailboat race in the bay by downtown. Corpus has a reputation for having lots of good sailing weather. For rentals, lessons, or cruises contact the **Corpus Christi Sailing Center** (✆ **361/881-8503**). It's located in the downtown marina at 200 S. Shoreline.

SEA KAYAKING   This is becoming wildly popular in the area, and is being combined with fishing or nature photography. Most of the interesting sites are near Rockport—see the next section in this chapter.

SURFING   Port Aransas is the surfing capital of this area. It's described later in this chapter.

WINDSURFING   Corpus's reputation for good breezes also draws a lot of windsurfers. Annual windsurfing regattas are held here. An ideal place to windsurf or take lessons is at Bird Basin in the Padre Island National Seashore, which is described later in this chapter. You'll find a lot of outfits in Corpus that will rent or give lessons; one is **Wind and Wave Watersports** at 10721 S.P.I.D. (✆ **361/937-9283**).

WHOOPING CRANE TOURS   The world-famous whooping cranes inhabit the Aransas National Wildlife Preserve from mid-November to mid-April. The best place to buy a ticket on a tour boat is Rockport, which lies closest to the preserve. You can also rent kayaks there and paddle around the shore of the preserve, but under no circumstances are you allowed to set foot on land. For more info, see the Rockport section.

WHERE TO STAY

Among the numerous national chain motels in Corpus Christi are **Best Western Garden Inn,** 11217 I-37, Exit 11B (✆ 800/937-8376 or 361/241-6675); **Comfort Suites,** 3925 S.P.I.D. (✆ 800/228-5150 or 361/225-2500); **Days Inn,** 4302 Surfside Blvd. (✆ 800/325-2525 or 361/882-3297); **Embassy Suites Hotel,** 4337 S.P.I.D. (✆ 800/362-2779 or 361/853-7899); **La Quinta,** 5155 I-37, Exit 3A (✆ 800/687-6667 or

361/888-5721); **Motel 6,** 845 Lantana St., I-37 Exit 4B (© 800/466-8356 or 361/289-9397); and **Travelodge,** 910 Corn Products Rd., I-37, Exit 5 (© 800/578-7878 or 361/289-5666). A reasonably priced independent motel is the **Sea Shell Inn,** 202 Kleberg Place (© 361/888-5291), with rates for two of $50 to $125. Room tax adds 15% to rates, and the highest rates in the Corpus Christi area are in the summer.

George Blucher House Bed & Breakfast Inn 𝕮𝕮𝕮
This wonderful B&B combines the ambience of an elegant historic home with modern amenities, including private bathrooms and plush robes. Built in 1904 for George and Alice Von Blucher, this 5,000-square-foot inn was purchased in 1999 by history buff Tracey Smith, who thoroughly researched the home's past before beginning restoration. After about a year of work, the B&B opened with six rooms, each named after one of the Blucher children. The ultrafeminine Pearl's Room is pink, with American and French antiques, a queen-size bed, and a private balcony with views of downtown; and Nellie's Room is decorated in a floral motif, with American and French country furnishings and two twin beds. Most rooms are on the second floor, but one ground-level unit, Jasper's Room, is wheelchair accessible.

The attention to detail that Ms. Smith showed in restoring the house also shows in her management of the B&B. The bed linens are first rate and coffee is readily available. Breakfasts here are a splendid event, and might include entrees such as chicken pecan quiche or eggs Benedict with artichokes, spinach, and cream cheese; and a fruit dish such as baked apple with maple syrup and pecans and wrapped in a puff pastry. A library has a comfortable sitting area and chess, dominos, backgammon, and other games. In addition, the inn is across the street from **Blucher Park,** a prime bird-watching area. Smoking is not permitted inside.

211 N. Carrizo, Corpus Christi, TX 78401. © **866/884-4884** or 361/884-4884. Fax 361/884-4885. www.georgeblucher house.com. 6 units. $100–$175 double. Rates include full breakfast. Holiday and special event weekends require a minimum 2-night stay. MC, V. Children older than 12 accepted with prior approval. *In room:* A/C, TV/VCR, Wi-Fi and dataport, hair dryers, iron.

Omni Corpus Christi Hotel 𝕮𝕮
The best choice in Corpus Christi for those seeking a full-service hotel, the Omni consists of two towers, Bayfront and Marina, overlooking Corpus Christi Bay. I prefer the Bayfront. The spacious rooms are simply appointed in a modern hotel style, and all have private balconies. Standard rooms have two doubles or one king-size bed, large working desks, plush chairs, large closets, and several telephones. The basic king rooms come with floor-to-ceiling windows that offer spectacular views of the Gulf, particularly from the upper floors of the 20-story Bayfront Tower. One of the three on-site restaurants is the highly rated Republic of Texas Bar & Grill (p. 224). Because this hotel gets a lot of weekday business travelers, you'll get especially good rates on weekends.

900 and 707 N. Shoreline Blvd., Corpus Christi, TX 78401. © **800/843-6664** or 361/887-1600. Fax 361/887-6715. www.omnihotels.com. 821 units. $154–$198 double; suites from $300. Golf packages available. AE, DC, DISC, MC, V. Free covered parking. **Amenities:** 3 restaurants; 2 heated indoor/outdoor pools; nearby golf course; nearby lit tennis courts; fully equipped health club; Jacuzzi; dry sauna; airport shuttle; salon; limited room service; massage; laundry service. *In room:* A/C, TV, dataport, hair dryer, iron.

CAMPING
RVers have plenty of camping choices in the Corpus Christi area, and although many of the RV parks will accept tenters, the rates are often the same as for sites with RV hook-ups; those in tents will be surrounded by RVs. Tenters should camp at nearby

Padre Island National Seashore or one of the other public parks in the area, which are listed elsewhere (p. 233) in this chapter.

Among RV parks here, the best is **Colonia del Rey**, 1717 Waldron Rd., near the entrance to Padre Island (*C* **800/580-2435** for reservations, or 361/937-2435; www. gocampingamerica.com/coloniadelrey), which has a swimming pool, Jacuzzi, and all the other usual amenities, and can accommodate rigs up to 85 feet long. Some sites have telephones, and rates are $21 to $23 for full hook-ups, including cable TV.

WHERE TO DINE

For a quick bite, you can try a burger from the chain that began here in Corpus— **Whataburger.** At least you won't have trouble finding one here; they're everywhere, and they're generally open late.

La Playa *(★★ (Finds* TEX-MEX   Part of the enjoyment of hanging out in South Texas is the excellent Tex-Mex food. This place has some great food and a menu large enough to meet everyone's tastes. The fajitas garner most of the attention here, but I think the restaurant's forte might be the enchiladas, of which there are several kinds. Especially good are the Tex-Mex with the traditional chili gravy or the green enchiladas with a nicely done tangy sauce. Something that's different on the menu (and very popular) is the deep-fried stuffed avocado. Order it if you dare. For dessert try the sopapillas or the flan. A second location is at 7118 S.P.I.D.

4201 S.P.I.D. *C* **361/980-3909.** Main courses $8–$16. AE, MC, V. Mon–Sat 11am–10pm; Sun 11am–9pm.

Republic of Texas Bar & Grill *(★★ (Moments* STEAK   This is the spot to celebrate a special occasion. Located on the 20th floor of the Omni Bayfront hotel, the Republic of Texas Bar & Grill is expensive and special. It has a unique terraced dining room, which, from every table, affords breathtaking views of the bay and the city through extra-tall plate-glass windows. Appetizers include a giant portobello mushroom, stuffed with sweet sausage and garlic herb cheese. This is primarily a steakhouse, and all beef is top USDA premium choice corn-fed that is hand cut and grilled over a fire of oak and mesquite. The menu usually also offers several game dishes, such as mesquite-grilled quail, and seafood. Sides include huge baked Idaho potatoes and garlic mashed potatoes, which are fine, but the house specialty hash browns are exquisite. There is also an extensive wine list. Service is excellent.

At the Omni Bayfront Hotel, 900 N. Shoreline Blvd. *C* **361/886-3515.** www.omnihotels.com/republic. Reservations recommended. Main courses $20–$40. AE, DISC, MC, V. Mon–Sat 5:30–10:30pm; Sun 5:30–9pm.

Water Street Seafood Company *(★★★* SEAFOOD   Considered by most locals to be the best seafood restaurant in Corpus Christi, this restaurant and its sister, the Water Street Oyster Bar, pack in the customers for dinner. What brings them in is the mesquite-grilled fish or the pecan-crusted oysters (which are something special). The cooking combines Southern and Mexican styles. I really enjoyed the Gulf crab cakes served with a spicy rémoulade and mango salsa. The specials on the chalkboard are quite yummy, too. Everything at Water Street is prepared fresh, and the staff is accommodating about making substitutions, meeting individuals' dietary needs, or providing smaller portions (at a lower price!).

309 N. Water St. *C* **361/882-8683.** Reservations not accepted but you can call ahead to be put on the waiting list. Main courses $5.95–$18. AE, DISC, MC, V. Sun–Thurs 11am–10pm; Fri–Sat 11am–11pm. Closed Thanksgiving and Dec 25.

4 Rockport ★★

35 miles NE of Corpus Christi; 182 miles SW of Houston; 161 miles SE of San Antonio

Rockport and its sister town, Fulton, are on the other side of the bay from Corpus, on the mainland coast facing out toward San Jose Island, which encloses Aransas Bay. The two towns have a combined population of 9,000. Rockport has more character than its neighbor and has become an art town, with resident artists, galleries, and the Rockport Art Center. The old downtown area is small and charming, with shops, galleries, and restaurants. But Rockport isn't in danger of becoming a fancy place; it's comfortable and feels lived in. Old-style motel courts, still the most common lodging option here, are testament to a time not so long ago when Rockport was a summer retreat for Texans looking for a quiet, economical place to enjoy the water. That's changing. A modern subdivision marina community has developed between the two towns, a Wal-Mart is going up, and a Holiday Inn Express has opened.

This part of the coast is particularly lovely. Notable are the many windswept oak trees, which are a favorite subject for artists and have become emblematic of the area. Of course, water is everywhere. A large protected wetlands area to the north, the Aransas National Wildlife Refuge, is the winter home to the only natural colony of whooping cranes in the world. But this is only one of several natural areas in the region. Birding and fishing are two of the major draws here. But if a beach is what you're looking for, the best ones are out on the barrier islands described in the next two sections.

ESSENTIALS
GETTING THERE & AROUND
Rockport is 45 minutes from Corpus Christi. Take Tex. 35 over the Harbor Bridge towards Portland and just keep going. Well after the Aransas Pass turnoff take the exit labeled MARKET ST. (FM 1069). Both Rockport and Fulton are on Bus. 35, which continues north over the Copano Bay Causeway to the Aransas National Wildlife Refuge.

VISITOR INFORMATION
For maps or info contact the **Rockport–Fulton Area Chamber of Commerce,** 404 Broadway, Rockport, TX 78382 (© **800/826-6441** or 361/729-6445; www.rockport-fulton.org).

FAST FACTS   The nearest full-service hospital, with a 24-hour emergency room, is **North Bay Hospital,** 11 miles south of Rockport at 1711 W. Wheeler Ave., Aransas Pass (© **361/758-8585**). The **post office,** located at 1550 FM 2165 in Rockport, is open Monday through Friday from 9am to 4:30pm, Saturday from 9am to noon.

WHAT TO SEE & DO
THE TOP ATTRACTION
This region is among the nation's premier bird-watching destinations, and the best spot for birding here is the **Aransas National Wildlife Refuge** ★★. More then 300 species of birds have been spotted here, but the whooping crane, which winters here from November to April (see sidebar), is the big draw.

In addition to birds, the refuge is home to about 30 species of snakes (only four are poisonous), turtles, lizards, and the refuge's largest reptile, the American alligator. Mammals commonly seen include white-tailed deer, javelina, wild boars, raccoons,

Whooping Cranes: Back from the Brink of Extinction

By and large, there are two kinds of tourists who come to the Rockport area in winter: winter Texans fleeing the harsh cold of their northern homes and nature enthusiasts who come to visit another sort of winter Texan, the magnificent whooping cranes. The largest birds in America, these cranes fly in from northwest Canada in October/November and leave again in the spring. An adult male stands 5 feet high and can have a wingspan of 8 feet. They are elegant, too: Elongated legs and throat give them dramatic lines, and the plumage has a classic appeal that never goes out of fashion—solid white with black wing tips, black eyeliner, and just a touch of red accent on the top of the head. It would be a tremendous blow to lose these creatures to oblivion, but that is almost what happened, and their comeback story is probably the most famous of all the cases of wildlife conservation.

Before the arrival of the Europeans, these birds inhabited the Gulf and Atlantic shores in winter and northern Midwest and Canada in summer. But hunting and loss of habitat dwindled the population until, by 1941, only 15 birds survived. All were members of the flock that winters here on the central Texas coast. A concerted effort requiring the efforts of many dedicated biologists and field workers was begun to save them. The team first pushed for laws preserving the summer and winter nesting grounds and all the major stopover points along the 2,400 miles of the migration route. The cranes were slow to come back, but through protection and public education, their mortality rates decreased and the population began to grow. This was difficult and took time because these cranes are slow to mature and don't reproduce until their fourth year. And even then the female lays only two eggs and raises only one chick. Worried that with only one flock the species was vulnerable, biologists began stealing the second eggs and hatching them elsewhere. They have established a nonmigrating population in southcentral Florida and another population that they've been "teaching" to migrate between Wisconsin and western Florida. So far it's working, but the Aransas flock is still the largest and only natural population of "whoopers" in the world. This year their numbers hit an all-time high of 224.

The best way to view the birds is from the deck of a boat. Several boats specialize in birding and whooping crane tours. They skirt along the coast of the refuge, which is the favorite feeding grounds for the cranes. A few are listed below.

eastern cottontail rabbits, and nine-banded armadillos. Also present, but only occasionally seen, are bobcats and opossums.

A 16-mile paved auto tour loop meanders through a variety of habitats, offering access to a 40-foot observation tower, a boardwalk that leads through a salt marsh to the coastline, and other viewing areas. The refuge has nine walking trails, ranging from .1 to 1.4 miles, a picnic area, and an impressive Wildlife Interpretive Center with information, exhibits, a bookstore, and administration offices. There are also seasons for hunting and saltwater fishing access. Camping is not permitted.

For more information, contact the Aransas National Wildlife Refuge at (✆ **361/ 286-3559**, or visit http://southwest.fws.gov. It's located about 36 road miles northeast of Rockport via Tex. 35, FM 774, and FM 2040. The refuge is open daily from just before sunrise to just after sunset, and the Wildlife Interpretive Center is open daily from 8:30am to 4:30pm. Admission to the refuge costs $5 per vehicle ($3 if there's only one person). Binoculars are available to borrow at the Wildlife Interpretive Center. Insect repellent is recommended year-round.

OUTDOOR ACTIVITIES

FISHING   There are public fishing piers in Fulton Harbor and at Rockport Beach Park, as well as numerous other areas. Fishing guides offer bay and deep-sea fishing trips, and rates vary considerably. Contact **Gold Spoon Charters** (✆ **361/727-9178;** www.goldspooncharters.com), **Green Hornet Fishing Guide Service** (✆ **361/749- 5904**), and **Hook Line & Sinker** (✆ **866/993-3131** or 361/727-0910).

KAYAKING   All the different bays around Rockport are well sheltered by the barrier islands. In some places the water gets quite shallow and is broken into narrow channels by mangroves. One such place is called Lighthouse Lakes. This is perfect territory for kayaking, which you can combine with birding, fishing, or nature photography. The important thing is to find renters who have a big enough selection that they can fit you with the appropriate kayak for your needs. You might talk to the people at **Rockport Kayak Outfitters** at 106 S. Austin St. (✆ **361/729-1505**). They offer rentals and tours. Tours require a minimum of four people, but you might be able to hook up with another group or get a self-guided tour on your own with one of their maps. They can haul you and your kayaks to a drop-off spot and pick you up later.

PARKS   Anglers and birders especially like **Goose Island State Park** (✆ **361/729- 2858;** www.tpwd.state.tx.us/park/goose), which is home to The Big Tree, a giant live oak with seemingly countless twisting branches that is estimated to be more than 1,000 years old. It's more than 35 feet in circumference, 44 feet high, and has a crown spread of 90 feet. The park has a short paved hiking and biking path, two playgrounds, picnic tables and grills, a boat ramp, and a lighted fishing pier. Fish caught here include speckled trout, redfish, flounder, and sheepshead. Crabbing and oystering are also popular. There are 102 campsites with water and electric hook-ups and 25 sites with water only, and the park also has restrooms with showers and an RV dump station. Entrance to the park costs $5 per person age 13 and older per day, and camping costs an additional $10 to $15 per night, with reservations available (✆ **512/ 389-8900**). The park is about 12 miles from Rockport. Follow Tex. 35 north 10 miles to Park Road 13, which you follow 2 miles east to the park entrance. There are several preserves and wildlife sanctuaries in and about the area, which make for good birding. You can ask at the Chamber of Commerce visitor center or go to their web page (see "Visitor Information," above).

WHOOPING CRANE TOURS/DOLPHIN TOURS   A number of companies offer whooping crane and birding tours from November through March. They use shallow-draft boats that go out usually for 3 to 4 hours. Cost is about $35 per person, with discounts for children and seniors, but several companies will take small groups at a flat rate of $150 to $200. Some guarantee that you'll see whooping cranes. Among those that charge per person are **Captain Billy Gaskins** (✆ 866/729-2997 or 361/ 729-2997); **Captain Ted's Whooping Crane Tours** (✆ 800/338-4551 or 361/729- 9589); and **Captain Eddy Polhemus Pisces** (✆ 361/729-7525). Most of these boats leave out of Fulton harbor, so you might want to go down and check out the boats for yourself and find one with a convenient departure time. Several do dolphin tours as well. Those offering the flat rate option for up to four people include **Captain Sally's Reel Fun Charters** (© 361/729-9095; www.captainsally.com). **Aransas Bay Birding Charters** (© 361/727-2689) offers 6-hour tours for up to six people for $300. Check with the Rockport–Fulton Area Chamber of Commerce (see "Visitor Information," above) for information on land-based birding tours.

INDOOR ATTRACTIONS

Fulton Mansion ✿   Constructed between 1874 and 1877 by cattle baron George Fulton, this mansion is the local architectural landmark. The site is managed by the Texas Parks and Wildlife Department, which offers hourly tours (except at noon) from 9am to 3pm Wednesday to Saturday. Built in French Empire style, it was notable in its day for having indoor plumbing and other modern conveniences. The materials used are rich and varied, and the interiors are impressive.

316 S. Fulton Beach Rd. © **361/729-0386**. Admission $5. By tour only. Wed–Sat 9, 10, 11am, 1, 2, and 3pm. Closed major holidays.

Rockport Center for the Arts ✿   Part of the charm of Rockport is that its small downtown area is such an inviting place to hang about and relax. And this center is a good place to begin. The Main Gallery presents about 10 changing exhibits each year that range from local to international artists. There are often displays of students' work, and sometimes hands-on exhibits, in the Garden Gallery. The Members Gallery presents an eclectic selection of works by members of the Rockport Art Association, which manages the center. The Rockport Art Association sponsors the Rockport Art Festival each summer, in late June and/or early July; and also sponsors a series of art classes, workshops, and concerts (call for the current schedule).

902 Navigation Circle, Rockport. © **361/729-5519**. www.rockportartcenter.com. Free admission. Tues–Sat 10am–4pm; Sun 1–4pm.

Texas Maritime Museum   From pirates to shipbuilding to offshore oil drilling, this excellent small museum brings to life the story of the Texas Gulf Coast, with lots of hands-on exhibits, historic fishing gear, and old strange-looking outboard motors. Among its changing and permanent exhibits, you'll see artwork, such as the *Lighthouses of Texas* watercolors by Harold Phenix, and a life-size ship's bridge where you can imagine yourself on the high seas. On the museum grounds are a survival capsule (used to escape offshore oil rigs in emergencies), a 26-foot-long lifeboat, and a replica of a scow sloop fishing boat. Allow at least 1 hour.

1202 Navigation Circle, Rockport. © **361/729-1271**. www.texasmaritimemuseum.org. Admission $5 adults, $4 seniors 60 and older, $2 children ages 6–12, free for children 5 and younger. Tues–Sat 10am–4pm; Sun 1–4pm. Closed major holidays.

WHERE TO STAY

Among the national chain motels in the Rockport and Fulton areas are the **Best Western Inn by the Bay,** 3902 N. Tex. 35, Fulton (© **800/235-6076** or 361/729-8351); **Days Inn,** 1212 E. Laurel St. (at Tex. 35), Rockport (© **800/329-7466** or 361/729-6379); and **Holiday Inn Express,** 901 Hwy. 35 N., Rockport (© **888/727-2566** or 361/727-0283).

Crane House ✿✿✿ *Moments*   As a travel writer, you sometimes see so many hotels, condos, and other lodgings that it all becomes a blur, and if you don't take notes you begin confusing them. There is no danger of that happening with this place; it's truly one of a kind. Crane House is an attractive and comfortable house with two bedrooms (one king and two twins), two bathrooms, a full kitchen, and a large screened porch. But it could have been a shack with bunk beds and an outhouse, and it would still have been special because it offers those rare commodities of privacy, solitude, and natural beauty, all in abundance. It sits alone on 824 acres bordering the Aransas National Wildlife Refuge, with a mile of coastline on St. Charles Bay (use of kayak included). The owners are in partnership with the Texas Nature Conservancy to protect more than 200 acres of wetlands that are part of the property. And, as if that weren't enough, a pair of whooping cranes are daily visitors to the backyard, and to view or photograph them you have to go no farther than the porch. And how many establishments have a guard horse looking after the place?

911 S. Water St., Rockport, TX 78382 (for reservations). ℂ 361/729-7239. www.cranehouseretreat.com. 1 unit. $195–$250. No credit cards. Pets accepted. **Amenities:** Full kitchen; kayak. *In room:* A/C.

Hoope's House ★★   With some B&Bs, you know the second you walk in that you're looking at a labor of love. That's what this beautiful B&B feels like. The owners have taken great pains in restoring the house and furnishing the rooms. The house has four garden rooms and four rooms in the house. The garden rooms are larger and offer more privacy (I like the San Jose and the Aransas), but the rooms in the house have more character and are absolutely charming (I like the Live Oak and the Blackjack). The pool is great, the grounds are immaculate, and the innkeepers are easygoing, down-to-earth types.

417 N. Broadway, Rockport, TX 78382. ℂ 800/924-1008 or 361/729-8424. Fax 361/790-9288. www.hoopeshouse. com. 8 units. $140 double. Rates include full breakfast. AE, MC, V. **Amenities:** Pool; Jacuzzi; bikes; tour info; in-room massage; fishing equipment. *In room:* A/C, TV, dataport, hair dryer, iron.

The Lighthouse Inn ★★   For a full-service hotel, this new, independently owned property right on the water is your best choice. All rooms have balconies with a view of the bay and a couple of rocking chairs from which to enjoy it. Pelicans like to fish right off the shore. Standard rooms are medium size, immaculate, and comfortably furnished. They come with two queen-size beds. The suites have a full kitchen, a completely separate sitting area, and two TVs.

200 S. Fulton Beach Rd., Rockport, TX 78382. ℂ 866/790-8439 or 361/790-8439. Fax 361/790-7393. www.lighthouse texas.com. 78 units. $129–$199 double; $169–$209 captain's suite; $299–$399 2-bedroom suite. AE, DC, DISC, MC, V. **Amenities:** Restaurant; bar; outdoor pool; Jacuzzi; fitness room; tour info; room service until 10pm; babysitting; coin-op laundry. *In room:* A/C, TV/DVD, coffeemaker, hair dryer, iron, microwave.

Village Inn Motel *Finds*   This well-maintained two-story older motel—some parts are pre-1930—is an excellent choice for those seeking economical, comfortable lodging within walking distance of Rockport's beach, piers, attractions, and restaurants. Inside the bright yellow exterior are a wide variety of simply but attractively decorated units. The rooms are larger than average, with modern furnishings and from one to four beds. Several standard rooms have small refrigerators and microwaves; there are also kitchenette units and several two-bedroom apartments with full kitchens. Twelve units have shower only; the rest have shower/tub combos.

503 N. Austin St., Rockport, TX 78382. ℂ 800/338-7539 for reservations, or 361/729-6370. www.village-inn-motel. com. 26 units. Summer $55–$65 double, $60–$75 kitchenette units, $100–$110 2-bedroom apartments; winter $52–$55 double, $55–$65 kitchenette units, $95 2-bedroom apartments. AE, DC, DISC, MC, V. Pets accepted ($10 per pet per day). **Amenities:** Outdoor pool. *In room:* A/C, TV, kitchen and fridge in some units.

WHERE TO DINE

For light sandwich-type food or for takeout, try **Tony Legner's Culinary Productions** in downtown Rockport at 1003 E. Concho (℡ **361/729-6395**). This deli/restaurant makes excellent pizza that you can eat there or take back to your hotel. It's open Tuesday to Saturday 11am to 6pm.

Latitude 28°02' ⟨⟨ SEAFOOD   It's always great to eat at a restaurant where the owner is the chef, but it's especially rewarding when that restaurant serves locally caught seafood where a little attention in dealing with local suppliers ensures quality and freshness. This is the case here, and there's no shortage of appealing dishes on the menu in addition to the nightly chef's specials. There are nonseafood dishes as well, including beef, chicken, and vegetarian options. The dining room is simple, comfortable, and attractive. The tables are well separated, and the walls serve as gallery space, holding works by local artists.

105 N. Austin St. ℡ 361/727-9009. Reservations recommended. Main courses $15–$27. AE, DISC, MC, V. Tues–Sun 5–10pm.

Los Comales ⟨ MEXICAN/TEX-MEX   An unpretentious Mexican food joint just a few blocks from Rockport's downtown area, Los Comales serves up some excellent dishes from a fairly large menu. All the standards, such as fajitas, and the sides, such as borracho beans, are done really well. One of the dishes that this place is known for is the stuffed, deep-fried avocado. Also terrific are the Enchiladas Tarascas, which have a tangy green sauce. You can also ask for some uncommon vegetarian options such as spinach and mushroom enchiladas.

431 Hwy. 35. ℡ 361/729-3952. Main courses $5–$15. AE, DISC, MC, V. Mon–Sat 11am–10pm; Sun 11am–9pm.

5 Port Aransas ⟨★

30 miles NE of Corpus Christi; 155 miles S of San Antonio

Port Aransas is a funky Texas-style beach town located on the north end of Mustang Island. It has nearly 4,000 permanent residents, but at any given time at least a couple of thousand island condo dwellers descend on the town for groceries, a beer, and such. Unlike Corpus and Rockport, Port Aransas is situated on open water. (Actually, it's open water in one direction, and the bay in the other.) Hence you get big, broad, sandy beaches, and some watersports that the other destinations don't offer. The town is different from Rockport also in that Rockport has other economic activities besides tourism. That's not really true for Port A (as the locals call it), which depends on winter Texans, fishing enthusiasts, surfers, and sun worshippers for its existence. This is why the town has a little more party spirit, which you can easily discern if you go barhopping here. That said, the perfect time *not* to come here is during spring break, when college students fill the town and disrupt the calm, small-town feel of the place.

ESSENTIALS

GETTING THERE & AROUND

Port Aransas is a little more than 30 minutes from Corpus Christi. The quickest way to get here is probably to take South Padre Island Drive (S.P.I.D.) out to Mustang Island and then drive north. But you can also get here by taking Tex. 35 north, as you would go to Rockport, but take the exit for Aransas Pass (Hwy. 361) and keep going until you see signs for the ferry. The ferry is free and is a very short ride that drops you off in the middle of town. Port Aransas is compact, and most of the watersports activities can be found by just walking around the town's harbor.

VISITOR INFORMATION

Just after you get off the ferry, you'll see the visitor center on your right at 421 W. Cotter (© 800/452-6278 or 361/749-5919; www.portaransas.org). The staff is very helpful.

FAST FACTS   The nearest full-service hospital, with a 24-hour emergency room, is **North Bay Hospital** at 1711 W. Wheeler Ave., Aransas Pass (© 361/758-8585).

WHAT TO SEE & DO

BEACHCOMBING   Okay, so maybe you want a beach that's completely free of cars and all signs of human settlement, where you can walk along in perfect communion with nature. If so, the obvious choice is San Jose Island, right across from Port A. It's privately owned by a Texas oil family and kept pristine. Transporting people to the island is the Jetty Boat ($10 per adult, $5 per child round-trip), which makes 10 trips daily. Visit **Fisherman's Wharf** at 900 N. Tarpon St. (© 800/605-5448 or 361/749-5760). *Note:* Whatever you might need on the island, you'll have to bring with you. This island is also a good place to collect seashells.

BEACH CRUISING   Texas beaches tend to be broad and flat and extend for miles. Driving is permitted on most beaches, and cruising is one of the favorite pastimes of the vacationing Texan. The idea is to pack a cooler in the car filled with picnic supplies; take along other essentials such as towels, beach chairs, and perhaps a beach umbrella; and then drive to the beach and slowly cruise along until you find your spot. Always go very slow (it's a matter of courtesy) and stay on the packed sand; don't get into the loose stuff. The beach on the Gulf side of Mustang Island is miles long, but isn't continuous; there are places where you have to get back on the road. But somewhere along there, you're going to find your spot. One possibility is at **Mustang Island State Park** 🎣🎣 (© 361/749-5246; www.tpwd.state.tx.us/park/mustang), which has more than 5 miles of wide, sandy beach, with fine sand, few rocks and broken shells, and almost enough waves for surfing.

BIKE RENTAL   Port A is nice town to explore on bike. The best-maintained rental bikes are at **Island Bikes** at 736 Tarpon St. (© 361/749-2453). Cost is about $15 per day.

DOLPHIN TOURS   **Dolphin Watch** runs dolphin and nature tours on its boat, the *Mustang.* Call © 361/749-6969 or just ask at Woody's Sports Center, listed below.

FISHING   A lot of fishermen complain that the bay around Port A is overfished. Still, I've run into a few boats that have had good luck. The town has more than 200 fishing guides. If you want to try deep-sea fishing from a party boat (rather than chartering your own boat), see the guys at Fisherman's Wharf, listed above. They have two large boats that go out regularly. If you want to charter, try **Woody's Sports Center** at 136 W. Cotter (© 361/749-5271 or 361/749-5252; www.gulfcoastfishing.com).

GAMBLING   All over town you'll see flyers and coupons for the *Texas Treasure,* a casino boat that heads out to the 9-mile limit before letting the dice fly. The boat docks at the same mainland pier as the ferry. For info and reservations call © 866/468-5825 or check out www.txtreasure.com.

HORSEBACK RIDING   For riding on the beach, contact **Mustang Riding Stables** (© 361/991-7433), located just south of Mustang Island State Park.

KAYAKING   The protected side of Mustang Island has lots of sloughs and cuts and coves that teem with wildlife and that are perfect for exploring by kayak. Contact **Wet Heads** (© **888/749-7111**) for rentals and guided and self-guided trips. They're located on the Port Aransas main beach at marker #9.

SURFING   Yes, there is surf on the Texas Gulf Coast, particularly when storms and hurricanes come this way. **Pat Magees Surf Shop,** 124 Ave. G (© **361/749-4177;** www.patmagees.com), has vintage surfboards and old Hawaiian shirts for sale.

WHERE TO STAY

There are a number of motels in town, but only one belongs to a national chain, **Best Western Ocean Villa** at 400 E. Ave. G (© **800/WESTERN**). Some local motels I like are **Alister Square Inn** at 122 S. Alister St. (© **888/749-3003**), and **Captain's Quarters Inn** at 235 W. Cotter (© **888/272-6727**).

Condos are the most popular form of lodging on the island. The beach condos in the town area are smaller buildings, but as you drive south you pass large condo properties on the beach, which are scattered along several miles of shore. Condo owners will contract with agencies to rent these out by the week, and these agencies advertise a lot in town and on the Web. I had dealings with one agency, **Starkey Properties** (© **888/951-6381;** www.starkeyproperties.com), which proved very professional.

For RVs, try Mustang Island State Park. For reservations, call © **512/389-8900.** They also have campsites. For a nice location closer to town, try **On the Beach RV Park** at 907 Beach Access Rd. (© **361/749-4909**).

Balinese Flats *(Value*   This stylish little establishment in the middle of town offers attractive two-bedroom apartments with full kitchens for a good price. In addition to the apartments, the owners are building a couple of single hotel rooms. All the units are comfortable and beautifully decorated with Mexican tiles, furniture, and accents. The bedrooms come with two queen beds, one queen, or two twins. Three units come with a full-size fridge; three come with a half-size fridge. Make sure to bring your cocktail fixin's so that you can enjoy the upstairs veranda with drink in hand. The same property management company owns another property that has views of the water from the protected side of the island. It's called Balinese Piers.

121 Cut-off Rd., Port Aransas, TX 78373. © **888/951-6381** or 361/749-1880. Fax 361/749-3592. www.balinese flats.com. 6 units. 2-bedroom apt summer $155–$175; spring and fall $115–$175; winter $65–$75. DISC, MC, V. *In room:* A/C, TV/DVD, Wi-Fi, full kitchen, coffeemaker, hair dryer.

The Tarpon Inn *(**   This is a lovely old two-story hotel that dates from 1886. It's well conserved and has plenty of character. Standard rooms are pretty small; I would go for one of the premium rooms, or better still, one of the two suites, which are extra large and comfortable. The FDR suite (no, he didn't sleep here; he just fished here) has a large sitting room, a kitchen, dining room, and a private porch. More romantic is the upstairs corner suite with a marvelous queen bed and a large tub in the bedroom. If these are over your budget, I like room 21, a premium queen that's spacious and has a large bathroom.

200 E. Cotter, Port Aransas, TX 78373. © **800/365-6784** or 361/749-5555. Fax 361/749-4305. www.thetaponinn. com. 24 units. $69–$99 double; $79–$110 premium; $125–$250 suite. 2-night minimum stay on weekends. AE, MC, V. **Amenities:** Outdoor pool; in-room massage; fishing guides and charters. *In room:* A/C, no phone.

WHERE TO DINE

Port Aransas has a surprising number of good restaurants for a town of its size. Here I list the three I think most interesting.

La Playa 😋😋 MEXICAN/SEAFOOD   This establishment has no connection with the restaurant in Corpus that shares its name. It's run by a Houston man who has been in the restaurant business for years. The food is extremely fresh and nicely prepared. Try the excellent fish tacos, a tangy *Campechana* (Mexican-style seafood cocktail), and rich seafood enchiladas. Other dishes that deserve mention are the Tex-Mex enchiladas, the chicken al chipotle, and the margaritas. Vegetarian specials are available. The setting is casual, the service is excellent, and the furniture is comfortable. You can't reserve a table, but you can call ahead just before leaving for the restaurant to get your name on the waiting list.

222 Beach St. ✆ 361/749-0022. Reservations not accepted. Main courses $7–$15. No credit cards. Tues–Thurs 5–9pm; Fri–Sat 5–10pm; Sun 5–9pm. Open a half-hour later during summer.

Shells 😋😋 STEAK/SEAFOOD/PASTA   The owner of this restaurant had a hand in creating and running several of Austin's most highly acclaimed restaurants. He has settled into Port A to take it easy and cook only as much as he enjoys. A chalkboard lists all offerings for that particular day. Lunch items are mostly sandwiches and salads. Dinner entrees are much more elaborate affairs. On my recent visits, the owner was serving, among other tempting items, prime center-cut sirloin with a caramelized garlic glaze, sirloin medallions on top of grilled focaccia with a Gorgonzola sauce, and seared amberjack with a chile-lime sauce. The appetizers included Chinese dumplings, Thai spring rolls, and sushi. ***Note:*** This restaurant is very small, and it's common to have to wait for a table.

522 E. Ave. G. ✆ 361/749-7621. Reservations not accepted. Main courses $13–$23. DISC, MC, V. Daily 11:30am–2:30pm and 5–9pm. (Hours are not strictly kept; don't show up at the last minute, you might find the restaurant has stopped serving.)

Venetian Hot Plate 😋😋 NORTHERN ITALIAN   This restaurant's curious name owes its existence to an error in translation, and by the time the Italian owners were made aware of their mistake, it was too late to change it. The food, however, needs no translation. Wonderful pasta dishes and a grilled polenta with bits of crumbled Gorgonzola are things to consider. There are nightly specials, and the set menu changes seasonally. The owners care a lot about wine and price it reasonably. The dining room is comfortable and peaceful.

232 Beach St. ✆ 361/749-7617. Reservations recommended. Main courses $13–$17. AE, DISC, MC, V. Tues–Sat 5–9 or 10pm. Open Sun during busy weekends.

6 Padre Island National Seashore ⭐

37 miles SE of Corpus Christi; 180 miles S of San Antonio; 414 miles S of Dallas

Some 70 miles of delightful white-sand beach, picturesque sand dunes, and warm ocean waters make Padre Island National Seashore a favorite year-round playground along the Texas Gulf Coast. One of the longest stretches of undeveloped coastline in America, this is an ideal spot for swimming, sunbathing, fishing, beachcombing, windsurfing, and camping. It also offers excellent bird-watching opportunities and a chance to see several species of rare sea turtles. The island was named for Padre José Nicolás Balli, a Mexican priest who, in 1804, founded a mission, settlement, and ranch about 26 miles north of the island's southernmost tip.

Padre Island is a barrier island, essentially a sand bar that helps protect the mainland from the full force of ocean storms. Like other barrier islands, one of the constants of Padre Island is change; wind and waves relentlessly shape and re-create the island, as grasses and other hardy plants strive to get a foothold in the shifting sands. Padre Island's Gulf side, with miles of beach accessible only to those with four-wheel-drive vehicles, offers wonderful surf fishing; while the channel between the island and mainland—the Laguna Madre—offers excellent windsurfing and a protected area for small power and sailboats.

ESSENTIALS

GETTING THERE   From Corpus Christi take Tex. 358 (South Padre Island Dr.) southeast across the JFK Causeway to Padre Island, and follow Park Road 22 south to the national seashore. The drive takes 45 minutes to an hour.

VISITOR INFORMATION   For information, contact **Padre Island National Seashore,** P.O. Box 181300, Corpus Christi, TX 78480-1300 (© **361/949-8068;** www.nps.gov/pais). The Park Service also maintains a recorded beach and road condition information line (© **361/949-8175**). The park is open 24 hours a day.

The **visitor center complex,** along Park Road 22 at Malaquite Beach, has an observation deck, a bookstore, and a variety of exhibits, including one on the endangered Kemp's ridley sea turtle. In the same complex is a store, **Padre Island Park Company** (© **361/949-9368**), that sells camping and fishing supplies and gift items, and rents chairs, umbrellas, body boards, and other beach toys. The visitor center is open from 8:30am to 6pm Memorial Day through Labor Day weekend, and from 8:30am to 4:30pm the rest of the year (closed Dec 25), and the store is usually open similar hours.

FEES & REGULATIONS   Entry for up to 7 days costs $10 per vehicle (good for 7 days) or $5 per individual on foot or bike. In addition, there is a $5 user fee at Bird Island Basin. Regulations here are much like those at other National Park Service properties, which essentially require that visitors not disturb wildlife or damage the site's natural features and facilities. Pets must be leashed and are not permitted on the swimming beach in front of the visitor center. Although driving off road is permitted on some sections of beach, the dunes, grasslands, and tidal flats are closed to all vehicles.

WHEN TO GO   Summer is the busiest time here, although it is generally hot (highs in the 90s/30s Celsius) and very humid. Sea breezes in late afternoon and evening help moderate the heat. Winters are generally mild, with highs from the 50s to the 70s (teens to the 20s Celsius), and lows in the 40s and 50s (single digits to the teens Celsius). Only occasionally does the temperature drop below 40°F (4°C), and a freeze is extremely rare. Hurricane season (June–Oct) is the rainiest time of the year and also has the highest surf. September to November is a good time to visit Padre Island, when it is still usually warm enough for swimming but not nearly as hot or crowded as summer.

SAFETY   Swimmers and those walking barefoot on the beach should watch out for the Portuguese man-of-war, a blue jellyfish that can cause an extremely painful sting. There are also poisonous rattlesnakes in the dunes, grasslands, and mud flats.

RANGER PROGRAMS   Various **interpretive programs** are held year-round, ranging from guided beach or birding walks to talks outside the visitor center and evening campground campfire programs. These programs usually last from 30 to 45 minutes and cover subjects such as migrating or resident birds, seashells, the island's plant life or animals, or things that wash up on the beach. There's also a **Junior Ranger Program** for kids 5 to 13, who answer questions in a free booklet and talk with rangers about the national seashore to earn certificates, badges, and sea-turtle stickers.

WHAT TO SEE & DO
EXPLORING THE HIGHLIGHTS BY CAR
Padre Island National Seashore has an 8½-mile paved road, with good views of the Gulf and dunes, that leads to the visitor center complex. In addition, most of the beaches are open to licensed street-legal motor vehicles; some sections have hard-packed sand that makes an adequate roadbed for two-wheel-drive vehicles while most of the beach requires four-wheel-drive. See "Four-Wheeling," below.

OUTDOOR ADVENTURES
BEACHCOMBING   The best times for beachcombing are usually early mornings and especially immediately after a storm when you're apt to find a variety of seashells, seaweed, driftwood, and the like. These types of items can be collected, but live animals

The Race to Save the Sea Turtles

The Gulf of Mexico is home to five species of sea turtles, all of which are either endangered or threatened, including the Kemp's ridley, considered to be the most endangered sea turtle in the world with only about 3,000 in existence. Kemp's ridleys have almost circular shells, grow to about 2 feet long, and weigh about 100 pounds. Adults are olive green on top and yellow below, and their main food source is crabs. Their main nesting area historically is along a 16-mile stretch of beach at Playa de Rancho Nuevo in Tamaulipas, Mexico, and although females lay about 100 eggs at a time, only about 1% of the hatchlings survive to adulthood.

In the 1970s, an international effort was begun to establish a second nesting area at Padre Island National Seashore, using the theory that sea turtles always return to the beach where they were hatched to lay their eggs. More than 22,000 eggs were gathered from Playa de Rancho Nuevo between 1978 and 1988, placed in boxes containing Padre Island sand, and shipped to Texas where they were placed in incubators. After hatching, about 13,500 baby turtles were released on the beach at Padre Island National Seashore and allowed to crawl into the water for a quick swim. Fearing that the young turtles would become lunch for predators, National Park Service biologists captured them and sent them to a marine fisheries lab in Galveston, where they spent up to a year growing big enough to have a better chance of survival in the wild. They were then tagged and released into the Gulf of Mexico.

Since then some of the turtles have returned to Padre Island and other sections of the Texas Gulf Coast to nest, and Park Service workers have collected a number of eggs for incubation and eventual release. The eggs are collected in late spring and summer, and anyone seeing a nesting sea turtle is asked to not disturb it but to report its location to national seashore personnel. The public can attend releases of the hatchlings, which usually occur in June and August; for information on release dates call the **Hatchling Hotline** at ℂ **361/949-7163.**

and historical or archaeological objects should be left. Among shells sometimes found at Padre Island are lightning whelks, moon snails, Scotch bonnets, Atlantic cockles, bay scallops, and sand dollars. The best shell hunting is often in winter, when storms disturb the water and thrust shells ashore; and many of the best shells are often found on Little Shell and Big Shell beaches, accessible only to those with four-wheel-drive vehicles. Metal detectors are not permitted on the beach.

BIRDING & WILDLIFE VIEWING   More than 350 species of birds frequent Padre Island, and every visitor is bound to see and hear at least some of them. The island is a key stopping point for a variety of migratory species traveling between North and Central America, making spring and fall the best time for bird-watching. And, since a number of species winter at Padre Island, there's good birding almost year-round except for the summer. Additionally, this is the northern boundary of some Central American species, such as green jays and jacanas.

Birding here is very easy, especially for those with four-wheel-drive vehicles, who can move down the coast to the more remote stretches of beach. Experienced bird-watchers say it is best to remain in your vehicle because humans on foot scare off birds sooner than approaching vehicles. As would be expected by its name, Bird Island Basin is also a good choice for birders as long as the marshes have water. The most commonly observed bird is the laughing gull, which is a year-round resident. Other species to watch for include rare brown pelicans plus the more common American white pelicans, long-billed curlews, great blue herons, sandhill cranes, ruddy turnstones, Caspian and Royal terns, willets, Harris' hawks, reddish egrets, northern bobwhites, mourning doves, horned larks, great-tailed grackles, and red-winged blackbirds.

In addition to birds, the island is home to the spotted ground squirrel, which is often seen in the dunes near the visitor center, white-tailed deer, coyotes, black-tailed jackrabbits, lizards, and a number of poisonous and nonpoisonous snakes.

BOATING   A boat ramp is located at Bird Island Basin, which provides access to Laguna Madre, a protected bay that is ideal for small power- and sailboats. Boat launching is not permitted on the Gulf side of the island, except for sailboats and soft-sided inflatables. To rent a sailboard, contact **Worldwinds Windsurfing** (© 361/ 949-7472; www.worldwinds.net). Personal watercraft are not permitted in Laguna Madre (except to get from the boat ramp to open water outside the park boundaries) but are allowed on the Gulf side beyond the 5-mile marker.

FISHING   Fishing is great year-round. Surf fishing is permitted everywhere along the Gulf side, except at Malaquite Beach, and yields whiting, redfish, black drum, and speckled sea trout; while anglers in Laguna Madre catch flounder, sheepshead, and croaker. A Texas fishing license with a saltwater stamp is required. Licenses, along with current fishing regulations and some fishing supplies, are available at **Padre Island Park Company** (© 361/949-9368). For current license information, contact the Texas Parks and Wildlife Department (© 800/792-1112; www.tpwd.state.tx.us).

FOUR-WHEELING   Licensed and street-legal motor vehicles (but not ATVs) are permitted on most of the beach at Padre Island National Seashore (but not Malaquite Beach or the fragile dunes, grasslands, and tidal flats). Most standard passenger vehicles can make it down the first 5 miles of South Beach, but those planning to drive farther south down the island (another 55 miles are open to motor vehicles) will need four-wheel-drive vehicles. Markers are located every 5 miles, and those driving down the beach are advised to watch for soft sand and high water, and to carry a shovel, jack,

Tips **For Travelers with Disabilities**

Specially designed fat-tire wheelchairs for use in the sand, and even in the water, are available at no charge at the visitor center. They do require someone to push.

boards, and other emergency equipment. Unless otherwise posted, the speed limit on the beach is 15 mph. Northbound vehicles have the right of way.

HIKING   The national seashore has miles and miles of beach that are ideal for walking and hiking. There's also the paved and fairly easy **Grasslands Nature Trail,** a .8-mile self-guided loop trail that meanders through grass-covered areas of sand dunes. Numbered posts correspond with descriptions of plants and other aspects of the natural landscape in a free brochure available at the trail head or the visitor center. You'll need insect repellent to combat mosquitoes, and because western diamondback rattlesnakes also inhabit the area, stay on the trail and watch where you put your feet and hands.

SWIMMING & SURFING   Warm air and water temperatures make swimming practically a year-round activity here—January through March are really the only time it's too chilly—and swimming is permitted along the entire beach. The most popular swimming area is 4½-mile-long Malaquite Beach, also called Closed Beach, which is closed to motor vehicles. You have to jostle for a spot only at spring break and on summer weekends. Note that there are no lifeguards on duty here. Although waves here are not of the Hawaii or California size, they're often sufficient for surfing, which is permitted in most areas, but not at Malaquite Beach.

WINDSURFING   The Bird Island Basin area on Laguna Madre is considered one of America's best spots for windsurfing because of its warm water, shallow depth, and consistent, steady winds. **Worldwinds Windsurfing** (© 361/949-7472; www.worldwinds.net) sells and rents windsurfing equipment and wet suits here, and offers windsurfing lessons during the summer. Call for current fees and schedule.

WHERE TO STAY & DINE

The closest hotels and restaurants are in Corpus Christi; see section 3 in this chapter. If you want to stay in the park, you'll have to camp.

Padre Island National Seashore's developed **Malaquite Campground** ✦, about a half-mile north of the visitor center, is a great spot to bed down, with 50 sites ($8 per night) that are available on a first-come, first-served basis year-round. Sites, within 100 feet of the beach, have good views of the Gulf, and the campground has cold showers, restrooms, and picnic tables. There are no RV hook-ups, but there is a dump station. For those who don't mind its limitations, it's definitely the best place to camp; it gets crowded only during spring break and on summer weekends.

7 South Padre Island

286 miles S of San Antonio; 366 miles SW of Houston; 531 miles S of Dallas; 815 miles SE of El Paso

South Padre Island is a resort town at the southern tip of this long, long barrier island. Any farther south and you would be in Mexico. The beach is much like the beach on the northern portion of the island, but the water here often seems clearer. Padre Island is a great place to stretch out on the beach, feel the Gulf breeze blowing, and hear nothing but the wash of the surf. If you get bored, you can busy yourself with boat rides, watersports, or taking the kids to the popular local water park.

This part of the island is narrow—2 or 3 blocks wide—and the town starts at the southern tip and extends north for about 5 miles, with a good bit of vacant land the farther north you go. It's a small town. Most of it consists of stores, hotels, a small convention center, restaurants, condos, and vacation houses. Regular housing is in short supply because storm insurance and other costs make it prohibitive. Most of the locals commute from the mainland, either from Port Isabel or Brownsville.

South Padre Island gets a lot of families who make the trip by car or RV. Many come from northern Mexico, driving up from cities such as Monterrey and Saltillo. It also gets winter Texans. And it gets some convention business. Conventioneers and weekenders will often come by plane, via the airports at Harlingen or Brownsville. You'll find reasonably priced flights from major cities in Texas, mostly on Southwest Airlines or Continental Express. South Padre Island is famous for being a spring break destination. Hotels will fill up with college kids, often several to a room. It's a good time to be somewhere else.

ESSENTIALS
GETTING THERE
BY PLANE   The closest airports are the **Brownsville/South Padre Island International Airport** (℃ **956/542-4373;** www.flybrownsville.com) in Brownsville (about 28 miles southwest) and the Valley International Airport (℃ **956/430-8600;** www. flythevalley.com) in Harlingen (about 40 miles west). All of the major car-rental companies have desks at these airports.

BY CAR   From U.S. 77/83, which connects to Harlingen, McAllen, and Corpus Christi, take Tex. 100 east to Port Isabel and then across the Queen Isabella Causeway to the south end of South Padre Island. From Brownsville, take Tex. 48 northeast to Tex. 100.

GETTING AROUND
A car is handy on South Padre Island, and parking and traffic congestion are not usually a problem except during spring break and on summer weekends. The town's main street is Padre Boulevard. It runs north–south down the middle of the island. Running parallel 1 block on either side are Laguna Boulevard (west) and Gulf Boulevard (east). You don't have to drive much once you're here since many of the major hotels, restaurants, and beaches are within walking distance of each other. Also, there is a free year-round bus service called The Wave ℃ **956/761-1025**), which operates daily from 7am to 7pm. There are two different buses. Both run the length of the town, and one goes into Port Isabel (each is clearly marked). They pass every 30 minutes along Padre Boulevard.

VISITOR INFORMATION
Contact the **South Padre Island Convention and Visitors Bureau,** 600 Padre Blvd., South Padre Island, TX 78597 (℃ **800/767-2373** or 956/761-6433; www.sopadre. com), which operates a visitor center. The center is just a few blocks north of the entry point on the east side of the boulevard beside a Wells Fargo branch office. Hours are Monday to Friday 8am to 5pm and Saturday and Sunday from 9am to 5pm. On weekdays in the summer the office stays open an extra hour later. You can pick up maps or talk to the staff for suggestions and advice.

South Padre Island

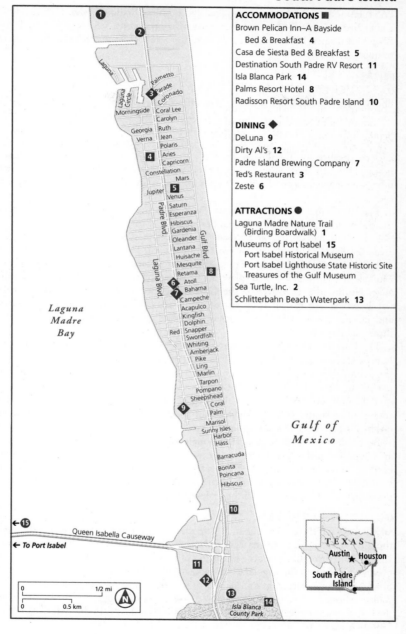

ACCOMMODATIONS ■
Brown Pelican Inn–A Bayside
  Bed & Breakfast **4**
Casa de Siesta Bed & Breakfast **5**
Destination South Padre RV Resort **11**
Isla Blanca Park **14**
Palms Resort Hotel **8**
Radisson Resort South Padre Island **10**

DINING ◆
DeLuna **9**
Dirty Al's **12**
Padre Island Brewing Company **7**
Ted's Restaurant **3**
Zeste **6**

ATTRACTIONS ●
Laguna Madre Nature Trail
  (Birding Boardwalk) **1**
Museums of Port Isabel **15**
  Port Isabel Historical Museum
  Port Isabel Lighthouse State Historic Site
  Treasures of the Gulf Museum
Sea Turtle, Inc. **2**
Schlitterbahn Beach Waterpark **13**

Laguna
Madre
Bay

Gulf of
Mexico

Queen Isabella Causeway

← To Port Isabel

0   1/2 mi
0   0.5 km

TEXAS
Austin ★ Houston
South Padre
Island

Isla Blanca
County Park

FAST FACTS   Health services are available at **Valley Regional Island Clinic,** 3000 Padre Blvd. (© **956/761-4524**). The **post office** (zip code 78597) is at 4701 Padre Blvd. and is open Monday through Friday from 8am to 4pm, Saturday from 10am to noon.

WHAT TO SEE & DO
DISCOVERING THE AREA'S PAST

Shipwrecks, tempests, and war, as well as some of the happier aspects of life along the southern Texas coast, are the focus of the **Museums of Port Isabel** ⟨✦⟩. Museum headquarters are in the Port Isabel Historical Museum, 317 E. Railroad Ave., Port Isabel (© **956/943-7602**; www.portisabelmuseums.com), which oversees this museum; another is called the Treasures of the Gulf Museum; and there's also a historic lighthouse. These are in downtown Port Isabel, are within easy walking distance of each other, and make for a good activity on a rainy day. Allow a half-hour to 1 hour to visit each one.

The **Port Isabel Historical Museum** ⟨✦⟩, located in a restored 1899 Victorian commercial building, houses exhibits that describe the history of the area from the time it was a supply depot during the Mexican-American War, through the Civil War, and the area's development as a shrimping and fishing capital. There are interactive exhibits, a large display of Mexican-American War artifacts, and a fascinating 1906 Victor Morales "Fish Mural." The displays about shipwrecks will interest kids and adults alike. Nearby, the **Treasures of the Gulf Museum** focuses on three Spanish shipwrecks which occurred in 1554 just off the coast. Exhibits include murals, artifacts, and various hands-on activities, including a children's discovery lab. There is also a theater and gift shop.

The **Port Isabel Lighthouse State Historic Site,** at the west end of the Queen Isabella Causeway, is hard to miss. This 72-foot-high lighthouse, which helped guide ships through Brazos Santiago Pass to Point Isabel from 1852 until 1905, now affords panoramic views of Port Isabel, South Padre Island, and as far as the eye can see out over the Gulf of Mexico. Also on the property is a replica of the lighthouse keeper's cottage made from the 1850 blueprints for the original. The cottage contains exhibits on the history of the lighthouse, and there's a picnic area.

Both museums are open Tuesday through Saturday from 10am to 4pm (last entry at 3:30pm), and the lighthouse and cottage are open daily from 9am to 5pm (last entry at 4pm). Admission to each site is $3 adults, $2 for seniors 55 and older, $1 for students with ID, and free for children younger than 5. Combination tickets for all three sites cost $7 for adults, $5 for seniors, and $2 for students.

OUTDOOR ACTIVITES

BIRD-WATCHING   More than 300 species of birds can be found during different times of the year. The **Laguna Madre Nature Trail** ⟨✦⟩, adjacent to the South Padre Island Convention Centre at the north end of town, is a boardwalk that meanders out over the wetlands of the Laguna Madre and around a freshwater pond. There are a few blinds where you can set up a scope and sit for hours unseen by the birds. The boardwalk is wheelchair accessible and open 24 hours, free of charge. For birding tours in the bay, contact George and Scarlet Colley of **Fins to Feathers Photo Safaris** (© **956/ 739-2473;** www.fin2feather.com). They take small groups out into the Laguna Madre for 3-hour trips.

DOLPHIN-WATCHING   Dolphin tours are a big activity on this island. For a great tour limited to small groups, contact **Fins to Feathers,** listed above. Scarlet Colley is a dolphin researcher and has filmed many hours of dolphin activity. The tour lasts 1½ hours. Another option is to take a large-boat tour, which you can sign up for at the marina, at the southern end of the island. There are a couple of companies that offer tours. The preferred one is **The Original Dolphin Watch** (© 956/761-4243).

FISHING   There have been record-setting catches made in the waters around South Padre Island: The state record blue marlin, at 876½ pounds, was taken offshore.

The beach and jetties are easily accessible and very popular with winter Texans (retired residents of the northern United States and Canada who spend at least part of the winter in the South Texas warmth). There are numerous local charter captains specializing in offshore big-game fishing, where anglers try for blue marlin, white marlin, sailfish, swordfish, wahoo, tuna, and mako shark. Offshore fishing also includes red drum, spotted sea trout, snapper, grouper, tarpon, and king mackerel.

The Laguna Madre, on average only 2 feet deep, is perfect for world-class light-tackle sport fishing. The lush carpet of sea grasses on its bottom provides good habitat and food for red drum, spotted sea trout, flounder, black drum, and snook, and locals brag that there are more of these fish per acre than in any other bay on the Texas Gulf.

The **Texas International Fishing Tournament (TIFT)** has been going strong for more than 60 years and attracts more than 1,000 participants each July. The 5-day event includes bay, offshore, and tarpon fishing divisions, and is open to anglers of all ages. Visit www.tift.org or contact the **South Padre Island CVB** (© 800/767-2373 or 956/761-6433; www.sopadre.com) for details.

SCHLITTERBAHN BEACH WATERPARK   This is operated by the same corporation that owns the highly popular water park in the German Hill Country town of New Braunfels—hence the German name. It has a wave pool and several water rides that require sturdy bathing suits. But it also has calmer facilities such as wading and floating pools that work well for those just trying to relax. My favorite feature is the river that connects the rides so that you don't have to spend all your time out of the water waiting in line. Admission prices are $35 adult, $28 children 3 to 11 years old. The park closes during the winter (mid-Sept to mid-Apr). It's located at 90 Park Rd., Hwy. 100. For information call © **956/772-7873** or visit www.schlitterbahn.com.

SUNBATHING & SWIMMING   The beaches of South Padre Island are some of the best on the Gulf: The sand is fine and white, and the water is warm and shallow. In town there are 23 access points with free parking, plus the county has a park at each end of town, with a $4 all-day parking fee, good at both parks. My favorite stretch of beach is in the county park north of town. Incidentally, although lined with hotels and condos, the shoreline and adjacent beaches are public and open to everyone.

WINDSURFING   With winds about 15 mph year-round, these waters are ideal for windsurfing. Spring and fall are best, usually with beautiful weather. Hurricane season runs from August to early November, but is not often a serious problem.

WHERE TO STAY

Room rates vary widely in South Padre Island over the course of the year, with the lowest rates usually in winter. There are more condo units on this island than there are regular hotel rooms. These will work for you if your plan is to stay here more than a few days. Most, but not all, rent by the week. Often there's a one-time cleaning fee

Tips   Face to Face with a Sea Turtle

Each of the seven worldwide species of sea turtles is either threatened or endangered, and five species are found in the Gulf of Mexico. Ila Loetscher, affectionately dubbed the "Turtle Lady," founded Sea Turtle, Inc., in 1977 to help protect the most endangered species of sea turtles, Kemp's ridley. The organization supports conservation and rehabilitation of all marine turtles, and operates a rehabilitation center where you can see four of the five Gulf of Mexico sea turtle species. Volunteers give presentations with live sea turtles Tuesday through Sunday at 10am, which help you identify the different species and explain how each of us can help protect them. Self-guided and guided tours of the facility, including the turtle tanks, are available at other times. **Sea Turtle, Inc.,** is located at 6617 Padre Blvd. (© **956/761-4511;** www.seaturtleinc.com), and admission costs $3 for adults and $1 for children. It's open Tuesday through Sunday from 10am to 4pm. Allow at least 45 minutes, and please buy something in the gift shop—all proceeds go to saving the sea turtles!

when you lease a condo, so it's a better deal the longer you stay. A complete list of condos is on the South Padre Island website: **www.sopadre.com**. Among the national chain motels in South Padre Island are **Days Inn,** 3913 Padre Blvd. (© **800/329-7466** or 956/761-7831); **Comfort Suites,** 912 Padre Blvd. (© **800/424-6423** or 956/772-9020); and **Super 8,** 4205 Padre Blvd. (© **800/800-8000** or 956/761-6300). Room tax adds about 13%.

Brown Pelican Inn—A Bayside Bed & Breakfast ☆   This peaceful two-story house on the bay with wraparound porches on both floors is a relaxing place to stay. Each room is decorated with American and English antiques and collectibles. Two rooms are downstairs: The Big Thicket room faces the bay and has a king-size bed and private entrance from the porch, and the Hill Country room is fully accessible for travelers with disabilities and has a queen-size bed. The upstairs rooms all have queen-size beds, and two face the bay, affording front seat views of stunning sunsets over the Laguna Madre. Seven rooms have showers only, one has a tub/shower combo. There are rocking chairs on the porches to entice you to sit back and relax. The homemade breakfast includes freshly baked pastries, a cooked dish, homemade granola, fresh fruit and juices, and gourmet coffee and tea. Smoking is permitted outside only.

207 W. Aries Dr. (P.O. Box 2667), South Padre Island, TX 78597. © 956/761-2722. Fax 956/761-8683. www.brown pelican.com. 8 units. $95–$150 double. Rates include full breakfast. AE, DISC, MC, V. Children younger than 12 not allowed. Reservations required. *In room:* A/C, TV.

Casa de Siesta Bed & Breakfast ☆   Attractive rooms connected by a broad, shaded breezeway encircle a leafy garden and patio. The design makes for privacy and relaxation. And on an island known as a family destination, it's nice to find an oasis for grown-ups. A small swimming pool completes the picture. The rooms are very large and decorated in a Mexican and Southwestern style: Saltillo tile floors, wrought-iron work, and folk art. You have a choice of two doubles or one king-size bed; three rooms come with four-poster beds. All have showers with attractive tile work. Smoking is allowed outside only.

4610 Padre Blvd., South Padre Island, TX 78597. © **956/761-5656.** Fax 956/761-1313. www.casadesiesta.com. 12 units. Nov–Jan $99 double; Mar and June–Aug $150 double; rest of year $125 double. Extra person $20. Holiday rates higher. Rates include full breakfast. AE, DISC, MC, V. Pets accepted with $15 per day fee. Children younger than 12 not allowed. **Amenities:** Pool. *In room:* A/C, TV, fridge.

The Palms Resort Motel *(Finds* Of the three traditional beach motels that still exist, this is the nicest. The property is well maintained and well managed. If you want to be on the beach, this is a great option. Rooms are attractive and spacious. Most come with a small dining area and have such extras as marble countertops and flat-screen TVs. Rooms on the southern side of the building are best. Bathrooms are attractive; some come with shower/tub combinations. In-room smoking is not permitted.

3616 Gulf Blvd., South Padre Island, TX 78597. © **800/466-1316** or 956/761-1316. Fax 956/761-1310. www.palms resortmotel.com. 29 units. $95–$125 double. AE, MC, V. **Amenities:** Restaurant; pool. *In room:* A/C, TV, fridge, coffee-maker, microwave.

Radisson Resort South Padre Island *(★* For a top-notch full-service hotel and the nicest beach in town, my vote goes to this Radisson. Two Catalina macaws—Rad and General—greet you as you enter the high-ceilinged lobby, and the birds seem quite at home, surrounded by tropical plants. The landscaping around the pools is lovely, with plenty of palm trees and flowers, and the popular public beach just outside the hotel is great. The cabanas—the "standard" rooms!—are colorfully decorated with floral bedspreads and artwork with a fish motif. Those with beach views are the best, and those with ocean views are the most expensive. The suites, which are actually two-bedroom condos, are large, handsomely appointed units with sleeping for up to six, two full bathrooms, a full kitchen, and a spacious living/dining room. Get one that is above the third floor for the sake of quiet.

500 Padre Blvd., South Padre Island, TX 78597. © **800/333-3333** or 956/761-6511. Fax 956/761-1602. www.radisson. com. 188 units. $100–$249 double; $205–$449 suite. AE, DC, DISC, MC, V. **Amenities:** Restaurant; bar; 2 outdoor pools (1 heated); 4 outdoor lit tennis courts; 3 Jacuzzis; in-room massage; limited room service. *In room:* A/C, TV w/pay movies, Wi-Fi, kitchen (in suites), coffeemaker, hair dryer, iron.

CAMPING

Isla Blanca Park *(★★* (© **956/761-5493**), on the southern tip of South Padre Island, is our choice for a developed campground on the island, with easy beach access. Part of the Cameron County Park System (P.O. Box 2106, South Padre Island, TX 78597), this well-maintained facility has 600 paved sites, many of which are pull-through, and more than half have full RV hook-ups. The park also offers restrooms with showers, a dump station, sandy beach, fishing jetty, boat ramp and marina, a playground, a bike trail, and beach pavilions with concessions. There is a primitive tent area right on the Laguna Madre. Rates are $21 to $26.

Those looking for a developed resort should head to **Destination South Padre RV Resort** (© **800/867-2373** or 956/761-5665; www.destinationsouthpadre.com), just south of the Queen Isabella Causeway on Padre Boulevard. It offers 190 gravel sites with full hook-ups, restrooms with showers, guest laundry, and security. There's a large heated pool, spa, boat dock, rec hall and game room, and numerous planned activities. Rates are $28 to $37. There are pet restrictions, and tents are not allowed.

WHERE TO DINE

If you're staying in a condo with a kitchen, and you have many mouths to feed, you'll be going to the grocery store in Port Isabel. Also, you'll find that Zeste, listed below, is a great resource for packaged foods not found anywhere else near here.

DeLuna 𝄐𝄐 *Finds* SEAFOOD/STEAKS   This two-story restaurant with great views of the bay offers the best, most creative cooking in South Padre Island. Chef/owner Julio DeLuna made a name for himself in Scottsdale, Arizona, before coming here to open his own place. Quality ingredients and freshness are points of pride with him. What doesn't come out of the Gulf is flown in on ice, such as Hawaiian walu and diver scallops. There are two menus. The downstairs menu is less expensive. From it I ordered the crab-encrusted mahimahi filet served with a lobster and brandy sauce. Friends ordered the filet mignon and the lobster salad. It was all excellently prepared, and I was left with the nagging feeling that I couldn't be in South Padre Island.

201 W. Corral. ℭ 956/761-1920. Reservations recommended. Main courses $17–$36. AE, MC, V. Daily 4:30–10pm.

Dirty Al's 𝄐 *Value* SEAFOOD   Al has been a fixture here for 20 years. Most of that time he was running a bait shop and serving tacos on the side just to fishermen. Now, his restaurant is what keeps him busy. The main attractions are the fried shrimp baskets, the stuffed crabs, the blackened fish, and the fried oyster baskets. Al fries up the best shrimp on the island here. And his prices are rock bottom. The restaurant/bait shop is beside the marina (which is south of the bridge). Picnic tables are scattered out in front for people to sit down while they wait for their name to be called (this place is crowded for dinner). Al has plans to add a second story soon, which might shorten wait times, but won't do much for the parking shortage.

1 Padre Blvd. ℭ 956/761-4901. Reservations not accepted. Main courses $7–$9. MC, V. Daily 11am–9pm.

Padre Island Brewing Company PUB GRUB   Brewpub fare (and some pretty decent beer, too) makes Padre Island Brewing Company a popular place. The cooked-to-order burgers and sandwiches such as the chicken fajita served on a French roll are the surest things. Entrees include steaks, baby back ribs, Texas quail, stuffed chicken breast, crab-stuffed flounder, and breaded beer batter shrimp. Eat outside on the second story deck for terrific views or inside, with a view of the brewing vats.

3400 Padre Blvd., at Bahama St. ℭ 956/761-9585. Main courses $7–$19. AE, DISC, MC, V. Tues–Sun 11:30am–10:30pm; Mon 5–10:30pm.

Ted's Restaurant *Value* AMERICAN   For breakfast or lunch, this homey establishment in a converted house offers decent food for a good price. The food is mostly the usual stuff for Texas. Breakfast dishes include eggs, pancakes, waffles, and *migas* (scrambled eggs with onions, tomatoes, chiles, cheese, and tortilla strips). The #4 breakfast (fajitas and eggs) is the local favorite. For lunch you can choose between fajitas, burgers, sandwiches, and salads. The staff takes pride in their fajitas. The tuna-and-avocado sandwich isn't bad either.

5717 Padre Blvd. ℭ 956/761-5327. Main courses $5–$8. MC, V. Daily 7am–3pm.

Zeste 𝄐 *Finds* DELI/GOURMET TAKEOUT   This new specialty market is an ideal addition to South Padre Island's dining options, and is positively heaven-sent for the condo renter in need of greater take-out options. Walking through the door, you're immediately in the mood for food when your nose catches a whiff of herbs and fresh-baked bread from the kitchen. Go to the food case and pick your entree and two sides, uncork a bottle and dine at leisure in the market's pleasant but small dining area, or take it all to go. The daily menu varies but usually offers Italian and Mediterranean entrees, as well as something such as an herb-roasted chicken or tenderloin, and vegetarian options (excellent appetizers, sides, soups, and desserts, too). You can order an entire picnic. The market section sells specialty foods, olives, wines, imported beers, coffees, and gourmet packaged foods.

3508 Padre Blvd. (C) **956/761-5555.** Plates $9–$15. AE, DISC, MC, V. Wed–Mon 11am–8pm. Extended summer hours.

AFTER DARK (OR PERHAPS AFTER NOON)

To have a cocktail while watching the sunset, head over to the bay side of the island to any of several places, including the bar at **DeLuna,** described above. Not far away are two that have ample deck space above the water. **Louie's Backyard,** 2305 Laguna Blvd. ((C) **956/716-6406**), is a large and popular establishment serving American food and operating a full bar. During high season, they have live music nightly. **Wahoo Saloon,** 201 W. Pike St. ((C) **956/761-5344**), is smaller and simpler. On Fridays during the summer, the city puts on a small fireworks show after dark, which can be enjoyed from any of these places.

When in need of a proper beach bar where you can work your toes into the sand while enjoying a cold beer, cross to the ocean side of the island and head to **Wanna-Wanna,** at the Island Inn motel, 5100 Gulf Blvd. ((C) **956/761-7677**).

7

San Antonio

by David Baird

San Antonio, home to the Alamo and the River Walk, has more character than any other big city in Texas. Indeed, it is often lumped together with New Orleans, Boston, and San Francisco as one of America's distinctive cities. And if you're looking for a destination for the whole family, you can't go wrong with San Antonio. It has a downtown area that is attractive and comfortable, a couple of large theme parks—SeaWorld and Fiesta Texas—and resorts that cater specifically to families.

For most of its history, San Antonio was the largest city in Texas, the "cosmopolitan" center, where multiple cultures came together and coexisted. In 1718 the native Coahuiltecan Indians were seeking protection from Apache raids, and invited the Spaniards to establish a mission here. A few years later, by order of the King of Spain, 15 families came from the Canary Islands to settle here. (The oldest families in San Antonio can trace their family tree back to these colonists.) The settlement grew and prospered. The church eventually built five missions along the San Antonio River. But during the fight for Mexican Independence and then Texan Independence (1821 and 1836, respectively), San Antonio was the site of several hard-fought battles, including the famous siege of the Alamo. This greatly reduced the population for more than a decade until it began to attract thousands of German settlers fleeing the revolutions in Europe. So many were to come that by 1860, German speakers in the city outnumbered both Spanish and English speakers. Throughout the following decades, these different immigrant groups would accommodate each other and forge a unique local culture.

The city continued to grow. In the early 1900s, it showcased the first skyscraper in Texas. But San Antonio wasn't growing fast enough to keep up with Houston or Dallas. By the 1920s, it had become Texas's third-largest city and had arrived at a crossroads. Was it to follow Houston and Dallas in their bull rush towards growth and modernism? Or was it to go its own way, preserving what it thought most valuable?

This crossroads manifested itself in the form of a political dispute over the meandering San Antonio River. A city commission recommended draining the riverbed and channeling the water through underground culverts to free up space for more downtown buildings. This outraged many locals. A group of women's clubs formed to save the river and create an urban green space along its banks. (And this was decades before anyone in Texas had ever heard of urban planning.) The women's campaign was multipronged and even included a puppet-show dramatization. They were victorious, and the rest, as they say, is history. The Paseo del Rio or River Walk eventually became the city's crowning feature and a point of local pride. It has contributed greatly to the dynamism of the downtown area and the city at large.

South-Central Texas

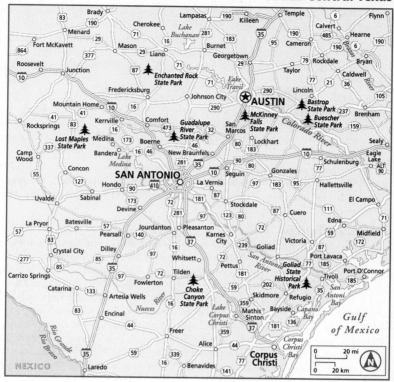

There is a richness in San Antonio that goes beyond the images often seen on the covers of guides and brochures. Visitors today will encounter a city with a strong sense of its own identity, a city whose downtown shows its age and its respect for the past.

1 Orientation

ARRIVING

BY PLANE The **San Antonio International Airport** (✆ **210/207-3411;** www.ci. sat.tx.us/aviation) is 7 miles north of downtown. It is compact, clean, well marked, and has two terminals.

GETTING TO & FROM THE AIRPORT Loop 410 and U.S. 281 south intersect just outside the airport. If you're renting a car here, it should take about 15 to 20 minutes to drive downtown via U.S. 281 south.

Most of the hotels within a radius of a mile or two offer **free shuttle service** to and from the airport (be sure to check when you make your reservation). If you're staying downtown, you'll most likely have to pay your own way.

VIA Metropolitan Transit's bus no. 2 is the cheapest ($1) way to get downtown but also the slowest; it'll take from 40 to 45 minutes.

SATRANS (© **800/868-7707** or 210/281-9900; www.saairportshuttle.com), with a booth outside each of the terminals, offers shared van service from the airport to the downtown hotels for $14 per person one-way, $24 round-trip. Vans run from about 7am until 1am; phone 24 hours in advance for van pickup from your hotel.

There's a **taxi** queue in front of each terminal. Airport taxis charge about $30 to get downtown.

BY TRAIN   San Antonio's train station is located at 350 Hoefgen St., in St. Paul's Square, on the east side of downtown near the Alamodome and adjacent to the Sunset Station entertainment complex. Cabs are readily available from here. Lockers are not available, but Amtrak will hold passengers' bags in a secure location for $2 per bag. Information about the city is available at the main counter.

BY BUS   San Antonio's bustling **Greyhound** station, 500 N. St. Mary's St. (© **210/ 270-5834**), is located downtown about 2 blocks from the River Walk. The station, open 24 hours, is within walking distance of a number of hotels, and many public streetcar and bus lines run nearby.

VISITOR INFORMATION

The main office of the **City of San Antonio Visitor Information Center** is across the street from the Alamo, at 317 Alamo Plaza (© **210/207-6748**). Hours are daily 9am to 5pm, except Thanksgiving, Christmas, and New Year's, when the center is closed.

The center offers visitors a free copy of the magazine *San Antonio Travel and Leisure Guide,* published semiannually by the **San Antonio Convention and Visitors Bureau (SACVB).** It has maps and listings and is something you can pour over during an idle moment. Also at the center are racks and racks of brochures that you can look through and some free magazines heavy on advertisements, such as *Fiesta,* with interesting articles about the city, and *Rio,* a tabloid focusing on the River Walk. You can find these last two publications at many of the downtown hotels and shops. Both list sights, restaurants, shops, cultural events, and some nightlife, though there's an obvious bias toward advertisers.

Also free—but more objective—is San Antonio's alternative paper, the *Current.* Though skimpy, it is a good source for nightlife listings. The *San Antonio Express-News* is the local newspaper. It's got a good arts/entertainment section called The Weekender, which comes out on Friday and is available around town.

CITY LAYOUT

San Antonio lies at the southern edge of the Texas Hill Country and is mostly flat. Streets, especially those in the old parts of town, are jumbled, while a number of the thoroughfares leading in and out of town follow old Spanish trails or 19th-century wagon trails.

MAIN ARTERIES & STREETS   Most of the major roads in Texas meet in San Antonio, where they form a rough wheel-and-spoke pattern. There are two loops: I-410 circles around the city, coming to within 6 to 7 miles of downtown in the north and east, and as far out as 10 miles in the west and south; and Highway 1604, which forms an even larger circle with a 13-mile radius. The spokes of the wheel are formed by highways I-35, I-10, I-37, U.S. 281, U.S. 90, and U.S. 87. Occasionally two or three highways will merge onto the same freeway, which will then carry the various designations. For example, U.S. 90, U.S. 87, and I-10 converge for a while in an east–west direction just south of downtown, while U.S. 281, I-35, and I-37 run together on a north–south route to the east; I-10, I-35, and U.S. 87 bond for a bit going north–south to the west of downtown.

Among the most major of the minor spokes are Broadway, McCullough, San Pedro, and Blanco, all of which lead north from the city center into the most popular shopping and restaurant areas of town. Fredericksburg goes out to the Medical Center from just northwest of downtown. You may hear locals referring to something as being "in the loop." That doesn't mean it's privy to insider information, but rather, that it lies within the circumference of I-410, and is therefore in central San Antonio.

Downtown is bounded by I-37 to the east, I-35 to the north and west, and U.S. 90 (which merges with I-10) to the south. Within this area, Durango, Commerce, Market, and Houston are the important east-west streets. Alamo on the east side and Santa Rosa (which turns into South Laredo) on the west side are the major north–south streets.

THE NEIGHBORHOODS IN BRIEF

The older areas described here, from downtown through Alamo Heights, are all "in the loop" (410). The Medical Center area in the Northwest lies just outside it, but the rest of the Northwest, as well as North Central and the West, are expanding beyond even Loop 1604.

Downtown Site of San Antonio's original Spanish settlements, this area includes the Alamo and other historic sites, along with the River Walk, the Alamodome, the convention center, the Rivercenter Mall, and many high-rise hotels, restaurants, and shops. It's also the center of commerce and government, so many banks and offices, as well as most city buildings, are located here. Downtown is fun and vibrant. The River Walk is the centerpiece, but there's a lot more that can be seen and appreciated that takes a bit of exploring.

King William The city's first suburb, this historic district directly south of downtown was settled in the mid- to late 1800s by wealthy German merchants who built some of the most beautiful mansions in town. It began to be yuppified in the 1970s, and, at this point, you'd never guess it had ever been allowed to deteriorate. Only two of the area's many impeccably restored homes are generally open to the public, but a number have been turned into bed-and-breakfasts. As you can imagine, the location is ideal for those who want to explore the central city.

Southtown Alamo Street marks the border between King William and Southtown, an adjoining commercial district. Long a depressed area, it's slowly becoming trendy thanks to a Main Street refurbishing project and the opening of the Blue Star arts complex. You'll find a nice mix of Hispanic neighborhood shops and funky coffeehouses and galleries here, but few hotels worth staying in.

South Side The old, largely Hispanic southeast section of town that begins where Southtown ends (there's no agreed-upon boundary, but I'd say it lies a few blocks beyond the Blue Star arts complex) is home to four of the city's five historic missions. Thus far, it hasn't been experiencing the same gentrification and redevelopment as much of the rest of the city—but that could change when the hike-and-bike trail along a stretch of the San Antonio River here is completed.

Monte Vista Area Immediately north of downtown, Monte Vista was established soon after King William by a conglomeration of wealthy cattlemen, politicos, and generals who moved "on to the hill" at the turn of the century. A number of the area's large houses have been split into apartments for students of nearby Trinity University and

San Antonio Community College, but many lovely old homes have been restored in the past 30 years. It hasn't reached King William status yet, but this is already a highly desirable (read: pricey) place to live. Monte Vista is close to the once thriving, but now less lively, restaurant and entertainment district along North St. Mary's Street between Josephine and Magnolia known locally as **The Strip.**

Fort Sam Houston Built in 1876 to the northeast of downtown, Fort Sam Houston boasts a number of stunning officers' homes. Much of the working-class neighborhood surrounding Fort Sam is now run-down, but renewed interest in restoring San Antonio's older areas is beginning to have some impact here, too.

Alamo Heights Area In the 1890s, when construction in the area began, Alamo Heights was at the far northern reaches of San Antonio. This is now home to San Antonio's well-heeled residents and holds most of the fashionable shops and restaurants. **Terrell Hills** to the east, **Olmos Park** to the west, and **Lincoln Heights** to the north are all offshoots of this area. The latter is home to the Quarry, once just that, but now a ritzy golf course and popular shopping mall. Shops and restaurants are concentrated along two main drags: Broadway and, to a lesser degree, New Braunfels. Most of these neighborhoods share a single zip code ending in the numbers "09"—thus the local term "09ers," referring to the area's affluent residents. The Witte Museum, San Antonio Botanical Gardens, and Brackenridge Park are all in this part of town.

Northwest The mostly characterless neighborhoods surrounding the South Texas Medical Center (a large grouping of healthcare facilities referred to as the **Medical Center**) were built relatively recently. The area includes lots of condominiums and apartments, and much of the shopping and dining is in strip malls (the trendy, still-expanding Heubner Oaks retail center is an exception). The farther north you go, the nicer the housing complexes get. The high-end Westin La Cantera resort, the exclusive La Cantera and Dominion residential enclave, several tony golf courses, and the Shops at La Cantera, San Antonio's fanciest new retail center, mark the direction that development is taking in the far northwest part of town, just beyond Six Flags Fiesta Texas and near the public Friedrich Park. It's becoming one of San Antonio's prime growth areas.

North Central San Antonio is inching toward Bulverde and other Hill Country towns via this major corridor of development clustered from Loop 410 north to Loop 1604, east of I-10 and west of I-35, and bisected by U.S. 281. The airport and many developed industrial strips line U.S. 281 in the southern section, but the farther north you go, the more you see the natural beauty of this area, hilly and dotted with small canyons. Recent city codes have motivated developers to retain trees and native plants in their residential communities.

West Although SeaWorld has been out here since the late 1980s, and the Hyatt Regency Hill Country Resort settled here in the early 1990s, other development was comparatively slow in coming. Now the West is booming with new midprice housing developments, strip malls, schools, and businesses. Road building hasn't kept pace with growth, however, so traffic can be a bear.

2 Getting Around

If you're staying in downtown, a car is more of a hindrance than an asset: Traffic and parking are a pain, and public transportation is good. If you're bunking anywhere else in San Antonio, however, you'll definitely want wheels—and you might as well rent them at the airport, where all the major car-rental companies are represented at each of the terminals.

BY PUBLIC TRANSPORTATION

BY BUS   VIA Metropolitan Transit Service offers regular bus service for $1, with an additional 15¢ charge for transfers. Express buses cost $2. You'll need exact change. Call ✆ **210/362-2020** for transit information, check the website at **www.viainfo.net**, or stop in one of VIA's many service centers. The most convenient for visitors is the downtown center, 260 E. Houston St., open Monday to Friday 7am to 6pm, Saturday 9am to 2pm. A helpful bus route is the no. 7, which travels from downtown to the San Antonio Museum of Art, Japanese Tea Garden, San Antonio Zoo, Witte Museum, Brackenridge Park, and the Botanical Garden. *Tip:* During large festivals such as Fiesta and the Texas Folklife Festival, VIA offers many Park & Ride lots that allow you to leave your car and bus it downtown.

BY STREETCAR   In addition to its bus lines, VIA offers four convenient downtown streetcar routes that cover all the most popular tourist stops. The streetcars cost $1 (exact change required; drivers carry none). The trolleys, which have signs color-coded by route, display their destinations.

BY CAR

If you can avoid driving downtown, by all means do so. The pattern of one-way streets is confusing and parking is extremely limited. It's not that the streets in downtown San Antonio are narrower or more crowded than those in most old city centers, but it's that there's no need to bother when public transportation is so convenient.

Rush hour lasts from about 7:30 to 9am and 4:30 to 6pm Monday through Friday. The crush may not be bad compared with that of Houston or Dallas, but it's getting worse all the time. Because of San Antonio's rapid growth, you can also expect to find major highway construction or repairs going on somewhere in the city at any given time. Feeder roads into Loop 410 will be particularly hard hit in the next few years, especially the Loop 410/U.S. 281 interchanges, where construction began in spring 2005 and is not scheduled to be completed until 2008. For the gory details, log on to the Texas Department of Transportation's website at **www.dot.state.tx.us**.

PARKING   Parking meters are not plentiful in the heart of downtown, but you can find some on the streets near the River Walk and on Broadway. The cost is $1 per hour (which is also the time limit) in San Fernando Plaza and near the courthouse, 75¢ in other locations. There are some very inexpensive (2 hr. for $1) meters at the outskirts of town but the real trick is to find one. If you don't observe the laws, you'll be quickly ticketed. *Note:* Although very few signs inform you of this fact, parking at meters is free after 6pm Monday through Saturday and free all day Sunday except during special events.

BY RIVER TAXI

Rio Taxi Service (✆ **800/417-4139** or 210/244-5700; www.riosanantonio.com) operates daily from 9am to 9pm. Its 39 pickup locations are marked by Rio Taxi signs with black-and-yellow checker flags. You buy your tickets once you board. At $4 one-way, $10 for an all-day pass, or $25 for a 3-day pass, it's more expensive than ground transport, but it's a treat.

BY TAXI

Cabs are available outside the airport, near the Greyhound and Amtrak terminals (only when a train is due, however), and at most major downtown hotels, but they're next to impossible to hail on the street; most of the time, you'll need to phone for one in advance. The best of the taxi companies in town (and also the largest, because it represents the consolidation of two of the majors) is **Yellow-Checker Cab** (© 210/222-2222), which has an excellent record of turning up when promised. The base charge on a taxi is $1.70; add $1.80 for each mile.

FAST FACTS: San Antonio

American Express The office is located at 9000 Wurzbach Rd. (© 210/593-0084).

Dentist To find a dentist near you in town, contact the San Antonio District Dental Society, 3355 Cherry Ridge, Suite 214 (© 210/732-1264).

Doctor For a referral, contact the Bexar County Medical Society at 6243 W. Ih 10, Suite 600 (© 210/301-4368; www.bcms.org), Monday through Friday from 8am to 5pm.

Drugstores Most branches of CVS (formerly Eckerd) and Walgreens, the major chain pharmacies in San Antonio, are open late Monday through Saturday. There's a CVS downtown at 211 Losoya/River Walk (© 210/224-9293). Call © 800/925-4733 to find the Walgreens nearest you; punch in the area code and the first three digits of the number you're phoning from and you'll be directed to the closest branch.

Hospitals The main downtown hospital is Baptist Medical Center, 111 Dallas St. (© 210/297-7000). Christus Santa Rosa Health Care Corp., 333 N. Santa Rosa St. (© 210/704-2011), is also downtown. Contact the San Antonio Medical Foundation (© 210/614-3724) for information about other medical facilities in the city.

Hot Lines Contact the National Youth Crisis Hot Line at © 800/448-4663; Rape Crisis Hot Line at © 210/349-7273; Child Abuse Hot Line at © 800/252-5400; Mental Illness Crisis Hot Line at © 210/227-4357; Bexar County Adult Abuse Hot Line at © 800/252-5400; and Poison Control Center at © 800/764-7661.

Newspapers & Magazines The *San Antonio Express-News* is the only main-stream source of news in town. See "Visitor Information," earlier in this chapter, for magazine recommendations.

Police Call © 911 in an emergency. The Sheriff Department's 24-hour non-emergency number is © 210/335-6000, and the Texas Highway Patrol can be reached at © 210/531-2220.

Safety The crime rate in San Antonio has gone down in recent years, and there's a strong police presence downtown (in fact, both the transit authority and the police department have bicycle patrols); as a result, muggings, pickpocketings, and purse snatchings in the area are rare. Still, use common sense as you would anywhere else: Walk only in well-lit, well-populated streets. Also, it's generally not a good idea to stroll south of Durango Avenue after dark.

Taxes The sales tax here is 8.25%, and the city surcharge on hotel rooms increases to a whopping 16.75%.

3 Where to Stay

San Antonio has the greatest number of historic hotels of any city in Texas. Those who enjoy staying in hotels that capture the feel of yesterday will have a lot to choose from. Even low-end hotel chains are reclaiming old buildings—many examples are covered in this chapter—so don't judge a place only by its affiliation. All of these, as well as most of the new luxury accommodations, are in the downtown area, which is where you'll likely want to be whether you're here for pleasure or business. Prices in this prime location tend to be high, especially for hotels on the river, but you'll likely be happy with your accommodations. And if you're willing to forgo your own wheels for a bit, you'll economize by eliminating car-rental and parking fees. Most of the city's tourist attractions are within walking distance or are accessible by efficient and inexpensive public transportation, and many restaurants favored by locals are within a short cab ride from downtown.

In recent years, a number of the old mansions in the King William and Monte Vista historic districts—both close to downtown—have been converted into bed-and-breakfasts; several of them are reviewed in this chapter. For information about additional bed-and-breakfasts in these areas and in other neighborhoods around the city, check out www.sanantoniobb.org, the website of the **San Antonio Bed & Breakfast Association.** Several of San Antonio's inns can also be booked via **Historic Accommodations of Texas,** P.O. Box 203, Vanderpool, TX 78885 (© **800/HAT-0368;** www. hat.org).

Expect most downtown hotels to fall into the Very Expensive or Expensive range, especially if they sit right on the river. With a few notable exceptions, detailed below, only chain hotels on the outskirts of downtown tend to be Moderate or Inexpensive. You'll do better to stay in a B&B in a historic area near downtown (the Monte Vista neighborhood gives especially good value), so you won't have to give up many amenities. Although they're not formally called concierges, B&B owners and innkeepers also do far more to guide their guests around town than employees given that title in many large city hotels. You can also expect B&Bs to provide fax and other business services, and these days most offer high-speed and/or wireless Internet connections.

With a few other exceptions, detailed here, the vast majority of the other lodgings around town are low-priced chains. The most convenient are clustered in the northwest near the Medical Center and in the North Central area, around the airport. For a full alphabetical listing of the accommodations in the city, mapped by area and including rate ranges as well as basic amenities, phone the **San Antonio Convention and Visitors Bureau** (© **800/447-3372**) and request a lodging guide. The "Accommodations" section of **www.sanantoniovisit.com** is also a good resource.

Greater San Antonio Accommodations, Dining & Attractions

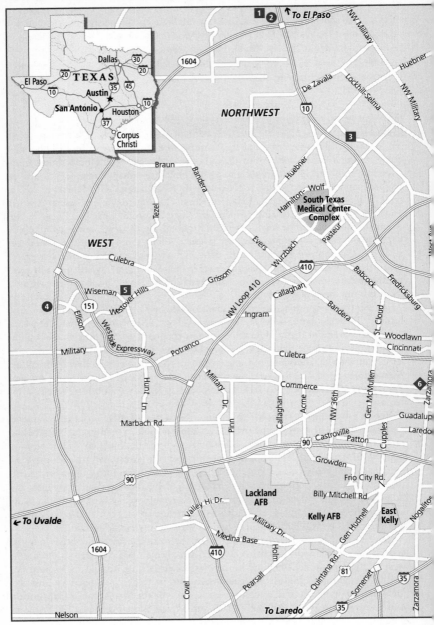

To El Paso

NW Military

Huebner

NW Military

Lockhill-Selma

De Zavala

NORTHWEST

Braun

Bandera

Tezel

Huebner

Hamilton Wolf

South Texas
Medical Center
Complex

Pasteur

WEST

Culebra

Evers

Wurzbach

410

Babcock

Fredericksburg

Grissom

Wiseman

Westover Hills

NW Loop 410

Callaghan

Bandera

St. Cloud

151

Ingram

Woodlawn
Cincinnati

Ellison

Westside Expressway

Potranco

Culebra

Military

Hunt Ln.

Military Dr.

Commerce

Callaghan

Acme

NW 36th

Gen McMullen

Cupples

Guadalupe
Laredo

Marbach Rd.

Pinn

90

Castroville

Patton

Growden

Frio City Rd.

90

Valley Hi Dr.

Lackland
AFB

Billy Mitchell Rd.

Kelly AFB

East
Kelly

To Uvalde

Medina Base

Military Dr.

Gen Hudnell

Quintana Rd.

Nogalitos

1604

410

Holm

81

Somerset

35

Covel

Pearsall

35

Zarzamora

Nelson

To Laredo

South Texas
Medical Center
Complex

TEXAS
Dallas
El Paso
Austin
San Antonio
Houston
Corpus
Christi
30
20
20
45
35
10
10
37

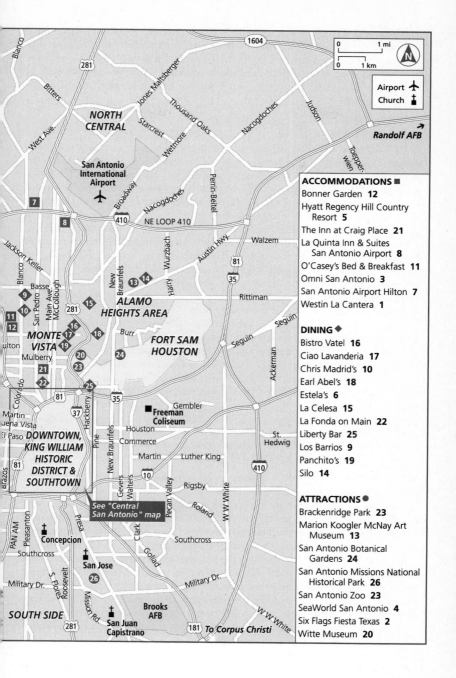

ACCOMMODATIONS ■
Bonner Garden **12**
Hyatt Regency Hill Country Resort **5**
The Inn at Craig Place **21**
La Quinta Inn & Suites San Antonio Airport **8**
O'Casey's Bed & Breakfast **11**
Omni San Antonio **3**
San Antonio Airport Hilton **7**
Westin La Cantera **1**

DINING ◆
Bistro Vatel **16**
Ciao Lavanderia **17**
Chris Madrid's **10**
Earl Abel's **18**
Estela's **6**
La Celesa **15**
La Fonda on Main **22**
Liberty Bar **25**
Los Barrios **9**
Panchito's **19**
Silo **14**

ATTRACTIONS ●
Brackenridge Park **23**
Marion Koogler McNay Art Museum **13**
San Antonio Botanical Gardens **24**
San Antonio Missions National Historical Park **26**
San Antonio Zoo **23**
SeaWorld San Antonio **4**
Six Flags Fiesta Texas **2**
Witte Museum **20**

Wherever you decide to stay, try to book as far in advance as possible—especially if the property is located downtown. And don't even think about coming to town during Fiesta (the third week in Apr) if you haven't reserved a room 6 months in advance.

In the following reviews, price categories are based on rates for a double room in high season, and don't factor in the 16.75% room tax. Often, rates will be a little higher for Fiesta.

DOWNTOWN
VERY EXPENSIVE

Hotel Contessa   This is the newest hotel on the river, and its location makes you wonder why someone waited for so long to build here. Fronting the property is a massive cypress tree crowning a small circle of land that juts out into the river. The building is attractive. The architecture follows what is by now a familiar model—rooms surrounding a soaring atrium. Glass elevators take you up the 12 stories to the rooms, all of them suites. The first thing you see upon entering a suite is a sitting room of good size. It's furnished in more traditional style than the common areas of the hotel, with Southwestern accents. Both the furniture and the lighting are more comfortable than most of the hotels in this category. The bathroom is attractive and ample, but nothing special for this category of hotel. The next door leads to the bedroom, which comes with either a river or a city view. The best river views are down low, at level with the cypress trees, and the best city views are up high. All rooms are nonsmoking. Each comes with either a king-size or two double beds.

Hotel operations are handled by Benchmark, which in my experience does a commendable job at providing services and running properties. But this could change—new hotels often will hire a professional management company until they feel capable of running the place. Also highly changeable are the rates and policies, which are always fluid during the first 2 years of a hotel's existence. But, all things remaining the same, I would prefer staying here to the Westin, next door. The matter would depend largely on the rates.

306 W. Market St. (at Navarro), San Antonio, TX 78205. ℂ **866/435-0900** or 210/229-9228. Fax 210/229-9228. www.thehotelcontessa.com. 265 units. $209–$269 suite; executive suites from $309. AE, DC, DISC, MC, V. Valet parking $25. **Amenities:** Restaurant; bar; outdoor heated pool; Jacuzzi; gym; spa; concierge; business center; room service until 10pm; laundry/dry cleaning. *In room:* A/C, TV, Wi-Fi, minibar, coffeemaker, hair dryer, iron, safe.

Hotel Valencia Riverwalk   It's easy to see why the Valencia is considered the hottest new lodging in town. The rooms are super chic—lots of contrasts, retro lamps, and tongue-in-cheek touches, such as the faux mink throw on the bed—and very techie-friendly. The on-site **Vbar** and **Citrus** restaurant are übertrendy and the panoply of colors and sounds (a splashing waterfall, music wafting through the halls) that you encounter as you enter the hotel is stimulating. But the entryway, on a busy street with a limited area for luggage (or vehicle) drop-off, is a tad *too* stimulating (as in chaotic), whether or not the remote Palm Pilot check-in is in operation. The hallways leading to the guest quarters are narrow and dark, and the rooms themselves have too many individual dimmer switches and lighting devices, and not enough space. The priciest rooms offer river views from narrow balconies. If you're looking for a slightly edgy ambience, the Valencia is a great environment. But if you're regular folk seeking a stress-free getaway, this may not be your place.

150 E. Houston St. (at St. Mary's), San Antonio, TX 78205. ℂ **866/842-0100** or 210/227-9700. Fax 210/227-9701. www. hotelvalencia.com. 213 units. $309–$389 double, suites from $599. Leisure, corporate, and Internet rates available.

Central San Antonio Accommodations, Dining & Attractions

ACCOMMODATIONS ■

Beckmann Inn and Carriage House **38**
Best Western Sunset Suites **30**
Brackenridge House **35**
The Columns on Alamo **39**
Comfort Inn Alamo/Riverwalk San Antonio **7**
Crockett Hotel **21**
Drury Inn & Suites San Antonio Riverwalk **12**
Emily Morgan **17**
Havana Riverwalk Inn **3**
Hotel Contessa **24**
Hotel Valencia Riverwalk **8**
Menger Hotel **28**
Ogé House Inn on the River Walk **33**
Omni La Mansión del Rio **13**
The Watermark Hotel & Spa **11**

DINING ◆

Acenar **10**
Azuca **34**
Biga on the Banks **23**
Boudro's **25**
Demo's **1**
Guenther House **37**
Le Rêve **14**
Little Rhein Steak House **27**
Mi Tierra **4**
Paesano's Riverwalk **16**
Rosario's **36**
Schilo's **26**
Sushi Zushi **22**
Taco Heaven **40**

ATTRACTIONS ●

The Alamo **20**
HemisFair Park **32**
La Villita National Historic District **31**
Market Square **4**
Museo American Smithsonian **5**
Plaza Wax Museum & Ripley's Believe It or Not **19**
Ripley's Haunted Adventure, Guinness World Records Museum, and Davy Crockett's Tall Tales Ride **18**
The River Walk **15**
San Antonio Children's Museum **9**
San Antonio IMAX Theater Rivercenter **29**
San Antonio Museum of Art **2**
Spanish Governor's Palace **6**

AE, DC, DISC, MC, V. Valet parking $27. **Amenities:** Restaurant; bar; exercise room; spa; concierge; business center; Wi-Fi in public areas; 24-hr room service; laundry/dry cleaning. *In room:* A/C, TV w/pay movies, high-speed Internet and Wi-Fi access, minibar, hair dryer, iron.

Omni La Mansión del Río ★★   This hotel is pure San Antonio and is the favorite choice of Texan out-of-towners. The core of the building was constructed in 1852 for a seminary, and renovations and expansions have kept the character of the original. Rooms have local flavor, with many featuring Mexican tile floors, beamed ceilings, and wrought-iron balconies. Unlike many of the other big hotels on the river, this one is not a high-rise (six floors). Rooms with a river view are level with the tall cypress trees that line the river bank, and the hotel's location on a central, yet relatively quiet, section of the River Walk is ideal. Interior rooms are also enjoyable, looking out, as they do, over landscaped courtyards. Since the Omni chain took over management in 2006, all the rooms have been remodeled. Most are large and are decorated with highly textured plush fabrics to set off the rustic elements of the room. The layout of the grounds is a bit mazelike—the directionally challenged, like me, may find themselves wandering in circles.

112 College St. (between St. Mary's and Navarro), San Antonio, TX 78205. ✆ **800/830-1400** or 210/518-1000. Fax 210/226-0389. www.omnilamansion.com. 337 units. $259–$429 double; suites from $1,039. AE, DC, DISC, MC, V. Valet parking $28. Pets under 20 lb. accepted for $25 per pet per day. **Amenities:** Restaurant; outdoor heated pool; fitness room; concierge; complimentary transportation around downtown business district; business center; 24-hr. room service; laundry/dry cleaning. *In room:* A/C, TV w/pay movies, dataport, high-speed Internet access, minibar, coffeemaker, hair dryer, iron.

The Watermark Hotel & Spa ★★★   The latest entry into the River Walk luxury hotel sweepstakes, the Watermark is a big-time winner. The welcoming Western-style lobby pays tribute to the historic L. Frank Saddlery Building, which once occupied this site. The rooms are some of the nicest in downtown (make that the city). Bright, with high ceilings, they've got a Texas-meets-Tokyo elegance. The marble bathrooms offer jetted tubs. And, outside of the resorts on the outskirts of town, this hotel has the city's best spa and beauty salon. And, oh, the service. There will be no stressful encounters with the front desk when you arrive. Instead, you're escorted to your room—where your minifridge has been stocked with goodies that you requested in advance—to complete the check-in process. What with the spa, the soothing guest quarters, and the staff attentiveness, you'd have to have the personality of Woody Allen not to relax in this place. All rooms are nonsmoking.

212 W. Crockett St. (at St. Mary's), San Antonio, TX 78205. ✆ **866/605-1212** or 210/396-5800. Fax 210/226-0389. www.watermarkhotel.com. 99 units. $339–$469 double; $939 suite. AE, DC, DISC, MC, V. Valet parking $28. **Amenities:** Restaurant; cafe; outdoor pool; whirlpool; health club; spa; concierge; business center; salon; 24-hr. room service; dry cleaning. *In room:* A/C, TV w/pay movies, dataport, high-speed Internet access, minifridge, coffeemaker, hair dryer, iron, safe.

EXPENSIVE

Emily Morgan ★★ *Value*   Located just a musket shot from the Alamo, the Emily Morgan was named after the mulatto slave mistress of Mexican general Santa Anna, who was reputed to have spied on him for the Texas independence fighters. It resides in a 1926 Gothic Revival–style medical arts center, replete with gargoyles, said to have been placed there to help the doctors ward off diseases. But there's little to suggest either battlefields or things medicinal inside. As a result of a recent extreme makeover, the rooms have a light, contemporary feel, designed to appeal to a young and affluent crowd who go for the pared-down look popularized by the W chain. Any industrial chic coldness is offset by lots of dark, burnished wood and such touches as a lit votive candle at turndown. For all its perks—250-count sheets, Aveda bath products, CD players, 27-inch TVs, and (in 115 of the rooms) jetted tubs—this place is considerably less expensive than many comparable hotels on the river. The hotel has a very liberal pet policy and even includes cat and dog treats on the room service menu. Smoking is not permitted in any of the guest rooms.

705 E. Houston St. (at Ave. E), San Antonio, TX 78205. ℂ 800/824-6674 or 210/225-5100. Fax 210/225-7227. www. emilymorganhotel.com. 177 units. $189–$229 double; $259–$289 suite. Corporate, promotional rates available. AE, DC, DISC, MC, V. Valet parking $18. Pets permitted with no extra charge or deposit. **Amenities:** Restaurant; outdoor heated pool; exercise room; Jacuzzi; sauna; concierge; Wi-Fi in public areas; 24-hr. room service; laundry/dry cleaning. *In room:* A/C, TV w/pay movies, dataport, high-speed Internet access, minifridge, coffeemaker, hair dryer, iron.

Menger Hotel ⟨★⟩   In the late 19th century, no one who was anyone would consider staying anywhere but the Menger, which opened its doors in 1859 and has never closed them. Ulysses S. Grant, Sarah Bernhardt, and Oscar Wilde were among those who walked—or, rumor has it, in the case of Robert E. Lee, rode a horse—through the halls, ballrooms, and gardens. Successfully combining the original, restored building with myriad additions, the Menger now takes up an entire city block. The hotel's location is terrific—smack between the Alamo and the Rivercenter Mall, a block from the River Walk. And its public areas, particularly the Victorian Lobby, are gorgeous. The **Menger Bar** is one of San Antonio's historic taverns. The Menger also has a small spa, still a relative rarity in San Antonio hotels. Ask for one of the recently refurbished rooms, as those that haven't been redone are somewhat tired. Decor ranges from ornate 19th-century to modern. If you want one of the antiques-filled Victorian rooms, be sure to request it when you book.

204 Alamo Plaza (at Crockett St.), San Antonio, TX 78205. ℂ 800/345-9285 or 210/223-4361. Fax 210/228-0022. www.historicmenger.com. 316 units. $215 double; $250–$495 suite. AE, DC, DISC, MC, V. Valet parking $25. **Amenities:** Restaurant; bar; outdoor pool; fitness room; spa; Jacuzzi; shopping arcade; limited room service; laundry/dry cleaning. *In room:* A/C, TV w/pay movies, high-speed Internet access, fridge rental ($25), hair dryer, iron.

MODERATE

Comfort Inn Alamo/Riverwalk San Antonio ⟨Value⟩   I'm no expert on the Comfort Inn chain, but I've been in enough of the lodgings to know that this one is nothing like the rest. First and foremost, it occupies the old Bexar (pronounced *Bear*) County Jail, and is a regular hotel with indoor corridors and a front desk at the entrance. But what really impressed me about the place was the cleanliness and the comfort of the rooms. The bathrooms were also a surprise—a little larger and much more attractive than the usual at this price level, with touches like polished granite countertops. The largest rooms come with two queen beds, and are quite comfortable. Other options are a king bed and the studio king. All rooms are nonsmoking. Service here is friendly and attentive.

120 Camaron St. (between Houston and Commerce), San Antonio, TX 78205. ℂ 800/223-4990 or 210/281-1400. Fax 210/228-0007. www.comfortinnsanantonio.com. 82 units. $109–$189 double. Rates include continental breakfast. AE, DC, DISC, MC, V. Off-site parking (1 block away) $6. **Amenities:** Outdoor heated pool; Jacuzzi; business center; laundry/dry cleaning; coin-op washer/dryer. *In room:* A/C, TV, high-speed Internet access, fridge, microwave, coffeemaker, hair dryer, iron.

Crockett Hotel ⟨★⟩ ⟨Value⟩   This hotel comes by its name honestly, unlike many of the places that bank on Davy Crockett's moniker. The famed Alamo hero definitely walked the land on which the hotel rose in 1909, as it—the land, that is—served as the Alamo's battleground. The property is a bit of a hybrid, consisting of the original historical landmark building (expanded in 1927) and several low-slung, motel-style units that surround what may be downtown's nicest swimming pool and a tropical landscaped courtyard. Rooms in both sections of the hotel are attractive, with lots of vibrant Southwest colors and allusions to Texas history (regional artwork, pine beds with Lone Star headboards, and the like). Look for deals; rooms here are discounted for every imaginable reason. The location is excellent, by the Alamo and the River-center Mall and close by the river.

320 Bonham St. (at Crockett St.), San Antonio, TX 78205. (℃ 800/292-1050 or 210/225-6500. Fax 210/225-7418. www.crocketthotel.com. 204 units. Rooms $129–$145; suites from $375. Various discounts (including Internet booking and specials). AE, DC, DISC, MC, V. Valet parking $21. Pets accepted; $100 deposit required ($50 refundable). **Amenities:** Restaurant; lounge; unheated outdoor pool and hot tub; limited room service; coin-op laundry; same-day dry cleaning (weekdays). *In room:* A/C, TV w/pay movies, dataport, high-speed Internet access, coffeemaker, hair dryer, iron.

Drury Inn & Suites San Antonio Riverwalk (Value)

One of San Antonio's most recent River Walk conversions, the one-time Petroleum Commerce Building is now a comfortable modern lodging. The polished marble floors and chandeliers in the lobby and the high ceilings and ornate window treatments in the guest rooms hearken back to a grander era, also evoked in business-traveler perks such as free hot breakfasts, free evening cocktails and snacks, free local phone calls, and 1 hour of free long distance per day. Guests also appreciate the 24-hour business center. Anyone who wants to economize on meals will also like the fact that many of these attractive Southwest-style rooms are equipped with refrigerators and microwaves.

201 N. St. Mary's St. (at Commerce St.), San Antonio, TX 78205. (℃ 800/DRURY-INN or 210/212-5200. Fax 210/352-9939. www.druryhotels.com. 150 units. $129–$154 double; $160–$185 suite. AE, DC, DISC, MC, V. Self-parking $12. Small pets accepted. **Amenities:** Restaurant; outdoor pool; exercise room; Jacuzzi; 24-hr. business center; Wi-Fi in public areas; dry cleaning. *In room:* A/C, TV, dataport, high-speed Internet access, fridge and microwave (in king rooms and suites), coffeemaker, hair dryer, iron.

Havana Riverwalk Inn (𝒦)

Decked out to suggest travelers' lodgings from the 1920s, this intimate inn—built in 1914 in Mediterranean Revival style—oozes character. All the guest quarters are delightfully different, with a safari hat covering a temperature control gauge here, an old photograph perched over a toilet paper roll there, gauzy curtains draped on a canopy bed, wooden louvers on the windows, and so on. Touches such as fresh flowers and bottled water add to the charm, and modern amenities such as irons have not been ignored. Not all rooms have closets, however, so be prepared to have your clothes (ironed or not) hanging in public view if you plan to invite anyone to your room. Singles will absolutely want to hit the hotel's happening cigar bar, **Club Cohiba.** Rooms are nonsmoking.

1015 Navarro (between St. Mary's and Martin sts.), San Antonio, TX 78205. (℃ 888/224-2008 or 210/222-2008. Fax 210/222-2717. www.havanariverwalkinn.com. 28 units. $159–$179 double; $399–$599 suite. AE, DC, DISC, MC, V. Self-parking $10. Only children ages 15 and older accepted. **Amenities:** Restaurant; bar; concierge; business center; secretarial services; limited room service; laundry/dry cleaning. *In room:* A/C, TV, dataport, high-speed Internet access, hair dryer, iron.

INEXPENSIVE

Best Western Sunset Suites–Riverwalk (𝒦) (Value)

Don't be put off by the fact that this all-suites hotel is located on the wrong side of the tracks, er, highway. In a converted turn-of-the-century building you'll find some of the nicest rooms in downtown San Antonio for the price—large, with custom-made Arts and Crafts–style furnishings, including comfy, clean-lined lounge chairs and faux Tiffany lamps. They're also some of the best-equipped rooms around: All offer sleeper sofas, microwaves, minifridges, and 27-inch TVs. And talk about deals: If you don't want to move your car from its free parking spot or take a 10-minute walk to the heart of downtown, you can ride the public trolley bus that passes by the hotel.

1103 E. Commerce St. (at Hwy. 281), San Antonio, TX 78205. © **866/560-6000** or 210/223-4400. Fax 210/223-4402. www.bestwesternsunsetsuites.com. 64 units. $129 double. AE, DC, DISC, MC, V. Free parking. **Amenities:** Health club; business center. *In room:* A/C, TV w/pay movies, dataport, Wi-Fi, kitchenette, coffeemaker, hair dryer, iron.

KING WILLIAM HISTORIC DISTRICT
EXPENSIVE

Ogé House Inn on the River Walk ★★   One of the most glorious of the mansions that grace the King William district, this 1857 Greek revival–style property is more of a boutique inn than a bed-and-breakfast. You'll still get the personalized attention you would expect from a host home, but it's combined here with the luxury of a sophisticated small hotel. All rooms are impeccably decorated in high Victorian style, yet feature modern conveniences such as small refrigerators; many rooms also have fireplaces and views of the manicured, pecan-shaded grounds, and one looks out on the river from its own balcony. The units downstairs aren't as light as those on the upper two floors, but they're less expensive and offer private entrances. A bountiful gourmet breakfast is served on individual white-clothed tables set with the finest crystal and china. You'll also find such modern touches as Wi-Fi throughout and high-speed Internet access in the rooms.

209 Washington St. (at Turner St.), San Antonio, TX 78204. © **800/242-2770** or 210/223-2353. Fax 210/226-5812. www.ogeinn.com. 10 units. $179–$250 double; suites from $259. Rates include full breakfast. Corporate rates available for single business travelers. 2-night minimum stay on weekends; 3 nights during holidays and special events. AE, DC, DISC, MC, V. Free off-street parking. **Amenities:** Wi-Fi in public areas. *In room:* A/C, TV, dataport, high-speed Internet access, fridge, hair dryer, iron.

MODERATE

Beckmann Inn and Carriage House   Sitting on the lovely wraparound porch of this 1886 Queen Anne home, surrounded by quiet, tree-lined streets on an underdeveloped stretch of the San Antonio River, you can easily imagine yourself in a kinder, gentler era. In fact, you can still see the flour mill on whose property the Beckmann Inn was originally built. The illusion of time travel won't be dispelled when you step through the rare Texas red-pine door into the high-ceilinged parlor. The house is filled with antique pieces that do justice to the setting, such as the ornately carved Victorian beds in each of the guest rooms. The owners are adding a new room for 2007, which they tell me will be larger than the rest, with a king bed and an extra-large bathroom. Smoking is prohibited in the rooms, but allowed in outdoor common areas. A full breakfast—perhaps cranberry French toast topped with orange twist—is served in the formal dining room, but you can also enjoy your coffee on a flower-filled sun porch.

222 E. Guenther St. (at Madison St.), San Antonio, TX 78204. © **800/945-1449** or 210/229-1449. Fax 210/229-1061. www.beckmanninn.com. 6 units. $109–$199. Rates include full breakfast. AE, DC, DISC, MC, V. Free off-street parking. **Amenities:** Wi-Fi in public areas. *In room:* A/C, TV, dataport, Wi-Fi, fridge, hair dryer, iron.

Brackenridge House *(Finds*   These days many B&Bs are beginning to resemble boutique hotels, with an almost hands-off approach on the part of the hosts. If you seek out B&Bs because you prefer warmer, more traditional treatment, this King William abode is likely to suit you. It's not just that the house is homey rather than fancy—although it's got its fair share of antiques, you don't feel as though they're too priceless to approach—but that owners Sue and Bennie (aka the King of King William)

Kids Family-Friendly Hotels

Hyatt Regency Hill Country Resort (p. 264)   In addition to its many great play areas (including a beach with a shallow swimming area), and its proximity to SeaWorld, this hotel offers Camp Hyatt—a program of excursions, sports, and social activities for children 3 to 12. The program fills up fast during school breaks and other holidays, when reservations are mandatory.

O'Casey's Bed & Breakfast (p. 263)   Usually B&Bs and family vacations are a contradiction in terms, but O'Casey's is happy to host well-behaved kids. *Best bet:* Stay in the separate guesthouse with the foldout bed, and then join the main-house guests for breakfast in the morning.

Omni San Antonio (p. 264)   This hotel's proximity to the theme parks as well as in-room Nintendo and various other Omni Kids features makes the Omni appealing to families.

Westin La Cantera (p. 264)   It's close to Six Flags Fiesta Texas, it's got two pools just for children, and it offers the Enchanted Rock Kids Club—an activities program for ages 5 through 12—from May through Labor Day.

Blansett instantly make you feel welcome. All rooms have TVs with HBO and Showtime, as well as minifridges, microwaves, and coffeemakers. And if you're really antisocial (or traveling with kids and/or a pet), you can always book the separate carriage house, a few doors down from the main house.

230 Madison St. (off Beauregard St.), San Antonio, TX 78204. (C) **800/221-1412** or 210/271-3442. www.brackenridge house.com. 6 units. $111–$145 double; $126–$145 suites and carriage house. Rates include breakfast (full in main house, continental in carriage house). Corporate, state, and federal rates; extended stay plans available for the carriage house. 2-night minimum stay required on weekend. AE, DC, DISC, MC, V. Free off-street parking. Small pets accepted in carriage house. **Amenities:** Outdoor heated pool; hot tub; Wi-Fi in public areas. *In room:* A/C, TV, dataport, Wi-Fi, fridge, microwave, coffeemaker, hair dryer, iron.

The Columns on Alamo ♺   You're spoiled for choice at this gracious B&B. You can stay in the 1892 Greek revival mansion, in an adjacent guesthouse built 9 years later, or in a new limestone cottage built in a rustic, early-1880s style. The mansion, where the innkeepers live, is the most opulent and offers unusual walk-through windows leading to a veranda, while the guesthouse—which houses most of the lodgings—affords more privacy if you're uncomfortable with the idea of staying in someone else's home. Those who really want to hole up should book the Honeymoon and Anniversary cottage, attached to the guesthouse, or the separate Rock House cottage in the back; it's large enough for four.

All the rooms are light, airy, and very pretty, although this is not the place for those allergic to pastels and frills; pink dominates many of the accommodations, and even the darker-toned Imari Room has lace curtains. (The Rock House, done in more casual country style, is the exception.) Several of the units boast two-person Jacuzzis and gas-log fireplaces. Rooms are nonsmoking, but there are designated areas outside. Hosts Ellenor and Arthur Link are extremely helpful, and their breakfasts are all you could ask for in morning indulgence.

1037 S. Alamo (at Sheridan, 5 blocks south of Durango), San Antonio, TX 78210. © 800/233-3364 or 210/271-3245. www.columnssanantonio.com. 13 units. $95–$172 double; $178–$258 cottage. Rates include full breakfast. Extended stay discounts. 2-day minimum stay required for Fri or Sat. AE, DC, DISC, MC, V. Free off-street parking. **Amenities:** Wi-Fi in public areas. *In room:* A/C, TV, dataport, Wi-Fi, fridge, hair dryer, iron.

MONTE VISTA HISTORIC DISTRICT
MODERATE
The Inn at Craig Place 🏵 This 1891 mansion-turned-B&B appeals to history, art, and architecture buffs alike. It was built by one of Texas's most noted architects, Alfred Giles, for H. E. Hildebrand, a major public figure at the time. The living room holds a mural by Julian Onderdonk, an influential Texas landscape artist, who grew up in Monte Vista in the 1880s. But that's all academic. More to the point, this place is gorgeous, with forests of gleaming wood and clean Arts-and-Crafts lines, as well as cushy couches and a wraparound porch. Rooms are at once luxurious—all have working fireplaces and hardwood floors, and come with robes, slippers, feather pillows, and down comforters—and equipped for modern needs. Among the romantic getaway packages offered are the "Pampering Perfected" and the "Romantic Rendezvous." And for those desperate to be forgiven your wrongdoings, whisk your beloved here for the "Honey, I'm Sorry" package, perks of which include a personalized note of apology and a rose waiting for you on the bed.

117 W. Craig Place (off N. Main Ave.), San Antonio, TX 78212. © 877/427-2447 or 210/736-1017. Fax 210/737-1562. www.craigplace.com. 5 units. $115–$215. Corporate rates available. Rates include full breakfast. AE, DC, DISC, MC, V. Free off-street parking. No children younger than 12 years old. *In room:* A/C, TV w/DVD, Wi-Fi, hair dryer, iron, no phone.

INEXPENSIVE
Bonner Garden 🏵 *Value* Those who like the charm of the bed-and-breakfast experience but aren't keen on Victorian froufrou should consider the Bonner Garden, located about a mile north of downtown. Built in 1910 for Louisiana artist Mary Bonner, this large, Italianate villa has elegantly appointed rooms that steer clear of the cluttered look. It also has something not commonly found at B&Bs: a large 45-foot swimming pool. The Portico Room, in which guests can gaze up at a painted blue sky with billowing clouds, enjoys a private poolside entrance. Most of the rooms feature European-style decor, but Mary Bonner's former studio, separate from the main house, is done in an attractive Santa Fe style. A rooftop deck affords a sparkling nighttime view of downtown. Smoking is permitted in outdoor areas.

145 E. Agarita (at McCullough), San Antonio, TX 78212. © 800/396-4222 or 210/733-4222. Fax 210/733-6129. www.bonnergarden.com. 6 units. $99–$150 double. Rates include full breakfast. Extended-stay discount (minimum 3 nights) and corporate rates available. 2-night minimum stay on weekends. AE, DISC, MC, V. Free off-street parking. **Amenities:** Outdoor pool. *In room:* A/C, TV/VCR, dataport, Wi-Fi, hair dryer, iron (in some rooms).

O'Casey's Bed & Breakfast *Value* *Kids* If there's a twinkle in John Casey's eye when he puts on a brogue, it's because he was born on U.S. soil, not the auld sod. But he and his wife Linda Fay exhibit a down-home friendliness that's no blarney. This Irish-themed B&B is one of the few around that welcomes families and is well equipped to handle them. One suite in the main house has a sitting area with a futon large enough for a couple of youngsters; another has a trundle bed for two kids in a separate bedroom. Studio apartments in the carriage house both offer full kitchens. All of this is not to suggest that accommodations are utilitarian—far from it. Rooms in the main house, a gracious structure built in 1904, feature hardwood floors and antiques, and many bathrooms display claw-foot tubs. There's a wraparound balcony upstairs, too. All guest rooms are nonsmoking; smoking is permitted in outdoor areas.

225 W. Craig Place (between San Pedro Ave. and Main St.), San Antonio, TX 78212. ℂ **800/738-1378** or 210/738-1378. www.ocaseybnb.com. 7 units. $85–$110 double (single-night stays on weekends may be slightly higher). Rates include full breakfast. Extended-stay discounts sometimes available. DISC, MC, V. Street parking. Pets allowed in apts only; $10 for up to a week. **Amenities:** Wi-Fi in public areas. *In room:* A/C, TV, Wi-Fi, kitchen (in apts).

NORTHWEST
VERY EXPENSIVE

Westin La Cantera ✰✰✰ *Kids*   With its knockout facilities, sprawling, gorgeous grounds, and loads of Texas character, the Westin is an all-around winner. It proximity to Six Flags and excellent children's programs make it family-friendly; its two championship courses plus a professional golf school appeal to duffers; and its gorgeous views from one of the highest points in San Antonio make this a romantic retreat, too. Casual elegant rooms, beautifully decorated in muted earth tones and subtle florals, are likely to be abandoned for the resort's myriad recreation areas. The indigenous plant life and animal life—deer, rabbits, and wild turkeys come out at dusk—should have you oohing and aahing. So will the Southwest cuisine (speaking of game . . .) and the sundown vistas of Francesca's at Sunset, the resort's excellent fine dining room.

16641 La Cantera Pkwy., San Antonio, TX 78256. ℂ **800/WESTIN-1** or 210/558-6500. Fax 210/641-0721. www.westinlacantera.com. 508 units. $259–$349 double; suites from $380; casitas from $350. AE, DISC, MC, V. Free self-parking; valet parking $12. Take the La Cantera Pkwy. Exit off I-10 and turn left; resort entrance is ¾ mile ahead, on the right. **Amenities:** 3 restaurants; 2 bars; outdoor heated pool; 2 golf courses; 2 lit tennis courts; health club; spa; Jacuzzi; children's center; video arcade; concierge; business center; 24-hr. room service; massage; dry cleaning. *In room:* A/C, TV w/pay movies, dataport, minibar, coffeemaker, hair dryer, iron, safe.

EXPENSIVE

Omni San Antonio ✰ *Kids*   This polished granite high-rise off I-10 west is convenient to SeaWorld, Six Flags Fiesta Texas, the airport, and the Hill Country, and the shops and restaurants of the 66-acre Colonnade complex are within easy walking distance. The lobby is soaring and luxurious, and guest rooms are well-appointed in a traditional but cheery Continental style. The proximity to the theme parks as well as in-room Nintendo and various other Omni Kids features make this hotel as appealing to families as it is to business travelers, who appreciate its exercise facilities, better than most in San Antonio and definitely the best in this part of town. Guests can also get treadmills brought into their rooms as part of the Omni "Get Fit" program. Although the hotel sees a lot of tourist and Medical Center traffic, service here is prompt and courteous.

9821 Colonnade Blvd. (at Wurzbach), San Antonio, TX 78230. ℂ **800/843-6664** or 210/691-8888. Fax 210/691-1128. www.omnihotels.com. 326 units. $169 double; suites from $300. A variety of discount packages available. AE, DC, DISC, MC, V. Free self-parking; valet parking $10. Pets 25 lb. or less permitted; $50 nonrefundable fee. **Amenities:** Restaurant; bar; indoor pool; outdoor pool; health club; Jacuzzi; sauna; concierge; free airport shuttle; business center; Wi-Fi in public areas; limited room service; laundry/dry cleaning; club-level rooms. *In room:* A/C, TV w/pay movies, dataport, Wi-Fi, minibar, coffeemaker, hair dryer, iron.

WEST
VERY EXPENSIVE

Hyatt Regency Hill Country Resort ✰✰✰ *Kids*   The setting, on 200 acres of former ranch land on the far-west side of San Antonio; the resort's low-slung native limestone buildings, inspired by the architecture of the nearby Hill Country; and the on-site activities, ranging from golf to yoga to tubing on the 950-foot-long Ramblin' River, all make this resort a top choice. The spa, boasting all the latest treatments, is one of the best pampering palaces in this part of Texas. The rooms underwent a major revamp in 2004–05, morphing from country cute to haute Dallas: neutral-toned rugs, dark-wood furnishings, silks and brocades in shades of mocha and taupe, and cushy new bedding. Many offer French doors that open out onto wood-trimmed porches. And 9 more Arthur Hill–designed holes of golf are in the offing (bringing the total up to 27 holes).

The resort is also extremely family-friendly. SeaWorld sits at your doorstep, there are free laundry facilities and a country store for supplies, and every room has a refrigerator (not stocked with goodies, alas). When you're tired of all that family bonding, the Hyatt Kids Club will keep the youngsters happily occupied while you spend some quality time relaxing on Ramblin' River.

9800 Hyatt Resort Dr. (off Hwy. 151, between Westover Hills Blvd. and Potranco Rd.), San Antonio, TX 78251. ℂ 800/ 55-HYATT or 210/647-1234. Fax 210/681-9681. http://hillcountry.hyatt.com. 500 units. $285–$400 double; $450–$2,550 suite. Rates lower late Nov to early Mar; packages available. AE, DC, DISC, MC, V. Free self-parking; valet parking $10. **Amenities:** 6 restaurants; 2 bars; 4 outdoor pools; golf course; 3 tennis courts (1 lit); 24-hr. health club; spa; 5 Jacuzzis; bikes on loan; children's programs; youth spa; game room; concierge; business center; Wi-Fi in public areas; room service; laundry/dry cleaning; free washer/dryer; club-level rooms. *In room:* A/C, TV w/pay movies, dataport, Wi-Fi and high-speed Internet access, fridge, hair dryer, iron, safe.

NORTH CENTRAL (NEAR THE AIRPORT)
EXPENSIVE
San Antonio Airport Hilton ⟨★⟩ You'll go straight from the airport to the heart of Texas if you stay at this friendly hotel, where the cheerful lobby has a bull-rider mural. Such nongeneric features as an outdoor putting green also help make your stay enjoyable. But while this hotel may be playful, it also knows how to get down to business. A $5-million renovation, completed in February 2005, added comfy pillow-top beds to the guest quarters, and gave them a more elegant, understated look than they had before. Pretty spiffy—but I for one am going to miss the cowboy lamps and Lone Star–pattern chairs. Don't mess with Texas.

611 NW Loop 410 (San Pedro exit), San Antonio, TX 78216. ℂ 800/HILTONS or 210/340-6060. Fax 210/377-4674. www.hilton.com. 386 units. $169–$199 double; suites from $175. Romance, weekend packages available. AE, DC, DISC, MC, V. Free covered parking. **Amenities:** Restaurant; bar; outdoor pool; putting green; Jacuzzi; sauna; video arcade; courtesy car; business center; Wi-Fi in public areas; 24-hr. room service; same-day dry cleaning; club-level rooms. *In room:* TV w/pay movies, dataport, Wi-Fi, high-speed Internet access, coffeemaker, hair dryer, iron.

INEXPENSIVE
La Quinta Inn & Suites San Antonio Airport Bunched up around the intersection of Highway 281 and Loop 410 are a number of airport hotels. Among them is this property, which is nicely located so that it doesn't front either freeway. It's still easy to find, has an airport shuttle that can also take you to any restaurant in a 2-mile radius, and has easy access to Hwy. 281 south, which leads to downtown. The property is only 5 years old and is well maintained. Guest rooms are plain but are comfortable and functional. And the bathrooms are a cut above the competition in this category in that they have a little more room and better lighting.

450 Halm Blvd., San Antonio, TX 78216. ℂ 800/642-4271 or 210/342-3738. Fax 210/348-9666. www.lq.com. 276 units. $95–$155 double. Rates include free breakfast buffet. AE, DC, DISC, MC, V. Free parking. Pets accepted for free. **Amenities:** Outdoor pool; airport shuttle; laundry/dry cleaning. *In room:* A/C, TV, dataport, high-speed cable Internet access, coffeemaker, hair dryer, iron.

4 Where to Dine

It's easy to eat very well in San Antonio; there's something to satisfy every taste and budget. The downtown dining scene, especially that found along the River Walk, is the one most visitors will become familiar with. I've devoted a good deal of space to restaurants in this area. However, many of these restaurants can be overpriced and overcrowded. And parking is either tough to find or expensive. You'll also find some good restaurants in Southtown, but most prime places to chow down are scattered throughout the north. By far the most fertile ground for outstanding San Antonio dining is on and around Broadway, starting a few blocks south of Hildebrand, extending north to Loop 410, and comprising much of the posh area known as Alamo Heights. Brackenridge Park, the zoo, the botanical gardens, and the Witte and McNay museums are all situated in this part of town, so you can combine your sightseeing with some serious eating.

DOWNTOWN
VERY EXPENSIVE
Biga on the Banks ✺✺ NEW AMERICAN   The setting and the cooking at this River Walk establishment are bold and contemporary. Clean lines, high ceilings, and gleaming wood floors are the scene for chef/owner Bruce Auden's intriguing, innovative cuisine with a subtle Texas influence. The starters include Asian spring rolls filled with minced venison, buffalo, ostrich, and pheasant accompanied by two spicy dipping sauces. The bone-on tenderloin steak with beer-battered onion rings and habanero ketchup raises comfort cuisine to new heights, and the variations on a theme in the Paseo de Chocolate dessert will send you happily into sugar shock, international-style. All this, yet the food is not nearly as dazzling as it used to be. Still, it's way above average, and if you're willing to eat before 6:30pm or after 9pm, you can sample a three-course meal for $35 per person, or four courses for $43.

International Center, 203 S. St. Mary's St./River Walk. ✆ 210/225-0722. www.biga.com. Reservations recommended. Main courses $19–$36; brunch $32 adults, $17 ages 12 and younger. AE, DC, DISC, MC, V. Sun–Thurs 5:30–10pm; Fri–Sat 5:30–11pm.

Le Rêve ✺✺✺ FRENCH   This restaurant is for serious diners, for whom fine dining is one of the ultimate expressions of civilized life. The chef/owner Andrew Weissman is originally from San Antonio but has spent many years honing his craft in France and elsewhere. His exacting method of cooking has garnered lavish praise and won many awards from the national food press. The menu items vary depending upon availability of ingredients. When they're on the menu, scallop dishes as well as beef tournedos dishes are good choices. The caramelized onion tart is a perennial. Try it. There is a tasting menu (with or without wine) and five-, four-, and three-course menus available, too. The attention to detail extends to the choice of wines, the small size and arrangement of the dining room, and the manner of service—all is aimed at complementing the food without being imposing or distracting.

152 E. Pecan St. at St. Mary's. ✆ 210/212-2221. www.restaurantlereve.com. Reservations required. Jacket required for men. Tasting menu $100, $165 with wine; prix-fixe 3 courses $80, 4 courses $90, 5 courses $100. AE, DC, DISC, MC, V. Tues–Sat 5:30–11pm (last reservation taken for 8:30pm seating).

Little Rhein Steak House AMERICAN/STEAKS   Built in 1847 in what was then the Rhein district, the oldest two-story structure in San Antonio has hosted an elegant steakhouse abutting the river and La Villita since 1967. Antique memorabilia decks the indoor main dining room, and a miniature train surrounded by historic replicas runs overhead. Leafy branches overhanging the River Walk patio are draped in little sparkling lights. The choice USDA Prime steaks from the restaurant's own meat plant are tasty, but recent competition from chains such as The Palm and Morton's nearby has resulted in a price hike. Now everything here—a baked potato, creamed spinach—is a la carte. The restaurant can also get quite noisy. That said, this is still one of the few family-owned steakhouses around, and it offers a unique River Walk dining experience.

231 S. Alamo at Market. (🄫 210/225-2111. www.littlerheinsteakhouse.com. Reservations recommended. Main courses $21–$42. AE, DC, DISC, MC, V. Daily 5–10pm.

EXPENSIVE

Boudro's 🄬 NEW AMERICAN   Locals tend to look down their noses at River Walk restaurants—with the long-running exception of Boudro's. The kitchen uses fresh local ingredients and the preparations and presentations do them justice. The setting is also out of the ordinary, boasting a turn-of-the-century limestone building with hardwood floors and a handmade mesquite bar. You might start with the guacamole, prepared tableside and served with tostadas, or the pan-fried Texas crab cakes. The prime rib, blackened on a pecan-wood grill, is deservedly popular, as is the pork chop with sun-dried cherry and chili marmalade. The food may be innovative, but portions are hearty nevertheless. For dessert, the whisky-soaked bread pudding is fine, and the lime chess pie with a butter pastry crust is divine. Service is very good despite the volume of business and the time the servers spend mixing up guacamole.

421 E. Commerce St./River Walk. (🄫 210/224-8484. www.boudros.com. Reservations strongly recommended. Main courses $15–$28. AE, DC, DISC, MC, V. Sun–Thurs 11am–11pm; Fri–Sat 11am–midnight.

Paesano's Riverwalk 🄬 ITALIAN   This River Walk incarnation of a longtime San Antonio favorite relinquished its old Chianti bottle–kitsch decor for a soaring ceiling, lots of inscrutable contemporary art, and a more up-to-date menu. But the one thing the restaurant couldn't give up, at the risk of a local insurrection, was the signature shrimp Paesano's. The crispy crustaceans are as good as their devotees claim, as are the reasonably priced pizzas. Other good values are the hearty southern Italian staples such as lasagna with meat sauce. Locals tend to go to the newer—and somewhat quieter—Paesano's, across from the Quarry Golf Club at 555 Basse Rd., Suite 100 (🄫 **210/828-5191**).

111 W. Crockett, Suite 101/River Walk. (🄫 210/227-2782. www.paesanosriverwalk.com. Reservations accepted for 10 or more only. Pizzas $14; pastas $8.95–$19; main courses $17–$29. AE, DC, DISC, MC, V. Sun–Thurs 11am–10pm; Fri–Sat 11am–11pm.

MODERATE

Acenar 🄬🄬 (Value) MEXICAN   When Lisa Wong (Rosario) and Bruce Auden (Biga), two longtime darlings of the San Antonio dining scene, collaborate on a restaurant, you figure the food and the atmosphere are going to be creative. Their "modern Tex-Mex" fare and the seemingly endless series of wildly colorful dining rooms (one on the river) in which it's served don't disappoint. In fact, both the food and the service exceed expectations, given the (over) size of this place and the crowds that immediately began to throng to it.

It's hard to go wrong with any of the dishes, but standouts include the crepes with duck in a tamarind-cherry-grilled-onion sauce, and the tacos filled with crabmeat *tinga* (a kind of stew with onions, tomatoes, and chipotle chiles) served with avocado.

You can eat well and still leave with money in your pocket if you go for something other than the specialty dishes, which are pricier but can be worth the splurge.

146 E. Houston St. (next to the Hotel Valencia). © 210/222-CENA. www.acenar.com. Reservations not accepted (priority seating for large parties). Lunch $6.75–$10 (specialties $10–$16); dinner $12–$15 (specialties $16–$30). AE, DC, MC, V. Mon–Thurs 11am–10pm, Fri–Sat 11am–11pm; bar Mon–Wed 4–10pm, Thurs–Sat 4pm–2am.

Sushi Zushi *Value* JAPANESE *Value* For a Japanese food fix in a congenial atmosphere, you can't beat this clean, well-lighted place. You'll find sushi in all its incarnations here, including a My Spurs roll—yellowtail, cilantro, avocado, chives, and *serro* chiles. There are rice bowls, soba noodle bowls, soups, teppanyakis, tempuras—in fact, a mind-boggling array of food choices, not to mention a long list of sakes. Two more branches of Sushi Zushi are in the Northwest at the Colonnade Shopping Center, 9901 W I-10 (© 210/691-3332), and in the Northeast at Stone Oak Plaza II, 18720 Stone Oak Pkwy. at Loop 1604 (© 210/545-6100).

203 S. Saint Mary's St. (The International Center). © 210/472-2900. www.sushizushi.com. Reservations recommended on weekends. Sushi rolls and sashimi $4–$15; bowls, tempuras, and other hot entrees $8–$17. AE, DISC, MC, V. Mon–Thurs 11:30am–10pm; Fri 11:30am–11pm; Sat 12:30–11pm; Sun 5–9pm.

INEXPENSIVE
Mi Tierra *Moments* If you've come to San Antonio with the idea of tasting traditional Tex-Mex as it is cooked day in and day out, come to Mi Tierra's. This Market Square institution is popular with both tourists and locals. The atmosphere is great and unselfconsciously so San Antonio. You can start with the botanas platter, which offers a good smattering of dishes, such as flautas and mini tostadas. The top-shelf margarita will make a nice accompaniment. Then move on to the classic Tex-Mex enchiladas bathed in chili gravy. The on-site bakery produces all the baked sweet breads of Mexico collectively known as *pan dulce*. Try one along with a cup of coffee or Mexican hot chocolate.

218 Produce Row (Market Sq.). © 210/225-1262. www.mitierracafe.com. Reservations accepted for large groups only. Breakfast $6.25–$9.75; lunch and dinner plates $8–$19. AE, MC, V. Open 24 hr.

Schilo's *Value* *Kids* GERMAN/DELI This place has been here since long before San Antonio started attracting tourists. It's on the river not far from the Alamo and makes for a good place to stop and rest your feet and enjoy a hearty bowl of split-pea soup or a piece of the signature cherry cheesecake. The large, open room with its worn wooden booths is classic. The waitresses—definitely not "servers"—wear dirndl-type outfits, and live German bands play on Saturday from 5 to 8pm. The menu has a large kid-friendly selection and retro low prices.

424 E. Commerce St. © 210/223-6692. Reservations for large groups for breakfast and dinner only. Sandwiches $3.25–$4.75; hot or cold plates $4.75–$5.45; main dishes (served after 5pm) $7–$8.95. AE, DC, DISC, MC, V. Mon–Sat 7am–8:30pm.

KING WILLIAM/SOUTHTOWN
EXPENSIVE
Azuca *Value* NUEVO LATINO Anyone familiar with the late, great Latina singer Celia Cruz knows that her signature shout was "Azuca!"—roughly, "Sweetie!" This Southtown restaurant pays tribute to the Cuban-born salsa queen in ways other than its name and the pop images of her that hang in one of the dining rooms (the one with the stage and the bar, naturally).

Just as Celia appealed to a wide array of Latin American (and American) tastes, so too do such well-prepared, creatively updated dishes as Bolivian empanadas, Caribbean *carrucho* (conch meat with olives, onion, and lime), and Peruvian-style rabbit stew with Inca corn. The glass art pieces from the studio next door and brightly hued walls create visual excitement—as Celia's performances did. And the live tango shows, the merengue and Latin bands (Wed–Sat), the warm, friendly service . . . well, come on by, sugar, you'll have a blast.

713 S. Alamo. © 210/225-5550. www.azuca.net. Reservations recommended. Lunch (salads and sandwiches) $7–$9.50; main courses $14–$27. AE, DC, DISC, MC, V. Mon–Thurs 11am–9:30pm (bar until 11pm); Fri–Sat 11am–10:30pm (bar until 2am).

MODERATE

Rosario's ⋆ MEXICAN   This longtime Southtown favorite, one of the first restaurants to establish a hip culinary presence in the area, has toned its menu down a bit; maybe owner Lisa Wong's adventurous urges have found an outlet in Acenar (see "Downtown," above). But the airy room, with its Frida Kahlo and Botero knockoffs and abundant neon, is as fun as ever. And contemporary Tex-Mex fare, prepared with superfresh ingredients, makes this a great choice for visitors to San Antonio. You might start with the chicken or chorizo quesadillas with guacamole or the fresh-tasting *ceviche fina* (white fish, onions, and jalapeños marinated in lime juice), and then go on to the delicious chile relleno, with raisins and potatoes added to the chopped beef stuffing. The large size of the room means that you generally don't have to wait for a table, but it also means that the noise level can make conversation difficult. I like to go to at midafternoon when the place is usually empty.

910 S. Alamo. © 210/223-1806. www.rosariossa.com. Reservations not accepted. Lunch $6–$9; main courses $8–$23. AE, DC, DISC, MC, V. Mon 11am–3pm; Tues–Thurs 11am–10pm; Fri–Sat 11am–11pm (bar until 2am Fri).

INEXPENSIVE

Guenther House ⋆ *Value* AMERICAN   If you're not staying in a King William B&B, this is your chance to visit one of the neighborhood's historic homes. And the food is a winner. Hearty breakfasts and light lunches are served both indoors—in a pretty Art Nouveau–style dining room added on to the Guenther family residence (built in 1860)—and outdoors on a trellised patio. The biscuits and gravy are a morning specialty, and the chicken salad (made with black olives) at lunch is excellent, but you can't go wrong with any of the wonderful baked goods made on the premises, either. Adjoining the restaurant are a small museum, a Victorian parlor, and a mill store featuring baking-related items, including mixes for lots of the Guenther House goodies. The house fronts a lovely stretch of the San Antonio River.

205 E. Guenther St. © 210/227-1061. www.guentherhouse.com. Reservations not accepted. Breakfast $3.95–$7.50; lunch $6.50–$7.25. AE, DC, DISC, MC, V. Daily 7am–3pm (house and mill store Mon–Sat 8am–4pm; Sun 8am–3pm).

MONTE VISTA AREA
MODERATE

La Fonda on Main ⋆ *Value* *Kids* MEXICAN/REGIONAL MEXICAN   One of San Antonio's oldest continually operating restaurants, established in 1932, has spiffed up both its menu and premises. The lovely red-tile-roof residence is cheerful and bright—almost as inviting as the garden-fringed outdoor patio. The menu is divided between classic Tex-Mex, featuring giant combination plates such as the La Fonda Special (two cheese enchiladas, a beef taco, a chicken tamale, guacamole, Mexican rice, refried beans) and a "Cuisines of Mexico" section, including such traditional dishes as *mojo de ajo* (Gulf shrimp with garlic butter served with squash).

2415 N. Main. ☎ 210/733-0621. www.lafondaonmain.com. Reservations recommended for 6 or more. Main courses $8–$11. AE, DC, MC, V. Sun–Thurs 11am–3pm and 5–9:30pm; Fri–Sat 11am–3pm and 5–10:30pm; Sun brunch 11am–3pm.

Liberty Bar NEW AMERICAN For years, this former bar and brothel—it dates back to 1890—has been an informal hangout spot for locals. The building leans a bit. It's definitely noticeable, and the curious effect it produces in most who view it is the desire for a drink. That's what the bar is counting on. The atmosphere here is quite cheerful. The food is good, too. You'll find comfort food—rib-eye steaks, crab cakes, and the like, as well as salads and sandwiches. The entrees on the daily menu often show a good bit of flare.

328 E. Josephine St. ☎ 210/227-1187. Reservations recommended. Main courses $6.95–$19. AE, DISC, MC, V. Sun–Thurs 11:30am–10:30pm; Fri–Sat 11:30am–midnight; Sun brunch 10:30am–2pm (bar until midnight Sun–Thurs, 2am Fri–Sat).

Los Barrios MEXICAN This very popular Tex-Mex joint has been around since the '70s, when it first opened in a former Dairy Queen. The Tex-Mex enchiladas, made of red tortillas and cheese bathed in a hearty chili gravy, are great. Or you could go for the five-enchilada plate with one of every variety served here. Departures from Tex-Mex include *cabrito* (goat) in salsa and the *milanesa con papas,* described on the menu (accurately) as a Mexican-style chicken-fried steak. Mondays and Tuesdays are popular for Fajita Nights, when you can get a pound of fajitas with all the sides for $10 ($16 regular price). Wednesdays are Margarita Nights, and on Thursdays there's a special on longnecks.

4223 Blanco Rd. ☎ 210/732-6017. Reservations accepted for large groups only. Dinners $7–$12. AE, DC, DISC, MC, V. Mon–Thurs 10am–10pm; Fri–Sat 10am–11pm; Sun 9am–10pm.

INEXPENSIVE

Chris Madrids BURGERS It's hard to drop much money at this funky gas-station-turned-burger-joint, but you might lose your shirt—over the years, folks have taken to signing their Ts and hanging them on the walls. An even more popular tradition is trying to eat the macho burger, as huge as its name might indicate. Several burgers are made with a Tex-Mex twist, adding refried beans, hot sauce, or jalapeños to the mix. The kid-friendly menu includes burgers, nachos, fries, and various combinations of these. The casual atmosphere and down-home cooking keep the large outdoor patio filled.

1900 Blanco Rd. ☎ 210/735-3552. www.chrismadrids.com. Reservations not accepted. Main courses $4–$6. AE, DC, DISC, MC, V. Mon–Sat 11am–10pm.

Demo's GREEK Located across the street from a Greek Orthodox church, Demo's a favorite among members of the local Greek community here. You can dine either on the airy patio or in the dining room decorated with murals of Greek island scenes. The menu includes gyros, Greek burgers, dolmas, spanakopita, and other Mediterranean specialties. Occasionally you'll see a belly-dancing show. In addition to this location, there's the original (but more characterless) restaurant at 7115 Blanco Rd. (☎ 210/342-2772) near Loop 410 across from what used to be Central Park Mall, and a third location farther out at Blanco and Loop 1604 (☎ 210/798-3840).

2501 N. St. Mary's St. ☎ 210/732-7777. www.demosgreekfood.com. Reservations accepted for parties of 10 or more only. Main courses $6–$12. AE, DC, DISC, MC, V. Mon–Thurs 11am–9pm; Fri–Sat 11am–midnight.

Kids Family-Friendly Restaurants

Chris Madrids (p. 270)   The kid-friendly menu includes burgers, nachos, fries, and various combinations thereof, and the casual atmosphere and down-home cooking make it popular with families.

Earl Abel's (p. 272)   The menu's so large—and the prices so low—at this bustling diner-type restaurant that everyone's bound to find something they like at a price that won't break the budget.

La Fonda on Main (p. 269)   With its friendly staff and inexpensive children's plates, this restaurant is a great place to introduce your kids to Mexican food. (Anglo options are available as well.)

Schilo's (p. 268)   A high noise level, a convenient location near the River Walk (but with prices far lower than anything else you'll find there), and a wide selection of familiar food make this German deli a good choice for the family.

ALAMO HEIGHTS AREA
EXPENSIVE
Bistro Vatel *★★ Value* FRENCH   Talk about a pressure cooker: In 1671, the great French chef Vatel killed himself out of shame because the fish for a banquet he was preparing for Louis XIV wasn't delivered on time. Fortunately, his descendant, Damian Watel, has less stress to contend with in San Antonio, where diners are very appreciative of the chef's efforts to bring them classic French cooking at comparatively reasonable prices. You can't go wrong with the rich escallop of veal with foie gras and mushrooms, and fans of sweetbreads will be pleased to find them here beautifully prepared in truffle crème fraîche sauce. Your best bet is the prix-fixe dinner, where you can choose one each from four appetizers (perhaps shrimp *vol au vent*) and entrees like roasted quail and enjoy the dessert of the day.

218 E. Olmos Dr. at McCullough. (C) 210/828-3141. www.bistrovatel.com. Reservations recommended on weekends. Main courses $15–$27; prix-fixe dinner $26. AE, MC, V. Tues–Fri 11:30am–1:30pm; Tues 5:30–9pm; Wed–Sat 5:30–10pm.

Silo *★★* NEW AMERICAN   For my money, this is the best place for fine dining if you you're wanting something other than French food. In contrast with other chic restaurants in town, it has quietly gone about its business, focusing on creating dishes that satisfy the palate and deliver something new. The last couple of meals I had here were perfect. Memorable dishes included the chipotle-marinated pork tenderloin with white-cheddar andouille grits and peach chutney, the crab spring rolls with shitake mushrooms and tantalizing dipping sauces, some pan-seared scallops treated very simply, and some wonderful mango-wasabi crab cakes. The amiable waitstaff could answer most of the questions put to them.

1133 Austin Hwy. (C) 210/824-8686. www.siloelevatedcuisine.com. Reservations recommended. Main courses $17–$35; prix fixe (salad, entree, dessert) $18 (5:30–6:45pm nightly). AE, DC, DISC, MC, V. Sun 11am–2:30pm (lunch and brunch menu available) and 5:30–9pm; Tues–Thurs 11am–2:30pm and 5:30–10pm; Fri–Sat 11am–2:30pm and 5:30–11pm.

Local Favorites: *Tacquerías*

Everyone has a favorite *taquería* (taco joint). A couple of high-ranking ones near downtown are **Estela's,** 2200 W. Martin St. (📞 **210/226-2979**), which has musical (salsa, mariachi) breakfasts on Saturday and Sunday from 10am to noon, as well as a great conjunto/Tejano jukebox; and **Taco Haven,** 1032 S. Presa St. (📞 **210/533-2171**), where the breakfast *migas* (hearty egg and tortilla dish) or *chilaquiles* (tortillas layered with meats, beans, and cheese) will kick-start your day. In Olmos Park, **Panchito's,** 4100 McCullough (📞 **210/821-5338**), has hungry San Antonians lining up on weekend mornings for *barbacoa* (Mexican-style barbecue) plates, heaped with two eggs, potatoes, beans, and homemade tortillas.

MODERATE

Ciao Lavanderia ⭐⭐ *Value* ITALIAN   Goodbye Laundromat, hello great dining deal. When the owner of Bistro Vatel (see above) opened a casual Italian eatery just a few doors down from his French restaurant, he stuck with his winning good-food-at-good-prices formula—and then some. In this open, cheery storefront, with its tongue-in-cheek tributes to the business that used to reside here (exposed ductwork, an old washing machine), you select from dishes in three price categories. For $6 you can get minestrone, a salad, or sauté; for $12 you can sample one of the pastas, thin-crust pizzas, or lighter seafood and chicken dishes; while for $16 you might enjoy such hearty entrees as a quail and mushroom risotto or pork loin scaloppine parmigiana. Daily specials such as *osso buco* tend to fall into these price categories, too. Everything's fresh and delicious, and the portions are geared toward a normal human appetite, not supersize. A nice selection of (mostly) Italian wines enhances an already optimal experience.

226 E. Olmos Dr. 📞 210/822-3990. Reservations accepted for large parties only. Pastas and pizzas $12; main courses $16. AE, DC, DISC, MC, V. Mon–Fri 11am–2pm and 5–10pm; Sat 5–10pm.

La Calesa ⭐ *Value* REGIONAL MEXICAN   Tucked away in a small house just off Broadway—look for Earl Abel's large sign across the street—this family-run restaurant cooks up great dishes from interior Mexico. All are good. The owners are from Mexico, but they will serve Tex-Mex, too, because, hey, this is San Antonio. The last time I was there I enjoyed the *mole,* a dish made from dried chiles, roasted tomatoes, ground nuts, herbs, spices, broth, and a bit of chocolate. The *cochinita pibil,* pork cooked slowly with *achiote* and sour orange, served with marinated onions, was wonderful, as was the pork cooked in a tasty green sauce. You can eat indoors in one of three cozy dining rooms, decorated with Mexican art prints and tile work, or outside on the small flower-decked wooden porch.

2103 E. Hildebrand (just off Broadway). 📞 210/822-4475. www.lacalesa.com. Reservations required for 6 or more. Main courses $5.95–$16. AE, DC, DISC, MC, V. Mon–Thurs 11am–9:30pm; Fri 11am–10:30pm; Sat 11:30am–10:30pm; Sun 11:30am–8pm.

INEXPENSIVE

Earl Abel's *Kids* AMERICAN   Earl Abel opened his first restaurant on Main Street in 1933. An organist for silent-film theaters in the 1920s, he had to find something else to do when the talkies took over. But his old Hollywood pals didn't forget him, and Bing Crosby and Gloria Swanson always dropped into Earl's place when they blew through San Antone.

Earl's granddaughter now runs the restaurant, which moved to Broadway in 1940, and the menu is much like it was more than 50 years ago, when what is now called comfort food was simply chow. The restaurant is no longer open 24 hours, but you can still come in after midnight for a cup of coffee and a thick slice of lemon meringue pie. The bargain daily specials and fried chicken remain the all-time favorites, but lots of folks come around for a hearty breakfast of eggs, biscuits and gravy, and grits.

4210 Broadway. (C) 210/822-3358. Reservations not accepted. Sandwiches $5.50–$6.75; main courses $5.25–$20 (daily specials $7–$8). AE, DC, DISC, MC, V. Daily 6:30am–1am.

5 Seeing the Sights

San Antonio has a wide selection of attractions that can satisfy a variety of interests. You could easily fill your time hitting each one on your list, but I would suggest that you set aside at least a little time for aimlessly strolling about the city's downtown.

Before you visit any of the paid attractions, stop in at the **San Antonio Visitor Information Center,** 317 Alamo Plaza ((C) 210/207-6748), across the street from the Alamo, and ask for their *SAVE San Antonio* discount book; it includes coupons for everything from the large theme parks to some city tours and museums. Many hotels also have a stash of discount coupons for their guests.

THE TOP ATTRACTIONS
DOWNTOWN AREA

The Alamo ✿✿   When most visitors see the Alamo for the first time, their common reaction is "Hmmm, I thought it would be bigger." Though the shape of the facade of the Alamo is widely recognized, most folks think of it as a large fortress. This only underscores how heroic and desperate were the actions of the Alamo's defenders who in 1836 held off a siege by a large Mexican army for 13 days. Among the defenders were famous men of their day, such as Davy Crockett and Jim Bowie, and the idea of their sacrifice for Texas independence gave added meaning to the struggle almost immediately. "Remember the Alamo!" became the battle cry at San Jacinto when the Texans finally defeated the Mexican army and captured its general, López de Santa Anna.

The Alamo's original name was Mission San Antonio de Valero, and many converted Indians from a variety of tribes lived and died here. The complex was secularized by the end of the 18th century and leased out to a Spanish cavalry unit; however, by the time the famous battle took place, it had been abandoned.

The outlying buildings of the original mission are gone. Only the **Long Barrack** (formerly the *convento,* or living quarters for the missionaries) and the much-photographed **mission church** are still here. The former houses a museum detailing the history of Texas in general and the battle in particular, and the latter includes artifacts of the Alamo fighters, along with an information desk and a small gift shop. The exhibit doesn't do the best job of explaining how the battle developed. If you want to understand more, see the IMAX show in the nearby Rivercenter Mall. A larger **museum** and gift shop are at the back of the complex. A peaceful **garden** and an excellent **research library** (closed Sun) are also on the grounds. Interesting historical presentations are given every half-hour by Alamo staffers; for private, after-hour tours, phone (C) 210/225-1391, ext. 34.

300 Alamo Plaza. (© 210/225-1391. www.thealamo.org. Free admission (donations welcome). Mon–Sat 9am–5:30pm; Sun 10am–5:30pm. Closed Dec 24–25. Streetcar: Red or Blue lines.

King William Historic District ⋆   San Antonio's first suburb, King William was settled in the late 19th century by prosperous German merchants who displayed their wealth through extravagant homes and named the 25-block area after Kaiser Wilhelm of Prussia. The area has gotten so popular that tour buses have been restricted after certain hours. But it's much more pleasant to be on foot here than in a tour bus. You can stroll down tree-shaded King William Street and admire the old houses and their beautifully landscaped yards. Stop at the headquarters of the San Antonio Conservation Society, 107 King William St. (© **210/224-6163;** www.saconservation.org), and pick up a self-guided walking tour booklet outside the gate. If you go at a leisurely pace, the stroll should take about an hour. Only the Steves Homestead Museum, 509 King William St. (© **210/225-5924**), built in 1876 for a lumber magnate, and the Guenther House (p. 269) are open to the public.

East bank of the river just south of downtown. Streetcar: Blue line.

La Villita National Historic District ⋆   Developed by European settlers along the east bank of the San Antonio River in the late 18th and early 19th centuries, La Villita was revitalized in the late 1930s by artists and craftspeople and the San Antonio Conservation Society. Now boutiques, crafts shops, and restaurants occupy this historic district, which resembles a Spanish/Mexican village, replete with shaded patios, plazas, brick-and-tile streets, and some of the settlement's original adobe structures, including the house of General Cós, the Mexican military leader who surrendered to the Texas revolutionary army in 1835. It'll take you only about 20 minutes to do a quick walk-through, unless you're an inveterate shopper—in which case, all bets are off.

Bounded by Durango, Navarro, and Alamo sts. and the River Walk. © 210/207-8610. www.lavillita.com. Free admission. Shops daily 10am–6pm. Closed Thanksgiving, Dec 25, and Jan 1. Streetcar: Red, Purple, or Blue lines.

Market Square ⋆   It may not be quite as colorful as it was when live chickens squawked around overflowing, makeshift vegetable stands, but Market Square will still transport you south of the border. Stalls in the indoor El Mercado sell everything from onyx paperweights and manufactured serapes to high-quality crafts from the interior of Mexico. Across the street, the Farmers' Market, which formerly housed the produce market, has carts with more modern goods.

Bring your appetite along with your wallet: In addition to two Mexican restaurants, almost every weekend sees the emergence of food stalls selling specialties such as *gorditas* (chubby corn cakes topped with a variety of goodies) or funnel cakes (fried dough sprinkled with powdered sugar). Most of the city's Hispanic festivals are held here, and mariachis usually stroll the square. The Museo Americano Smithsonian (MAS; see "More Attractions," later in this chapter) provides a historic context to an area that can seem pretty touristy—though no more so than any Mexican border town.

Bounded by Commerce, Santa Rosa, Dolorosa, and I-35. © 210/207-8600. http://tavernini.com/mercado. Free admission. El Mercado and Farmers' Market Plaza summer daily 10am–8pm; winter daily 10am–6pm; restaurants and some shops open later. Closed Thanksgiving, Dec 25, Jan 1, and Easter. Streetcar: Red, Purple, or Yellow lines.

The River Walk (Paseo del Río) ⋆⋆⋆   Just a few steps below the streets of downtown San Antonio is another world, alternately soothing and exhilarating, depending on where you venture. The quieter areas of the 2½ paved miles of winding riverbank, shaded by cypresses, oaks, and willows, exude a tropical, exotic aura. The River Square and South Bank sections, chockablock with sidewalk cafes, tony restaurants, bustling bars, high-rise hotels, and even a huge shopping mall, have a festive, sometimes frenetic feel. Tour boats, water taxis, and floating picnic barges regularly ply the river, and local parades and festivals fill its banks with revelers.

Although plans to cement over the river after a disastrous flood in 1921 were stymied, it wasn't until the late 1930s that the federal Works Project Administration (WPA) carried out architect Robert Hugman's designs for the waterway, installing cobblestone walks, arched bridges, and entrance steps from various street-level locations. And it wasn't until the late 1960s, when the River Walk proved to be one of the most popular attractions of the HemisFair exposition, that its commercial development began in earnest. There's a real danger of the River Walk becoming overdeveloped but plenty of quieter spots still exist. And if you're caught up in the sparkling lights reflected on the water on a breeze-swept night, you might forget there was anyone else around.

San Antonio Museum of Art ★★   This attraction may not be top-listed by everyone, but I enjoy doable (read: not overwhelmingly large) museums with interesting architecture and collections related to the cities in which they're located—and this one definitely fits the bill on all those counts. Several castlelike buildings of the 1904 Lone Star Brewery were gutted, connected, and transformed into a visually exciting exhibition space in 1981. Although holdings range from early Egyptian, Greek, Oceanic, and Asian to 19th- and 20th-century American, it's the Nelson A. Rockefeller Center for Latin American Art, opened in 1998, that is the jewel of the collection. This 30,000-square-foot wing hosts the most comprehensive collection of Latin American art in the United States, with pre-Columbian, folk, Spanish colonial, and contemporary works. You'll see everything here from magnificently ornate altarpieces to a whimsical Day of the Dead tableau. The newly opened Lenora and Walter F. Brown Asian Art Wing represents another major collection, the largest Asian art collection in Texas and one of the largest in the Southwest.

200 W. Jones Ave. ℰ 210/978-8100. www.samuseum.org. Admission $8 adults, $7 seniors, $5 students with ID, $3 children 4–11, free for children younger than 4. Free general admission Tues 4–9pm (fee for some special exhibits). Tues 10am–8pm; Wed–Sat 10am–5pm; Sun noon–6pm. Closed Thanksgiving Day, Dec 25, Jan 1, Easter, and Fiesta Fri. Bus: 7, 8, 9, or 14.

ALAMO HEIGHTS AREA
Marion Koogler McNay Art Museum ★★   Well worth a detour from downtown, this museum is one of my favorite spots. It's got a knockout setting on a hill north of Brackenridge Park with a forever view of the city, and it's in a sprawling Spanish Mediterranean–style mansion (built in 1929) so picturesque that it's constantly used as a backdrop for weddings and photo shoots. The McNay doesn't have a world-class art collection, but it has a good one, with at least one work by most American and European masters of the past 2 centuries. You can see works by Van Gogh, Manet, Gauguin, Degas, O'Keefe, Hopper, Matisse, Modigliani, Cézanne, and Picasso, to name just a few of the artists. And the Tobin Collection of Theatre Arts, including costumes, set designs, and rare books, is outstanding. The McNay also hosts major traveling shows. It'll take you at least an hour to go through this place at a leisurely pace, longer if it's cool enough for you to stroll the beautiful 23-acre grounds dotted with sculpture and stunning landscaping.

6000 N. New Braunfels Ave. © 210/824-5368. www.mcnayart.org. Free admission ($5 suggested donation; fee for special exhibits). Tues–Sat 10am–5pm; Sun noon–5pm. Docent tours 2pm Sun Oct–May. Closed Jan 1, July 4, Thanksgiving, and Dec 25. Bus: 14.

Witte Museum ⚜ *Kids*   A family museum that adults will enjoy almost as much as kids, the Witte focuses on Texas history, natural science, and anthropology, with occasional forays as far afield as the Berlin Wall. Your senses will be engaged along with your intellect: You might hear bird calls as you stroll through the Texas Wild exhibits, or feel rough-hewn stone carved with Native American pictographs beneath your feet. Children especially like exhibits devoted to mummies and dinosaurs, as well as the EcoLab, where live Texas critters range from tarantulas to tortoises. But the biggest draw for kids is the terrific HEB Science Treehouse, a four-level, 15,000-square-foot science center that sits behind the museum on the banks of the San Antonio River; its hands-on activities are geared to all ages. Also on the grounds are a butterfly and hummingbird garden and three restored historic homes. *Note:* Several years ago the museum acquired the wonderful Herzberg Circus Collection, and parts of it are regularly incorporated into the museum's exhibits.

3801 Broadway (adjacent to Brackenridge Park). © 210/357-1900. www.wittemuseum.org. Admission $7 adults, $6 seniors, $5 children 4–11, free for children younger than 4. Free Tues 3–8pm. Tues 10am–8pm; Mon and Wed–Sat 10am–5pm; Sun noon–5pm. Closed 3rd Mon in Oct, Thanksgiving, and Dec 24–25. Bus: 7, 9, or 14.

SOUTH SIDE
San Antonio Missions National Historical Park ⚜⚜   The Alamo was just the first of five missions established by the Franciscans along the San Antonio River to Christianize the native population. The four other missions, which now fall under the aegis of the National Park Service, are still active parishes, run in cooperation with the Archdiocese of San Antonio. But the missions were more than churches: They were whole communities. The Park Service has assigned each mission an interpretive theme to educate visitors about the roles they played in early San Antonio society. You can visit them separately, but if you have the time, see them all; they were built uncharacteristically close together and—now that you don't have to walk there or ride a horse—it shouldn't take you more than 2 or 3 hours to see them. If your time is limited, definitely visit San José and try to make it to San Francisco, even though it's the farthest from downtown.

Concepción, 807 Mission Rd. at Felisa, was built in 1731, is the oldest unrestored Texas mission—it looks much as it did 200 years ago. **San José** ⚜⚜, 6701 San José Dr. at Mission Road, established in 1720, was the largest, best known, and most beautiful of the Texas missions. It was reconstructed to give visitors a complete picture of life in a mission community. Popular mariachi masses are held here every Sunday at noon (come early if you want a seat). Moved from an earlier site in east Texas to its present location in 1731, **San Juan Capistrano,** 9101 Graf at Ashley, doesn't have the grandeur of the missions to the north, but the original simple chapel and the wilder setting give it a peaceful, spiritual aura. The southernmost mission in the San Antonio chain, **San Francisco de la Espada** ⚜, 10040 Espada Rd., also has an ancient, isolated feel, although the beautifully maintained church shows just how vital it still is to the local community.

Headquarters: 2202 Roosevelt Ave. Visitors Center: 6701 San José Dr. at Mission Rd. © 210/932-1001. www.nps.gov/saan. Free admission (donations accepted). All the missions open daily 9am–5pm. Closed Thanksgiving, Dec 25, and Jan 1. National Park Ranger tours daily. Bus: 42 stops at Mission San José (and near Concepción).

FAR NORTHWEST

Six Flags Fiesta Texas ⊛ *Kids*   In 2004, Tornado, an extremely wet and wild tunnel and funnel tubing experience, joined the Superman Krypton Coaster, nearly a mile of twisted steel with six inversions; the Rattler, one of the world's highest and fastest wooden roller coasters; the 60-mph-plus Poltergeist roller coaster; and Scream!, a 20-story space shot and turbo drop, to name just a few. Laser games and virtual reality simulators complete the technophile picture. Feeling more primal? Wet 'n' wild attractions include the Lone Star Lagoon, the state's largest wave pool; the Texas Treehouse, a five-story drenchfest whose surprises include a 1,000-gallon cowboy hat that tips over periodically to soak the unsuspecting; and Bugs' White Water Rapids. If you want to avoid both sogginess and adrenaline overload, there is a vast variety of food booths, shops, crafts demonstrations, and live shows. This theme park still has some local character, dating back to the days when it was plain old Fiesta Texas: Themed areas include a Hispanic village, a western town, and a German town.

17000 I-10W (corner of I-10W and Loop 1604). ℂ 800/473-4378 or 210/697-5050. www.sixflags.com/parks/fiesta texas. Admission $47 adults, $34 seniors 55 and older, $32 children less than 48 in., free for children younger than 3. Discounted 2-day and season passes available. Parking $10 per day. The park opens at 10am; closing times vary depending on the season, as late as 10pm in summer. The park is generally open daily late May to mid-Aug; Sat–Sun Mar–May and Sept–Oct; closed Nov–Feb. Call ahead or visit website for current information. Bus: 94 (summer only). Take exit 555 (La Cantera Pkwy.) on I-10W.

WEST SIDE

SeaWorld San Antonio ⊛ *Kids*   Leave it to Texas to provide Shamu, the performing killer whale, with his most spacious digs: At 250 acres, this SeaWorld is the largest of the Anheuser-Busch-owned parks, which also makes it the largest marine theme park in the world. If you're a theme park fan, you're likely to find the walk-through habitats where you can watch penguins, sea lions, sharks, tropical fish, and flamingos do their thing fascinating, but the aquatic acrobatics at such stadium shows as Shamu Adventure, combining live action and video close-ups, and Viva, where divers and synchronized swimmers frolic with whales and dolphins, might be even more fun.

You needn't get frustrated just looking at all that water because there are loads of places here to get wet. The Lost Lagoon has a huge wave pool and water slides aplenty, and the Texas Splashdown flume ride and the Rio Loco river-rapids ride also offer splashy fun; younger children can cavort in Shamu's Happy Harbor and the L'il Gators section of the Lost Lagoon. Nonaquatic activities include the Steel Eel, a huge "hyper-coaster," and The Great White, the Southwest's first inverted coaster—which involves going head over heels during 2,500 feet of loops (don't eat before either of them).

10500 SeaWorld Dr., 16 miles northwest of downtown San Antonio at Ellison Dr. and Westover Hills Blvd. ℂ 800/ 700-7786. www.seaworld.com. 1-day pass $43 adults, $3 off adult price for seniors (55 and older), $33 children 3–9, free for children younger than 3. Discounted 2-day and season passes available. Internet purchase discounts. Parking $10 per day. Open early Mar to late Nov. Days of operation vary. Open at 10am on operating days, closing times vary. Call ahead or check website for current information. Bus: 64. From Loop 410 or from Hwy. 90W, exit Hwy. 151W to the park.

MORE ATTRACTIONS
DOWNTOWN AREA

Museo Americano Smithsonian   Anyone who's visited Market Square in the past few years has seen the bland white structure at its entryway, the Centro des Artes, turn vivid shades of raspberry and lime. The building is slated to open in April 2007, as a showcase of Hispanic arts and culture in Texas. It's appropriate that among the first exhibits of this Smithsonian affiliate is "Our Journeys/Our Stories: Portraits of Latino Achievements," a traveling show created by the Smithsonian. Using photographs and biographical profiles of 24 individuals (from Nobel Laureate Mario Molina to singer Celia Cruz) and one family, the exhibit traces Latino experiences, traditions, and ideals in the U.S. Check the website or phone closer to the opening date to find out what else there is to see—and what the museum's hours are.

101 S. Santa Rosa Blvd. (at Commerce, in Market Sq.). © 210/299-4300. www.thealameda.org. Admission $6 adults, $3 children. Call for hours. Streetcar: Red, Purple, or Yellow lines.

San Fernando Cathedral ✦ Construction of a church on this site, overlooking what was once the town's central plaza, was begun in 1738 by San Antonio's original Canary Island settlers and completed in 1749. Part of the early structure is incorporated into the magnificent Gothic revival–style cathedral built in 1868. Jim Bowie got married here, and General Santa Anna raised the flag of "no quarter" from the roof during the siege of the Alamo in 1836.

115 Main Plaza. © 210/227-1297. www.sfcathedral.org. Free admission. Daily 6am–7pm; gift shop Mon–Fri 9am–4:30pm, Sat until 5pm. Streetcar: Purple or Yellow lines.

Spanish Governor's Palace ✦ *Finds* Never actually a palace, this 1749 adobe structure formerly served as the residence and headquarters for the captain of the Spanish presidio. It became the seat of Texas government in 1772, when San Antonio was made capital of the Spanish province of Texas and, by the time it was purchased by the city in 1928, it had served as a tailor's shop, barroom, and schoolhouse. The building, with high ceilings crossed by protruding viga beams, is beautiful in its simplicity, and the 10 rooms crowded with period furnishings paint a vivid portrait of upper-class life in a rough-hewn society.

105 Plaza de Armas. © 210/224-0601. www.sanantonio.gov/sapar/spanishgovernorspalace.asp. Admission $1.50 adults, 75¢ children 7–13, free for children younger than 7. Mon–Sat 9am–5pm; Sun 10am–5pm. Closed Jan 1, San Jacinto Day (Apr 21), Thanksgiving, and Dec 25. Streetcar: Purple line.

PARKS & GARDENS

HemisFair Park *Kids* Built for the 1968 HemisFair, an exposition celebrating the 250th anniversary of the founding of San Antonio, this urban oasis boasts **water gardens** and a **wood-and-sand playground** constructed by children (near the Alamo St. entrance). Among its indoor diversions are the **Institute of Texan Cultures** and the **Tower of the Americas. The Schultze House Cottage Garden** ✦, 514 HemisFair Park (© 210/229-9161), created and maintained by Master Gardeners of Bexar County, is also worth checking out for its heirloom plants, varietals, tropicals, and xeriscape area. Look for it behind the Federal Building.

Bounded by Alamo, Bowie, Market, and Durango sts. No phone. www.sanantonio.gov/sapar/hemisfair.asp. Streetcar: Blue, Yellow, or Purple lines.

San Antonio Botanical Gardens ✦ Take a horticultural tour of Texas at this gracious 38-acre garden, encompassing everything from south Texas scrub to Hill Country wildflowers. Fountains, pools, paved paths, and examples of Texas architecture provide visual contrast to the flora. The formal gardens include a garden for the blind, a Japanese garden, an herb garden, a biblical garden, and a children's garden. Perhaps most outstanding is the $6.9-million Lucile Halsell Conservatory complex, a series of greenhouses replicating a variety of tropical and desert environments. The 1896 Sullivan

Carriage House, built by Alfred Giles and moved stone by stone from its original downtown site, serves as the entryway to the gardens.

555 Funston. (C) 210/207-3250. www.sabot.org. Admission $6 adults; $4 seniors, students, and military; $3 children 3–13; free for children younger than 3. Daily 9am–5pm. Closed Dec 25 and Jan 1. Bus: 7, 9, or 14.

ESPECIALLY FOR KIDS

Without a doubt, the prime spots for kids in San Antonio are SeaWorld and Six Flags Fiesta Texas. In addition to these sights, detailed in "The Top Attractions" and "More Attractions" sections above, there's the **San Antonio IMAX Theater Rivercenter** ⭐, 849 E. Commerce St., in the Rivercenter Mall ((C) **800/354-4629** for recorded schedule information, or 210/247-4629; www.imax-sa.com). Having kids view "Alamo: The Price of Freedom" on a six-story-high screen with a stereo sound system is a sure-fire way of getting them psyched for the historical battle site just across the street.

Adults may get the bigger charge out of the waxy stars and some of the oddities collected by the globetrotting Mr. Ripley at the nearby **Plaza Wax Museum & Ripley's Believe It Or Not,** 301 Alamo Plaza ((C) **210/224-9299;** www.plazawaxmuseum.com), just down the block, but there's plenty for kids to enjoy at this twofer attraction. The walk-through wax Theater of Horrors usually elicits some shudders and at Believe It Or Not, youngsters generally get a kick out of learning about people around the world whose habits are even weirder than their own. Just down the block is the city's newest attraction, the threefer **Ripley's Haunted Adventure, Guinness World's Record Museum, and Davy Crockett's Tall Tales Ride,** 329 Alamo Plaza ((C) **210/ 226-2828**). There's something for everyone at this multimillion-dollar entertainment complex, whether you like getting spooked by high-tech haunts, marveling at the odd things people will do to break records, or hearing about the world according to Davy Crockett—as reported by his friend, the bear.

Also downtown, the **San Antonio Children's Museum** ⭐⭐, 305 E. Houston St. ((C) **210/21-CHILD;** www.sakids.org), provides a wonderful introduction to the city for the pint-size and grown-up alike. San Antonio history, population, and geography are all explored through such features as a miniature River Walk, a multicultural grocery store—even a miniature dentist's office. See also "San Antonio After Dark," below, for the **Magik Theatre.**

If the family gets overheated, head to Splashtown, 3600 N. I-35 ((C) **210/227-1100;** www.splashtownsa.com), which includes a huge wave pool, hydro tubes nearly 300 feet long, a Texas-size water bobsled ride, more than a dozen water slides, and a two-story playhouse for the smaller children.

ORGANIZED TOURS

San Antonio's organized tours basically provide you with an efficient way to get around and pick up some local lore. **San Antonio City Tours,** 1331 N. Pine ((C) **800/ 868-7707** or 210/228-9776; www.sacitytours.net), serves up a large menu of guided bus excursions, covering everything from San Antonio's missions and museums to shopping forays south of the border. The **Alamo Trolley Tour,** 216 Alamo Plaza ((C) **210/247-0238;** http://sacitytours.net/trolleytours.html), touches on all the downtown highlights, plus two of the missions in the south. If you want to get off at any of these sights, you can pick up another trolley (they run every 45 min.) after you're finished. To get up close and personal with the River Walk, try a **Rio San Antonio River Cruise.** This amusing, informative tour, lasting from 35 to 40 minutes, will take you more than 2 miles down the most built-up sections of the Paseo del Río, with interesting sights pointed out along the way. Ticket offices are at the Rivercenter Mall and at the River Walk, under the Market St. Bridge (© **210/244-5700;** www.rio sanantonio.com).

6 Sports & Outdoor Activities

Most San Antonians head for the hills—that is, nearby Hill Country—for outdoor recreation. Some suggestions of sports in or around town follow; see the section "Hill Country Side Trips from San Antonio" for more.

BIKING   With the creation and continuing improvements of the biking paths along the San Antonio River, part of the larger **Mission Trails** project, local and visiting cyclists will finally have a good place within the city to spin their wheels (it's not quite there yet, but soon . . .). Other options within San Antonio itself include **Bracken-ridge Park; McAllister Park** on the city's north side, 13102 Jones-Maltsberger (© **210/ 207-PARK** or 207-3120); and around the area near **SeaWorld of Texas.** If you didn't bring your own, **Charles A. James Bicycle Company,** 329 N. Main Ave. (© **210/ 224-8717;** www.charlesajamesbicycle.com), will deliver bikes to your door free if you're staying downtown. Perhaps the best resource in town is the website of the San Antonio Wheelmen, **www.sawheelmen.com**, with details on local organized rides and links to bicycle shops in the area.

GOLF   Golf has become a big deal in San Antonio, with more and more visitors coming to town expressly to tee off. Of the city's six municipal golf courses, two of the most notable are **Brackenridge,** 2315 Ave. B (© **210/226-5612**), the oldest (1916) public course in Texas, featuring oak- and pecan-shaded fairways; and northwest San Antonio's $4.3-million **Cedar Creek,** 8250 Vista Colina (© **210/695-5050**), repeatedly ranked as South Texas's best municipal course in golfing surveys. For details on both and other municipal courses, log on to www.sanantonio.gov/sapar/golf.asp. Other options for unaffiliated golfers include the 200-acre **Pecan Valley,** 4700 Pecan Valley Dr. (© **210/333-9018**), which crosses the Salado Creek seven times and has an 800-year-old oak near its 13th hole; the high-end **Quarry,** 444 E. Basse Rd. (© **800/ 347-7759** or 210/824-4500; www.quarrygolf.com), on the site of a former quarry and one of San Antonio's newest public courses; and **Canyon Springs,** 24405 Wilderness Oak Rd. (© **888/800-1511** or 210/497-1770; www.canyonspringsgc.com), at the north edge of town in the Texas Hill Country, lush with live oaks and dotted with historic rock formations. There aren't too many resort courses in San Antonio because there aren't too many resorts, but the two at the **Westin La Cantera,** 16401 La Cantera Pkwy. (© **800/446-5387** or 210/558-4653; www.lacanteragolfclub.com), have knockout designs and dramatic hill-and-rock outcroppings to recommend them. To get a copy of the free *San Antonio Golfing Guide,* call © **800/447-3372.**

HIKING   The 240-acre **Friedrich Wilderness Park,** 21480 Milsa (© **210/698-1057;** http://wildtexas.com/parks/fwp.php), operated by the city of San Antonio as its only nature preserve, is crisscrossed by 5.5 miles of trails that attract bird-watchers as well as hikers; a 2-mile stretch is accessible to people with disabilities.

RIVER SPORTS   For tubing, rafting, or canoeing along a cypress-lined river, San Antonio river rats head 35 miles northwest of downtown to the 2,000-acre **Guadalupe River State Park,** 3350 Park Rd. 31 (© **830/438-2656;** www.tpwd.state.tx.us/park/guadalup), near Boerne. Five miles north of Highway 46, just outside the park, you can rent tubes, rafts, and canoes at the **Bergheim Campground,** FM 3351 in Bergheim (© **830/336-2235**).

TENNIS With a reservation you can play at the 22 lighted hard courts at the **McFarlin Tennis Center,** 1503 San Pedro Ave. (© **210/732-1223**), for the very reasonable fees of $2.50 per hour per person ($1 for students and seniors), $3.50 ($2) after 5pm.

SPECTATOR SPORTS
BASKETBALL Spur madness hits San Antonio every year from mid-October through May (and these days, more often than not, June), when the city's only major-league franchise, the **San Antonio Spurs,** shoots hoops at the state-of-the-art AT&T Center. Ticket prices range from $10 for nosebleed-level seats to $100 for seats on the corners of the court. Tickets are available at the Spurs Ticket Office in the AT&T Center, which is at One AT&T Center Pkwy. (© **210/444-5819**), or via Ticketmaster San Antonio (© **210/224-9600;** www.ticketmaster.com).

GOLF The **AT&T Championship,** an Official Senior PGA Tour Event, is held each October at the Oak Hills Country Club, 5403 Fredericksburg Rd. (© **210/698-3582**). One of the oldest professional golf tournaments, now known as the **Valero Texas Open,** showcases the sport in September at the Resort Course at La Cantera Golf Club, 16401 La Cantera Pkwy. (© **201/345-3818**).

RODEO If you're in town in early February, don't miss the chance to see 2 weeks of Wild West events such as calf roping, steer wrestling, and bull riding at the annual **San Antonio Stock Show and Rodeo.** You can also hear major live country-and-western talent. Call © **210/225-5851,** or log on to www.sarodeo.com for information on schedules.

7 Shopping
San Antonio offers the shopper a nice balance of large malls and little enclaves of specialized shops. You'll find everything here from the utilitarian to the unusual: a huge Sears department store, a Saks Fifth Avenue fronted by a 40-foot pair of cowboy boots, a mall with a river running through it, and some lively Mexican markets.

You can count on most shops around town being open from 9 or 10am to 5:30 or 6pm Monday through Saturday, with shorter hours on Sunday. Malls are generally open Monday through Saturday 10am to 9pm and on Sunday noon to 6pm. Sales tax in San Antonio is 8.25%.

GREAT SHOPPING AREAS
Most out-of-town shoppers will find all they need **downtown,** between the large Rivercenter Mall, the boutiques and crafts shops of La Villita, the colorful Mexican wares of Market Square, the Southwest School of Art and Craft, and assorted retailers and galleries on and around Alamo Plaza. More avant-garde boutiques and galleries, including Blue Star, can be found in the adjacent area known as Southtown.

Most San Antonians prefer to shop in the malls along Loop 410, especially North Star, Heubner Oaks, and Alamo Quarry Market. The city's newest large scale mall, **Shops at La Cantera,** is out along the outer loop (Loop 1604). This is now the fanciest mall in town, having secured the city's only Neiman Marcus and only Nordstrom, and it has plenty of smaller retail stores to match the same well-heeled customer base. More up-market retail outlets can be found closer to downtown in the fancy strip centers that line Broadway, where it passes through Alamo Heights (the posh Collection and Lincoln Heights are particularly noteworthy).

ART

ArtPace, in the northern part of downtown, and the **Blue Star Arts Complex,** in Southtown), are the best venues for cutting-edge art, but **Finesilver Gallery,** 816 Camaron St., Suites 1 and 2, just north of downtown (© 210/354-3333; www.finesilver. com), is a good alternative. Downtown is home to several galleries that show more established artists. Two of the top ones are **Galería Ortiz,** 102 Concho, in Market Sq. (© 210/225-0731), San Antonio's premier place to buy Southwestern art; and **Nanette Richardson Fine Art,** 555 E. Basse Rd. (© 210/930-1343; www.nanette richardsonfineart.com), with a wide array of oils, watercolors, bronzes, ceramics, and handcrafted wood furnishings.

For more details on these and other galleries, pick up a copy of the **San Antonio Gallery Guide,** at the San Antonio Convention and Visitors Bureau, 317 Alamo Plaza (© 800/447-3372 or 210/207-6000). You can also check out the art scene online at the Office of Cultural Affairs' website, **www.sanantonio.gov/art/website,** with links to several local galleries.

CRAFTS/FOLK ART

Mexican folk art and handicrafts make wonderful take-homes from San Antonio, and several of the best places to find them are in Southtown. They include **San Angel Folk Art,** 1404 S. Alamo, Suite 410, in the Blue Star Arts Complex (© 210/226-6688; www.sanangelfolkart.com), chock-a-block with colorful, whimsical, and well-made wares; and **Tienda Guadalupe Folk Art & Gifts,** 1001 S. Alamo (© 210/226-5873), where you can pick up a Day of the Dead T-shirt, or anything else you can think of relating to the early November holiday celebrated with great fanfare in San Antonio. Just north of downtown, near Monte Vista, the two-level **Alamo Fiesta,** 2025 N. Main at Ashby (© 210/738-1188; www.alamofiesta.com), catering to local Hispanic families, has a huge selection of crafts at extremely reasonable prices. If you like to see the creative process in progress, come to **Garcia Art Glass, Inc.,** 715 S. Alamo St. (© 210/354-4681; www.garciaartglass.com), to see beautiful glass bowls, wall sconces, mobiles, and more come into being. Not everything is very portable, but the bracelets and other pretty baubles made out of glass beads definitely are. Or stop by **Glassworks,** 6350 N. New Braunfels Ave. (© 210/822-0146), where their goal is to show that in addition to being gorgeous, blown glass can also be formed into items that are interesting—a golf putter, for example—affordable, and accessible.

MALLS & SHOPPING CENTERS

Although it's officially **Alamo Quarry Market,** 255 E. Basse Rd. (© 210/824-8885; www.quarrymarket.com), no one ever calls this relative newcomer to the mall scene anything but "The Quarry"—in large part because from the early 1900s until 1985 the property was in fact a cement quarry. This unenclosed mall has a series of large emporiums (such as Borders and Old Navy) and smaller upscale boutiques (Laura Ashley and Aveda). Starring Saks Fifth Avenue–the one fronted by the huge pair of cowboy boots—and upscale shops such as Abercrombie & Fitch and Williams-Sonoma,

North Star Mall, Loop 410, between McCullough and San Pedro (© **210/340-6627;** www.northstarmall.com), is the crème de la crème of the San Antonio indoor malls. But there are many sensible shops here, too, including a Mervyn's department store. Both the Quarry and North Star Mall are about 15 minutes from downtown. At the light-filled, bustling **Rivercenter Mall,** 849 E. Commerce (© **210/225-0000;** www.shoprivercenter.com), you can pick up a ferry from a downstairs dock, listen to bands play on a stage surrounded by water, or visit the IMAX theater and a comedy club. The 130-plus shops, anchored by Dillard's and Foleys, run the price gamut, but tend toward upscale casual. Upscale shoppers migrate to the far northwest part of town, where the **Shops at La Cantera,** 16401 La Cantera Pkwy., hosts the city's only Neiman Marcus and Nordstrom—among other high-end retail. Check **www.shopla cantera.com** for details.

WESTERN WEAR

A one-stop shopping center for all duds Western, **Boot Hill** at Rivercenter Mall, 849 E. Commerce, Suite 213 (© **210/223-6634;** www.boothillusa.com), is one of the few left in town that's locally owned. At **Lucchese Gallery,** 255 E. Basse, Suite 800 (© **210/828-9419;** www.lucchese.com), footwear is raised to the level of art. If it ever crawled, ran, hopped, or swam, these folks can probably put it on your feet. Lucchese is far better known than **Little's Boots,** 110 Division Ave. (© **210/923-2221;** www. davelittleboots.com), but this place—established in 1915—uses as many esoteric leathers and creates fancier footwear designs. If you're willing to wait a while, you can get anything you like hand-customed for you. The late Pope John Paul II, Prince Charles, and Dwight Yoakam all had headgear made for them by **Paris Hatters,** 119 Broadway (© **210/223-3453;** www.parishatters.com), in business since 1917 and still owned by the same family. About half of the sales are special order, but the shelves are stocked with high-quality ready-to-wear hats.

MARKETS

Two large indoor markets, **El Mercado** and the **Farmers' Market**—often just called, collectively, the Mexican market—occupy adjacent blocks on Market Square at 514 W. Commerce St., near Dolorosa (© **210/207-8600**). Competing for your attention are more than 100 shops and pushcarts and an abundance of food stalls. The majority of the shopping booths are of the border-town sort, filled with onyx chess sets, cheap sombreros, and the like, but you can also find a few higher quality boutiques. Come here for a bit of local color, good people-watching, and food.

8 San Antonio After Dark

San Antonio has its symphony and its Broadway shows, and you can see both at one of the most beautiful old movie palaces in the country. But much of what the city has to offer is not quite so mainstream. Latin influences lend spice to some of the best local nightlife. Don't forget San Antonio is America's capital for Tejano music, a unique blend of German polka and northern Mexico ranchero sounds (with a dose of pop added for good measure). You can sit on one side of the San Antonio River and watch such colorful dance troupes as **Ballet Folklórico** perform on the other. And Southtown, with its many Hispanic-oriented shops and galleries, celebrates its art scene with the monthly First Friday, a kind of extended block party.

For the most complete listings of what's on while you're visiting, pick up a free copy of the weekly alternative newspaper, the *Current,* or the Friday "Weekender" section of the *San Antonio Express-News.* You can also check out the website of **San Antonio Arts & Cultural Affairs:** www.sanantonio.gov/art. There's no central office in town for tickets, discounted or otherwise. You'll need to reserve seats directly through the theaters or clubs, or, for large events, through **Ticketmaster** (✆ **210/224-9600;** www.ticketmaster.com). Generally, box office hours are Monday to Friday 10am to 5pm, and 1 to 2 hours before performance time. The **Majestic** (see below) and **Empire** (see below) also have hours on Saturday 10am to 3pm.

THE PERFORMING ARTS

The San Antonio Symphony is the city's only resident performing arts company of national stature, but smaller, less professional groups keep the local arts scene lively, and cultural organizations draw world-renowned artists. The city provides them with some unique venues—everything from standout historic structures such as the Majestic, Empire, Arneson, and Sunken Garden theaters to the state-of-the-art AT&T Center. Because, in some cases, the theater is the show and, in others, a single venue offers an eclectic array of performances, I've included a category called "Major Arts Venues," below.

MAJOR ARTS VENUES

If you're visiting San Antonio from May to August, be sure to see something at the **Arneson River Theatre,** La Villita (✆ **210/207-8610;** www.lavillita.com/arneson), built by the Works Projects Administration (WPA) in 1939 as part of architect Robert Hugman's design for the River Walk. This unique theater stages shows—with a mostly south-of-the-border flair—on one side of the river while the audience watches from an amphitheater on the other.

The baroque Moorish/Spanish revival–style **Majestic Theatre,** 230 E. Houston (✆ **210/226-3333;** www.majesticempire.com), hosts some of the best entertainment in town—the symphony, major Broadway productions, big-name solo performers.

There's always something happening at the **Guadalupe Cultural Arts Center,** 1300 Guadalupe (✆ **210/271-3151;** www.guadalupeculturalarts.org), the main locus for Latino cultural activity in San Antonio. Visiting or local directors put on six or seven plays a year; the Xicano Music Program celebrates the popular local conjunto and Tejano sounds; and the CineFestival, running since 1977, is one of the town's major film events.

Smaller than its former rival the Majestic (see above), just down the block, the **Empire Theatre,** 226 N. St. Mary's St. (✆ **210/226-5700;** www.majesticempire.com), hosts a similarly eclectic array of acts, including musical performance, lectures, and literary events.

CLASSICAL MUSIC

The **San Antonio Symphony,** 222 E. Houston St. (✆ **210/554-1000** or 554-1010 box office; www.sasymphony.org), is one of the finest in the United States. Founded in 1939, the orchestra celebrated its 50th anniversary by moving into the Majestic Theatre, the reopening of which was planned to coincide with the event. The symphony offers two major annual series, classical and pops. The classical series showcases the talents of music director emeritus Christopher Wilkens and a variety of guest performers, while for the pops series, you might find anyone from banjo virtuoso Buddy

Wachter to Tito Puente, Jr., to Three Dog Night. Tickets range from $11 to $90, $11 to $62 for pops.

THEATER

The big production, Broadway shows turn up at the Majestic Theatre, but several smaller local troupes are worth checking out. The community-based **Josephine Theater,** 339 W. Josephine St. (© **210/734-4646;** www.josephinetheatre.org), puts on an average of five productions a year—mostly musicals—at the Art Deco–style Josephine Street Theater, only 5 minutes from downtown. Whether it's an original piece by a member of the company or a work by a guest artist, anything you see at the **Jump-Start Performance Company,** 108 Blue Star Arts Complex, 1400 S. Alamo (© **210/227-JUMP;** www.jump-start.org), is likely to push the social and political envelope. This is the place to find the big-name performance artists such as Karen Finley or Holly Hughes who tour San Antonio. The only professional family theater in town, the popular **Magik Theatre,** Beethoven Hall, 420 S. Alamo in HemisFair Park (© **210/227-2751;** www.magiktheatre.org), features a daytime series with light fare for ages 3 and older, and evening performances, recommended for those 6 and older, that may include weightier plays. About half the plays are adaptations of published scripts, while the other half are originals, created especially for the theater. San Antonio's first public theater, the **San Pedro Playhouse,** 800 W. Ashby (© **210/733-7258;** www.san pedroplayhouse.com), presents a wide range of plays in a neoclassical-style performance hall built in 1930. For information on other small theaters in San Antonio and links to many of those listed in this section, log on to the website of the **San Antonio Theater Coalition** at www.satheatre.com.

THE CLUB & MUSIC SCENE

The closest San Antonio comes to having a club district is the stretch of North St. Mary's between Josephine and Magnolia—just north of downtown and south of Brackenridge Park—known as **the Strip.** This area was hotter about 15 years ago, but it still draws a young crowd to its restaurants and lounges on the weekend. The River Walk clubs tend to be touristy, and many of them close early because of noise restrictions.

In addition to the **Alamodome,** 100 Montana St. (© **210/207-3663;** www.san antonio.gov/dome), the major concert venues in town include **Verizon Wireless Amphitheater,** 16765 Lookout Rd., north of San Antonio just beyond Loop 1604 (© **210/657-8300;** www.vwatx.com), and, when the Spurs aren't playing there, downtown's **AT&T Center,** One AT&T Center Pkwy (© **210/444-5000;** www.nba.com/spurs).

COUNTRY & WESTERN

John T. Floore, the first manager of the Majestic Theatre, opened up **Floore's Country Store,** 14664 Old Bandera Rd., 2 miles north of Loop 1604 (© **210/695-8827;** www.liveatfloores.com), in 1942. A couple of years later, he added a cafe and a dance floor—at half an acre, the largest in south Texas—and since then, it's hosted country greats such as Willie Nelson, Hank Williams, Sr., and more recently, Lyle Lovett and Dwight Yoakam. The lively 1880s-style **Leon Springs Dancehall,** 24135 I-10, Boerne Stage Road exit (© **210/698-7072;** www.leonspringsdancehall.com), can pack some 1,200 people into its 18,000 square feet. Lots of folks come with their kids when the place opens at 7pm. Some of the best local country-and-western talent is showcased here on Friday and Saturday nights, the only 2 nights the dance hall is open.

ROCK

Loud and not much to look at—low ceilings, red-vinyl booths, garage pinup calendars stapled to the ceiling—tiny **Taco Land,** 103 W. Grayson St. (② 210/223-8406), is nevertheless the hottest alternative music club in San Antonio, showcasing everything from mainstream rock to surf punk. Some of the bands that turn up may seem less than impressive, but, hey, you never know: Nirvana played here before they hit the big time. **White Rabbit,** 2410 N. St. Mary's St. (② 210/737-2221; www.sawhite rabbit.com), attracts a mostly young crowd to its black-lit recesses.

JAZZ & BLUES

If you like big bands and Dixieland, there's no better place to listen to music downtown than **The Landing,** Hyatt Regency Hotel, River Walk (② 210/325-2495; www. landing.com), one of the best traditional jazz clubs in the country. You might have heard cornetist Jim Cullum on the airwaves: His American Public Radio program,

---

Conjunto: An American Classic

Although conjunto is one of our country's original contributions to world music, for a long time few Americans outside Texas knew much about it.

It evolved at the end of the 19th century, when South Texas was swept by a wave of German immigrants who brought with them popular polkas and waltzes. These sounds were easily incorporated into—and transformed by—Mexican folk music. The newcomer accordion, cheap and able to mimic several instruments, was happily adopted, too. With the addition at the turn of the century of the *bajo sexto,* a 12-string guitarlike instrument used for rhythmic bass accompaniment, conjunto was born.

San Antonio is to conjunto music what Nashville is to country. The most famous *bajo sextos,* used nationally by everyone who is anyone in conjunto and Tejano music, were created in San Antonio by the Macías family—the late Martín and now his son, Alberto. The undisputed king of conjunto, **Flaco Jiménez**—a mild-mannered triple-Grammy winner who has recorded with the Rolling Stones, Bob Dylan, and Willie Nelson, among others—lives in the city. And San Antonio's **Tejano Conjunto Festival,** held each May, is the largest of its kind, drawing aficionados from around the world—there's even a conjunto band from Japan.

Most of the places to hear conjunto and Tejano are off the beaten tourist path, and they come and go fairly quickly. Those that have been around for a while—and are visitor-friendly—include **Arturo's Sports Bar & Grill,** 3310 S. Zarzamora St. (② 210/923-0177), and **Cool Arrows,** 1025 Nogalitos St. (② 210/227-5130). For live music schedules, check the Tejano/Conjunto section under "Entertainment" and "Music" of www.mysanantonio.com, the website of the *San Antonio-Express News.* You can also phone **Salute!** (see above) to find out which night of the week they're featuring a Tejano or conjunto band. Best yet, just attend one of San Antonio's many festivals—you're bound to hear these rousing sounds.

Riverwalk, Live from the Landing, is now broadcast on more than 160 stations nationwide. The live jazz at tiny **Salute!**, 2801 N. St. Mary's St. (© **210/732-5307;** www.saluteinternationalbar.com), tends to have a Latin base, but you never know what you're going to find here—anything from synthesized '70s sounds to conjunto. A friendly music garden, **Kingston Tycoon Flats,** 2926 N. St. Mary's St. (© **210/731-9838**), is a fun place to kick back and listen to blues, rock, acoustic, or jazz. The burgers and Caribbean dishes are good, too. Bring the kids—an outdoor sandbox is larger than the dance floor.

THE BAR SCENE

A MICROBREWERY   Preppie and gallery types don't often mingle, but the popularity with college kids of the **Blue Star Brewing Company,** 1414 S. Alamo, no. 105 (© **210/212-5506**), in the Blue Star Arts Complex demonstrates the transcendent power of good beer (the pale ale is especially fine).

A SEE-AND-BE-SEEN BAR   These days, San Antonio's young fashionistas mingle at the L.A.-style **Zen Bar,** 221-223 Houston St. (© **210/271-7472;** www.zenbar.com). The Buddha at the entryway and lots of intimate couches and lounges whisper Asian serenity but the music—international, funk, salsa—shouts get your groove on. There's no smoking indoors, but the patio out back is puffer-friendly. It's worth a visit for the peek-a-boo bathrooms alone.

A HISTORIC BAR   More than 100 years ago, Teddy Roosevelt recruited men for his Rough Riders unit at the dark, wooded **Menger Bar,** Menger Hotel, 204 Alamo Plaza (© **210/223-4361**); they were outfitted for the Spanish-American War at nearby Fort Sam Houston. Constructed in 1859 on the site of William Menger's earlier successful brewery and saloon, the bar was moved from its original location in the Victorian hotel lobby in 1956, but 90% of its historic furnishings remain intact. You can still see an "X" on the bar put there by prohibitionist Carrie Nation, and Spanish Civil War uniforms hang on the walls.

LOCAL FAVORITE   During the week, lawyers and judges come to unwind at the **Cadillac Bar & Restaurant,** 212 S. Flores (© **210/223-5533**), in a historic stucco building near the Bexar County Courthouse and City Hall; on weekends, singles take the stand.

A SPORTS BAR   If you want to hang with the Spurs, come to **Tex's,** San Antonio Airport Hilton and Conference Center, 611 NW Loop 410 (© **210/340-6060**), regularly voted San Antonio's best sports bar in the *Current* readers' polls. Among Tex's major array of exclusively Texas sports memorabilia are a signed Nolan Ryan jersey and one of George Gervin's basketball shoes—the other is at the newer Tex's on the River, at the Hilton Palacio del Rio.

THE GAY SCENE

Tina Turner, Deborah Harry, and LaToya Jackson—the real ones—have all played the **Bonham Exchange,** 411 Bonham (© **210/271-3811;** www.bonhamexchange.com), a high-tech dance club near the Alamo. While you may find an occasional cross-dressing show here, the mixed crowd of gays and straights, young and old, come mainly to move to the beat under wildly flashing lights. Main Street just north of downtown has three gay men's clubs in close proximity (it's been nicknamed the "gay bar mall"). **Pegasus,** 1402 N. Main (© **210/299-4222**), is your basic cruise bar. **The Silver Dollar,** 1418

N. Main (© **210/227-2623**), does the country-and-western thing. And **The Saint,** 1430 N. Main (© **210/225-7330**), caters to dancing fools. Covers are low to non-existent at all three. Popular lesbian bars include **Bermuda Triangle,** 119 El Mio (© **210/ 342-2276**), and **Petticoat Junction,** 1812 N. Main (© **210/737-2344**).

9 Hill Country Side Trips from San Antonio

San Antonio lies at the southern edge of the Hill Country, Austin at its eastern edge. The interstate highway I-35 that runs between these two cities parallels a geological feature called the Balcones Escarpment, which is a fault zone that was created when the Edwards Plateau, a thick shelf of limestone, was gently pushed up about 1,500 feet above the coastal plains. This plateau extends for hundreds of miles north and west of San Antonio and Austin; the part closest to these cities is called the Hill Country. The extra elevation makes the climate a little milder, and the water pouring through the limestone creates an abundance of natural springs (and lots of caverns and caves, too).

In the 19th century, these features attracted many German and Czech settlers who were fleeing the social upheavals in Europe. They established small towns that now dot the area and add a little contrast to the prevailing cowboy culture. The mild climate, rolling hills, and abundant springs continue to attract visitors to this part of the state, with summer camps, guest ranches, and resorts serving a public that comes here to enjoy the outdoors.

BOERNE ⭑

From downtown San Antonio, it's a straight shot north on I-10 to Boerne (rhymes with "journey"). Boerne's a good base for travelers, as it's near both a big city (just 30 miles from San Antonio) and some very rural areas. A popular health resort in the 1880s, the little (2¼-mile-long) town near Cibolo Creek was first settled 30 years earlier by freedom-seeking German intellectuals, including firebrand journalist Ludwig Börne, for whom it was named. A gazebo with a Victorian cupola in the center of the main plaza often hosts concerts by the Boerne Village Band, the oldest continuously operating German band in the world outside Germany (it first tuned up in 1860). A number of the town's 19th-century limestone buildings house small historical museums, boutiques, and restaurants, and old-fashioned lampposts and German street signs add atmosphere. But Boerne's biggest draw is the crafts and antiques shops lining the *Hauptstrasse,* or main street. For details, stop in at the **Greater Boerne Chamber of Commerce,** 126 Rosewood Ave., Boerne, TX 78006 (© **888/842-8080** or 830/249-8000; www.boerne.org).

One of the most popular nearby attractions is **Cascade Caverns** (© **830/755-8080;** www.cascadecaverns.com); drive about 3 miles south of Boerne on I-10, take exit 543, and drive 2¼ miles east. This active cave boasts huge chambers, a 100-foot underground waterfall, and comfortable walking trails; guides provide 45-minute to 1-hour interpretive tours every 30 minutes. It's open Memorial Day through mid-August daily 9am to 6pm; off season Monday through Friday 10am to 4pm, Saturday and Sunday 9am to 5pm. Admission is $13 adults, $7.95 children.

WHERE TO STAY

Now an appealing B&B in the heart of town, **Ye Kendall Inn,** 128 W. Blanco, Boerne, TX 78006 (© **800/364-2138** or 830/249-2138; www.yekendallinn.com), opened as a stagecoach lodge in 1859. The rooms ($120–$150) and suites ($160–$210)

A Taste of Alsace in Texas

For a town just 20 miles west of San Antonio (via U.S. 90 W.), Castroville has maintained a rural atmosphere. Henri Castro, a Portuguese-born Jewish Frenchman who received a 1.25-million-acre grant from the Republic of Texas in exchange for his commitment to colonize the land, founded it on a scenic bend of the Medina River in 1842. Second only to Stephen F. Austin in the number of settlers he brought over, Castro recruited most of his 2,134 immigrants from the Rhine Valley, especially from the French province of Alsace. A few of the oldest citizens still can speak Alsatian, a dialect of German, though the language is likely to die out in the area when they do.

Get some insight into the town's history at the **Landmark Inn State Historic Site,** 402 E. Florence St., Castroville, TX 78009 (✆ **830/931-2133;** www.tpwd.state.tx.us/landmarkinn), which also counts a nature trail, an old gristmill, and a stone dam among its attractions. The park's centerpiece, the **Landmark Inn** offers eight simple rooms decorated with early Texas pieces dating up until the 1940s.

For a delicious taste of the past, visit **Haby's Alsatian Bakery,** 207 U.S. 90 E. (✆ **830/931-2118**), owned by the Tschirhart family since 1974 and featuring apple fritters, strudels, stollens, breads, and coffeecakes.

For additional information, contact the **Castroville Chamber of Commerce,** 802 London St., P.O. Box 572, Castroville, TX 78009 (✆ **800/778-6775** or 830/538-3142; www.castroville.com), where you can pick up a walking-tour booklet of the town's historical buildings, as well as a map that details the local boutiques and antiques shops.

Note: Castroville tends to close down on Monday and Tuesday, and some places are shuttered on Wednesday and Sunday as well. If you want to find everything open, come on Thursday, Friday, or Saturday.

are individually—and attractively—decorated, some with Victorian antiques, others with American rustic pieces. Historic cabins ($140–$190) transported to the grounds are available, too.

The **Guadalupe River Ranch Resort and Spa,** P.O. Box 877, Boerne, TX 78006 (✆ **800/460-2005;** www.guadaluperiverranch.com), was owned by actress Olivia de Havilland in the 1930s, and served as an art colony for a time. This gorgeous spread offers abundant activities ranging from river rafting and porch sitting to getting wrapped and polished at the spa. The rooms—arrayed in a variety of buildings, including stone cottages and an adobe hacienda—range from $104 to $234, double.

WHERE TO DINE

The Limestone Grill, in Ye Kendall Inn (see above), 128 W. Blanco (✆ **830/249-9954**), sets an elegant tone for its eclectic Southwestern/American menu. An adjoining wine bar made the scene in late 2004. The more casual **Bear Moon Bakery,** 401 S. Main St. (✆ **830/816-BEAR**), is ideal for a hearty breakfast or light lunch. Organic ingredients and locally grown produce enhance the flavor of the inventive soups, salads, sandwiches, and wonderful desserts. The food is mix and match—a variety of portion sizes and ethnic origins—and somewhat hit-and-miss at the **Dodging Duck Brewhaus,** 402 River Rd. (© **830/248-DUCK**), but you can't beat the views of Cibolo Creek from the front deck, and the beer, handcrafted on the premises, is top-notch.

BANDERA

Bandera is a slice of life out of the Old West, a town that could serve as a John Ford film set. Established as a lumber camp in 1853, this popular guest-ranch center still has the feel of the frontier. Not only are many of its historic buildings intact, but people are as genuinely friendly as any you might imagine from America's small-town past. True, the roads are getting more crowded each year, but once you hunker down, you're unlikely to need to do much driving around.

WHAT TO SEE & DO

Interested in delving into the town's roots? Pick up a self-guided tour brochure of historic sites—including **St. Stanislaus** (1855), the country's second-oldest Polish parish—at the **Bandera County Convention and Visitors Bureau,** 1206 Hackberry St., Bandera, TX 78003 (© **800/364-3833** or 830/796-3045; www.banderacowboycapital. com). Or explore the town's living traditions by strolling along Main Street, where a variety of crafters work in the careful, hand-hewn style of yesteryear. Shops include **Kline Saddlery** (© **830/460-4303**), featuring belts, purses, briefcases, and flask covers as well as horse wear; the **Stampede** (© **830/796-7650**), a good spot for Western collectibles; and the huge **Love's Antique Mall** (© **830/796-3838**), a one-stop shopping center for current local crafts as well as things retro. Off the main drag, buy beautiful customized belt buckles, spurs, and jewelry at **Hy O Silver,** 715 13th St. (© **830/ 796-7961**). Naturally, plenty of places in town such as **The Cowboy Store,** 302 Main St. (© **830/796-8176**), can outfit you in Western duds.

THE GREAT OUTDOORS

You don't have to go farther than **Bandera Park** (© **830/796-3765**), a 77-acre green space within the city limits, to enjoy nature, whether you want to stroll along the River Bend Native Plant Trail or picnic by the Medina River. Or you can canter through the **Hill Country State Natural Area,** 10 miles southwest of Bandera (© **830/796-4413;** www.tpwd.state.tx.us/park/hillcoun), the largest state park in Texas allowing horseback riding. A visit to the nonprofit **Brighter Days Horse Refuge,** 682 Krause Rd., Pipe Creek, about 9 miles northeast of Bandera (© **830/ 510-6607;** www.brighterdayshorserefuge.org), will warm any animal lover's heart. The price of admission to this rehabilitation center for abandoned and neglected horses is a bag of carrots or apples; donations are also very welcome.

STAYING AT A GUEST RANCH

For the full flavor of the region, plan to stay at one of Bandera's many guest ranches (you'll find a full listing of them, as well as of other lodgings, on the Bandera website). Note that most of them have a 2-night (or more) minimum stay.

At the **Dixie Dude Ranch,** P.O. Box 548, Bandera, TX 78003 (© **800/375-YALL** or 830/796-7771; www.dixieduderanch.com), a longtime favorite retreat, you're likely to see white-tailed deer or wild turkeys as you trot on horseback through a 725-acre spread. The down-home, friendly atmosphere keeps folks coming back year after year. Tubing on the Medina River and soaking in a hot tub are among the many activities at the **Mayan Ranch,** P.O. Box 577, Bandera, TX 78003 (© **830/796-3312** or 460-3036; www.mayanranch.com). The ranch provides plenty of additional Western fun for its guests during high season—things like two-step lessons and trick-roping exhibitions. The owner of **Silver Spur Guest Ranch,** 9266 Bandera Creek Rd., Bandera, TX 78003 (© **830/796-3037** or 460-3639; www.ssranch.com), used to be a bull rider, so the equestrian expertise of the staff is especially high. So is the comfort level. The rooms in the main ranch house and the separate cabins are individually decorated, with styles ranging from Victorian pretty to country rustic. The ranch, which abuts the Hill Country State Natural Area, also boasts the region's largest swimming pool, some roaming buffalo, and a great kids' play area.

WHERE TO DINE

Those not chowing down at a guest ranch might want to put on the feed bag on Main Street's **O.S.T.** (© **830/796-3836**), named for the Old Spanish Trail that used to run through Bandera. Serving up down-home Texas and Tex-Mex victuals since 1921, this cafe has a room dedicated to The Duke and other cowboy film stars. **Billy Gene's,** 1105 Main St. (© **830/460-3200**), lays on huge platters of down-home country standards such as chicken-fried steak or meatloaf for seriously retro prices. Less health-defying dishes such as huge salads are available here, too. The setting, in a motel at the edge of town, is nothing special, but the **Bandera Star Steakhouse,** 700 State Hwy. 16 S. (© **830/796-3093**), serves some of the best big meat in town. Small meat too: Half-size portions of, say, pork chops, come with all the sides (salad, veggies, rolls) but aren't as hard on the wallet or waistline. It's not easy to find a seat inside **Mac and Ernie's,** a quirky, semigourmet eatery in a shack some 12 miles west of Bandera in Tarpley (© **830/562-3250**). But that's okay, because the picnic tables out back are the perfect setting for the outstanding steaks, catfish, and specials like quail in ancho honey, served on paper plates.

SOME LOCAL HONKY-TONKS

Don't miss **Arkey Blue & The Silver Dollar Bar** ⭐⭐ (© **830/796-8826**), a genuine spit-and-sawdust cowboy honky-tonk on Main Street usually called Arkey's. No one who tends toward the P.C. should enter the tiny **11th Street Cowboy Bar,** 307 11th St. (© **830/796-4849**), what with all the bras hanging off the rafters. But you can always just listen to Cajun and country bands. At the **Bandera Saloon,** 401 Main St. (© **830/796-3699**), the deck is out front and overlooks the town's main drag, but the boot-scootin' to live rockabilly and country music takes place inside the large barnlike structure.

8

Austin

by David Baird

In almost anything you read or hear about Austin, you will be told that it is a laid-back city. "Laid-back" has become Austin's defining trait. First-time visitors get here and expect to find a city whose denizens all move about and express themselves in the unhurried manner of Willie Nelson. They must feel a little put upon when they drive into town only to find bearish traffic and pushy drivers and a downtown that is looking uncomfortably similar to Houston or Dallas.

Over the years Austin has gotten bigger and busier, but it hasn't lost its essential nature. Stay here for a couple of days and you'll feel the laid-back quality you've heard about. Austinites are personable, gracious, and open, and for them the enjoyment of the simple pleasures of life holds a great deal more attraction than the rat race. At times it seems that everyone you meet is either a musician, a massage therapist, or has some other sort of alternative career.

Austinites of all walks of life enjoy the outdoors. Barton Springs is the preferred spot for a swim; the popular hike-and-bike trail that encircles Town Lake is a favorite place for either a leisurely walk or a serious run. The city streets and bike lanes are filled with Austin's many cyclists. Just outside of town are several parks and nature preserves and rivers and lakes that can be enjoyed. Hand in hand with this love of the outdoors is a strong environmental consciousness, which is reflected in the local government. Austin leads the nation in green energy production, has the most aggressive recycling and energy conservation programs in the state, and, though starting late, has instituted programs to reduce traffic and urban sprawl.

Finally, one can't talk about Austin for very long without mentioning the rather large university at its center. The University of Texas has brought thousands of bright, young students here, who, once they get their degrees, decide that they don't want to leave. They stay and add to a large pool of educated people looking for a livelihood. This has attracted large high-tech companies who seek a large educated workforce. Austin has also been fertile grounds for a lot of native start-up companies in all kinds of fields.

Austin is now big enough to be many things to many people. But to me it's the creative center and the social and environmental conscience of Texas.

1 Orientation

ARRIVING

BY PLANE   The $581-million **Austin-Bergstrom International Airport** (© 512/530-ABIA; airport code **AUS**) opened in 1999 on the site of the former Bergstrom Air Force Base, just off Highway 71 (Ben White Blvd.) and only 8 miles southwest of the Capitol, is the town's transportation darling. It's even got a geek's dream of a website, www.ci.austin.tx.us/austinairport, featuring a virtual reality tour of the terminal, flight schedules, links to airlines and car-rental companies, descriptions of concessions, the latest bulletins on noise-pollution control, and more. For those wanting nonvirtual data, there's an information booth on the lower level of the terminal open daily from 7am to 11pm.

Taxis from the major companies in town usually form a line outside the terminal, though occasionally you won't find any waiting. To ensure off-hour pickup in advance, phone **American Yellow Checker Cab** (© 512/452-9999) before you leave home. The ride between the airport and downtown costs around $25.

If you're not in a huge rush to get to your hotel, **SuperShuttle** (© 800/BLUE VAN or 512/258-3826; www.supershuttle.com) is a less expensive alternative to cabs, offering comfortable minivan service to hotels and residences. Prices range from $10 one-way ($18 round-trip) for trips to a downtown hotel to $14 ($24 round-trip) for trips to a central hotel and $18 ($26) for trips to a hotel in the northwestern part of town. The drawback is that you often must share your ride with several others, who may be dropped off first. You don't have to book in advance for pickups at the airport, but you do need to phone 24 hours ahead of time to arrange for a pickup if you're leaving town.

For 50¢ you can go from the airport to downtown or the university area on a city bus called the **Airport Flyer** (Rte. 100). It runs until about midnight. The passenger pickup is outside the arrival gates, close to the end of the concourse. Buses depart about every 40 minutes. You can grab a route schedule from the city's visitor information office, by the baggage carrousels. Or you can download it from the **Capital Metro Transit** website (www.capmetro.org). Most of the major car-rental companies have outlets at the airport. The trip from the airport to downtown by car or taxi can take anywhere from 20 to 45 minutes, much more if you're headed to north Austin. During rush hour, there are often backups all along Highway 71. Be sure to slot in extra time when you need to catch a flight.

BY TRAIN   The **Amtrak** station (© 512/476-5684) is at Lamar and West First Street, in the southwest part of downtown. There are generally a few cabs waiting to meet the trains, but if you don't see one, you'll find a list of phone numbers of taxi companies posted near the pay phones. Some of the downtown hotels offer courtesy pickup from the train station. A cab ride shouldn't run more than $5 or $6 (there's a $3 minimum charge).

BY BUS   The **bus terminal** is near Highland Mall, about 10 minutes north of downtown and just south of the I-35 motel zone. There are some hotels within walking distance, and many others a short cab ride away; a few taxis usually wait outside the station. If you want to go downtown, you can catch either bus no. 7 (Duval) or bus no. 15 (Red River) from the bus stop across the street. A cab ride downtown—about 10 minutes away on the freeway—should cost around $10.

VISITOR INFORMATION

The **Austin Visitor Center** is downtown at 209 E. 6th St. (© 866/GO-AUSTIN; www.austintexas.org) and is open Monday through Friday from 9am to 5pm and Saturday and Sunday from 9am to 6pm (closed Thanksgiving, Christmas, and Easter). You can pick up tourist information pamphlets downtown at the **Old Bakery and Emporium,** 1006 Congress Ave. (© 512/477-5961), open Monday to Friday 9am to 4pm, and the first two Saturdays in December 10am to 3pm. The **Capitol Visitors**

Center, 112 E. 11th St. (© **512/305-8400;** www.texascapitolvisitorscenter.com), a Texas Department of Transportation travel center, dispenses information on the entire state; it's open Monday through Saturday 9am to 5pm, Sunday noon to 5pm, and closed major holidays.

For entertainment listings, pick up the free alternative newspaper, the *Austin Chronicle,* distributed to stores, hotels, and restaurants around town every Thursday. It's got a close rival in *XLent,* the free weekend entertainment guide put out by the city's daily newspaper, *Austin-American Statesman,* which also comes out on Thursday.

Inside Line (© **512/416-5700**) can clue you in about Austin information from the essential to the esoteric—everything from weather forecasts and restaurant reviews to financial news and bat facts. Dial extension 4636 for instructions on how to use the system.

CITY LAYOUT

In 1839, Austin was laid out in a grid on the northern shore of the Colorado River, bounded by Shoal Creek to the west and Waller Creek to the east. The section of the river abutting the original settlement is now known as Town Lake, and the city has spread far beyond its original borders in all directions. The land to the east is flat Texas prairie; the rolling Hill Country begins on the west side of town.

MAIN ARTERIES & STREETS   I-35, forming the border between central and east Austin (and straddling the Balcones Fault Line), is the main north–south thorough-fare; Loop 1, usually called Mo-Pac (it follows the course of the Missouri-Pacific rail-road, although some people like to say it got its name because it's "mo' packed"), is the west-side equivalent. Highway 290, running east and west, merges with I-35 where it comes in on the north side of town, briefly reestablishing its separate identity on the south side of town before merging with Highway 71 (which is called Ben White Blvd. between 183 and Lamar Blvd.). Highway 290 and Highway 71 split up again in Oak Hill, on the west side of town. Not confused enough yet? Highway 2222 changes its name from Koenig to Northland and, west of Loop 360, to Bullcreek, while, in the north, Highway 183 is called Research Boulevard. (Looking at a map should make all this clear as mud.) Important north–south city streets include Lamar, Guadalupe, and Burnet. If you want to get across town north of the river, use Cesar Chavez (once known as First St.), 15th Street (which turns into Enfield west of Lamar), Martin Luther King, Jr., Boulevard (the equivalent of 19th St., and often just called MLK), 38th Street, or 45th Street.

THE NEIGHBORHOODS IN BRIEF

Although Austin, designed to be the capital of the independent Republic of Texas, has a planned, grand city center similar to that of Washington, D.C., the city has spread out far beyond those original boundaries. These days, with a few exceptions, detailed below, locals tend to speak in terms of landmarks (the University of Texas) or geographical areas (East Austin) rather than neighborhoods.

Downtown The original city, laid out by Edwin Waller in 1839, runs roughly north from the Colorado River. The river has been dammed in several places, forming a series of lakes. By downtown it is called Town Lake. The first street on the north shore of Town Lake used to be called 1st Street, now it's called **Cesar Chavez Street.** Downtown extends north up to 11th Street, where the Capitol Building is. The main north–south street is **Congress Avenue.** It runs from the river to the Capitol. Downtown's eastward limit is the I-35 freeway, and its westward limit is Lamar Boulevard. This is a prime sightseeing (it includes the Capitol and several historic districts), and a hotel area, with music clubs, restaurants, shops, and galleries. There are a lot of clubs on and around **6th Street,** just east of Congress, and in the **Warehouse District,** centered on 3rd and 4th streets just west of Congress, and also in the **Red River District,** on (where else?) Red River, between 6th and 10th streets.

South Austin For a long time not a lot was happening south of Town Lake. This was largely a residential area—a mix of working class and bohemians lived here. **South Congress,** the sleepy stretch of Congress Avenue running through the middle of South Austin, was lined with cheap motels. Then in the 1980s it started taking off. The area became attractive to store and restaurant owners who liked the proximity to downtown without the high rents. Trendy shops moved into the old storefronts. Yuppies started buying houses in the adjoining neighborhoods. And now South Austin is one of the preferred places to live. **Fairview Park** and **Travis Heights,** adjoining neighborhoods between Congress and I-35, are perhaps the most popular. They were Austin's first settlements south of the river. At the end of the 19th century, the bluffs on the south shore of the river became desirable as Austin residents realized they were not as likely to be flooded as the lower areas on the north bank. Farther south and west, toward the Lady Bird Johnson Wildflower Center, south Austin begins to reassert its rural roots.

Central Austin This is a larger area that includes downtown and the university campus. It's not a precisely defined area. If you were to travel north from Town Lake through the downtown area and past the Capitol, you would come across a complex of state government office buildings (on and around 15th St.). Past that would be the UT campus (19th–26th sts.). Farther north, you get to the **Hyde Park** neighborhood (35th–51st sts.). Hyde Park got its start in 1891 as one of Austin's first planned suburbs; renovation of its Victorian and early craftsman houses began in the 1970s, and now there's a real neighborhood feel to this pretty, tree-lined area. Beyond Hyde Park numbered streets disappear. You pass through a couple of neighborhoods, and eventually you come to Research Blvd. For a lot of Austinites this is where Central Austin ends and north Austin begins. Central Austin doesn't extend East of I-35, but it does extend west of the Mo-Pac Freeway. Central Austin also includes the neighborhoods west of Lamar. One of these is **Clarksville,** a formerly black community founded in the 1870s by freed slaves. It's now a neighborhood of small old houses that command high prices. To the west of Clarksville, on the other side of Mo-Pac, is an even more expensive neighborhood called **Tarrytown.**

East Side This section is east of I-35, between Town Lake and 12th Street. Predominantly Hispanic, the neighborhood has many Mexican food restaurants and markets. You'll also find a number of African-American heritage sites (there is a black community just north of the Hispanic community), including Huston-Tillotson College, Metropolitan African Methodist Episcopal Church, and the George Washington Carver Museum; the French Legation Museum and state cemetery are also in this area. The quiet, tree-lined **French Place,** just east of I-35 between Manor and 38½ streets, is beginning to vie with South Congress for yuppie/artist ingress. The warehouses near MLK are increasingly being occupied by art galleries and turned into residential spaces for those likely to frequent them. Naturally, new restaurants are arriving to feed all the hungry artistes.

I-35 Corridor Austin has grown around the heavily traveled connector area between Central and the Northwest, where the airport used to be located. Lined with chain hotels and restaurants, it's as charmless as it sounds, but it's convenient to both downtown and the north. The old airport is now being converted into mixed-use space for condos, retail, and affordable housing.

West Austin Upstream from downtown, the Colorado River flows from north to south. On the west bank

across from Tarrytown is West Austin. This is an affluent suburban area that includes the communities of **Rollingwood** and **Westlake Hills.** There's another dam, and the river here is called Lake Austin. Far beyond that is another, larger dam that creates Lake Travis. Here's where you find **Lakeway,** as well as the more charming, low-key **Bee Cave.** But you don't have to live here to play here: This is also where those who live in Central Austin come to splash around and kick back on nice weekends.

Northwest This is where most of the high-tech industry is located. It is largely suburban. It includes the Arboretum, a large mall, and surrounding shopping area. Farther north are the bedroom communities of Round Rock and Cedar Park.

2 Getting Around

BY PUBLIC TRANSPORTATION

Austin's public transportation system, **Capital Metropolitan Transportation Authority** (www.capmetro.org), operates more than 50 bus. A day pass on Metro costs $1; express service from various Park & Ride lots costs $2. You'll need exact change or fare tickets (see below) to board the bus. Call © **800/474-1201** or 512/474-1200 (TTY 512/385-5872) from local pay phones for point-to-point routing information.

The seven free 'Dillo routes—Blue, Gold, Orange, Red, Silver, and the latest, Moonlight and Starlight—make it simple as well as economical for visitors to troll the tourist sights. Routes include the most popular—and most parking challenged—sections of downtown, as well as the University of Texas, the South Congress shopping district, and historic East Austin. The Orange and Silver 'Dillos are particularly geared toward sightseeing, while the Starlight and Moonlight rides, available Thursday through Saturday from 6pm to 3am, shuttle you around downtown's hottest nightspot and restaurant areas.

BY CAR

With its lack of traffic planning, driving in Austin is, to put it mildly, a challenge. Don't fall into a driver's daze anywhere in town; you need to be as vigilant on the city streets as you are on highways. The former are rife with signs that suddenly insist LEFT LANE MUST TURN LEFT or RIGHT LANE MUST TURN RIGHT—generally positioned so they're noticeable only when it's too late to switch. A number of major downtown streets are one-way; many don't have street signs or have signs so covered with foliage they're impossible to read. Driving is particularly confusing in the university area, where streets like "32½" suddenly turn up. Multiply the difficulties at night, when you need X-ray vision to read the ill-lit street indicators.

The highways are no more pleasant. I-35—nicknamed "the NAFTA highway" because of the big rigs speeding up from Mexico—is mined with tricky on-and-off ramps and, around downtown, a confusing complex of upper and lower levels; it's easy to miss your exit or find yourself exiting when you don't want to. The rapidly developing area to the northwest, where Highway 183 connects I-35 with Mo-Pac and the Capital of Texas Highway, requires particular vigilance, as the connections occur very rapidly. There are regular lane mergers and sudden, precipitous turnoffs.

PARKING   Unless you have congressional plates, you're likely to find the selection of parking spots downtown extremely limited during the week (construction isn't making the situation any better); as a result, lots of downtown restaurants offer valet parking (with hourly rates ranging from $4–$6). There are a number of lots around the area, costing anywhere from $5 to $7 per hour, but the most convenient ones tend to fill up quickly. If you're lucky enough to find a metered spot, it'll run you 75¢ per hour, with a 2-hour limit, so bring change. Although there's virtually no street parking available near the Capitol before 5pm during the week, there is a free visitor garage on 15th and San Jacinto (2-hr. time limit). *Tip:* If you're willing to forgo your own wheels for a bit, park in one of the free Park & Ride lots serviced by the Red, Gold, and Silver 'Dillo lines and take advantage of Austin's excellent free public transport (see "By Public Transportation," above).

In the university area, trying to find a spot near the shopping strip known as the Drag can be just that. However, cruise the side streets and you're eventually bound to find a pay lot that's not filled. The two most convenient on-campus parking garages are located near San Jacinto and East 26th streets and off 25th Street between San Antonio and Nueces. There's also a (free!) parking lot near the LBJ Library, but it's far from the central campus. Log on to **www.utexas.edu/business/parking/resources** for additional places to drop off your car.

BY TAXI

The major cab companies in Austin are **Austin Cab** (© **512/478-2222**) and **American Yellow Checker Cab** (© **512/452-9999**). The flag-drop charge is $2.05, and it's $2.05 for each mile after that.

FAST FACTS: Austin

American Express The branch at 10710 Research Blvd., Suite 328 (© **512/452-8166**; www.americanexpress.com), is open Monday to Friday 9am to 5:30pm, Saturday 10am to 2pm.

Dentist Call the Dental Referral Service at © **800/917-6453**.

Doctor The Medical Exchange (© **512/458-1121**) and Seton Hospital (© **512/324-4450**) both have physician referral services.

Drugstores You'll find many Walgreens, Eckerd, and Randalls drugstores around the city; most HEB grocery stores also have pharmacies. Several Walgreens are open 24 hours. Have your zip code ready and call © **800/925-4733** to find the Walgreens branch nearest you.

Emergencies Call © **911** if you need the police, the fire department, or an ambulance.

Hospitals Brackenridge, 601 E. 15th St. (© **512/324-7000**); St. David's, 919 E. 32nd St. at I-35 (© **512/397-4240**); and Seton Medical Center, 1201 W. 38th St. (© **512/324-1000**), have good and convenient emergency-care facilities.

Internet Most links of Schlotzsky's Deli, a chain that originated in Austin, offer free Internet access via computer stations; you're limited to 20 minutes, but that should give you enough time to check your e-mail. Several Schlotzsky's also offer free wireless network access. Of course, much of downtown is wireless. And in the rest of Austin, you're likely to find coffee shops that offer free Wi-Fi. The Austin Visitor Center (see the "Visitor Information" section, earlier in this chapter) offers free Internet access, and all of Austin's Starbucks and city parks are Wi-Fi friendly.

Newspapers & Magazines The daily *Austin American-Statesman* (www.austin 360.com) is the only large-circulation, mainstream newspaper in town. The *Austin Chronicle* (www.auschron.com), a free alternative weekly, focuses on the arts, entertainment, and politics. Monday through Friday, the University of Texas publishes the surprisingly sophisticated *Daily Texan* (www.dailytexan online.com) newspaper, covering everything from on-campus news to international events.

Police The nonemergency number for the Austin Police Department is © **512/ 974-5000.**

Post Office The city's main post office is located at 8225 Cross Park Dr. (© **512/ 342-1252**); more convenient to tourist sights are the Capitol Station, 111 E. 17th St., in the LBJ Building, and the Downtown Station, 510 Guadalupe St. For information on other locations, phone © **800/275-8777.**

Safety Austin has been ranked one of the five safest cities in the United States, but that doesn't mean you can throw common sense to the wind. It's never a good idea to walk down dark streets alone at night, and major tourist areas always attract pickpockets, so keep your purse or wallet in a safe place. Although 6th Street itself tends to be busy, use caution on the side streets in the area.

Taxes The tax on hotel rooms is 15%. Sales tax, added to restaurant bills as well as to other purchases, is 8.25%.

Transit Information Call Capital Metro Transit (© **800/474-1201** or 512/474-1200 from local pay phones; TTY 512/385-5872).

Weather Check the weather at © **512/451-2424** or www.news8austin.com/ content/weather.

3 Where to Stay

Unlike San Antonio, Austin doesn't have a huge pool of downtown hotel rooms dependent on large conventions, so it can sometimes be difficult to find a discounted room downtown. When you look on the Internet for bargains, you're more often than not pointed toward properties in the southeast corner of the city, near the intersection of

I-35 and Highway 71, where a large number of properties sit. This location is not a good choice for exploring the city, but the difference in rates may be too good to pass up.

In looking for discounts, keep in mind the calendars of the state legislature and the University of Texas. Lawmakers and lobbyists converge on the capital from January through May of odd-numbered years, so you can expect tighter bookings. The beginning of fall term, graduation week, and football weekends—UT's football stadium seats 80,000—draw thousands of out-of-towners.

The busiest season, however, is the month of March, when the South by Southwest music festival occurs. It is designed to coincide with UT's spring break, usually the third week of the month. SxSW is the largest gathering of the year for the music industry. It attracts more than a hundred bands, plus fans, producers, and music company execs. And now there's a film and media festival the week before the music begins, bringing thousands more to town. To make matters worse, Austin often hosts regional playoffs for NCAA basketball, and the university likes to take advantage of spring break by hosting several academic conferences. Of course, there are a few other spots in the calendar when the city is busier than usual, such as in late September for the Austin City Limits Music Festival. This festival has caught on in a big way and attracts thousands now.

You'll get a far better feel for what makes Austin special if you stay somewhere in central Austin. The verdant Town Lake area includes both downtown near the Capitol and the resurgent South Congress area. The areas near the University of Texas, including west campus and the Hyde Park neighborhood, are ideal for those willing to trade some modern perks for hominess and character. Those with a penchant for playing on the water or putting around should consider holing up near the lakes and golf courses to the west.

Austin has some glitzy high-rises but only a few historic hotels, so if it's character you're after, you might opt for one of the town's bed-and-breakfasts. In addition to those listed, I'd recommend other members of the **Austin Area B & B Association.** Call ✆ **866/972-2333** or 512/371-1115 or log on to www.austinareabandb.com for more info. For Austin inns that belong to Historic Accommodations of Texas, check the website at www.hat.org or contact the organization at P.O. Box 139, Fredericksburg, TX 78624 (✆ **800/HAT-0368**).

The prices listed below are based on full rack rates, the officially established, undiscounted tariffs that you should never have to pay. Most hotels catering to business travelers offer substantially lower prices on weekends, while some bed-and-breakfasts offer reduced rates for weekdays. If you don't mind changing rooms once, you can get the best of both discount worlds. Note that rates listed below do not include the city's 15% hotel sales tax.

Incidentally, wherever you bunk in Austin, you're likely to be in high-tech heaven. Even B&B rooms offer high-speed wireless Internet connections these days, and many hotels also offer WebTV, enabling you to retrieve e-mail and cruise the Internet via the tube.

DOWNTOWN
VERY EXPENSIVE

The Driskill ✰✰✰   Opened in 1886, the Driskill is Austin's original grand hotel. It has seen its share of history and is, in fact, a national historic landmark. Lyndon Johnson managed the final days of his presidential campaign from here and received the election results. The Daughters of the Republic of Texas, the saviors of the Alamo, met

Greater Austin Accommodations, Dining & Attractions

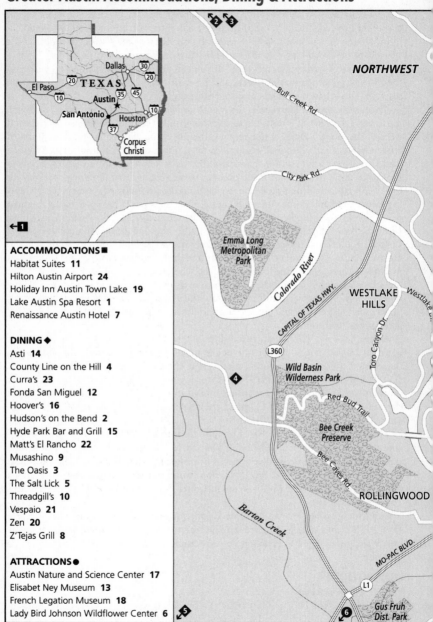

NORTHWEST

Bull Creek Rd.

City Park Rd.

Emma Long Metropolitan Park

Colorado River

CAPITAL OF TEXAS HWY.

WESTLAKE HILLS

Westlake Dr.

Toro Canyon Dr.

L360

Wild Basin Wilderness Park

Red Bud Trail

Bee Creek Preserve

Bee Caves Rd.

ROLLINGWOOD

Barton Creek

MO-PAC BLVD.

L1

Gus Fruh Dist. Park

ACCOMMODATIONS ■
Habitat Suites **11**
Hilton Austin Airport **24**
Holiday Inn Austin Town Lake **19**
Lake Austin Spa Resort **1**
Renaissance Austin Hotel **7**

DINING ◆
Asti **14**
County Line on the Hill **4**
Curra's **23**
Fonda San Miguel **12**
Hoover's **16**
Hudson's on the Bend **2**
Hyde Park Bar and Grill **15**
Matt's El Rancho **22**
Musashino **9**
The Oasis **3**
The Salt Lick **5**
Threadgill's **10**
Vespaio **21**
Zen **20**
Z'Tejas Grill **8**

ATTRACTIONS ●
Austin Nature and Science Center **17**
Elisabet Ney Museum **13**
French Legation Museum **18**
Lady Bird Johnson Wildflower Center **6**

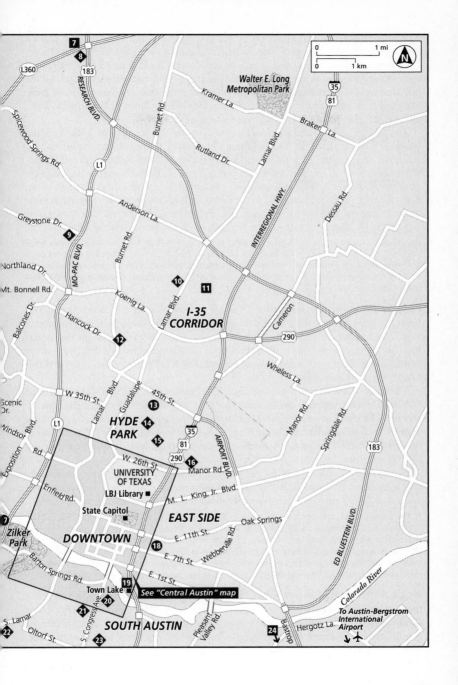

here to agree on their plan of action. It was here, too, that the Texas Rangers plotted their ambush on Bonnie and Clyde. Indeed, all kinds of plots have been hatched here.

Over time the hotel has weathered ups and downs. Right now it's living a golden age. A hugely expensive renovation project put the "grand" back into the hotel. All the public areas have been refurbished to give them an impressive old-and-expensive look. Off the lobby, you'll find the **1886 Café;** the **Driskill Grill,** for fine dining (p. 309); and a cushy piano bar; plus a small but well-equipped spa.

The Driskill offers guests a choice between rooms in the original 1886 building (labeled "historic") or in the 1928 addition ("traditional"); the latter are the better deal, especially those on the 12th floor, which have higher ceilings. Rooms are well lit, distinctively decorated, and furnished with period pieces. Bathrooms in both buildings are attractive and come with several amenities, including plush bathrobes. This hotel is on Austin's lively 6th Street, and some of the rooms with balconies can be noisy. Also, some of the traditional king rooms are small and so dominated by the bed that there's little room to move about. It's a good idea to check room size before settling in.

604 Brazos St. (at E. 6th St.), Austin, TX 78701. © 800/252-9367 or 512/474-5911. Fax 512/474-2214. www.driskill hotel.com. 188 units. $320–$340 double; suites from $465. AE, DC, DISC, MC, V. Valet parking $18. Pets less than 25 lb. accepted with $50 fee per pet per stay. **Amenities:** 2 restaurants; bar; health club; spa; concierge; business center; 24-hr. room service; laundry service/dry cleaning. *In room:* A/C, TV w/pay movies, dataport, high-speed Internet access, WebTV, hair dryer, safe.

Four Seasons Austin 🏨🏨🏨 *Kids*

Though it may be pricey, it's hard to beat this hotel. It's got a great location on Town Lake, near all the downtown tourist attractions; large, comfortable rooms; an excellent restaurant, **The Café,** which is also the toniest roost in town for watching bats stream out of the Congress Avenue Bridge; and the best health club and spa in the downtown area. But it's the service that really sets this hotel apart from all others.

The look of the place is part modern, part traditional, and part Texas. Polished sandstone floors, deep easy chairs, a cowhide sofa, and Western art should give you the picture. The guest rooms are plush and conservative with muted colors, light floral patterns, rich woodwork, and house plants. The city views are fine, but the ones of the lake are finer still. The hotel is located on Austin's popular hike-and-bike trail, so you can jog right out the door.

If you're traveling with toddlers, the staff can provide necessary gear such as strollers and baby seats. For older kids there are complimentary things such as popcorn and soda or milk and cookies if you notify the hotel when you make your reservations.

98 San Jacinto Blvd. (at 1st/Cesar Chavez St.), Austin, TX 78701. © 800/332-3442 or 512/478-4500. Fax 512/478-3117. www.fourseasons.com/austin. 291 units. $345–$430 double; suites from $505. Lower rates on weekends; bed-and-breakfast and romance packages available. AE, DC, MC, V. Self-parking $12; valet parking $20. Pets no taller than 12–15 inches accepted; advance notice to reservations department required. **Amenities:** Restaurant; bar; outdoor pool; health club; spa; bike rentals; concierge; car-rental desk; secretarial services; 24-hr. room service; same-day laundry service/dry cleaning. *In room:* A/C, TV w/pay movies, dataport, high-speed Internet access, minibar, hair dryer, iron, safe.

Hyatt Regency Austin on Town Lake 🏨🏨

Austin's Hyatt Regency brings the outdoors indoors, with a signature atrium lobby anchored by a Hill Country tableau of a limestone-banked flowing stream, waterfalls, and oak trees. It's impressive, but the genuine article outside is more striking. The hotel sits on Town Lake's south shore. The north-facing rooms have watery vistas with the downtown skyscrapers as a backdrop. The wealth of outdoor recreation opportunities makes this hotel a good choice. Bat tours and other Town Lake excursions depart from a private dock, where you can

Central Austin Accommodations, Dining & Attractions

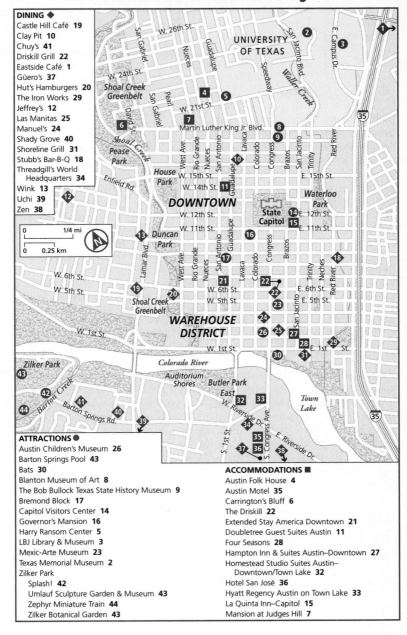

DINING ◆
Castle Hill Café **19**
Clay Pit **10**
Chuy's **41**
Driskill Grill **22**
Eastside Café **1**
Güero's **37**
Hut's Hamburgers **20**
The Iron Works **29**
Jeffrey's **12**
Las Manitas **25**
Manuel's **24**
Shady Grove **40**
Shoreline Grill **31**
Stubb's Bar-B-Q **18**
Threadgill's World
    Headquarters **34**
Wink **13**
Uchi **39**
Zen **38**

ATTRACTIONS ●
Austin Children's Museum **26**
Barton Springs Pool **43**
Bats **30**
Blanton Museum of Art **8**
The Bob Bullock Texas State History Museum **9**
Bremond Block **17**
Capitol Visitors Center **14**
Governor's Mansion **16**
Harry Ransom Center **5**
LBJ Library & Museum **3**
Mexic-Arte Museum **23**
Texas Memorial Museum **2**
Zilker Park
    Splash! **42**
    Umlauf Sculpture Garden & Museum **43**
    Zephyr Miniature Train **44**
    Zilker Botanical Garden **43**

ACCOMMODATIONS ■
Austin Folk House **4**
Austin Motel **35**
Carrington's Bluff **6**
The Driskill **22**
Extended Stay America Downtown **21**
Doubletree Guest Suites Austin **11**
Four Seasons **28**
Hampton Inn & Suites Austin–Downtown **27**
Homestead Studio Suites Austin–
    Downtown/Town Lake **32**
Hotel San José **36**
Hyatt Regency Austin on Town Lake **33**
La Quinta Inn–Capitol **15**
Mansion at Judges Hill **7**

also rent paddle boats and canoes. Rooms have recently been remodeled. They have good beds and a modern-functional look that is comfortable and seems geared more to the business traveler. Those on higher floors facing Town Lake are the most coveted.

208 Barton Springs Rd. (at S. Congress), Austin, TX 78704. © **800/233-1234** or 512/477-1234. Fax 512/480-2069. www.hyatt.com. 446 units. $249–$314 double; $345–$650 suite. Weekend specials, corporate and government rates available. AE, DC, DISC, MC, V. Self-parking $9; valet parking $13. **Amenities:** Restaurant; bar; outdoor pool; health club; Jacuzzi; bike rentals; business center; room service; laundry service/dry cleaning; club-level rooms. *In room:* A/C, TV, dataport, Wi-Fi, coffeemaker, hair dryer, iron.

EXPENSIVE

Doubletree Guest Suites Austin (★ (Kids)   Lobbyists sock in for winter legislative sessions at this tony all-suites high-rise, a stone's throw from the state Capitol. It would be hard to find more comfortable temporary quarters. At 625 square feet, the standard one-bedroom suites are larger than a typical New York apartment, and all are decorated in attractive Western style with Texas details, offering cushy foldout sofas and large mirrored closets, and spacious bathrooms, too. Many rooms have small balconies with capital Capitol views, and the windows open. Full-size appliances with all the requisite cookware allow guests to prepare meals in comfort. Obviously, these suites with kitchens appeal to families with mouths to feed, but beyond that, the sturdy and practical way the rooms are furnished and decorated seems particularly apt for people with younger kids.

303 W. 15th St. (at Guadalupe), Austin, TX 78701. © **800/222-TREE** or 512/478-7000. Fax 512/478-3562. www. doubletree.com. 189 units. 1-bedroom suite $169–$219; 2-bedroom suite $229–$309. Corporate, extended-stay, Internet, and other discounts available. Children younger than 18 stay free in parent's room. AE, DC, DISC, MC, V. Self-parking $10; valet parking $15. Pets less than 25 lb. accepted for $25 per day. **Amenities:** Restaurant; outdoor pool; health club; Jacuzzi; sauna; concierge; business center; secretarial services; Wi-Fi in public areas; room service; dry cleaning/laundry; coin-op laundry. *In room:* A/C, TV w/pay movies, dataport, high-speed Internet access, full-size kitchen, hair dryer, iron.

Hampton Inn & Suites Austin-Downtown (★ (Value)   This conventioneer hotel, opened in 2003, may be part of a chain but it's definitely a cut above cookie-cutter. Rooms, done in clean-lined Western style with wood headboards, polished stone floors, and wrought-iron curtain rods, are very attractive. The hot breakfast buffet, included in the room rate, is generous. Perks include free local phone calls and no surcharge for using a calling card, as well as a coin-op laundry. The location, a block from the convention center and close to all of downtown's sights, restaurants, and nightlife, is hard to beat.

200 San Jacinto Blvd. (at 2nd St.), Austin, TX 78701. © **800/560-7809** or 512/472-1500. Fax 512/472-8900. www. hamptoninn.com. 209 units. $179–$249 double. Corporate, AAA discounts available. Children younger than 18 stay free in parent's room; rates include breakfast buffet and happy hour (Mon–Thurs). AE, DC, DISC, MC, V. Valet (only) parking $14. **Amenities:** Heated outdoor pool; fitness room; business center; room service; guest laundry. *In room:* AC, TV, dataport, Wi-Fi, minifridge, coffeemaker, hair dryer, iron.

MODERATE

Holiday Inn Austin Town Lake (Kids)   The most upscale Holiday Inn in Austin, this high-rise is also the best situated on the north shore of Town Lake, at the edge of downtown, and just off I-35. Many of the units have sofa sleepers, which can translate into real family savings, especially since kids stay free (and if they're younger than 12, eat free at the hotel restaurant, too). Other amenities include a rooftop pool large enough for lap swimming, happy-hour specials, and a big-screen TV in the lounge. The hotel is planning a thorough renovation of guest rooms for early 2007. It will be upgrading beds, furniture, and bathrooms. All rooms will soon be nonsmoking.

20 N. I-35 (exit 233, Riverside Dr./Town Lake), Austin, TX 78701. ☎ **800/HOLIDAY** or 512/472-8211. Fax 512/472-4636. www.holiday-inn.com/austintownlake. 320 units. $159–$199 double. Weekend and holiday rates, corporate discounts. Children younger than 18 stay free. AE, DC, DISC, MC, V. Valet parking $12. **Amenities:** Restaurant; bar; outdoor pool; exercise room; unstaffed business center; secretarial services; Wi-Fi; room service; laundry/coin-op laundry/dry cleaning; executive floors. *In room:* AC, TV w/pay movies, dataport, Wi-Fi, coffeemaker, hair dryer, iron.

La Quinta Inn–Capitol *(Value)* Practically on the grounds of the state Capitol, this is a great bargain for both business and leisure travelers. Rooms are more attractive than those in your typical motel: TVs are large, the rich-toned furnishings are far from cheesy, and perks such as free local phone calls, free high-speed Internet access, and free continental breakfasts keep annoying extras off your bill. The sole drawback is the lack of a restaurant on the premises.

300 E. 11th St. (at San Jacinto), Austin, TX 78701. ☎ **800/NU-ROOMS** or 512/476-1166. Fax 512/476-6044. www.laquinta.com. 150 units. $92–$119 double; $119–$169 suite. Rates include continental breakfast. Children younger than 18 stay free in parent's room. AE, DC, DISC, MC, V. Valet parking $10. Pets accepted (no deposit or extra fee). **Amenities:** Outdoor pool; secretarial services; laundry service/dry cleaning. *In room:* A/C, TV w/pay movies, dataport, high-speed Internet access, coffeemaker, hair dryer, iron.

SOUTH AUSTIN
EXPENSIVE
Hotel San José Opened in the late 1990s, this revamped 1930s motor court is the epitome of SoCo cool. It's got retro appeal, with small porches and a small pool, and it's right across the street from the famed Continental Club, which means lots of musicians and their handlers stay here. There are nods to local design—red Spanish tile roofs, cowhide throw rugs, and Texas pine beds—but the dominant theme is Zen, with Japanese-style outdoor landscaping and rooms so stripped down they border on the stark, though they do have the Austin high-tech basics of high-speed Internet access plus VCRs and/or DVD players and CD players. Book a room in the back to avoid the Congress Avenue traffic noise.

1316 S. Congress Ave. (south of Nelly, about a half-mile south of Riverside), Austin, TX 78704. ☎ **800/574-8897** or 512/444-7322. Fax 512/444-7362. www.sanjosehotel.com. 40 units. $95 (for 3 rooms with shared bathroom); $165–$175 double; $185–$315 suite. Corporate and entertainment discounts available; lower rates during the week. AE, DC, MC, V. Free parking. Dogs accepted for $10 per dog per day. **Amenities:** Bar/lounge; coffee shop; outdoor pool; bike rentals; breakfast-only room service; dry cleaning. *In room:* TV/VCR, dataport., high-speed Internet access, CD player.

INEXPENSIVE
Austin Motel *(Value)* It's not only nostalgia that draws repeat guests to this Austin institution, established in 1938 on what used to be the old San Antonio Highway and in the current owner's family since the 1950s. A convenient (but not quiet) location on trendy South Congress Avenue and reasonable rates help, too. Other assets are a classic kidney-shaped pool, a great neon sign, free HBO, free coffee in the lobby, and **El Sol y La Luna,** a good Latin restaurant. It's also got one of those rarities: real single rooms, so those traveling on their own don't have to pay for a bed they're not sleeping in. All rooms are different and some are more recently renovated than others, so ask to look before settling in.

1220 S. Congress St. (south of Nelly, about a half-mile south of Riverside), Austin, TX 78704. ☎ **512/441-1157.** Fax 512/441-1157. www.austinmotel.com. 41 units. $60–$90 single; $80–$122 double; $143–$153 suite. AE, DC, DISC, MC, V. Free parking. Limited number of rooms for pets; one-time $10 fee. **Amenities:** Outdoor pool. *In room:* A/C, TV, fridge (some), coffeemaker, hair dryer, iron, safe.

It Pays to Stay

If you're planning to settle in for a spell, two downtown accommodations at prime locations will save you major bucks. Rooms at **Extended Stay America Downtown,** 600 Guadalupe (at 6th St.), Austin, TX 78701 (✆ **800/EXT-STAY** or 512/457-9994; www.extstay.com), within easy walking distance of both the Warehouse District and the Lamar and 6th shops, and at **Homestead Studio Suites Austin–Downtown/Town Lake,** 507 S. First St. (at Barton Springs), Austin, TX 78704 (✆ **888/782-9473** or 512/476-1818; www.homesteadhotels. com), near the Barton Springs restaurant row and the hike-and-bike trail, will run you from $400 to $500 per week. Full kitchens and coin-op laundries at both bring your costs down even more.

CENTRAL
EXPENSIVE
Mansion at Judges Hill 🏵🏵   All the rooms in this boutique hotel are furnished and decorated with much more character than you'll find at any of the local chain hotels. This is as true of the rooms in the modern building at the rear of the property as it is for the ones in the original mansion. The rooms that are the most fun are the second-story signature rooms, which all open onto a sweeping upstairs porch and have tall ceilings and large bathrooms with special amenities (including L'Occitane toiletries and bathrobes). Beds have particularly good mattresses and linens. The third-floor rooms are a little smaller, but lovely. The first floor holds the bar and the restaurant. The modern building offers rooms far from the traffic sounds coming from MLK. Despite being modern, the rooms vary quite a bit. Most come without tubs. The deluxe king rooms are the nicest (particularly room 212). All rooms are nonsmoking. The West Campus location is convenient to the university and to downtown.

1900 Rio Grande (at MLK Blvd. [19th St.]), Austin, TX 78705. ✆ **800/311-1619** or 512/495-1800. www.mansionat judgeshill.com. 48 units. $139–$199 North Wing; $169–$299 Mansion. Rates go higher for special events. AE, DC, DISC, MC, V. Free off-street parking. Pets accepted with restrictions. **Amenities:** Restaurant; bar; limited room service; limited laundry service; in-room massage; babysitting. *In room:* A/C, TV, dataport, Wi-Fi, coffeemaker, hair dryer, iron, CD player.

MODERATE
Austin Folk House 🏵🏵 *Value*   You get the best of both worlds at this appealing B&B where old-time charm is combined with new plumbing. When it was transformed from a tired apartment complex at the beginning of the new millennium, this 1880s house near the University of Texas got a complete interior overhaul, but maintained such integral traditional assets as the comfy front porch. The sunny rooms have cheerfully painted walls and the wiring to accommodate megachannel cable TVs, private phone lines, broadband cable access, and radio/alarms with white noise machines. At the same time, nice antiques and such amenities as fancy bedding and towels, candles, robes, expensive lotions, and soaps make you feel like you're in a small luxury inn. The lavish breakfast buffet served in a dining room decorated with the folk art for which the B&B is named does nothing to dispel that idea. Prices are more than

reasonable for all this, while the free off-street parking, near the heart of UT, puts this place at a premium all by itself. Local phone calls are gratis.

506 W. 22nd St. (at Nueces), Austin, TX 78705. © **866/472-6700** or 512/472-6700. www.austinfolkhouse.com. 9 units. $110–$195 double; Internet specials sometimes available. Rates include full breakfast. AE, DISC, MC, V. Free off-street parking. **Amenities:** Bike rentals; Wi-Fi in public areas; video library. *In room:* A/C, TV/VCR, dataport, Wi-Fi and high-speed cable, hair dryer, iron.

Carrington's Bluff *(★*   Occupying a verdant acre on a rise at the end of a quiet street near the University of Texas, this 1877 house exudes country charm. But that doesn't mean it's lacking citified amenities. The antiques-filled rooms keep business as well as leisure travelers happy. Both houses offer access to full kitchens, including refrigerators stocked with Bluebell ice cream.

1900 David St. (at 22nd St.), Austin, TX 78705. © **888/290-6090** or 512/479-0638. www.carringtonsbluff.com. 8 units. $105–$189 double. Higher rates for special events. Rates include breakfast. AE, DISC, MC, V. Free off-street parking. *In room:* A/C, TV/VCR, dataport, Wi-Fi, coffeemaker, hair dryer, iron.

I-35 CORRIDOR
MODERATE
Habitat Suites *(★★ (Finds (Kids*   Don't be put off by the generic name and nonde-script location on the outskirts of Highland Mall: This detail-obsessive "ecotel" offers Kukicha twig tea, at least one vegan and macrobiotic entree at breakfast, a swimming pool that uses a salt generator (the better to avoid chlorine), solar-paneled buildings, and a book of Buddha's teaching in the bedside-table drawer. Lush gardens (tended without chemical fertilizers) and little front porches or decks add to the comfort. The rooms themselves don't have much character, but they're extremely large (the two-bed-room duplex suites have separate entrances) and offer full kitchens, as well as real fire-places and windows that actually open. Chemically sensitive? Every room is cleaned with citric oil, and no other harsh chemicals are used.

500 E. Highland Mall Blvd. (take exit 222 off I-35 to Airport Blvd., take a right to Highland Mall Blvd.), Austin, TX 78752. © **800/535-4663** or 512/467-6000. Fax 512/467-6000. www.habitatsuites.com. 96 units. $137 1-bedroom suite; $197 2-bedroom suite. Lower weekend rates; extended-stay rates available. Rates include full breakfast and (Mon–Sat) afternoon beer and snacks. AE, DC, DISC, MC, V. Free parking. **Amenities:** Outdoor pool; Jacuzzi; Wi-Fi in public areas; coin-op laundry/environmentally sound dry cleaning. *In room:* A/C, TV, dataport, Wi-Fi in some suites, kitchen, fridge, coffeemaker, hair dryer, iron.

NORTHWEST
EXPENSIVE
Renaissance Austin Hotel   Anchoring the upscale Arboretum mall on Austin's northwest side, the Renaissance caters to executives visiting nearby high-tech firms. But on weekends, when rates are slashed, even underlings can afford to take advantage of the hotel's many amenities, including an excellent health club, a nightclub, and direct access to the myriad allures of the mall (movie theaters among them). Guest rooms, redone in 2003 with a Hill Country look—warm russets, browns, and greens, dark wood, and leather chairs—are all oversize and offer comfortable sitting areas. Suites include extras such as wet bars and electric shoe buffers. Another perk: Not only can you check in with Fido free of charge, but the chef whips up some mean dog biscuits.

9721 Arboretum Blvd. (off Loop 360, near Research Blvd.), Austin, TX 78759. © **800/HOTELS-1** or 512/343-2626. Fax 512/346-7945. http://marriott.com. 478 units. $259–$279 double; suites from $289. Weekend packages available. AE, DC, DISC, MC, V. Free self-parking; valet parking $10. Pets accepted. **Amenities:** 3 restaurants; bar; nightclub; indoor pool; outdoor pool; health club; Jacuzzi; sauna; concierge; car-rental desk; business center; secretarial services;

(Kids) Family-Friendly Hotels

Doubletree Guest Suites (p. 304) and **Habitat Suites** (p. 307) That "suites" in the name of these properties says it all. These accommodations offer spacious not-in-your-face quarters, plus the convenience (and economy) of kitchen facilities, so you don't have to eat out all the time.

Four Seasons Austin (p. 302) Tell the reservations clerk that you're traveling with kids, and you'll be automatically enrolled in the free amenities program, which offers age-appropriate snacks—cookies and milk for children younger than 10, popcorn and soda for those older—along with various toys and games that will be waiting for you when you arrive. And you don't have to travel with all your gear because the hotel will provide such items as a car seat, stroller, playpen, bedrails, disposable pacifiers, a baby bathtub, shampoo, powder and lotions, bib, bottle warmers, and disposable diapers.

Holiday Inn Austin Town Lake (p. 304) You're near lots of the outdoor play areas at Town Lake, and kids stay and (younger than 12) eat free. It's hard to beat that!

Lakeway Inn (p. 309) There's plenty for kids to do here, and this property offers a Family Playdays Package, which includes a $100 credit toward recreational activities (such as boat rentals and tennis), plus a free meal and dessert for children 12 and younger with the purchase of adult entree. Prices vary depending on the time of year.

Wi-Fi in public areas; 24-hr. room service; babysitting; same-day laundry/dry cleaning; club-level rooms. *In room:* A/C, TV w/pay movies, dataport, high-speed Internet access, fridge (some), coffeemaker, hair dryer, iron.

WESTLAKE/LAKE TRAVIS
VERY EXPENSIVE

Lake Austin Spa Resort 🌸🌸🌸 If you had to create the quintessential Austin spa, it would be laid-back, be located on a serene body of water, offer lots of outdoor activities, and feature superhealthy food that lives up to high culinary standards. You'll sign off on every item of that wish list here. The spa takes advantage of its proximity to the Highland Lakes and the Hill Country by offering such activities as combination canoe/hiking trips and excursions to view the wildflowers. The aromatic ingredients for soothing spa treatments such as a honey-mango scrub are grown in the resort's garden. Guest rooms, many in cottages with private gardens, fireplaces, and hot tubs, are casually elegant, with all-natural fabrics and locally crafted furniture. The coup de grâce is the 25,000-square-foot LakeHouse spa.

1705 S. Quinlan Park Rd. (5 miles south of Hwy. 620), Austin, TX 78732. © **800/847-5637** or 512/372-7300. Fax 512/266-1572. www.lakeaustin.com. 40 units. 3-day packages available for $1,455 per person (assuming double occupancy). Rates include all meals, classes, and activities. Spa treatments/personal trainers are extra. AE, DC, DISC, MC, V. Free parking. Dogs accepted in Garden Cottage rooms; $250 pet guest fee. Children 14 and older only. **Amenities:** Restaurant; indoor pool; 2 outdoor pools; health club; spa; kayaks; canoes; hydrobikes; room service; laundry service. *In room:* A/C, TV/DVD, dataport, Wi-Fi, hair dryer, CD player.

EXPENSIVE

Lakeway Inn *(Value (Kids*   This conference resort in a planned community on Lake Travis is for those seeking traditional recreation at prices that won't require a second mortgage. There's something for everyone: a marina, with pontoons, ski boats, sculls, sailboats, water-skis, WaveRunners, fishing gear, and guides; a 32-court tennis complex; and a 36-hole of golf course along with the Jack Nicklaus–designed Academy of Golf. The main lodge of this older property was razed and rebuilt at the end of the 1990s, but, oddly, the rooms were reincarnated with a rather dark and staid 1970s look. Still, they're spacious and comfortable, with all the requisite conference attendee business amenities and, in many cases, lake views.

101 Lakeway Dr., Austin, TX 78734. ⓒ 800/LAKEWAY or 512/261-6600. Fax 512/261-7322. www.lakewayinn.com. 239 units. $139–$269 double. Romance, golf, spa, B&B, and family packages available. AE, DC, DISC, MC, V. Free self-parking; valet parking $12. **Amenities:** Restaurant; bar; 2 outdoor pools; health club; spa; watersports rentals; concierge; business center; room service. *In room:* A/C, TV w/pay movies, dataport, high-speed Internet access in most rooms, coffeemaker, hair dryer, iron.

AT THE AIRPORT
MODERATE

Hilton Austin Airport *(★*   This Hilton's circular shape gives Austin's only full-service airport hotel, formerly the headquarters of Bergstrom Air Force Base, a distinctively spaceshiplike look. Although the hotel retains few of the features that made it one of three bunkers where the President of the United States might be spirited in the event of a nuclear attack, the building remains rock-solid—and blissfully soundproof. These days, the dome serves as a skylight for a bright and airy lobby. The theme throughout is Texas Hill Country, with lots of limestone and wood and plenty of live plants for good measure. Large, comfortable rooms are equipped with all the amenities.

9515 New Airport Dr. (half-mile from the airport, 2 miles east of the intersection of Hwy. 183 and Hwy. 71), Austin, TX 78719. ⓒ 800/445-8667 or 512/385-6767. Fax 512/385-6763. www.hilton.com. 263 units. $139–$199 double; suites from $190. Weekend, online, and parking discounts. AE, DC, DISC, MC, V. Self-parking $8; valet parking $14. **Amenities:** Restaurant; lounge; outdoor pool; health club; business center; 24-hr. room service; laundry service/dry cleaning; club-level rooms. *In room:* A/C, TV w/pay movies, dataport, high-speed Internet access, minibar, coffeemaker, hair dryer, iron.

4 Where to Dine

You would expect to eat well in a town where lawmakers schmooze power brokers, academics can be tough culinary graders, and techies and musicians require high-grade fuel. Austin doesn't disappoint. Chic industrial spaces vie for diners' dollars with gracious 100-year-old houses and plant-filled hippie shacks.

If you're staying in the downtown or University of Texas area, consider taking a cab (or on the weekend, a free 'Dillo) when you go out to dinner. It's hard to find a metered spot for your car, and you won't pay much more for a taxi than you would for valet parking or an independent lot.

DOWNTOWN
VERY EXPENSIVE

Driskill Grill *(★★* NEW AMERICAN   Chef David Bull—named one of *Food & Wine's* Best New Chefs in 2003 and winner of Austin dining awards out the wazoo—works wonders on American standards such as broiled lobster and braised beef ribs. He has a knack for winning combinations of taste and adding just the right number of new ingredients to the dishes to pleasantly surprise the diner without leaving him/her with the feeling of being a test subject. The menu changes, but just to give you an idea, here are some examples of what your might find: prawns with bits of grilled chorizo, charred tomatoes, corn butter and coriander; or rack of lamb with wild-mushroom risotto, a rich broth flavored with oregano, and garlic chips. Mark Chapman, the Driskill's pastry chef, is also a creative talent. His chocolate silk tart, seasoned with ancho chiles and shaved ginger, is amazing.

604 Brazos St., The Driskill. ⓒ 512/391-7162. www.driskillgrill.com. Reservations recommended. Main courses $32–$44 (occasionally higher); prix fixe $65 per person; chef's 6-course tasting menu $90 ($125 paired with wine); chef's 9-course tasting $125 ($175 with wine). AE, DC, DISC, MC, V. Tues–Sat 5:30–10:30pm.

EXPENSIVE

Castle Hill Café 🖈🖈 *Value* NEW AMERICAN   This restaurant, located in the popular district of shops clustered around the intersection of Lamar and West 6th Street, is one of my favorites. The dining room is comfortable and relaxed without being trendy or trying to impress. And the food shares these qualities. The menus change every few weeks, but there's almost always something inspired by Mexico, some kind of pasta dish, something with Italian taste, a few vegetarian options, and a few tantalizing crossover dishes. Entree prices have crept up in recent years, but lunches are still a good deal. The entree salads such as the chile-lime grilled chicken with guacamole relish and two blue-corn empanadas, perhaps preceded by something such as a cup of spicy duck and sausage gumbo, will fill you up. You certainly won't go away hungry.

1101 W. 5th St. ⓒ 512/476-0728. Reservations accepted for parties of 4 or more only. Main courses $17–$23. AE, DISC, MC, V. Mon–Fri 11am–2:30pm; Mon–Sat 6–10pm.

Shoreline Grill 🖈 SEAFOOD/NEW AMERICAN   Fish is the prime lure at this tony grill, which looks out over Town Lake and the Congress Avenue Bridge, but from late spring through early fall, bats run a close second. Thousands of Mexican free-tailed bats emerge in unison from under the bridge at dusk, and patio tables for viewing the phenomenon are at a premium. When they're not admiring the view, diners focus on such starters as semolina-crusted oysters or venison chorizo quesadillas. Drum, a moist, meaty fish from the Gulf, is worth trying however it's prepared, and the roast salmon with tequila-lime butter is excellent, too. Nonseafood dishes include Parmesan-crusted chicken with penne pasta and prime rib with horseradish potatoes. In recent years this restaurant has been neglected by locals for newer, trendier spots, but the Shoreline Grill is still an excellent downtown dining spot.

98 San Jacinto Blvd. ⓒ 512/477-3300. www.shorelinegrill.com. Reservations recommended (patio seating can't be guaranteed but requests are taken). Main courses $16–$38. AE, DC, DISC, MC, V. Mon–Fri 11am–10pm; Sat–Sun 5–10pm.

MODERATE

Clay Pit 🖈 *Value* INDIAN   An elegant setting—a historic building with wood floors and exposed limestone walls, lit with soft lamps and votive candles, and sumptuous recipes, including creative curries and other sauces rich with nuts, raisins, and exotic spices—raise this brainchild of a husband-and-wife team and a New Delhi–trained chef to gourmet status. The starter of perfectly cooked coriander calamari is served with a piquant cilantro aioli. For an entree, consider *khuroos-e-tursh,* baked chicken breast stuffed with nuts, mushrooms, and onions and smothered in a cashew-almond cream sauce, or one of the many dazzling vegetarian dishes. A bargain buffet and a variety of wraps made with nan make this a great lunch stop while touring the nearby Capitol.

1601 Guadalupe St. ℭ **512/322-5131.** www.claypit.com. Reservations recommended. $6.95 lunch buffet; main courses $9–$16. AE, DC, DISC, MC, V. Mon–Thurs 11am–2pm and 5–10pm; Fri 11am–2pm and 5–11pm; Sat–Sun 5–11pm.

INEXPENSIVE

Hut's Hamburgers *Value* AMERICAN   This classic burger shack is very Austin. It opened its doors as Sammie's Drive-In in 1939, serving the traditional-style Texas burger with lettuce and onions. Now it offers 19 types of burgers, including a vegetarian garden burger (which is very Austin, too). As you might expect, you can also get fries and shakes, the usual burger complements, but you mustn't forget the onion rings, which are done beautifully. Also on the menu are blue-plate specials of meatloaf, chicken-fried steak, and catfish. The decor is sports pennants and '50s memorabilia.

807 W. 6th St. ℭ **512/472-0693.** Sandwiches and burgers $4–$7; plates $7–$10. AE, DISC, MC, V. Daily 11am–10pm.

The Iron Works BARBECUE   Some of the best barbecue in Austin is served in one of the most unusual settings. Until 1977, this building housed the ironworks of the Weigl family, who came over from Germany in 1913. You can see their ornamental craft all around town, including at the State Capitol. Cattle brands created for Jack Benny ("Lasting 39"), Lucille Ball, and Bob Hope are displayed in front of the restaurant. The fall-off-the-bones-tender beef ribs are the most popular order, with the brisket running a close second. Lean turkey breast and juicy chicken are also smoked to perfection.

100 Red River (at E. 1st St.) ℭ **800/669-3602** or 512/478-4855. www.ironworksbbq.com. Reservations accepted for large parties only. Sandwiches $3–$5; plates $6–$12; by the lb. $5–$11. AE, DC, MC, V. Mon–Sat 11am–9pm.

Las Manitas *Moments* MEXICAN   Las Manitas has reached "iconic" status in Austin. No one is quite sure what this means or what rights it confers, but the tag has been bestowed and accepted universally and is not in dispute. Unfortunately, Las Manitas is facing closure. The owners of the land want a developer to build a Marriott hotel on this site, which is one of the last blocks of Congress Avenue that hasn't surrendered to the march of progress. There have been hearings at city hall, at which someone came up with the notion of "iconic businesses"—places that make Austin *Austin*. There will be more hearings, but it's unclear whether anything will come of them. If it is, you should check it out. It's got the kind of hominess that you can't fake, that comes only with years of being a community venue.

If you manage to get here, just about anything on the menu is good. For lunch I gravitate towards the enchiladas Michoacán or the enchiladas rojas. For breakfast, I enjoy the *chilaquiles verdes* (tortilla strips cooked in green sauce, with Jack cheese, and onions), which remind me of some I used to have in Mexico.

211 Congress Ave. ℭ **512/472-9357.** Reservations not accepted. Breakfast $4–$7; lunch $4–$9. AE, DC, DISC, MC, V. Mon–Fri 7am–4pm; Sat–Sun 7am–2:30pm.

SOUTH AUSTIN
EXPENSIVE

Uchi ASIAN/JAPANESE   Last year chef/owner Tyson Cole was named one of America's best new chefs by *Food and Wine* magazine. He loves to play with ingredients Texans are familiar with to create Asian dishes that are beautifully presented and exciting to Austin's tastes. His Uchiviche—citrus-marinated whitefish and salmon mixed with tomato, peppers, cilantro, and chiles—will make a believer out of you. It's not only the seafood that gets the culinary crossover treatment: Brie, pumpkin, shiitake mushrooms, and asparagus are among the food items that you can order tempura-style. And the skewered Kobe beef should satisfy those who eschew vegetables and fish. Choose from a long list of cold sakes—especially the rare upmarket brands—for the perfect complement.

801 S. Lamar Blvd. ⦅€⦆ 512/916-4808. www.uchiaustin.com. Reservations accepted (and strongly recommended) for Mon–Thurs 5:30–9pm and Fri–Sat 5:30–6:30pm. Sushi (per piece) $2.50–$4.50; sashimi, hot and cold plates $5–$25. AE, DISC, MC, V. Mon–Thurs 5–10pm; Fri–Sat 5–11pm.

Vespaio ⦅★⦆ ITALIAN   Still one of Austin's trendiest restaurants, Vespaio doesn't quite draw the long lines that it did when it first opened in the late 1990s, but the weird policy for reservations—they're accepted only for early hours on off days—ensures that the see-and-be-seen bar is always packed. The setting is fun, and the food is worth waiting for, but you can drop quite a bit of dough on expensive wines while you're doing so. The spaghetti alla carbonara is super, as is the veal scaloppine with mushrooms. In the mood for a go-for-baroque pizza? Try the *boscaiola*, topped with wild-boar sausage and Cambozola cheese. Among the 10 chalkboard specials offered nightly, the mixed meat and seafood grills are usually top-notch.

1610 S. Congress Ave. ⦅€⦆ 512/441-6100. Reservations accepted for Tues–Thurs and Sun 5:30–6:30pm only. Pizzas and pastas $14–$21; main courses $14–$29. AE, DC, DISC, MC, V. Tues–Sun 5:30–10:30pm (bar 5pm–midnight).

MODERATE

Curra's Grill ⦅★★⦆ ⦅Kids⦆ REGIONAL MEXICAN   You're likely to find this plain, unassuming restaurant packed at any time of day, but it's worth the wait for the best interior Mexican food in South Austin. A couple of breakfast tacos and a cup of special Oaxacan dark roast coffee are a great way to jump-start your day. For either lunch or dinner, choices are abundant. The Mexican tamales come in several flavors and are quite good, with moist spongy masa. You can build your own enchiladas from a selection of sauces and fillings—I like the *mole* and the chile *pasilla*. The Yucatecan *cochinita pibil* (pork baked in a marinade of achiote, sour orange and herbs and spices) is tender and complex. The tortillas are handmade. For dessert, the flan can't be beat. Curra's has a north Austin location, 6801 Burnet Rd. (⦅€⦆ 512/451-2560), and a far north location, at 6301 W. Parmer Lane (⦅€⦆ 512/457-2500).

614 E. Oltorf. ⦅€⦆ 512/444-0012. Reservations recommended for large parties. Main courses $8–$15. AE, DISC, MC, V. Daily 7am–10pm.

Güero's ⦅★⦆ ⦅Kids⦆ MEXICAN/REGIONAL MEXICAN   Although the menu listings at this sprawling converted feed store, which serves as the unofficial center of the SoCo scene, are stylishly tongue-in-cheek—the entry for one pork dish describes it as being the same as the beef version "except piggish"—the food is good, and the service both efficient and friendly. You can enjoy health-conscious versions of Tex-Mex standards as well as dishes from the interior of Mexico: snapper *a la veracruzana* (with tomatoes, green olives, and jalapeños), say, or the small and wonderfully seasoned tacos al pastor. The corn tortillas are handmade. Come Sunday afternoon for a live music bonus. My gripe with this place is that it's too noisy and too popular.

1412 S. Congress. ⦅€⦆ 512/447-7688. www.guerostacobar.com. Reservations not accepted. Main courses $7–$19. AE, DC, DISC, MC, V. Mon–Fri 11am–11pm; Sat–Sun 8am–11pm.

Matt's El Rancho MEXICAN   Opened in downtown in 1952, this old landmark restaurant has a large, faithful body of customers. Owner Matt Martinez later moved his restaurant to South Austin in 1986, and now his son, Matt, Jr., runs the show. The restaurant does a huge business with customers seeking dependable old-school Tex-Mex dishes such as enchiladas in chili gravy, flautas, or fajitas. The chiles rellenos and shrimp Mexicana (smothered with peppers, onions, tomato, ranchero sauce, and Jack cheese) are perennial favorites. You might have to wait for an hour on weekend nights, especially if there's a university event in town. You can lounge out on the terrace sipping a fresh lime margarita to pass the time. The restaurant get a mixed crowd—mostly families, long-time Austinites, not a lot of students.

2613 S. Lamar Blvd. ℂ 512/462-9333. www.mattselrancho.com. Reservations not accepted for after 6pm on weekends, except for large groups. Dinners $8.50–$18. AE, DC, DISC, MC, V. Sun–Mon and Wed–Thurs 11am–10pm; Fri–Sat 11am–11pm.

The Salt Lick 🏃 *Kids* BARBECUE   It's 12 miles from the junction of 290 West and FM 1826 to The Salt Lick, but you'll start smelling the smoke during the last 5 miles of your trip. Moist chicken, beef, and pork, as well as terrific homemade pickles—not to mention the pretty, verdant setting—more than justify the drive. If you indulge in the all-you-can-eat family-style platter of beef, sausage, and pork ribs, you might have to pass on the fresh-baked peach cobbler, which would be a pity. In warm weather, seating is outside at picnic tables under oak trees; in winter, fireplaces blaze in a series of large, rustic rooms. The Salt Lick prides itself on its sauce, which has a sweet-and-sour tang. If you like your barbecue with a brew, you'll need to tote your own in a cooler, because Hays County is dry. Kids younger than 4 eat free. But you don't have to drive all the way out to the country for a smoked-meat fix: The Salt Lick's airport branch is convenient and quick.

18300 FM 1826, Driftwood. ℂ 512/858-4959 or 888/SALT-LICK (mail order). http://saltlickbbq.com. Reservations for large parties only. Sandwiches $7–$8; plates $7–$15. No credit cards. Daily 11am–10pm.

INEXPENSIVE

Chuy's *Kids* MEXICAN   One of the row of low-priced, friendly restaurants that line Barton Springs Road just east of Zilker Park, Chuy's stands out for its determinedly wacky decor—hubcaps lining the ceiling, Elvis memorabilia galore—and its sauce-smothered Tex-Mex food. You're not likely to leave hungry after specials such as Chuy's special enchiladas, piled high with smoked chicken and cheese and topped with sour cream, or one of the "big as yo' face" burritos, stuffed with ground sirloin, say, and cheese and beans. This has been a local landmark since long before presidential daughter Jenna Bush got busted here for underage drinking (the margaritas *are* tempting . . .).

1728 Barton Springs Rd. ℂ 512/474-4452. www.chuys.com. Reservations not accepted. Main courses $6–$12. AE, DC, DISC, MC, V. Sun–Thurs 11am–10:30pm; Fri–Sat 11am–11pm.

Shady Grove 🏃 AMERICAN   If your idea of comfort food involves chiles, don't pass up Shady Grove, one of Austin's quintessential relaxed restaurants. The inside dining area, with its Texas kitsch roadhouse decor and cushy booths, is plenty comfortable, but most people head for the large, tree-shaded patio when the weather permits. When your appetite is whetted by a day of fresh air at nearby Zilker Park, a hearty bowl of Freddie's Airstream chili might be just the thing. All the burgers are made with high-grade ground sirloin, and if you've never had a Frito pie (Fritos topped with Airstream chili and cheese), this is the place to try one. Large salads—among them, noodles with Asian vegetables—or the hippie sandwich (grilled eggplant, veggies, and cheese with pesto mayonnaise) will satisfy the less carnivorous.

1624 Barton Springs Rd. ℂ 512/474-9991. www.theshadygrove.com. Reservations not accepted. Main courses $8–$11. AE, DC, DISC, MC, V. Sun–Thurs 11am–10pm; Fri–Sat 11am–11pm.

Zen (Value) (Kids) JAPANESE The food is flavorful, healthy, and inexpensive, the pared-down room light and welcoming—if you're looking for a nice, quick bite, it's hard to beat Zen. The poultry in such dishes as chicken teriyaki and veggies, for example, is steroid-free, 25¢ gets you brown instead of white rice with your order, and the menu has so many heart-healthy symbols on it that it resembles a Valentine's card. Most of the food is typically Japanese—sushi, udon noodles, rice bowls, and teriyaki dishes—except, for some reason, for the Madison Mac & Cheese. No doubt it's a tongue-in-cheek touch, like the light fixtures that look like Chia pet doormats. Two newer locations are at 2900 W. Anderson Lane, Suite 250 (© **512/451-4811**), and 3423 N. Guadalupe (© **512/300-2633**).

1303 S. Congress Ave. © 512/444-8081. www.eatzen.com. Reservations not accepted. $3.80–$7.95. DISC, MC, V. Daily 11am–10pm.

CENTRAL
VERY EXPENSIVE

Jeffrey's ★★ NEW AMERICAN In keeping with the tone set by the surrounding Clarksville neighborhood, the bistro is cozy, comfortable, and informal. The house signature appetizer, crispy oysters on yucca chips topped with habanero honey aioli, is a perennial favorite. Main courses, such as beef tenderloin with vanilla potatoes and smoked chile crab sauce or duck and shrimp with black lentils and an orange-ginger glaze tend to have so many flavors inserted them that the diner is sometimes left wondering whether the composition will hold together at all. In my experience Jeffrey's pulls it off, but I'm still left wondering about the dishes I didn't order. If you're wanting comfort food, try some other establishment.

1204 W. Lynn. © 512/477-5584. www.jeffreysofaustin.com. Reservations strongly recommended. Main courses $19–$44; tasting menu $76, with wines $112. AE, DC, DISC, MC, V. Mon–Thurs 6–10pm; Fri–Sat 5:30–10:30pm; Sun 6–9:30pm.

EXPENSIVE

Fonda San Miguel ★ REGIONAL MEXICAN This is the most famous interior Mexican restaurant in Austin and perhaps the entire state. It serves classic preparations such as *mole poblano* and *cochinita pibil,* which are both prepared beautifully. However, most knowledgeable diners won't find a lot of surprises on the menu; it's mainly just the standards. Customers come to dine on dishes that they know, and they come because the dining experience taken as a whole is thoroughly enjoyable. There's something about the oversized rooms, the rich colors of the walls, the dampened background music, and the harmonious lighting that makes for a charming evening. For the pleasure of this experience, though, you pay quite a bit, much more than at other Mexican restaurants. I would say the food is overpriced, but if you're looking for a location for a special evening, you won't go wrong here. Also expensive, but with a more interesting variety of dishes (such as fruit gazpacho and chilaquiles), is the Sunday brunch.

2330 W. North Loop. © 512/459-4121 or 459-3401. www.fondasanmiguel.com. Reservations recommended. Main courses $18–$31. AE, DC, DISC, MC, V. Mon–Thurs 5:30–9:30pm; Fri–Sat 5:30–10:30pm (bar opens 30 min. earlier); Sun brunch 11am–2pm.

Wink ★★ (Finds) NEW AMERICAN One of the darlings of the local foodie scene is a spare but attractive 17-table eatery in an unlikely strip center. Chef/owners Stewart Scruggs and Mark Paul are fresh-ingredient fanatics and they train their staff well. Your server should be able to fill you in on every detail of the menu, down to the organic farm where the arugula and fennel in your rabbit confit salad came from. Expect a mix

Kids   Family-Friendly Restaurants

Curra's (p. 312), **Güero's** (p. 312), **Hoover's** (p. 316), **Threadgill's** (see below), and **Zen** (p. 314) all have special menus for ages 12 and younger, not to mention casual, kid-friendly atmospheres and food inexpensive enough to feed everyone without taking out a second mortgage. **Chuy's** (p. 313) is great for teens and aspiring teens, who'll love the cool T-shirts, Elvis kitsch, and green iguanas crawling up the walls. **The Salt Lick** (p. 313) serves all-you-can-eat family-style platters, and kids younger than 4 eat free.

of such typical New American suspects as seared scallop on pancetta with baby sweet potatoes and more adventurous dishes such as braised boar belly with apple-cider sauce. The tasting menus, which include some off-menu surprises, are worth the splurge. Save some room (and dough) for such desserts as the dreamy lemon curd cups.

1014 N. Lamar Blvd. ✆ 512/482-8868. www.winkrestaurant.com. Reservations strongly recommended. Main courses $19–$28; 5-course tasting menu $65 ($95 with wine); 7-course tasting menu $85 ($125 with wines). AE, DC, DISC, MC, V. Mon–Thurs 6–11pm; Fri–Sat 5: 30–11pm.

MODERATE

Asti ✪ *Value* ITALIAN   This is the Italian place everyone wants in their neighborhood: casual, consistently good, and reasonably priced. An open kitchen and retro Formica-topped tables create a hip, upbeat atmosphere. The designer pizzas make a nice light meal, and northern Italian specialties such as the Calabrese-style trout and the pan-seared halibut with green beans are winners. Save room for such desserts as the creamy espresso sorbet or the amazing bittersweet chocolate cannoli. For a little restaurant, Asti has an unexpectedly large and well-selected wine list.

408C E. 43rd St. ✆ 512/451-1218. www.astiaustin.com. Reservations recommended Thurs–Sat. Pizzas, pastas $7.50–$16; main courses $15–$16. AE, DC, DISC, MC, V. Mon–Thurs 11am–10pm; Fri 11am–11pm; Sat 5–11pm.

Hyde Park Bar and Grill *Value* AMERICAN   In the Hyde Park neighborhood's little enclave of restaurants along Duval Street is the Hyde Park Bar & Grill, easy to spot due to the landmark giant fork out front. Not only is it easy to find, it's easy to get to, it's easy to park your car, and, at least during off hours, it's easy to get a table here. If you do have to wait, then it's easy to have a drink at the bar. On weekends this place is popular, especially when there are events at the university. In addition to the chicken-fried steak and more healthful options, such as the roast chicken or any one of the various salads, people come here for the battered french fries, which are perennially voted best fries in Austin. The atmosphere at Hyde Park—a one-story former home now divided into different dining rooms—is cozy, and the service is quick and unobtrusive.

4206 Duval St. ✆ 512/458-3168. Reservations not accepted. Salads and sandwiches $6–$9; main courses $9–$16. AE, DC, DISC, MC, V. Daily 11am–midnight.

INEXPENSIVE

Threadgill's ✪ *Kids* AMERICAN/SOUTHERN   If you want a hit of music history along with heaping plates of down-home food at good prices, this Austin institution is for you. When Kenneth Threadgill obtained Travis County's first legal liquor license after the repeal of Prohibition in 1933, he turned his Gulf gas station into a club. His

Wednesday-night shows were legendary in the 1960s, with such performers as Janis Joplin turning up regularly. In turn, the Southern-style diner that was added on in 1980 became renowned for its huge chicken-fried steaks, as well as its vegetables. You can get fried okra, broccoli-rice casserole, garlic-cheese grits, black-eyed peas, and the like in combination plates or as sides. Unlike the original location, the South Austin branch at 301 W. Riverside (© 512/472-9304), known as Threadgill's World Headquarters, lays on a Sunday brunch buffet and, during the week, a "howdy" hour. Both branches still double as live music venues.

6416 N. Lamar Blvd. © 512/451-5440. www.threadgills.com. Reservations not accepted. Sandwiches and burgers $6–$8; main courses $8–$15. DISC, MC, V. Mon–Sat 11am–10pm; Sun 11am–9pm.

EAST SIDE
MODERATE

Eastside Cafe AMERICAN   This was one of the earliest eateries to open in this rapidly changing area just east of the university, on the other side of the I-35 freeway. Eastside Cafe remains popular with student herbivores and congressional carnivores alike. Diners enjoy eating on a tree-shaded patio or in one of a series of small, homey rooms in a classic turn-of-the-century bungalow. You can get half orders of such pasta dishes as the artichoke manicotti, of the mixed field green salad topped with warm goat cheese, and of entrees such as the sesame-breaded catfish. Many of the main courses have a Southern comfort orientation—pork tenderloin with cornbread stuffing, say—and all come with soup or salad and a vegetable. Each morning, the gardener informs the head chef which of the vegetables in the restaurant's large organic garden are ready for active duty.

2113 Manor Rd. © 512/476-5858. www.eastsidecafeaustin.com. Reservations recommended. Pastas $9–$14; main courses $13–$28. AE, DC, DISC, MC, V. Mon–Thurs 11:15am–9:30pm; Fri 11:15am–10pm; Sat 10am–10pm; Sun 10am–9:30pm (brunch Sat–Sun 10am–3pm).

INEXPENSIVE

Hoover's *Finds* *Kids* AMERICAN/SOUTHERN   Whether you call it down-home, Southern, or soul, the victuals heaped on your plate in this low-key East Side eatery will leave you feeling content. When native Austinite Alexander Hoover, long a presence on the local restaurant scene, opened up his own place near the neighborhood where he grew up, he looked to his mother's farm-grown recipes—a smidge of Cajun, a dollop of Tex-Mex—for inspiration. Fried catfish, meatloaf, gravy-smothered pork chops, sides of mac and cheese or jalapeño-creamed spinach, peach cobbler—it's all authentic and it's all tasty.

2002 Manor Rd. © 512/479-5006. www.hooverscooking.com. Reservations not accepted. Sandwiches (with 1 side) $6.50–$7.50; plates (with 2 sides) $7–$12. DC, DISC, MC, V. Mon–Fri 11am–10pm; Sat–Sun 8am–10pm.

NORTHWEST
EXPENSIVE

Z'Tejas Southwestern Grill *Value* SOUTHWEST   An offshoot of a popular downtown eatery at 1110 W. 6th St., this Arboretum restaurant is notable not only for its zippy Southwestern cuisine but also for its attractive dining space, featuring floor-to-ceiling windows, a soaring ceiling, and Santa Fe–style decor. Grilled shrimp and guacamole tostada bites make a great starter, and if you see it on a specials menu, go for the smoked chiles rellenos made with apricots and goat cheese. Entrees include a delicious horseradish-crusted salmon and a pork tenderloin stuffed with chorizo, cheese, onions, and poblano chiles. Even if you think you can't eat another bite, order a piece of ancho chile fudge pie. It will miraculously disappear.

9400-A Arboretum Blvd. ℭ **512/346-3506.** www.ztejas.com. Reservations recommended. Main courses $11–$25. AE, DC, DISC, MC, V. Mon–Thurs 11am–10pm; Fri 11am–11pm; Sat–Sun 10am–11pm.

MODERATE

Musashino ℛ JAPANESE   This place has the freshest, best-prepared sushi in town—which is why, in spite of its inauspicious location (on the southbound access road of Mo-Pac in northwest Austin) and less-than-stunning setting (beneath a Chinese restaurant called Chinatown), it's always jammed. A combination of Musashino's local star status and its policy of not accepting reservations means you're likely to have to wait awhile for a table. If you don't mind not having the entire menu at your disposal, the cozy upstairs area, which has a sushi bar and table service, but a shorter menu, is a good substitute. Be sure to ask your server what's special before you order; delicacies not listed on the regular menu are often flown in.

3407 Greystone Dr. ℭ **512/795-8593.** http://musashinosushi.com. Reservations not accepted. Sushi $2–$12 (including rolls); main courses $14–$28. AE, DC, DISC, MC, V. Mon–Fri 11:30am–2pm; Tues–Thurs and Sun 5:30–10pm; Fri–Sat 5:30–10:30pm.

WESTLAKE/LAKE TRAVIS
VERY EXPENSIVE

Hudson's on the Bend ℛℛ NEW AMERICAN   If you're game for game, served in a very civilized setting, come to Hudson's. Soft candlelight, fresh flowers, fine china, and attentive service combine with outstanding and out-of-the-ordinary cuisine to make this worth a special-occasion splurge. Sparkling lights draped over a cluster of oak trees draw you into a series of romantic dining rooms, set in an old house some 1½ miles southwest of the Mansfield Dam, near Lake Travis. The chipotle cream sauce was sufficiently spicy so that it was hard to tell whether the diamondback rattlesnake cakes tasted like chicken; but they were very good, as were the duck confit *gordita* (thick corn tortilla) and wild game tamale starters. Pecan-smoked duck breast and a mixed grill of venison, rabbit, quail, and buffalo are among the excellent entrees I've sampled. One caveat to be aware of is that the charming but acoustically poor setting can make Hudson's indoor dining rooms noisy on weekends. Opt for the terrace if the weather permits.

3509 Hwy. 620 N. ℭ **512/266-1369.** www.hudsonsonthebend.com. Reservations recommended, essential on weekends. Main courses $26–$45. AE, DC, DISC, MC, V. Sun 6–9pm; Mon–Thurs 6–9:30pm; Fri–Sat 5:30–10pm.

MODERATE

The Oasis AMERICAN/MEXICAN   This is the required spot for Austinites to take out-of-town guests at sunset. From the multilevel decks nestled into the hillside hundreds of feet above Lake Travis, visitors and locals alike cheer as the fiery orb descends behind the hills on the opposite shores. No one ever leaves unimpressed by the sunset. The food is another matter entirely: At best, it's erratic. Although different owners have tried over the years, so far no one has succeeded in getting it right all the time. Keep it simple—nachos, burgers (as opposed to, say, the crawfish étouffée enchiladas)—and you'll be okay. Then add a margarita, and kick back. It doesn't get much mellower than this.

6550 Comanche Trail, near Lake Travis. ℭ **512/266-2442.** www.oasis-austin.com. Reservations not accepted. Main courses $12–$20. AE, DC, DISC, MC, V. Mon–Thurs 11:30am–10pm; Fri 11:30am–11pm; Sat 11am–11pm; Sun 11am–10pm (brunch 11am–2pm); closing an hour earlier in fall/winter.

ONLY IN AUSTIN
MUSICAL BRUNCHES

For a religious experience on Sunday morning that doesn't require entering a more traditional place of worship, check out the gospel brunch at **Stubb's Bar-B-Q,** 801 Red River St. (© **512/480-8341**). The singing is heavenly, the pork ribs divine. At **Threadgill's World Headquarters** (p. 315), you can graze at a Southern-style buffet while listening to live inspirational sounds; find out who's playing at www.threadgills. com. If you worship at the altar of the likes of Miles Davis, the Sunday jazz brunches at **Manuel's,** 310 Congress Ave. (© **512/472-7555;** www.manuels.com), let you enjoy eggs with venison chorizo or corn gorditas with garlic and cilantro while listening to smokin' traditional or Latin jazz.

5 Seeing the Sights

I have two pieces of advice for visitors to Austin. First, don't hesitate to ask locals for directions or suggestions. Austinites are friendly and approachable. The locals have a relaxed attitude toward life, and it's common practice here for complete strangers to engage in conversation. And second, take full advantage of the city's Visitor Information Center at 209 E. 6th Street. It offers free walking tours, has pamphlets for self-guided tours, and is the point of departure for the motorized city tours. Also, you can pick up plenty of maps and brochures, including a map of the 'Dillo routes—free buses that circulate around downtown and the Capitol area for free.

What sets Austin apart from most cities, and what puts it on all the "most livable" lists is, in addition to many historic attractions and museums, the amount of green space and outdoor activities available linked with an attitude among locals bordering on nature worship. From bats and birds to Barton Springs, from the Highland Lakes to the hike-and-bike trails, Austin lays out the green carpet for its visitors. You'd be hard-pressed to find a city that has more to offer fresh-air enthusiasts.

THE TOP ATTRACTIONS
DOWNTOWN

Blanton Museum of Art ℱ   Austin finally has a serious art museum. For years the lack of one has been a source of embarrassment to those who promote the city as a haven for culture and wish for Austin to assume its place among the major cities of the country. The new Blanton fills that niche, though it comes through the efforts of the University of Texas and not the city's leading citizens. The university's art collection is ranked among the top in the United States. Most notable is the Suida-Manning Collection, a superb gathering of Renaissance works by such masters as Veronese, Rubens, and Tiepolo that was sought after by the Metropolitan museum, among others. Other permanent holdings include the Mari and James Michener collection of 20th-century American masters, a large collection of Latin American art, and a collection of 19th-century plaster casts of monumental Greek and Roman sculpture. A big success so far, the Blanton is already producing its first major show—the works of Renaissance painter Luca Cambiaso.

On the first Friday of every month the museum hosts "B scene," a social evening that mixes art with live music, wine, finger foods, and socializing.

Martin Luther King at Congress. © **512/471-7324.** www.blantonmuseum.org. $5 adults, $4 seniors (65 and older), $3 youth (13–25), free for children 12 and younger. Admission is free Thurs. Parking is $3 with validation. Tues–Sat 10am–5pm (until 8pm Thurs); Sun 1–4pm. Closed university holidays. Bus: UT Shuttle.

(Kids) Going Batty

Austin has the largest urban bat population in North America—much to the delight of Austinites. Some visitors are dubious at first, but it's impossible not to be impressed by the sight of 1.5 million of the creatures emerging en masse from under the Congress Avenue Bridge.

Each March, free-tailed bats migrate from central Mexico to various roost sites in the Southwest. In 1980, when a deck reconstruction of Austin's bridge created an ideal environment for bringing up babies, some 750,000 pregnant females began settling in every year. Each bat gives birth to a single pup, and by August these offspring take part in nightly forays east for bugs, usually around dusk. Depending on the size of the group, they might collectively munch on anywhere from 10,000 to 30,000 pounds of insects a night. By November, these youngsters are old enough to hitch rides back south with their group on the winds of an early cold front.

Bat Conservation International (© 512/327-9721; www.batcon.org), has lots of information. Log on to the website or phone 800/538-BATS for a catalog. To find out what time the bats are going to emerge from the bridge, call the *Austin American-Statesman* **Bat Hot Line** (© **512/416-5700**, category 3636).

The Bob Bullock Texas State History Museum 🌟 *Value* *Kids* You'll get a quick course in Texas 101 at this museum, opened near the state Capitol in 2001 and designed to echo some of its elements. Three floors of exhibits are arrayed around a rotunda set off by a 50-foot, polished granite map of Texas. It's an impressive building, and the permanent displays—everything from Stephen F. Austin's diary to Neil Armstrong's spacesuit—and rotating exhibits are interesting enough but, for all the interactive video clips and engaging designs (lots of different rooms to duck into; varied floor surfaces), the presentations didn't strike me as dramatically different from those in other history museums. The real treat is the multimedia, special-effects Spirit Theater, the only one of its kind in Texas, where you can experience the high-speed whoosh of the great Galveston hurricane and feel your seats rattle as an East Texas oil well hits a gusher. Austin's only IMAX theater, with 3-D capabilities, is pretty dazzling too, though the films don't necessarily have a direct relation to Texas history. If you do everything, plan to spend at least 2½ to 3 hours here.

1800 N. Congress Ave. © 512/936-8746. www.thestoryoftexas.com. Exhibit areas: $5.50 adults, $4.50 seniors 65 and older, $3 ages 5–18 (youth), free for children 4 and younger. IMAX theater: $7 adults, $6 seniors, $5 youth, $5 child. Texas Spirit Theater: $5 adults, $4 seniors, $3.50 youth, $3.50 child ages 3–4. Combination tickets: Exhibits and IMAX $10/$8/$6/$5; exhibits and Spirit Theater $8.50/$6.50/$5/$3.50; exhibits and both theaters $14/$11/ $8.50/$6.50 (children younger than 3 free to theaters if they sit in a parent's lap). Parking $8 (IMAX parking free after 6pm). Mon–Sat 9am–6pm; Sun noon–6pm. Phone or check website for additional IMAX evening hours. Closed Jan 1, Easter, Thanksgiving, and Dec 24–25. Bus: Orange or Blue 'Dillo.

State Capitol 🌟🌟 *Value* The largest state capitol in the country, second only in size to the U.S. Capitol—but measuring 7 feet taller—this 1888 building covers 3 acres of ground. A $188-million revamp restored the Capitol building and grounds to their former glory and added a striking new underground annex, which connects the Capitol and four other state buildings by tunnels. The legislative sessions are open to the public; go up to the third-floor visitors' gallery if you want see how politics are conducted Texas-style. Include the Capitol Visitors Center (p. 321), and figure on spending 2 hours, minimum, here. *Tip:* Wear comfortable shoes; you'll be doing a lot of walking.

11th and Congress sts. © 512/463-0063. www.tspb.state.tx.us. Free admission. Mon–Fri 7am–10pm; Sat–Sun 9am–8pm; hours extended during legislative sessions (held in odd years, starting in Jan, for 140 straight calendar days). Closed all major holidays. Free guided tours Mon–Fri 8:30am–4:30pm; Sat 9:30am–3:30pm; Sun noon–3:30. Bus: multiple bus lines; Orange, Red, Gold, or Blue 'Dillo.

CENTRAL
Barton Springs Pool ✦✦ *(Kids)*   If the University of Texas is the seat of Austin's intellect, and the state Capitol is its political pulse, Barton Springs is the city's soul. The Native Americans who settled near here believed these waters had spiritual powers, and today's residents still place their faith in the abilities of the spring-fed pool to soothe and cool. Each day, approximately 32 million gallons of water from the underground Edwards Aquifer bubble to the surface here; it maintains a constant 68°F (20°C) temperature year-round. Lifeguards are on duty for most of the day, and a large bathhouse operated by the Parks and Recreation Department offers changing facilities and a gift shop. The Splash! interactive exhibit, which demonstrates how the aquifer was formed and how it is sustained, is on-site.

Zilker Park, 2201 Barton Springs Rd. © 512/476-9044. www.ci.austin.tx.us/parks/bartonsprings.htm. Admission $3 adults, $2 ages 12–17, $1 seniors and children 11 and younger (admission charged only after 9am Mar 13–Oct; free for early birds). Daily 5am–10pm except during pool maintenance (Thurs 9am–7pm). Lifeguard on duty Apr–Sept 8am–10pm; Oct to early Nov 8am–8pm; mid-Nov to Mar 9am–6pm. Gift shop and Splash! Tues–Fri noon–6pm; Sat–Sun 10am–6pm. Bus: 30 (Barton Creek Sq.).

LBJ Library and Museum ✦ *(Value)*   A presidential library may sound like a big yawn, but this one's almost as interesting as the 36th president to whom it's devoted. Here, the story of Johnson's long political career, starting with his early days as a state representative and continuing through to the Kennedy assassination and the groundbreaking Great Society legislation, is told through a variety of documents, mementos, and photographs. Johnson loved political cartoons, even when he was their butt, and examples from his large collection are among the museum's most interesting rotating exhibits. Other exhibits might include anything from photographs from the American Civil Rights era to a display of presidential holiday cards. Adults and kids alike are riveted by the animatronic version of LBJ. A large, free parking lot next to the library makes it one of the few UT campus sights that's easy to drive up to.

University of Texas, 2313 Red River. © 512/721-0200. www.lbjlib.utexas.edu. Free admission. Daily 9am–5pm. Closed Dec 25. Bus: 15; Blue or Orange 'Dillo; UT Shuttle.

SOUTH AUSTIN
Lady Bird Johnson Wildflower Center ✦✦✦   Talk about fieldwork! The researchers at this lovely, colorful complex have 178 acres of wildflowers for their personal laboratory. The main attractions are naturally the display gardens—among them, one designed to attract butterflies—and the wildflower-filled meadow, but the native stone architecture of the visitor center and observation tower is attention grabbing, too. Free lectures and guided walks are usually offered on the weekends—it's best to phone or check the website for current programs. It'll take you about a half-hour to drive here from central Austin, so plan to eat lunch here and spend a leisurely half-day.

4801 La Crosse Ave. © 512/292-4200. www.wildflower.org. Admission $7 adults, $6 students and seniors 60 and older, $3 ages 5–12, free for children younger than 5. Tues–Sat 9am–5:30pm; Sun noon–5pm. (Mar–Apr rates go up to $7/$5 and grounds are open Mon.) Take Loop 1 (Mo-Pac) south to Slaughter Lane; drive ¾ mile to La Crosse Ave.

MORE ATTRACTIONS
DOWNTOWN

Bremond Block ✦ In the mid-1860s, Eugene Bremond, an early Austin banker, started investing in land on what was once Block 80 of the original city plan. In 1874, he moved into a Greek revival home made by master builder Abner Cook. By the time he was through, he had created a family compound, purchasing and enlarging homes for himself, two sisters, a daughter, a son, and a brother-in-law. Some were destroyed, but those that remain on what is now known as the Bremond Block are exquisite examples of elaborate late-19th-century homes.

Between 7th, 8th, San Antonio, and Guadalupe sts. Bus: Silver 'Dillo.

Capitol Visitors Center ✦ The Capitol wasn't the only important member of the state complex to undergo a face-lift: Texas also spent $4 million to gussy up its oldest surviving office building, the 1857 General Land Office. If the imposing German Romanesque structure looks a bit grand for the headquarters of an administrative agency, keep in mind that land has long been the state's most important resource. Among the employees of this important—and very political—office was the writer O. Henry, who worked as a draftsman from 1887 to 1891. He based two short stories on his experiences here.

112 E. 11th St. (southeast corner of Capitol grounds). © 512/305-8400. www.texascapitolvisitorscenter.com. Free admission. Daily 9am–5pm. Bus: Gold, Orange, Red, or Blue 'Dillo.

The Driskill Col. Jesse Driskill was not a modest man. When he opened a hotel in 1886, he named it after himself, put busts of himself and his two sons over the entrances, and installed bas-relief sculptures of longhorn steers—to remind folks how he had made his fortune. Nor did he build a modest property. The ornate four-story structure, which originally boasted a sky-lit rotunda, has the largest arched doorway in Texas over its east entrance. It's so posh that the state legislature met here while the 1888 Capitol was being built. The hotel has had its ups and downs over the years, but it was restored to its former glory in the late 1990s.

604 Brazos St. © 512/474-5911. Bus: Silver, Blue, or Red 'Dillo.

Governor's Mansion ✦ Although this is one of the oldest buildings in the city (1856), this opulent house is far from a mere symbol or museum piece. State law requires that the governor live here whenever he or she is in Austin.

That isn't exactly a hardship, although it was originally built by Abner Cook without any indoor toilets (there are now seven). Among the many historical artifacts on display are a desk belonging to Stephen F. Austin and portraits of Davy Crockett and Sam Houston. Only a limited number of visitors are allowed to tour the mansion, so make your required advance reservations as soon as you know when you're planning to visit—and at least 1 business day ahead of time.

1010 Colorado St. © 512/463-5516 (recorded information) or 463-5518 (tour reservations). www.txfgm.org. Free admission. Tours generally offered every 20 min. Mon–Thurs 10am–noon (last tour starts 11:40am). Closed Fri, weekends, some holidays, and at the discretion of the governor; call the 24-hr. information line to see if tours are offered the day you want to visit. Bus: Red, Blue, Gold, or Orange 'Dillo.

MEXIC-ARTE Museum The first organization in Austin to promote multicultural contemporary art when it was formed in 1983, MEXIC-ARTE has a small permanent collection of 20th-century Mexican art, including photographs from the Mexican revolution and a fascinating array of masks from the state of Guerrero. It's supplemented by visiting shows—including some from Mexico, such as a recent survey of south-of-the-border contemporary art—and a back gallery of works of local Latino artists.

419 Congress Ave. (C) 512/480-9373. www.mexic-artemuseum.org. Admission $5 adults, $4 seniors and students, $1 children younger than 12. Mon–Thurs 10am–6pm; Fri–Sat 10am–5pm; Sun noon–5pm. Bus: Red 'Dillo.

6th Street   Formerly known as Pecan Street, 6th Street was once the main connecting road to the older settlements east of Austin. During the Reconstruction boom of the 1870s, the wooden wagon yards and saloons of the 1850s and 1860s began to be replaced by the more solid masonry structures you see today. After the new state Capitol was built in 1888, the center of commercial activity began shifting toward Congress Avenue, and by the middle of the next century, 6th Street had become a skid row. Restoration of the 9 blocks designated a National Register District began in the late 1960s. In the 1970s, the street started thriving as a live-music center. Austin's former main street is now lined with restaurants, galleries, bars, and shops. On any night you'll find a mostly young crowd walking the sidewalks looking for just the right bar.

Between Lavaca Ave. and I-35. Bus: Silver 'Dillo.

CENTRAL

Elisabet Ney Museum ⚘   Strong-willed and eccentric, German-born sculptor Elisabet Ney nevertheless charmed Austin society in the late 19th century. When she died, her admirers turned her Hyde Park studio into a museum. In the former loft and working area—part Greek temple, part medieval battlement—visitors can view plaster replicas of many of the artist's sculptures. Drawn toward the larger-than-life figures of her age, Ney had created busts of Schopenhauer, Garibaldi, and Bismarck by the time she was commissioned to make models of native Texas heroes Stephen F. Austin and Sam Houston for an 1893 Chicago exposition.

304 E. 44th St. (C) 512/458-2255. www.ci.austin.tx.us/elisabetney. Free admission. Wed–Sat 10am–5pm; Sun noon–5pm. Bus: 1 or 5.

Harry Ransom Humanities Research Center ⚘   The special collections of the HRC contain approximately 1 million rare books (including a Gutenberg Bible); 30 million literary manuscripts (including those by James Joyce, Ernest Hemingway, and Tennessee Williams); 5 million photographs, including the world's first; and more than 100,000 works of art, with several pieces by Diego Rivera and Frida Kahlo. Most of this wealth remains in the domain of scholars, although anyone can request a look at it, but since two new galleries were opened in 2003, visitors are treated to select portions of it in excellent rotating exhibitions.

University of Texas, Harry Ransom Center, 21st and Guadalupe sts. (C) 512/471-8944. www.hrc.utexas.edu. Free admission. Galleries Tues–Wed and Fri 10am–5pm; Thurs 10am–7pm; Sat–Sun noon–5pm; call for reading-room hours. Closed university holidays. Bus: Blue 'Dillo; UT Shuttle.

Texas Memorial Museum *(Kids*   This museum, opened in 1936 to guard the natural and cultural treasures of the state, is now devoted to the natural sciences alone. Despite a major revamp in the early 2000s, it still seems oddly old-fashioned in parts, especially the lifeless dioramas and weird stuff in jars on the fourth floor. But kids will like first-floor Hall of Geology, with its huge Texas Pterosaur—the largest flying creature ever found—suspended from the ceiling.

University of Texas, 2400 Trinity St. (C) **512/471-1604**. www.texasmemorialmuseum.org. Free admission (donations appreciated). Mon–Fri 9am–5pm; Sat 10am–5pm; Sun 1–5pm. Closed major holidays. Bus: 7, 103, 110, 127, 171, or 174; Orange 'Dillo.

EAST SIDE

French Legation Museum   The oldest residence still standing in Austin was built in 1841 for Count Alphonse Dubois de Saligny, France's representative to the fledgling Republic of Texas. Although his home was extravagant for the then-primitive capital, the flamboyant de Saligny didn't stay around to enjoy it for very long: He left town in a huff after his servant was beaten in retaliation for making bacon out of some pigs that had dined on the diplomat's linens. In the back of the house, considered the best example of French colonial–style architecture outside Louisiana, is a re-creation of the only known authentic Creole kitchen in the United States.

802 San Marcos. (C) **512/472-8180**. www.frenchlegationmuseum.org. Admission $4 adults, $3 seniors, $2 students/ teachers, free for children 5 and younger. Tours Tues–Sun 1–4:30pm. Bus: 4 and 18 stop nearby (at San Marcos and 7th sts.); Silver 'Dillo. Go east on 7th St., then turn left on San Marcos St.; the parking lot is behind the museum on Embassy and 9th sts.

GREEN SPACES

Zilker Botanical Garden ★ *Kids*   There's bound to be something blooming at the Zilker Botanical Garden from March to October, but no matter what time of year you visit, you'll find this a soothing outdoor oasis to spend some time in. The Oriental Garden, created by the landscape architect Isamu Taniguchi when he was 70 years old, is particularly peaceful. A butterfly garden attracts gorgeous winged visitors during April and October migrations, and you can poke and prod the many plants in the herb garden to get them to yield their fragrances. One-hundred-million-year-old dinosaur tracks, discovered on the grounds in the early 1990s, are part of the 1.5-acre Hartman Prehistoric Garden, which includes plants from the Cretaceous Period and a 13-foot bronze sculpture of an Ornithomimus dinosaur.

2220 Barton Springs Rd. (C) **512/477-8672**. http://zilkergarden.org. Free admission. Grounds dawn–dusk. Garden center Mon–Fri 8:30am–4pm; Sat 10am–5pm (Jan–Feb 1–5pm); Sun 1–5pm (sometimes open earlier on weekends for special garden shows; phone ahead). Bus: 30.

Zilker Park ★ *Kids*   Comprising 347 acres, the first 40 of which were donated to the city by the wealthy German immigrant for whom the park is named, this is Austin's favorite public playground. Its centerpiece is Barton Springs Pool (see "The Top Attractions," earlier in this chapter), but visitors and locals also flock to the Zilker Botanical Garden, the Austin Nature Preserves, and the Umlauf Sculpture Garden and Museum. See also the "Especially for Kids" and "Staying Active" sections for details about the Austin Nature and Science Center, the Zilker Zephyr Miniature Train, and Town Lake canoe rentals. In addition to its athletic fields (nine for soccer, one for rugby, and two multiuse), the park hosts a 9-hole disk (Frisbee) golf course and a sand volleyball court.

2201 Barton Springs Rd. (C) **512/476-9044**. www.ci.austin.tx.us/zilker. Free admission. Daily 5am–10pm. Bus: 30.

ESPECIALLY FOR KIDS

The Bob Bullock Texas State History Museum (p. 319) and the **Texas Memorial Museum** (p. 322), are child-friendly, but outdoor attractions are still Austin's biggest draw for children. There's lots of room for children to splash around at **Barton Springs,** and even youngsters who thought bats were creepy are likely to be converted on further acquaintance with the critters.

In addition, kids enjoy the **Austin Children's Museum** 𝒶𝒶, Dell Discovery Center, 201 Colorado St. (℗ **512/472-2499;** www.austinkids.org), a rambling state-of-the-art facility that's got everything from low-key but creative playscapes for tots to studio sound-stage replicas for teens. Bats, bees, and crystal caverns are among the subjects of the Discovery Boxes at the 80-acre **Austin Nature and Science Center** 𝒶, Zilker Park, 301 Nature Center Dr. (℗ **512/327-8181**), which also abounds with interactive exhibits involving rescued animals. The Dino Pit is a lure for budding paleontologists. The scenic 25-minute ride on the narrow-gauge **Zilker Zephyr Miniature Train,** 2100 Barton Springs Rd., just across from the Barton Springs Pool (℗ **512/478-8286**), goes at a leisurely pace through Zilker Park along Barton Creek and Town Lake.

ORGANIZED TOURS

The aquatically inclined might consider taking one of the electric-powered **Capital Cruises** (℗ **512/480-9264;** www.capitalcruises.com), which ply Town Lake March through October. Options include bat-viewing cruises, fajita dinner cruises, and afternoon sightseeing excursions. Similar itineraries are offered by **Lone Star River Boat** (℗ **512/327-1388**), but they go farther upstream and add narration. Both companies depart from the dock near the Hyatt Regency Hotel. Can't decide between sea and land? Board one of the six-wheel-drive amphibious vehicles operated by **Austin Duck Adventures** (℗ **512/4-SPLASH;** www.austinducks.com). After exploring Austin's historic downtown and scenic west side, you'll splash into Lake Austin. Tours board in front of the Austin Convention & Visitors Bureau, 209 E. 6th St. See "Austin After Dark," below, for details on touring the Austin City Limits studio.

WALKING TOURS

Whatever price you pay, you won't find better guided walks than the informative and entertaining **tours** 𝒶𝒶 offered free of charge by the **Austin Convention and Visitors Bureau (ACVB;** ℗ **866/GO-AUSTIN** or 512/454-1545; www.austintexas.org) from March through November. Ninety-minute tours of the historic Bremond Block leave every Saturday and Sunday at 11am; Congress Avenue/East 6th Street is explored for 1½ hours on Thursday, Friday, and Saturday starting at 9am, Sunday at 2pm. The hour-long Capitol Grounds tour is conducted on Saturday at 2pm and Sunday at 9am. All tours depart promptly from the south entrance of the Capitol, weather permitting. Be warned, though: Come even a few minutes late and you'll miss out.

6 Staying Active

OUTDOOR FUN

BIKING   A city that has a "bicycle coordinator" on its payroll, Austin is a cyclist's dream. Contact **Austin Parks and Recreation,** 200 S. Lamar Blvd. (℗ **512/974-6700;** www.ci.austin.tx.us/parks), for information on the city's more than 25 miles of scenic paths, the most popular of which are the Barton Creek Greenbelt (7.8 miles) and the Town Lake Greenbelt (10 miles). The **Veloway,** a 3.1-mile paved loop in Slaughter Creek Metropolitan Park, is devoted exclusively to bicyclists and in-line skaters.

You can rent bikes and get maps and other information from **University Cyclery,** 2901 N. Lamar Blvd. (℗ **512/474-6696;** www.universitycyclery.com). A number of downtown hotels rent or provide free bicycles to their guests. For information on weekly road rides, contact the **Austin Cycling Association,** P.O. Box 5993, Austin, TX 78763 (℗ **512/282-7413;** www.austincycling.org), which also publishes a monthly newsletter, *Southwest Cycling News,* though only local calls or e-mails are returned. For rougher mountain-bike routes, try the **Austin Ridge Riders.** Their website, www. austinridgeriders.com, will have the latest contact information.

CANOEING   You can rent canoes at **Zilker Park,** 2000 Barton Springs Rd. (© **512/ 478-3852;** www.fastair.com/zilker), for $10 an hour or $30 all day (daily Apr–Sept; only weekends, holidays, weather permitting, Oct–Mar). **Capital Cruises,** Hyatt Regency boat dock (© **512/480-9264;** www.capitalcruises.com), also offers hourly rentals on Town Lake. If your paddling skills are a bit rusty, check out the instructional courses of UT's **Recreational Sports Outdoor Program** (© **512/471-3116**).

GOLF   For information about Austin's six municipal golf courses, call © **512/974- 9350** or log on to www.ci.austin.tx.us/parks/golf.htm. Each offers pro shops and equipment rental, and their greens fees are very reasonable. Among them are the 9-hole **Hancock,** which was built in 1899 and is the oldest course in Texas, and the 18-hole **Lions,** where Tom Kite and Ben Crenshaw played college golf for the University of Texas.

HIKING   Austin's parks and preserves abound in nature trails; see "Austin Outdoors" in the "More Attractions," section earlier in this chapter, for additional information. Contact the **Sierra Club** (© **512/472-1767;** www.texas.sierraclub.org/ austin) if you're interested in organized hikes. **Wild Basin Wilderness Preserve** (© **512/327-7622;** www.wildbasin.org) is another source for guided treks, offering periodic "Haunted Trails" tours along with its more typical hikes.

SWIMMING   The best known of Austin's natural swimming holes is **Barton Springs Pool** (see "The Top Attractions," earlier in this chapter), but it's by no means the only one. Other scenic outdoor spots to take the plunge include **Deep Eddy Pool,** 401 Deep Eddy Ave. at Lake Austin Boulevard (© **512/472-8546**), and **Hamilton Pool Preserve,** 27 miles west of Austin, off Texas 71 on FM 3238 (© **512/264-2740**).

For lakeshore swimming, consider **Hippie Hollow** on Lake Travis, 2½ miles off FM 620 (www.co.travis.tx.us/tnr/parks/hippie_hollow.asp), where you can let it all hang out in a series of clothing-optional coves, or **Emma Long Metropolitan Park** on Lake Austin (© **512/346-1831** or 512/346-3807).

You can also get into the swim at a number of **free neighborhood pools;** contact the City Aquatics Department (© **512/476-4521;** www.ci.austin.tx.us/parks/aquatics. htm) for more information.

SPECTATOR SPORTS

There are no professional teams in Austin, but a minor-league baseball team and a new arena football team have captured local attention. College sports are very big, particularly when the **University of Texas (UT) Longhorns** are playing. The most comprehensive source of information on the various teams is www.texassports.com, but you can phone the **UT Athletics Ticket Office** (© **512/471-3333**) to find out about schedules and **UTTM Charge-A-Ticket** (© **512/477-6060**) to order tickets.

BASEBALL   The **University of Texas** baseball team goes to bat February through May at Disch-Falk Field (just east of I-35, at the corner of Martin Luther King, Jr., Blvd. and Comal). Many players from this former NCAA championship squad have gone on to the big time, including two-time Cy Young award winner Roger Clemens.

Baseball Hall-of-Famer Nolan Ryan's **Round Rock Express,** a Houston Astros farm club, won the Texas League championship in 1999, their first year in existence (they now compete in the Pacific Coast League). See them play at the Dell Diamond, 3400

E. Palm Valley Rd. in Round Rock (© **512/255-BALL** or 244-4209; www.roundrock express.com), an 8,688-seat stadium where you can choose from box seats or stadium seating—and an additional 3,000 fans can sit on a grassy berm in the outfield. Tickets range from about $6 to $12.

BASKETBALL   The **University of Texas** Longhorn and Lady Longhorn basketball teams, both former Southwest Conference champions, play in the Frank C. Erwin, Jr., Special Events Center (just west of I-35 on Red River between Martin Luther King, Jr., Blvd. and 15th St.) November through March.

FOOTBALL   It's hard to tell which is more central to the success of an Austin Thanksgiving: the turkey or the UT–Texas A&M game. Part of the Big 12 Conference, the **University of Texas** football team often fills the huge Darrell K. Royal/Texas Memorial Stadium (just west of I-35 between 23rd and 21st sts., E. Campus Dr., and San Jacinto Blvd.) during home games, played August through November.

Fans of smaller-field, indoor professional football welcomed the **Austin Wranglers** (© **512/491-6600;** www.austinwranglers.com) to the ranks of the Arena Football League in 2004. The Wranglers play at the Erwin Center (see "Basketball," above).

GOLF   Initiated in 2003 and boasting a $1.6-million purse, The **FedEx Kinko's Classic** (© **512/732-2666;** www.fedexkinkosclassic.com), is part of the PGA's Champions Tour, and is held at the Hills Country Club at Lakeway Resort.

HOCKEY   The **Austin Ice Bats** hockey team (© **512/927-PUCK;** www.icebats. com) has been getting anything but an icy reception from its Austin fans. This typically rowdy team plays at the Travis County Exposition Center, 7311 Decker Lane (about 15 min. east of UT). Tickets, which run from $10 to $35, are available at any UTTM outlet or from **Star Tickets** (© **888/597-STAR** or 512/469-SHOW; www. startickets.com). The team generally plays on weekends mid-October through late March; a phone call will get you the exact dates and times.

7 Shopping

THE SHOPPING SCENE
When it comes to items intellectual, musical, or ingestible, Austin is a match for cities twice its size. Shopping here may not quite have evolved into an art as it has in glitzier Texas towns like Houston or Dallas, but Austin has a more than satisfying range of ways to spend your money, plus several unique retail niches.

Specialty shops in Austin tend to open around 9 or 10am, Monday through Saturday, and close at about 5:30 or 6pm; many have Sunday hours from noon until 6pm. Malls tend to keep the same Sunday schedule, but Monday through Saturday they don't close their doors until 9pm. Sales tax in Austin is 8.25%.

GREAT SHOPPING AREAS
Downtown, specialty shops and art galleries are filtering back to the renovated 19th-century buildings along **6th Street** and **Congress Avenue.** A little to the west, around 6th Street and Lamar Boulevard, the **Market District,** anchored by a huge new Whole Foods Complex, is accelerating its expansion. Below Town Lake, **South Congress Avenue** is still attracting trendy art galleries, boutiques, and antiques stores, but the funkier, less expensive shops are cropping up on the (currently) lower-rent **South 1st Street** and **South Lamar Boulevard.** In the vicinity of Central Market, between West

35th and 40th streets and Lamar and Mo-Pac, such small shopping centers as Jefferson Square are similarly charming. Many stores on **the Drag**—the stretch of Guadalupe Street between Martin Luther King Jr. Boulevard and 26th Street, across from the University of Texas campus—are student oriented, but a wide range of clothing, gifts, toys, and, of course, books can also be found here.

Much of Austin's shopping has moved out to the malls. One of the newer growth areas is in the northwest, where three upscale shopping centers, **The Arboretum, The Arboretum Market,** and the **Gateway Shopping Centers** (consisting of Gateway Courtyard, the Gateway Market, and Gateway Square) have earned the area the nickname "South Dallas."

THE GOODS A TO Z
ART

It's not exactly SoHo, but the area just northwest of the Capitol and south of the University of Texas—specifically, the block bounded by Guadalupe and Lavaca to the west and east and 17th and 18th streets to the south and north—has a large concentration of galleries. They include the group clustered in the **Guadalupe Arts Building,** 1705 Guadalupe, as well as Women & Their Work (see below).

Austin's commitment to music makes it a perfect location for **Wild About Music,** 115 E 6th St. (© **512/708-1700;** www.wildaboutmusic.com), a gallery and shop strictly devoted to arts and crafts with a musical theme. Come see the multimedia prints by Texas musician Joe Ely, the instrument-shaped furniture, and the unique Texas music T-shirt collection. Winning the nod for Best Gallery from the *Austin Chronicle* in 2006, **Women & Their Work,** 1710 Lavaca St. (© **512/477-1064;** www. womenandtheirwork.org), highlights more than visual art—it also promotes and showcases women in dance, music, theater, film, and literature. "Outsider" art, created in the rural South, usually by the poor and sometimes by the incarcerated, is not for everyone, but for those interested in contemporary American folk art, **Yard Dog Folk Art,** 1510 S. Congress Ave. (© **512/912-1613;** www.yarddog.com), is not to be missed. Colorful hand-woven cloth from Guatemala, intricate weavings from Peru, glassware, jewelry, and tinwork from Mexico—all these and more are available at **Tesoros,** 209 Congress Ave. (© **512/479-8377;** www.tesoros.com), which (in addition to its high-quality folk art) also offers a limited selection of furniture, dishes, and housewares from Latin America. A dazzling panoply of hand-painted furniture, pottery, and art—new and old—from around the world is beautifully presented at **Eclectic,** 700 N. Lamar Blvd. (© **512/477-1816**).

FOOD

Not only can you buy every imaginable edible item at **Central Market,** 4001 N. Lamar (© **512/206-1000;** www.centralmarket.com), fresh or frozen, local or imported, but you can also enjoy the cooking of a top-notch chef in the restaurant section. Prices are surprisingly reasonable. The newer Westgate Shopping Center branch, 4477 S. Lamar, in South Austin (© **512/899-4300**), is as impressive as the original. The first link in what is now the world's largest organic and natural foods supermarket, **Whole Foods Market,** 525 N. Lamar (© **512/476-1206**), celebrated its 25th birthday in early 2005 by opening an 80,000-square-foot store near its original downtown location, creating a 600-seat amphitheater, a playscape, gardens, on-site massages, a cooking school, and more. The northwest store in Gateway Market, 9607 Research Blvd. (© **512/345-5003**), was not subjected to an extreme makeover.

In addition to hosting some of the nation's most impressive mega-groceries, Austin also has an abundance of farmers' markets. Perhaps the most notable of them, **Austin Farmers' Market,** held downtown at Republic Square Park, 4th Street at Guadalupe, every Saturday from 9am to 1pm March through November (© **512/236-0074;** www.austinfarmersmarket.com), not only features food products but also live music, cooking demonstrations, kids' activities, and workshops on everything from organic gardening to aromatherapy.

MUSIC
Carrying a huge selection of sounds, **Waterloo Records and Video,** 600A N. Lamar Blvd. (© **512/474-2500;** www.waterloorecords.com), is always the first in town to get the new releases. The store has a popular preview listening section, offers compilation tapes of Austin groups, and sells tickets to all major-label shows around town.

RUNNING GEAR
Owned by the footwear editor for *Runner's World* magazine and serving as the official wear-test center for that publication, **Run-Tex,** 422 W. Riverside Dr. (© **512/472-3254;** www.runtex.com), not only has a huge inventory of shoes and other running gear, but also does everything it can to promote healthful jogging practices, even offering free running classes and a free injury-evaluation clinic. There's also a larger Run-Tex in Gateway Market, 9901 Capital of Texas Hwy. (© **512/343-1164**), a location at 2201 Lake Austin Blvd. (© **512/477-9464**), and the related **WalkTex,** 4001 N. Lamar (© **512/454-WALK**), but the downtown store is right near the Austin runner's mecca, Town Lake.

TEXAS SOUVENIRS
Over the years, visitors have admired—sometimes excessively—the intricately designed door hinges of the Capitol. The gift shop at the **Capitol Visitors Center,** 112 E. 11th St. (© **512/305-8400;** www.texascapitolvisitorscenter.com), sells brass bookends made from the original model used, during the Capitol's renovation, to cast replacements for hinges that were cadged over the years. Other Texana includes local food products and historical books. See also **Wild About Music,** listed under "Art" above.

WESTERN WEAR
Name notwithstanding, **Allen's Boots,** 1522 S. Congress (© **512/447-1413**), sells a lot more than footwear. Come here too for hats, belts, jewelry, and other boot-scootin' accouterments (bring the youngins, too). The custom-made boots of the **Capitol Saddlery,** 1614 Lavaca St. (© **512/478-9309;** www.capitolsaddlery.com), were immortalized in a song by Jerry Jeff Walker. This three-level store, in the same family for 7 decades, is a bit chaotic, but you can't beat it for authentic cowboy gear.

8 Austin After Dark

It's hard to imagine an itch for entertainment, high or low, that Austin couldn't scratch. For starters, live music is found everywhere and in just about every genre. And the level of virtuosity is impressive. Many famous musicians such as the Dixie Chicks and Shawn Colvin call Austin home and frequently perform here. But there is also a large number of lesser known but great performers, who for one reason or another are content to stay in Austin and enjoy a comfortable and modest level of success.

The live music scene is also extremely inexpensive. Some really good bands play for tips on weekdays and for starving-artist pay at other times. This has been true for years, and it makes you feel that the city is getting a lot more from this arrangement than it's having to put out. Not that Austin doesn't try to support its local musicians. Some group or other is always organizing benefit concerts or free public concerts to promote the local talent.

Keep an eye out for these kinds of performances by checking out the *Austin Chronicle* and *XLent,* the entertainment supplement of the *Austin-American Statesman.* Both are available in hundreds of outlets every Thursday.

Unbeknownst to a lot of people, there is more to the performing arts here than just the club scene. Theater and dance have strong community support. You can call the **Austin Circle of Theaters Hot Line** (𝄢 **512/416-5700,** ext. 1603; www.acotonline. org) to find out what's on the boards each week. If you want to know who's kicking around, phone **Danceline** (𝄢 **512/416-5700,** ext. 3262).

The University of Texas brings many touring performances to town and also hosts local concerts and productions. You can reach Texas Box Office at www.texasboxoffice. com or 𝄢 **512/477-6060;** there are also outlets in most HEB grocery stores.

Some of the concerts at La Zona Rosa, the Backyard, and Austin Music Hall, and selected shows at the Paramount Theatre, can be booked through **Star Tickets Plus** (𝄢 **888/597-STAR** or 512/469-SHOW; http://premier.ticketsplus.net), with outlets in most Albertson's grocery stores.

The **Austix Box Office,** 3423 Guadalupe (𝄢 **512/474-8497** or 416-5700, ext. 1603; www.austix.com), handles phone charges for many of the smaller theaters in Austin, as well as half-price ticket sales. Call for a recorded listing of what's currently being discounted, then pick up tickets at the Austix Box Office or at the **Austin Visitors Center,** 209 E. 6th (at the corner of Brazos) Tuesday through Thursday from noon to 6pm, Friday and Saturday from noon to 7pm. Half-price tickets are also on sale at **Bookpeople,** 603 N. Lamar Blvd. (𝄢 **512/472-5050**), on Thursday from 4 to 7pm.

The newest ticket service in town, **Front Gate Tickets** (𝄢 **512/389-0315;** www. frontgatetickets.com), handles Austin City Limits Festival tickets as well as those for some of the larger shows at Stubb's, Antone's, La Zona Rosa, the Parish, and the Vibe.

THE PERFORMING ARTS

Austin has its own symphony, theater, ballet, lyric opera, and modern dance companies, but it also draws national and international talent to town. Much of the action, local and imported, takes place at the University of Texas's **Performing Arts Center** (PAC), but many of the performances will move to a new venue in the summer of 2008. A civic association promoting the performing arts has collected millions of dollars in donations and is busy at work building a new complex to be called the **Long Center.** It will hold a large concert hall, a theater, and other facilities. The building is located on the south side of Town Lake at Riverside Drive between South First and Lamar, and looks to be a striking piece of architecture.

OPERA & CLASSICAL MUSIC

A resident in Austin since 1911, the **Austin Symphony,** 1101 Red River St. 𝄢 **888/4-MAESTRO** or 512/476-6064; www.austinsymphony.org), performs most of its classical works at Bass Concert Hall. The city's first professional opera company, **Austin Lyric Opera,** 901 Barton Springs Rd. (𝄢 **800/31-OPERA,** or 512/472-5992 for box office; www.austinlyricopera.org), presents three or four productions annually. **The Austin Chamber Music Center,** 4930 Burnet Rd., Suite 203 (© **512/454-7562** or 512/454-0026; www.austinchambermusic.org), features an Intimate Concert series, open to the public but held at elegant private homes, and hosts visiting national and international artists.

THEATER

The **State Theater Company,** 719 Congress Ave. (© **512/472-5143** or 472-7134; www.austintheatre.org), which performs at the beautiful old theater for which it is named, is Austin's most professional troupe, and their recent repertoire ran the gamut from Judith Ivey's *Women on Fire* to a dramatization of Orwell's *1984.* Austin's oldest theater, incorporated in 1933, the **Zachary Scott Theatre Center** (© **512/476-0541** [box office] or 476-0594; www.zachscott.com), makes use of two adjacent venues at the edge of Zilker Park: the John E. Whisenhunt Arena at 1510 Toomey Rd., and the theater-in-the-round Kleburg at 1421 W. Riverside Dr.

DANCE

The two dozen professional dancers of **Ballet Austin** (© **512/476-2163** [box office] or 476-9051; www.balletaustin.org) leap and bound in such classics as *The Nutcracker* and *Swan Lake,* as well as in the more avant-garde pieces of the trendsetting *Director's Choice* series, which pairs the work of various contemporary choreographers with the music of popular local Latin musicians and singer-songwriters. When in town, the troupe performs at Bass Concert Hall or the Paramount Theatre.

THE CLUB & MUSIC SCENE

The appearance of country-and-western "outlaw" Willie Nelson at the Armadillo World Headquarters in 1972 united hippies and rednecks in a common musical cause, and is often credited with the birth of the live-music scene on Austin's **6th Street.** The city has since become an incubator for a wonderfully vital, crossbred alternative sound that mixes rock, country, folk, blues, punk, and tejano. Although the Armadillo is now defunct, live music in Austin is very much alive, just more geographically diffuse. There's always something happening downtown on 6th Street or in the **Warehouse District,** and, most recently, on the stretch of **Red River** between 6th and 10th streets.

CLUB/DANCE

A series of narrow black-and-white rooms with retro minimalist furnishings, **Oslo,** 301 W. 6th St (© **512/480-9433**), is *the* place to see and be seen in Austin, with lines out the door. The club plays host to a strong roster of the city's finest DJs, as well as live performers such as regular Tuesday-night torch singer, Hedda Layne.

FOLK & COUNTRY

The Broken Spoke, 3201 S. Lamar Blvd. (© **512/442-6189;** www.brokenspoke austintx.com), is the genuine item, a Western honky-tonk dating from 1964 with a wood-plank floor and a cowboy-hatted, two-steppin' crowd. Still, it's in Austin, so don't be surprised if the band wears Hawaiian shirts, or if tongues are firmly in cheek for some of the songs. Although it also showcases rock, rockabilly, and new wave sounds, the **Continental Club,** 1315 S. Congress Ave. (© **512/441-2444;** www.continental club.com), holds on to its roots in traditional country, celebrating events such as Hank Williams's birthday. A small, smoky club with high stools and a pool table in the back room, this is a not-to-be-missed Austin classic.

JAZZ & BLUES

Although Willie Nelson and crossover country-and-western bands such as the Austin Lounge Lizards have been known to turn up at **Antone's,** 213 W. 5th St. (© 512/ 320-8424; www.antones.net), the club has always been synonymous with the blues. Stevie Ray Vaughan used to be a regular and when major blues artists like Buddy Guy or Etta James venture down this way you can be sure they'll either be playing Antone's or stopping by for a surprise set. Stars on location in Austin mingle with T-shirted students and well-dressed older aficionados at the **Elephant Room,** 315 Congress Ave. (© 512/473-2279; www.natespace.com/elephant), an intimate space that's as dark and smoky as a jazz club should be.

ROCK

Austin's last word in alternative music, **Emo's,** 603 Red River St. (© 512/477-EMOS; www.emosaustin.com), draws acts of all sizes and flavors, from Gang Green to Green Day. It primarily attracts college kids, but you won't really feel out of place at any age. Another good representative of the hot new music scene along Red River north of 6th Street, the **Red-Eyed Fly,** 715 Red River St. (© 512/474-1084; www.redeyedfly.com), showcases Texas's top hard-rock, pop, and punk bands—as well as national touring acts—at its great outdoor stage. Inside, the jukebox rocks with local sounds.

SINGER/SONGWRITER

A small, dark cavern with great acoustics and a fully stocked bar, the **Cactus Café,** Texas Union, University of Texas campus (24th and Guadalupe; © 512/475-6515; www.utexas.edu/student/txunion/ae/cactus), is singer/songwriter heaven. The attentive listening vibes attract the likes of Alison Krauss and Suzanne Vega, along with well-known acoustic combos. The adjacent **Texas Union Ballroom** (© 512/475-6645) draws larger crowds with big names like the Dixie Chicks.

Located in the parking garage of an apartment building, **Ego's,** 510 S. Congress Ave. (© 512/474-7091), is dark, smoky, seedy, and loads of fun. Locals throng here for the strong drinks and live nightly music, from piano to honky-tonk country. You'll recognize the **Saxon Pub,** 1320 S. Lamar Blvd. (© 512/448-2552; www.thesaxon pub.com), a long-standing home to South Austin's large community of singer/ songwriters, by the giant knight in shining armor in the parking lot. The walk down a dark alley in the Warehouse District to reach the multilevel **Speakeasy,** 412 Congress Ave. (© 512/476-8086; www.speakeasyaustin.com), is all part of the 1920s Prohibition theme, which, mercifully, is not taken to an obnoxious extreme. Rather, a swanky atmosphere is created by lots of dark wood and red-velvet drapes on the side of the stage. The romantic Evergreen terrace affords a nice view of downtown.

ECLECTIC

A terrific sound system and a casual country atmosphere have helped make **The Backyard,** Tex. 71 West at R.R. 620, Bee Cave (© 512/263-4146; www.thebackyard.net), one of Austin's hottest venues. Since it opened in the early 1990s, the Allman Brothers, Elvis Costello, Norah Jones, kd lang, and Bonnie Raitt have all played the terraced outdoor amphitheater. An Austin classic, **La Zona Rosa,** 612 W. 4th St. (© 512/263-4146; www.lazonarosa.com), has departed from its funky roots a bit to feature bigger names and bigger covers than in the past. But this renovated garage filled with kitschy memorabilia is still a prime spot to listen to good bands. Within the rough limestone walls of **Stubb's,** 801 Red River St. (© 512/480-8341; www.stubbsaustin.com), you'll find great barbecue, three friendly bars, and terrific music ranging from singer/songwriter solos to hip-hop open mics to all-out country jams. Out back, the Waller Amphitheatre hosts some of the bigger acts. The Sunday gospel brunches are fast becoming an Austin institution.

THE BAR SCENE
A HISTORIC BAR

Since 1866, when councilman August Scholz first opened his tavern near the state Capitol, every Texas governor has visited **Scholz Garten,** 1607 San Jacinto Blvd. (© **512/474-1958**), at least once (and many quite a few more times). An extensive menu combines barbecue favorites with traditional bratwurst and sauerkraut; a state-of-the-art sound system cranks out polka tunes; and patio tables and a few strategically placed TV sets help Longhorn fans cheer on their team. All in all, a great place to drink in some Austin history.

GAY BARS

Its name notwithstanding, **Oilcan Harry's,** 211 W. 4th St. (© **512/320-8823;** www.oilcanharrys.com), attracts a clean-cut, upscale Warehouse District crowd, while **The Rainbow Cattle Co.,** 305 W. 5th St. (© **512/472-5288;** www.rainbowcattleco.com), is Austin's prime gay country-and-western dance hall. It's about 75% male, but also attracts a fair share of lesbian two-steppers, especially on Thursday, which is Ladies Night. For more venues, log on to **http://austin.about.com/cs/gaynightlife.**

LOCAL FAVORITES

The **Cedar Door,** 201 Brazos (© **512/473-3712;** www.cedardooraustin.com), remains Austin's favorite neighborhood bar, drawing a group of potluck regulars ranging from hippies to journalists and politicos. At **Club de Ville,** 900 Red River St. (© **512/457-0900**), you can settle in on one of the couches inside—the low red light is both atmospheric and flattering—or lounge under the stars, where a natural limestone cliff creates a private walled patio.

9 Hill Country Side Trips from Austin

The following destinations in Texas's Hill Country, one of the state's prettiest regions, can be visited on day trips from Austin, but you'll get more of the region's leisurely flavor with a sleepover. Trips to the areas detailed here can easily be combined with those described in the "Hill Country Side Trips from San Antonio" section in chapter 7. To locate these towns, see the "South-Central Texas" map on p. 247.

FREDERICKSBURG ✦

Fredericksburg may have become fairly touristy, but it also remains devoted to its European past. Baron Ottfried Hans von Meusebach was one of 10 nobles who formed a society designed to help Germans resettle in Texas, where they would be safe from political persecution and economic hardship. In 1846, he took 120 settlers in ox-drawn carts from New Braunfels to this site, which he named for Prince Frederick of Prussia. The town's mile-long main street is still wide enough for a team of oxen to turn around in (although that hasn't been tested lately). The permanent peace treaty Meusebach negotiated with the Comanches in 1847, claimed to be the only one in the United States that was ever honored, and the gold rush of 1849—Fredericksburg was the last place California-bound prospectors could get supplies—both helped the town thrive. Fredericksburg became and remains the seat of Gillespie County, the largest peach-producing county in the state—which explains the many roadside stands selling the fruit from late May through mid-August, and the profusion of peachy products found around this area.

SEEING THE SIGHTS

The **Visitor Information Center,** 302 E. Austin St., Fredericksburg, TX 78624 (© **888/ 997-3600** or 830/997-6523), can direct you to the many points of interest in the town's historic district. These include a number of little **Sunday Houses,** built by German settlers in distant rural areas because they needed a place to stay overnight when they came to town to trade or attend church.

The unusual octagonal **Vereins Kirche (Society Church)** in Market Square once functioned as a town hall, school, and storehouse. A 1935 replica of the original 1847 building now holds the archives of the Gillespie County Historical Society. The Historical Society also maintains the **Pioneer Museum Complex,** 309 W. Main St., anchored by the 1849 Kammlah House, which was a family residence and general store until the 1920s. Among the other historical structures here are a one-room schoolhouse and a blacksmith's forge. The 1852 Steamboat Hotel, originally owned by the grandfather of World War II naval hero Chester A. Nimitz, is now part of the **National Museum of the Pacific War** ✸✸, 311 E. Austin St. (© **830/997-4379;** www.nimitz-museum.org), a 9-acre Texas State Historical Park and the world's only museum focusing solely on the Pacific theater. In addition to the exhibits in the steamboat-shaped hotel devoted to Nimitz and his comrades, there are also the Japanese Garden of Peace, a gift from the people of Japan; the Memorial Wall, the equivalent of the Vietnam wall for Pacific War veterans; the life-size Pacific Combat Zone (2½ blocks east of the museum), which replicates a World War II battle scene; and the George Bush Gallery, where you can see a captured Japanese midget submarine and a multimedia simulation of a bombing raid on Guadalcanal.

Nearby

Take FM 965 some 18 miles north to reach **Enchanted Rock State Natural Area** ✸✸ (© **325/247-3903;** www.tpwd.state.tx.us/park/enchantd), a 640-acre, pink-granite dome that draws hordes of hikers. The creaking noises that emanate from it at night— likely caused by the cooling of the rock's outer surface—led the area's Native American tribes to believe that evil spirits inhabited the rock. Because of the rock's popularity, a limit is placed on visitors. It's best to call in advance.

WHERE TO STAY

Perhaps even more than for its shopping, Fredericksburg is well known for its appealing accommodations. In addition to the usual rural motels, the town boasts more than 300 bed-and-breakfasts and *gastehauses* (guest cottages). If you choose one of the latter, you can spend the night in anything from an 1865 homestead with its own wishing well to a bedroom above an old bakery or a limestone Sunday House. Unlike the typical B&B, these places ensure privacy because either breakfast is provided the night before—the perishables are left in a refrigerator—or guests are given coupons to enjoy breakfast at a local restaurant. *Gastehauses* are comparatively reasonable; for about $110 to $175, you can get loads of history and charm. The five main services that book this type of lodging are **Be My Guest,** 110 N. Milam (© **866/997-7227** or 830/ 997-7227; www.bemyguestfredericksburgtexas.com); **First Class Bed & Breakfast**

Reservation Service, 909 E. Main (© **888/991-6749** or 830/997-0443; www. fredericksburg-lodging.com); **Gästehaus Schmidt,** 231 W. Main St. (© **866/427-8374** or 830/997-5612; www.fbglodging.com); **Hill Country Lodging & Reservation Service,** 215 W. Main St. (© **800/745-3591** or 830/990-8455; www.fredericksburg bedbreakfast.com); and **Main Street B&B Reservation Service,** 337 E. Main (© **888/ 559-8555** or 830/997-0153; www.travelmainstreet.com). Specializing in the more familiar type of B&B is **Fredericksburg Traditional Bed & Breakfast Inns** (© **800/ 494-4678;** www.fredericksburgtrad.com).

Opened in 2004, the **Hangar Hotel,** 155 Airport Rd., Fredericksburg, TX 78624 (© **830/997-9990;** www.hangarhotel.com), lends some variety to Fredricksburg's mix of B&Bs and motels. It banks on nostalgia for the World War II flyboy era. Located, like the name suggests, at the town's tiny private airport, this hotel hearkens back to the 1940s with its clean-lined art-moderne-style rooms, as well as an officer's club (democratically open to all) and retro diner. Rates—which include one $5 "food ration," good at the diner, per night—run from $139 to $149 on weekends, $109 during the week.

WHERE TO DINE

Fredericksburg's dining scene is very diverse, catering to the traditional and the trendy alike. The former tend to frequent the **Altdorf Biergarten,** 301 W. Main St. (© **830/ 997-7865**), and **Friedhelm's Bavarian Inn,** 905 W. Main St. (© **830/997-6300**), both featuring moderately priced, hearty schnitzels, dumplings, and sauerbraten, and large selections of German beer. The **Fredericksburg Brewing Co.,** 245 E. Main St. (© **830/997-1646**), offers its own home brews and, in addition to the typical pub food, dishes up lots of lighter selections. For blue-plate specials and huge breakfasts of eggs, biscuits, and gravy, locals converge on **Andy's Steak & Seafood Grill,** 413 S. Washington St. (© **830/997-3744**), open since 1957.

LYNDON B. JOHNSON COUNTRY

Welcome to Johnson territory, where the forebears of the 36th president settled almost 150 years ago. Here you'll find LBJ's boyhood home and the sprawling ranch that became known as the Texas White House.

From Fredericksburg, take U.S. 290 east for 16 miles to the entrance of the **Lyndon B. Johnson State and National Historical Parks at LBJ Ranch** ✯, near Stonewall, jointly operated by the Texas Parks and Wildlife Department (© **830/644-2252;** www.tpwd.state.tx.us/park/lbj) and the National Park Service (© **830/868-7128;** www.nps.gov/lyjo). Tour buses depart regularly from the visitor center to the still-operating Johnson Ranch. On the other side of the Pedernales River, a reconstructed version of the former president's modest birthplace lies close to his final resting place. Also part of the state park is the **Sauer-Beckmann Living History Farm,** where costumed interpreters give visitors a look at typical Texas-German farm life at the turn of the 20th century. As interesting as Colonial Williamsburg, this is a terrific place to come with kids. Nearby are nature trails, a swimming pool (open only in summer), and lots of picnic spots. Admission is $6 per adult for bus tours, the only way to see the ranch; all other areas are free.

It's 14 miles farther east along U.S. 290 to **Johnson City,** a pleasant agricultural town named for founder James Polk Johnson, LBJ's first cousin once removed. The modest white clapboard **Boyhood Home** ✯, where Lyndon was raised after age 5, is the centerpiece of this unit of the national historical park. Before exploring, stop at the **visitor center** (© 830/868-7128)—take F Street to Lady Bird Lane and you'll see the signs—to see an educational film and to get details about touring the Boyhood Home. The Boyhood Home and visitor center are open from 8:45am to 5pm daily; admission is free.

BEYOND LBJ: WHAT TO DO, WHERE TO EAT & STAY
Johnson City has attractions that have little to do with the 36th president or history, although, you can claim that shopping for antiques is also a history-oriented activity. Several low-key antiques shops dot Main Street; perhaps the best is the **Old Lumber Yard,** 209 E. Main St. (© 830/868-2381), selling reasonably priced items from a variety of eras, including the present one. One of the highlights of the complex is the **Silver K Café** (© 830/868-2911), where soups, salads, and sandwiches are served at lunchtime from Monday to Saturday. From Thursday through Saturday evenings, you might dine on Gulf Coast cioppino, perhaps, or pan-grilled top sirloin with mustard sauce. Prices range from moderate to expensive. If you prefer your meats more portable, visit **Whittington's,** 602 Hwy. 281 S. (© 877/868-5501), renowned around Texas for its beef and turkey jerky (just drop in for a sample; fresh jerky bears little resemblance to the convenience store kind).

The area's top place to dine—and to bed down—isn't in Johnson City, however, but about 16 miles to the west. You'll drive down a rural back road to reach **Rose Hill Manor,** 2614 Upper Albert Rd., Stonewall, TX 78671 (© 877/ROSEHIL or 830/644-2247; www.rose-hill.com), a reconstructed Southern manse. Light and airy accommodations—four in the main house, and six in separate cottages—are beautifully but comfortably furnished with antiques. All offer porches or patios and great Hill Country views. Rates run from $145 to $165. The inn's New American cuisine, served Wednesday through Sunday evenings in an ultraromantic dining room, is outstanding. Reservations are essential; prices are expensive.

The **Johnson Chamber of Commerce and Tourism Bureau,** 604 Hwy. 281 S., Johnson City, TX 78636 (© 830/868-7684; www.johnsoncity-texas.com), can provide information about other local dining, lodging, and shopping options.

NEW BRAUNFELS & GRUENE
New Braunfels sits at the junction of the Comal and Guadalupe rivers. German settlers were brought here in 1845 by Prince Carl of Solms-Braunfels, the commissioner general of the Society for the Protection of German Immigrants in Texas, the same group that later founded Fredericksburg. Although Prince Carl returned to Germany within a year to marry his fiancée, who refused to join him in the wilderness, his colony prospered. By the 1850s, New Braunfels was the fourth-largest city in Texas after Houston, San Antonio, and Galveston. Although you have to look a little to find its quainter side today, this is a good place to enjoy a bit of Germanic history—and a lot of watersports.

EXPLORING NEW BRAUNFELS
At the **New Braunfels Chamber of Commerce,** 390 S. Seguin, New Braunfels, TX 78130 (© 800/572-2626 or 830/625-2385; www.nbjumpin.com), you can pick up a pamphlet detailing the 40-point **historic walking tour** of midtown. Highlights include the Romanesque-Gothic Comal County Courthouse (1898) on Main Plaza; the nearby Jacob Schmidt Building (193 W. San Antonio), built on the site where William Gebhardt, of canned chili fame, perfected his formula for chili powder in

1896; and the 1928 Faust Hotel (240 S. Seguin), believed by some to be haunted by its owner.

Several small museums are worth a visit. Prince Carl never did build a planned castle for his sweetheart, Sophia, on the elevated spot where the **Sophienburg Museum,** 401 W. Coll St. (© **830/629-1572;** www.nbtx.com/sophienburg), now stands, but it's nevertheless an excellent place to learn about the history of New Braunfels and other Hill Country settlements. The **Museum of Texas Handmade Furniture** (★, 1370 Church Hill Dr. (© **830/629-6504;** www.nbheritagevillage.com), also sheds light on local domestic life of the 19th century with its beautiful examples of Texas Biedermeier by master craftsman Johan Michael Jahn. They're displayed at the gracious 1858 Breustedt-Dillon Haus. The 11-acre Heritage Village complex also includes an 1848 log cabin and a barn that houses a reproduction cabinetmaker's workshop.

HISTORIC GRUENE (★★

Get a more concentrated glimpse of the past at Gruene (pronounced "Green"), 4 miles northwest of downtown New Braunfels. First settled by German farmers in the 1840s, Gruene was virtually abandoned during the Depression in the 1930s. It remained a ghost town until the mid-1970s, when two investors realized the value of its intact historic buildings and sold them to businesses rather than raze them. These days, tiny Gruene is crowded with day-trippers browsing the specialty shops in the wonderfully restored structures, which include a smoked-meat shop, lots of cutesy gift boutiques, and several antiques shops.

The **New Braunfels Museum of Art & Music** (★, 1259 Gruene Rd., on the river behind Gruene Mansion (© **800/456-4866** or 830/625-5636), focuses on popular arts in the West and South (as opposed to, say, high culture and the classics). Subjects of recent exhibits, which change quarterly and combine music and art components, have included Texas accordion music, central Texas dance halls, and cowboy art and poetry. Live music throughout the year includes an open mic on Sunday afternoons, and the recording of *New Braunfels Live* radio show of roots music on Thursday evenings. A brochure detailing the town's retailers, restaurants, and accommodations is available from the New Braunfels Chamber of Commerce (see above) or at most of Gruene's shops. You can also get information on the town's website, **www.gruene texas.com**.

WATERSPORTS

Gruene also figures among the New Braunfels area's impressive array of places to get wet, most of them open only in summer. Outfitters who can help you ride the Guadalupe River rapids on raft, tube, canoe, or inflatable kayak include **Rockin' R River Rides** (© **800/553-5628** or 830/629-9999; www.rockinr.com) and **Gruene River Company** (© **888/705-2800** or 830/625-2800; www.toobing.com), both on Gruene Road just south of the Gruene Bridge. You can go tubing, too, at **Schlitterbahn** (★, Texas's largest water park and one of the best in the country, 305 W. Austin St. in New Braunfels (© **830/625-2351;** www.schlitterbahn.com). Those who like their water play a bit more low-key might try downtown New Braunfels's **Landa Park** (© **830/608-2160**), where you can either swim in the largest spring-fed pool in Texas or calmly float in an inner tube down the Comal River.

Want to buy your own toys—and learn how to use them? The 70-acre **Texas Ski Ranch,** 6700 I-35 N. (© **830/627-2843;** www.texasskiranch.com), is paradise for those interested in wake, skate, and motor sports. Features of this expanding complex include a cable lake, boat lake, skate park, and motor track—at all of which you can test the equipment you want to purchase or rent (you can also bring your own), and show off the latest athletic clothing, sold here, too. Training clinics and private lessons for a variety of sports are offered.

WHERE TO STAY IN NEW BRAUNFELS & GRUENE
A prime downtown location, tree-shaded courtyard, and gorgeously florid, high Victorian–style sleeping quarters have put accommodations at the **Prince Solms Inn,** 295 E. San Antonio St., New Braunfels (© **800/625-9169** or 830/625-9169; www.princesolmsinn.com), in great demand. Three Western-themed rooms in a converted 1860 feed store next door are ideal for families. Rates range from $125 to $175.

For a river view, consider the **Gruene Mansion Inn,** 1275 Gruene Rd., New Braunfels (© **830/629-2641;** www.gruenemansioninn.com). The barns that once belonged to the opulent 1875 plantation house were converted to rustic elegant cottages with decks; some also offer cozy lofts. Rooms range from $149 to $169 per night. Two separate lodges, suitable for families, are available, too ($209–$229).

The nearby **Gruene Apple Bed and Breakfast,** 1235 Gruene Rd. (© **830/643-1234;** www.grueneapple.com), was built expressly to serve as an inn. Many of the 14 luxurious theme rooms—from Wild West to the more decorous 1776—look out on the river from private balconies. On-site recreation includes a natural stone swimming pool, hot tub, pool table—even a small movie theater. Doubles range from $160 to $210.

WHERE TO DINE IN NEW BRAUNFELS & GRUENE
The **New Braunfels Smokehouse,** 140 Hwy. 46 S., at I-35 (© **830/625-2416;** www.nbsmokehouse.com), opened in 1951 as a tasting room for the meats it started hickory smoking in 1943. Savor it in platters or on sandwiches, or have some shipped home as a savory souvenir. The far newer **Huisache Grill,** 303 W. San Antonio St. (© **830/620-9001;** www.huisache.com), has an updated American menu that draws foodies from as far as San Antonio. An even more recent arrival on downtown's fine dining scene, **Myron's,** 136 Castell Rd. (© **830/624-1024;** myronsprimesteakhouse.com), serves perfectly prepared Chicago prime steak in a retro swank dining room (a converted 1920s movie palace).

In Gruene, the **Gristmill River Restaurant & Bar,** 1287 Gruene Rd. (© **830/625-0684;** www.gristmillrestaurant.com), a converted 100-year-old cotton gin, includes burgers and chicken-fried steak as well as healthful salads on its Texas-casual menu. Kick back on one of its multiple decks and gaze out at the Guadalupe River.

NEW BRAUNFELS & GRUENE AFTER DARK
Lyle Lovett and Garth Brooks are just a few of the big names who have played **Gruene Hall** ★★, Gruene Road, corner of Hunter Road (© **830/629-7077;** www.gruenehall.com), the oldest country-and-western dance hall in Texas and still one of the state's most outstanding spots for live music.

9

West Texas

by Eric Peterson

This is the real Texas: vast open spaces; longhorn cattle; pickup trucks lined up in front of roadside honky-tonks; and deeply tanned cowboys with sweat-stained hats, slim-cut jeans, and muddy boots. While most of Texas has become quite metropolitan—the vast majority of the state's residents live in cities—the plains of West Texas retain much of the Old West flavor. Communities here are generally small and far apart, residents seldom lock their doors, and even the region's biggest city, El Paso, feels like an overgrown small town. For those willing to take the time and effort, this area is filled with gems: a wide range of people, attractions, and activities amid a landscape that's alternately bleak and beautiful.

The region's history comes alive at numerous museums and historic sites, such as Spanish missions from the 17th and 18th centuries, several restored frontier forts, and the combination courtroom and saloon used in the late 1800s by Judge Roy Bean, the self-styled "Law West of the Pecos." West Texas also offers some surprises, including one of America's most beautiful caves; the state's oldest winery; a replica of William Shakespeare's famed Globe Theatre; an avant-garde installation art complex in the much-hyped town of Marfa; and numerous lakes, including 67,000-acre Lake Amistad, a national recreation area along the U.S.–Mexico border that is a joint project of both countries.

1 El Paso

43 miles SE of Las Cruces, New Mexico; 564 miles NW of San Antonio; 617 miles W of Dallas

Here, in the sun-swept, mountainous desert of Texas's westernmost corner, is El Paso, the state's sixth-largest city. Built between two mountain ranges on the shores of the Rio Grande, the city is an urban history book, with chapters dedicated to Spanish conquistadors, ancient highways, gunfighters, border disputes, and modern sprawl.

El Paso's rich history is a result of its geography. The Franklin Mountains, which now border the downtown area and occupy the city's heart, offered natural defense for the American Indians who inhabited the area for more than 10 millennia; the Rio Grande offered water. As the mountains slope into a vast canyon, the Spanish explorers who first crossed the Rio Grande in the 16th century saw it as an ideal north–south route, one that soon became known as the "Camino Real" (or "King's Highway") and served as a principal trade route for nearly 300 years.

With the 17th century came an influx of Catholic missionaries, a group that established numerous missions that survive today. But Spain saw its grip weaken, and a Mexican flag flew over El Paso when independence was established in 1821. This era

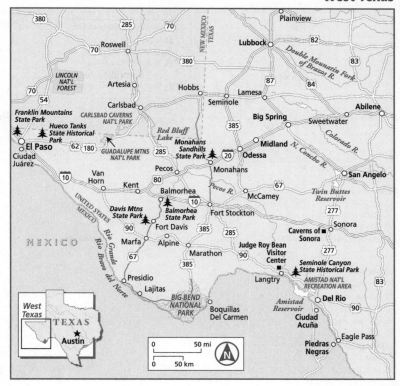

was short-lived, as Mexico ceded the land north of the Rio Grande to the United States following the Mexican-American War (1846–48). After the railroad arrived in 1881, El Paso earned the nickname "Sin City," thanks to the saloons, brothels, and casinos that lined every major street. Many notorious gunfighters—including Billy the Kid and John Wesley Hardin—called the city home.

El Paso boomed in the early 20th century and again following World War II, entrenching itself as a center for agriculture, manufacturing, and international trade. The city's relationship with Ciudad Juárez has been symbiotic for centuries, even more so since the resolution of a century-old border dispute in the 1960s and the signing of the North American Free Trade Agreement in 1994.

In comparison with the relative wealth and glitz of Santa Fe or Tucson, El Paso is in many ways the authentic Southwest—unpolished, undiluted, and honest. Separated by a swath of the Rio Grande, El Paso and Ciudad Juárez each represent their country's largest border city, and the local culture, a fusion of Mexican and American traditions, is distinct and unique in comparison to the way of life in eastern Texas. A day or two of exploration is worthwhile; take the time to wander downtown, enjoy a Tex-Mex meal, and gain a better understanding of what a border town is all about.

El Paso

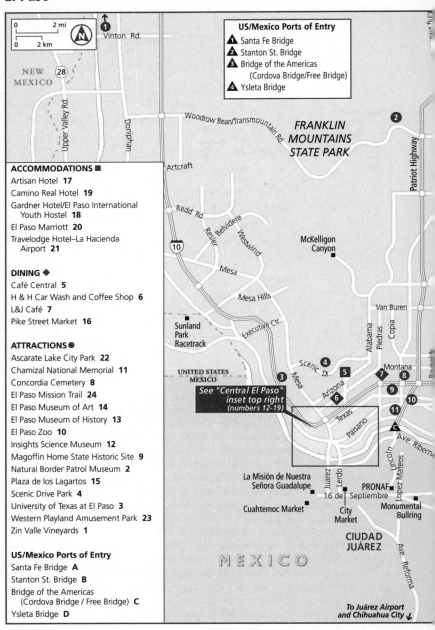

See "Central El Paso" inset top right (numbers 12-19)

US/Mexico Ports of Entry
1. Santa Fe Bridge
2. Stanton St. Bridge
3. Bridge of the Americas
   (Cordova Bridge/Free Bridge)
4. Ysleta Bridge

FRANKLIN MOUNTAINS STATE PARK

NEW MEXICO

UNITED STATES
MEXICO

MEXICO

CIUDAD JUÁREZ

McKelligon Canyon

Sunland Park Racetrack

La Misión de Nuestra Señora Guadalupe

Cuahtemoc Market

City Market

PRONAF
16 de Septiembre

Monumental Bullring

To Juárez Airport and Chihuahua City

ACCOMMODATIONS ■
Artisan Hotel **17**
Camino Real Hotel **19**
Gardner Hotel/El Paso International
    Youth Hostel **18**
El Paso Marriott **20**
Travelodge Hotel–La Hacienda
    Airport **21**

DINING ◆
Café Central **5**
H & H Car Wash and Coffee Shop **6**
L&J Café **7**
Pike Street Market **16**

ATTRACTIONS ●
Ascarate Lake City Park **22**
Chamizal National Memorial **11**
Concordia Cemetery **8**
El Paso Mission Trail **24**
El Paso Museum of Art **14**
El Paso Museum of History **13**
El Paso Zoo **10**
Insights Science Museum **12**
Magoffin Home State Historic Site **9**
Natural Border Patrol Museum **2**
Plaza de los Lagartos **15**
Scenic Drive Park **4**
University of Texas at El Paso **3**
Western Playland Amusement Park **23**
Zin Valle Vineyards **1**

US/Mexico Ports of Entry
Santa Fe Bridge **A**
Stanton St. Bridge **B**
Bridge of the Americas
    (Cordova Bridge / Free Bridge) **C**
Ysleta Bridge **D**

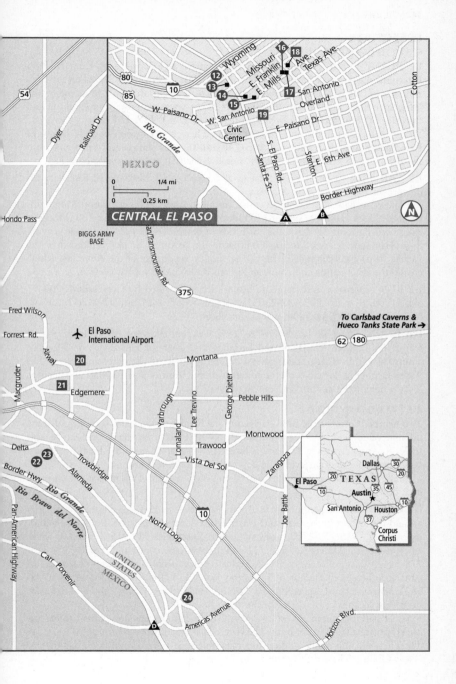

CENTRAL EL PASO

Wyoming
Missouri
E. Franklin
E. Mills Ave.
Texas Ave.
San Antonio
Overland
W. Paisano Dr.
W. San Antonio
E. Paisano Dr.
Civic Center
E. 6th Ave.
Santa Fe St.
S. El Paso Rd.
Stanton
Border Highway
Cotton

Rio Grande
MEXICO

0   1/4 mi
0   0.25 km

Hondo Pass
Dyer
Railroad Dr.

BIGGS ARMY BASE

an/Transmountain Rd.

375

Fred Wilson
Forrest Rd.
El Paso International Airport

To Carlsbad Caverns &
Hueco Tanks State Park →

62 180

Macgruder
Airway
Montana

Edgemere
Yarbrough
Lee Trevino
George Dieter
Pebble Hills

Lomaland
Trawood
Vista Del Sol
Montwood
Zaragoza

Delta
Trowbridge
Alameda
North Loop
Joe Battle

Border Hwy. Rio Grande
Rio Bravo del Norte
Pan-American Highway
Carr Porvenir

UNITED STATES
MEXICO

Americas Avenue
Horizon Blvd.

TEXAS
Dallas
30
20
El Paso
20
10
Austin
35
45
San Antonio
Houston
10
37
Corpus Christi

341

ESSENTIALS
GETTING THERE
BY PLANE   Over 125 commercial flights arrive and depart daily from **El Paso International Airport,** located a mile north of I-10 via Airway Boulevard on the city's east side (℡ **915/780-4749;** www.elpasointernationalairport.com). Most major airlines, including **Aerólitoral** (℡ **800/800-2376;** www.aerolitoral.com/english) and **Frontier** (℡ **800/432-1359;** www.frontierairlines.com), serve El Paso.

The major car-rental agencies are represented here; see "Getting Around," below. **El Paso/Juárez Shuttle Service** (℡ **915/740-4400**) offers shuttle service to and from the airport (a 15-min. trip each way); a one-way trip downtown costs about $25.

BY CAR   The main artery to the east and west is I-10, bisecting El Paso between downtown and the Franklin Mountains.

From Carlsbad Caverns (160 miles from El Paso) and Guadalupe Mountains National Parks to the east (about 130 miles), visitors arrive via U.S. 62/180 (Montana Ave.), which eventually skirts the north side of downtown El Paso. For those arriving from Alamogordo, New Mexico (80 miles to the north), U.S. 54 (also known as the Patriot Fwy.) runs through El Paso's east side to the Bridge of the Americas, which crosses the Rio Grande and connects El Paso with Ciudad Juárez, Mexico.

BY BUS   Interstate and intrastate bus service is provided by **Greyhound,** 200 W. San Antonio Dr. (℡ **915/532-2365;** www.greyhound.com), and **TNM&O,** 201 W. Main Dr. (℡ **915/532-3404;** www.tnmo.com).

BY TRAIN   **Amtrak** (℡ **800/872-7245;** www.amtrak.com) offers westward rail service on Tuesday, Thursday, and Saturday and eastward rail service on Monday, Thursday, and Saturday. Trains go east to Chicago (via San Antonio) and west to Los Angeles; other major cities on the routes include Houston and Tucson. The depot is located downtown at 700 San Francisco St.

GETTING AROUND
Two natural features—the Rio Grande and the Franklin Mountains—have guided the urban development of El Paso for more than 400 years, so getting around can be a bit tricky for the newcomer. The city is essentially U-shaped, with the Franklin Mountains occupying the center and the downtown area at the bottom.

While El Paso has a public bus system, cars are the norm. Parking is rarely an issue, even downtown.

BY CAR   There are numerous car-rental agencies in El Paso, clustered primarily around the airport in the east, and North Mesa Street on the city's west side, including **Avis** (℡ 915/779-2700; www.avis.com); **Enterprise** (℡ 915/779-2260; www.enterprise.com); **Dollar** (℡ 915/772-4255; www.hertz.com); and **Thrifty** (℡ 915/778-5445; www.dollar.com). The **American Automobile Association (AAA)** maintains an office in El Paso at 655 Sunland Park Dr. (℡ 800/765-0766 or 915/778-9521; www.aaa.com), open Monday through Friday from 9am to 6pm and Saturday from 9am to 1pm.

Street parking is free almost everywhere in El Paso except downtown, where the meters must be fed 25¢ per hour. The covered garages downtown charge $3 to $6 per day. There are also many outdoor lots that are geared toward tourists on day trips to Ciudad Juárez. These usually run $2 to $5 per day.

BY BUS   El Paso's bus system, **Sun Metro** (© **915/533-1220;** www.sunmetro.org), operates one of the world's largest fleets of natural gas–powered buses. The main transfer station is downtown on San Jacinto Plaza at Mesa and Main streets. There are also trolleys that run between the University of Texas El Paso (UTEP) campus and downtown. Buses run from 5am to 9pm on weekdays, with slightly shorter hours on weekends and holidays; the fare is $1 for adults and 50¢ for children, students, and those with disabilities, and 30¢ for seniors.

BY TAXI   Both **Yellow Cab** (© **915/533-3433**) and **Sun City Cab** (© **915/544-2211**) offer 24-hour service in El Paso and the surrounding area.

ON FOOT   Downtown El Paso is well suited for a walking tour, and it is popular to park downtown and walk across the Santa Fe Bridge into Ciudad Juárez. *Note:* Be sure to carry your passport with you if you cross the border. While photo ID has been traditionally sufficient for reentry into the United States, all land crossings into Mexico will require a passport as of January 2008.

VISITOR INFORMATION

The **El Paso Convention & Visitors Bureau** is located at One Civic Center Plaza, next to the El Paso Convention and Performing Arts Center (© **800/351-6024** or 915/534-0600; www.visitelpaso.com) and also operates information centers at the airport and Fort Bliss. *El Paso: The Official Visitor's Guide* is a good publication to request before your trip.

There is also a **Texas Travel Information Center,** with an excellent selection of brochures, maps, and other visitor resources located 20 miles northwest of El Paso in Anthony (I-10, Exit 0), at the Texas–New Mexico border.

For information on Ciudad Juárez, contact **Fiprotur Chihuahua,** Av. de las Americas #2551, Ciudad Juárez, Chihuahua, Mexico (© **888/654-0394;** www.visitajuarez.com).

FAST FACTS: El Paso

American Express Sun Travel American Express, 3100 N. Mesa St., Suite B (© **915/532-8900**), offers American Express services Monday through Friday from 8am to 5pm.

Babysitters Front desks at major hotels often can make arrangements on your behalf.

Dentists Contact **1-800-DENTIST** (© **800/336-8478**).

Doctors Call **El Paso County Medical Society** (© **915/533-0981**).

Drugstores **Walgreens Drug Stores** has a 24-hour prescription service at 1831 N. Lee Trevino Dr. (© **915/594-1129**).

Emergencies For police, fire, and medical emergencies, call © **911.** To reach the **Poison Center,** dial © **800/764-7661** or 915/544-1200.

Hospitals Full-service hospitals, with 24-hour emergency rooms, include **Sierra Medical Center,** 1625 Medical Center Dr. (© **915/747-4000**), just northwest of downtown, and **Del Sol Medical Center,** 10301 Gateway W. (© **915/595-9000**), on the east side of the city.

Newspapers & Magazines The *El Paso Times* (www.elpasotimes.com) is the city's only daily English-language newspaper, and an El Paso edition of *El Diario de Juárez* (www.eldiario.com.mx) is published in Spanish daily. *El Paso Scene* (www.epscene.com) is the city's free monthly arts-and-entertainment paper. *El Paso Inside & Out* (www.elpasoinsideandout) is a monthly magazine focusing on arts, culture, and regional issues.

Post Office The main post office, located downtown at 219 E. Mills Ave., is open Monday through Friday from 8:30am to 5pm, Saturday from 8:30am to noon.

Safety While El Paso has among the lowest crime rates of any major U.S. city, it is far from crime-free, and drugs and auto theft are two preeminent problems. It's important to keep aware of your surroundings at all times and ask at your hotel or a visitor center about the safety of a given neighborhood, especially after dark. *Note:* When visiting Mexico, it is important to remember that Ciudad Juárez is one of the world's most active drug-smuggling centers, but crime against tourists is rare.

Taxes In the city of El Paso, the total sales tax is 8.25% and 15.5% for lodging.

Time Zone El Paso is in the Mountain Standard Time zone, like nearby New Mexico but unlike the rest of Texas, which is in the Central Standard Time zone. Set your clock back 1 hour if you enter El Paso from the east.

WHAT TO SEE & DO
THE TOP ATTRACTIONS
Chamizal National Memorial 🏛 When the Mexican-American War ended in 1848, the two countries agreed upon a border: the center of the deepest channel of the Rio Grande. However, as historian Leon C. Metz once wrote, "Rivers are never *absolutely* permanent. They evaporate, flood, change channels, shrink, expand, and even disappear. Rivers are, by nature, capricious." After the war, the Rio Grande gradually shifted southward, resulting in a diplomatic stalemate between Mexico and the United States over the boundary's location. This impasse lasted until 1967, finally ending when presidents Lyndon B. Johnson and Adolfo López Mateos signed the Chamizal Treaty. Parcels of land were exchanged, residents and businesses uprooted, and a permanent, concrete channel was constructed to signify a more predictable boundary.

The 55-acre park at the Chamizal National Memorial commemorates the dispute's settlement with a bevy of facilities: 2 miles of foot trails, an outdoor amphitheater that hosts many free concerts, and a visitor center/museum (expect to spend 30 min. touring the museum). It's a nice open space that's more accessible and greener than the Franklin Mountains and larger than the other municipal parks. There is also a walkway to the adjacent Bridge of the Americas leading to the memorial's Mexican counterpart, **Parque Chamizal,** with an anthropology museum and an amusement park in Ciudad Juárez.

800 S. San Marcial Dr., at Paisano Dr. and U.S. 54 (Patriot Fwy.). © **915/532-7273.** www.nps.gov/cham. Free admission, with fees for some events in the amphitheater. Park daily 5am–10pm. Visitor center daily 10am–5pm.

El Paso Mission Trail 🏛 First established in the 17th and 18th centuries, three historic Spanish missions provide a link to El Paso's colonial past. All three are among the

El Paso's Alligator Art

In El Paso's downtown San Jacinto Plaza, the **Plaza de los Lagartos,** a fiber-glass fountain comprised of snarling alligators, basks in the sun. The lively 1993 piece by pop artist (and El Paso native) Luis Jimenez harks back to the gators that called the plaza home for nearly a century. In the 1880s, El Paso's mayor first deposited the reptiles in the plaza's fountain as something of a joke; surprisingly, they thrived amid the hustle and bustle of the growing city until they were deemed a potential hazard and removed in the 1960s. (It's located in San Jacinto Plaza, bordered on the east and west by Mesa and Oregon sts., and north and south by Main and Mills sts.)

oldest continually active missions in the country, and warrant a visit for their architectural and historic merit. But if you only have time to hit only one, drive out to San Elceario; unlike Ysleta and Socorro, it's removed from the modern urban development and still feels like it's from a different era and culture.

From I-10, exit Zaragosa Road (Exit 32) and head south 3 miles to **Mission Ysleta,** 9501 Socorro Rd. at Zaragosa Road (www.ysletamission.org), established in 1682 in what was then Mexico. The silver-domed chapel here was built in 1851 after floods shifted the Rio Grande and washed away all of the previous structure, save the foundation.

Heading southeast on Socorro Road for 3 miles takes you to **Mission Socorro** (© **915/859-7718**), established in 1682, 1 day after Mission Ysleta. The original adobe chapel (1692) was washed away by a flood in the 1740s, rebuilt, destroyed again in 1829, and finally replaced in 1843 by the current restored structure.

Presidio Chapel San Elceario (© **915/851-2333**), established at its present location in 1789 as a Spanish military outpost, sits 6 miles south of Mission Socorro on Socorro Road. Parishioners built the present-day church in 1877 as the centerpiece of the village plaza, which retains its historic charm to this day. This structure is the largest of the three missions, and an excellent example of the merging of American Indian and Spanish architectural styles with majestic arches and a pressed tin ceiling. The surrounding village has been gaining fame in recent years as the site of "The First Thanksgiving," said to have taken place in 1598, 23 years before the Plymouth Thanksgiving.

Visitors are welcome to tour the missions on their own; expect to spend at least 3 hours if you visit all three. Bus tours are offered by the **El Paso-Juárez Trolley Company** (© **915/544-0062**).

An 8-mile stretch of Zaragosa and Socorro roads, southeast of downtown El Paso via I-10. © **915/534-0630.** Free admission.

El Paso Museum of Art ☆☆   Once regarded as lacking a regional focus, the El Paso Museum of Art has recently turned that criticism on its head: The stunning landscapes and personal portraits on display here evoke the region's look, and more importantly, its feel. Of the five permanent galleries, three are dedicated to the cultures that have commingled in El Paso for the last 400 years: One is dedicated to Mexican art of the 17th to 19th centuries, one to European art from the 13th to 18th centuries, and one to American works dating from 1800 to the mid-1900s. Seasonal exhibits often feature edgier contemporary works. The museum begs for an unhurried hour of your time.

1 Arts Festival Plaza. © **915/532-1707.** www.elpasoartmuseum.org. Free admission. Tues–Sat 9am–5pm (until 9pm Thurs); Sun noon–5pm.

MORE ATTRACTIONS

Oenophiles will want to take a side trip to **Zin Valle Vineyards,** 7315 Hwy. 28, Canutillo (© **915/877-4544;** www.zinvalle.com), where the tasting room is open from noon to 5pm Friday to Monday and by appointment at other times. A new **El Paso Museum of History** has been slated to open by winter 2007, downtown at 510 Santa Fe St. (© **915/858-1928;** www.elpasotexas.gov/history).

Ascarate Lake City Park   Centered on a 44-acre artificial lake, this municipal park consists of 400 acres of undeveloped terrain crisscrossed by trails. While swimming in the lake is prohibited, recreational opportunities include fishing (the lake is stocked with channel catfish and rainbow trout) and golfing at the park's 27-hole golf course. There's also an aquatics center with an indoor Olympic-size pool and ball fields.

6900 Delta Dr., between Alameda Ave. and Border Hwy. © **915/772-3941.** Free admission to park, although some attractions have fees, including the golf course and Western Playland Amusement Park. Daily dawn–dusk.

Concordia Cemetery   El Paso's "Boot Hill," Concordia is the final resting place of numerous infamous outlaws who met their maker in the city's wilder days. The gravestones here, which mostly date to the second half of the 19th century, remain haunting reminders of El Paso's storied past. Near the northern gate, the most notable grave is that of notorious John Wesley Hardin, known as "The Fastest Gun in the West." After his 1895 assassination in downtown El Paso, Hardin was put to rest here alongside other gunslingers (including Hardin's killer) and a generation of law-abiding citizens. Hardin's grave is said to be El Paso's most-visited attraction.

Copia St. and I-10. © **915/562-7062.** Free admission. Daily 24 hr. Immediately north of I-10 via Copia St. (Exit 22A).

El Paso Zoo 🐾 *Kids*   Home to some 1,700 animals from 240 different species in natural habitat exhibits, the El Paso Zoo is one of the state's best. The focus is on American and Asian wildlife, with a monkey island, reptile house, Asian Grasslands exhibit, and Americas Aviary. Among the crowd favorites are sun bears, black jaguars, tigers, and Asian elephants. There is also a restaurant, gift shop, and a replica of a "Paraje," the 16th-century equivalent of a rest stop on the Camino Real. Allow at least 1 hour.

4001 E. Paisano Dr. (across from the El Paso County Coliseum). © **915/521-1850.** www.elpasozoo.org. Admission $5 adults, $4 seniors 62 and older, $3 children ages 3–12, free for children younger than 3. Mon–Fri 9:30am–4pm year-round; Sat–Sun 9:30am–4pm winter, 9:30am–5pm summer. Closed Thanksgiving, Dec 25, and Jan 1.

Magoffin Home State Historic Site   Built in 1875 for Joseph Magoffin, a pioneer leader who helped guide the city through its chaotic Wild West days, this is El

---

(Fun Fact **Live by the Gun . . .**

Notorious gunslinger John Wesley Hardin, who claimed to have killed 40 men, was shot in the back of the head in a saloon in 1895. At the time, Hardin was planning to embark on a law career (he had even gone as far as printing business cards), despite the fact that he spent more than three-quarters of his last 20 years in prison.

(Tips) Scenic Drive Park

Located high above downtown atop the cliffs of the Franklin Mountains, this municipal park (on Scenic Dr. between Rim Rd. and Alabama Ave.) offers amazing views, day and night. With the naked eye or coin-op telescopes, you can see downtown El Paso, across the Rio Grande to Juárez, and even parts of New Mexico.

Paso's only historical house museum open to the public. A recommended hour-long stop for the history buff, the house is a prime example of Territorial architecture, with an adobe structure and Greek revival accents. Many original furnishings are still in place: The Victorian parlor is unique due to its Mexican accents, the oldest part of the home still sports a viga ceiling (thatched and exposed), and one bedroom is outfitted with a 13-foot half-canopy bed and furnishings purchased at the 1884 World's Fair in New Orleans.

1120 Magoffin Ave. (©) 915/533-5147. Admission $3 adults, free for children younger than 13. Thurs–Sun 9am–4pm and by appointment Wed.

National Border Patrol Museum   The only museum dedicated to the U.S. Border Patrol, this facility does a good job presenting displays on all aspects of the federal agency, founded in El Paso in 1924. Allow about a half-hour to peruse such highlights as the Lady Liberty exhibit, a Statue of Liberty replica and text and diaries about the immigrant experience; and two former Border Patrol aircraft: a Piper Super Cub plane and a Hughes OH-6A helicopter. There are also exhibits on Border Patrol dogs, electronics, and ground vehicles.

4315 Transmountain Dr. (©) 915/759-6060. www.borderpatrolmuseum.com. Free admission (donations accepted). Tues–Sat 9am–5pm. Closed major holidays.

ESPECIALLY FOR KIDS

Insights Science Museum (flag) (Kids)   This downtown museum is a winner for young minds curious about the inner workings of nature. There are interactive exhibits on topics ranging from energy and optics to health and biology. Kids get a big jolt of fun out of the Tesla coil that courses with 500,000 volts several times a day. Another favorite is the exhibit on sound, with an Echo Tube and displays on sonic waves. A comprehensive tour requires about an hour.

505 N. Santa Fe St. (©) 915/534-0000. www.insightselpaso.org. Admission $6 adults; $5 students, seniors, and military; $4 children 4–11; free for children younger than 4. Mon–Sat 9am–5pm; Sun noon–5pm.

Western Playland Amusement Park (Kids)   The longtime local amusement park relocated to Sunland Park, New Mexico, in 2006, taking with it the El Bandito roller coaster and opening several new thrill rides. Concession stands and picnic areas fill the needs of the hungry and thirsty.

1249 Futurity Dr., across from Sunland Park Race Track and Casino. (©) 915/772-3914. www.westernplayland.com. Admission $15–$17 for a pass for unlimited rides. Open Mar–Nov; call for current hours.

ORGANIZED TOURS

The **El Paso–Juárez Trolley Company** (flag) ((©) **915/544-0062;** www.borderjumper.com) offers trolley tours that venture into Mexico, New Mexico, and historic El Paso for $10 to $20, depending on the package. Juárez tours depart hourly from One Civic Center Plaza from 10am to 4pm year-round. Call for information on other tours, which are offered seasonally. **Si! El Paso Tours** (© **800/658-6742** or 915/541-1308; www.sielpasotours.com) offers tours and transportation on both sides of the border. The **El Paso CVB** (© **915/534-0600;** www.visitelpaso.com) can provide travelers with informative brochures that detail self-guided historic walking tours of both El Paso and Ciudad Juárez.

OUTDOOR ACTIVITIES

At nearly 24,300 acres, **Franklin Mountains State Park** is the largest urban wilderness park in the United States and a favorite destination of El Pasoans looking to hike, bike, or climb. Rugged and speckled by cacti and ocotillo, the mountains are populated by small mammals, birds, reptiles, deer, and the occasional mountain lion. At 7,192 feet, the summit of North Franklin Mountain is about 3,000 feet higher than the city below.

The mountains, the final southern ridge of the geological phenomenon that created the Rockies, are home to about 40 miles of developed hiking and mountain biking trails; floods in 2006 washed many trails out, so call for current information. The hikes are primarily moderate to difficult; try the 1.2-mile round-trip to the Aztec Caves or the more difficult 9.2-mile round-trip to the peak of North Franklin Mountain.

If you don't want to break a sweat, take the **Wyler Aerial Tramway** (© **915/566-6622**) to the summit of Ranger Peak ($7 adults, $4 children 12 and younger). Beyond the trails and the tram, the park is also a renowned rock-climbing spot and home to an outdoor amphitheater (see "The Performing Arts," p. 353).

It takes about 20 minutes to reach the park by car from downtown El Paso. There are numerous primitive campsites, but no water or electricity in the park. Fees are $4 for day use (free to children younger than 13) and $8 for camping, and the park is open from 8am to 5pm year-round (campers receive a combination to the gate so they can come and go after day-use hours). For more information, contact Franklin Mountains State Park, 1331 McKelligon Canyon Rd., El Paso, TX 79930 (© **915/566-6441**).

Hueco Tanks State Historic Site, located 30 miles northeast of El Paso via U.S. 62/180 and Ranch Road 2775, is another popular rock-climbing destination. It is a world-class bouldering site, among the best on the planet. Centered on three small, rocky outcroppings that loom above the surrounding desert, the park gets its name from the *huecos* (depressions) that catch rainwater and attract life. Many of the rocks are marked by lively pictographs, the work of native tribes over the last 10,000 years. Tours of these fragile sites are offered at 9am and 11am in the summer and 10:30am and 2pm in the winter; reservations are recommended.

Other than climbing, hiking and camping are popular activities at the park. There are 6.5 miles of trails and a campground with 20 back-in sites (3 with water only, 17 with water and electricity) and showers. Campsite availability is dependent on volunteers; call ahead to see if the campground is open. The park charges $4 for day use and $12 to $16 for campsites. Bikes are not permitted. For more information, contact Hueco Tanks State Historic Site, 6900 Hueco Tanks Rd. #1, El Paso, TX 79938 (© **915/857-1135**).

GOLF The 27-hole **Painted Dunes Desert Golf Course,** located 9 miles northeast of I-10 via U.S. 54 at 12000 McCombs St. (© **915/821-2122;** www.painteddunes. com), is one of the top municipal courses in the entire country. Nonresident greens fees range from $35 to $43, cart included. Lee Trevino began his illustrious professional golf career at **Emerald Springs Golf and Conference Center,** 20 miles east of town at 16000 Ashford St. (© **915/852-9110**). Greens fees are $30 to $35, cart included. There is also **Ascarate Golf Course** in Ascarate Lake City Park

---

> (*Fun Fact* **Calling All Pros**
>
> El Paso is the most populous American city that is not home to a major-league
> sports franchise (MLB, NHL, NFL, or NBA).

(© **915/772-7381**), with greens fees of $13 to $16 (carts: $10) and **Cielo Vista Golf Course,** 1510 Hawkins Blvd. (© **915/591-4927**), with greens fees of $21 to $25 (carts: $11).

HIKING   The top hiking areas in and around El Paso are at **Franklin Mountains State Park** and **Hueco Tanks State Historic Site** (see above).

MOUNTAIN BIKING   **Franklin Mountains State Park** (see above) is by far the most popular mountain-biking destination in the El Paso area. There are about 40 miles of bike-accessible trails, but many were damaged by heavy rain in 2006; call for current information.

SPECTATOR SPORTS

BASEBALL   The **El Paso Diablos,** an independent team in the Central League, play a May-to-August schedule at 10,000-seat Cohen Stadium, 9700 Gateway Blvd. N. Single-game tickets are $5 to $7. Call © **915/755-2000** or visit www.diablos.com for schedules.

BASKETBALL   The University of Texas at El Paso (UTEP) fields a Conference USA team, the **Miners,** that plays from December to March at the Don Haskins Center, 2801 N. Mesa St. Tickets range from $5 to $15 for single games. Call © **915/747-5234** or visit www.utepathletics.com to purchase tickets or for more information.

FOOTBALL   The **UTEP Miners** football squad plays a Conference USA schedule from September to December on campus at the Sun Bowl. Single-game tickets are $10 to $50. Also, the stadium hosts the second-oldest New Year's bowl game in the nation. Call © **915/747-5234** or visit www.utepathletics.com for schedules or to purchase tickets.

HORSE RACING   There is live horse racing just outside of western El Paso (actually in New Mexico) at **Sunland Park Racetrack and Casino,** 1200 Futurity Dr. (© **505/874-5200;** www.sunland-park.com). The racing season runs from December to April (simulcast racing from around the country is featured year-round). There are also restaurants, lounges, and a casino on-site.

RODEO   The **Southwestern International PRCA Rodeo** is held every September at Cohen Coliseum, 9700 Gateway N. Call © **915/755-2000** or visit www.elprodeo. com for schedules and ticket information.

SHOPPING

El Paso's main shopping district is downtown—targeting both Mexican and American shoppers—and there are several enclosed malls scattered around the city. The area is known for Western wear, Southwestern art, and Mexican imports.

The three-story **Galeria San Ysidro,** 801 Texas Ave. (© **915/544-4444;** www.galeria sanysidro.com), is more than just an antiques store, housing an impressive selection of art, furniture, and decor from all over the world. Renowned for the talent that it represents, **Adair Margo Gallery,** 415 E. Yandell Dr. (© **915/533-0048;** www.adair margo.com), specializes in sculpture and paintings by local and regional artists, including Tom Lea and James Magee. **Cowtown Boots,** 11401 Gateway W. (© **915/ 593-2929;** www.cowtownboots.com), claims to be the world's largest Western wear store, with 40,000 square feet of boots (alligator to ostrich), jeans, clothing, and accessories. If you want some custom boots that are leather works of art, make an appointment at **Rocketbuster Boots,** 115 S. Anthony St. (© **915/541-1300;** www.rocketbuster. com), but you'll need at least $750 for a pair. For tongue-searing delicacies, we love the **El Paso Chile Company,** 909 Texas Ave. (© **888/4-SALSAS** or 915/544-3434; www.elpasochile.com), for its sauces (with such fiery names as "Hellfire & Damnation") and all things spicy.

Shopping centers include **Sunland Park Mall,** 750 Sunland Park Dr. (© **915/ 833-5595**), and **Cielo Vista Mall,** 8401 Gateway W. (© **915/779-7070**). Located where Pancho Villa and General Pershing once negotiated, **Placita Santa Fe,** 5034 Doniphan Rd., features 20 quaint shops, specializing in art, designer clothing, antiques, and jewelry.

WHERE TO STAY

You'll find numerous hotels and motels in El Paso, but little in the way of B&Bs and resorts. Most of the accommodations are chain franchises, with a few exceptions, located either near the airport or adjacent to I-10. The city's room taxes add about 15.5% to lodging bills.

In addition to the properties described below, there are numerous hotels and motels located off I-10 near El Paso International Airport, including **Best Western Airport Inn,** 7144 Gateway E. (© **800/528-1234** or 915/779-7700), with a double rate of $64, and **Comfort Inn,** 900 Yarbrough Dr. (© **800/228-5150** or 915/594-9111), with a double rate of $89. Downtown, there is the **Holiday Inn Express** at 409 E. Missouri St. (© **888/465-4329** or 915/544-3333), offering doubles for $99 to $110. In the Sunland Park area, the pick of the litter is the **Holiday Inn Sunland Park,** 900 Sunland Park Dr. (© **800/658-2744** or 915/833-2900), with a double rate of $99 to $129.

EXPENSIVE

Camino Real Hotel 🅵🅵   El Paso's finest hotel—and one of a handful downtown— is the only Camino Real hotel or resort outside of Mexico. However, it's just 6 blocks north of the border, adjacent to the El Paso Convention and Performing Arts Center and within easy walking distance of all of the downtown attractions. Listed on the National Register of Historic Places, the hotel effortlessly meshes El Paso's past and present.

Formerly known as the Hotel Paso del Norte, the property first opened in 1912, awing guests with its lavish marble and cherrywood lobby under a stunning glass dome from Tiffany's in New York. While the dome remains in place above a splendid bar and fine-dining restaurant, almost everything else has changed in the time since as a result of numerous renovations. In 1986, a modern 17-story tower was built next to the old Paso del Norte, expanding the lobby and more than doubling the hotel's capacity.

Tastefully decorated with reproductions and contemporary furnishings, the oversize rooms have two doubles, two queen-size, or one king-size bed, the decor punctuated great downtown views. Elegant suites have Victorian and Southwestern motifs.

101 S. El Paso St., El Paso, TX 79901. © **800/769-4300** or 915/534-3000. Fax 915/534-3024. www.caminoreal.com. 359 units. $99–$160 double; $170–$1,000 suite. AE, DC, DISC, MC, V. Underground parking $5 daily. **Amenities:**

3 restaurants; bar; outdoor heated pool; exercise room; sauna; courtesy car; business center; 24-hr. room service. *In room:* A/C, cable TV w/pay movies, dataport, coffeemaker, hair dryer, iron.

El Paso Marriott ☆   This modern chain property is a solid lodging option for those flying in or out of El Paso. The lobby, centered about a large comfortable seating area, was stylishly refurbished in a renovation, not to mention the thick-walled rooms, which are reliable and contemporary, embellished with a nice range of amenities. The place is aimed at the business traveler, but it more than fills the needs of tourists and it's a bargain on the weekend.

1600 Airway Blvd. (a quarter-mile south of El Paso International Airport), El Paso, TX 79925. ✆ **800/228-9290** or 915/779-3300. Fax 915/779-4591. 296 units. $199–$199 double ($79–$89 on weekends); $399 suite. AE, DC, DISC, MC, V. **Amenities:** Restaurant; bar; 2 pools (1 indoor, 1 outdoor); exercise room; fitness center; Jacuzzi; sauna; shopping arcade; concierge; business center; spa; salon; limited room service; coin-op washers and dryers; dry cleaning. *In room:* A/C, cable TV w/pay movies, complimentary Wi-Fi, coffeemaker, hair dryer, iron.

MODERATE

Artisan Hotel *Finds*   Opened in February 2007, the Artisan Hotel—one of a boutique chain with similar properties in Las Vegas and Memphis—revels in over-the-top flamboyance. The lobby's walls and ceiling are clad in oversized reproductions of classics by da Vinci, van Gogh, and other masters; it also features a central fountain and bronze statues. The rooms, with one king bed or two queens, also feature reproduction prints (one master per room) on jet-black walls, with great city and mountain views. Also of note: the candlelit lobby bar, all leather and dark wood, and the chic outdoor pool deck on the fifth floor with the best views in town.

325 Kansas St., El Paso, TX 79901. ✆ **915/225-9100.** Fax 915/225-0050 www.artisanelpaso.com. 120 units. $129 double. AE, DISC, MC, V. **Amenities:** Restaurant; bar; outdoor heated pool. *In room:* A/C, cable TV, complimentary Wi-Fi, minibar, coffeemaker, hair dryer, iron, safe.

Travelodge Hotel—La Hacienda Airport ☆ *Value* *Kids*   Some roadside motels surprise you with their attention to detail—this is definitely one of them. Situated northeast of downtown off busy Montana Avenue, the grounds here are a world apart, centered on a shady courtyard surrounding a heated pool. The rooms are housed in 10 different brick buildings, with exterior entry through hand-painted wooden doors. Some of the accommodations in the older buildings are on the small side, albeit well maintained and comfortable, while the larger rooms in the newer structures are a notch above the norm, with blue-and-white decor and exposed wooden-beamed ceilings. We like the eight Jacuzzi rooms, featuring a picture window that separates the tub from the bedroom, and the family suites, amusingly decorated with plenty of room.

6400 Montana Ave., El Paso, TX 79925. ✆ **800/772-4231** or 915/772-4231. Fax 915/779-2918. www.the.travelodge. com/elpaso05473. 91 units. $49–$75 double; $85 suite; $95 Jacuzzi room. Rates include continental breakfast. AE, DC, DISC, MC, V. Pets accepted with $10 per night fee. **Amenities:** Restaurant; bar; outdoor heated pool; exercise room; Jacuzzi; business center; limited room service; coin-op washers and dryers. *In room:* A/C, cable TV w/pay movies, complimentary Wi-Fi, fridge, coffeemaker, hair dryer, iron, safe.

INEXPENSIVE

Gardner Hotel/El Paso International Youth Hostel *Value*   A downtown mainstay since 1922, the Gardner Hotel has a storied history—infamous gangster John Dillinger stayed here in the 1930s while on the run. The public areas are well kept, especially the attractive lobby, which has been restored to its original condition with a marble staircase, mauve carpeting, and historic photographs. There are two shared hostel rooms—one for males and one for females—each with two bunk beds and desks. There is also a wide range of private accommodations—some with no frills, some with the original antique furnishings. Hostel guests share bathrooms and an equipped kitchen, and also have access to a television, pool table, and a pay Internet kiosk. The private rooms have private bathrooms.

311 E. Franklin St., El Paso, TX 79901. ℂ 915/532-3661. www.gardnerhotel.com. 50 units. $20 dormitory bunk; $30–$80 private rooms. MC, V. **Amenities:** Coin-op washers and dryers. *In room:* A/C.

CAMPING

Several primitive campsites are available at Franklin Mountains State Park, and there are also tent and RV sites at Hueco Tanks State Historic Site; see "Outdoor Activities," above.

El Paso–West RV Park   Located just west of the Texas–New Mexico state line, this clean campground is nicely treed (for the desert, that is), with laundry facilities, free Wi-Fi, handicap-accessible showers, and a small store with groceries and RV supplies. An 18-hole golf course is located right across the street.

1415 Anthony Dr., Anthony, NM 88021. ℂ 800/754-1543 for reservations or 505/882-7172. 100 sites with full hookups, including 70 pull-throughs. $20 nightly. MC, V. 10 miles west of El Paso city limits (I-10, Exit 162 in New Mexico).

WHERE TO DINE
Note: Smoking is not allowed in El Paso's restaurants.

EXPENSIVE
Café Central CONTEMPORARY ECLECTIC   Worth the splurge, Café Central is an anomaly in a town dominated by Tex-Mex: a sleek urban bistro serving sophisticated international cuisine. There are three seating areas—a gracious dining room, a sleek lounge, and a breezy patio out front. The menu changes daily, but always offers a wide range of standout fare (most notably the creative Southwestern interpretations of traditional continental dishes). On a given night, you might start with Dos Equis–steamed clams with tomatoes, garlic, jalapeños, and cilantro; follow with a cup of cream of green-chile soup; and then enjoy a tantalizing main course of sautéed calamari and shellfish on a capellini bed; a grilled white veal chop with a revelation of a side dish in the green-chile risotto; or possibly luscious guyamas shrimp with a zesty tequila-cilantro sauce. The award-winning wine list is one of the city's best, with more than 300 bottles, and the desserts include the best *leches* (Mexican milk cakes) in all of Texas.

109 N. Oregon St., in the lobby of the Texas Tower (One Texas Court). ℂ 915/545-2233. Reservations recommended. Main courses $7–$28 lunch, $13–$35 dinner. AE, DC, DISC, MC, V. Mon–Thurs 11am–10pm; Fri–Sat 11am–11pm. Closed Sun and major holidays.

MODERATE/INEXPENSIVE
The local microbrewery, **Jaxon's,** has four locations: 1135 Airway Blvd. (ℂ **915/778-9696**), 4799 N. Mesa St. (ℂ 915/544-1188), 7410 Remcon Cir. (ℂ 915/845-6557), and 12111 Montwood Dr. (ℂ 915/857-6677). For coffee or a plump sandwich, hit the Seattle-themed **Pike Street Market,** 207 Mills St. (ℂ **915/545-1010**), a downtown hangout popular with suits and slackers alike.

H&H Car Wash and Coffee Shop *Finds* TEX-MEX/COFFEE SHOP   A dinky coffee shop straight out of the 1960s, the H&H is a bit weathered, noisy, and not much to look at. It doesn't matter—the place is home to some of the best inexpensive Tex-Mex in town. It's packed with locals from open to close, scarfing down such specialties as *carne picada* (diced sirloin with jalapeños, tomatoes, and onions), huevos rancheros, and chiles rellenos. Proprietor Kenneth Haddad does one heckuva job, using only the freshest ingredients and sticking with tradition. For hungry road-trippers with dirty cars and tight budgets, you can't get any more convenient than the H&H: Gas up, get your car washed, and have a bite to eat, all in one fell swoop. The car wash operates from 9am to 5pm during the week and from 9am to 3pm on Saturdays, charging $10 to $25 for a complete hand cleaning, inside and out.

701 E. Yandell Dr. at Ochoa St. © 915/533-1144. Reservations not accepted. Main courses $4–$7. AE, DISC, MC, V. Mon–Sat 7am–3pm. North of I-10, exit Cotton St. (20).

L&J Café 🔆🔆 TEX-MEX   Nicknamed "The Old Place by the Graveyard" because of its proximity to the Concordia Cemetery (p. 346), the L&J is an El Paso landmark. Owned and operated by the Duran family since it first opened in 1927, the L&J served as a casino and speakeasy during Prohibition and packs them in today for transcendental Tex-Mex. We're hooked on the chicken enchiladas, which approach perfection, but the chile con queso and *caldillo* (beef and potato stew with a green chile and garlic kick) are as good as you'll find anywhere. There are also healthy versions of many entrees, prepared with less cheese and tortillas that aren't fried. It doesn't hurt that the salsa is spicy, the beer is cold, and the service is quick and friendly, even when the place is filled to capacity—as it is most of the time.

3622 E. Missouri St. © 915/566-8418. Reservations not accepted. Main courses $5–$10. AE, DC, DISC, MC, V. Mon–Fri 10am–8pm; Sat 10am–6pm (bar open later). North of I-10, exit Copia St. (22A).

EL PASO AFTER DARK

El Paso's entertainment scene is spread throughout the city, and remarkably diverse. The El Paso Performing Arts Center, the beautifully restored Plaza Theatre, the McKelligon Canyon Amphitheatre, the outdoor and indoor stages at Chamizal National Memorial, and the facilities at University of Texas at El Paso all host regular performances. Fans of rock, country, Tejano, and jazz will likely find what they're looking for at the city's bars and clubs. The UTEP college scene is centered on Mesa and Cincinnati streets.

The free, monthly *El Paso Scene* and its online counterpart, **www.epscene.com**, are the best places to start for exploring arts-and-entertainment opportunities. The Friday *El Paso Times* (www.elpasotimes.com) also features performance listings, as does *The Prospector*, UTEP's student newspaper. Tickets for many events are available through **Ticketmaster** (© 915/544-8444; www.ticketmaster.com).

THE PERFORMING ARTS

El Paso Opera, 1035 Belvidere St., Suite 100 (© 915/581-5534; www.epopera.org), produces spring and fall shows annually, with a Thursday and Saturday performance of each held at the Plaza Theatre downtown. Spanish and English subtitles are projected for every performance. Tickets run $10 to $80 for a single event. **El Paso Pro-Musica,** 6557 N. Mesa St. (© 915/833-9400; www.elpasopromusica.org), presents several concerts a year, including the El Paso Chamber Music Festival every January. Concerts are held at numerous locations with ticket prices of $5 to $20. **El Paso Symphony Orchestra,** 1 Civic Center Plaza (© 915/535-3776; www.epso.org), puts on about a dozen different concerts annually. Tickets for single performances are $10 to $35, with discounts for children and seniors. At Franklin Mountains State Park, the outdoor **McKelligon Canyon Theatre,** 2 McKelligon Canyon Rd. (© 915/565-6900), annually hosts **Viva! El Paso** from late May to late August.

The **El Paso Playhouse,** 2501 Montana Ave. (© 915/532-1317; www.elpaso playhouse.org), stages a new production almost every month. There's also a children's company, Kids-N-Co., which produces timeless fairy tales and other light fare. Tickets are usually less than $10. The **University of Texas at El Paso Dinner Theatre,** Union Ballroom on the UTEP campus (© **915/747-6060** or 915/747-5234; www.utep.edu/ udt), is a tradition, producing student musicals since 1983. Today, the theater presents plays Wednesday through Sunday at 7pm during the school year. Dinner might include prime rib, baked potato, and a cookie sundae. Recent productions have included *The Full Monty, The Rocky Horror Show,* and *Joseph and the Amazing Technicolor Dreamcoat.* Tickets run about $35, except for Sunday matinees (2:30pm), which are $20, but don't include dinner.

THE CLUB & LIVE MUSIC SCENE

Blu, 209 S. El Paso St. (© **915/351-8258**), is a downtown dancing hot spot featuring both DJs and local and national musical acts. **Stampede,** 5500 Doniphan Rd. (© **915/833-6397**), is an El Paso country-and-western institution that features recorded and live music.

THE BAR SCENE

Serving cayenne-spiced Cajun dishes and daily $1 beer specials, **Crawdaddy's,** 212 Cincinnati St. (© **915/533-9332**), is a cozy-but-rowdy haunt favored by the UTEP crowd. It's located amid a strip of bars and restaurants on Cincinnati Street, one of the city's livelier blocks at midnight. One of the most regal places in the Southwest to sip a cocktail, **Dome Bar,** 101 S. El Paso St. in the Camino Real Hotel (© **915/534-3000**), is light years beyond a typical hotel bar. **Rosa's Cantina,** 3454 Doniphan Dr. (© **915/833-0402**), was made famous by country legend Marty Robbins in his 1959 hit "El Paso"—or perhaps merely inspired by it after the fact.

A SIDE TRIP TO CIUDAD JUÁREZ

El Paso's sister city, Ciudad Juárez, is the fourth-largest city in Mexico with approximately 3 million residents. Together, the cities form the largest binational population in the world. Juárez is a regional manufacturing center, due to cheap, abundant labor, and companies such as General Motors and Sony have facilities in the city. Juárez is seedy in the same way as other border cities such as Nogales and Tijuana, but it is more of a real Mexican city, not one that is built on tourism alone. Juárez's history and authenticity, in our opinion, make it an interesting stop for an afternoon, or even an entire day. (If you're headed specifically to Marfa or Big Bend, however, it probably isn't worth the diversion.)

Like El Paso, Juárez's modern history begins with Spanish conquistador Juan de Oñate crossing the Rio Grande in 1581. The oldest structure on the border, **La Misión de Nuestra Señora Guadalupe (Our Lady of Guadalupe Mission),** was completed in 1668 and remains in remarkably good condition today. The city played important roles in the Mexican-American War and the Mexican Revolution, and was once frequented by Pancho Villa.

Today, the city's booming manufacturing industry is complemented by tourism, with many visitors crossing the border to take in the colorful outdoor markets, historic missions, and lively nightlife. Tourists often drive across the five bridges scattered around El Paso, park in downtown El Paso and walk across, or else take a taxi or a trolley tour. The bridges, aside from the "Free Bridge" (or Cordova Bridge) south of I-10 via U.S. 54, all charge nominal tolls, even to pedestrians, of 25¢ to $2. The most convenient points of entry are the two downtown bridges, at Stanton Street and Santa Fe Street. U.S. currency is welcome practically everywhere in Juárez.

> **_Tips_ A Note About Safety**
>
> Although most visitors to Juárez have an enjoyable time without incident, the city sees its fair share of drug trafficking, pickpocketing, and violence. Tourists have not been targeted by violence, but have been victims of theft. It is especially important to remain aware of your surroundings when visiting the city.

ESSENTIALS

VISITOR INFORMATION   Contact **Fiprotur Chihuahua,** Av. de las Americas No. 2551, Ciudad Juárez, Chihuahua, Mexico (© **888/654-0394;** www.visitajuarez. com). The **El Paso Convention & Visitors Bureau,** One Civic Center Plaza, El Paso, TX 79901 (© **800/351-6024** or 915/534-0601; www.elpasocvb.com), can also provide information and advice on trips across the border. If you're on foot, pick up the excellent _Downtown Historic Walking Tour of Juárez_ brochure. **_Note:_** Be sure to bring your passport if you cross the border. As of January 2008, passports will be required for reentry into the U.S.

TROLLEY TOURS   We strongly recommend taking one of the tours offered by the **El Paso–Juárez Trolley Company** (© **915/544-0062;** www.borderjumper.com). Riders board in front of the El Paso Convention and Performing Arts Center downtown and can leave the train to shop or eat at any of eight different stops, then catch another trolley later in the day to return to El Paso. The trolleys run daily from 10am to 4pm year-round. Tickets cost $13 for adults, $9 for children ages 4 to 12, and free for kids younger than 4.

WHAT TO SEE & DO
See the "El Paso" map on p. 340 to locate these attractions.

The Top Attractions
Juárez Museum of Art   Poorly funded but often artistically inspired, this contemporary, cone-shaped concrete structure is a worthwhile stop for people particularly interested in Mexican art. The museum has three main galleries, with the central structure surrounded by a moat and connected to the others via bridges, and visitors should expect to spend a little less than an hour exploring them. Exhibits change about six times annually, and include historic and contemporary pieces by local artists with a special emphasis on plastic arts.

Av. Lincoln and Av. Ignacio Mejia, in the PRONAF Center area. © 011-52/16-13-17-08. Free admission. Tues–Sun 11am–7pm.

La Misíon de Nuestra Señora Guadalupe   Originally built between 1662 and 1668 by Mexican, Spanish, and Indian labor, this is the oldest surviving church in the area and remains an active chapel today. It is considered a prime example of Indian baroque architecture, influenced by Arab tradition, and is adorned with 18th-century sculptures and oil paintings. Next door is a contemporary cathedral; behind the mission is a bronze statue of the founder, Fray Garcia of San Francisco.

Av. 16th de Septiembre, 2 blocks west of Av. Juárez.

Shopping
Browsing the outdoor markets and specialty stores in Juárez is a favorite pastime of the city's visitors.

Prices are rock bottom for the usual Mexican knickknacks—tapestries, sculptures, and souvenirs—and a bit less than their U.S. counterparts for liquor and food. Bargaining is part of the game at almost every shop in Juárez—it's not bad form to haggle at all. The markets are open daily from morning to evening, but exact hours are up to individual shopkeepers.

Geared toward tourists, the **Juárez City Market,** at Agustin Melgar Street and Avenida 16th de Septiembre, is a fun—although not particularly upscale—shopping spot. The two-story building is loaded with an endless array of velvet paintings, plaster of Paris statues, jewelry, and other standard-issue Mexican souvenirs. If your tastes tend towards posh, try **Decor,** at the intersection of Avenida Ignacio Mejia and Avenida Lincoln, a three-story retail standout chock-full of furniture, glass, ceramics, and jewelry. Other popular shopping spots include the **duty-free stores** at Av. Juárez #378 and Av. 16th de Septiembre #531 for liquor, porcelain, crystal, and perfumes; and **Avenida Juárez,** just south of the Santa Fe Street Bridge, lined with street merchants, souvenir shops, and pharmacies, culminating in the local's market, **Cuauhtemoc Market,** on the south side of the main plaza.

WHERE TO DINE

Ajuua!! ✦ AUTHENTIC MEXICAN   A onetime house converted into a splashy restaurant, Ajuaa!!—the Mexican equivalent of "Yahoo!"—is a massive art project that's a local standby for parties and entertaining out-of-town guests. Serving a wide variety of Mexican fare (from a menu at night and buffets at lunch and breakfast), the food is predominately beef, chicken, and seafood dishes with traditional Mexican preparations, and the drink of choice is tequila—the bar stocks 200 varieties, and margarita flavors run the gamut from mango to celery. There is nightly entertainment during dinner and live bands later on weekend nights.

162 N. Efren Ornelas. ℂ **011-52/16-16-69-35.** Main courses $4–$14. AE, DISC, MC, V. Daily 8am–midnight.

Nuevo Martino ✦ CONTINENTAL/MEXICAN   The atmosphere is thick at Nuevo Martino, straight from the jet-set days of the 1940s. A favorite of tourists and well-heeled locals, this intimate downtown cafe is dimly lit with red-leather booths, a fully stocked bar, and mirrored walls. White-jacketed waiters serve a full Continental menu, with dishes ranging from quail to octopus to chateaubriand (prepared tableside), as well as a selection of authentic Mexican entrees. Our favorites: the filet *tampiqueño,* a tender cut of beef covered with green chiles and soft Jack cheese, served with soup, salad, beans, tacos, and an enchilada; and the black bass medallions Mexicana with minispuds in a rich and spicy red-pepper sauce. The prices beat what you'll find north of the border, and the potent margaritas are not to be missed.

Av. Juárez #643. ℂ **011-52/12-33-70.** Main courses $14–$25. MC, V. Sun and Tues–Thurs noon–10pm; Fri–Sat 11am–11pm.

CIUDAD JUAREZ AFTER DARK

Juárez is a popular after-dark destination for El Pasoans, and there are numerous bars geared toward tourists on Avenida Juárez downtown and, to the east, Avenida Lincoln. Many of the bars are actually strip clubs, although there are sports bars and nightclubs as well. The can't-miss nightspot is the **Kentucky Club,** 629 Av. Juárez, swank in a Juárez sort of way. You can't do any better if you're looking to spend an afternoon over margaritas—legend has it that the drink was invented here in 1946 by a longtime bartender, the late Lorenzo Garcia. And Hollywood types once frequented this bar: Marilyn Monroe bought the bar a round after a quickie divorce from Arthur Miller.

The Copper Canyon

El Paso is often a jumping-off point for trips to the Copper Canyon in north-western Mexico. If you are interested in seeing a rugged and beautiful land; if you're interested in taking one of the most remarkable train trips in the world; if you're interested in hiking or riding horseback through remote areas to see an astonishing variety of flora and fauna; or if you're curious about a land still populated by indigenous people living pretty much the way they have for centuries, the Copper Canyon is the place to go.

Most often, when people say "Copper Canyon," they are referring to a section of the Sierra Madre known commonly in Mexico as the Sierra Tarahumara (after the Indians who live there). The area was formed through violent volcanic uplifting, followed by a slow, quiet process of erosion that carved a vast network of canyons into the soft volcanic stone.

Crossing the Sierra Tarahumara is the famed **Chihuahua al Pacífico (Chi-huahua to the Pacific)** railway. Acclaimed as an engineering marvel, the 390-mile railroad has 39 bridges (the highest is more than 1,000 ft. above the Chinipas River) and 86 tunnels. It climbs from Los Mochis, at sea level, up nearly 8,000 feet through some of Mexico's most magnificent scenery—thick pine forests, jagged peaks, and shadowy canyons—before descending again to its destination, the city of Chihuahua.

It's easier than ever to get to the region, but it's trickier than ever to travel through it on your own—hotel rooms can be hard to come by, and there have been numerous changes in the operation of the Copper Canyon train. Consequently, this is not the place to do casual, follow-your-nose trav-eling. A number of tour operators and packagers book trips to the Copper Canyon. The easiest thing is to contract with an agency that will plan your trip from El Paso. **San Diego Leisure** (© 800/605-1257; www.tourcopper canyon.com) sets up trips for any number of people using regular bus serv-ice and the Copper Canyon train. Or, you can take a bus to Chihuahua and contact a travel agency there that will book a trip into the canyon. This would be the cheapest and most flexible way to do it. I recommend **Turismo al Mar** (© 877/228-1288; www.copper-canyon.net).

Another option is to go with a custom tour operator; travel through these companies generally allows you more time in the canyon and a bet-ter experience. The best of the bunch is **Columbus Travel** (© 800/843-1060; www.canyontravel.com), which is pretty much in a class by itself. It has lined up some beautiful small lodges in the canyons and staffed them with tal-ented local guides. Another operator that provides good service is the El Paso–based **Native Trails** (© 800/884-3107; www.nativetrails.com).

For more information on traveling in the Copper Canyon, pick up a copy of *Frommer's Mexico* or check out www.frommers.com/destinations/the coppercanyon.

—David Baird

2 Small Towns of Central West Texas ⊛

Travelers crossing West Texas pass through a smattering of communities where they'll find a variety of roadside motels and restaurants. But those who only grab some Zs or a quick bite to eat will be missing out on some fun things to see and do. While most of the areas discussed in this section would not be our choice as a vacation destination in and of themselves, they are definitely worth a stop, and one could easily spend anywhere from a few hours to a few days in each place.

FORT DAVIS & DAVIS MOUNTAINS STATE PARK
205 miles SE of El Paso; 23 miles NE of Alpine; 110 miles NW of Big Bend National Park

A charming small town surrounded by dramatic scenery and steeped in Old West lore, Fort Davis is one of those rare places that can please both city and country types. The town itself is teeming with boutiques and B&Bs, and to the north, outdoors buffs will appreciate Davis Mountains State Park.

The town's origins are tied to Fort Davis, the identically named U.S. Army post established in 1854. The town was initially a ranching center, but the fort's 1891 abandonment and the railroads' decision to bypass the community led to an economic bust. After the fort was designated a National Historic Site in 1961, traffic increased and helped create the tourism-heavy landscape in place today.

ESSENTIALS
Getting There
Fort Davis is located on Tex. 17 between Balmorhea and Marfa. From the north, the town is accessed via I-10 by taking either Exit 192 or Exit 206 and driving south on the highway for about 40 miles. Tex. 118 also runs through the town, from Kent (on I-10) to the northwest and to Alpine to the southeast. The nearest major commercial airports are 170 miles north in Midland and 205 miles to the northwest in El Paso.

Getting Around
Fort Davis is centered on the town square and historic courthouse. Most of the businesses, lodging establishments, and restaurants are located on Main Street (Tex. 118), which runs north–south through the town square. You can stroll around town, but not to any of the attractions discussed below.

Visitor Information
The **Fort Davis Chamber of Commerce,** 4 Memorial Sq. (Box 378), Fort Davis, TX 79734 (℗ **800/524-3015** or 432/426-3015; www.fortdavis.com), provides brochures, advice, and other information.

FAST FACTS   Big Bend Regional Medical Center, 2600 Tex. 118 N. in Alpine (℗ **432/837-3447**), has 24-hour emergency services. The **post office,** located on the town square on Main Street, is open Monday through Friday from 8am to 4pm.

WHAT TO SEE & DO
The Top Attractions
Fort Davis National Historic Site ⊛   One of the best remaining examples of a frontier military post, Fort Davis was established in 1854, named after then-secretary of war Jefferson Davis. Surrounded by geological formations that offered natural defense as well as beauty, six companies of the Eighth U.S. Infantry first occupied the fort to battle hostile Comanches, Kiowas, and Apaches. Confederate soldiers controlled the fort for a spell in 1861; afterward, the fort sat vacant until 1867. It rose again as a

stronghold in the Indian wars of the late 19th century, pitting the African-American 10th U.S. Cavalry and other soldiers against the Apaches, until it was abandoned once and for all in 1891. Ten structures have since been restored, five of which are furnished with period antiques. Most of the Texas forts are either run-down or sitting in the middle of a barren plain, so this one—well manicured with a stunning rocky backdrop— is a standout. Expect to spend a little more than an hour if you tour all 10 structures.

Tex. 17/118, 1 mile north of Fort Davis. © 432/426-3224. www.nps.gov/foda. Admission $3 adults, free for children younger than 16. Daily 8am–5pm.

McDonald Observatory ☆ *Kids* Operated by the University of Texas and free from urban light pollution, McDonald Observatory is one of the word's leading astronomical research facilities. Start at the visitor center and take in the 12-minute orientation video: It will provide you with perspective both historical and interstellar. Guided tours depart the center several times daily and last about an hour. Twice daily, the visitor center hosts solar-viewing activities, where guests can get a glimpse of sunspots, flares, and other solar activity. If your schedule allows, visit during a nighttime "Star Party" ($10 adults, $8 children) held Tuesday, Friday, and Saturday at times determined by the season. These events allow guests to view celestial objects and constellations through the observatory's high-powered telescopes. Serious stargazers can join as members ($50 and up) in order to stay in the Astronomer's Lodge on-site ($70 per person per night, meals included).

Tex. 118 North, 16 miles northwest of Fort Davis. © 877/984-STAR (7827) for recorded information, or 432/426-3640. www.mcdonaldobservatory.org. Daytime pass (includes guided tour) $8 adults, $7 children younger than 13, $30 maximum per family. Daily 10am–5:30pm. Guided tours are conducted at 11am and 2pm daily.

Outdoor Activities
Fort Davis's outdoor recreation is centered on **Davis Mountains State Park,** located 4 miles northwest of town via Tex. 118 (© 432/426-3337). The second-highest range in all of Texas, the Davis Mountains reach their pinnacle at the peak of the 8,382-foot Mount Livermore. Hiking is our activity of choice here; try the moderate, 8-mile round-trip that leads to the Fort Davis National Historic Site. On or off the trails, the park is a great place for wildlife viewing and bird-watching. It's one of the few places in the United States that you might spot a Montezuma quail, and javelina (the wild boars that roam the Southwest), tarantulas, horned frogs, and pronghorn antelope also live in the park. The entrance fee is $3 for adults, free for children younger than 13. Campsites run $18 for full hook-ups, $14 for water and electric hook-ups only, and $8 to $10 for tent and primitive sites.

WHERE TO STAY
Hotel Limpia ☆ Spread out over 10 historic buildings, the individually decorated rooms at the Hotel Limpia are outfitted with quilted queen-size beds, rocking chairs, and modern bathrooms. The gorgeous 1,100-square-foot master suite in the vine- and stone-clad main building opens from a glassed veranda into a delightful garden area, but if you're looking for privacy, try one of the secluded cottages, located nearly a mile away from the main buildings. (Some of the units have kitchenettes.) There's also a great gift shop with Texas-flavored curios, books, and decor, the county's only bar, and a good restaurant.

101 Memorial Square (P.O. Box 1341), Fort Davis, TX 79734. © 800/662-5517 or 432/426-3237. Fax 432/426-3983. www.hotellimpia.com. 50 units, including 25 suites. $89–$109 double; $119–$250 suite. AE, DISC, MC, V. **Amenities:** Restaurant; bar. *In room:* A/C, TV, kitchenette (in some units), hair dryer.

Indian Lodge   Located at the base of a gentle slope adjacent to Davis Mountains State Park, this hotel is actually a state park in and unto itself—Indian Lodge State Park. Built in the 1930s by the Civilian Conservation Corps, Indian Lodge's architects drew inspiration from Indian pueblos, resulting in 18-inch-thick adobe walls and thatched viga ceilings fashioned from river cane and wooden beams. The original rooms are decorated the same as the day the place opened, with hand-carved cedar chairs, dressers, and bed frames, all with engraved petroglyphs, as well as decorative fireplaces and ornate stonework. A renovation, completed in 2006, undid a 1960s "modernization." All of the rooms are set off from a sunny central patio with a wishing well and rock gardens.

Tex. 118 North, at Davis Mountains State Park (P.O. Box 1707), Fort Davis, TX 79734. ✆ **432/426-3254**. Fax 432/ 426-2022. 39 units. $80–$115 double. DISC, MC, V. **Amenities:** Restaurant; outdoor heated pool. *In room:* A/C, TV.

Old Schoolhouse Bed and Breakfast   Situated in a shady grove of 32 pecan trees at the foot of Sleeping Lion Mountain, this B&B served as Fort Davis's schoolhouse from 1904 into the 1930s. It was then a private residence until 1999, when Carla and Steve Kennedy converted it into a charming inn where guests come from Texas's big cities to "decompress." The quaint rooms are scholastically themed: The spacious Reading Room has a king-size bed, a sleeper sofa, and a private entrance; the smaller 'Riting and 'Rithmetic rooms share a bathroom and feature antique furnishings. You won't want to skip the breakfasts here; you'll miss tempting home-cooked entrees such as corn-tortilla quiche, apple-baked oatmeal, or baked eggs with ham and three cheeses.

401 N. Front St. (P.O. Box 1221), Fort Davis, TX 79734. ✆ **432/426-2050**. Fax 432/426-2509. www.schoolhouse bnb.com. 3 units, 2 with shared bathroom, 1 guesthouse. $85–$95 double; $195 guesthouse. Rates include full breakfast. MC, V. *In room:* A/C, complimentary Wi-Fi, hair dryer, iron, no phone.

WHERE TO DINE

If you're looking for a quick bite, your best bet is **Murphy's Pizzeria & Café,** at the junction of Tex. 17 and Tex. 118 on the south end of town (✆ **432/462-2020**), serving up better-than-expected pizzas ($8 and up), as well as pasta, sandwiches, and salads. The **Hotel Limpia Dining Room,** 100 State St. (✆ **432/426-3241**), is upscale; main courses are $10 to $25. Upstairs is Sutler's Club, the only watering hole in the traditionally dry county. Membership ($2–$3 for 3 days) is required.

BALMORHEA STATE PARK ★★

185 miles E of El Paso; 32 miles N of Fort Davis

One of the lesser-seen jewels of the Texas State Park system (and one of the smallest, at 45 acres), **Balmorhea State Park,** 9207 Tex. 17 S. (✆ **432/375-2370;** www.tpwd. state.tx.us/park/balmorhe), is centered on a massive, 1¾-acre swimming pool that is fed by San Solomon Springs. It holds 3.5 million gallons of water at a fairly constant 74°F (23°C). Size aside, this is no ordinary pool: The water teems with fish, and the floor is covered in rocks. The Civilian Conservation Corps built the V-shaped pool in the 1930s, surrounding it with shady trees and a 200-foot circle of limestone and flagstone. Swimming is popular, as are snorkeling and scuba diving. You might see the occasional (nonpoisonous) water snake or turtle in it. A canal system crosscuts the park, leading from the pool to other areas, and providing a habitat for many native fish species, two of which—the Comanche Springs pupfish and Pecos Gambusia—are endangered. There are changing areas with showers and two diving boards at the pool, which is open daily from 8am until a half-hour before sunset. Next door, the **Toyahvale Desert**

A Side Trip to Candelaria

West of Presidio, FM 170 continues for 48 miles as a paved road to Candelaria. The drive is scenic, off the beaten path, and highly recommended. The commercial operations are few and far between, save a few cantinas and **Chinati Hot Springs,** Box 67 Candelaria Route, Marfa, TX 79843 (**© 432/229-4165;** www.chinatihotsprings,org), a rustic resort centered on the 109°F (43°C) water of the eponymous springs. Regardless, you'll find many photo opportunities and get a sense of the border as a real place and not an imaginary line.

Oasis, 9225 Tex. 17 S. (**© 432/375-2572**), provides swimwear, snorkel rentals, and scuba equipment rentals and air fills from 10am to 6pm daily.

A reconstructed *cienega* (desert wetland) is another notable attraction in Balmorhea State Park. Located near the campground, the San Solomon Cienega is a good spot to look for native wildlife: You might see a Texas spiny soft-shelled turtle, a blotched water snake, or a green heron from the raised wooden platform, or spot a channel catfish through the underwater viewing window. A path system allows viewing of the fish, reptiles, and amphibians in the canals.

The park has 38 campsites, most with water and electrical hook-ups, for $11 to $17 a night, in addition to the $5 entrance fee. Additionally, there is a small motel on the park's grounds, with standard double rooms for $55 to $65 and kitchenettes for $70 nightly. For groceries, you'll need to head into town, as the gift shop at the visitor center stocks mainly souvenirs and books. The park is located 5 miles south of the town of Balmorhea on Tex. 17.

MARFA
115 miles NW of Big Bend National Park; 193 miles SE of El Paso; 21 miles S of Fort Davis

Named after a character in Dostoevski's *The Brothers Karamazov* by a railroad exec's wife, this town of 2,000 residents is on the brink of one of the last American frontiers. Surrounded by rugged terrain, Marfa is, to say the least, remote. Once an Old West saloon-and-casino outpost, the predominantly Mexican town has evolved into a haven for contemporary artists, its nucleus being the avant-garde Chinati Foundation. This phenomenon makes for some interesting contrasts: 10-gallon hats and berets, wine bars and feed stores, cowboys and intellectuals, all coexisting in the same small town. There's a lot of buzz about Marfa being "the next Santa Fe," but it remains more than a little bit sleepy—and that's a big part of its charm.

ESSENTIALS
Getting There
Marfa is located at the junction of U.S 67, U.S. 90, and Tex. 17, 60 miles north of Big Bend Ranch State Park. If you're arriving from the east, take I-10, Exit 248, and proceed 82 miles on U.S. 67 through Alpine. From the west, Marfa is located 78 miles southeast of Van Horn on U.S. 90; from the north, it's 60 miles south of I-10, Exit 206, on Tex. 17. The nearest major commercial airport is nearly 200 miles away in El Paso.

Getting Around

Tex. 17 (Lincoln St.) is the main north–south artery and U.S. 90 (San Antonio St.) is the main east–west route. The town square and Presidio County Courthouse are located at Lincoln and Highland streets. You can stroll around downtown Marfa, but in general, a car is necessary to check out the Marfa lights and other attractions.

Visitor Information

Contact the **Marfa Chamber of Commerce,** 207 N. Highland Ave. (P.O. Box 635), Marfa, TX 79843 (© 800/650-9696 or 432/729-4942; www.marfacc.com), for visitor information. The website **www.marfatx.com** is another good resource.

FAST FACTS   The nearest hospital is 35 miles west in Alpine, the **Big Bend Regional Medical Center,** 2600 Tex. 118 N. (© 432/837-3447). The **post office,** 100 N. Highland Ave., is open Monday through Friday from 8am to 4:30pm.

THE TOP ATTRACTIONS

Chinati Foundation ✸✸ *Finds*   Housed in 15 buildings at a former U.S. Army post, this decidedly different arts facility is the centerpiece of Marfa's fertile contemporary arts scene. Founded in 1985 by the late Donald Judd, the permanent collection consists of numerous works of minimalist and avant-garde art in mediums ranging from paper to steel, from fluorescent light to concrete. Defying artistic expectations, the pieces are all about context; each is strongly tied to architecture and landscape. There are also temporary displays and exhibitions by an international group of artists-in-residence. Guided tours last about 4 hours, starting at 10am, breaking for lunch, and continuing at 2pm. The foundation hosts a major open house every October. Marfa's population momentarily doubles during the event, selling out every hotel within a 100-mile radius.

U.S. 67 (a half-mile south of Marfa). © 432/729-4362. www.chinati.org. Admission $10 adults, $5 students and seniors, free for children younger than 12. No public admission except by guided tours, which are offered Wed–Sun at 10am and 2pm.

Marfa and Presidio County Museum   Housed in the historic Victorian adobe Humphris-Humphreys House, this museum focuses on the area since 1883, with exhibits on ranching, mining, and military history. We recommend it mainly for the excellent collection of black-and-white photographs shot by Frank Duncan in the first half of the 20th century, and a natural history exhibit on the surrounding Chihuahuan Desert. Allow 1 hour.

110 W. San Antonio St. © 432/729-4140. Free admission, donations accepted. Mon–Fri 2–5pm; Sat by appointment.

Presidio County Courthouse   Built in 1885 for $60,000—and magnificently restored in 2001 for $2.5 million—this courthouse is one of West Texas's most impressive, with its magnificent domed roof and classical Victorian woodwork. The architectural style is Second Empire with Italianate details such as overhanging eaves, decorative brackets, and windows that delineate the floors. A "Statue of Justice" stands atop the dome, sans the traditional scales. According to local legend, a convicted cowboy shot the scales out of the statue's hands in the 1890s, proclaiming, "There is no justice in this country." If you have the time, climb to the fifth floor for the view of Marfa and the surrounding countryside.

Lincoln St. and Highland Ave. © 432/729-4942 for information. Free admission. Building Mon–Fri 9am–5pm; grounds 24 hr.

Marfa's Mystery Lights

In 1883, an illumination flickered on the horizon east of Marfa, spooking a young cowhand by the name of Robert Ellison. Fearing the lights were Apache campfires, Ellison left behind the cattle he was herding and searched the terrain on horseback. He found nothing. Ever since, the **"Marfa Ghost Lights"** have puzzled thousands of eyewitnesses, as they appear, disappear, and reappear in an area where there are no roads, no houses, and no human inhabitants. Some observers insist the lights are the work of super-natural beings or visiting aliens, while others point to electrostatic discharge, car headlights, campfires, or swamp gas as the real cause, but no one has definitively solved the mystery.

There is a nifty viewing area 9 miles east of Marfa on U.S. 90. The lights are best viewed between 2 and 4 hours after sundown: Look to the northeast, just to the right of the mountains, along the horizon for the sporadic flickers of light. If there's a crowd, it's a scene straight out of *Close Encounters of the Third Kind.* If the lights really pique your interest, don't miss the annual **Marfa Lights Festival,** a Labor Day weekend celebration with a parade, street dances, concerts, and arts-and-crafts sales.

WHERE TO STAY

Cibolo Creek Ranch ⭐⭐⭐   Tucked under the Chinati Mountains in some of the most wide-open country in all of Texas, this is a getaway for the most special of occasions, and accordingly priced. Situated on a 32,000-acre ranch that's a world away from the outside world (and home to bison, elk, and Texas longhorns), the ranch is centered on a restoration of a historic 19th-century private fort, the domain of trader and cattle baron Milton Faver until the 1880s. The idyllic setting plays host today to a first-class resort, featuring picture-perfect guest rooms with red-tile floors, adobe walls, and sumptuous border decor. The recreation is as impressive as the scenery: Horseback rides and Humvee tours are available for a fee. Trails crisscross the property. Natural springs feed canals that fill an idyllic lake, complete with fish to lure and paddleboats to paddle. Gourmet meals, served family style, are part of the package at the remote ranch.

P.O. Box 44, Shafter, TX 79850. ℂ **432/229-3737.** Fax 432/229-3653. www.cibolocreekranch.com. 32 units. $450 double; $75 per additional person. Rates include all meals and many recreational activities. AE, DISC, MC, V. **Amenities:** Restaurant; bar; outdoor heated pool; exercise room; Jacuzzi; activities desk. *In room:* A/C, coffeemaker, no phone. Located 32 miles south of Marfa off U.S. 67.

The Hotel Paisano ⭐⭐   After years of semi-hibernation, this glorious 1930s-era hotel was rescued in 2001 by the proprietors of the Hotel Limpia in nearby Fort Davis. A comprehensive restoration later, the property has reclaimed its former status as the premiere hotel between El Paso and San Antonio. The building itself is stunning, a renowned hybrid of prairie and mission architecture that's listed on the National Register of Historic Places. Inside, the rooms balance history and modernity, with comfortable new furnishings and a myriad of arches, stained-glass windows, and other subtle details. And there's some serious Hollywood lore: The cast and crew of the epic *Giant* stayed here during production in the 1950s. James Dean's onetime room is the most popular, but Rock Hudson's corner suite, with a full kitchen and a massive balcony overlooking the courtyard pool, is our favorite.

Texas St. and Highland Ave. (P.O. Box Z), Marfa, TX 79843. ☎ **866/729-3669** or 432/729-3669. Fax 432/426-3779. www.hotelpaisano.com. 40 units, including 9 suites. $99–$109 double; $119–$250 suites. AE, DISC, MC, V. **Amenities:** Restaurant; bar; outdoor heated pool. *In room:* A/C, kitchen, no phone.

The Thunderbird Hotel ☆☆ This onetime roadside motel became a hip work of minimalist art during a 2004 renovation. Centered on an outdoor pool and a gravel parking lot, the U-shaped structure's rooms are starkly contemporary with Western details (for example, cowhide rugs atop painted concrete floors) and such modern perks as iPod docking stations. The pool and adjacent fire-pit area have wireless Internet access, and the rooms are wired. Available for rental here: cruiser bikes ($20 a day), vintage record players ($10 a stay), DVDs from a well-chosen library ($2 a night), and a typewriter (free).

601 W. San Antonio St. and Highland Ave., Marfa, TX 79843. ☎ **432/729-1984.** Fax 432/729-1989. www.thunderbird marfa.com. 24 units. $115–$175 double. AE, DISC, MC, V. **Amenities:** Bar; outdoor heated pool; bike rentals. *In room:* A/C, cable TV/DVD, dataport, minibar, hair dryer.

WHERE TO DINE

Beyond the greasy spoons, there are a few high-end restaurants in Marfa, including **Jett's Grill** at the Hotel Paisano, Texas Street and Highland Avenue (☎ **432/729-3838**). Named after James Dean's character in *Giant,* the restaurant serves dinner and Sunday brunch only and features Continental fare spiced with a south-of-the-border twist. Main courses run $9 to $25. Another upscale option is **Maiya's,** 103 N. Highland Ave. (☎ **432/729-4410**), offering a creative selection of northern Italian fare in a very sleek, very red space. It's open Wednesday through Saturday evenings, with most dishes between $15 and $30.

SHOPPING

The best bookstore in the entire region is the sophisticated **Marfa Book Co.,** 105 S. Highland Ave. (☎ **432/729-3906**), which features a coffee and wine bar and a deep inventory of art and architecture titles.

ALPINE

80 miles N of Big Bend National Park; 26 miles E of Marfa; 23 miles SE of Fort Davis

The home of Sul Ross State University, Alpine is nicknamed "The Hub of the Big Bend." Long the commercial center of vast Brewster County, this town of 6,500 has numerous amenities that make it a good jumping-off point to Big Bend National Park, or a nice stopover while en route to other area destinations: a vibrant Main Street with plenty of galleries and funky retailers, excellent hiking in all directions, an active railroad depot on the Southern Pacific line, and festivals and museums that are pure West.

ESSENTIALS
Getting There

Alpine is located at the junction of U.S 67/90 and Tex. 118, just 80 miles north of Big Bend National Park. If you're arriving from the east, take I-10, Exit 248, and proceed 56 miles on U.S. 67. From the west, Alpine is located 55 miles south of Balmorhea (I-10, Exit 206). **Amtrak** (☎ **800/872-2745**) serves the train station at 102 W. Holland St., the closest such facility to Big Bend National Park.

Getting Around

U.S. 67/90 (Holland St.) is the main east–west artery and Tex. 119 (5th St.) is the main north–south route; downtown is centered on the intersection of the two. Rental cars are available through **Alpine Auto Rental** (© **800/894-3463** or 432/837-3463; www.alpineautorental.com).

Visitor Information

Contact the **Alpine Chamber of Commerce,** 106 N. 3rd St., Alpine, TX 79830 (© **800/561-3735** or 432/837-2326; www.alpinetexas.com).

FAST FACTS   The **Big Bend Regional Medical Center,** 2600 Tex. 118 N. (© **432/ 837-3447**), has the only 24-hour emergency room in the region. The **post office,** 901 W. Holland Ave., is open Monday through Friday from 8am to 4pm, and Saturday 10am to 1pm.

THE TOP ATTRACTIONS

Museum of the Big Bend ☆   This excellent facility tracks the Big Bend region's history, from American Indian cultures (points that date back more than 3,000 years) to the "Conquistador to Cowboy" exhibit, telling the story of European settlers. Among the other highlights are replicas of pterosaur bones excavated from Big Bend National Park (the critter had a 40-ft. wingspan!) and an outdoor cactus garden. Expect to spend about an hour.

On the campus of the Sul Ross State University. © **432/837-8143**. www.sulross.edu/~museum. Free admission. Tues–Sat 9am–5pm; Sun 1–5pm.

Elephant Mountain Wildlife Management Area   While hiking and camping are available, the prime activity here is a 15-mile round-trip driving tour that provides

Gallery Hopping in the Big Bend

Marfa might be one of the most buzzed-about art towns in the West, but— outside of the Chinati Foundation—it has only a handful of galleries. Art aficionados can cover Marfa's gallery scene proper in a few hours, but a day can be made visiting galleries in not only Marfa, but Alpine and Marathon as well. Here are our favorites.

Marfa   We like **Ballroom Marfa,** an installation-oriented space at 108 E. San Antonio St. (© **432/729-3600**), that also hosts film screenings, lectures, and musical performances; and the photography-laden **Highland Gallery,** 119 N. Highland Ave. (© **432/729-3000**).

Alpine   Keri Artzt's **Kiowa Gallery,** 105 E. Holland Ave. (© **432/837-3067**), is our favorite in the region, with an eclectic collection of mostly regional work, ranging from elegant to oddball. **Ivey's Emporium,** 109 E. Holland Ave. (© **432/837-7474**), has a wide range of artworks and gifts.

Marathon   **Baxter Gallery,** 209 W. U.S. 90 (© **432/386-4041**), specializes in landscapes and wildlife sculptures by local artisans. The fine art photography at **Evans Gallery,** 21 S. 1st St. (© **432/386-4366**), is alternately sublime and stunning.

99 *Luftballons* over Alpine

Well, maybe not quite 99, but you can see at least a few dozen balloons launch near the Casparis Airport, 2 miles north of Alpine off Highway 118, during Labor Day weekend. The **Big Bend Balloon Bash** is 3 days of balloons and other aerial pursuits. Arrive before 9am to see the balloons, or go see them glow Saturday night. Call (C) **432/837-7486** or log on to www.bigbendballoonbash.com.

excellent wildlife-viewing opportunities. The area is home to a herd of desert bighorn, as well as mule deer, javelina, and dozens of reptile and bird species. Morning is the best time to spot the critters in this mountainous desert environment. There are primitive campsites with fire rings available at no cost.

26 miles south of Alpine via Tex. 118. (C) **432/837-3251.** Free admission. Portions of the area are open year-round; driving tour May 1–Aug 30.

WHERE TO STAY

Holland Hotel   Originally opening on Alpine's main drag in the 1920s, the Holland Hotel has seen a good deal of work in recent years and has a wide variety of lodgings to choose from. No room here is exactly the same as another, ranging from newly retouched suites (with hardwood floors, antique furnishings, and jetted tubs) to the cozy fourth-floor Crow's Nest, complete with a private rooftop deck. There are four modern lofts in a nearby rental, the largest of which is more than 1,000 square feet. On the ground floor is the Edelweiss Brewery and Restaurant.

209 W. Holland Ave., Alpine, TX 79830. (C) **800/535-8040** or 432/837-3844. Fax 432/837-7346. www.hollandhotel. net. 27 units, including 5 suites and 4 lofts. $50–$135 double; $65–$150 suite; $115–$195 suite. AE, DC, DISC, MC, V. **Amenities:** Restaurant (German/microbrewery). *In room:* A/C, cable TV w/pay movies, coffeemaker, no phone (some).

The Maverick Inn ⊀   A retro-minded update of a roadside motel—down to the new old-fashioned neon sign—the Maverick Inn took cues from the Gage Hotel and other historic desert tourist outposts. Studies in masculine Texas chic, the woody, adobe-walled rooms have Saltillo tile floors with cowhide rugs. The small, bean-shaped pool is an oasis, bordered by desert flora and a shaded patio.

1200 E. Holland Ave., Alpine, TX 79830. (C) **432/837-0628.** Fax 432/837-0825. www.themaverickinn.com. 18 units. $75–$125 double. AE, DISC, MC, V. **Amenities:** Outdoor heated pool. *In room:* A/C, cable TV, complimentary Wi-Fi, kitchenettes, microwave, fridge, coffeemaker, hair dryer, iron.

WHERE TO DINE

Named for a ranch in *Giant,* the **Reata Restaurant,** 203 N. 5th St. ((C) **432/837-9232;** www.reata.net), serves Texas nouveau and some of the meanest steaks in the Big Bend; main courses average $10 for lunch and $20 for dinner. **Alicia's,** 708 E. Gallego Ave. ((C) **432/837-2802**), is a standby for big burritos and hearty breakfasts ($3–$8). **Texas Fusion,** 200 W. Murphy Ave. ((C) **432/837-1214**), is locals' new favorite, serving barbecue, Mexican, burgers, and steaks; main courses are $4 to $13.

3 Midland-Odessa

300 miles E of El Paso; 135 miles S of Lubbock

Welcome to oil country, where the ups and downs of the petroleum industry have long defined these twin cities, 21 miles apart on I-20. Midland-Odessa sits in the geographic center of the Permian Basin, the home of the country's richest oil fields—about 20% of the United States' reserves. Today, only Alaska produces more oil than the Permian Basin.

The area saw the first of several oil booms in the 1920s. However, less than a decade later, the Great Depression brought on the first of several busts. Production increased during World War II, but foreign competition brought on another bust by 1970s. The pendulum again swayed in the boom direction until 1982, when the bottom suddenly fell out of the oil market: Wells were capped, new houses went unsold, and banks failed. In the time since, the economy has diversified and recovered, but Midland-Odessa remains the heart and soul of the Permian Basin's oil industry. As it goes, so does Midland-Odessa.

The onetime home of two presidents—George H. W. Bush and his son George W.—the cities are home to a handful of noteworthy attractions and offer an educational glimpse at the rewards and the ravages of a volatile, oil-heavy economy. But Midland-Odessa is by no means a tourist destination—it's really an overnight stopover on the dusty and dry West Texas plains.

ESSENTIALS
GETTING THERE
Midland is located on the north side of I-20, accessible via exits 136 and 138. Tex. 349 runs north–south through the city. Odessa is located 21 miles west of Midland on the north side of I-20, accessible via exits 112 through 121. U.S. 385 (Grant Ave.) bisects the city north–south, through downtown and to I-20.

Midland International Airport, located between Midland and Odessa at 9506 La Force Blvd. (© 432/560-2200; www.flymaf.com), is the primary commercial airport in the area. Car-rental companies are on-site.

GETTING AROUND
Laid out on a fairly standard grid that parallels I-20, Midland is a relatively easy city to navigate by car. Most of the accommodations are located on the west side of town on **Wall Street (Business 20),** which continues east through downtown. **Loop 250** circumnavigates the city.

Odessa's busiest street is **Grant Avenue (U.S. 385, also known as Andrews Hwy.),** which runs north–south through downtown. **42nd Street** becomes **Tex. 191** and continues east to Midland. **Loop 338** circles the city.

VISITOR INFORMATION
The **Midland Convention and Visitors Bureau,** 109 N. Main St., Midland, TX 79701 (© **800/624-6435** or 432/683-3381; www.visitmidlandtx.com), and the **Odessa Convention and Visitors Bureau,** 700 N. Grant Ave., Suite 200, Odessa, TX 79761 (© **800/780-4678** or 432/333-7871; www.odessacvb.com), can provide additional information on the cities.

FAST FACTS   Midland Memorial Hospital, 2200 W. Illinois Ave. (© **432/685-1111**), has a 24-hour emergency room; Midland's **downtown post office** is at 100 E. Wall St. **Medical Center Hospital,** 500 W. 4th St. (© **432/640-4000**), is Odessa's largest full-service hospital; the **main post office** is located at 200 N. Texas St.

WHAT TO SEE & DO
THE TOP ATTRACTIONS
Fans of roadside kitsch surely will appreciate two Odessa landmarks: The world's largest jackrabbit is located on 8th Street and Sam Houston Avenue; and on the campus of the

University of Texas of the Permian Basin at 4901 E. University Blvd. sits a 70% scale replica of Stonehenge.

American Airpower Heritage Museum 🎯 With a "Ghost Squadron" of more then 130 planes and choppers, this museum is home to the world's largest collection of vintage World War II aircraft. It's worth an hour or two for aviation and history buffs. The planes are housed in an adjacent 60,000-square-foot hangar, with about 15 on display at any given time. There are also multimedia exhibits and nice collections of war artifacts and aviation nose art. The museum's operators sponsor the annual AIRSHO each October, featuring dramatic re-creations of World War II events.

9600 Wright Dr. at Midland International Airport. ✆ 432/563-1000 or 432/567-3009. www.airpowermuseum.org. Admission $10 adults, $9 teens and seniors, $7 children 6 to 12, free for children younger than 6. Mon–Sat 9am–5pm; Sun and holidays noon–5pm.

The Globe of the Great Southwest *Finds* A replica of London's Globe Theatre (William Shakespeare's old haunt) down to the octagonal design and jutting stage surrounded by seating, the resident company produces about eight plays annually; the emphasis is on Shakespeare. The theater also hosts touring productions and concerts.

2308 Shakespeare Rd., Odessa. ✆ 432/332-1586. www.globesw.org. Admission $5. Tickets for performances $10–$12. Mon–Fri 10am–6pm. Tours available by appointment only.

Museum of the Southwest 🎯 *Kids* Occupying the stately Turner Mansion (1934), this museum does a nice job displaying art and archaeological artifacts. We were impressed by the quality of the museum's permanent collection, with pieces by several Taos Society members and a wide range of indigenous art. Also on-site: a children's museum, with interactive exhibits on art and science and a kid-size town, and a planetarium. Shows are usually held on Friday nights at 8pm. Expect to spend an hour or two here.

Midland's Famous Son, George

Born in New Haven, Connecticut, on July 6, 1946, George Walker Bush—aka "Dubya"—was on the plains of West Texas by the time he was 2 years old. His father (and our 41st president), George H. W. Bush, moved the family west to seek fortune in the oil business. The first stop was Odessa, but in 1950, the family moved to Midland, where they lived until 1959. It was this time—young George's formative years—that made the biggest impression on this president-to-be, and in 1975 he returned as an adult to make Midland his home and make his own name in the oil business.

One of the Bush family's Midland homes, where they lived from 1957 to 1959, still stands at 2703 Sentinel Ave. In addition, the Bushes lived at 405 E. Maple Ave. (from 1950–51) and 1412 W. Ohio Ave. (between 1951–55). The Ohio Avenue home has been restored to its 1950s appearance and is open to the public. For additional information, contact the **George W. Bush Childhood Home,** 1412 Ohio Ave. (✆ 432/682-1111; www.bushchildhoodhome.org). Additionally, the **Presidential Museum** in Odessa (✆ 432/363-7737) relocated the Bush home in Odessa to its grounds and also restored it for the public.

1705 W. Missouri Ave., Midland. (432/683-2882. www.museumsw.org. Free admission (donations welcome). Planetarium shows $3 adults, $2 children ages 12 and younger. Tues–Sat 10am–5pm; Sun 2–5pm.

Odessa Meteor Crater and Museum   The second-largest meteor crater in the United States (bested only by Sunset Crater near Flagstaff, Arizona) is about 50,000 years old, born when a flaming hunk of asteroid collided with the West Texas plains. A National Natural Landmark, the crater was once 550 feet wide and 100 feet deep, but sediment has obscured it substantially. It's still big enough to encompass a short nature trail, marked with interpretive signs detailing the initial impact and the subsequent study. The museum houses chunks of the actual meteorite among its displays. Expect to spend 45 minutes here.

Meteor Crater Rd. (9 miles southwest of Odessa via I-10, Exit 108). (432/381-0946. Free admission. Tues–Sat 10am–5pm; Sun 1–5pm.

The Permian Basin Petroleum Museum   Midland, being the center of both the Permian Basin (geographically) and the American oil business (economically), is the ideal location for a museum dedicated to "black gold." Requiring a little more than an hour of time to investigate, the displays here are a tad dated and often come off as P.R. for the Texas oil industry. Nonetheless, the museum interprets both the prehistoric basis for the rich oil field—West Texas was a tropical sea 230 million years ago—and the industry's modern history.

1500 I-20 West (Exit 136), Midland. (432/683-4403. www.petroleummuseum.org. Admission $8 adults, $6 ages 12–17 and seniors, $5 children 6–11, free for children younger than 6. Mon–Sat 9am–5pm; Sun 2–5pm.

The Presidential Museum   Whereas many museums detail the life and times of one president, this is one of a few museums dedicated to the office of the U.S. presidency itself. The permanent collection of campaign memorabilia is exhaustive and fascinating, with scores of buttons, posters, and stickers hyping candidates from every imaginable party. Expect to spend an hour or two.

4919 E. University Blvd., Odessa. (432/363-7737. $8 adults, $5 students and seniors, free for children younger than 5. Tues–Sat 10am–5pm. Closed major holidays.

OUTDOOR ACTIVITIES & SPECTATOR SPORTS
Midland has two public golf courses: the 27-hole **Hogan Park Golf Course,** 3600 N. Fairground Rd. ((**432/685-7360**), and the 18-hole **Nueva Vista Golf Club,** 6101 W. Wadley Ave. ((**432/520-0500**). Greens fees for 18 holes range from $25 to $37, cart included. In Odessa, **Sunset Country Club,** 9301 Andrews Hwy. ((**432/366-1061**), is an 18-hole course open to the public year-round. Greens fees are $14 to $19, and carts are $11.

Baseball fans can get their fix in the form of the **Midland RockHounds** ((**432/520-2255;** www.midlandrockhounds.org), the AA Texas League affiliate of the Oakland Athletics. The RockHounds play 70 home dates from April to August at the new First American Bank Ballpark, 5514 Champions Dr. Tickets cost $5 to $14. The Central Hockey League's **Odessa Jackalopes** ((**432/552-7825;** www.jackalopes.org) play an October-to-March schedule at the Ector County Coliseum, 42nd Street and Andrews Highway. Tickets run $13 to $23.

WHERE TO STAY
Hilton Midland Plaza   If you're looking for luxury at a reasonable price, look no further than this full-service hotel, located at ground zero of the American oil business in downtown Midland. The hotel consists of two 11-story towers on either side of a

courtyard pool. Graced with a three-level atrium, the lobby is relaxing and inviting, and the guest rooms are spacious and comfortable. Every room has plush chairs, a pair of two-line phones, and a 27-inch television. Some of the rooms on the concierge level have balconies.

117 W. Wall St., Midland, TX 79701. ℂ **432/683-6131.** Fax 432/683-0958. www.midland.hilton.com. 249 units. $109–$229 double; $300–$450 suite. AE, DC, DISC, MC, V. **Amenities:** 4 restaurants; 2 bars; outdoor heated pool; exercise room; Jacuzzi; spa; concierge; limited room service; laundry service; dry cleaning; executive level. *In room:* A/C, TV w/pay movies, dataport, coffeemaker, hair dryer, iron.

MCM Elegante ⚸   This former Radisson reopened as an independent in 2002 under the tag, "tropical elegance in the desert." With a lobby boasting multihued floral carpeting, stained-glass chandeliers, and a large aquarium, the hotel is a bit over the top, but it hits the mark more often than not. With nice city views from wall-length windows, crown molding, and red-hued wood furnishings, the rooms go beyond what you'd expect in a chain, with plenty of perks. (One example: The smallish bathrooms are stocked with bottled water—guests readily pay the $3.50 price tag once they get a taste of what's on tap.) The recreational facilities are dynamite, including a jogging track, putting/chipping green, seasonally domed pool area, and several sports fields.

5200 E. University Blvd., Odessa, TX 79762. ℂ **866/368-5885** or 432/368-5885. Fax 432/362-8958. www.mcm elegante.com. 191 units, including 4 suites. $169 double; $199–$299 suite. AE, DC, DISC, MC, V. **Amenities:** Restaurant; bar; outdoor pool; exercise room; spa; Jacuzzi; car-rental desk; courtesy car; salon; limited room service; dry cleaning; executive level. *In room:* A/C, TV w/pay movies, complimentary Wi-Fi, coffeemaker, hair dryer, iron.

WHERE TO DINE

Our pick for a quick bite in the area is **Manuel's Crispy Tacos,** 1404 E. 2nd St., Odessa (ℂ **432/333-2751**), a fun family joint known for its namesake dish. Main courses are $5 to $16.

Wall Street Bar and Grill ⚸ BISTRO   With a stock ticker over the front entrance, this restaurant caters to the wheelers and dealers of Midland's business community, but history buffs will find other things to gawk at while they dine. The 1910 building, originally a saddle shop, still features the original pressed tin ceiling, and the cherry-stained mahogany bar and back bar received a commendation from the Texas Historical Foundation for their restoration. The menu, conversely, is contemporary, with tastily creative offerings such as seafood rellenos with chipotle-tomatillo sauce, pecan-crusted trout, and charbroiled pork chops. The crawfish étouffée, rich and thick, is just about as good as it gets.

115 E. Wall St., Midland. ℂ **432/684-8686.** Main courses $9–$21. AE, DC, DISC, MC, V. Mon–Fri 11am–2:30pm; Sun–Thurs 5:30–10pm; Fri–Sat 5:30–11pm; Sun brunch 10:30am–2:30pm.

DUNE SLEDDING IN MONAHANS SANDHILLS STATE PARK
30 miles W of Odessa

When Spanish explorers first stumbled upon these sand hills in the mid–16th century, they labeled them "perfect miniature Alps of sand." Perpetually changing geologic and geometric wonders, the 3,840 acres of dunes at **Monahans Sandhills State Park,** I-20 Exit 86 (ℂ **432/943-2092;** www.tpwd.state.tx.us/park/monahans), represent the only public access to a 200-mile range of dunes that stretches from eastern New Mexico into the Permian Basin of West Texas.

Start at the visitor center, where you can watch a short orientation video, check out exhibits on all things sandy, and trek through the dunes on a .25-mile interpretive trail. The center rents plastic disks and toboggans for West Texas–style sledding, down dune-slopes that top out at 70 feet in height. Besides sledding them, you can explore the dunes on foot or horseback. (You'll need to bring your own horse to the 600-acre equestrian area; no stables are on-site.)

The dunes are far from barren. Many plants thrive here, including the shin oak, an unusually small oak with unusually large acorns that comprise a "Lilliputian Jungle" in the park. Other native inhabitants are deer, coyote, possum, and bobcats. For the human guests, there are 24 back-in campsites with water and electricity for $13 a night; the day-use fee is $2 (free for children younger than 13). The park is open daily from 8am to 10pm.

If you're a Coca-Cola fanatic, stop in at **Big Burger and Coca-Cola Museum,** 1016 Stockton St. in Monahans, off of I-20 Exit 80 (C **432/943-5655**), an all-American burger joint plastered with every imaginable piece of Coke memorabilia. Menu items range from $4 to $8; the fried catfish dinners merit a detour.

4 San Angelo

224 miles NW of Austin; 111 miles SE of Midland; 64 miles N of Sonora

First known as "the town over the river" from Fort Concho, San Angelo was the prototypical rollicking, gun-slinging Wild West outpost during the late 1860s and 1870s. During these early days, the soldiers from the fort and cowhands from the field would cross the Concho River to get to the brothels, casinos, and saloons that dominated the town on the other side.

A city of about 100,000 residents, modern San Angelo is a more than adequate stopover on a cross-Texas road trip. Its rowdy past can be revisited in the form of Historic Concho Avenue, now lined with boutiques and jewelers instead of casinos and bordellos, and old Fort Concho, a National Historic Landmark. The city is also one of the few oases of West Texas, with the Concho snaking through town and five reservoirs within 40 miles, and home to a noteworthy arts scene.

ESSENTIALS
GETTING THERE
The largest city in Texas not located on an interstate, San Angelo lies at the junction of three U.S. highways: 67, 87, and 277. U.S. 87 crosses I-20 at Big Spring, and U.S. 67 and U.S. 277 are both accessible from I-20 near Abilene. From the south, U.S. 67 diverges from I-10 at Fort Stockton and U.S. 277 crosses the interstate at Sonora.

San Angelo Regional Airport/Mathis Field, located about 8 miles south of the city at 7654 Knickerbocker Rd. (C **325/659-6409;** www.mathisfield.com), is the only commercial airport in the Concho River Valley and is served by **Continental** (C **800/523-3273**) and **American** (C **800/433-7300**). Car rentals are available at the airport from **Avis, Budget,** and **Hertz.**

GETTING AROUND
With the confluence of the north and south forks of the Concho River marking the city center, bridges seem to be everywhere and can often make navigation by car a bit tricky. **Bryant Boulevard** (U.S. 87/277) is the major north–south street, but it splits into two one-way streets (the northbound **Koenigheim St.** and southbound **Abe St.**) in the middle of the city. **Chadbourne Street,** just a few blocks east of Bryant Boulevard, runs through the historic part of the city, skirting downtown and **Historic Concho Avenue** en route to Fort Concho and other attractions.

The **civic bus system** (© **325/947-8729**) operates five routes from the Historic Santa Fe Depot at 703 S. Chadbourne St., from 6:30am to 5:30pm Monday through Friday and from 9:30am to 5:30pm Saturday. Fare is $1 for adults, 50¢ for students and seniors, and free for any accompanying children under 5.

VISITOR INFORMATION

The **San Angelo Convention and Visitors Bureau,** 418 W. Ave. B., San Angelo, TX 76903 (© **800/375-1206** or 325/655-4136; www.sanangelo.org), operates a visitor center, open Monday through Friday from 9am to 5pm, Saturday 10am to 5pm, and Sunday noon to 4pm.

FAST FACTS   San Angelo has two 24-hour emergency rooms: **San Angelo Community Medical Center,** 3501 Knickerbocker Rd. (© **325/949-9511**), and **Shannon Medical Center,** 120 E. Harris Ave. (© **325/653-6741**). The **main post office,** 1 N. Abe St., is open Monday through Friday from 8am to 5:30pm, Saturday from 9am to 4:30pm.

WHAT TO SEE & DO
THE TOP ATTRACTIONS

Worth a peek is **Paint Brush Alley,** between Concho and Twohig avenues downtown, an imaginative reinvention of an alley as an urban gallery of murals by different artists.

Fort Concho National Historic Landmark   Established in 1867 as a means of pioneer defense, Fort Concho provided the impetus for San Angelo's original development. Originally 40 buildings on 1,000 acres, this U.S. Army post, once commanded by William "Pecos Bill" Shafter, was active until 1889, with black Buffalo Soldiers making up a considerable portion of the men stationed here. The post is now one of the jewels of the old Texas forts, with 17 restored buildings and 5 rebuilt structures. Some of the buildings are fully furnished with period artifacts, including a barracks outfitted to an 1870s T, down to the last checker on the board. There are exhibits in two of the restored officers' quarters (one is a small museum on telephony, featuring one of Alexander Graham Bell's originals) and the old post headquarters. Expect to spend a little more than an hour here.

630 S. Oakes St. © 325/481-2646. www.fortconcho.com. Admission $3 adults, $2 seniors, $1.50 students, free for children younger than 6. Tues–Sat 10am–5pm; Sun 1–5pm.

River Walk   Thanks to the River Beautification Project, which kicked off in 1986, the Concho River is now a splendid centerpiece for the entire city of San Angelo. It sports a 4-mile walking/jogging trail, bountiful outdoor gardens and water displays, a great playground, and even a 9-hole golf course (© **325/657-4485**) on the River Walk's acres (greens fees $8–$10). Celebration Bridge crosses the river behind the San Angelo Museum of Fine Arts (see below), right past a bronze statue of a mermaid, "Pearl of the Conchos." Between the bridge and the old downtown plaza (El Paseo de Santa Angela) sits the Bill Aylor, Sr., Memorial RiverStage, an outdoor venue that is a focus of San Angelo's performing arts scene. The River Walk provides easy access to the San Angelo Museum of Fine Arts, Historic Concho Avenue, and Fort Concho. Along the banks of the Concho River.

San Angelo Museum of Fine Arts 🜇   From its eye-catching home on the Concho River, this standout museum is a must-see for lovers of art and architecture, demanding a stop of 45 minutes or more. The permanent collection focuses on contemporary American ceramics, with 150 such pieces, and every year from April to

Fun Fact The Concho Pearl

The word *concho* pops out from every other corner in San Angelo, from Concho Avenue to Fort Concho to the Concho River. If you're not from the area, it probably doesn't mean much, but if you're a San Angelo jeweler, it means a great deal. The Concho River Valley is home to a dozen species of freshwater mussels in the *Unionacea* family that produce the rare concho pearl, tinted luminous pink, deep purple, or rich lavender by Mother Nature. Some of the earliest known examples of the pearls were Spanish crown jewels in the 16th century. If you want to try to harvest one yourself, you'll need a permit from the **Texas Parks and Wildlife Department** (© **800/792-1112**; www.tpwd.state.tx.us). You can avoid wading in the river, however, if you're willing to plunk down some cash at a local jeweler.

June, the museum features the country's top ceramics show, with a national competition in even-numbered years. Another nice perk: The museum has an open back office that allows visitors to see how the facility is managed and get a glimpse into the storage areas. The award-winning building is a work of art in itself, consisting of native limestone, in-grain mesquite flooring, and a curving, copper-clad roof.

1 Love St. on the Concho River. © 325/653-3333. www.samfa.org. Admission $2 adults, $1 seniors, free for students and children. Tues–Sat 10am–4pm; Sun 1–4pm. Closed major holidays.

OUTDOOR ACTIVITIES

When it comes to outdoor recreation, San Angelans are blessed with the Concho River, two reservoirs, and an excellent civic park system. The highlight is **San Angelo State Park** ✵, 3900-2 Mercedes St. (© **325/949-4757**), at O. C. Fisher Lake on the city's northwest side, attracting mountain bikers, hikers, boaters, anglers, and equestrians. The park sits at the nexus of four distinct geographical areas—Hill Country, Trans-Pecos, the rolling plains to the east, and the high plains to the north—in an area that has been inhabited by humans for over 10,000 years. Admission to the park is $2 per adults and free for children younger than 13. The day-use hours are from 8am to 10pm.

The park's trail system is one of the best in all of West Texas, with more than 50 miles of multiuse trails (hiking, biking, horseback riding). Certain trails provide access to the only ride-in, equestrian campsites between El Paso and San Antonio. The trails connect the north and south shores of the reservoir and range from flat and smooth to rocky and rugged; a detailed map is available at the entrance. There are ample opportunities for birding and wildlife watching, with 300 avian and 50 mammal species (including pelicans, cormorants, Texas longhorn cattle, and buffalo), and a significant population of horned lizards. In season, hunting and fishing are popular.

On guided tours, visitors can take a look at the petroglyphs in the park, go on a 3-mile hike to fossilized footprints, or learn about the history of buffalo and Texas longhorn. The tours are informative, engaging, and offered on demand (fees are charged).

There are 79 campsites with water and electric hook-ups here, and over 100 primitive tent camping areas. The campground on the north shore, shaded by massive pecan trees, is especially isolated and attractive, while the southern campgrounds are closer to the reservoir and playground. Nightly camping fees, in addition to park entrance fees, are $8 to $18. There are also a few simple cabins that can accommodate six guests for $45 a night.

Six miles south of downtown via Knickerbocker Road, the city-owned **Lake Nasworthy** is a fishing, hiking, and boating hot spot. Below the nearly 1,600 surface acres of fresh water, two non-native saltwater species (hybrid trout-corvina and red drum) have thrived alongside native bass and catfish. **Spring Creek Marina and RV Park,** 45 Fisherman's Rd. (© **800/500-7801** or 325/944-3850; www.springcreekmarina-rv. com), has campsites with full hook-ups ($26–$32 nightly), boat rentals, and a convenience store.

The **San Angelo Nature Center** at Lake Nasworthy, 7409 Knickerbocker Rd. (© **325/942-0121**), is a small museum with a garden, library, and a short interpretive trail system. The center is open Tuesday through Saturday from noon to 5pm.

The **Pictographs of Painted Rocks,** called a "museum, library, and art gallery" of ancient American Indians, is another noteworthy excursion near San Angelo. Located 22 miles southeast of the city near the town of Paint Rock, the site features a natural limestone wall adorned with more than 1,600 pictographs. On the winter solstice, rays of light reflect off of an ornate, otherwise invisible painting known as "Sun Dagger." For information on tours, call © **325/732-4376.**

The municipal park system in San Angelo is a cut above average, with the **River Walk** (p. 372) and **Civic League Park,** West Beauregard and Park streets, featuring the International Water Lily Garden. This garden displays lily species from all over the globe that bloom both day and night during the spring and summer. Call **San Angelo Park Headquarters** at © **325/657-4279** for additional information on the city's park system.

BOATING & FISHING   In addition to O. C. Fisher Lake and Lake Nasworthy (see above), there are three other reservoirs within a 40-mile radius of San Angelo: **Twin Buttes Reservoir** (© **325/657-4206**), located immediately west of Lake Nasworthy; **Lake E. V. Spence** (© **325/453-2061**), known for its striped bass, situated 35 miles north of San Angelo via Tex. 208 and Tex. 158; and **Lake O. H. Ivie** (© **325/267-6341**), the largest body of water in the region at nearly 20,000 surface acres, located 40 miles east of the city via farm roads 765 and 2134.

GOLF   The 7,171-yard **Quicksand Golf Course,** 2305 Pulliam St. (© **325/482-8337**), is one of Texas's best (and toughest) 18-hole courses, with greens fees around $30 to $40, cart included. There's also the 18-hole **Riverside Golf Course,** 900 W. 29th St. (© **325/653-6130**), with greens fees of $21 to $27.

HIKING   The top hiking area in the region is **San Angelo State Park,** with 50 miles of trails. The trails are easy to difficult, with the loops between the north and south shores and the hike to the **Highland Range Scenic Lookout** (less than a mile) being the most popular.

MOUNTAIN BIKING   The most popular mountain biking spots in the San Angelo area are the trails at **San Angelo State Park** and around **Twin Buttes Reservoir.** Bike rentals are not available in town.

SPECTATOR SPORTS

The **San Angelo Colts** (© 325/942-6587; www.sanangelocolts.com) play in the AA Central Baseball League from early May to early September at Foster Field, 1600 University Ave. Single-game tickets are $6 to $10. The **San Angelo Stock Show and Rodeo Association** (© **325/653-7785**) organizes several annual roping and rodeo events.

SHOPPING

Historic Concho Avenue, downtown between Oakes and Chadbourne streets, is a melting pot of boutiques, jewelers, and antiques shops. Among its highlights are **J. Wilde's,** 20 E. Concho Ave. (© 325/655-0878), a boutique with fashions and furnishings best described as Western chic (which doesn't quite do them justice); and **Legend Jewelers,** 18 E. Concho Ave. (© 888/655-4367 or 325/653-0112), purveyors of the luminous concho pearl. The top shopping center is **Sunset Mall,** 4001 Sunset Dr., at Loop 306 (© 325/949-1947).

San Angelo is home to a vibrant arts community, typified by the Texas hippie vibe at the **Old Chicken Farm Art Center** ℱ, 2505 N. Martin Luther King Blvd. (© 325/653-4936; www.chickenfarmartcenter.com), a local landmark since 1971. Formerly an abandoned chicken farm, this funky artist's compound is home to 12 studios that are open at various times, displaying a wide range of pottery, metalwork, and paintings. The main **StarKeeper Gallery** houses the contemporary handmade ceramics of Roger Allen, the center's founder and proprietor; it's open Tuesday through Saturday from 10am to 5pm. The Art Center hosts resident artist's openings on the first Saturday of each month. There's also an on-site B&B, the **Inn at the Art Center** (see below).

WHERE TO STAY

San Angelo has a nice variety of lodging available, with a handful of B&Bs and numerous chain motels and hotels. Most of the properties are located along Bryant Boulevard or near the convention center on Rio Concho Drive. Of the independents, we recommend **Inn of the Conchos,** 2021 N. Bryant Blvd. (© 800/621-6041 or 325/658-2811; www.inn-of-the-conchos.com), with double rates of $60 to $70.

Inn at the Art Center ℱ *Finds*   If you like your B&B a bit on the unusual side, look no further. In place of Victorian architecture and antiques, you'll find rooms in what once were chicken coops and feed silos at the Old Chicken Farm Art Center (see "Shopping," above). Our favorite: the Artist's Loft, situated within two cylindrical silos (the bedroom in one, a sitting area and bathroom in the other) connected via arched doorways and decorated with interesting murals and mosaics. There are also the themed Santa Fe and French rooms in the old coop. Outside, you can get a firsthand look at artists at work or relax in one of the many shady nooks and crannies on the property, including a sculpture-laden courtyard and a covered patio. The restaurant, the Silo House, serves prix-fixe dinners by reservation on Thursday, Friday, and Saturday evenings.

2503 Martin Luther King Blvd., San Angelo, TX 76903. © 866/557-5337 or 325/659-3836. www.chickenfarmartcenter. com. 3 units. $90–$110 double. Rates include full breakfast. AE, DISC, MC, V. **Amenities:** Restaurant. *In room:* A/C, cable TV/VCR, complimentary Wi-Fi, coffeemaker.

San Angelo Inn and Conference Center ℱ *Kids*   This solid property is our pick for a night in San Angelo for several reasons: a quiet location, surrounded by trees and parkland near the banks of the Concho River and the River Walk; reliable rooms with typical hotel-room decor (that is, white walls and floral spreads) as well as powerful air-conditioning; and a full range of amenities. It's a good bet for families, with a kid's menu in the restaurant, in-room video games, and a small indoor pool.

441 Rio Concho Dr., San Angelo, TX 76903. © 800/784-7839 or 325/658-2828. Fax 325/658-8741. 148 units, including 6 suites. $79–$109 double; $114 suite. AE, DC, DISC, MC, V. **Amenities:** Restaurant; bar; indoor heated pool; exercise room; Jacuzzi; limited room service; dry cleaning. *In room:* A/C, cable TV w/PlayStation, complimentary Wi-Fi, fridge, coffeemaker, hair dryer, iron.

CAMPING

The best campgrounds are at **San Angelo State Park** (✆ 325/949-4757) and **Spring Creek Marina and RV Park** (✆ 800/500-7801 or 325/944-3850) at Lake Nasworthy. See "Outdoor Activities," above.

WHERE TO DINE

Armenta's *(Finds* TEX-MEX   The proprietors of this festive eatery did not hold back one iota when it came to decoration, transforming a once-standard diner into a feast for the eyes with an armada of colorful parrot sculptures, strings of chile-pepper lights, and Mexican pottery. They don't hold back with the first-rate food, either, which is every bit as spicy as the scenery. Specialties include fiery *guizo*—sautéed beef with onions, tomatoes, and peppers—and the *camarones a la diabla*—shrimp spiced for the most inflammable of taste buds. The homemade salsa packs a similar punch.

1325 S. Oakes St. (1 mile south of downtown). ✆ 325/653-1954. Main courses $1–$3 breakfast; $5–$11 lunch and dinner. AE, DISC, MC, V. Mon–Sat 8am–10pm. Closed major holidays.

El Mejor (Mejor que Nada) *(Kids* MEXICAN/STEAKS   Opening as a small convenience store in 1986, demand for this eatery's homemade Mexican food sent the establishment into expansion mode. First came picnic tables, then an enclosed patio (with a fountain and margarita bar), then an addition to the front room, and so on. Now the place is a big, bustling restaurant, dishing out enticing Mexican fare and thick, juicy steaks. Our personal favorite is Mejor's chicken enchilada, jammed with onions and peppers and covered in a zesty, sweet-hot tomatillo salsa. Carnivores will delight in the steaks and fajitas, calorie watchers can order the Karla (vegetarian Mexican stir-fry), and kids can play in the arcade.

1911 S. Bryant Blvd. ✆ 325/655-3553. Main courses $6–$15. AE, DISC, MC, V. Mon–Thurs 11am–9pm; Fri–Sat 11am–10:30pm.

Miss Hattie's Café and Saloon STEAKS/SEAFOOD   Named after the infamous proprietor of one of San Angelo's now-defunct bordellos, Miss Hattie's is one of the city's culinary standouts. Housed in a brick edifice that dates from 1884, the dining room is full of Victorian frills and antiques, with lace-sheathed tables under the original pressed-tin ceiling. The cuisine is a nice match for the atmosphere: tender steaks, daily seafood specials, salads, and pastas. Our recommendation: Start with the chicken and corn fritters as an appetizer and move on to the Southwestern Carpetbagger (a rib-eye stuffed with spiced crabmeat) for the main course. The lunch menu sports a nice selection of gourmet sandwiches and salads and heartier fare such as meatloaf and chicken with dumplings. Two doors down is **Miss Hattie's Bordello Museum,** 18½ E. Concho Ave. The restored brothel offers tours Thursday through Saturday every hour from 1 to 4pm; admission is $5 per person.

26 E. Concho Ave. ✆ 325/653-0570. www.misshatties.com. Main courses $6–$11 lunch, $10–$30 dinner. AE, MC, V. Mon–Thurs 11am–9pm; Fri–Sat 11am–10pm.

SAN ANGELO AFTER DARK

San Angelo has a strong performing arts culture for a city its size. The **San Angelo Symphony** performs about a half-dozen classical and pops shows a year at various venues (✆ 325/658-5877; www.sanangelosymphony.org). Single tickets are $20 for adults and $6 to $8 for children and students. The **Angelo Civic Theatre,** 1936 Sherwood Way (✆ 325/949-4400; www.angelocivictheatre.com), the oldest community theater in the state, produces about five musicals, comedies, and dramas a year at its

230-seat playhouse. Tickets run $8 to $12. The city is also home to the **Cactus Jazz Series** (© 325/653-6793; www.sanangeloarts.com) at the historic Cactus Hotel, 36 E. Twohig Ave., culminating in the annual Cactus Jazz and Blues Festival in September.

A SIDE TRIP TO THE CAVERNS OF SONORA

Hidden in the middle of nowhere, some 75 miles from San Angelo, are the delightful **Caverns of Sonora.** Designated a Registered Natural Landmark by the National Park Service in 1966, these truly magnificent caves are privately owned and can be explored only on guided tours. You'll see glistening draperies, miles of puffy popcorn, millions of helictites and soda straws, reflecting pools, plus all the usual stalagmites and stalactites in a wildly fascinating collage of formations. The caverns' signature formation is an unusual helictite shaped like a butterfly. The tour is 2 miles long and takes about 2 hours; call for current admission prices

The caverns are open daily from 8am to 6pm March through Labor Day, and from 9am to 5pm the rest of the year, except Christmas Day. From San Angelo, go south on U.S. 277 64 miles to the small town of Sonora, then 8 miles west on I-10 to Exit 392, then follow signs south to the caverns. For additional information, contact **Caverns of Sonora** (© 325/387-3105; www.cavernsofsonora.com).

Camping in an attractive tree-shaded campground is available at the caverns. Other than that, the nearest lodging, dining, and other services are in Sonora. For information, contact the **Sonora Chamber of Commerce,** 707 N. Crockett Ave., P.O. Box 1172, Sonora, TX 76950-1172 (© 325/387-2880; www.sonoratx-chamber.com).

5 Del Rio & Amistad National Recreation Area 🖈

156 miles S of San Angelo; 154 miles W of San Antonio; 268 miles NW of Corpus Christi; 392 miles SW of Dallas

For our money, this pleasant little city of about 35,000 people is the nicest border town you'll find from Texas to California. Situated along the U.S.–Mexico border across the Rio Grande from Ciudad Acuña, Del Rio is a great base for watersports enthusiasts visiting Amistad National Recreation Area, and also has an excellent museum where you can learn about Judge Roy Bean, one of the most colorful judges in the history of the American West, who became both famous and infamous as "The Law West of the Pecos."

The site of Del Rio was originally called San Felipe del Rio by Spanish missionaries, who unsuccessfully tried to start a mission here in 1635 but were thwarted by hostile American Indians. The name survived, however, and was in use in the mid-1800s when the reliable water source of San Felipe Springs helped the area begin to develop as a farming community. The springs also were a watering stop for the short-lived U.S. Army Camel Corps, in which camels imported from North Africa were used on the Western frontier as a substitute for horses. The name of the community was shortened to Del Rio in 1883.

In the late 1960s, a dam was built on the Rio Grande near Del Rio, creating a 67,000-acre lake that provides flood protection and irrigation water, as well as a huge water playground in what is generally an arid and rocky land of cactus and sagebrush.

ESSENTIALS
GETTING THERE

Del Rio is located at the junction of U.S. highways 90 and 277/377, along the U.S.-Mexico border. The **Amtrak** station is at 100 N. Main St. (© 800/872-2745), along the Sunset Limited route.

Fun Fact Creature of the Night

In 1963, groundbreaking disc jockey **Wolfman Jack** got his start at XERF, a super-powerful 500,000-watt radio station in Ciudad Acuña, after he helped commandeer the station during a gunfight. From there, the Wolfman offered mainstream America its first taste of black music: A B. B. King record was his first spin, and James Brown once paid a visit and climbed XERF's legendary tower.

VISITOR INFORMATION

The **Del Rio Chamber of Commerce,** 1915 Veterans Blvd., Del Rio, TX 78840 (© **800/889-8149** or 830/775-3551; www.drchamber.com), operates a visitor center and can mail information before your trip. In Ciudad Acuña, **Comite Turistico de Acuña** (© **877/717-9966**) is your best source of tourism info.

FAST FACTS   Val Verde Regional Medical Center, 801 Bedell Ave. (© **830/775-8566**), has a 24-hour emergency room. The **post office,** 2001 N. Bedell Ave., is open Monday through Friday from 8:30am to 4:30pm, Saturday from 9am to 11am.

THE TOP ATTRACTIONS

In addition to the attractions discussed below, there are a number of handsome **historic buildings** in Del Rio. A free brochure that describes and locates some three dozen buildings constructed between 1869 and 1929 is available at the chamber of commerce's visitor center (see "Visitor Information," above). **San Felipe Springs** offers a nice walk along crystal-clear water; the best access point is at the **Creekwalk** at Moore Park, Calderon Boulevard and De La Rosa Street, where you'll find a spring-fed swimming pool and a small amphitheater.

Many visitors to Del Rio take an excursion across the border to **Ciudad Acuña,** a small Mexican city where you'll find a main street lined with shops offering a variety of leather goods, pottery, woven items, jewelry, and other products, plus a number of good restaurants. As with most border towns, American currency is welcome at practically all businesses in Ciudad Acuña. Driving isn't a problem, but walking is a bit of a struggle, especially on hot days. If you want to leave your car in the U.S., catch a ride with **City Taxi** (© **830/775-6344**). *Note:* Be sure to carry your passport if you cross the border. As of January 2008, passports are required for reentry into the U.S.

Alamo Village   Built by John Wayne and company for his epic 1959 film *The Alamo*—and used for dozens of Westerns since—this attraction meshes Western and Hollywood history into one fun attraction. Beyond the mockup of the Alamo, there is an entire Wild West village, complete with a cantina (food, not beer), gift shops, and a roving herd of Texas longhorn. From Memorial Day to Labor Day, actors face off in mock gunfights and country musicians play in the cantina. Expect to spend an hour or two.

FM 674, 7 miles north of Brackettville (30 miles east of Del Rio via U.S. 90). © **830/563-2580**. www.alamovillage. com. Admission $9 adults, $5 children 6–11, free for children younger than 6. Daily 9am–5pm.

Fort Clark Springs   A notable army and cavalry post from 1852 to 1946, Fort Clark has since evolved into a unique real-estate development and resort with good amenities for the traveler. There are 1,600 acres of wilderness here, populated by whitetail deer and wild turkeys, crosscut by miles of nature trails, and featuring a behemoth spring-fed swimming pool (Texas's third largest) and two golf courses. There's also a museum, a basic motel (about $60 for a double), and an RV park (about $20 for a site with full hook-ups). The Villa Del Rio also rents a pair of guest quarters here for $145 to $185 double.

U.S. 90, Brackettville (30 miles east of Del Rio). (②) **830/563-2493**. www.fortclark.com. Free admission. Activity prices vary. Open daily.

Val Verde Winery   Established in 1883 by Italian immigrant Frank Qualia, Val Verde Winery, the state's oldest bonded winery, is now the pride and joy of third-generation vintner Thomas Qualia. Using grapes from the adjacent vineyards and other Texas vineyards, the winery produces from six to eight varieties of wine, including its award-winning Don Luis Tawny Port, which is aged in French oak barrels for 5 years. Short, informative guided tours are available at no charge, followed or substituted by free tastings. Wines are available by the bottle (usually $8–$25). Allow 20 minutes for your visit.

100 Qualia Dr. (near its intersection with Hudson St.). (②) **830/775-9714**. www.valverdewinery.com. Free admission. Mon–Sat 10am–5pm.

Whitehead Memorial Museum ℛ (Kids)   This above-average small-town museum really does have something for everyone. Covering more than 2 acres, exhibits include a furnished log cabin, a blacksmith shop, a 1919 American LaFrance fire engine, and the early-20th-century office of Dr. Simon Rodriguez, the community's first Hispanic physician, who is credited with delivering more than 3,000 babies in the area. The graves of Roy Bean and one of his sons are also on the property. The star of the museum, however, is the fantastic Cadena Nativity—a 32×20-foot Nativity scene that contains more than 600 figurines of people and animals plus another 600-plus miniature buildings, trees, bushes, and the like. Allow 1 to 2 hours.

1308 S. Main St. (②) **830/774-7568**. www.whitehead-museum.com. Admission $5 adults, $4 seniors, $3 youths 13–18, $2 children 6–12, free for children younger than 6. Tues–Sat 9am–4:30pm; Sun 1–5pm; check for possible holiday closures.

WHERE TO STAY IN DEL RIO

Veterans Boulevard, the main drag through town (U.S. highways 90/277/377), is lined with chain motels. Choices here include **Best Western Inn of Del Rio,** 810 Veterans Blvd. (② **800/336-3537** or 830/775-7511), and **Ramada Inn,** 2101 Veterans Blvd. (② **800/272-6232** or 830/775-1511). Room tax adds 13%.

Villa del Rio Bed & Breakfast ℛℛ   For anyone who appreciates the old-world ambience of a historic mansion, a bit of pampering, and a creative and tasty breakfast, Villa del Rio is the place to stay while visiting the Del Rio area. This luxurious bed-and-breakfast is a Mediterranean-style villa—actually a mix of Italian and Mexican styles with an Alamo motif—built in 1887 that still has the beautiful original hand-painted Italian tile floors. You'll also find a series of original murals that depict the area's rich history, and a plethora of painstakingly restored details. Outside is a delightful sitting area around a tiled fountain and 2 acres of subtropical vegetation, including palm, magnolia, and century-old pecan trees.

There are three rooms on the second floor of the main house, all with queen-size beds and decorated with a mix of new and antique furnishings. The spacious and colorful Peacock Suite has a private bathroom, a screened sun porch, and a small sitting room with a day bed. The other two rooms—named for Judge Roy Bean and his unrequited

The Legend of Roy Bean

Judge Roy Bean, the self-styled "Law West of the Pecos," was by all accounts an eccentric character, and definitely the stuff of which legends are made. Born Phantly Roy Bean in Kentucky, probably around 1825, as a teenager he followed his two older brothers west, to California and then New Mexico. Although his brothers were mostly successful and respectable, Roy always seemed to be in trouble, usually related to gambling and women, and occasionally would leave town just a few steps ahead of the hangman.

During the Civil War, Bean reportedly smuggled supplies from Mexico to Confederate troops in Texas. After the war he ended up in San Antonio, where he cemented his already dubious reputation. There he married and had four children before abandoning the family about 16 years later, when he followed a rail-construction crew west to Vinegarroon. It's believed Bean then opened a saloon in a tent, before somehow getting appointed as the local justice of the peace in 1882.

Several years later Bean moved north to a small settlement along the railroad tracks that came to be called Langtry. Bean claimed he had named the town after the beautiful English actress of the day Lillie Langtry, with whom he was quite infatuated, although the town likely garnered its name earlier from a construction foreman. Bean wrote to Miss Langtry several times, asking her to visit the town "named in her honor."

Bean was elected and reelected as justice of the peace on and off for about 20 years—he reportedly was briefly thrown out of office when it became evident that he had received more votes than there were eligible voters. Bean's Langtry courtroom, which he called the Jersey Lillie after Miss Langtry, was also his saloon and home, and he often chose his juries from the saloon's customers.

beloved, Lillie Langtry—have traditional and white-wicker furniture, respectively, and share a connecting bathroom. Behind the main house and across a lawn is the Pancho Villa Adobe Cottage, with a full kitchen and room for a family.

The homemade breakfasts are hearty, Southwest-style cooking, such as jalapeño crepes served with a thick ham steak and an amazing fruit plate. Proprietor Jay J. Johnson-Castro's advice is hearty, too: He's an artist of note with great knowledge of the region's galleries, as well as its history, culture, and recreation.

123 Hudson Dr., Del Rio, TX 78840. © 800/995-1887 or 830/768-1100. Fax 830/768-0768. www.villadelrio.com. 4 units. $85–$215 double. Rates include full breakfast. AE, MC, V. Well-behaved older children welcome in the main house; all children welcome in the cottage. *In room:* A/C, no phone.

WHERE TO DINE IN DEL RIO

As with lodging, you'll find scads of national chains located along Del Rio's Veterans Boulevard. You'll be better served (in more ways than one) by seeking out one of Del Rio's locally owned restaurants, such as the **Avanti Authentic Italian Restaurant** ⭐, 600 E. 12th St. (© **830/775-3363**). Although West Texas doesn't usually come to

Numerous stories about Bean's sometimes bizarre rulings have been told, and it's often difficult to tell fact from fiction. When a railroad worker was charged with killing a Chinese laborer, Bean said that although it was against the law to kill your fellow man, he could find no law against killing a "heathen Chinaman," so the case was dismissed. The killer was, however, required to pay for the funeral. Another generally accepted story is the case of a dead man found to have a gun and gold coins worth about $40 in his pockets. Bean promptly fined the corpse $40 for carrying a concealed weapon. But he gained perhaps his greatest notoriety for staging a heavyweight championship fight in 1896. At the time, prizefighting was illegal in Texas as well as in Mexico, so Bean staged the fight on a sandbar in the Rio Grande, a no-man's land between the two. He also made a tidy profit at his saloon selling drinks to the spectators.

Although there are also stories of Bean being a "hanging judge," there is no proof that he ever sentenced anyone to hang. But then, Bean kept no records at all of what transpired in his courtroom. Bean died in his saloon on March 16, 1903, supposedly after a binge of heavy drinking in Del Rio. A few months later, Lillie Langtry, who was performing in the region, finally made it to Langtry, spending 30 minutes there during a train stopover.

To learn more about Bean, drive out to Langtry (60 miles west of Del Rio via U.S. 90) to Bean's restored saloon at the **Judge Roy Bean Visitor Center** (© **432/291-3340**), where dioramas and displays in this official state visitor center tell the story of Bean's life. The visitor center and saloon are open daily from 8am to 5pm and admission is free. Allow about an hour.

mind when you think of great Italian food, it will after a visit to Avanti. It offers genuine homemade lasagna, ravioli, and other Italian specialties—mostly northern Italian—prepared with fresh ingredients and cooked to order. Avanti is open Monday to Friday for lunch and dinner, and dinner only on Saturday; main courses range from $8 to $20.

If you want to get a true (and inexpensive) taste of the region, head south to Ciudad Acuña. (Call **City Taxi** at © **830/775-6344** for a ride.) Our picks: **Manuel's,** Morelos #130 (© **011-52/87-72-59-15**), an upscale Mexican restaurant with good steaks and rellenos; **La Cabañita,** Galena #267 E. (© **011-52/87-72-14-67**), a fun, funky space with a menu for meat lovers; and the local favorite, **Tacos Grill,** Guerrero #1490 S. (© **011-52/87-72-40-41**). There's also a legendary watering hole, **The Corona Club,** 2 blocks south of the downtown crossing bridge at Hidalgo #200 (www.thecoronaclub.com). A location in the movie *Desperado,* this classic border dive opens into a spectacular courtyard that is the best music venue in the area.

AMISTAD NATIONAL RECREATION AREA ⊛

A beautiful spot for boating, fishing, water-skiing, scuba diving, and swimming, this is a rare international reservoir, created by the United States and Mexico with the construction of a 6-mile-long dam across the Rio Grande at the international border. Amistad Reservoir—*amistad* is Spanish for friendship—provides electric generation, water storage, flood control, and most important to anglers and watersports enthusiasts, a huge lake as a U.S. National Recreation Area.

The water here is a beautiful blue color, caused by the lakebed's limestone character and lack of loose soil. The 67,000-acre lake is actually at the confluence of three rivers, and runs 74 miles up the Rio Grande, 24 miles up the Devils River, and 14 miles up the Pecos River. Shoreline measures 890 miles: 540 miles in Texas and the rest in Mexico.

There are about a dozen boat ramps spread throughout the recreation area, with three developed boat launching areas. **Diablo East** is 10 miles northwest of Del Rio via U.S. 90, **Rough Canyon** is 23 miles north of Del Rio via U.S. 90 and U.S. 277/377, and **Pecos** is 44 miles northwest of Del Rio via U.S. 90. Boat and slip rentals and sales of supplies are available at Diablo East and Rough Canyon. Motorized boat use passes cost $4 per day or $40 per year.

At Diablo East, **Lake Amistad Marina,** HCR-3 U.S. 90, P.O. Box 420635, Del Rio, TX 78842 (*C* **800/255-5561** or 830/774-4157; www.foreverresorts.com), rents a variety of boats, ranging from fishing boats and runabouts costing $125 per 8-hour day to luxurious 65-foot houseboats that sleep 10 and rent for over $3,000 for a 3-day/2-night weekend in summer. Boat rentals are also available at **Rough Canyon Marina,** P.O. Box 420845, Del Rio, TX 78842 (*C* **830/775-8779**). Kayaking and canoeing have been growing in popularity in recent years; contact **Ruthie's Rentals,** HCR 1 (*C* **830/774-5377**), for a rental.

There is a swimming area (no lifeguards) at Governors Island, and swimming is permitted in most undeveloped areas. Water temperatures range from a chilly 54°F (12°C) in winter to a pleasant 86°F (30°C) in summer. Water-skiing is permitted in open water (away from mooring areas, channels, and swimming beaches) during daylight hours only.

Forty-pound catfish have been pulled from the lake, as have record striped bass. Among other species caught are largemouth bass, yellowbelly and bluegill sunfish, white and black crappie, and alligator gar. Fishing is permitted from boats and from shore anywhere except in marinas, at boat ramps, and designated swimming beaches. There are also fishing docks and fish-cleaning stations at several locations. A Texas fishing license (available at convenience stores and most shops along U.S. 90) is required on the U.S. side of the border, and a Mexican fishing license is required in Mexican waters. A list of licensed fishing guides is available at the headquarters.

Among the wildlife you're likely to see are white-tailed deer, javelina (also called collared peccaries), black-tailed jackrabbits, rock squirrels, and nine-banded armadillos. Campers might also see ringtails, which usually only venture out at night. The recreation area is also home to poisonous snakes including several species of rattlesnakes, plus poisonous scorpions, spiders, and stinging insects. Birds to watch for include white-winged doves, sandpipers, great blue herons, great egrets, American coots, killdeer, roadrunners, black vultures, ravens, and an occasional bald or golden eagle. One particularly good spot to bird-watch is the San Pedro Campground, where you're also likely to see a lot of butterflies. Rangers lead morning birding walks the third Saturday of the month from September through May; the group meets at park visitor center at 8am.

American Indian peoples are believed to have come to this area about 12,000 years ago, but it was not until about 4,000 years ago, when a different group inhabited the area, that the creation of the spectacular rock art we can see today in several areas in and near the recreation area began. These pictographs—designs painted on rocks

---

(Tips) **The Mouth of the Pecos**

On the east rim of the 300-foot cliffs above the Pecos River, there is an over-look before the U.S. 90 bridge over the Pecos that is one of the region's best photo opportunities. Heading west on the highway from Del Rio, take the left immediately before the bridge for the most scenic views of the vast surround-ing badlands and the untamed Pecos snaking into the Rio Grande below.

---

using colors created from ground iron ore and other minerals mixed with animal fat—are difficult to get to, but well worth the effort.

One of the best rock art sites is **Panther Cave,** at the confluence of the Rio Grande and Seminole Canyon, which is usually accessible by boat and a steep climb up stairs. It has numerous figures that resemble humans or animals, including what looks like a 9-foot panther. Another good site, accessible by boat at average lake levels and by a stren-uous hike through tall brush at low-water levels, is **Parida Cave,** located on the Rio Grande. See also the section on Seminole Canyon State Park & Historic Site, below.

The recreation area has four campgrounds, with a total of about 60 primitive sites. Campgrounds are generally open, with brush and some low trees, but little shade, and have vault toilets, covered picnic tables, and grills. **Governors Landing Campground,** with 15 sites overlooking the lake, is the only campground with drinking water (water is available along the Diablo East entrance road, where there is also an RV dump sta-tion). **San Pedro Campground** has 21 sites and **Spur 406** and **277 North** camp-grounds each have about a dozen sites. There is also a dispersed camping area at Spur 406 with rooms for about a dozen sites. Camping is first-come, first-served, and is limited to 14 consecutive days, or 60 days in a 12-month period. Backcountry camp-ing from boats is permitted along the lakeshore, except at marinas and other devel-oped areas. Camping costs $4 to $8 per night.

Rangers present a variety of programs, including evening programs at the amphithea-ter at the visitor center; and kiosks with displays on natural history, recreation, and water safety are scattered throughout the recreation area. Pets are permitted, but must be leashed at all times. Rangers warn that limestone, which is abundant along the shore, can cut the pads of dogs' feet, and they add that pets need to be protected from fleas, ticks, and heartworm (spread by mosquitos) at the lake.

Facilities in the Mexican part of the lake include a swimming beach and a boat ramp near the west end of the dam. Boaters who touch land in Mexico are required to pass through U.S. Customs (in Del Rio) when they return to the United States.

Admission to the park, which is open 24 hours, is free. About 10 miles west of Del Rio off U.S. 90, the park visitor center, with information, a small bookstore, and a few displays, is open daily from 8am to 5pm, except Thanksgiving, Christmas, and New Year's. The first lake access is about 10 miles west of the visitor center. For informa-tion, contact **Amistad National Recreation Area,** U41211V Veterans Blvd., Del Rio, TX 78840 (© **830/775-7491;** www.nps.gov/amis).

SEMINOLE CANYON STATE PARK & HISTORIC SITE

Adjacent to Amistad National Recreation Area, about 45 miles northwest of Del Rio via U.S. 90, this state park provides opportunities to take guided hikes to see what many consider the best pictographs in North America, possibly 4,000 years old. In addition, Seminole Canyon offers a short nature trail, camping, hiking through a rugged limestone terrain, wildlife viewing and bird-watching, and a museum.

Although it is believed that humans lived in this area at the end of the last ice age, some 12,000 years ago, they left few signs of their presence. Then, about 7,000 years ago, a different culture arrived, and within 3,000 years of their arrival they began to paint designs on sheltered rock walls. State park rangers lead hiking tours to several of the rock art sites.

The **Fate Bell Cave Dwelling Tour** is offered Wednesday through Sunday at 10am and 3pm. Cost is $5 per person, $2 for children ages 6 to 12, and reservations are not required. This is a moderately rated 2-mile round-trip hike that leads into Seminole Canyon to a huge rock shelter where participants will see hundreds of pictographs. The state park also has two guided tours that are offered only about a half-dozen times a year, by advance reservation through the park office (see below). The 1¾-mile round-trip **Upper Canyon Tour,** which costs $12 per person and takes 2 hours, leads to a normally closed area of the park in the upper section of the canyon to see pictographs and some railroad sites from 1882; and the 8-mile round-trip **Presa Canyon Tour,** which costs $25 per person, is an all-day hike into the lower canyon to see rock art sites that are normally off-limits to the public.

The park has a 6-mile round-trip **hiking/biking trail** along the top of the canyon that leads to a bluff from which you can see Panther Cave, and its namesake painted panther, across Lake Amistad (see the section on Amistad National Recreation Area, above). Bring your binoculars for a better view. The trail has little elevation change, but is rocky with little shade. No one is allowed to go down into the canyon except on guided tours.

The **Windmill Nature Trail,** just behind the visitor center/museum, is an easy, although not shaded and therefore hot, .7-mile loop. It meanders through a harsh environment of ocotillo, cacti, yucca, juniper, Texas mountain laurel, and other desert plants to its namesake windmill—actually the remains of two windmills, one from the 1890s and one from the 1920s.

The species of birds and animals to watch for in the park are much the same as at the adjacent Amistad National Recreation Area, and include birds such as great blue herons, black and turkey vultures, scaled quail, killdeer, white-winged and mourning doves, greater roadrunners, and northern mockingbirds. Also watch for great-tailed grackles, northern cardinals, pyrrhuloxia, ash-throated flycatchers, ladder-backed woodpeckers, and black-chinned hummingbirds. Mammals here include desert cottontails, black-tailed jackrabbits, coyotes, raccoons, white-tailed deer, striped skunks, and javelina.

The small campground, with 31 sites, sits on an open knoll covered with mesquite, creosote bush, yucca, cacti, and other desert plants. There are hot showers and a dump station. Sites with water only cost $10 per night and those with water and electricity cost $14 per night. Campsites can be reserved, with a credit card, by contacting **Texas State Parks** (✆ **512/389-8900;** www.tpwd.state.tx.us).

The park is open 24 hours a day year-round, except for 1 week in November and 1 week in December when it is open only to properly licensed hunters. The visitor center, with its excellent museum containing exhibits on the area's ancient inhabitants as well as its more recent history, is open daily from 8am to 5pm. Admission to the park costs $3 adults, $2 seniors, free for children younger than 13. For information, contact **Seminole Canyon State Park & Historic Site,** P.O. Box 820, Comstock, TX 78837 (✆ **432/292-4464;** www.tpwd.state.tx.us/park/seminole).

Big Bend & Guadalupe Mountains National Parks

by Eric Peterson

You'll find Texas's most spectacular mountain scenery, as well as absolutely wonderful opportunities for hiking and other forms of outdoor recreation, at Big Bend and Guadalupe Mountains national parks. These parks also have an abundance of wildlife and both prehistoric and historic sites. Big Bend National Park is bounded by the Rio Grande, as it defines the U.S.-Mexico border, while Guadalupe Mountains National Park boasts the highest peak in Texas and a canyon that

we believe has the prettiest scenery in the state, especially in the fall.

In addition to these two national parks in Texas, a third, Carlsbad Caverns National Park, is just over the state line in New Mexico. This easy side trip from Guadalupe Mountains National Park offers some of the world's most beautiful cave formations, and, if you're so inclined, the thrill of a true caving experience, as you crawl belly-to-rock through dirty, narrow, and dark underground passages.

1 Big Bend National Park ★ ★

Vast and wild, Big Bend National Park is a land of extremes—and a few contradictions. Its rugged terrain harbors thousands of species of plants and animals—some seen practically nowhere else on earth—and a visit here can be a hike into the sun-baked desert, a float down a majestic river through the canyons, or a trek among high mountains where bears and mountain lions rule.

Millions of years ago, an inland sea covered this area. As it dried up, sediments of sand and mud turned to rock; mountains were created and volcanoes roared. The resultant canyons and rock formations that we marvel at today—red-, orange-, yellow-, white-, and brown-hued—make for one of the most spectacular landscapes in the Southwest. This is not a fantasyland of delicate shapes and intricate carvings, like Bryce Canyon National Park in Utah, but a powerful and dominating terrain. Although the greatest natural sculptures are in the park's three major river canyons—the Santa Elena, Marsical, and Boquillas—throughout Big Bend you'll find spectacular and majestic examples of what nature can do with this mighty yet malleable building material we call rock.

Visitors to Big Bend National Park will also discover a wild, rugged wilderness, populated by myriad desert and mountain plants and animals; box turtles, black-tailed jackrabbits, funny-looking javelina, powerful black bears, and mountain lions are all known to roam here. The park is considered a birder's paradise, with more bird species than at any other national park. It's also a wonderful spot to see wildflowers and the delightfully colorful display of cactus blooms.

For hikers, there are all kinds of trails, from easy walks to rugged backcountry routes that barely qualify as trails at all. There are also opportunities to let the Rio Grande do the work as it carries rafts, canoes, and kayaks among canyons carved through 1,500 feet of solid rock. Drivers of 4×4s enjoy exploring the backcountry roads, and history buffs find a number of historical attractions and cultural experiences. Because of the vastness of this park, you'll need to schedule at least 2 full days here, though 3 or 4 would be better.

ESSENTIALS

GETTING THERE   Big Bend National Park is not really close to anything except the Rio Grande and Mexico. There is no public transportation to or through the park, so to get to the park you'll need a car. Park headquarters is 108 miles southeast of Alpine via Tex. 118, and 69 miles south of Marathon via U.S. 385. From El Paso, 328 miles northwest of the park, take I-10 east 121 miles to Exit 140, follow U.S. 90 southeast 99 miles to Alpine, then turn south on Tex. 118 for 108 miles to park headquarters.

There is train and bus service to Alpine, where the nearest hospital is located. For information contact the **Alpine Chamber of Commerce** (© **800/561-3735** or 432/837-2326; www.alpinetexas.com).

The nearest commercial airports are **Midland International** (© **432/560-2200;** www.flymaf.com), 235 miles north, and **Del Rio International Airport** (© **830/774-8538**). From Midland-Odessa, take I-20 west about 50 miles to Exit 80 for Tex. 18, which you follow south about 50 miles to Fort Stockton. There take U.S. 385 south 125 miles through Marathon to park headquarters. From Del Rio, you take U.S. 90 west 175 miles to Marathon, and U.S. 385 south 70 miles to park headquarters.

VISITOR INFORMATION   For advance information, contact the **Superintendent,** P. O. Box 129, Big Bend National Park, TX 79834 (© **432/477-2251;** www. nps.gov/bibe). For information on nearby attractions, as well as places to stay and eat, contact the **Big Bend Area Travel Association** (© **877/244-2363;** www.visitbig bend.com).

Books, maps, and videos are available from the **Big Bend Natural History Association** (© **432/477-2236;** www.bigbendbookstore.org). The free park newspaper, *The Big Bend Paisano,* published seasonally by the National Park Service, is a great source of current information on special programs, suggested hikes, kids' activities, and local facilities, with telephone numbers inside and outside the park.

There are five visitor centers in the park: **Panther Junction Visitor Center** (open year-round) is centrally located at park headquarters; **Persimmon Gap Visitor Center** (open year-round) is at the North Entrance to the park on U.S. 385; **Rio Grande Village Visitor Center** (open Nov–Apr) is on the river in the eastern part of the park; **Castolon** (open Nov–Apr) is near the river in the southwestern end of the park; and **Chisos Basin Visitor Center** (open year-round) is in the Chisos Mountains in the middle of the park, at 5,401 feet in elevation. All visitor centers provide information, backcountry permits, books, and maps, and have exhibits; there is an impressive display on mountain lions at Chisos Basin and informative exhibits focusing on the park's cultural history at Castolon. Bulletin boards with schedules of ranger programs, notices of animal sightings, and other information are located at each of the visitor centers.

FEES, REGULATIONS & PERMITS   Entry into the park for up to a week costs $20 per passenger vehicle, and $5 per person on foot or bicycle. A $10 camping permit,

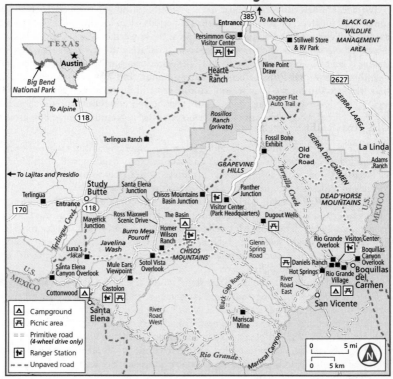

available at any visitor center, is required for all backcountry camping and good for 2 weeks; permits are also required for all river-float trips (see "Camping" and "River Running," later in this chapter).

Wood or ground fires are prohibited in the park, and caution is advised when using camp stoves, charcoal grills, and cigarettes. Smoking is prohibited on all trails in the Chisos Basin. Check at the visitor centers for current drought conditions and any restrictions that may be in effect when you visit. Horses are not permitted on any paved roads in the park.

WHEN TO GO   Weather here is generally mild to hot, although because of the vast range of elevations—from about 1,800 feet at the eastern end of Boquillas Canyon to 7,825 feet on Emory Peak in the Chisos Mountains—conditions can vary greatly throughout the park at any given time. Essentially, the higher you go, the cooler and wetter you can expect it to be, although no section of the park gets a lot of precipitation.

Summers are hot, often well over 100°F (38°C) in the desert in May and June, and afternoon thunderstorms are common July through September. Winters are usually mild, although temperatures occasionally drop below freezing, and light snow is possible, especially in the Chisos Mountains. Fall and spring are usually warm and pleasant.

Average annual visitation is just over 300,000. Although the park is relatively uncrowded much of the year, there are several periods when lodging and campgrounds are full: college spring break (usually the 2nd and 3rd week in Mar), Easter weekend, Thanksgiving weekend, and the week between Christmas and New Year's Day. Park visitation is generally highest in March and April, and lowest in August and September.

Although the park's visitor centers, campgrounds, and other developed facilities may be taxed during the busy season, visitors can still be practically alone simply by seeking out lesser-used hiking trails. Those seeking solitude should discuss their hiking skills and expectations with rangers, who can offer suggestions on the best areas to escape the crowds.

SAFETY   Watch for wild animals along the roads, especially at night when they may be blinded by your vehicle's headlights and stunned into standing still in the middle of the road. Feeding wildlife is strictly prohibited—not only to minimize the risk of injuries to park visitors, but because it's bad for the animals.

The Basin Road Scenic Drive into the Chisos Mountains has sharp curves and steep grades and is not recommended for trailers longer than 20 feet or motor homes longer than 24 feet. The **Ross Maxwell Scenic Drive** to Castolon is fine for most RVs and trailers but might present a problem for those with insufficient power to handle the steep grade. These roads require extra caution by all users—drivers of motor vehicles, pedestrians, and bicyclists alike.

Desert heat can be dangerous. Hikers should carry at least 1 gallon of water per person per day; wear a hat, long pants, and long sleeves; and use a good sunscreen. Don't depend on springs as water sources, and avoid hiking in the middle of the day in summer. Early mornings and evenings are best. Talk to rangers about your plans before heading out; they can help you plan a hike in accordance with your ability and time frame. They can also advise you on expected weather conditions—sudden summer thunderstorms are common and can cause flash flooding in usually dry washes and canyons.

Swimming is not recommended in the Rio Grande, even though it may look tantalizingly inviting on a hot summer day. Waste materials and waterborne microorganisms have been found in the river and can cause serious illness. Also, strong undercurrents, deep holes, and sharp rocks in shallow water are common.

RANGER PROGRAMS & SPECIAL EVENTS   Park ranger naturalists offer a variety of programs year-round. Illustrated evening programs take place at the 5,400-foot **Chisos Basin amphitheater** year-round. From November to April, evening programs are offered regularly in the amphitheater at **Rio Grande Village** and occasionally at Cottonwood Campground. Subjects include the park's geology, plants, animals, and human history. We especially like the ranger-led **nature walks** ☆☆, and rangers also occasionally lead driving tours. Workshops are also planned, on subjects such as adobe construction or photography. Look for weekly schedules on the bulletin boards scattered about the park.

The park has a **Junior Ranger Program** for children of all ages. Kids learn about the park through a variety of activities, and earn stickers, certificates, badges, and patches. Pick up Junior Ranger Activity Books ($1) at any visitor center.

The **Big Bend Natural History Association** (see "Visitor Information," above) offers a variety of seminars. Cost is about $50 per day and most seminars are for 1 or 2 days. Subjects could include black bears, archaeology, bats, birds, cacti, photography, and wildflowers.

WHAT TO SEE & DO
EXPLORING THE HIGHLIGHTS BY CAR

The park has several paved roads. In addition, there are several unimproved roads requiring high clearance or 4×4 vehicles.

There are two scenic drives in the park, both with sharp curves and steep inclines and not recommended for certain RVs and trailers (see "Safety," above).

The 7-mile **Chisos Basin Drive,** which takes at least a half-hour, climbs up Green Gulch to Panther Pass before dropping down into the basin. Near the pass there are some sharp curves, and parts of the road are at a 10% grade. The views are wonderful any time of the year, and particularly when the wildflowers dot the meadows, hills, and roadsides. The best months for wildflowers are March and April, and even later on the highest mountain trails.

When you've breathed your fill of clear mountain air, head back down and turn west toward the **Ross Maxwell Scenic Drive** through the Chihuahuan Desert and finally to the Rio Grande. This drive, which will take an hour or so plus stops, winds through the desert on the west side of the Chisos Mountains, providing a different perspective. Afterward, it passes through Castolon, and then continues along and above the river to **Santa Elena Canyon.** Here you should park and hike the trail, which climbs above the river, offering great views into the steep, narrow canyon (see "Hiking," below).

Another worthwhile drive, recommended for all vehicles, begins at **Panther Junction Visitor Center** and goes to Rio Grande Village. Allow a half-day. From the visitor center, head southeast through the desert toward the high mountains that form the skyline in the distance. The first half of the drive passes through desert grasses, finally making a comeback after severe overgrazing in the decades before the establishment of the park in 1944. Recovery is slow in this harsh climate, but it is beginning to revegetate.

As the elevation gradually decreases, you progress farther into the desert, and the grasses give way to lechugilla and ocotillo, cacti, and other arid-climate survivors. Off to the south is the long, rather flat **Chilcotal Mountain,** named for the chilicote, or mescal-bean bushes, growing near its base. The chilicote's poisonous red bean is used in Mexico to kill rats. Several miles farther the River Road turns off and heads southwest toward Castolon, more than 50 miles away. This is a primitive road for high-clearance vehicles only.

Tips Don't Cross the Rio Grande!

Increased national security following the September 11, 2001, terrorist attacks has put a stop to the once popular informal trips to Mexico that many visitors to Big Bend National Park used to make. Although there are no authorized border crossing points within the national park, for years Mexican citizens would use rowboats to ferry park visitors across the Rio Grande to several small Mexican villages, where the Americans could shop and eat genuine Mexican food. But Homeland Security officials have announced that those informal border crossings are no longer permitted, and anyone entering the United States from Mexico in the park is subject to a fine of up to $5,000 and imprisonment of up to 1 year.

If you feel adventurous, take the **Hot Springs** turnoff about a mile beyond the Tornillo Creek Bridge. The road follows a rough wash to a point overlooking the convergence of Tornillo Creek and the Rio Grande. A trail along the riverbank leads to several springs. The foundation of a bathhouse is a remnant of the town of Hot Springs, which thrived here about 20 years before the park was established.

Back on the paved road, you'll soon pass through a short tunnel in the limestone cliff, beyond which is a parking area for a short trail to a view point overlooking **Rio Grande Village.** It's just a short drive from here to Rio Grande Village, your destination, where you can take a .75-mile nature trail ending at a high point above the Rio Grande, offering terrific views up and down the river.

HISTORIC SITES

There is evidence that prehistoric American Indians and later Apaches, Kiowas, and Comanches occupied this area. Throughout the park you can find **petroglyphs, pictographs,** and other signs of early human presence, including ruins of **stone shelters.** There are pictographs along the Hot Spring Trail (see "Hiking," below), and along the river. Watch for **mortar holes** scattered throughout the park, sometimes a foot deep, where Indians would grind seeds or mesquite beans.

Also within the park boundaries are the remains of several early-20th-century communities, a mercury mine, and projects by the Civilian Conservation Corps.

The **Castolon Historic District,** located in the southwest section of the park just off the Ross Maxwell Scenic Drive, includes the remains of homes and other buildings, many stabilized by the National Park Service, that were constructed in the early 1900s by Mexican-American farmers, Anglo settlers, and the U.S. Army. The first is the **Alvino House,** the oldest surviving adobe structure in the park, dating from 1901. Nearby is **La Harmonia Store,** built in 1920 to house cavalry troops during the Mexican Revolution, but never actually used by soldiers because the war ended. Two civilians converted it into a general store and then purchased the building, calling it La Harmonia for the harmony and peaceful relations they hoped to encourage among area residents. The store continues to operate, selling snacks, groceries, and other necessities.

The village of **Glenn Springs,** located in the southeast section of the park and accessible by dirt road off the main park highway, owes its creation to having a reliable water source in an otherwise arid area. It was named for rancher H. E. Glenn, who grazed horses in the area until Indians killed him in the 1880s. By 1916 there were several ranches, a factory that produced wax from the candelilla plant, a store, a post office, and a residential village divided into two sections—one for the Anglos and the other for the Mexicans. But then Mexican bandit revolutionaries crossed the border and attacked, killing and wounding a number of people, looting the store, and partially destroying the wax factory. Within 3 years, the community was virtually deserted. Today, the spring still flows, and you can see the remains of several adobe buildings and other structures.

Remains of a small health resort can be seen at the **Hot Springs,** accessible by hiking trail or dirt road, along the Rio Grande west of Rio Grande Village in the park's southeast section. Construction of the resort began in 1909 under the auspices of J. O. Langford, who was forced to leave during the Mexican Revolution. However, Langford returned and completed the project in the 1920s, advertising the Hot Springs as "The Fountain of Youth that Ponce de León failed to find." Today you'll see the ruins of a general store/post office, other buildings, and a foundation that fills with natural mineral water, at about 105°F (41°C), creating an almost natural hot tub.

To get to the **Marsical Mine** you will likely need a four-wheel-drive or high-clearance vehicle. Located in the south-central part of the park, it is most easily accessed by River Road East, which begins 5 miles west of Rio Grande Village. The mine operated on and off between 1900 and 1943, producing 1,400 76-pound flasks of mercury, which was almost one-quarter of the total amount of mercury produced in the United States during that time. Mining buildings, homes, the company store, a kiln, foundations, and other structures remain in what is now a National Historic District.

Also in the park you can see some excellent examples of the work done by the **Civilian Conservation Corps** in the 1930s and early 1940s. These include stone culverts along the Basin Road, the Lost Mine Trail, and several buildings, including some stone-and-adobe cottages that are still in use at the Chisos Mountains Lodge.

OUTDOOR ADVENTURES

Local companies that provide equipment rentals and a variety of guided adventures both in the park and the general area include **Desert Sports** (*©* **888/989-6900** or 432/371-2727; www.desertsportstx.com), located on FM 170, 5 miles west of the junction of FM 170 and Tex. 118, and **Far Flung Outdoor Center,** FM 170 (P. O. Box 377), Terlingua, TX (*©* **800/839-7238** or 432/371-2633; www.ffoc.net).

Bird-Watching & Wildlife Viewing 𝕒𝕒

There is an absolutely phenomenal variety of wildlife at Big Bend National Park. About 450 species of birds can be found here over the course of the year—that's more than at any other national park and nearly half of all those found in North America. At latest count there were also about 75 species of mammals, close to 70 species of reptiles and amphibians, and more than three dozen species of fish.

This is the only place in the United States where you'll find the Mexican long-nosed bat, listed by the federal government as an endangered species. Other **endangered species** that make their homes in the park include the black-capped vireo and a tiny fish—the Big Bend gambusia, which we hope prospers and multiplies because its favorite food is mosquito larvae.

Birders consider Big Bend National Park a key bird-watching destination, especially for those looking for some of America's more unusual **birds.** Among the park's top bird-watching spots are Rio Grande Village and Cottonwood campgrounds, the Chisos Basin, and the Hot Springs. Species to watch for include the colorful golden-fronted woodpecker, which can often be seen year-round among the cottonwood trees along the Rio Grande; and the rare colima warbler, whose range in the United States consists solely of the Chisos Mountains at Big Bend National Park. Among the hundreds of other birds that call the park home (at least part of the year) are scaled quail, spotted sandpipers, white-winged doves, greater roadrunners, lesser nighthawks, white-throated swifts, black-chinned and broad-tailed hummingbirds, acorn woodpeckers, northern flickers, western wood-pewees, ash-throated flycatchers, tufted titmice, bushtits, cactus and canyon wrens, loggerhead shrikes, Wilson's warblers, and Scott's orioles.

Mammals you may see in the park include desert cottontails, black-tailed jackrabbits, rock squirrels, Texas antelope squirrels, Merriam's kangaroo rats, coyotes, gray foxes, raccoons, striped skunks, mule deer, and white-tailed deer. There are occasional sightings of mountain lions, usually called panthers here, in the Green Gulch and Chisos Basin areas. Four attacks on humans have occurred at the park, with no fatalities. Black bears, which were frequently seen in the area until about 1940, were mostly killed off by area ranchers who saw them as a threat to their livestock. However, with the protection provided by national park status, they began to return in the mid-1980s and have now established a small population.

There are a number of **reptiles** in the park, including some poisonous snakes, such as diamondback, Mojave, rock, and black-tailed rattlesnakes, plus the trans-pecos copperhead. Fortunately, it is unlikely you will see a rattler or copperhead, since they avoid both the heat of the day and busy areas. You are more apt to encounter nonpoisonous western coachwhips, which are often seen speeding across trails and roadways. Sometimes called "red racers," they're reddish, sometimes bright red, and among America's fastest snakes. Other nonpoisonous snakes that inhabit the park include Texas whipsnakes, spotted night snakes, southwestern black-headed snakes, and black-necked garter snakes.

Among the **lizards** you may see scurrying along desert roads and trails is the southwestern earless lizard—adult males are green with black and white chevrons on their lower sides, and often curl their black-striped tails over their backs. You'll also see various whiptail lizards in the desert, but in the canyons and higher in the mountains, watch for the crevice spiny lizard, which is covered with scales and has a dark collar. Although rare, there are also **western box turtles** in the park, as well as several types of more common water turtles.

Hiking 🐾🐾🐾

Big Bend National Park is a wonderful park for hikers, with a wide variety of trails, most of which are easy or moderate. There are a number of short, easy interpretive nature walks, either with booklets available at the trail heads or signs along the trail. One example is the **Panther Path,** which is 50 yards round-trip, outside the Panther Junction Visitor Center, offering a walk through a garden of cacti and other desert plants. We also enjoy the **Window View Trail,** which is .3 miles round-trip and is accessible via the Chisos Basin Trailhead. This level, paved, and wheelchair-accessible self-guided nature trail runs along a low hill and offers beautiful sunset views through the Window, a V-shaped opening in the mountains to the west. The **Rio Grande Village Nature Trail** 🐾 .75-mile round-trip starts at the southeast corner of Rio Grande Village Campground across from site 18 and is a good choice for sunrise and sunset views. It climbs from the surprisingly lush river floodplain about 125 feet into desert terrain to a hilltop that offers excellent panoramic vistas.

Those who want to see historic structures should try the easy 1-mile **Hot Springs Trail,** which is at the end of an improved dirt road to Hot Springs, off the road to Rio Grande Village. An interpretive booklet available at the trail head describes the sights, including a historic health resort and homestead (see "Historic Sites," above), along this loop. Fairly substantial ruins remain of a general store/post office, other buildings, and a foundation that fills with natural mineral water at about 105°F (41°C), creating an inviting hot tub. Also along the trail are pictographs left by ancient Indians, and panoramic views of the Rio Grande and Mexico.

Among other easy hikes is the **Tuff Canyon Trail** (.75 mile round-trip), which is accessed from the Ross Maxwell Scenic Drive, 5 miles south of the Mule Ears Overlook access road. This walk leads into a narrow canyon, carved from soft volcanic rock called tuff and offers several canyon overlooks. The 1.6-mile **Chisos Basin Loop Trail** (access at the Chisos Basin trail head) is a fairly easy walk that climbs about 350 feet into a pretty meadow and leads to an overlook that offers good views of the park's mountains, including Emory Peak, the highest point in the park at 7,825 feet; more adventurous hikers can continue here to the breathtaking South Rim for a 12-mile round trip. The easy **Grapevine Hills Trail,** which is 2.2 miles round-trip, begins about 6 miles down the unpaved Grapevine Hills Road. It has an elevation change of about 240 feet as it follows a sandy wash through the desert, among massive granite boulders, ending at a picturesque balancing rock.

Among shorter, moderately rated trails, we heartily recommend the .8-mile one-way **Santa Elena Canyon Trail** 𝕬𝕬𝕬, which you'll find at the end of Ross Maxwell Scenic Drive. You may get your feet wet crossing a broad creek on this trail, which also takes you up a series of steep steps; it's one of the most scenic short trails in the park, leading along the canyon wall, with good views of rafters on the Rio Grande, and down among the boulders along the river. Interpretive signs describe the canyon environment. Beware of flash flooding as you cross the Terlingua Creek, and skip this trail if the creek is running swiftly. Another good moderate hike is the **Boquillas Canyon Trail** 𝕬, which is 1.4 miles round-trip and starts at the end of Boquillas Canyon Road. This hike begins by climbing a low hill and then drops down to the Rio Grande, ending near a shallow cave and huge sand dune. There are good views of the scenic canyon and the Mexican village of Boquillas, across the Rio Grande.

Among longer trails, we suggest the moderately rated 3.8-mile round-trip **Mule Ears Spring Trail** 𝕬, which you'll find at the Mule Ears Overlook parking area along the Ross Maxwell Scenic Drive. This relatively flat desert trail crosses several arroyos and then follows a wash most of the way to Mule Ears Spring. It offers great views of unusual rock formations, such as the Mule Ears, and ends at a historic ranch house and rock corral. At 4 miles round-trip the moderate **Pine Canyon Trail** takes you from desert grasslands dotted with sotols into a pretty canyon with dense stands of pinyon, juniper, oak, and finally bigtooth maple and ponderosa pine. At the higher elevations (it climbs 1,000 ft.), you'll also see Texas madrones—evergreen trees with smooth reddish bark that is shed each summer. At the end of the trail is a 200-foot cliff, which becomes a picturesque waterfall after heavy rains. This trail is located at the end of unpaved Pine Canyon Road (check on road conditions before going).

Horseback Riding

Horses are permitted on most dirt roads and many park trails (check with rangers for specifics), and may be kept overnight at many of the park's primitive campsites, although not at the developed campgrounds. The **Government Springs Campsite,** located 3½ miles from Panther Junction, is a primitive campsite with a corral that accommodates up to eight horses. It can be reserved up to 10 weeks in advance (© 432/477-2241). Those riding horses in the park must get free stock use permits, which should be obtained in person up to 24 hours in advance at any of the park's visitor centers.

Although there are no commercial outfitters offering guided rides in the park as of this writing, there are opportunities for rides just outside the park on private land, such as nearby Big Bend Ranch State Park and across the river in Mexico. **Lajitas Stables** (© 800/887-4331 or 432/371-2212; www.lajitasstables.com) offers a variety of guided trail rides, lasting from 2 hours to all day to 5 days. Some trips follow canyon trails; others visit ancient Indian camps, ghost towns, or cross the border into Mexico. Typical rates are $60 for 2 hours, $85 for 4 hours, and $130 for a full day; multiday trips are usually about $150 per day, and include all meals and camping equipment, as well as the horse. There are also combination riding/rafting expeditions.

Mountain Biking

Bikes are not permitted on hiking trails, but are allowed on the park's many established dirt roads. Mountain bikes are available for rent from **Desert Sports** (see above), at a cost of $30 per day, $150 for 6 to 7 days, and $20 for each additional day after 7 days. The company also offers 1-day and multiday guided trips, including a combination mountain-biking and float trip in the park—3 days for $450.

River Running 🐟

The Rio Grande follows the southern edge of the park for 118 miles, and extends another 127 miles downstream as a designated Wild and Scenic River. The river offers mostly calm float trips, but it does have a few sections of rough white water during high-water times. It can usually be run in a raft, canoe, or kayak. You can either bring your own equipment, or rent equipment near the park (none is available in the park), but for novices it's safest to take a trip with one of several river guides approved by the National Park Service.

Those planning trips on their own must obtain $10 permits at a park visitor center, in person only and no more than 24 hours before the trip. Permits for the lower canyons of the Rio Grande Wild and Scenic River are available at the **Persimmon Gap Visitor Center,** and a self-serve permit station located there when the visitor center itself is closed. Permits for the section of river through Santa Elena Canyon can also be obtained at the **Barton Warnock Environmental Education Center,** 1 mile east of the community of Lajitas, Texas, about 20 miles from the park's west entrance. Park rangers, however, strongly advise that everyone planning a river trip check with them beforehand to get the latest river conditions. A river-running booklet with additional information is available at park visitor centers and from the **Big Bend Natural History Association** (see "Visitor Information," earlier in this chapter).

Rafts, inflatable kayaks, and canoes can be rented from **Desert Sports** (© 888/ 989-6900 or 432/371-2727; www.desertsportstx.com). Rafts cost $25 per person per day (three-person minimum) with discounts for trips longer than 4 days; inflatable kayaks cost $35 per day for one person and $45 per day for two people; and canoes cost $45 per day, with discounts for multiday rentals. The company also provides shuttle services and offers guided 1-day and multiday canoe and raft trips, where you can either grab a paddle and take an active role, or sit back and let your boatman and the river do the work. Typical prices are $280 per person for 2 days on the river through Santa Elena Canyon; and $475 per person for 3 days on the river through Marsical Canyon, considered the most remote canyon in the national park. Desert Sports also offers trips that combine a float trip with hiking or mountain biking. Also see "Mountain Biking," above.

Another company that provides guided trips on the Rio Grande is **Big Bend River Tours** (© 800/545-4240 or 432/371-3033; www.bigbendrivertours.com), which has daily raft trips year-round. Trips range from a delightful half-day float for about $65 per person to 10-day excursions for over $1,500 per person. Among the company's most popular trips is the 21-mile float through beautiful Santa Elena Canyon, which offers spectacular scenery and wonderful serenity, plus the excitement of a challenging section of rapids called the Rockslide. There are also often opportunities to see wildlife. The canyon can be explored on a day trip (about $130 per person), a 2-day trip (about $285 per person), or a 3-day trip (about $425 per person), with varying rates based on the number of people making the trip. The longer trips include a stop in a side canyon with waterfalls and peaceful swimming holes. Big Bend River Tours also offers guided canoe and inflatable kayak trips, provides a shuttle service, and rents equipment.

The third outfitter on the Rio Grande in the Terlingua/Study Butte area is **Far Flung Outdoor Center** (© **800/839-7238** or 432/371-2633; www.ffoc.net), offering raft and canoe trips for $63 per person for a half-day, and about twice that for a full day canyon float. The company also offers jeep and ATV tours of the region.

WHERE TO STAY

This is an isolated area, so don't expect to find your favorite chain motel or restaurant right around the corner. Make lodging reservations well in advance, especially in winter—the high season here—when rates are highest.

IN THE PARK

Chisos Mountains Lodge ⟨★⟩ The best place to stay while exploring Big Bend, Chisos Mountains Lodge offers a variety of accommodations ranging from simple motel rooms to our preference, the historic stone cottages. Built by the Civilian Conservation Corps in the 1930s, the six delightful cottages have a rustic feel that seems right for a national park setting. They have stone floors, wooden furniture, three double beds, and covered porches. Book as far in advance as possible.

The lodge units, which are also a bit on the rustic side, have one double and one single bed, wood furnishings, and painted brick walls with Western and/or Southwestern art. The lodge's motel rooms are small and simply decorated, with two double beds and terrific views of the Chisos Mountains. The Casa Grande Motor Lodge, also part of the Chisos Mountains Lodge, offers spacious and more modern motel rooms, attractively furnished, with two beds and private balconies. The restaurant here serves three meals a day, including a breakfast buffet. All rooms are nonsmoking.

Chisos Basin, Big Bend National Park, TX 79834-9999. © **432/477-2291.** Fax 432/477-2352. www.chisosmountains lodge.com. 72 units. $89–$105 double. AE, DC, DISC, MC, V. **Amenities:** Restaurant; coin-op washers and dryers. *In room:* A/C (in motel and Casa Grande units), fridge, coffeemaker, no phone.

THE STUDY BUTTE–TERLINGUA AREA

Just outside the national park's west entrance, this is the closest community to the park with lodging and other services. Here you'll find the **Big Bend Motor Inn,** at the junction of Tex. 118 and FM 170 (P. O. Box 336), Terlingua, TX 79852 (© **800/ 848-BEND** or 432/371-2218), offering simple but comfortable and well-maintained modern motel rooms, with rates of $85 to $90 for doubles, and about $100 for kitchenette rooms. A restaurant and convenience store are on-site. The **Chisos Mining Co. Motel,** on FM 170 about ¾ mile west of Tex. 118 (P. O. Box 228), Terlingua, TX 79852 (© **432/371-2254;** www.cmcm.cc), is an attractive, well-maintained property. It has standard motel units ($50–$65 double) as well as cabins and houses ($70–$140).

Ten Bits Ranch ⟨★★⟩ Located about 10 miles north of Study Butte, this isolated lodging is one of a kind, a re-creation of an old Western town, replete with boardwalks and storefronts masking the guest rooms. Hosting their first guests in late 2004, the individually decorated options—the Bank, the Gunsmith, the Schoolhouse, and the General Store—are named for their corresponding storefronts, and decorated with a sense of desert chic. The ranch is sustainable and off the grid, meaning water use is limited and modern amenities few—you can really get away from it all here. Owners Jennifer and Steve Wick are well acquainted with the Big Bend area as a former travel agent and park ranger, respectively. Steve, a budding paleontologist and archaeologist, offers special dinosaur excavation getaways on the ranch's 125 acres, which are a trove of fossils.

6000 N. County Rd. (P. O. Box 293), Terlingua, TX 79852. ℂ 866/371-3110. www.tenbitsranch.com. 4 units. $128–$199 double, with a 2-night minimum stay Oct–May. Rates include continental breakfast. AE, DISC, MC, V. **Amenities:** Guest kitchen. *In room:* No phone.

MARATHON

Gage Hotel 🏵🏵   Located 50 miles north of the park boundary, the historic Gage Hotel opened in 1927 as the social hub for area ranchers and miners, but fell into shambles under the desert sun in the ensuing decades. But that period is long over: The current owners restored the old redbrick's many charms in the early 1980s, melding history and an eye for Texas chic. The historic rooms have cow-skin rugs, hardwood floors, Navajo blankets, and oodles of personality; those with shared bathrooms are a bit on the smallish side, but those with private bathrooms are our personal favorites. With outdoor entrances closer to the magnificent pool and courtyards, the larger Los Portales rooms are part of an addition completed in 1992 and have adobe floors and expanded amenities (coffeemakers, phones, hair dryers, and irons). The restaurant, Café Cenizo, serves steaks and gourmet Southwestern cuisine.

U.S. 90 (P. O. Box 46), Marathon, TX 79842. ℂ 800/884-GAGE or 432/386-4205. www.gagehotel.com. 39 units (9 with shared bathroom), including 1 suite and 2 guesthouses. $76 double with shared bathroom; $98–$182 double with private bathroom; $208 suite; $303–$330 guesthouse. AE, DISC, MC, V. **Amenities:** Restaurant; bar; outdoor heated pool; exercise room; spa; Jacuzzi; in-room massage. *In room:* A/C, no phone.

LAJITAS

Lajitas, the Ultimate Hideout 🏵🏵   Remote to say the least, Lajitas is a historic village–turned–luxury resort presided over by Mayor Clay Henry, a beer-swilling billy goat. (There's a heckuva story here, but it's a long one.) The guest rooms—which range from former officer's quarters on a onetime cavalry post to more modern rooms in the central hotel—are uniformly posh, and the amenities and facilities extensive. There's a lot going on here: a real estate development, an 18-hole golf course (19 holes if you count the par 1 with the green across the Rio Grande in Mexico), galleries and shops, a private runway, and 25,000 acres of mostly pristine property. The rates are definitely on the high end; regardless, Lajitas is a great getaway for the golf lover who appreciates luxury.

HC 70, Box 400, Lajitas, TX 79852. ℂ 877/525-4827 or 432/424-5000. Fax 432/424-5001. www.lajitas.com. 92 units. $245–$370 double; $430–$900 suite. AE, DISC, MC, V. Located 20 miles west of the park's west entrance. **Amenities:** 3 restaurants; 2 bars; outdoor pool; 18-hole golf course; spa; concierge; activity desk; shopping arcade; in-room massage. *In room:* A/C, satellite TV w/DVD player, minibar, coffeemaker, hair dryer, iron, safe.

WHERE TO DINE
IN THE PARK

The restaurant at **Chisos Mountain Lodge** (see "Where to Stay," earlier in this chapter) is your only dining option while within park boundaries.

THE STUDY BUTTE–TERLINGUA AREA

For barbecue and steaks ($8.50–$14), **La Kiva,** FM 170 (ℂ 432/371-2250), is a cavelike establishment on Terlinuga Creek. **Phat Café,** FM 170 (ℂ 432/371-2520), serves one nightly seating of Asian fusion at 7pm.

Starlight Theatre 🏵🏵 MEXICAN/NEW AMERICAN   A 1930s movie palace abandoned when the mines in Terlingua went bust in the following decade, the Starlight Theatre was reborn as an eatery and watering hole in 1991. The stage is still here, but the silver screen takes a backseat to the food (especially the trademark enchiladas, filet mignon, and sautéed chicken), drink (namely Texas beers and prickly pear margaritas), and desserts (the cobbler for two is legendary). The funky West Texan decor—featuring numerous requisite longhorn skulls—is a contrast for the unexpectedly diverse menu, which features a number of vegetarian and seafood options. The theater still occasionally hosts movie nights, as well as plays and live music.

In Historic Terlingua Ghost Town, off U.S. 90. © 432/371-2326. www.starlighttheatre.com. Main courses $6–$22; Sunday brunch $5–$13. AE, MC, V. Daily 5–10pm; Sun also 10am–2pm. Bar open later.

LAJITAS

Ocotillo ★★ WILD GAME   For our money the best restaurant on the entire Texas-Mexico border, Ocotillo specializes in wild game with Mexican-inspired sauces; the interplay between the two is a revelation. Executive Chef Blas Gonzales brought 20 years of experience from Austin, and his seasonal menu typically includes a few stalwarts: melt-in-your-mouth elk, topped with Maine lobster in a guava-sour cherry sauce; a heavenly corn pudding; and, for dessert, the best *tres leches* cake on the border, made by Gonzales's wife. You might also come across interesting nightly specials—say, wild boar in a jalapeno-mango sauce or ostrich with guajillo-pepper sauce. Everything is fresh: Seafood is flown in daily from both coasts, and many ingredients are grown in a terrace garden on-site. Housed in a reinvented Wild West trading post, the glass windows overlook the Rio Grande, the room is accented by contemporary art and sculpture, and the bar has a staircase leading up to a fourth-story lookout.

At Lajitas, the Ultimate Hideout. © 432/424-5000. Reservations accepted. Main courses $21–$41. AE, DISC, MC, V. Tues–Sat 6–9pm.

CAMPING

A $10 camping permit, available at any visitor center, is required for use of the primitive backcountry roadside and backpacking campsites. All are open year-round.

In the Park

There are three developed campgrounds run by the National Park Service (no showers, laundry facilities, or RV hook-ups; $10 per night), and an RV park run by a concessionaire. A limited number of campsites in Rio Grande Village and the Chisos Basin campgrounds accept reservations from November 15 to April 15; call © 877/444-6777 or visit **www.reserveusa.com**.

Rio Grande Village Campground is the largest, with 100 sites, flush toilets, running water, and a dump station. It has numerous trees, many with prickly pear cacti growing up around them, and thorny bushes everywhere. Sites are either graveled or paved and are nicely spaced for privacy. Sites are often taken by 1pm in winter (the busy season). One area is designated a "No Generator Zone." Separate but within walking distance is **Rio Grande Village Trailer Park** (© 432/477-2293), a concessionaire-operated RV park with 25 sites with full hook-ups. It looks like a parking lot in the midst of grass and trees, fully paved with curbs and back-in sites (no pull-throughs). Cost is $21 per night. Tents are not permitted. A small store has limited camping supplies and groceries, a coin-operated laundry, showers for a fee, propane, and gasoline.

Chisos Basin Campground ★★, although not heavily wooded, has small piñon and juniper trees and 65 well-spaced sites. The highest-elevation campground in the park at 5,400 feet, it's nestled around a circular road in a bowl below the visitor center. There is a dump station, flush toilets, and running water. The access road to the campground is steep and curved, so take it slowly. The campground is not recommended for trailers over 20 feet or motor homes over 24 feet.

Cottonwood Campground is named for the huge cottonwood trees that dominate the scene. The 31 first-come, first-served sites in this rather rustic area are spacious and within walking distance of the river. There are pit toilets, and generators may not be used.

Near the Park

About 7 miles east of the park's North Entrance on FM 2627 is **Stillwell Store and RV Park,** HC 65, Box 430, Alpine, TX 79830-9752 (© **432/376-2244;** www.freeranger.com/stillwell), a casual RV park in desert terrain that's open year-round. There are two areas across the road from each other. The west side has full hook-ups, while the east has water and electric only, but the east side also features horse corrals and plenty of room for horse trailers. There are 80 RV sites ($15–$18 per night) plus almost unlimited space for tenters, who are charged $5 per person. There's a dump station, showers, a self-serve laundry, and a public phone. The park office is at the Stillwell Store, where you can get groceries, limited camping supplies, and gasoline. There is also a small museum (donations accepted), with exhibits from the Stillwell family's pioneer days.

2 Guadalupe Mountains National Park

Once a long reef below the ocean's surface, then a dense forest, Guadalupe Mountains National Park is today a rugged wilderness of tall Douglas firs and lush vegetation rising out of a vast desert. Here you will find varied hiking trails, panoramic vistas, the highest peak in Texas, plant and animal life unique in the Southwest, and a canyon that many believe is the prettiest spot in all of Texas.

As you approach from the north, the mountains seem to rise gradually from the landscape, but seen from the south they stand tall and dignified. El Capitan, the southern tip of the reef escarpment, watches over the landscape like a sentinel. In the south-central section of the park, Guadalupe Peak, at 8,749 feet the highest mountain in Texas, provides hikers with incredible views of the surrounding mountains and desert.

Within its 86,416 acres of land, the park has several hubs of human activity and distinct ecological zones. Park headquarters and the visitor center are at Pine Springs, along the park's southeast edge, where you'll also find a campground and several trail heads, including one with access to the Guadalupe Peak Trail, the park's premier mountain hike. Nearby, a short dirt road leads to historic Frijole Ranch, with a museum and more trail heads. A horse corral is nearby for those traveling with their steeds. The McKittrick Canyon section of the park, near the northeast corner, gets our vote as the most beautiful spot in Texas, especially in the fall when its oaks, maples, ash, and walnut trees produce a spectacular show of color. A day-use area only, McKittrick Canyon has a delightful although intermittent stream, a wide variety of plant and animal life, several trail heads, and historic buildings. Along the park's northern boundary, practically in New Mexico, is the secluded and forested Dog Canyon.

Particularly impressive about Guadalupe Mountains National Park is its vast variety of flora and fauna. You'll find species here that don't seem to belong in West Texas, such as the maple and oak, which produce the wonderful fall colors in McKittrick Canyon. Scientists say these seemingly out-of-place plants and animals are leftovers from a time when this region was cooler and wetter. As the climate changed and the

Guadalupe Mountains National Park

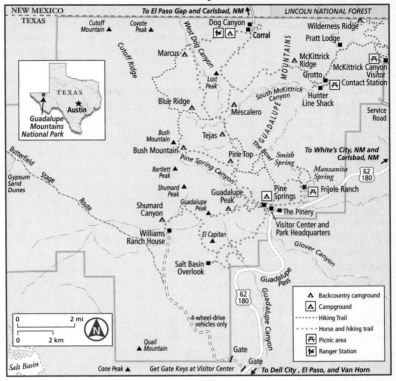

desert spread, some species were able to survive in these mountains, where conditions remained somewhat cooler and moister. At the base of the mountains, at lower elevations, you'll find desert plants such as sotol, agave, and prickly pear cactus; but as you start to climb, especially in stream-nurtured canyons, expect to encounter ponderosa pine, ash, walnut, oak, and ferns. Wildlife abounds, including mule deer, elk, and all sorts of birds and the occasional snake.

It takes several days to fully explore this park, but just a half-day trip to McKittrick Canyon would be well worth your time.

ESSENTIALS

GETTING THERE   Located on the border of New Mexico and Texas, the park is 55 miles southwest of Carlsbad, New Mexico, along U.S. 62/180. From El Paso drive east 110 miles on U.S. 62/180 to the Pine Springs Visitor Center.

Air travelers can fly to **Cavern City Air Terminal** (© 505/887-1500), at the south edge of the city of Carlsbad, which has commercial service from Albuquerque with **Mesa Airlines** (© 505/885-0245), plus Hertz car rentals. The nearest major airport is **El Paso International** (© 915/780-4749; www.elpasointernationalairport.com) in central El Paso just north of I-10, with service from most major airlines and car-rental companies; see chapter 9 for more information.

VISITOR INFORMATION   Contact **Guadalupe Mountains National Park,** 400 Pine Canyon Rd., Salt Flat, TX 79847 (© **915/828-3251;** www.nps.gov/gumo). Books and maps can be ordered from the **Carlsbad Caverns Guadalupe Mountains Association,** 727 Carlsbad Caverns Hwy. (P. O. Box 417), Carlsbad, NM 88221 (© **505/785-2486;** www.ccgma.org).

Park headquarters and the main visitor center are located at Pine Springs just off U.S. 62/180. There are three other access points along this side of the park: Frijole Ranch, about a mile east of Pine Springs and a mile north of the highway; McKittrick Canyon (day use only), about 7 miles east and 4 miles north of the highway; and Williams Ranch, about 8 miles south of Pine Springs and 8 miles north of the highway on a four-wheel-drive road. (*Note:* Keys to locked gates can be checked out at park headquarters.)

The **Pine Springs Visitor Center,** open daily year-round except Christmas, has natural history exhibits, a bookstore, and an introductory slide program. **McKittrick Canyon** has a visitor contact station with outdoor exhibits and an outdoor slide program on the history, geology, and natural history of the canyon. On the north side of the park is **Dog Canyon Ranger Station** (© **505/981-2418**), at the end of N. Mex. 137, about 70 miles from Carlsbad and 110 miles from park headquarters. Information, restrooms, and drinking water are available.

FEES, REGULATIONS & PERMITS   Entry into the park runs $5 per person. Backcountry camping is free, but a permit is required. Corrals are available for those who bring their horses to ride in the park; although use is free, permits are required. All permits are available at the Pine Springs Visitor Center and Dog Canyon Ranger Station and must be requested in person, either the day before or the day of use. Horses are prohibited in the backcountry overnight.

Visitors to McKittrick Canyon, a day-use area, must stay on the trail; entering the stream is not permitted. The McKittrick Canyon **entrance gate** opens at 8am daily, and closes at 4:30pm Mountain Standard Time and at 6pm Mountain Daylight Time. Neither wood nor charcoal fires are allowed anywhere in the park.

WHEN TO GO   In general, summers in the Guadalupe Mountains are hot (highs in the 80s and 90s/upper 20s and 30s Celsius, and lows in the 60s/upper teens Celsius) and winters are mild (highs in the 50s and 60s/teens Celsius and lows in the upper 20s and 30s/around 0 Celsius), but there can be sudden and extreme changes in the weather at any time. In winter and spring, high winds can whip down the mountain slopes, sometimes reaching 100 mph; on hot summer days, thunderstorms can blow up quickly. The sun is warm even in winter, and summer nights are generally cool no matter how hot the afternoon. Clothing that can be layered is best, comfortable and sturdy walking/hiking shoes are a must, a hat and sunscreen are highly recommended, and plenty of drinking water is essential for hikers.

Overall, Guadalupe Mountains National Park is one of America's less-visited national parks, with attendance of only about 225,000 each year. This is partly because it is primarily a wilderness park, where you'll have to tackle rugged hiking trails to get to the best vistas, but also because of its isolation. The only time the park might be considered even slightly crowded is during spring-break time, usually in March, when students from area colleges bring their backpacks and hit the trails. Quite a few families visit during the summer, but even then the park is not usually crowded, and visitation drops considerably once schools open in late August.

An exception is McKittrick Canyon, renowned throughout the Southwest for its beautiful fall colors, at their best in late October and early November. The one road into McKittrick Canyon is a bit busy then, but once you get on the trails you can usually walk away from the people.

SAFETY   This is extremely rugged country, with sometimes unpredictable weather, and hikers need to be well prepared, with proper hiking boots and plenty of water. Because the park's backcountry trails often crisscross each other and can be confusing, rangers strongly recommend that hikers carry topographical maps.

RANGER PROGRAMS   On summer evenings, rangers offer programs at the campground amphitheater.

WHAT TO SEE & DO
EXPLORING THE HIGHLIGHTS BY CAR
This is not the place for the vehicle-bound. There are no paved scenic drives traversing the park; roads here are simply means of getting to historical sites and trail heads.

HISTORIC SITES
The Pinery was 1 of 200 stagecoach stations along the 2,800-mile Butterfield Overland Mail Coach Route. The stations provided fresh mules every 20 miles and a new coach every 300 miles, in order to maintain the grueling speed of 5 mph 24 hours a day. John Butterfield had seen the need for overland mail delivery between the Eastern states and the West Coast, so he designed a route and the coaches, and acquired a federal contract to deliver the St. Louis mail to San Francisco in 25 days. In March 1857 this was a real feat, and the remaining rock walls at the ruins of The Pinery, which you can see on The Pinery Trail (see "Hiking," below) commemorate Butterfield's achievement.

Located in McKittrick Canyon, **Pratt Lodge** was built by Wallace E. Pratt in 1931 and 1932, of stone quarried from the base of the Guadalupe Mountains, using heart-of-pine from east Texas for rafters, collar beams, and roof supports. Pratt, a geologist for the Humble Oil Co. (now ExxonMobil), and his family came for summer vacations when the heat in Houston became unbearable. He finally retired here in 1945. In 1957, the Pratts donated 5,632 acres of their 16,000-acre ranch to the federal government to begin the national park. In addition to the grand stone lodge, there are several outbuildings, stone picnic tables, and a stone fence.

Williams Ranch House rests at the base of a 3,000-foot rock cliff on the west face of the Guadalupe Mountains. The 7⅓-mile access road, navigable only by high-clearance 4×4s, follows part of the old Butterfield Overland Mail Route for about 2 miles. The road crosses private land and has two locked metal gates, for which you must sign out keys at the visitor center.

History is unclear on exactly who built the house and when, but it's believed to have been built around 1908, and it is fairly certain that the first inhabitants were Henry and Rena Belcher. For almost 10 years, they maintained a substantial ranch here, at times with close to 3,000 head of longhorn cattle. Water was piped from Bone Spring down the canyon to holding tanks in the lowlands. James Adolphus Williams acquired the property around 1917, and with the help of an Indian friend, ranched and farmed the land until moving to New Mexico in 1941. After Williams's death in 1942, Judge J. C. Hunter bought the property, adding it to his already large holdings in the Guadalupes.

Another historic site is **Frijole Ranch,** which was a working ranch from when it was built in the 1870s until 1972. Inside the ranch house is a museum with exhibits on the cultural history of the Guadalupe Mountains, including prehistoric Indians, the later Mescalero Apaches, Spanish conquistadors, and ranchers of the 19th and 20th centuries. On the grounds are several historic buildings, including a schoolhouse.

OUTDOOR ADVENTURES
Hiking 𝕽𝕽

This is a prime hiker's park, with more than 80 miles of trails that range from easy walks to steep, strenuous, and sometimes treacherous adventures. Among shorter trails, try the **Indian Meadow Nature Trail** 𝕽, with access from Dog Canyon Campground (walk south from the water fountain). This exceptionally easy .6-mile round-trip stroll follows a series of numbered stops keyed to a free brochure, available at the trail head. You'll learn about the native vegetation and cultural history of the area as you ramble along this virtually level dirt trail. The name comes from early settlers, who told of seeing Indian tepees in this lovely meadow. The **McKittrick Canyon Nature Trail** 𝕽, rated moderate due to a rocky trail, is .9 mile round-trip, and begins at the McKittrick Canyon contact station. A great way to discover the variety of plants and animals that inhabit the canyon, this trail, which has some steep climbs, posts numerous educational signs along the path telling you why rattlesnakes are underappreciated and how the cactus supplies food and water for wildlife.

The easy .75-mile round-trip **Pinery Trail** (paved and accessible by wheelchair) gives visitors a brief introduction to the low-elevation environment at the park. Interpretive signs discuss the plants along the trail and the history of the area. About .25 miles from the visitor center the trail makes a loop around the ruins of an old horse-changing station, left over from the Butterfield Stage Route (see "Historic Sites," above). The trail head is by the Pine Springs Visitor Center, or from the parking area on U.S. 62/180, located 1 mile north of the visitor center entrance road.

Among the park's longer trails, our favorite is the moderate-to-difficult **McKittrick Canyon Trail** 𝕽𝕽𝕽, which is 5.1 miles one-way, with access at the McKittrick Canyon Trail head. We think McKittrick Canyon is the most beautiful spot in all of Texas, and this trail explores the length of it. The first 2.3 miles to the Pratt Lodge are moderate because of rocky trail conditions; the following 1.2 miles to the Grotto gain 340 feet in elevation and are also considered moderate; and the strenuous climb to the Notch rises nearly 1,300 feet in just 1.6 miles. Even so, this is one of the most popular hikes in the park, though not everyone makes it to the Notch.

The canyon is forested with conifers and deciduous trees. In fall the walnut and ash trees burst into color, painting the world in bright colors set off by the brown of the oaks and the rich variety of the evergreens. The stream in the canyon, which appears and disappears several times in the first 3 miles of the trail, is a permanent stream with reproducing trout. Hikers may not drink from, wade in, or disturb the stream in any way.

The first part of the trail is wide and seems quite flat, crossing the stream twice on its way to Pratt Lodge, which is wonderfully situated at the convergence of North and South McKittrick canyons. About a mile from the lodge a short spur veers off to the left to the Grotto, a recess with odd formations that look like they belong in an underground cave. This is a great spot for lunch at one of the stone picnic tables. Continuing down the spur trail to its end, you reach the Hunter Line Cabin, which served as temporary quarters for ranch hands of the Hunter family. Beyond the cabin, South

McKittrick Canyon has been preserved as a Research Natural Area with no entry. Return to the main trail and continue toward the Notch, or head back down the canyon to your car. In another .5 miles, the trail begins switchbacking up the side of South McKittrick Canyon for the steepest ascent in the park, until it slips through the Notch, a distinctive narrow spot in the cliff. Sit down and rest while you absorb the incredible scenery. The view down the canyon is magnificent and quite dazzling in autumn. You can see both Hunter Line Cabin and Pratt Lodge in the distance. Remember to start down in time to reach your car well before the gate closes (see "Fees, Regulations & Permits," above).

To stand at the highest point in Texas, hike the strenuous **Guadalupe Peak Trail** ⭐⭐, which goes 4.2 miles from the trail head in Pine Springs Campground to the top of 8,749-foot-high Guadalupe Peak, where the magnificent views make the almost 3,000-foot climb worthwhile. If you have only 1 day to explore this park, and you are an average or better hiker, this is the hike you should choose. Start early, take plenty of water, and be prepared to work. When you've gone about halfway, you'll see what seems to be the top not too far ahead, but beware: This is a false summit. Study the changing life zones as you climb from the desert into the higher-elevation pine forests—this will take your mind off your straining muscles and aching lungs. A mile short of the summit, a campground lies in one of the rare level spots on the mountain. If you plan to spend the night, strongly anchor your tent, as the winds can be ferocious up here, especially in spring.

From the summit, the views are stupendous. To the north are Shumard Peak and Bush Mountain, the next two highest points in Texas, with respective elevations of 8,615 and 8,631 feet. The Chihuahuan Desert stretches to the south, interrupted only by the Delaware and Sierra Diablo mountains. This is one of those "on a clear day you can see forever" spots—sometimes all the way to 12,003-foot-high Sierra Blanca, near Ruidoso, New Mexico, 100 miles north.

Horseback Riding

About 60% of the park's trails are open to horses for day trips, but horses are not permitted in the backcountry overnight. There are **corrals** at Frijole Ranch (near Pine Springs) and Dog Canyon (see "Visitor Information," above). Each set of corrals contains four pens that can accommodate up to 10 horses. There are no horses or other pack animals available for hire in or near the park. Park rangers warn that horses brought into the park should be accustomed to steep, rocky trails.

Wildlife Viewing

Because of the variety of habitats here, and also because these canyons offer some of the few water sources in West Texas, Guadalupe Mountains National Park offers excellent wildlife viewing and bird-watching possibilities. **McKittrick Canyon** and **Frijole Ranch** are considered among the best wildlife viewing spots, but a variety of species can be seen throughout the park. Those spending more than a few hours will likely see mule deer, and the park is also home to a herd of some 50 to 70 elk, which are sometimes seen in the higher elevations or along the highway in winter. Other **mammals** include raccoons, striped and hog-nosed skunks, gray foxes, coyotes, gray-footed chipmunks, Texas antelope squirrels, black-tailed jackrabbits, and desert cottontails. Black bears and mountain lions also live in the park, but are seldom seen.

About two dozen varieties of **snakes** make their home in the park, including five species of rattlesnakes. There are also numerous **lizards,** which are usually seen in the

---

> **Tips** **Leaf Peepin'**
>
> McKittrick Canyon's beautiful display of fall colors usually takes place between
> late October and early November. It varies, though, so call before going.

---

mornings and early evenings. These include the collared, crevice spiny, tree, side-blotched, and Texas horned lizards, and Chihuahuan spotted whiptails. The most commonly seen is the prairie lizard, identified by the light-colored stripes down its back.

More than 200 species of **birds** are known to spend time in the park, including peregrine falcons, golden eagles, turkey vultures, and wild turkeys. You are also likely to encounter rock wrens, canyon wrens, black-throated sparrows, common nighthawks, mourning doves, rufous-crowned sparrows, mountain chickadees, ladder-backed woodpeckers, solitary vireos, and western scrub jays.

WHERE TO STAY & DINE

There are no accommodations or restaurants within the park. The closest communities offering lodging and dining are in New Mexico: **White's City,** 35 miles from the park, and **Carlsbad,** 55 miles from the park, which are discussed below in the section on Carlsbad Caverns National Park.

CAMPING
In the Park

There are two developed vehicle-accessible campgrounds in the park. Both are open year-round, cost $8 per night, and have restrooms and drinking water, but no showers or RV hookups. **Pine Springs Campground** ✦ is near the visitor center and park headquarters just off U.S. 62/180. There are 19 spaces for RVs, 20 very attractive tent sites, and two group campsites (call park headquarters for information). About a half-mile inside the north boundary of the park is **Dog Canyon Campground,** accessible from N. Mex. 137. Here there are nine tent sites and four RV sites. Although reservations are not accepted, you can call ahead to check on availability of sites (© **915/828-3251**). Camp stoves are allowed, but wood and charcoal fires are prohibited.

The park also has 10 designated **backcountry campgrounds,** with from five to eight sites each. Be sure to pick up free permits at the Pine Springs Visitor Center or Dog Canyon Ranger Station the day of or the day before your backpacking trip. Water is available at trail heads, but is not available in the backcountry. All trash, including toilet paper, must be packed out. Fires are strictly prohibited; use cook stoves only. You can only camp in designated campgrounds.

Near the Park

Nothing is actually nearby, but you'll find commercial camping in New Mexico at **White's City RV Park** in White's City (35 miles from the park), which is discussed below in the section on Carlsbad Caverns National Park.

3 A Side Trip to Carlsbad Caverns National Park

One of the largest and most spectacular cave systems in the world, Carlsbad Caverns National Park comprises more than 100 known caves that snake through the porous limestone reef of the Guadalupe Mountains. Fantastic and grotesque formations fascinate visitors, who find every shape imaginable (and unimaginable) naturally

Carlsbad Caverns National Park

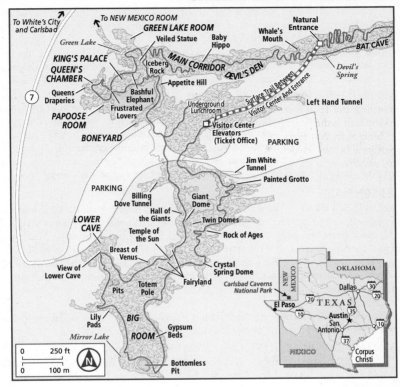

sculpted in the underground—from frozen waterfalls to strands of pearls, soda straws to miniature castles, draperies to ice-cream cones. Plan to spend a full day.

Formation of the caverns began some 250 million years ago, when a huge inland sea covered this region. Then, about 20 million years ago, a reef that was once undersea moved upwards, ultimately breaking free of thousands of feet of sediment enshrouding it. As tectonic forces pushed the buried rock up, erosion wore away softer minerals, leaving behind the Guadalupe Mountains. Brine from gas and oil deposits mingled with rainwater, creating sulfuric acid that dissolved limestone and created cave passages.

Once the caves were hollowed out, nature became artistic, decorating the rooms with a vast variety of fanciful formations. Very slowly, water dripped down through the rock into the caves, dissolving more limestone and absorbing the mineral calcite and other materials on its journey. Each drop of water then deposited its tiny load of calcite, gradually creating the cave formations we see today.

Although American Indians had known of Carlsbad Cavern (the park's main cave) for centuries, it was not discovered by settlers until ranchers in the 1880s were attracted by sunset flights of bats emerging from the cave. The first reported trip into the cave was in 1883, when a man supposedly lowered his 12-year-old son into the cave entrance. A cowboy named Jim White, who worked for mining companies that collected bat droppings for use as a fertilizer, began to explore the cave in the late 1800s. Fascinated by the formations, White shared his discovery with others, and soon word of this magical belowground world spread.

Carlsbad Cave National Monument was created in October 1923. In 1926, the first electric lights were installed, and in 1930 Carlsbad Caverns gained national park status.

Underground development at the park has been confined to the famous Big Room, one of the largest and most easily accessible of the caverns, with a ceiling 25 stories high and a floor large enough to hold six football fields. Visitors can tour parts of it on their own, aided by a state-of-the-art portable audio guide, and explore other sections and several other caves on guided tours. The cave is also a summer home to about 300,000 Mexican free-tailed bats, which hang from the ceiling of Bat Cave during the day, but put on a spectacular show each evening as they leave the cave in search of food, and again in the morning when they return for a good day's sleep.

ESSENTIALS

GETTING THERE   The main section of Carlsbad Caverns National Park, with the visitor center and entrance to Carlsbad Cavern, the park's main cave, is located about 35 miles from Guadalupe Mountains National Park. From Guadalupe Mountains National Park take U.S. 62/180 northeast to White's City, and turn left onto N. Mex. 7, the park access road. You enter the boundary of Carlsbad Caverns National Park almost immediately and reach the visitor center in about 7 miles. From the city of Carlsbad, head 30 miles southwest on U.S. 62/180 and then 7 miles on N. Mex. 7 to the visitor center.

For airport information, see the "Getting There" section under "Guadalupe Mountains National Park," earlier in this chapter.

VISITOR INFORMATION   Contact **Carlsbad Caverns National Park,** 3225 National Parks Hwy., Carlsbad, NM 88220 (© **505/785-2232;** www.nps.gov/cave). Books and maps can be ordered from the **Carlsbad Caverns Guadalupe Mountains Association,** 727 Carlsbad Caverns Hwy. (P. O. Box 417), Carlsbad, NM 88221 (© **505/785-2486;** www.ccgma.org).

The visitor center is open daily from 8am to 7pm from Memorial Day to Labor Day; and self-guided cave tours can be started from 8:30am to 5pm. The rest of the year the visitor center is open from 8am to 5pm, with self-guided cave tours from 8:30am to 3:30pm. Tour times and schedules may be modified during slower times in the winter. The park is closed on Christmas Day.

At the visitor center are displays depicting the geology and history of the caverns, bats and other wildlife, and a three-dimensional model of Carlsbad Cavern. You can get information about the tours available and other park activities, both above- and belowground. There is also a well-stocked bookstore, a restaurant, and a gift shop.

FEES   Admission to the visitor center and aboveground sections of the park is free. The basic cavern entry fee, which is good for 3 days and includes self-guided tours of the Natural Entrance and Big Room, is $6 for adults and free for children younger than 16. Holders of Golden Eagle, Golden Age, Golden Access, and National Parks passes, plus their immediate families, are admitted free. Audio guide rentals cost an additional $3.

A general cave admission ticket is required in addition to tour fees for all guided cave tours except those to Slaughter Canyon Cave and Spider Cave. Reservations are required for all guided tours. Holders of Golden Age and Golden Access passports receive 50% discounts on tours. The King's Palace guided tour costs $8 for adults, $4 for children ages 6 to 15, and is free for children ages 4 and 5 with an adult—younger children are not permitted. Guided tours of Left Hand Tunnel, limited to those 6 and older, cost $7 for adults and $3.50 for children 6 to 15. Guided tours of Spider Cave, Lower Cave, and Hall of the White Giant are limited to those 12 and older, and cost $20 for adults and $10 for youths 12 to 15. Slaughter Canyon Cave tours, for those 6 and older, cost $15 for adults and $7.50 for children 6 to 15. You can make reservations for cave tours up to 3 months in advance by phone or online (© **800/967-CAVE;** http://reservations.nps.gov).

REGULATIONS & PERMITS   As you would expect, damaging the cave formations in any way is prohibited. What some people do not understand is that they should not even touch the formations, walls, or ceilings. This is not only because many of the features are delicate and easily broken, but also because skin oils will both discolor the rock and disturb the mineral deposits that are necessary for growth.

All tobacco use is prohibited underground. In addition, food, drinks, candy, and chewing gum are not allowed on the underground trails. Those making wishes should not throw coins or other objects into the underground pools.

Cave explorers should wear flat shoes with rubber soles and heels, because of the slippery paths. Children younger than 16 must remain with an adult at all times while in the caves. Although strollers are not allowed for younger children, child backpacks are a good idea, but beware of low ceilings and doorways along the pathways.

No photography is permitted at the evening Bat Flight programs without a special permit.

Pets are not permitted in the caverns, on park trails, or in the backcountry, and because of the hot summer temperatures pets should not be left unattended in vehicles. There is a kennel (© **505/785-2281**) available at the visitor center. It has cages in an air-conditioned room, but no runs, and is primarily used by pet owners for periods of 3 hours or so while they are on cave tours. Pets are provided with water, but not food, and there are no grooming or overnight facilities. Reservations are not necessary; cost is $4 per pet.

Free permits, available at the visitor center, are required for all overnight hikes into the backcountry.

WHEN TO GO   The climate aboveground is warm in the summer, with highs often in the 90s and sometimes exceeding 100°F (38°C), and evening lows in the mid-60s (teens Celsius). Winters are mild, with highs in the 50s and 60s (teens Celsius) in the day and nighttime lows usually in the 20s and 30s (around 0°C). Summers are known for sudden intense afternoon and evening thunderstorms; August and September see the most rain. Underground it's another story entirely, with a year-round temperature that varies little from its average temperature of 56°F (13°C), making a jacket or sweater a welcome companion.

Crowds are thickest in summer, and on weekends and holidays year-round, so visiting on weekdays between Labor Day and Memorial Day is the best way to avoid them. January is the quietest month.

Visiting during the park's off season is especially attractive because the climate in the caves doesn't vary regardless of the weather on top, where the winters are generally mild and summers warm to hot. The only downside to an off-season visit is that you won't be able to see the bat flights. The bats head to Mexico when the weather starts to get chilly, usually by late October, and don't return until May. There are also fewer guided cave tours off season, although those tours will have fewer people. The best time to see the park might well be in September, when you can still see the bat flights but there are fewer visitors than during the peak summer season.

RANGER PROGRAMS In addition to the cave tours, which are discussed below, rangers give a talk on bats at sunset each evening from mid-May to October at the cavern's Natural Entrance (times change; check at the visitor center or call © **505/ 785-3012**). Rangers also offer a variety of demonstrations, talks, guided nature walks, and other programs daily. Especially popular are the climbing programs, where rangers demonstrate caving techniques. In recent years there has also been a series of stargazing programs presented by graduate students from New Mexico State University. The park also offers a **Junior Ranger Program,** in which kids can earn badges by completing various activities. Details are available at the visitor center.

On the second Thursday in August (usually), a "bat flight breakfast" from 5 to 7am encourages visitors to watch the bats return to the cavern after their night of insect-hunting. Park rangers prepare breakfast for early-morning visitors for a small fee and then join them to watch the early morning return flight. Call the park for details.

WHAT TO SEE & DO
EXPLORING THE HIGHLIGHTS BY CAR

No, you can't take your car into the caves, but for a close-up as well as panoramic view of the Chihuahuan Desert, head out on the **Walnut Canyon Desert Drive,** a 9½-mile loop. You'll want to drive slowly on the one-way gravel road, both for safety and to thoroughly appreciate the dramatic scenery. Passenger cars can easily handle the tight turns and narrow passage, but the road is not recommended for motor homes or cars pulling trailers. Pick up an informational brochure at the visitor center bookstore.

CAVING ADVENTURES 🐾🐾🐾

Carlsbad Cavern (the park's main cave), Slaughter Canyon Cave, and Spider Cave are open to the general public. All guided tours must be reserved and have individual fees in addition to the general cave entry fee (see "Fees," above). Guided tours are sometimes fully booked weeks in advance, so reserve early.

Most park visitors head first to Carlsbad Cavern, which has elevators, a paved walkway, and an underground rest area. A 1-mile section of the Big Room self-guided tour is accessible to those in wheelchairs (no wheelchairs are available at the park), though it's best to have another person along to assist. Pick up a free accessibility guide at the visitor center.

The Big Room Tour, Natural Entrance Route, and King's Palace Guided Tour are the most popular trails, and all of them are lighted, paved, and have handrails. However, the Big Room is the only one of the three that's considered easy. The formations along these trails are strategically lit to display them at their most dramatic. This also means that today's visitors can see much more of the cave than early explorers, who were limited by their weak lanterns.

The **Big Room Self-Guided Tour** 🐾🐾🐾 is an easy 1-mile loop that you get to by taking the visitor center elevator to the Underground Rest Area or via the Natural Entrance Route (see below). Considered the one thing that all visitors to Carlsbad Caverns National Park must do, this easy trail meanders through a massive chamber—it isn't called the Big Room for nothing—where you'll see some of the park's most spectacular formations and likely be overwhelmed by the enormity of it all. Allow about 1 hour.

The **Natural Entrance Route,** also 1 mile, is considered moderate to difficult, and is accessed outside the visitor center. This fairly strenuous hike takes you into Carlsbad Cavern on the same basic route used by its early explorers. You leave the daylight to enter a big hole, and then descend more than 750 feet into the cavern on a steep and narrow switchback trail, moving from the "twilight zone" of semidarkness to the depths of the cave, which would be totally black without the electric lights conveniently provided by the Park Service. The self-guided tour takes about 1 hour and ends near the elevators, which can take you back to the visitor center. However, we strongly recommend that from here you proceed on the Big Room Self-Guided Tour if you have not already been there.

The **King's Palace Guided Tour** 🐾🐾 is a moderate 1-mile loop that you get to by taking the visitor center elevator to the underground rest area. This 1½-hour ranger-led walk wanders through some of the cave's most scenic chambers, where you'll see wonderfully fanciful formations in the King's Palace, Queen's Chamber, and Green Lake Room. Watch for the delightful Bashful Elephant formation between the King's Palace and Green Lake Room. Along the way, rangers discuss the geology of the cave and early explorers' experiences. Although the path is paved, there is an 80-foot elevation change.

Ranger-Led Cave Tours

In addition to the popular self-guided and guided tours discussed above, there are a number of ranger-led tours to less-developed sections of Carlsbad Cavern that provide more of the experience of exploration and genuine caving than the above tours over well-trodden trails. These caving tours vary in difficulty, but all include a period of absolute darkness or "blackout," which can make some people uncomfortable. Because some tours involve walking or crawling through tight spaces, people who suffer from claustrophobia should discuss specifics with rangers before purchasing tickets.

Left Hand Tunnel starts in the visitor center near the elevator. The easiest of the caving tours, in this one you actually get to walk (rather than crawl) the entire time! Hand-carried lanterns (provided by the Park Service) light the way, and the trail is dirt but relatively level. You'll see a variety of formations, fossils from Permian times, and pools of water. Open to those 6 and older, this tour takes about 2 hours. The moderate **Lower Cave Tour,** which is 1-mile round-trip, starts at the visitor center near the elevator. This 3-hour trek involves descending or climbing over 50 feet of ladders, and an optional crawl. It takes you through an area that was explored by a National Geographic Society expedition in the 1920s, and you'll see artifacts from that and other explorations. In addition, you'll encounter a variety of formations, including cave pearls, which look a lot like the pearls created by oysters and can be as big as golf balls. This tour is open to those 12 and older only. Four AA batteries are required for the provided headlamp; sturdy hiking boots and gloves are recommended.

The **Hall of the White Giant Tour,** which starts at the visitor center, is only .5-mile (one-way), but it is strenuous and will take 3 to 4 hours as you crawl through narrow, dirty passageways and climb up slippery rocks. The highlight is, of course, the huge formation called the White Giant. Only those in excellent physical condition should consider this tour; children must be at least age 12. Four AA batteries for the provided headlamp and sturdy hiking boots are required; and kneepads, gloves, and long pants are strongly recommended.

More Cave Tours

It takes some hiking to reach the other caves in the park, so carry drinking water, especially on hot summer days. All children younger than age 16 must be accompanied by an adult; other age restrictions apply as well. Each tour includes a period of true and total darkness or "blackout."

The **Slaughter Canyon Cave Tour** 🐾🐾 is 1.25 miles round-trip and is considered moderate. The parking area is about a 45-minute drive from Carlsbad and is reached via U.S. 62/180, going south 5 miles from White's City to a marked turnoff that leads 11 miles to the parking lot. Discovered in 1937, this cave was mined for bat guano (used as fertilizer) until the 1950s. It consists of a corridor 1,140 feet long with many side passageways. This highly recommended guided tour lasts about 2 hours, plus at least another half-hour to hike up the steep trail to the cave entrance. No crawling is involved, although the smooth flowstone and old bat guano on the floor can be slippery, so hiking boots are recommended. You'll see a number of pristine cave formations, including the crystal-decorated Christmas Tree, the 89-foot-high Monarch, and the menacing Klansman. Open to children 6 and older, participants must take D battery flashlights.

The 4-hour tour of **Spider Cave** is a very strenuous 1-mile loop (plus a half-mile hike to and from cave). Meet at the visitor center and follow a ranger to the cave. This tour is ideal for those who want the experience of a rugged caving adventure as well as some great underground scenery. Highlights include climbing down a 15-foot ladder, squeezing through very tight passageways, and climbing on slick surfaces—all this after a fairly tough half-mile hike to the cave entrance. But it's worth it. The cave has numerous beautiful formations—most much smaller than those in the Big Room—and picturesque pools of water. Children must be at least 12 years old. Participants need four AA batteries for the provided headlamps and good hiking boots. Kneepads, gloves, and long pants are strongly recommended.

BATS, BIRDS & OTHER WILDLIFE VIEWING

At sunset, from mid-May to October, a crowd gathers at the Natural Entrance to watch hundreds of thousands of **bats** take off for a night of insect hunting. An amphitheater in front of the Natural Entrance provides seating, and ranger programs are held each evening (exact times vary; check at the visitor center or call ✆ 505/785-3012) during the bats' residence at the park (the bats winter in Mexico). The most bats will be seen in August and September, when baby bats born earlier in the summer join their parents and migrating bats from the north, on the nightly forays. Early risers can also see the return of the bats just before dawn.

However, bats aren't the only wildlife at Carlsbad Caverns. The park has a surprising number of **birds**—more than 300 species—many of which are seen in the Rattlesnake Springs area. Among species you're likely to see are turkey vultures, red-tailed hawks, scaled quail, killdeer, lesser nighthawks, black-chinned hummingbirds, vermilion flycatchers, northern mockingbirds, and western meadowlarks. In addition, each summer several thousand cave swallows usually build their mud nests on the ceiling just inside the Carlsbad Cavern Natural Entrance (the bats make their home farther back in the cave).

Among the park's **larger animals** are mule deer and raccoons, which are sometimes spotted near the Natural Entrance at the time of the evening bat flights. The park is also home to porcupines, hog-nosed skunks, desert cottontails, black-tailed jack rabbits, rock squirrels, and the more elusive ringtails, coyotes, and gray fox. These are sometimes seen in the late evenings along the park entrance road and the Walnut Canyon Desert Drive.

WHERE TO STAY & DINE

There are no accommodations within the park, but there are two concessionaire-operated restaurants (✆ 505/785-2281). A family-style full-service restaurant at the

visitor center serves three meals daily in the $4 to $8 range. The restaurant is open from 8:30am to 5pm most of the year, with extended hours from Memorial Day to mid-August and on Labor Day weekend. The **Underground Rest Area,** located inside the main cavern 750 feet belowground, has a cafeteria-style eatery offering snacks and box lunches. Its hours are coordinated with cave hours.

The closest lodging properties are 7 miles east of the visitor center at White's City, which contains a variety of businesses under one management, including two motels, restaurants, shops, a museum, gas station, and an RV park. The **Best Western Cavern Inn,** 17 Carlsbad Cavern Hwy. at N. Mex. 7 (© **800/228-3767** or 505/785-2291; www.whitescity.com), plus its sister property across the street, offer spacious rooms with Southwestern decor. Double rates are $72 to $80. The White's City arcade also contains a couple of restaurants, a post office, a small grocery store, a gift shop, a museum, and a theater for weekend melodramas.

The next closest services are in and near the city of Carlsbad, 30 miles northeast of White's City on U.S. 62. Here you'll find several chain and franchise motels and a number of independent and chain restaurants. Motels on the southwest edge of the city, on the road to Carlsbad Caverns, include **Best Western Stevens Inn,** 1829 S. Canal St. (© **800/730-2851** or 505/887-2851), with double rates of $70 to $90. Also in this area are the **Comfort Inn,** 2429 W. Pierce St. (© **800/228-5150** or 505/887-1994); **Days Inn,** 3910 National Parks Hwy. (© **800/325-2525** or 505/887-7800); and **Super 8 Motel,** 3817 National Parks Hwy. (© **800/800-8000** or 505/887-8888), with similar rates.

For more information, contact the **Carlsbad Chamber of Commerce,** P. O. Box 910, Carlsbad, NM 88220 (© **800/221-1224** or 505/887-6516; www.carlsbadchamber. com), or stop at the visitor center at 302 S. Canal St.

CAMPING

There are no developed campgrounds or vehicle camping of any kind in the national park. Backcountry camping, however, is permitted in some areas; pick up free permits at the visitor center.

The closest camping is **White's City RV Park,** 17 Carlsbad Cavern Hwy. at N. Mex. 7 (© **800/228-3767** or 505/785-2291), located in the White's City complex at the eastern edge of the park boundary, about 7 miles east of the visitor center. In addition to RV sites with hook-ups and shade shelters, the campground has practically unlimited tent camping. There's a dump station and a clean bathhouse. Because the campground is part of the White's City complex, campers have access to its pools, restaurants, and other services. Rates for both RVs and tents are $20 to $25 per night.

11

The Panhandle Plains

by Eric Peterson

A wide-open sea of prairie, the high plains of northern Texas might well be the nation's crossroads: The small-town charm of the Great Plains, the spice of the Southwest, and the polite twang of the South are all present in equal measures. Beyond this cultural intersection, highways have crisscrossed the region since the 1930s, fostering a brood of cheap motels and kitschy roadside Americana.

Inhabited by nomadic tribes for much of the last 12,000 years, the Panhandle Plains are distinguished by a high mesa—3,000 feet above sea level—that tapers downhill to the south and east, bordered by spectacular canyons and unique geological formations. In 1541, when Vásquez de Coronado ventured north in his quest for the fabled Seven Cities of Gold, he pounded stakes into the ground to claim the land for Spain—as well as mark his route for a return trip through the mostly featureless flatlands. Thus, the "Llano Estacado," Spanish for "staked plains," was born. Today, Lubbock inhabits the center of the mesa that Coronado staked out; Amarillo sits on its northern edge.

The late 19th century brought significant change to the area: Ranchers began to graze cattle here, railroads crisscrossed the mesa in all directions, and agriculture took hold as the predominant industry. Million-acre ranches became the norm. During the fall and winter of 1874 and 1875, the indigenous tribes battled the U.S. Army in the Red River War, culminating with the dispersal of Comanches, Kiowas, and Southern Cheyennes to reservations in Oklahoma.

The landscape was irrevocably altered again by the discovery of oil in the 1920s, when ranchers found themselves sitting on "black gold" mines. The Dust Bowl days of the 1930s dampened development, but the area recovered and saw tremendous growth following World War II.

At first glance, the Panhandle Plains might appear monotonous, but the region is actually worth a closer look than you'll get from behind the wheel. The magnificent palette of Palo Duro Canyon, the lively nightlife in Lubbock, and Amarillo's ranching heritage—from cattle to Cadillacs—are unexpected diversions that make this area a worthy stopover on a cross-country trip.

1 Amarillo

122 miles N of Lubbock; 267 miles E of Albuquerque, New Mexico

The commercial center of the Texas Panhandle, Amarillo arose when the Fort Worth and Denver City Railway started laying track in the area in 1887, a decade after ranchers began to graze their cattle on the buffalo grass–speckled plains. When the town was formally incorporated, the name Amarillo—meaning "yellow" literally and "wild

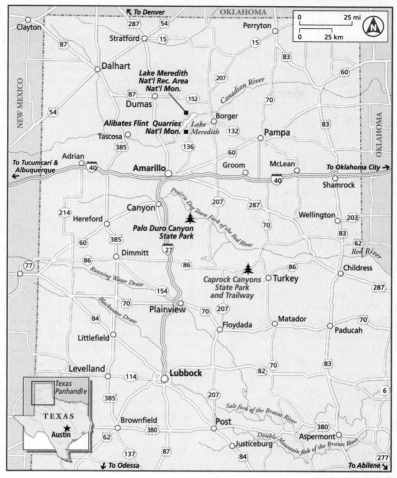

horse" figuratively—was adopted from a nearby lake. In a little over a decade, the combination of the railroad and the ranchland led to the establishment of Amarillo's long-standing status as a cattle-shipping capital. To this day, the city "smells like money" most when the Amarillo Livestock Auction is in full swing.

While its agricultural roots remain the cornerstone of the local economy, Amarillo's location on a major east–west highway—Route 66 until 1970 and I-40 thereafter—has long made it a popular stopover for tourists, with a plethora of motels and restaurants catering to the cross-country crowd. Amarillo is fairly low-key and nondescript at first glance, but it's a pleasant, inexpensive spot for an overnight stay. Several of its attractions are must-see tourist traps, namely the roadside kitsch of Cadillac Ranch and the Big Texan steakhouse. As a destination, Amarillo can be a fun place to spend a weekend, especially for those with a taste for cowboy culture.

ESSENTIALS
GETTING THERE
BY PLANE More than 50 commercial flights take off or land daily from **Rick Husband Amarillo International Airport** (© 806/335-1671), off I-40 Exit 76 (Lakeside Dr.), 7 miles east of downtown. Airlines serving Amarillo include **American Eagle** (© 800/433-7300), **Continental Express** (© 800/525-0280), **Southwest** (© 800/435-9792), and **Great Lakes Aviation** (© 800/554-5111). Car rentals are available from **Avis** (© 806/335-2313), **Hertz** (© 806/335-2331), **Enterprise** (© 806/335-9443), **Budget** (© 806/335-1696), and **National** (© 806/335-2311).

BY CAR Coming from east or west, Amarillo can be accessed via I-40, exits 62 (Hope Rd.) through 75 (Lakeside Dr.). The primary downtown exit is 70 (Taylor/Buchanan sts.) and the airport is located northeast of Exit 75. Coming from the north by car, you'll likely enter Amarillo via U.S. 87/287, which takes you through downtown and continues south to Canyon and Lubbock as I-27. If you are coming from the northwest, Texas FM 1061 can be used as a shortcut from U.S. 385; it becomes Tascosa Road as it enters Amarillo. U.S. 60 is the primary route northeast to Pampa and southwest to Hereford, and U.S. 287 veers east beyond the city, to Childress, and, beyond that, Wichita Falls and Fort Worth.

ORIENTATION
I-40 cuts through the heart of Amarillo, skirting the south side of downtown. The city's primary north–south artery is U.S. 87, which splits into four one-way, north–south streets in the downtown area. (From the west, these streets are Taylor, Fillmore, Pierce, and Buchanan.) South of I-40, U.S. 87 becomes I-27, which leads to Canyon and Lubbock. The northern boundary of downtown is 1st Avenue, the southern boundary I-40. The Route 66 Historic District begins at 6th Avenue and Georgia Street and continues west along 6th Avenue for a mile to Western Street. Amarillo Boulevard is a major east–west route through the northern stretch of the city. Along with Georgia Street, Ross-Mirror and Washington streets are among the busiest north–south roads in Amarillo. Loop 335 is comprised of four roads (Soncy Rd., FM 1719, Lakeside Dr., and Hollywood Rd.) that circumnavigate the city.

GETTING AROUND
Aside from some one-way streets downtown, Amarillo is a snap to navigate by car, with relatively little traffic. (Instead of a rush hour, locals like to say they have a "rush minute.")

   Amarillo City Transit (© 806/378-3095) operates a bus system Monday through Saturday from 6:15am to 7pm. The main transfer point is located downtown at 3rd Avenue and Fillmore Street. Eight different routes run from downtown to the major shopping centers and Harrington Regional Medical Center. Ride tickets are 75¢ for adults, 60¢ for children ages 6 to 12 and students, and 35¢ for seniors and travelers with disabilities.

   Taxi service is provided by **Ace's Taxi** (© 806/676-7263), **Airport Taxi** (© 806/358-8350), and **Bob's Taxi** (© 806/373-1171).

VISITOR INFORMATION
The **Amarillo Convention & Visitor Council** maintains an information center at 401 S. Buchanan St. (© 800/692-1338 or 806/374-8474; www.visitamarillotx.com), open 7 days a week. For statewide information, visit the **Texas Travel Information Center** on the city's east side; it's located on the south frontage road just west of I-40 Exit 75.

Amarillo

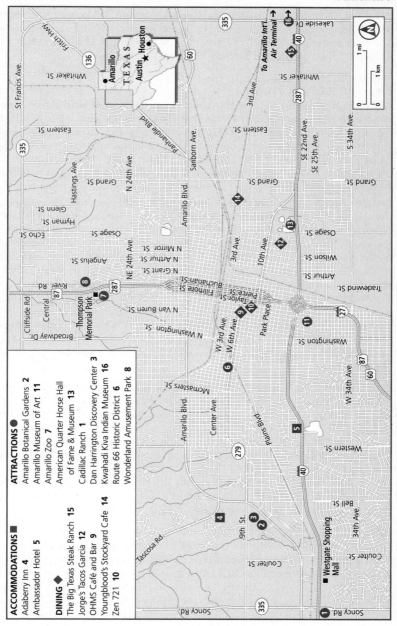

ACCOMMODATIONS ■
Adaberry Inn **4**
Ambassador Hotel **5**

DINING ◆
The Big Texas Steak Ranch **15**
Jorge's Tacos Garcia **12**
OHMS Café and Bar **9**
Youngblood's Stockyard Cafe **14**
Zen 721 **10**

ATTRACTIONS ●
Amarillo Botanical Gardens **2**
Amarillo Museum of Art **11**
Amarillo Zoo **7**
American Quarter Horse Hall
  of Fame & Museum **13**
Cadillac Ranch **1**
Dan Harrington Discovery Center **3**
Kwahadi Kiva Indian Museum **16**
Route 66 Historic District **6**
Wonderland Amusement Park **8**

FAST FACTS   The **Northwest Texas Hospital** is at 1501 S. Coulter Dr. (✆ **806/ 354-1000**), just north of I-40 on the Harrington Regional Medical Center campus. The main **post office** is located at 2301 S. Ross St. and is open Monday through Friday from 7:30am to 6pm and Saturday from 9am to 2pm.

WHAT TO SEE & DO
THE TOP ATTRACTIONS

Dedicated to the history of the equine breed named for its speed when racing a quarter-mile, the **American Quarter Horse Hall of Fame & Museum,** 2601 I-40 E. at Quarter Horse Dr. (✆ **806/376-5181;** www.aqha.org), offers a comprehensive look at the animals and the culture surrounding them, with live equestrian events during the summer at an onsite arena. The museum closed in early 2006 for a makeover (including the installation of new state-of-the-art exhibits) and, at press time, was slated to reopen by mid-2007.

Cadillac Ranch ✿   One of the more recognizable and bizarre roadside attractions in the country, Cadillac Ranch consists of 10 vintage Cadillacs (dating 1949–64) buried up to their backseat in a wheat field west of Amarillo, rising out of the earth at the same angle as Cheops Pyramid in Egypt. Conceived and funded by Amarillo's Stanley Marsh 3, the eccentric grandson of one of the Panhandle's most successful oilmen, Cadillac Ranch was constructed in 1974 by the Ant Farm, a San Francisco–based art collective, and relocated west in 1997 to its present site to escape the shadow of Amarillo's growth. Cadillac Ranch is also interactive: Marsh freely allows visitors to add their creative touches with spray paint, a marker, or a key. (For more on Stanley Marsh 3's artistic exploits in the Amarillo area, see "Unanticipated Rewards" on p. 418.)

I-40 W., on the south frontage road between exits 60 (Arnot Rd.) and 62 (Hope and Holiday roads). Free admission. Daily 24 hr.

Route 66 Historic District   This colorful area west of downtown Amarillo preserves about a mile of old Route 66, aka the "Mother Road." Once a suburb accessible by trolley car, the district has evolved into a hub for the city's nightlife and shopping. Buildings that once housed drugstores and theaters are now home to eateries, antiques stores, and specialty shops. The area is a bit run-down in spots, but it's not all that touristy and it's fun as a glimpse into the glory days of Route 66. The surrounding neighborhood, known as Old San Jacinto, might have once been a suburb, but, in many ways, it is now the heart of the city. During the summer, the district hosts several festivals, with street dances, live entertainment, and art displays.

6th Ave. between Western and Georgia sts. Call the Amarillo CVC at ✆ **806/374-8474** for additional information.

MORE ATTRACTIONS

Amarillo Botanical Gardens   Dedicated to the art, science, and enjoyment of horticulture, these outdoor gardens feature displays on flora indigenous to the high plains region and offer a pleasant, if unremarkable, spot to take a 30-minute break from the road. Of special note is a "scent garden" designed for patrons with sight impairments. An attractive new tropical conservatory opened in late 2006.

1400 Streit Dr., at Harrington Regional Medical Center. ✆ **806/352-6513.** www.amarillobotanicalgardens.org. Admission $4 adults, $3 seniors 60 and older, $2 children 4–12, and free for children younger than 4. Outdoor gardens daily dawn–dusk; indoor exhibits Mon–Fri 9am–5pm year-round, also Sat–Sun 1–5pm May–Sept.

Amarillo Museum of Art   The only accredited art museum within a 260-mile radius, this institution houses a worthwhile collection of paintings, photographic exhibits, and sculptures in its galleries. Requiring about 30 minutes to peruse, the permanent collection includes a good deal of regional 20th-century art and a nice Asian exhibit, thanks to a local patron with a passion for Far Eastern works. The museum hosts nearly 20 changing exhibits annually in its six galleries; recent programs included works by Georgia O'Keeffe, a former area resident, and displays that use art as a lens to explore the area's colorful history.

2200 S. Van Buren St., on the campus of Amarillo College. © 806/371-5050. www.amarilloart.org. Free admission. Tues–Fri 10am–5pm (until 9pm Thurs); Sat–Sun 1–5pm. Closed major holidays.

Amarillo Zoo   This accredited zoo is small and generally unspectacular, although it excels at preserving and displaying the High Plains' indigenous animals, termed "Texotic." The highlight is a 20-acre range populated by grazing bison; the mustang, the feral horse of the American West, is also in the collection, as are mountain lions, Texas longhorns, and spider monkeys. In all, the zoo is a good half-hour stop for families with children who've been cooped up in the back seat for far too long.

NE 24th St. and Fillmore sts., Thompson Memorial Park, about 1 mile north of downtown on U.S. 287. © 806/381-7911. www.amarillozoo.org. Free admission (donations accepted). Tues–Sun 9:30am–5pm. Closed major holidays.

Don Harrington Discovery Center *Kids*   The Texas Panhandle's preeminent children's science museum, the Discovery Center is home to more than 60 permanent displays, including an eye-popping exhibit on turbulent weather patterns and Tiny Town, a play area for kids 4 and younger. The center is also home to the innovative Space Theater, an all-digital system that shows a variety of productions. Out front is the space age Helium Monument, comprised of four helium-filled steel columns.

1200 Streit Dr. © 806/355-9547. www.dhdc.org. Admission $5.50 adults, $5 students and seniors, $4.50 children 3–12, free for children younger than 3. Tues–Sat 9:30am–4:30pm; Sun noon–4:30pm. Closed major holidays.

Kwahadi Kiva Indian Museum   At once a museum and a dance theater, this attractive new facility presents the story of the people native to the Panhandle through art and culture. Inside a Pueblo-inspired building, author and artist Thomas Mails' collection of paintings and artifacts is presented; out front, Kwahadi Dancers take to the stage for regular performances. Most performances are on summer weekend nights at 7:30 with ticket prices of $5 to $7, or $12 to $15 if you partake in the barbecue that precedes the show.

9151 I-40 E. © 806/335-3175. www.kwahadi.com. Admission $3 adults, $1.50 children. Summer Tues–Sat 11am–6pm, Sun 1–5pm; winter Tues–Sat noon–5pm, Sun 1–5pm. Call for the current schedule of the Kwahadi Dancers.

Wonderland Amusement Park *Kids*   An Amarillo landmark since the glory days of Route 66, Wonderland is the Panhandle's top amusement park, featuring more than 25 different nostalgic rides on a 15-acre chunk of Thompson Park. The amusements include three roller coasters, six water rides, a carousel, and several kiddie rides. My favorites: the double-loop "Texas Tornado" coaster and the "Shoot the Chutes" water ride. There is also a minigolf course and an arcade.

2601 Dumas Dr., at Thompson Memorial Park. © 800/383-4712 or 806/383-3344. www.wonderlandpark.com. Individual rides $1.50 each plus a $4 gate admission fee. Unlimited rides $11–$13 weeknights, $15–$19 weekends. Apr to Labor Day Sat–Sun 1–10pm; May Tues and Thurs–Fri 6:30–9:30pm; June to mid-Aug Mon–Fri 7–10:30pm. Closed Labor Day to Mar.

Unanticipated Rewards

Cadillac Ranch (p. 416) is just the tip of Amarillo's public art iceberg, which is in large part the product of the fervent imagination of Stanley Marsh 3 (he favors the Arabic "3" over the Roman "III").

The grandson of an early Texas oil millionaire, Marsh is also the man behind 200 signs on display at Amarillo homes and businesses. Looking very much like colorful municipal signs, they don't dispense traffic or parking rules, instead offering a variety of offbeat slogans. One reads "Strong drink." "What is a village without village idiots?" asks another. "'Either the well is very deep,' thought Alice, 'or I'm falling very slowly,'" reads yet another. While the signs are spread out around Amarillo and the surrounding towns, Old San Jacinto is the neighborhood where you'll see them in the highest concentration. The ever-enigmatic Marsh explained the signs, saying, "They are to be looked at. The signs are just there, like the Rock of Gibraltar or the Statue of Liberty. They are a system of unanticipated rewards."

Beyond Cadillac Ranch and the signs, Marsh's eccentric public art vision extends to the southern fringes of Lubbock, to the rural junction of I-27 and Sundown Lane, where a sculpture of a pair of disembodied legs greets passerby. (An absurd plaque explains that they are all that remains of a great statue of Ozymandias, "damaged by students from Lubbock after losing to Amarillo in a competition.") There's also "Floating Mesa," hundreds of sheets of plywood painted the color of a blue sky on the side of a mountain. Unless it is overcast, the resulting impression is that the summit is floating. It is located about 8 miles northwest of Amarillo on the west side of Tascosa Road.

While many are amused by the creations of Stanley Marsh 3, not every Amarillo resident finds them in good taste. Those disgusted by their presence have decried them as eyesores with little or no artistic value. In response, Marsh was once quoted as saying, "Art is a legalized form of insanity, and I do it very well."

OUTDOOR ACTIVITIES

Amarillo offers many opportunities for outdoor recreation, in the form of in-city golf courses, pools, and parks, as well as several lakes, reservoirs, and state parks in the surrounding area. The best recreation spot is **Palo Duro Canyon State Park** (see "Canyon & Palo Duro Canyon State Park," later in this chapter), about 27 miles southeast of the city.

The **Lake Meredith National Recreation Area** (© 806/857-3151; www.nps.gov/lamr), located 38 miles northeast of Amarillo via Tex. 136, is another outdoor hot spot, featuring opportunities for boating, fishing, hunting, horseback riding, camping, hiking, swimming, scuba diving, wildlife and bird viewing, and four-wheeling. The site is also home to **Alibates Flint Quarries National Monument** (www.nps.gov/alfl), the point of origin for a significant percentage of arrowhead points and flint tools found throughout the Great Plains. While the monument is closed to most recreational activity, guided tours are offered at 10am and 2pm during the summer and at other times of the year by reservation. Aside from boat-launching fees, access to Lake Meredith is free to the public.

Wildcat Bluff Nature Center, 2301 N. Soncy Rd. (© **806/352-6007;** www.wildcat bluff.org), is the best spot for hiking and wildlife viewing in the city itself, offering over 2 miles of moderate trails on its 600 acres of cottonwood-shaded hills. The center's wildlife population includes mule deer, horned toads, coyotes, and turkey vultures. Admission is $3 adults and $2 for kids and seniors.

The major city parks in Amarillo include: **Thompson Memorial Park,** at Dumas Drive and 24th Avenue, home to Wonderland Amusement Park and the Amarillo Zoo, as well as a 36-hole golf course, 1 mile of jogging/walking trails, a heated outdoor pool (open seasonally), ball fields, picnic sites with grills, and fishing ponds; **John S. Stiff Memorial Park,** at SW 48th Avenue and Bell Street, with ball fields, three indoor and eight outdoor tennis courts, an outdoor heated pool, and picnic sites; and **Southeast Regional Park,** at SE 46th Avenue and Osage Street, with an outdoor heated pool, ball fields, fishing ponds, and picnic areas. For more information on Amarillo's city parks, contact the Parks and Recreation Department at © **806/ 378-3036** or visit **www.amarilloparks.org.**

BOATING   Lake Meredith National Recreation Area is the Panhandle's top watersports destination. When full, the main lake occupies 12,000 of the area's 46,000 acres and draws in boaters, windsurfers, water-skiers, and even scuba divers. Boat rentals (from personal watercraft to houseboats) are available from **Forever Resorts** (© **806/865-3391;** www.marinaatlakemeredith.com) at the marina at Lake Meredith National Recreation Area. To launch a boat of any size into Lake Meredith, a $4 day-use fee is required.

FISHING   ** Catfish and bass are the fish of choice for anglers in the Texas Panhandle and several spots in and around Amarillo are quite popular. For no fee outside of the cost of a Texas state fishing license, visitors can fish in several ponds in Amarillo's city park system, including **Thompson Memorial Park at Dumas Drive and 24th Avenue, **Martin Road Park** at NE 15th Avenue and Mirror Street, **Southeast Regional Park** at SE 46th Avenue and Osage Street, and **Harrington Regional Medical Center Park** at SW 9th Avenue and Wallace Street. **Lake Meredith National Recreation Area** is another popular fishing spot for the Panhandle. At the lake's **marina** (© **806/865-3391**), patrons find basic fishing supplies, concessions, and a heated and cooled fishing house ($4 for 12 hr.). Fishing licenses can be obtained at local Wal-Marts and sporting good stores, including Big 5 Sporting Goods, 8004 I-40 W. (© **806/356-8115**).

GOLF   ** The City of Amarillo Parks and Recreation Department manages two golf courses: **Comanche Trail, 4200 S. Grand St. (© **806/378-4281**), with greens fees for 18 holes of $14 to $18; and **Ross Rogers Golf Course,** 722 NE 24th Ave. in Thompson Memorial Park (© **806/378-3086**), with greens fees of $15 to $22.

HIKING   ** Aside from the hiking opportunities at **Wildcat Bluff Nature Center, there are two hiking trails at **Lake Meredith National Recreation Area.** The Devil's Canyon Trail is a moderate one-way trail that leaves from Plum Creek on the north side of the lake and continues into the canyon for 1.5 miles. In city limits, the **Rock Island Rail Trail** runs from Coulter Street on the west side to 7th and Crockett streets near downtown, 4 miles of jogging/biking/walking terrain in all. Numerous foot trails also traverse **Palo Duro Canyon State Park** (see "Canyon & Palo Duro Canyon State Park," below).

HORSEBACK RIDING   There are several horse-friendly trails in **Lake Meredith National Recreation Area,** in McBride Canyon and alongside Plum Creek on the lake's north side. The National Park Service provides corrals at the Plum Creek and Mullinaw campgrounds, but riders need to bring their own horses. **Palo Duro Canyon State Park** also has horse trails and stables (see "Canyon & Palo Duro Canyon State Park," below).

MOUNTAIN BIKING   The closest mountain-biking trails to Amarillo are 27 miles away in **Palo Duro Canyon State Park** (see "Canyon & Palo Duro Canyon State Park," below). The 3-mile Devil's Canyon Trail at **Lake Meredith National Recreation Area** (see "Hiking," above) is also accessible to mountain bikers.

SPECTATOR SPORTS

BASEBALL   The **Amarillo 'Dillas** play in the United League at the Amarillo National Bank Dilla Villa, 3300 3rd St. on the north side of the Tri-State Fairgrounds (© **806/ 242-7825** for ticket information; www.amarillodillasbaseball.com). The schedule runs from mid-October to late March with single-game ticket prices ranging from $4 to $6.

HOCKEY   The **Amarillo Gorillas** play in the Central Hockey League at the Amarillo Civic Center (the "Jungle"), 801 S. Polk St. in downtown Amarillo (© **806/342-7825** for ticket information; www.amarillogorillas.com). The schedule runs from mid-October to late March with single-game ticket prices ranging from $11 to $21.

RACING   Motor-sports enthusiasts can get a fix of racing action at **Route 66 Motor Speedway,** located about 10 miles east of downtown Amarillo at 3601 E. Amarillo Blvd. (© **806/383-7223**). The oval dirt track is a half-mile long. Races are held on Saturday nights from April to September; admission is $6 to $20.

RODEO   The Working Ranch Cowboys Association (WRCA) holds its annual **World Championship Ranch Rodeo** in Amarillo during the second week of November. Real working cowboys compete in such events as wild-cow milking, bronco riding, and team penning at the Amarillo Civic Center, 401 S. Buchanan St. (© **806/ 378-3096** for tickets; www.wrca.org). In early June, there's **Cowboy Roundup USA** (© **806/372-4777**), with a ranch rodeo and a chuck wagon cook-off. Several other major equestrian events are held in town during the fall and winter; contact the **Amarillo CVC** (© **800/692-1338**) for details.

SHOPPING

Amarillo's biggest enclosed shopping center is the **Westgate Shopping Mall,** 7701 I-40 W., between the Coulter Drive and Soncy Road exits (© **806/358-7221;** www.westgatemalltx.com). The mall's stores include Dillard's, Gap, and Sears, as well as a movie theater and several restaurants. Westgate is open Monday through Saturday from 10am to 9pm, and Sunday from noon to 6pm. The **Historic Route 66 District** is an antiques buff's dream, with more than 100 stores on West 6th Avenue between Georgia and Western streets. New upscale retailers have staked a claim to **South Soncy Road.** Western wear is also big in Amarillo; head to **Cavender's Boot City,** 7920 I-40 W. at Coulter Drive (© **806/358-1400**), for a huge selection of boots, along with hats, belt buckles, jeans, jewelry, and practically every other Western wearable on the market.

WHERE TO STAY

Amarillo's location on I-40 makes it an ideal stopping point on cross-country trips. Several inexpensive mom-and-pop motels line Amarillo Boulevard (Loop 335) in northern Amarillo, but finding a good room in that area is a hit-or-miss proposition. A better bet is the I-40 corridor: You'll find dozens of chain motels located just off the interstate, including **Best Western Amarillo Inn,** 1610 Coulter Dr. (© 800/528-1234 or 806/358-7861); **Best Western Santa Fe Inn,** 4600 I-40 E. at Exit 73 (© 800/528-1234 or 806/372-1885); **Courtyard by Marriott,** 8006 I-40 W. (© 800/321-2211 or 806/467-8954); **Holiday Inn,** 1911 I-40 E. at Exit 71 (© 800/HOLIDAY or 806/372-8741); **Motel 6,** 6030 I-40 E. at Exit 66 (© 800/466-8356 or 806/359-7651); **Hampton Inn and Suites,** 6901 I-40 W. (© **800/HAMPTON** or 806/467-9997); and **Quality Inn and Suites,** 1803 Lakeside Dr. (© 800/847-6556 or 806/335-1561). Room taxes in Amarillo add about 15% to lodging bills.

Adaberry Inn ★★ *(Finds*   Constructed from scratch in 1997, the Adaberry Inn rose to national prominence when it served as Oprah Winfrey's home for 2 months in 1999 while she fought a defamation lawsuit brought on by Amarillo-area cattle ranchers. One look inside this thoroughly modern B&B and it's easy to see why the TV talk-show star chose to stay here. The uniquely decorated rooms are each themed after a particular city: Missoula features a Western motif, with cowboy hats, barn doors under the sink, and a mountainous mural on one wall; and Key West offers a more tropical setting with aquatic artwork, a latticed ceiling, and yellow walls. The best, though, is the Aspen suite (Oprah's room), which features a rock fireplace, a Jacuzzi for two, and ski-themed decorative touches.

Seven of the rooms have private balconies or patios. There's also a game room with a putting green and a pool table downstairs, adjacent to a state-of-the-art home theater. The inn's main balcony is an ideal place to watch sunsets over the Lost Canyon, a quiet wildlife refuge with walking trails right in the Adaberry's backyard. Smoking and pets are not permitted inside of the inn.

6818 Plum Creek Dr., Amarillo, TX 79124. © 806/352-0022. Fax 806/356-0248. www.adaberryinn.com. 9 units. $125 double; $195 suite. Rates include full breakfast and complimentary snacks and beverages. AE, DC, DISC, MC, V. Children older than 12 accepted. **Amenities:** Exercise room; game room; in-room massage; dry cleaning. *In room:* A/C, cable TV/VCR, complimentary Wi-Fi, coffeemaker, hair dryer, iron.

Ambassador Hotel ★★   The 10-story Ambassador is Amarillo's tallest hotel. It's also the city's best, a pleasant touch of class in cowboy country. The property underwent a $4-million renovation in 2006, and the results are impressive, stately European interiors accented by Texan style, with plenty of basket-weave wood, granite, and tooled leather. The 9th and 10th floors make up the concierge level, with brass fixtures, minibars, and complimentary breakfast and cocktails. Many of the upper rooms have great views of the pleasantly treed cityscape below—those facing east are the best in this regard. Decorated with gallery-caliber art and maps, the lobby is striking—a five-story atrium with a sloping glass enclosure over an excellent cafe and a small pool—and the service and amenities are the best in town.

3100 I-40 W. (Exit 68B on Georgia St.), Amarillo, TX 79102. © 800/817-0521 or 806/385-9869. Fax 806/385-9869. www.ambassadoramarillo.com. 265 units, including 3 suites. $129–$169 double; $249–$449 suite. Specials of up to 50% off often available. AE, DC, DISC, MC, V. **Amenities:** 2 restaurants; bar; indoor heated pool; privileges at a nearby health club; exercise room; indoor Jacuzzi; concierge; courtesy car; business center; limited room service; laundry service; dry cleaning; executive level. *In room:* A/C, cable TV w/pay movies and Nintendo, complimentary Wi-Fi, coffeemaker, hair dryer, iron.

CAMPING

Several camping options exist in and around Amarillo, with numerous RV campgrounds in the city as well as primitive camping opportunities at Lake Meredith National Recreation Area (see "Outdoor Activities," above). The recreation area does not have RV hook-ups, but it's free to stay here. See also "Canyon & Palo Duro Canyon State Park," below.

Amarillo KOA Located in a secluded spot near the airport on Amarillo's eastern fringe, this campground is well maintained and reliable. Facilities include a pet walk, a heated outdoor pool, free Wi-Fi, playground, game room, and gift shop with sundries and RV supplies. Also, a chuck wagon dinner is served nightly during the summer.

1100 Folsom Rd., Amarillo, TX 79108. (C) 800/562-3431 (reservations only) or 806/335-1792. Fax 806/335-3702. 123 sites, including 58 pull-throughs, 26 back-ins, 23 tent sites, and 5 cabins. $24–$35 campsites; $45–$60 cabins. DISC, MC, V. Located east of Lakeside Dr. (I-40 Exit 75) via U.S. 60.

WHERE TO DINE

The Big Texan Steak Ranch ☆ Kids STEAK   It is next to impossible to miss the Big Texan when you drive across the Panhandle on I-40: You'll see the first billboards touting the legendary deal—"Eat a 72-ounce steak dinner in an hour and get it for free!"—hours before you get to the restaurant. Beyond the hype, the Big Texan is a unique attraction in itself, with a gift shop, motel ($50–$90 for a double), old-fashioned shooting gallery, and extensive collection of taxidermy and kitsch. Costumed cowboy musicians perform every night, and dancing is a regular happening in the summer.

With so much going on, you might forget that the Big Texan is a restaurant, but its legendary steaks are what put the place on the map: They're actually quite good. Beyond the 72-ouncer (which, not so incidentally, sports a $72 price tag if you don't finish it), the restaurant also serves juicy prime rib, rib-eye, New York strip, and other steaks in a dinner that includes salad, bread, and two side dishes. A smattering of seafood and barbecue dishes also delights diners. Breakfast and lunch are comparable: all-American and ultrahearty.

For the record, some 40,000 people have tried to eat the 72-ounce steak since its introduction in 1959, and nearly 7,000 have succeeded. One—a wrestler named Klondike Bill—inhaled two of the dinners in the 1-hour time limit.

7701 I-40 E. (C) 800/657-7177 or 806/372-6000. www.bigtexan.com. Reservations accepted for large parties only. Main courses $5–$16 breakfast, $7.50–$30 lunch and dinner. AE, DC, DISC, MC, V. Daily 7:30am–10:30pm.

Jorge's Tacos Garcia TEX-MEX   Jorge's proprietor, George Veloz II, dreamed of opening a Tex-Mex restaurant since he was in middle school. Fittingly, Jorge's Tacos Garcia is the spitting image of his childhood vision, right down to the fountain out front. The "West Texas Tex-Mex" and New Mexican recipes are time-tested at Jorge's, from a family that has been in the restaurant business for half of a century. I like the batter-free rellenos, the *enchiladas de chile verde,* made with blue corn tortillas and topped with green chile, and the *taquitos de barbacoa,* grilled tacos loaded with "Mexican barbecue." Fans of the Mexican specialty *menudo* can indulge themselves with Jorge's special recipe at any time the restaurant is open. There are also a dozen combination plates, seafood dishes, daily specials, and a kids' menu.

1100 S. Ross St. (C) 806/371-0411. Reservations not accepted. Main courses $6–$14. AE, DISC, MC, V. Mon 10:30am–9:30pm; Tues–Sat 10:30am–10pm; Sun 10:30am–3:30pm.

OHMS Café and Bar ⚔ ECLECTIC   This is my pick for a lunch spot. The chalk-board menu changes daily at this pleasant downtown eatery, which doubles as a gallery for local artists. (Incidentally, OHMS stands for "On Her Majesty's Service," so named by the former owner, a native of the United Kingdom.) Lunch is served caf-eteria-style, with such regular offerings as a very British—and very good—shepherd's pie, linguine with fresh basil and brie, and herbed baked chicken, all with soup or salad (with tasty homemade dressings) and fresh bread. Dinner brings table service and higher prices, and healthier fare than the Amarillo norm; likely selections are pan-seared wild salmon, rosemary-mustard pork loin, ahi tuna, and elk tenderloin. Wine Lovers Wednesdays feature tapas matched with flights of wine. The art on display changes monthly, and live acoustic music is featured on a regular basis.

619 S. Tyler St. ℂ 806/373-3233. www.ohmscafe.com. Main courses $6–$8.50 lunch, $15–$25 dinner. AE, DC, DISC, MC, V. Mon–Fri 11:30am–1:30pm; Wed–Sat 6–10pm. Bar open later.

Youngblood's Stockyard Cafe *Finds* AMERICAN   Whereas the Big Texan is kitschy and Disney-esque, the Stockyard Cafe is the real deal: Diners just don't get any more cowboy than this. Tucked away at the site of one of the largest livestock auctions in the world, this restaurant is smoky, old-fashioned, and furnished with cowhides, burlap, and the requisite taxidermy. But it's the food that keeps those cattlemen com-ing, from the simple and fresh American breakfasts to the steaks, hamburgers, and sandwiches at lunch. Dinnertime in Amarillo means more steaks, and the Stockyard Cafe is no exception, serving the chicken-fried variety and 8-ounce sirloins. Every-thing on the menu is fresh and Texas-size.

100 S. Manhattan St., in the Amarillo Livestock Auction Bldg. ℂ 806/374-6024. Reservations not accepted. Main courses $4–$12. AE, DISC, MC, V. Mon–Sat 6:30am–2:30pm; Fri 5–8:30pm.

Zen 721 ⚔ ASIAN FUSION   An unexpectedly urbane eatery in downtown Amar-illo, Zen 721 eschews longhorn skulls, beer signs, and Texas flags for red velvet, mini-malist Asian art, and industrial chic, to good effect. Thanks to good service and creative fare from the open kitchen, the restaurant has quickly become a local favorite since opening in 2003. The menu has a few nods to French and Mexican cuisine, but relies on such Asian standards as sushi and yakitori skewers and entrées such as seared sea bass in lemon grass broth, wok-flashed stir fry, and pepper-crusted beef strip over rice and fresh vegetables.

614 S. Polk St. ℂ 806/372-1909. www.zen721.com Reservations accepted. Main courses $7–$14 lunch, $9–$25 dinner. AE, DISC, MC, V. Mon–Fri 11am–1:45pm; Tues–Thurs 5–10pm; Fri–Sat 5–11pm. Bar open later.

AMARILLO AFTER DARK
THE PERFORMING ARTS
Amarillo Little Theatre, 2019 Civic Circle (ℂ 806/355-9991; www.amarillolittle theatre.org), produces about 10 plays a year at two theaters southwest of downtown. The Mainstage focuses on musicals and lighter fare, whereas the Adventure Space pro-duces edgier, adult-oriented fare. Recent productions have included *The Odd Couple, Steel Magnolias,* and *Assassins.* Ticket prices range from $9 to $20.

The **Amarillo Opera** (ℂ 806/372-7464; www.amarilloopera.org) produces two main stage operas annually, one each in the fall and spring, and an annual spirituals concert on the first weekend of every February. The performances take place at the Globe-News Cen-ter for the Performing Arts, 400 S. Buchanan St., and tickets are priced from $25 to $100.

The **Amarillo Symphony** (℃ **806/376-8782;** www.amarillosymphony.org) performs classical and pops concerts year-round, also at the Globe-News Center; tickets for most concerts cost between $15 and $25.

Lone Star Ballet (℃ **806/372-2463;** www.lonestarballet.org) presents a season of local and guest performances from October to April at the Globe-News Center. The local company produces *The Nutcracker* annually on the second weekend of December, and occasionally performs joint performances with the Amarillo Symphony. Tickets are $15 to $40.

NIGHTCLUBS & BARS

The main nightlife district in Amarillo is **South Polk Street** downtown, between 7th and 8th avenues. **Bodega's,** 709 S. Polk St. (℃ **806/378-5790**), is a chic wine bar and jazz club. **Butlers Martini Lounge,** 703 S. Polk St. (℃ **806/376-8180**), and a music venue, the **Mayfair Club,** 701 S. Polk (℃ **806/367-9641**), are other slick standbys on the block. Rough and raw, the **Golden Light Cafe,** 2908 W. 6th Ave. (℃ **806/374-9237**), is a Route 66 landmark, open since 1946 with a grill and oodles of nostalgia. For country-and-western fans, there's **Midnight Rodeo,** 4400 S. Georgia St. (℃ **806/358-7083**), featuring a gargantuan dance floor centered on an oval bar. Another good venue for live music—primarily country—is the hubcap-laden **Route 66 Roadhouse,** 609 S. Independence St. (℃ **806/355-7399**), which also has pool tables and dartboards.

2 Canyon & Palo Duro Canyon State Park ★

16 miles S of Amarillo; 103 miles N of Lubbock

Founded as Canyon City in 1889, Canyon takes its name from the spectacular Palo Duro Canyon, which lies 12 miles to the west. The nomadic prehorse tribes of Apaches first inhabited the region, but by the 18th century Comanche and Kiowa horsemen used the canyon as a major campground. By the late 19th century, white ranchers began grazing cattle in the area: Charles Goodnight, the inventor of the chuck wagon, drove a herd into Palo Duro Canyon in 1876 and established the JA Ranch.

Today a city of 13,000 residents, Canyon is known primarily as the gateway to Palo Duro Canyon State Park and the home of West Texas State A&M University. The town is a good base camp for those who want to explore Palo Duro Canyon but don't want to spend their nights in a tent. The community also has a charming small-town vibe, and much of its colorful history is presented at the excellent Panhandle-Plains Historical Museum.

ESSENTIALS
GETTING THERE & AROUND

Canyon is located immediately south of the junction of I-27 and U.S. 87, about 16 miles south of downtown Amarillo. Once entering town, U.S. 87 becomes 23rd Street, one of Canyon's main commercial thoroughfares. Tex. 217, which runs east–west, becomes 4th Avenue in town and is accessible via I-27, Exit 106; head west 2 miles to get to Canyon proper or east 10 miles to get to Palo Duro Canyon State Park.

Canyon's small size makes it impossible to get lost. The streets run north–south and begin at 1st at the west side of town. The avenues run east–west and begin numerically in the north.

> ## *Tips* Texas
>
> More than 3 million people have attended the musical drama *Texas!* since per-
> formances began in 1966, making it the nation's biggest outdoor drama. It's
> been updated as *Texas,* a spectacle of choreography and song covering the
> Panhandle's storied past. Staged at Pioneer Amphitheatre in Palo Duro Canyon
> State Park, the 2-hour play takes place Tuesday through Saturday from early
> June to mid-August at 8:30pm. For tickets, call © **806/655-2181** or visit
> **www.texas-show.com**. Adult tickets range from $11 to $27; those for children
> younger than 12 are slightly cheaper. For an extra $7.50 ($6 for children), atten-
> dees can partake of a steak dinner at 6pm. The admission fee to Palo Duro
> Canyon State Park is waived at 5:30pm for all *Texas* ticket holders.

VISITOR INFORMATION

Open from 9am to 4:30pm weekdays, the **Canyon Chamber of Commerce,** 1518
5th Ave. (© **800/999-9481** or 806/655-7815; www.canyonchamber.org), can provide visitors with information and maps.

FAST FACTS   The closest hospitals are located 16 miles north in Amarillo, including **Northwest Texas Hospital,** 1501 S. Coulter Dr. (© **806/354-1000**). The **post
office** is at 1304 4th Ave., open Monday through Friday from 9am to 4:30pm.

WHAT TO SEE & DO
THE TOP ATTRACTIONS

Palo Duro Canyon State Park ★★ *Moments*   The 60-mile Palo Duro Canyon,
sculpted by the Prairie Dog Town Fork of the Red River over the last 90 million years,
presents a grand contrast to the ubiquitous treeless plains of the Texas Panhandle. Its
800-foot cliffs, striped with layers of orange, red, and white rock and adorned by
groves of juniper and cottonwood trees, present a stark beauty that make this the preeminent state park in all of Texas. Simply put, it is the one "can't miss" natural attraction in the region. Palo Duro, which is Spanish for "hard wood," is a geology buff's
dream: The base of the canyon is walled by red shales and sandstones from the Permian period (ca. 250 million B.C.); these are topped by colorful Triassic shales and
sandstones; and the top of the canyon is made of a pastiche of stones only a few million years old. Of the 200 species of animals that venture into the canyon, you're most
likely to see mule deer and wild turkeys. There's also the famed Pioneer Amphitheatre,
the venue for the musical drama *Texas;* several hiking, biking, and horseback riding
trails; and a visitor center/museum/bookstore with interpretive exhibits on the
canyon's formation, history, and wildlife.

11450 Park Rd. 5, Canyon, TX 79015. © **806/488-2227**. www.paloducanyon.com. Day use $4 adults, free for chil-
dren ages 12 and younger. Additional fees for campsites (see "Camping," below). Gates open daily 8am–10pm. 12
miles west of Canyon via Tex. 217.

Panhandle-Plains Historical Museum ★★ *Finds*   The largest history museum in
the entire state, the Panhandle-Plains Historical Museum is anything but a dusty collection of spurs and bits. Well thought out, engaging, and informative, the facility
stands out as the top museum in the Panhandle (and all of West Texas, for that matter) because it comprehensively covers so many subjects under one roof. "People of the

Old Route 66

The ghosts of speed demons behind the wheels of phantom hot rods, torching the highway between Chicago and Los Angeles, still cruise northern Texas's stretch of the fabled "Mother Road." However, the construction of I-40, completed in 1984 on a similar course as Route 66, irrevocably changed the landscape of cross-country travel. What was once Route 66 is now a patchwork of service roads, two-lane highways, and inaccessible stretches of dirt. As the interstate defined the course of the last several decades of development, many of the towns through which Route 66 once snaked lost a fair share of commercial traffic, but hordes of nostalgic travelers have given many of the old and offbeat roadside landmarks a much-needed boost in recent years.

OLD ROUTE 66 HIGHLIGHTS

Established in 1890 by an Irish sheep rancher, **Shamrock,** 100 miles east of Amarillo via I-40, is home to the **U Drop Inn,** located at the junction of U.S. 83 and Old Route 66. Built in 1936, this service station/coffee shop is one of the earliest examples of Art Deco architecture on the Texas plains. The motel was totally restored and reopened in 2004 as the new home of the **Shamrock Chamber of Commerce** (© 806/256-2501; www.shamrocktx.net). Aside from the U Drop Inn, the **Pioneer West Historical Museum,** 204 N. Madden St. (© 806/256-3941), is the prime tourist stop, with 25 rooms in the restored Reynolds Hotel (1925) devoted to historical artifacts and other displays, including objects on loan from NASA's Houston Space Center. It's open Tuesday through Friday from 10am to noon and 1 to 3pm, although hours are somewhat erratic; admission is free, but donations are accepted. Also, come March 17, Shamrock hosts a lively St. Patrick's Day celebration, with a street fair, parade, and other festivities. Shamrock has a number of restaurants and motels, including the **Irish Inn,** 301 I-40 E. (© 806/256-2106), with double rates from $65 to $80.

Plains" is a comprehensive history of the Panhandle's inhabitants, offering a glimpse into how people have adapted to the past and present challenges of water, food, and climate. The museum is largely hands-on and interactive: You can sit in a Mustang and listen to Buddy Holly tunes or try out a sidesaddle. Other wings cover the region's history in terms of petroleum, art, transportation, Western heritage, and paleontology/geology. New in 2006: a gallery spotlighting American Indian art. Allow 1 to 2 hours.

2503 4th Ave., on the campus of West Texas State A&M University. © 806/651-2244. www.panhandleplains.org. Admission $7 adults, $6 seniors, $3 children ages 4–12, free for children younger than 4. Sept–May Mon–Sat 9am–5pm; June–Aug Mon–Sat 9am–6pm; year-round Sun 1–6pm. Closed major holidays.

OUTDOOR ACTIVITIES

GOLF   Palo Duro Creek, 50 Country Club Dr. (© 806/655-1106), is an 18-hole course open to the public 365 days a year. Greens fees are $27 with cart for 18 holes.

In the small town of **McLean,** 16 miles west of Shamrock, you'll find the **Devil's Rope Museum,** at the junction of Old Route 66 and Kingsley Street (© **806/779-2225;** www.barbwiremuseum.com), a converted Sears bra factory now home to displays on the history and evolution of both barbed wire and Route 66. It's open Tuesday through Saturday from 10am to 4pm (shorter hours in inclement weather) with admission by donation.

The town of **Groom,** 25 miles west of McLean, is the home of one of the largest crosses in the world: **the Cross of Our Lord Jesus Christ,** located off of I-40, Exit 119 (© **806/665-7788;** www.crossministries.net). With about 1,000 visitors stopping daily, the 190-foot, 1,250-ton cross is truly monolithic. If for nothing else, cross-country travelers should stop to admire its sheer size.

Just east of Groom is another Route 66 landmark: the **Leaning Tower of Texas,** a water tower intentionally built to slant with one set each of short and long legs and the last remaining vestige of a long-gone truck stop. Like the cross in Groom and Cadillac Ranch in Amarillo, fans of roadside attractions will want to stop for this peculiar photo op.

By far the biggest Texas city on Old Route 66, **Amarillo** still houses a nicely preserved stretch of the restored highway in its Route 66 Historic District, between Western and Georgia streets on West 6th Avenue (p. 416).

About 45 miles west of Amarillo is the tiny town of **Adrian,** known as the "Midpoint of Route 66." The appropriately named **MidPoint Café** on Route 66 (© **806/538-6379;** www.uglycrustpies.com), a favorite of tourists, cowboys, and bikers alike, is a friendly diner open daily in the summer (8am–4:30pm) and Monday through Saturday in the winter (8:30am–3:30pm). Bedecked with Route 66 memorabilia and shelves of souvenirs, the menu includes hearty American breakfasts, burgers with the works, and daily specials, with most main courses coming in at about $5 to $10.

HIKING With 25 miles of trails, **Palo Duro Canyon State Park** is the best hiking spot in the entire Texas Panhandle. The most popular hike is to see the **Lighthouse,** an impressive "hoodoo" rock formation so named because of its towering appearance. The Lighthouse is accessible by two trails: Lighthouse Trail, a moderate 5.75-mile round-trip; or Running Trail, a more strenuous 11-mile round-trip that runs through gullies and flats, and over a ridge. Both trail heads begin near the Hackberry Camp Area.

HORSEBACK RIDING Many of the trails in **Palo Duro Canyon State Park** are horse-friendly, including the aforementioned Lighthouse Trail. Several equestrian campsites can also be found in the park. For those who do not have a horse of their own, **Old West Stables,** located inside the park (© **806/488-2180**), offers 1-hour guided tours on horseback for $20.

MOUNTAIN BIKING   Mountain bikes are permitted—and quite popular—on the myriad trails in **Palo Duro Canyon State Park**. However, bike rentals are not available in Canyon or Amarillo, so bringing your own is a prerequisite.

WHERE TO STAY

Canyon has a few mom-and-pop motels and a few B&Bs. For reliability and convenience, we like the new **Best Western Canyon Inn & Suites,** 2801 4th Ave. (© 800/ 937-8376 or 806/655-1818), which has an indoor pool and exercise room. Double rates are $65 to $79.

Hudspeth House ✦   This three-story B&B was a "kit home" ordered from a company back East, assembled in 1909, then relocated to its present location in 1913. The inn takes its name from a teacher at the college that became West Texas State A&M University, Miss Mary Elizabeth Hudspeth, a friend of Georgia O'Keeffe who also taught at the school in the 1910s. (The famed artist was a frequent dinner guest at the house in her time.) Outside, a shady wraparound porch and colorful gardens invite guests into a lively and elegant parlor. Current owners (and native Brits) John and Connie Okill bought the inn in 2004 and gave it a nice makeover, naming the rooms after their kids and grandkids in the process. Uniquely decorated all, two of the rooms are third-floor lofts; we like the spare woodsy charm of Benjamin's Cabin, and the large and stylish comfort of James' Loft.

1905 4th Ave., Canyon, TX 79015. © **800/655-9809** or 806/655-9800. www.hudspethinn.com. 8 units. $85–$139 double. Rates include full breakfast. AE, DISC, MC, V. *In room:* A/C, TV, complimentary Wi-Fi.

CAMPING

Palo Duro Canyon State Park   The park offers a wide variety of camping options, from primitive backpacking sites accessible only by foot to standard RV sites with water and electrical hook-ups. Several of the camping areas have showers and restrooms, as well as a dump station. For more substantial supplies, you'll want to hit a grocery store in Canyon first. The seven rustic, mission-style cabins were built in the 1930s, and since renovated. They can sleep two to four people and have varied facilities; they have no kitchens, but there are grills out front. Pets are permitted at all of the sites, but they must remain leashed at all times.

11450 Park Rd. 5, Canyon, TX 79015. © **512/389-8900,** or 512/389-8900 for reservations. 100 sites, including 7 pull-throughs, 75 back-ins, and 18 tent sites. Additional primitive sites, equestrian sites, and 7 cabins available. $12–$20 campsites; $55–$115 cabins. DISC, MC, V. Located 12 miles east of Canyon via Tex. 217.

WHERE TO DINE

A local favorite, **Pepito's,** 408 23rd St. (© **806/655-4736**), is a solid Tex-Mex restaurant with tiled, landscape-adorned tables and regional art. The specialties are fajitas and the restaurant is open for lunch and dinner Mondays through Saturdays.

A unique dining experience can be had with **Cowboy Morning** (© **800/ 658-2613**) in Claude, about 40 miles east of Canyon. The meals include a horse-drawn wagon ride to a canyon overlook and authentic chuck wagon cuisine. Cowboy Morning includes biscuits, scrambled eggs, sausage, potato casserole, cowboy coffee, and orange juice and is priced at $23 for adults, $18 for children ages 4 to 12, and free for children 3 and younger. The nighttime offering is Western Night in Palo Duro Canyon, including a jeep tour, barbecue dinner, a living history presentation, and stage show ($39 for adults, $30 for children ages 4 to 12, and free for children 3 and younger).

3 Lubbock

122 miles S of Amarillo; 100 miles SE of Clovis, New Mexico

When Capt. Randolph Marcy, one of the first Anglo explorers to happen onto the site of modern-day Lubbock, arrived, he was something less than impressed. "It was the dreaded Llano Estacado," he wrote, "a land where no man, either savage or civilized, permanently abides; it spreads forth into a treeless, desolate waste of uninhabited solitude, which has always been and must continue, uninhabited forever."

Certainly, Marcy would be in for a shock if he were to see Lubbock today: a city of over 200,000 residents, the home of a major university in Texas Tech, and the economic and cultural center of the surrounding South Plains. Self-labeled as "the nursery" for Austin's music scene, its musical heritage is legendary: Buddy Holly still reigns as the local king, but Tanya Tucker, Mac Davis, Waylon Jennings, and Dixie Chick Natalie Maines have also called the city home.

Named after Col. Thomas Lubbock, a Confederate officer, Lubbock was established in 1890 and grew rapidly, its economy built on cotton and cattle, and, later, oil and gas. The city has long been a regional hub; hence the nickname, "Hub City." Look at a map and the moniker's appropriateness becomes crystal clear: Lubbock is surrounded by dozens of small agricultural towns.

A bit rough around the edges, Lubbock is a fun stopover for a night because of its lively dining scene, college-town vibe, and happening nightlife with plenty of good music.

ESSENTIALS
GETTING THERE

BY PLANE   Lubbock International Airport, 5401 N. Martin Luther King Blvd. (✆ **806/775-2044;** www.flylia.com), sees 70 arrivals and departures daily. Three airlines serve the airport: **American Eagle** (✆ **800/433-7300**), **Continental** (✆ **800/ 525-0280**), and **Southwest** (✆ **800/435-9792**).

All the major car-rental agencies, including **Avis** and **Hertz,** have desks at the airport. **Royal Coach Towne Car Service** (✆ **806/795-3888**) offers airport transportation in Lincoln Town Cars into the city for $14 to $24.

BY CAR   Lubbock sits at the intersection of three major highways on the "Port to Plains" route. I-27 enters the city from the north and becomes U.S. 87 south of Lubbock. Cutting down from Clovis, New Mexico, northwest of the city, U.S. 84 continues southeast to I-20 near Abilene. U.S. 62/82 is the third major highway that runs through Lubbock, entering town from the southwest, where it is the primary route to and from Carlsbad and Roswell, New Mexico, and continuing through the plains to the east.

GETTING AROUND

Getting around Lubbock is fairly stress-free: It is laid out on a standard grid with few anomalies, with I-27 bisecting the city north–south and Loop 289, a major highway, circling it. Downtown is located just west of I-27, accessible via either Exit 3 (19th St.) or Exit 4 (4th St.). The east–west streets in central Lubbock are numbered, beginning with 1st in the north, and the north–south streets surrounding I-27 are arranged alphabetically, from Avenue A on the east side of the highway and continuing to Avenue Z on the west side of I-27.

CitiBus (© **806/712-2000;** www.citibus.com), Lubbock's mass transit system, operates 11 routes Monday through Friday from 5:45am to 7:15pm and Saturday from 7:15am to 7:35pm. No service is offered on Sunday. The main downtown transfer station is located at the intersection of Broadway and Buddy Holly Avenue (Ave. H). Fares are $1 for adults, 75¢ for children ages 6 to 12, 50¢ for seniors and those with disabilities, and free for children younger than 6. A $2 day pass allows for unlimited rides.

Taxi service is offered by **City Cab** (© **806/765-7777**) and **Yellow Cab** (© **806/ 765-7474**).

VISITOR INFORMATION
Visit Lubbock, the Convention and Visitors Bureau, 1500 Broadway, 6th floor (© **800/692-4035** or 806/747-5232; www.lubbocklegends.com), can provide visitors with local maps and information on lodging, dining, and attractions.

FAST FACTS **Highland Community Hospital,** 2412 50th St. (© **806/ 788-4100**); **University Medical Center,** 602 Indiana St. (© **806/775-8200**); and **Covenant Medical Center,** 3615 19th St. (© **806/725-1011**), operate 24-hour emergency rooms. The main **post office** is located downtown at 411 Ave. L and is open Monday through Friday from 8:30am to 5pm.

WHAT TO SEE & DO
THE TOP ATTRACTIONS
Buddy Holly Center 𝄞𝄞 Named for Lubbock's legendary rock pioneer, this gem of a museum is a must-visit if you're a rock-'n'-roll fan, and at least worth a quick look if you're not. The permanent exhibit about the life and music of Buddy Holly is the centerpiece of this facility, which also houses an art gallery and the Texas Musicians Hall of Fame. Though Holly died in a plane crash at the age of 23, his impact on the development of rock is undeniable—he influenced everyone from Elton John to the Grateful Dead. The center's collection includes such memorabilia as Holly's trademark horn-rimmed glasses (the pair recovered from the crash site) alongside his guitars, personal mementos, and interactive exhibits. Visitors should also view the 20-minute Holly documentary, if time allows. The Lubbock Fine Arts Gallery features rotating exhibits of all kinds, and the Texas Musicians Hall of Fame gives perspective on Lubbock's deep musical heritage. Acting as a regional arts center, the B.H.C. also hosts numerous courtyard concerts, classes, and "Cultural Conversations" on topics of regional artistic interest. The museum's breadth dictates that guests spend a bit more than an hour here. If you crave more Holly, ask for their handout with directions to his grave, birthplace, and other places of interest.

1801 Crickets Ave. in the Depot Entertainment District. © 806/775-3560. www.buddyhollycenter.org. $5 adults, $3 seniors, free for children 12 and younger. Tues–Fri 10am–6pm; Sat 11am–6pm. Closed major holidays.

Museum of Texas Tech University 𝄞 Housing some three million objects and artifacts, this museum is a well-rounded facility that covers a diverse, if not terribly focused, mix of subjects: Visual arts, natural and social sciences, and the humanities are all represented with both permanent and regularly rotating exhibits. The ethnology and textiles collection is among the best you'll find anywhere, comprised of objects made by people living in Texas, the Southwest, and the Great Plains. It also has galleries filled with Taos and sub-Saharan art, exhibits on wildlife, and full-size dinosaur skeletons. The temporary exhibits are routinely excellent. Also on-site is the

Lubbock

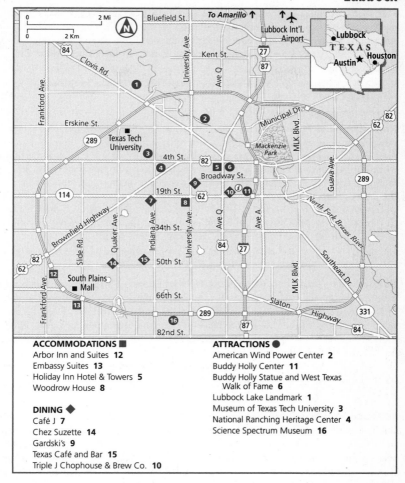

ACCOMMODATIONS ■
Arbor Inn and Suites **12**
Embassy Suites **13**
Holiday Inn Hotel & Towers **5**
Woodrow House **8**

DINING ◆
Café J **7**
Chez Suzette **14**
Gardski's **9**
Texas Café and Bar **15**
Triple J Chophouse & Brew Co. **10**

ATTRACTIONS ●
American Wind Power Center **2**
Buddy Holly Center **11**
Buddy Holly Statue and West Texas
  Walk of Fame **6**
Lubbock Lake Landmark **1**
Museum of Texas Tech University **3**
National Ranching Heritage Center **4**
Science Spectrum Museum **16**

Moody Planetarium (public shows are held daily for $2 adults, $1 for students and seniors, free for children younger than 5). Expect to spend between 1 and 2 hours here if you want to scratch the museum's surface.

4th St. and Indiana Ave. ℂ **806/742-2490.** www.museum.ttu.edu. Free admission. Tues–Sat 10am–5pm (until 8:30pm Thurs); Sun 1–5pm. Closed Mon and major holidays.

National Ranching Heritage Center As some of the country's largest and most storied ranches originated in the Panhandle area in the early 1900s, Lubbock is a natural for the home of a museum dedicated to preserving the history of ranching in the United States. However, the history buff short on time might skip this in favor of the more comprehensive Panhandle-Plains Historical Museum in Canyon (p. 425). The outdoor displays consist of nearly 40 relocated historic buildings; visitors can tour such structures as a *vaquero* corral (1783), a log cabin (1850), a "dugout" dwelling (1890), and the Victorian-style Barton House (1909). The center hosts several annual events, including a chuck-wagon dinner and concert in the spring, fiddle dances in the summer, and "Candlelight at the Ranch" in December. Allow a half-hour to an hour.

3121 4th St. at Indiana Ave. ℂ **806/742-0498.** www.ttu.edu/ranchingheritagecenter. Free admission. Mon–Sat 10am–5pm; Sun 1–5pm. Closed major holidays.

MORE ATTRACTIONS

American Wind Power Center *(Finds)*   Between 1850 and 1920, over 700 American companies manufactured windmills, but today a mere two U.S. businesses make these iconic machines. Such statistics provided an impetus for this unique and worthwhile museum, which displays a collection of 200 water-pumping windmills. Windmills of every size, shape, and color are displayed in the main gallery and outside on the museum's grounds, including a rare twin-wheel windmill, with a pair of 12-foot wheels on a single tower, and a 164-foot Vestas wind turbine—with 77-foot blades. (It powers the museum as well as 60 homes.) Indoors, the center houses many more unusual windmills, an art gallery, and a gift shop. Allow 1 hour.

1701 Canyon Lake Dr. ℂ **806/747-8734.** www.windmill.com. $5 suggested donation per person, or $10 per family. Tues–Sat 10am–5pm. Closed major holidays. Located 1 mile west of I-27 via 19th St.

Buddy Holly Statue and West Texas Walk of Fame   This shady urban isle just west of the Lubbock Civic Center pays tribute to Lubbock's most famous son, Buddy Holly, with an oversize statue of his likeness, guitar in hand. In 1979, Holly became the first inductee into the West Texas Walk of Fame that surrounds the statue. Other inductees include actor Barry Corbin *(WarGames)* and musicians Roy Orbison, Tanya Tucker, and Waylon Jennings. It's a pleasant spot to sit on a bench, enjoy the gardens, and reflect on the fleeting life and times of an American original. Come September, it's the locale of the annual Buddy Holly Festival.

Between 7th and 8th sts. at Ave. Q.

Lubbock Lake Landmark   A unit of the Museum of Texas Tech University, the Lubbock Lake Landmark consists of a 300-acre archaeological and natural history preserve, believed to be the only site in North America where a complete record of 12,000 years of human history has been uncovered. The nicely presented interpretive center features chronological displays on each group that has inhabited the region, from the nomadic hunters of the Paleo-Indian period to the pioneers of the late 1800s. The facility requires about 45 minutes to tour, and, if it's fresh air you're after, take an extra hour to explore 4 miles of nature trails and an outdoor sculpture garden with life-size bronzes depicting animals that once roamed the area, including a mammoth and a giant armadillo. Additionally, Lubbock Lake Landmark is home to an active archaeological program during the summer and children's programs throughout the year.

2401 Landmark Lane at Loop 289 and Clovis Hwy. (U.S. 84). ℂ **806/742-1116.** www.museum.ttu.edu/LLL/index.html. Free admission (donation requested). Tues–Sat 9am–5pm; Sun 1–5pm.

Fun Fact
"At least the first 40 songs we wrote were Buddy Holly–influenced."
—Former Beatle Paul McCartney

A Different Kind of Texas Tea

The images of herds of longhorn, oil pumps on the horizon, and endless cotton fields might be the enduring images of the northwestern Texas plains, but if the area's burgeoning wine industry has anything to do with it, the vineyard may just become another regional icon. The climate is close to ideal for the cultivation of grapes, with its moderate elevation, warm days, and cool nights. Within a 15-minute drive of Lubbock, there are three wineries that open their doors to tours.

Emerging from a grape-growing experiment on a shady Lubbock patio in 1976, **Llano Estacado Winery,** located 5 miles southeast of Lubbock on Tex. 1585 between U.S. 84 and U.S. 87 (© 806/745-2258; www.llanowine.com), is now one of the largest and best wineries in Texas: Its wines have won more awards than any other winery in the state. The tasting room is open from 10am to 5pm Monday through Saturday and from noon to 5pm Sunday. **Cap*Rock Winery,** 5 miles south of Lubbock at U.S. 87 South and Woodrow Road (© 806/863-2704; www.caprockwinery.com), uses vinifera grapes to produce chardonnays, cabernet sauvignons, and other wines. Free tours and samples are available from 10am to 5pm Monday through Saturday and from noon to 5pm Sunday. **Pheasant Ridge Winery** on Route 3, 12 miles northeast of Lubbock via I-27 (© 806/746-6033; www.pheasantridgewinery.com), is located on the site of one of Texas's oldest vineyards and offers tours and tastings Friday and Saturday from noon to 6pm and Sunday from 1 to 5pm. In the Depot Entertainment District, visit **La Diosa Cellars,** 901 17th St. (© 806/744-3600; www.ladiosacellars.com), the only winery within city limits. Its tasting room is actually a fantastic wine bar (serving tapas and featuring live acoustic music), open for lunch and dinner Tuesday through Saturday. The winery sources its fruit from Texas and produces about 2,000 cases a year.

Science Spectrum Museum *(Kids)*   This museum aims to educate children about science and technology, and hits the bull's-eye more often than not. With three floors and 200 exhibits that take 1 to 2 hours to explore, the subject matter runs the gamut from animals and aquariums to space and flight, and many of the displays are interactive. Also of note is the "Brazos River Journey," a permanent aquarium/terrarium exhibit detailing how the regional river ecosystem interacts with the hand of man, complete with rattlesnakes, largemouth bass, and sharks. The facility is also home to an Omni Theatre—with a 55-foot dome screen—and a gift shop.

2579 S. Loop 289 (between Indiana and University aves.). © 806/745-6299. www.sciencespectrum.com. Admission $5.50 adults, $4.50 seniors and children ages 3–12, free for children younger than 3. Additional tickets ($4–$5) necessary for the Omni Theatre. Mon–Fri 10am–5pm; Sat 10am–6pm; Sun 1:30–5pm.

OUTDOOR ACTIVITIES

Within the city limits of Lubbock, the 248-acre **Mackenzie Park,** located east of I-27 at 4th Street (© 806/775-2687), is the largest recreation area, with two golf courses—one traditional and one Frisbee—walking, jogging, and equestrian trails, and Prairie Dog Town, one of the few active colonies in the urban United States.

Caprock Canyons State Park and Trailway (𝒞 806/455-1492) is a 2½-hour drive from Lubbock, located to the northeast near Quitaque off Tex. 86. Like Palo Duro Canyon to the northwest, this 13,906-acre park offers a startling contrast to the plains in its jagged formations of red rocks and diverse vegetation. An abandoned railroad line was converted into a 65-mile trail system that travels along a canyon floor, through a one-time railroad tunnel, and up a steep incline onto the mesa of the High Plains. Hikers, bikers, and horses are permitted on the trail. Several other hiking opportunities exist in the park as well. Primitive backcountry campsites are available for $8 nightly as well as tent sites for $10 and sites with partial RV hook-ups for $12 to $20. Additionally, boaters and fishers can take advantage of Lake Theo, located on the south side of the park. The park charges a $3 day-use fee per person (free for kids younger than 13).

BOATING   Two boat ramps access the spring-fed **Buffalo Springs Lake,** Tex. 835, 5 miles east of Loop 289 (𝒞 806/747-3353; www.buffalospringslake.net). Gate fees are $4 adults, $2.50 children younger than 11, $1 seniors, and $5 per watercraft. Rentals are not available. Boating is also allowed at **Lake Alan Henry** (𝒞 806/775-2673; www.lakealanhenry.org), 65 miles southeast of Lubbock via U.S. 84 and FM 2458, a rugged-looking reservoir surrounded by a wildlife habitat area with several miles of hiking trails.

GOLF   Lubbock has several public 18-hole golf courses, including **Elm Grove Golf Course,** 3202 Milwaukee St. (𝒞 806/799-7801), with greens fees of $25 to $28 with a cart or $15 to $18 on foot; **Shadow Hills Golf Course,** 6002 3rd St. (𝒞 806/793-9700), with greens fees of $27 to $32 with a cart and $16 to $21 without; **Rawls Golf Course,** 1st and Indiana sts. on the campus of Texas Tech (𝒞 806/742-4635), with green fees of $48 to $55 with cart; and **Meadowbrook Golf Course,** 601 Municipal Dr. in Mackenzie Park (𝒞 806/765-6679), with two 18-hole courses and greens fees of $25 to $32 with cart or $20 to $25 without. Nearby, **The Mackenzie Park Disk Golf Course** is free, although you'll need your own Frisbee. It is a 21-hole course that includes a 470-yard shot over the Brazos River from a cliff.

HIKING   Four miles of nature trails snake around **Lubbock Lake Landmark** (p. 432), as well as the 6-mile trailway at **Caprock Canyons State Park.** Several miles of walking and jogging trails, many of which are horse-friendly, are within the city limits at **Mackenzie Park,** 4th Street and I-27 (𝒞 806/775-2687).

MOUNTAIN BIKING   There are a few trails at **Buffalo Springs Lake,** Tex. 835, 5 miles east of Loop 289 (see "Boating," above), but Lubbock's hard-core mountain bikers head north to **Palo Duro Canyon State Park** (see "Canyon & Palo Duro Canyon State Park," earlier in this chapter) and **Caprock Canyons State Park.**

SWIMMING   Lubbock is home to four municipal pools, all outdoor and open from late May to early August: **Clapp Municipal Swimming Pool,** 4500 Ave. U; **Mae Simmons,** 2300 Weber Dr.; **Maxey,** 4007 30th St.; and **Rogers,** 3200 Bates St. In season, each is open from 1 to 6pm daily with an admission fee of $2 adults, $1.50 children 17 and younger. For further information, call 𝒞 806/775-2673. **Buffalo Springs Lake** (see "Boating," above) boasts two beaches that are open to swimmers year-round. Aside from the admission fee ($4 adults, $2.50 children 11 and younger), there is no additional fee to swim. A year-round indoor pool is located at the **YWCA,** 3101 35th St. (𝒞 806/792-2723). A day pass is $5 for adults, $2.50 for kids.

SPECTATOR SPORTS

The Lubbock home crowd roots for the **Texas Tech Red Raiders,** who compete in Big 12 football, baseball, and men's and women's basketball. Call 🕾 888/462-4412 or 806/742-8324 for schedules and ticket information. A Central Hockey League team, the **Lubbock Cotton Kings** (🕾 806/747-7825; www.cottonkings.com), plays at Lubbock Municipal Coliseum, 272 Drive of Champions, between October and March. Tickets are $10 to $25.

SHOPPING

Lubbock is home to the region's largest mall, **South Plains Mall,** 6002 Slide Rd. at South Loop 289 (🕾 806/792-4653; www.southplainsmall.com), which houses more than 150 stores, including Gap, Abercrombie & Fitch, and many other department stores, specialty shops, and restaurants. The mall's hours are from 10am to 9pm Monday through Saturday and from noon to 6pm Sunday. The **Antique Mall of Lubbock,** 7907 W. 19th St. (🕾 806/796-2166), offers West Texas's largest selection of antiques, open daily from 10am to 6pm.

WHERE TO STAY

You'll find Lubbock's greatest concentration of hotels and motels in three areas: downtown; off I-27 between 50th Street and Loop 289; and in the city's southwest corner, off Loop 289 near Quaker and Indiana avenues. Among the city's chain properties are: **Clarion,** 505 Ave. Q (🕾 800/246-4234 or 806/747-0171), with double rates of $80 to $100; **Embassy Suites,** 5212 S. Loop 289 (🕾 806/771-7000), with suites for $109 to $159; and **Motel 6,** 909 66th St. (🕾 800/466-8356 or 806/745-5541), with double rates of $40 to $50. In Post, 36 miles southeast of Lubbock via U.S. 84, the historic 1915 **Hotel Garza,** 302 E. Main St. (🕾 806/495-3962; www.hotelgarza.com), offers individually decorated rooms and suites for $79 to $119 for two people. Room taxes in Lubbock add 13% to lodging bills.

Arbor Inn & Suites ⊛   Opening in 2005, this independent property impressed us with its attention to detail and excellent service. The rooms are fresh and spacious, averaging about 500 square feet, and have great bathrooms, with granite counters and plenty of space. Functional and stylish, all rooms have a sleeper couch and many have balconies; the suites have complete kitchens as well. Ultimately, we were won over by the breakfast, featuring do-it-yourself waffle stations with premeasured batter and a Texas-shaped griddle, and the spectacular outdoor pool, with a faux beach, waterfall, and fountains.

5310 Englewood Ave., Lubbock, TX 79424. 🕾 866/644-2319 or 806/722-2726. www.arborinnandsuites.com. 73 units, including 24 suites. $79–$89 double; $99 suite. AE, DC, DISC, MC, V. **Amenities:** Outdoor heated pool; exercise room; indoor Jacuzzi; business center; complimentary laundry machines. *In room:* A/C, cable TV w/DVD player, kitchens, microwave, fridge, coffeemaker, iron, safe.

Holiday Inn Hotel & Towers   The top downtown hotel in Lubbock, this early 1980s–era Holiday Inn is the city's largest lodging option, located adjacent to the Civic Center smack-dab in the middle of downtown. Well-maintained and comfortable, the rooms are pleasant if unremarkable, with off-white walls and beige furnishings. I like the east tower, six stories of rooms surrounding a wide-open atrium. The suites with west-facing windows are the best—guests are greeted every morning by the Buddy Holly statue on the West Texas Walk of Fame below. Other rooms overlook a treed central courtyard.

801 Ave. Q, Lubbock, TX 79401. © **800/HOLIDAY** or 806/763-1200. Fax 806/763-2656. www.holiday-inn.com/lubbock-civic. 293 units. $84–$94 double; $104–$125 suite. AE, DC, DISC, MC, V. **Amenities:** Restaurant; bar; small indoor pool; exercise room; indoor Jacuzzi; sauna; courtesy car; limited room service; coin-op laundry; dry cleaning. *In room:* A/C, TV w/pay movies, dataport.

Woodrow House ✿ The Southern Colonial architecture (complete with white pillars and a redbrick exterior) of this urban bed-and-breakfast belies its age: Built in 1995, the Woodrow House combines Texas tradition with modern amenities. The suite here—a retrofit Santa Fe caboose in the backyard—is a real eye-catcher, and my favorite room in town. It has a queen-size bed framed by wrought iron and a foldout futon, as well as a kitchenette. The old engineers' seats are now great spots to sit and read. Inside, visitors enjoy an elegant parlor and seven themed rooms. The Lone Star Room is a lot of fun: a framed Republic of Texas dollar, longhorn skulls, a Texas flag, and a king-size bed. But if your nostalgic leanings are a bit more modern, book the '50s Room, where images of Buddy Holly and Elvis abound.

2629 19th St., Lubbock, TX 79410. © **800/687-5236** or 806/793-3330. Fax 806/793-7676. www.woodrowhouse.com. 7 units. $115 double; $145 suite. Rates include full breakfast. AE, DISC, MC, V. **Amenities:** Babysitting; laundry service. *In room:* A/C, TV, kitchenette (in suite), complimentary Wi-Fi, fridge, coffeemaker, hair dryer, iron.

CAMPING

Buffalo Springs Lake, Tex. 835 (© **806/747-3353**), has one of the most scenic campgrounds in the area, with 33 shady sites and three tent areas. Camping fees are $10 for tents and $15 to $22 for full hook-ups. **Caprock Canyons State Park** (© **806/455-1492**) is another popular camping destination, with primitive back-country sites ($8) and tent sites ($10) as well as sites with partial RV hook-ups ($12–$20). See "Outdoor Activities," earlier in this chapter, for complete information on both parks.

WHERE TO DINE

Café J ✿ MEDITERRANEAN/ECLECTIC Hip yet homey, Café J has drawn raves for taking a fresh direction in Lubbock's dining scene. With a menu that includes a number of pastas and crepes (including the scrumptious Santa Fe Crepe, stuffed with ground beef and green chiles, and topped with pepper jack cheese) and a nice selection of lighter fare, including salads and grilled ahi tuna. More substantial entrees include soy-and-sake-glazed orange roughy and pistachio-crusted pork tenderloin. Thanks in part to its location directly across from the Texas Tech campus, the pair of bars here are among Lubbock's trendiest nightspots.

2605 19th St. © **806/743-5400.** Reservations accepted. Main courses $8–$26. AE, DC, DISC, MC, V. Sun and Tues–Fri 11am–2:30pm; Tues–Sun 5:30–11pm. Bars open later.

Chez Suzette ✿✿ *Finds* FRENCH/ITALIAN Almost hidden in a strip mall, Chez Suzette is Lubbock's most romantic dining spot. Black-and-red checkerboard floors, lattice, and dim lighting give the dining room an intimate, distinctly French feel, which carries over to the menu. Start with escargot or carpaccio and a salad, then move on to the main course: coq au vin; veal medallions topped with blue cheese and garlic sauce, served with zucchini pancakes; or ahi tuna with a balsamic reduction. Lighter selections include pastas and vegetarian plates. Lunches are similar but smaller, and the mouthwatering desserts—crème brûlée, bananas Foster, crepes, and pastries—are all made from scratch.

4423 50th St., in the Quaker Square Shopping Center. © **806/795-6796.** Reservations recommended. Main courses $9–$20. AE, DC, DISC, MC, V. Tues–Fri 11:30am–2pm; Mon–Sat 5:30 till closing.

Gardski's AMERICAN   A favorite of both students and suits, this landmark eatery near the campus of Texas Tech University is actually a converted Victorian home, abandoned by its residents after a close call with a tornado in 1970. The place serves some mighty mean sandwiches—I can't resist the Smokin' Mad Jack, plump with smoked ham, brown-sugar bacon, pepper jack, and red onions, with jalapeños on the side. A more upscale menu of lighter chicken and seafood plates is served at dinner; down-home favorites such as meatloaf, catfish, chicken-fried steak, and good burgers round out the menu.

2009 Broadway. ✆ **806/744-2391.** Reservations accepted for large parties only. Main courses $5.50–$7.50 lunch, $7.50–$16 dinner. AE, MC, V. Daily 11am–10pm.

Texas Café and Bar BARBECUE   This rowdy, smoky roadhouse, affectionately called "The Spoon" by locals, is pure Texas, from the local color seated at the bar and weathered tables to the Lone Star neon signs, longhorn skulls, and politically incorrect wooden Indian. The menu, too, is 100% Texan: spicy beef chili with Texas-shaped cornbread; barbecued turkey, beef, and sausage; Texas beans; and big, juicy burgers. If you want something that's a little different, try the Fajitas a la Brisket, barbecued beef brisket wrapped in a tortilla and served with pico de gallo salsa. Everything here is spicy, hearty, and just plain good. There's a poolroom in the back, and live music on weekends.

3604 50th St. ✆ **806/792-8544.** Reservations not accepted. Main courses $4.50–$11. AE, DC, DISC, MC, V. Daily 11am–10pm. Bar open later.

Triple J Chophouse & Brew Co. ⍟ STEAKS   In the former domain of the Hub City Brewery, this eatery and microbrewery is more upscale than its predecessor, but still ranks near the top of my Lubbock list. There are tables in a long seating area, below brick walls adorned with horns and Texas photography of all kinds, and a slick bar, which sits directly in front of the glass-enclosed brewing area. The menu focuses on beef, but also offers seafood, wood-fired pizzas, and some good ol' Texan comfort food (potpies, brisket, rib tips). The sides are creative (like parmesan creamed spinach and shoestring fries), but the terrific brews remain a key attraction: There are typically 8 to 10 of them on tap, including excellent German Kölsch-style beer. If you're feeling extra-carnivorous, you can "grab the bull by the horns" and order a hand-cut steak to the thickness you indicate tableside. Eaters of the thickest steak of the month win a prize.

1807 Buddy Holly Ave., in the Depot District. ✆ **806/747-6555.** Main courses $7–$23. AE, MC, V. Mon–Thurs 11am–10pm; Fri–Sat 11am–midnight; Sun 11am–3pm.

LUBBOCK AFTER DARK
THE PERFORMING ARTS

Built in 1938, the beautifully restored **Cactus Theater,** 1812 Buddy Holly Ave. (✆ **806/762-3233** for information; www.cactustheater.com), is now the centerpiece of Lubbock's performing arts scene. On Friday through Sunday, it features regular doo-wop and nostalgia shows, as well as other concerts and musicals. Popular productions include tributes to Buddy Holly and other music legends. Tickets run $15 to $40.

   Lubbock Symphony Orchestra, 1313 Broadway, Suite 2 (✆ **806/762-1688;** www.lubbocksymphony.org), performs 10 classical concerts and one pops concert every year at the Lubbock Civic Center Theater (at 6th St. and Ave. O), often featuring guest conductors and musicians from around the world. Ticket prices range from $10 to $50.

Established in 1926, the **Texas Tech University Theatre,** on the Texas Tech campus on 18th Street between Boston and Flint avenues (© **806/742-3603;** www.theatre.ttu.edu), has produced over 1,000 plays in the time since. Recent productions include *To Kill a Mockingbird, Macbeth,* and *Six Characters in Search of an Author.* The theater also hosts ballets, experimental plays, and one-act play festivals. Tickets are $10 to $12.

NIGHTCLUBS & BARS

Lubbock has a bustling nightlife, primarily due to the presence of 25,000 Texas Tech students. The vibrant **Depot Entertainment District,** located between Buddy Holly Avenue and I-27 around 19th Street, is where you'll find the highest concentration of clubs, including **The Blue Light,** 1806 Buddy Holly Ave. (© **806/762-1185**), known for its live music and hip, young crowd; and **Bleachers Sports Café,** 1719 Buddy Holly Ave. (© **806/744-7767**), a huge sports bar/music venue. Also in the neighborhood, you can line dance and two-step to live country music at **Wild West,** 2216 I-27 (© **806/741-3031**). **Cricket's Grill and Draft House,** 2412 Broadway (© **806/744-4677**), is a rowdy Texas Tech hangout with nearly 100 beers on draft. In Justiceburg, 50 miles southeast of Lubbock on U.S. 84, drop in on **Jessie Jane's** (no phone; www.jessiejanes.com) for rollicking music and good grub Wednesday through Saturday.

Many restaurants morph into bustling nightspots after sundown, including the **Texas Café and Bar** (p. 437) and **Café J** (p. 436). Just north of the Texas Tech campus, **Conference Cafe,** 3216 4th St. (© **806/747-7766**), is a rowdy college hangout. If you do imbibe in Lubbock, try the city's signature cocktail, the Chilton. Invented by a local doctor of the same name, the drink consists of vodka, fresh-squeezed lemon juice, and soda, in a salt-rimmed glass—the result is tart but refreshing.

Appendix:
Texas in Depth

by Neil E. Schlecht

Texas looms large, and not only in the imaginations of Texans. Once a separate nation, and today bigger than both England and France combined, it's a place that dreams big and walks tall, where the sky and ranches—and, Texans hope, the possibilities—are massive. The history of Texas is laced with events and heroes large and legendary, many of which have catapulted into state and national lore. In many ways Texas has come to symbolize the nation's westward expansion, its complicated struggle for independence, and the dearly held mystique of a land of opportunity and wide-open spaces. Texas's complex settlement pattern—the territory was claimed by Spain, France, and Mexico before becoming an independent republic and then the 28th state in the Union in 1845—supports its mythic status. "Six flags" really did famously fly over the state from the 16th to the 19th century, during which time there were eight changes of government. Even though the state has increasingly become one of immigrants from other states and other nations south of the border, Texans continue to exhibit a fiercely independent streak. The pages that follow explore the state's history and provide a primer on its unique culture.

1 History 101

EARLY NATIVE AMERICANS
In prehistoric times, central parts of the state were once submerged underwater, and about a hundred million years ago, massive dinosaurs, some of them unique to Texas, roamed the plains.

The first human occupation of the land dates from about 10,000 B.C. Traces of a prehistoric people today referred to as the Paleo-Indians have been found, though very little is known of these early hunters. Tribal groups emerged around 8,000 B.C., leaving behind murals of daily life and religious ceremonies in caves in what is now West Texas. As many as 30,000 different Native American tribes—including the Caddos, Coahuiltecans, Tonkawans, Apaches, and Comanches—occupied the land before the arrival of European settlers in the 16th century. Agriculturally oriented, Indians grew crops that would become

modern mainstays, such as cotton, corn, beans, squash, tomatoes, and potatoes. Even the name "Texas" can be traced to Native American tribes: *Tejas* is the Spanish pronunciation of the Caddo word for "friend."

ARRIVAL OF THE SPANIARDS
Unfortunately, the arrival of the Spaniards was hardly friendly. Many of the Native American tribes were quickly wiped out, killed either by disease or land-grabbing conquistadors. Along with opportunists in search of gold, glory, and land were missionaries in search of souls. Their objective was the Christianization of native tribes.

The first European to reach Texas shores is believed to have been Alonso Alvarez de Piñeda. In 1519, the Spanish explorer made a map of the Texas coast, establishing the basis for the first claim to the land and Spanish rule. Alvar Núñez Cabeza de Vaca landed in Galveston in 1528 in search of cities of gold, eventually finding his way several years later to Mexico City, where he told stories of seven such cities that lay just north of where his expeditions took him. His tall tales—the first of many that would emanate from Texas—prompted fellow explorer Coronado to venture north through Texas all the way to Kansas. Of course, he never found those elusive cities of gold, the so-called Seven Cities of Cíbola, but his explorations did fortify Spain's land claims.

In 1598, Juan de Oñate formally claimed Texas for Spain, though the first permanent settlement and official mission, Corpus Christi de la Isleta (near El Paso), didn't come for another 84 years. Spain held Texas for 300 years, and its influence, perhaps filtered through its Latin American colonies, is strongly felt; in reality, however, Spain did little more than raise a few missions and settlements along the coast.

UNDER THE FRENCH FLAG

The French claimed Texas based on a visit from Rene-Robert Cavelier, Sieur de la Salle, who sailed the Mississippi River down to the Gulf of Mexico in 1682. Back in France, La Salle received a royal commission to establish a French empire in the southwestern territories of North America. When he returned in 1685, the Frenchman miscalculated and landed 400 miles west of the mouth of the Mississippi, on the Texas coast near Matagorda Bay. Undaunted, he established Fort San Louis and raised the French flag. The French settlement lasted only a few years, victim of both disease and Indian attack (which felled the fort), and La Salle himself was killed by his own men.

Spaniards quickly responded to the French settlements in Texas and Louisiana, establishing their own new mission, San Francisco de los Tejas, in East Texas in 1690. Three decades later, the Mission of San Antonio de Valero—the Alamo—led to the founding of the city of San Antonio (which became the seat of Spanish government in Texas in 1772). Spain established missions across Texas, but its colonization of the territory proceeded slowly.

MEXICO'S TURN

Mexico won independence from Spain in 1821 and turned its sights to the immense territory north. The Mexican government granted authorization to Stephen F. Austin, who would become known as the "Father of Texas," to settle in southeast Texas with a colony of 300 families (the "Texas Original 300"). The Austin settlers weren't the first Anglo-Americans in

Dateline

- **10,000 B.C.–A.D. 1500** Prehistoric and Native American tribes occupy the territory between the Rio Grande in the south and the Red River in the north.
- **1519** A Spanish explorer, Alonso Alvarez de Piñeda, explores and maps the Texas coastline.
- **1528** Cabeza de Vaca shipwrecks on Galveston Island

and spends the next few years exploring Texas.
- **1682** Spanish missionaries establish the first two missions in present-day Texas, near El Paso.
- **1685** The Frenchman LaSalle establishes Fort St. Louis on the coast and lays claim to Texas for France.
- **1716–89** Spain establishes Catholic missions in Texas and the new towns San Antonio, Goliad, and Nacogdoches.

- **1821** Stephen F. Austin receives a grant from the Mexican government to begin colonization in Texas, and many thousands of Americans settle over the next 2 decades.
- **1835** Texans turn back Mexican troops at the Battle of Gonzales, instituting the Texas Revolution.
- **1836** The Texas Declaration of Independence is signed and an interim government

Texas, but the new colony, made up mostly of Tennesseans, marked the official beginning of Anglo-American colonization. Just 15 years later, nearly 50,000 people had settled in Texas.

American settlers had to accept Mexican citizenship and Roman Catholicism to remain in Texas. Mexico had a republican form of government, but states' rights, including those of Texas, were not defined, and the Mexican government did little to protect its colony. As more Americans settled there, Texas took on the shape of a U.S. outpost, despite the Mexican flag flying over it. Stephen Austin organized a militia, which would become the famous Texas Rangers, to protect the colony. Tensions grew, and Mexico denied the entry of additional American settlers in 1830. Other religious, political, and cultural clashes between Texans and the Mexican government ensued, and the self-proclaimed president of Mexico, Gen. António López de Santa Anna, bolstered his troops in Texas. Texans then requested the status of independent Mexican state. When their diplomatic initiative failed, Texans declared independence from Mexico on March 2, 1836.

War was imminent. Texas forces attacked San Antonio. In response, Santa Anna and his troops vastly outnumbered and then ruthlessly crushed the valiant

Texans, led by Davy Crockett and Jim Bowie, at the Alamo in a 2-week battle in March 1836. Mexican troops slaughtered more than 300 Texas prisoners at Goliad only days later, unwittingly giving rise to the battle cry of independence: "Remember the Alamo! Remember Goliad!" (though only the first defeat is now generally remembered). Six weeks later the Texans, led by Gen. Sam Houston's army, rebounded with a stunning and decisive victory over Santa Anna at the Battle of San Jacinto, winning their independence from Mexico on April 21, 1836.

THE REPUBLIC OF TEXAS & THE CONFEDERACY

The Lone Star flag flew triumphantly for nearly a decade, from 1836 to 1845, over the Republic of Texas, a nation that was officially recognized by the United States and Europe but not Mexico. Six different sites served as the Texas capital until the town of Austin finally won out in 1839. The government, based on the U.S. model, had a president, a senate, a house of representatives, and an army, navy, and militia. Yet the new republic faced some daunting problems, such as boundary disputes, debt, and concerns about Mexican attack. Unable to solve those by itself, the republic accepted U.S. annexation, and Texas became the 28th state in 1845, ceding some western lands (parts of modern-day

for the Republic of Texas is formed. A small Texan army is overwhelmed by the Mexican army during a 2-week siege at San Antonio's Battle of the Alamo. Nearly 400 Texans are executed by the Mexicans at the Goliad Massacre, under order of Santa Anna. Texans decisively defeat Mexican forces at the Battle of San Jacinto and win independence.

- **1845** U.S. president James Polk annexes Texas and signs

legislation making Texas the 28th state.
- **1846** The Mexican-American War erupts over boundary disputes, establishing Texas's southern boundary at the Rio Grande River.
- **1861** Texas secedes from the Federal Union and joins the Confederate States of America.
- **1870** The U.S. Congress readmits Texas into the Union.
- **1883** The University of Texas is inaugurated in Austin.

- **1888** The present state capitol in Austin, larger than the U.S. Capitol, is dedicated.
- **1925** Texas becomes the second state to elect a woman governor, Miriam Ferguson.
- **1963** President John F. Kennedy is assassinated in Dallas. Texan Lyndon B. Johnson is sworn in as president.
- **1964** The Space Center in Houston (now named for

continues

Oklahoma, New Mexico, and Colorado) to the Union. Mexico terminated diplomatic relations with the United States; the Mexican War ended with Mexico's surrender to the United States in 1848 and the Treaty of Guadalupe Hidalgo, which rejected Mexican claims on Texas and the Southwest.

But there was more tumult to come. Texas joined the Confederate States of America, seceding from the United States in January 1861. Texas sided with the Confederacy during the Civil War, though support was not unanimous among leaders. Gov. Sam Houston chose to resign rather than back the Confederate states. About 90,000 Texans saw military service, and the Texas economy was left in shambles. After the end of the Civil War, Texas—after ratifying the 13th, 14th, and 15th amendments—officially rejoined the Union in March 1870.

THE WILD WEST TO TODAY

Texas was still the Wild West and most of its settlers lived the frontier life. The dismal economy after the war and abundant longhorn cattle in southern Texas led to the great Texas trail drives to northern markets in the 1860s. The drives north from Texas to Kansas City, such as the famous Chisholm Trail, brought prosperity to ranchers and particularly the city of Fort Worth, the site of cattle auctions and

shipping companies, which grew as the railroads reached Texas at the end of the 19th century. The free-for-all, boomtown aspect of life in Texas became a natural haven to all sorts of opportunists and outlaws, among them Wild Bill Hickok, John Wesley Hardin, and Billy the Kid (and later, Bonnie Parker and Clyde Barrow).

In 1901, the Texas oil and gas boom exploded with the discovery of the Spindletop oil field near Beaumont, transforming the agricultural economy and bringing riches to many other Texans. The discovery of "black gold" produced a spate of new Texas boomtowns, with an influx of workers—known as wildcatters and mavericks—hoping that a little hard work in the oil fields would translate into rapid wealth.

Texas celebrated its centennial in 1936 with the Texas Centennial Exposition in Dallas at Fair Park. But the next real watershed event in Texas was a tragic one. On November 22, 1963, President John F. Kennedy was assassinated as his motorcade passed through downtown Dallas. Kennedy's vice president, Texas's own Lyndon B. Johnson, was sworn in as the 36th president aboard the presidential plane at Dallas's Love Field airport.

The urban areas of Texas have continued to grow, with Houston, San Antonio, and Dallas among the 10 largest cities in the United States. These cities

---

Lyndon B. Johnson) becomes permanent home to NASA.

- **1966** A gunman atop the tower at the University of Texas at Austin opens fire on students and faculty below, killing 17 before being killed by police.
- **1970s** Unprecedented population growth as Sunbelt seekers flood the state; oil industry is catalyst behind booming economy.

- **1980s** Bust hits the oil and gas industry; real estate prices plummet.
- **1993** A Waco cult, the Branch Davidians, enters into a 2-month standoff with federal officials from the Bureau of Alcohol, Tobacco, and Firearms.
- **1994** Texas becomes the second-most-populous state in the nation.

- **2000** After a prolonged and disputed election, Texas Governor George W. Bush is ushered into the presidency of the United States by the U.S. Supreme Court.
- **2001** Houston-based energy giant Enron—formerly the world's largest energy trading company—files for bankruptcy.
- **2002** Enron's demise erupts into a scandal of improper

and fast-growing, formerly suburban communities have successfully attracted firms that have relocated their headquarters from around the country. Texas has recently become a leader in the technology industry, and the capital, Austin, has been transformed from a government and university town to one of the nation's most important clusters of high-tech corporations and computer-chip makers.

2 Talk Like a Texan

It may be true that Texans talk differently, but it's tough to pin down a true Texas accent—a reality evident in virtually any Hollywood picture about the place. Most Texans don't speak with the southern drawl of the Deep South. It's more of a Western twang. And because Texas is such a big place, influenced by the language of adventurers heading west and newly arrived immigrants (Yankees from the north, Mexicans from south of the border), Texans have adopted a rich vocabulary and colorful manner of speaking.

It's not just how they say it, but what they say that makes Texans stand out. Their folksy language and homespun hyperbole seems to come effortlessly. Longtime CBS news anchor Dan Rather, a native of Wharton, Texas, was both ridiculed and celebrated for his colorful language; one election night he described a candidate who "tore through Dixie like a big wheel through a cotton field." Evocative phrases, such as "that dawg don't hunt," also spilled effortlessly from the sharp tongue of late former Texas governor

Ann Richards, who famously chided George Bush, Sr., for having been born "with a silver foot in his mouth." Another tried-and-true method of talkin' Texan is to sprinkle in Spanish words and Anglicize the Spanish names of towns and streets. Even non-Hispanic Texans liberally toss around phrases like "Hola," "Qué pasa?" and "Adiós, amigo" in their everyday patter. Keep an ear out for things like "Guada-loop" (for Guadalupe) and "Man-shack" (for Manchaca).

Here's some help to getting on linguistically in the Lone Star State.

GLOSS'RY

All the fixin's Accompaniments—beans, mashed potatoes, gravy, and the like—to go with your chicken-fried steak. The plate should groan under their weight.

Awl Texas's largest industry. As in, awl 'n' gas.

Big ol' Large; esteemed.

Buffalo chip What cowboys kick around out in the fields—cow dung.

accounting practices and fake "shell companies," prompting Justice Department inquiries, arrests, and the suicide of at least one former executive.

- **2004** Former Texas governor George W. Bush wins the election for a second term as president of the United States.
- **2005** People displaced by Hurricane Katrina in New

Orleans and along the Gulf Coast inundate Texas, finding temporary and permanent refuge in Houston, Dallas, and other cities. Texan cyclist and cancer survivor Lance Armstrong (born in Plano) wins a record seventh consecutive Tour de France, the world's most difficult cycling competition. Antiwar protester Cindy Sheehan, whose soldier son died in Iraq, holds

vigil outside President Bush's Crawford ranch.
- **2006** Former Texas Governor Ann Richards, as colorful and emblematic a Texan as LBJ, dies of cancer.

Coke Generic term for soft drink. Dr. Pepper, Pepsi, RC Cola—they're all just "Coke" to Texans.

Dadgummit and **dadburnit** Common expletives.

Fixin' to A general state of preparedness or intent to carry out an act. ("I'm fixin' to eat that chicken-fried steak of yours.")

Gimme cap Freebie baseball caps, with logos of awl 'n' gas and other companies on the bill; redneck uniform to be worn as an alternative to cowboy hat. The name is derived from the frequent request, "Gimme one them thar caps."

Give a holler A plea to call, write, or e-mail.

Good ol' boy A true Texan.

Gussied up The look necessary for going out in public: dolled up 'n' pretty.

Hook 'em The cry and hand signal (index finger and pinkie raised like horns) of UT graduates everywhere—as in, "Hook 'em, horns."

Howdy, y'all The one-size-fits-all greeting—singular, plural, who cares? Y'all is a contraction of "you all," but is actually just Texan for "you." Howdy is pronounced "high-dee."

I reckon The act of thinking out loud.

Kicker Cowboy who puts his pointy-toed boots to good use.

Over yonder Where you'll likely be when you give a holler.

Yankee A northerner; outsider; opponent of Texas statehood.

Yes, ma'am The polite way to respond to any woman over 20.

Yessir and **nossir** The polite way to respond to a Texan man.

3 Texan Style

Some Yankees and coastal snob-types might be inclined to think that "Texan style" is an oxymoron. And it's true, Texans are probably better known as world-class shoppers than arbiters of taste. But style? Texans have plenty of their own.

Beyond oil, championship sports teams, and roots music, Texas's greatest export is the classic Western cowboy style that the state seems to embody for people around the world. Everybody from Ralph Lauren to Madonna seems to have adopted cowboy duds as the very symbol of American cool and rugged independence. Outsiders may not pull it off with as much natural ease as Texans, but the basics of cowboy style aren't hard to master.

There's the fundamental **ranch-hand style,** which depends on clothes tough enough to withstand the demands of life on the range: long, snug-fitting boot-cut jeans (preferably Wrangler or Lee) that bunch up at the bottom, worn with a belt featuring a big ol' buckle, scuffed-up

calfskin cowboy boots, crisp Western shirt, and a cowboy hat (straw in summer, felt in winter). Taking the basic elements, you can gussy up the look as much as you wish. The **drugstore cowboy** or **rodeo queen** look adopts fun and fancy embellishments such as embroidered yokes and sterling silver collar tips. **Urban cowboys** in oil and banking simply throw more money at the basics, and don boots and hats with their pinstripes for business (and ranch-style gabardine twill pants in place of jeans on the weekends). The boots aren't made of regular old calfskin leather, but of such exotic skin as alligator, ostrich, or eel, preferably handmade and with elaborate uppers. The hat will be a top-of-the line number from a classic Western outfitter such as M. L. Leddy's in Fort Worth. The belt buckle (along with the tip and keeper) is sterling silver.

For a certain kind of woman in Texas—the kind that will only wear a

> **Fun Fact** **Texas Types**
>
> **The Wildcatter:** An independent oilman, a gambler at heart whose fortunes rise and fall with the oil and gas industry.
>
> **The Roughneck:** Laborer who operates the oil rigs. Often itinerant or immigrant—down and dirty and flush with cash. A Texas sailor.
>
> **The Maverick:** Originally denoted an unbranded calf, but came to be understood as a Texas archetype: the nonconformist, independent-thinking man (or woman!).

Western shirt if it is expensively studded with rhinestones and rubies—the classic look has long been the one created by upscale Dallas and Houston shopping mavens: big salon-coifed and frosted hair, a wide pearly smile, and an overly precious designer outfit, accented by a cornucopia of fur and jewelry. The Robert Altman film *Dr. T & the Women* got the Dallas upper-class look of professional shoppers down to a T.

BOOTS Cowboy boots date from the riding boots the Spanish conquistadors and *vaqueros* wore. They're the most fundamental element of the cowboy look, and almost everyone in Texas owns at least one pair. President Bush delights in showing his off to reporters. Real cowboys have everyday boots and dress-up or dance-floor boots. The basics are plain old black or brown calfskin boots, with either a roper (low heel) or a riding or semiwalking (high heel) style. The toes can be pointed, squared off, or gently rounded. The sharp pointed toe is the most authentic, though today many younger ropers go with the rounded style. The tops, which are generally calf-high, can be either V-shaped or straight, but should always have stitched-on pull straps. Boot stores stock a bewildering array of leathers: Besides basic (but smooth, rugged, and inexpensive) calfskin, you'll find showy and more delicate (and often vastly more expensive) exotic skins, such as lizard, eel, alligator,

ostrich, snake, stingray, water buffalo, and kangaroo. Generally the most expensive boots a shop will stock are horned-toe crocodile; a pair of those babies will set you back a couple of grand. Boot design can be no-nonsense or elaborately styled, with contrasting uppers, fancy stitching, and piping.

Even more important than look, though, is fit: A boot has to fit properly. It should be snug, requiring you to pull on with both straps and yank off with a touch of difficulty, but not tight. Your heel should snap into place but allow for a little movement. A good boot seller can help you determine the right fit. Don't buy unless you're sure. Texas brands to look for include Lucchese, Nocona, Justin, and Tony Lama.

HATS Cowboy hats are serious business. They're worn at all times and not taken off indoors; if you don't think so, check out a Western dance hall on a Friday night, where you'll find cowboys twirling about the dance floor with their best hats firmly in place. The classic Stetson, like the one LBJ wore on the ranch, dates from the 1850s. A cowboy's proper "beaver" dress hat can run $1,000 or more. The key to your new hat is getting it formed, or creased, for that perfect range or courthouse look. A real-life roper retires his white straw hat at the end of summer, opting for a sturdy felt sombrero for autumn and winter—a seasonal fashion dictum not unlike the one that demands that New Englanders banish white from their wardrobes after Labor Day.

WESTERN SHIRTS Most traditional and urban cowboys go for heavy, pressed-cotton Western shirts in plaids or solids. Fancy Western swing shirts with pearl snaps, contrasting yokes, and little "smile" or "arrow" pockets aren't that easy to find these days. If you want a singing cowboy or fancy honky-tonk shirt, you'll either need to go vintage or shell out big bucks for a high-end designer, such as Manuel of Hollywood (who dresses Dolly Parton and other flashy country-music stars). At its most basic, though, the Western shirt should have a reinforced Western yoke,

flap pockets, a full cut, and snapped cuffs. The shirttail is always worn tucked in.

ACCESSORIES The most important Western accessories are belt buckles, belts, hatbands, bolo ties, and bandannas. For the Texan man, hand-tooled belts (often with the wearer's name embossed), hatbands, and especially buckles—which range from obscenely large Texas state seals, oil derricks, and Jack Daniels emblems to simple, elegant silver buckles, tips, and keepers—allow him to express himself. A real Texan never buys a leather belt that comes stock with a buckle. Bolo ties, though still worn in some parts, are a little passé for the average Joe trying to adopt the cowboy look.

4 Texan Music

Neither country and western nor the blues originated in Texas, but both genres of roots music have been indelibly shaped by talented Texans. The state ranks alongside Tennessee or Louisiana for contributions to the Americana music scene, and the number of individual music greats that Texas has spawned is astonishing. They've come from such big cities as Houston, Austin, and Dallas, of course, but most remarkable is how many have rolled out of Lubbock. The barren lands of West Texas have proved incredibly fertile for the creation of homespun music. Texas has spawned so many musicians that a museum honoring their contributions to pop culture is in the works, most likely to be housed in Houston.

Most listeners think of country music when they think of Texas sounds, and the state was certainly instrumental in the form's early development, a product of cowboy songs and folk contributions from new immigrants. **Bob Wills and the Texas Playboys,** who emerged from Lubbock in the 1920s, introduced Western swing (or Texas swing), a combustible mix of hillbilly tunes, fiddle music, jazz, polka, cowboy ballads, and Mexican

ranchero music. Such Texas artists as **George Jones** in the 1950s popularized honky-tonk, characterized by steel guitars, fiddles, and plaintive vocals. Jones, one of country's finest voices, later became a balladeer and top-10 hit maker. Like **Kenny Rogers** of Conroe, Texas, he was more closely identified with Nashville than with Texas.

With characteristic independence, Texas musicians developed their own kind of country. Progressive and outlaw country fused hard-core honky-tonk, folk, rock, and blues. With country music reaching a national audience in the 1970s with the blandly orchestrated Nashville sound, a gang of Texas outlaws, led by **Willie Nelson, Waylon Jennings, Jerry Jeff Walker** (not a native Texan but closely identified with the scene), and **Kris Kristofferson** seized the stage with a gritty, maverick rejection of the slicker country being produced in Nashville. Waylon and Willie's "Luckenbach, Texas," a song about a town with two dozen people, became a state anthem. Nelson, the braided, bandanna-wearing iconoclast of Texas country, has evolved into one of Texas's most beloved contemporary figures. He began his career as a songwriter of hits for Patsy Cline ("Crazy") and others before positioning himself as a cult artist and finally a crossover country star, daring to dabble in all genres, from traditional country and ballads ("Blue Eyes Cryin' in the Rain") to potent country poetry and even reggae. Nelson is currently as into alternative fuels (marketing a biodiesel fuel called "BioWille," which is available in eight states, including 16 locations in Texas) as he is in exploring new musical genres.

Other Texas singer-songwriters, such as **Guy Clark** and **Townes Van Zandt,** less prone to the outlaw lifestyle but still resolutely independent, mined a territory of lyrical country-folk music. These unjustly overlooked artists laid the foundation for the current generation of Texas songwriters, including **Lyle Lovett, Jimmie Dale Gilmore,** and **Steve Earle,** musicians as at home in country as they are in rock, gospel, and the blues. Western swing has undergone a couple of rounds of revival, in the 1970s and again in the early 1990s. **Asleep at the Wheel,** a multipiece band that has gone through innumerable lineup changes, has been present for both. Current stars among Texas singer-songwriters with a touch of twang include **Nanci Griffith, Michelle Shocked,** and **Kelly Willis.** Expanding the horizons of Texas music are Dallas-area rockabilly bar-burners **Reverend Horton Heat** and Texas polka aficionados **Brave Combo,** originally from Denton.

Texas blues began with such legendary figures as **Blind Lemon Jefferson** (whose "Black Snake Moan" struck quite a chord in the 1920s) and **Blind Willie Johnson,** both of whom played the area around Deep Ellum in Dallas. **Robert Johnson** may have been from Mississippi, but he made his only known recordings in Dallas and San Antonio in the 1930s. **Sam "Lightning" Hawkins,** of Houston, created a blistering blues guitar style that influenced generations of rockers. Other notable Houston blues musicians include **B. B. King, Albert Collins,** and **Clarence "Gatemouth" Brown.**

Port Arthur's **Janis Joplin**'s raw vocals and blues-inflected rock (not to mention her heroin overdose and posthumous hit, "Me and Bobby McGee") made her an icon of the 1960s. **Stevie Ray Vaughan,** an incendiary guitar wizard from south Dallas, also became a blues-rock star before his light went out prematurely in a helicopter crash in 1990. Austin club regulars **Angela Strehli, Lou Ann Barton,** and **Toni Price** continue the Texas blues tradition.

Texas has produced its share of rock-'n'-roll pioneers, too. Lubbock's **Buddy Holly,** the bespectacled proto-rocker who with his band, the Crickets, influenced Elvis, the Beatles, and countless new-wavers with tunes like "Peggy Sue" and "That'll Be the Day," went down in a 1959 plane crash after just a couple of years at the top. **Roy Orbison,** from Vernon, Texas, began his career in rockabilly, but his high, haunting voice propelled a number of memorable mainstream hits in the 1960s, like "Only the Lonely" and "In Dreams." **ZZ Top,** from Houston, started out in swaggering blues-rock territory, singing about "Tush" and "LaGrange" before their belly-length beards and songs like "Legs" and "Tube Steak Boogie" made them MTV darlings. Current Texas faves on the alternative scene include the intellectual pop of **Spoon** (from Austin); the dusty, Neil Young–like **Centro-Matic** (Denton); the trippy instrumentalists **Explosions in the Sky** (Midland); and the costumed, unwieldy collective **The Polyphonic Spree** (Dallas).

With its Latino roots and large Hispanic population, Texas has given rise to yet another genre that reflects cross-cultural fertilization, Tex-Mex border sounds. Conjunto, *norteña,* and Tejano are all slightly different takes on this definitive Tex-Mex style, anchored by the accordion and 12-string Mexican guitar. The megastar **Selena** (Corpus Christie) brought Tejano to national Latino audiences before her death (she was murdered by the founder of her fan club), and reached a wider audience through films and books about her life. **Flaco Jiménez** is the leading conjunto proponent today. Another cross-cultural musical phenomenon in Texas is zydeco, a Creole stew that combines Afro-Caribbean, blues, and Cajun rhythms, and is especially popular in the Houston and Galveston areas (as well as Louisiana). **Los Lonely Boys,** three Mexican-American brothers from San Angelo, had a huge hit in 2004 with "Heaven" and their radio-friendly brand of Latino-tinged blues pop, which some have labeled "Texican."

In large part, Texas has proved such fecund musical ground because of its strong tradition of live performance. For a couple of decades now, Austin has immodestly declared itself the "Live Music Capital of the World," and its rollicking clubs have presented nightly diverse lineups of homegrown and imported live music acts. From Armadillo World Headquarters to Club Foot and Liberty Lunch, Austin has embraced a disproportionate share of legendary, beloved, and now-defunct live music venues. **Gilley's** and **Billy Bob's,** two huge, slick honky-tonks still going strong in Houston and Fort Worth, are important national showcases for traditional country and redneck rock bands, while classic small-town Texas dance halls such as **Gruene Hall** (in Gruene, pronounced "green," located south of Austin, smack in the middle of New Braunfels) keep the flame burning. Dancing to country music is a true Texas art, and while the popularity of individual dances—the Two-Step, Cotton-Eyed Joe, and line dancing (a kind of kickers' aerobics)—rises and falls with the latest hits, in Texas they have amazing staying power. The dance floors of local honky-tonks pack in young Billy Ray Cyrus look-alikes and single rodeo queens in tight jeans as well as nimble older folks boot-scootin' like there's no tomorrow.

5 Texan Cuisine

Texans are famous for their love of artery-clogging steaks the size of Volkswagens. Amarillo's Big Texan Steak Ranch restaurant features a 72-ouncer (eat it in under an hour and get it for free). Locals are rabidly fond of **chicken-fried steak.** This oddity is a thick slab of inexpensive beef beaten until tender and dipped in batter, deep-fried like chicken, buried under a puddle of cream gravy, doused with pepper, and served with a glob of mashed potatoes (skins on). Other home-style veggies such as okra and black-eyed peas are also worthy accompaniments. A good chicken-fried steak—crisp, light, and tender—is weirdly enjoyable, but an inferior one can be like gnawing on an old tire. Note to Yankees who don't want to get laughed out of town: Don't specify "medium" or "medium rare" when ordering a chicken-fried steak. It comes only one way: cooked.

But steak—whether broiled or chicken-fried—is only part of the story. The real holy trinity of Texas eats consists of three down-home staples no true Texan can do without for long: chili, barbecue, and Tex-Mex.

CHILI   A bowl of Texas red, hot, or hotter than hell is often thought of as Mexican or Tex-Mex. But it's as Texan as they come, with its origins in San Antonio in the late 1800s. Chili (not chile, which is Spanish for pepper) should be thick, meaty, and spicy, and served unadorned. Real Texas chili is made with beef (or occasionally rabbit or venison) but not beans. This standard has been relaxed, though, and plenty of Texans like pinto beans (never kidney beans) in their chili. There are annual chili cook-offs across the state; the most famous is held in the border town of Terlingua. Degrees of fire are usually designated as one-, two-, or three-alarm or indicated by an X, XX, or XXX. Four Xs means that bowl of devil's soup is guaranteed to scorch your tongue, lips, and entire digestive tract.

Weird food item: **Frito pie,** which is meaty chili, cheese, and diced onions poured over a plate of (or into a bag of) Frito's corn chips. Frito pie is a staple in Texas school cafeterias (or at least it was when I was growing up).

BARBECUE (BBQ) Vying with chili and chicken-fried steak for the honor of state dish is barbecue (even though Texans didn't invent it; the word comes from the Spanish, *barbacoa,* and the style originated in Spain and evolved in the Caribbean and Latin America). Still, the art of roasting meats over an open fire distinguishes Texans from, say, lesser humans. Texans slow cook (smoke) beef brisket and ribs (and to a lesser extent, pork, chicken, turkey, sausage, and *cabrito,* young goat) in pits over mesquite or hickory wood. The slow roasting and wood give it its unique, revered flavor. Texas barbecue, unlike its worthy regional competitors in such places as Memphis and the Carolinas, is almost wholly focused on beef, and it tends to be tangier and spicier than the sweeter pork popular in those places. A plate of brisket or ribs is served with heaps of tangy barbecue sauce (which is often also employed as a basting sauce), and side dishes such as potato salad, pinto beans, and coleslaw. A proper Texas barbecue will either be a down-and-dirty, ramshackle joint such as Sonny Bryan's in Dallas and Angelo's in Fort Worth, or a rustic place in the country with long picnic tables and a huge barbecue pit in full view, such as the Salt Lick in Driftwood, outside of Austin.

TEX-MEX Neither identifiably Mexican nor strictly Texan, Tex-Mex is, as the name indicates, a hybrid menu of simple dishes. A Texan gets homesick for authentic Tex-Mex cooking just as fast as she does for barbecue or chili. No Texan has ever had good Tex-Mex except in Texas; both barbecue and chili seem a bit easier to reproduce over state lines. Not spicy or intricate like authentic Mexican food, Tex-Mex is greasy, filling, tasty, and cheap, a step above addictive junk food. There is little distinction between dishes and ingredients. Almost all involve corn or flour tortillas, lots of white and yellow cheese, chili, hot sauce, and rice and refried beans—meaning that a good plate of Tex-Mex will lack for color. It will be essentially a uniformly muddy yellow-brown hue. Tex-Mex dishes can be spiced up with Tabasco sauce or scorcher jalapeño peppers, which young Texans learn to gobble up like pickles.

All Tex-Mex meals begin with tortilla chips and salsa (hot sauce) and guacamole for dipping. Enchiladas, chiles rellenos, *tacos al carbón,* and burritos have long been the standard-bearers for Tex-Mex, but in the past couple of decades **fajitas,** grilled beef or skirt steak rolled in flour tortillas and dolled up with guacamole, pico de gallo, and cilantro, have become the most popular dish. Less than authentic, but wildly popular, is the substitution of strips of barbecued chicken breast for beef.

BEVERAGES Texans wash down chili and barbecue with plastic glasses of **ice tea** (it's the rare Texan who says *iced* tea) the size of small oil drums and **Texas beer,** preferably longnecks of Lone Star, Pearl, and Shiner Bock, drunk straight from the bottle. Beverage choices shift slightly in Tex-Mex restaurants. While pitchers of ice tea are fine, the beer should be ice-cold *cerveza,* Mexican beer such as Corona, Tecate, Dos Equis, or Bohemia, usually served with a wedge of lime squeezed into the bottle or can. And the number-one libation for washing down a plate of Tex-Mex is the **margarita,** a tart concoction of tequila, lime juice, and triple sec, either served on the rocks or frozen. Most margaritas use cheap well tequila, but connoisseurs opt for "top-shelf" margaritas (served on the rocks), made with 100% blue agave tequilas. And the connoisseurs of connoisseurs drink aged tequilas—called *reposado* or *añejo*—straight, followed by a "tequila chaser," like the one served at Javier's restaurant in Dallas: a shot glass of orange juice, lemon juice, V8, pepper, salt, and Tabasco.

Texas also has a surprisingly robust roster of **wineries,** many in the Central Texas Hill Country around Fredericksburg and the High Plains near Lubbock. Llano Estacado and Pheasant Ridge are national award winners.

6 Larger Than Life: Famous Texans

You may already know that outsize personalities such as outlaws Bonnie Parker and Clyde Barrow, rock stars Buddy Holly and Janis Joplin, former president Lyndon B. Johnson, presidential hopeful H. Ross Perot, and model Jerry Hall hail from Texas. Below is a quick list of other famous folk with Texan roots—some of them might surprise you.

Lance Armstrong (Plano). Heroic cycling champion—record-holding all-time champion of the Tour de France—and inspirational survivor of testicular cancer. Wears a Texas Lone Star on his helmet and one of those ubiquitous "LiveStrong" yellow bracelets on his wrist. He lives in Austin.

Gene Autry (Tioga). A singin' cowboy and A-list film star who made it big with "The Yellow Rose of Texas" in the 1930s.

George W. Bush (Midland). He wasn't born on the prairies of Texas (rather, in blue-state Connecticut), but the former governor clings hard to his Texas heritage, with a ranch in Crawford, outside Waco. He grew up in the midst of the oil business, tried his hand at that, failed, and then went on to purchase the Texas Rangers baseball team before becoming governor of Texas and then president of the United States. His core of closest advisors, like Karl Rove and Karen Hughes, are Texans.

Joan Crawford (San Antonio). Hollywood's Mommie Dearest, from deep in the heart of Texas.

Michael Dell (Austin). This Houston-born whiz-kid and billionaire (he's the ninth-richest American) started Dell Computer Corporation, which today is one of the largest tech companies in the world, in his dorm room at UT in Austin. Though he dropped out of UT, Dell later gave the university $50 million.

Morgan Fairchild (Dallas). Big D principles—big hair and big boobs—come to cartoonish life.

Farrah Fawcett (Corpus Christi). 1970s bathing suit pinup, Charlie's hottest angel—the woman who created the wings hairstyle—and UT grad recently gone ditzy.

Phyllis George (Denton). Former Miss America, former morning show host, and former wife of the Kentucky governor.

Howard Hughes (Houston). Eccentric billionaire industrialist as famous for his reclusive and weirdo tendencies as his moneymaking prowess, which included planes, movies, and tools.

Terrence Malick (Austin). Inscrutable film director who's made four films in 3 decades—but what gems, including *Badlands, Days of Heaven,* and *The Thin Red Line.*

Steve Martin (Waco). Wild and crazy comedian turned occasionally serious author *(Shopgirl)* and art collector.

Larry McMurtry (Wichita Falls). Pulitzer prize–winning author of *Lonesome Dove,* a tale of the cattle drives of the late 1880s, and other novels made into Texas-based movies, including *The Last Picture Show* and *Terms of Endearment.*

Meat Loaf (Houston). Monster of a man with a big voice who recorded "Bat Out of Hell." He later slimmed down, cut his stringy locks, and translated his music video experience into an acting career (in *The Rocky Picture Horror Show* and B-grade action films).

Bill Moyers (Marshall). From student of religion to LBJ press secretary to soft-spoken PBS journalist investigating weighty matters like philosophy, iron men, and dying.

Madalyn Murray O'Hair (Austin). Strident atheist who roared tirelessly to separate church from all things state.

Roy Orbison (Wink). The man with the growl in his classic '60s song "Pretty Woman." Dark specs, amazing angelic voice, and even more amazing hair.

Dan Rather (Wharton). Serious newsman who made anchorman, with a penchant for odd signature sign-offs, down-home aphorisms, and bizarre episodes in his personal life. ("What's the frequency, Kenneth?")

Ginger Rogers (Fort Worth). Fred's favorite dance partner hailed from Cowtown; I bet she did a mean two-step. Née Virginia McMath.

Jaclyn Smith (Houston). Another Charlie's Angel and Kmart spokesperson.

Liz Smith (Fort Worth). Gossip queen and columnist.

Sissy Spacek (Quitman). Sometimes brilliant actress who went from *Badlands* to a *Coal Miner's Daughter* to *Missing.*

Lee Trevino (Dallas). Pro golfer—and serious rival of Nicklaus and Palmer—whose folksy language and links style made Tex-Mex cool in the mid-'70s.

Van Cliburn (Kilgore). Accomplished pianist (winner of Tchaikovsky competition in 1958) and namesake of international piano competition held annually in Fort Worth's Bass Performance Hall.

Index

AAA (American Automobile Association), 44–45, 49, 56, 342
Aardvark (Fort Worth), 150
AARP, 39–40
Above and Beyond Tours, 39
Access-Able Travel Source, 39
Access America, 36
Accessible Journeys, 39
Accommodations, 51–54
    best, 8–12
    surfing for, 42
Adair Margo Gallery (El Paso), 350
Adair's Saloon (Dallas), 18, 116
Adrian, 427
African American Museum (Dallas), 105
Ahab Bowen (Dallas), 113
AIDSinfo, 29
Airport security, 45
Air travel, 44, 49
Alamodome (San Antonio), 285
The Alamo (San Antonio), 20, 273–274
Alamo Fiesta (San Antonio), 282
Alamo Quarry Market (San Antonio), 282
Alamo Village (Ciudad Acuña, Mexico), 378
Alan Henry, Lake, 434
Alibates Flint Quarries National Monument, 418–419
Allen's Boots (Austin), 328
Alley Theatre (Houston), 196, 197
All In One Tour Services (Dallas), 108
Alpine, 5, 364–366
Alvino House (Big Bend National Park), 390
Amarillo, 5–6, 412–424, 427
    accommodations, 421–422
    getting around, 414
    nightlife, 423–424
    orientation, 414
    outdoor activities, 418–420
    restaurants, 422–423
    shopping, 420

    sights and attractions, 416–418
    spectator sports, 420
    traveling to, 414
    visitor information, 414
Amarillo Botanical Gardens, 416
Amarillo 'Dillas, 6, 420
Amarillo Gorillas, 420
Amarillo Little Theatre, 423
Amarillo Museum of Art, 417
Amarillo Opera, 423
Amarillo Symphony, 424
Amarillo Zoo, 417
American Airlines Vacations, 45
American Airpower Heritage Museum (Midland), 368
American Automobile Association (AAA), 44–45, 49, 56, 342
American Express, 56
    Austin, 297
    Dallas, 80
    El Paso, 343
    Houston, 162
    San Antonio, 252
    traveler's checks, 31
American Foundation for the Blind (AFB), 39
American Indians, 338
    Amistad National Recreation Area, 382–383
    history of, 439
    Kwahadi Kiva Indian Museum (Amarillo), 417
    petroglyphs, 373, 390
    pictographs, 276, 348, 374, 382–384, 390, 392
American Institute of Architects (AIA) Sandcastle Competition (Galveston), 33, 211
American Wind Power Center (Lubbock), 432
Amistad National Recreation Area, 381–383
Amon Carter Museum of Western Art (Fort Worth), 16, 140–141
Anderson Fair (Houston), 199
Angelika Film Center and Café (Houston), 198
Angelina National Forest, 203

Angelo Civic Theatre (San Angelo), 376–377
The Antique Colony (Fort Worth), 147
Antique Mall of Lubbock, 435
Antiques, Fort Worth, 147
Antone's (Austin), 4, 177, 331
Aquariums
    Dallas Aquarium at Fair, 105
    The Dallas World Aquarium, 107
    Downtown Aquarium (Houston), 184
    Moody Gardens (Galveston), 210
    Sea Center Texas (Brazosport), 215
    Texas State Aquarium (Corpus Christi), 220–221
Aransas National Wildlife Refuge (Rockport), 19, 225–227
Area codes, 56
Arkey Blue & The Silver Dollar Bar (Bandera), 18, 291
Arlington, 21, 118–119
Armstrong, Lance, 450
Arneson River Theatre (San Antonio), 284
Art Car Parade and Ball (Houston), 33
Artfunkles Vintage Boutique (Dallas), 113
Art galleries
    Alpine, 365
    Austin, 327
    Brazosport, 214
    El Paso, 349–350
    Marfa, 365
    San Angelo, 375
    San Antonio, 282
ArtPace (San Antonio), 282
Arturo's Sports Bar & Grill (San Antonio), 286
Ascarate Golf Course (El Paso), 348–349
Ascarate Lake City Park (El Paso), 346
Ashton Villa (Galveston), 210

Asian Cultures Museum
(Corpus Christi), 221
Atalanta (Jefferson), 204
AT&T Center (San Antonio), 285
AT&T Championship (San
Antonio), 281
AT&T Cotton Bowl Classic
(& Parade; Dallas), 32
ATMs (automated teller
machines), 30
Audubon Society, 47
Austin, 25, 292–337
accommodations, 298–309
arriving in, 292–293
getting around, 296–297
Hill Country side trips from,
332–337
layout of, 294
neighborhoods, 294–296
nightlife, 328–332
organized tours, 324
outdoor activities, 324–325
parking, 297
restaurants, 309–318
shopping, 326–328
sights and attractions, 318–324
spectator sports, 325–326
visitor information, 293–294
what's new in, 4
The Austin Chamber Music
Center, 330
Austin Children's Museum, 324
Austin Chronicle Hot Sauce
Festival, 34
Austin Circle of Theaters Hot
Line, 329
Austin Convention and Visitors
Bureau (ACVB), 324
Austin Ice Bats, 326
Austin Lyric Opera, 329–330
Austin Nature and Science
Center, 324
Austin Symphony, 329
Austin Wranglers, 326
Auto racing
Amarillo, 420
Dallas, 110
Fort Worth, 145
Autry, Gene, 450

Backyard (Austin), The, 331
Balcony Club (Dallas), 115
Ballet Austin, 330
Ballroom Marfa, 365
Balmorhea State Park, 22,
360–361
Bandera, 290
Bandera Park, 290
Bandera Saloon, 291

Barbecue (BBQ), 449
Barton Springs Pool
(Austin), 320
Baseball
Amarillo, 6, 420
Austin, 325
Corpus Christi, 221
Dallas, 110
El Paso, 349
Houston, 194
Midland-Odessa, 369
San Angelo, 374
Basin Road Scenic Drive, 388
Basketball
Austin, 326
Dallas, 110
El Paso, 349
Houston, 194
San Antonio, 281
Bass Performance Hall (Fort
Worth), 139, 148
Bats
Austin, 22, 319
Carlsbad Caverns National
Park, 410
Battleship *Texas* (Houston), 185
Bayfest! (Corpus Christi), 34
Bayou Bend (Houston), 191
Bayou Place (Houston), 198
Beachcombing
Padre Island National
Seashore, 235
Port Aransas, 231
Beach cruising, Port Aransas,
231
Beaches
Brazosport, 216
Galveston, 209
Matagorda Island, 218
Port Aransas, 231
South Padre Island, 241
Bean, Judge Roy, 380–381
Beaumont, 200
Belle Starr Carriages
(Lubbock), 108
Bermuda Triangle (San
Antonio), 288
Beverages, 449–450
Big Balls of Cowtown (Fort
Worth), 149
Big Bend Balloon Bash
(Alpine), 366
Big Bend National Park,
5, 15, 25, 385–398
accommodations, 395–396
camping, 397–398
exploring the highlights by
car, 389–390
fees, regulations, and permits,
386–387

historic sites, 390–391
outdoor adventures, 391–395
ranger programs and special
events, 388
restaurants, 396–397
safety, 388
seasons, 387–388
traveling to, 386
visitor information, 386
Big Bend River Tours, 394–395
Big Burger and Coca-Cola
Museum (Monahans), 371
Big Easy Social and Pleasure
Club (Houston), 199
Big Room Self-Guided Tour
(Carlsbad Caverns National
Park), 408
Big Thicket National Preserve,
19, 200
Biking and mountain biking
Amarillo, 420
Austin, 324–325
Big Bend National Park, 394
Dallas, 108–109
El Paso, 349
Fort Worth, 145
Houston, 193
Lubbock, 434
Palo Duro Canyon State
Park, 428
Port Aransas, 231
San Angelo area, 374
San Antonio, 280
Seminole Canyon State
Park, 384
Billy Bob's Texas (Dallas), 116
Billy Bob's Texas (Fort Worth),
18, 137, 149
Bird-watching, 47
Aransas National Wildlife
Refuge (Rockport), 225–227
Big Bend National Park, 391
Blucher Park, 223
Brazosport, 216
Carlsbad Caverns National
Park, 410
Corpus Christi, 222
Davis Mountains State
Park, 359
Goose Island State Park, 227
Guadalupe Mountains
National Park, 404
Gulf Coast, 215
Padre Island National
Seashore, 236
Quintana Beach, 216
San Angelo State Park, 373
South Padre Island, 240
whooping crane tours,
222, 226–228

Bishop's Palace (Galveston), 210
The Black Dog Tavern (Fort Worth), 150
Blanco's (Houston), 18, 199
Blanton Museum of Art (Austin), 4, 318
Bleachers Sports Café (Lubbock), 438
Blogs and travelogues, 42
Blu (El Paso), 354
Blucher Park, 223
The Blue Light (Lubbock), 438
Blue Star Arts Complex (San Antonio), 282
Blue Star Brewing Company (San Antonio), 287
Boating, 47. See also Canoeing; Kayaking
  Amarillo, 419
  Amistad National Recreation Area, 382
  Caddo Lake, 205
  Corpus Christi, 222
  Lubbock, 434
  Padre Island National Seashore, 236
  San Angelo, 374
Boat tours and cruises
  Austin, 324
  Caddo Lake, 205
  Galveston, 209
  San Antonio, 279–280
The Bob Bullock Texas State History Museum (Austin), 319
Bodega's (Amarillo), 424
Boerne, 288–290
Bohlin (Dallas), 113
Boingo, 43
The Bone (Dallas), 115
Bonham Exchange (San Antonio), 287
Books, recommended, 54–55
Boot Hill (San Antonio), 283
Boot Town (Dallas), 113
Boquillas Canyon Trail, 393
Botanical gardens
  Amarillo, 416
  The Dallas Arboretum & Botanical Garden, 19, 104
  Fort Worth Botanic & Japanese Gardens, 19, 141
  San Antonio, 278–279
  Zilker Botanical Garden (Austin), 323
Brackenridge golf course (San Antonio), 280
Brays Bayou (Houston), 193
Brazoria County Historical Museum (Brazosport), 214

Brazoria National Wildlife Refuge, 216
Brazosport, 213–218
Bremond Block (Austin), 321
Brighter Days Horse Refuge, 290
The Broken Spoke (Austin), 19, 330
Brooklyn (Dallas), 115
Buddies II (Dallas), 117
Buddy Holly Center (Lubbock), 430
Buddy Holly Statue (Lubbock), 432
Buffalo Bayou (Houston), 193
Buffalo Creek Golf Club (Dallas), 109
Buffalo Springs Lake, 434, 436
Bum Steer (Fort Worth), 147
Bush, George W., 450
  Childhood Home (Midland), 368
Business hours, 56
Butlers Martini Lounge (Amarillo), 424
Byron Nelson Classic (Dallas), 111
Byzantine Fresco Chapel Museum (Houston), 190–191

Cactus Café (Austin), 331
Cactus Jazz Series (San Angelo), 377
Cactus Theater (Lubbock), 437
Caddo Lake, 203–205
Caddo Lake State Park, 205
Caddo Lake Steamboat Co., 205
Cadillac Bar & Restaurant (San Antonio), 287
Cadillac Ranch (Amarillo), 416, 418
Café J (Lubbock), 438
Calendar of events, 32–35
Camping, 46–47
  Amarillo, 422
  Amistad National Recreation Area, 383
  Big Bend National Park, 397–398
  Carlsbad Caverns National Park, 411
  Corpus Christi, 223–224
  El Paso, 352
  Guadalupe Mountains National Park, 404
  Lubbock, 436

Padre Island National Seashore, 237
Palo Duro Canyon State Park, 428
Quintana Beach County Park, 217
San Angelo State Park, 373
South Padre Island, 243
Candelaria, 361
Canoeing
  Austin, 325
  Big Bend National Park, 394
  Big Thicket National Preserve, 200
  Caddo Lake, 205
Canyon, 6, 424–428
Canyon Springs golf course (San Antonio), 280
Capitol Saddlery (Austin), 18, 328
Capitol Visitors Center (Austin), 321, 328
Caprock Canyons State Park and Trailway, 434, 436
Cap*Rock Winery (near Lubbock), 433
Caravan of Dreams (Fort Worth), 150
Carlsbad Caverns National Park, 404–411
Car rentals, 49–50
  surfing for, 42
Car travel, 44–45, 49
Casa Mañana Theater (Fort Worth), 148
Casa Ramírez (Houston), 195
Cascade Caverns (near Boerne), 288
Casino, Port Aransas, 231
Castolon Historic District (Big Bend National Park), 390
Castroville, 289
Cattle Raisers Museum (Fort Worth), 141
Cavender's Boot City
  Amarillo, 420
  Dallas, 113
The Cavern (Dallas), 115
Caverns of Sonora, 377
Caves and caving
  Carlsbad Caverns National Park, 408–410
  Cascade Caverns (near Boerne), 288
  Caverns of Sonora, 377
  Seminole Canyon State Park, 383, 384
Cedar Creek golf course (San Antonio), 280

Cedar Door (Austin), 332
Cellphones, 44
The Center for the Arts & Sciences (Brazosport), 16, 214
Centers for Disease Control and Prevention, 37
Central Market (Austin), 327
Centre at Post Oak (Houston), 196
Chamizal National Memorial (El Paso), 344
Chicken-fried steak, 448
Chihuahua al Pacífico (Chihuahua to the Pacific) railway, 357
Children. See Families with children
Children's Museum of Houston, 187
Chili, 448–449
Chilicotal Mountain, 389
Chinati Foundation (Marfa), 362
Chinati Hot Springs, 361
Chinatown (Houston), 195
Chisos Basin Campground, 397–398
Chisos Basin Drive, 389
Chisos Basin Loop Trail, 392
Christmas in the Stockyards (Fort Worth), 35, 137
Cielo Vista Golf Course (El Paso), 349
Cielo Vista Mall (El Paso), 350
City Streets (Fort Worth), 148
Ciudad Acuña (Mexico), 378
Ciudad Juárez (Mexico), 343, 354–356
Civic League Park (San Angelo), 374
Civil War, 442
    Texas Civil War Museum (Fort Worth), 2
Cliburn, Van, 451
Climate, 31
Club de Ville (Austin), 332
Commemorative Air Force Annual AIRSHO (Midland), 34
Concepción mission (San Antonio), 276
Concho pearls, 373
Concho River Valley, 373
Concordia Cemetery (El Paso), 346
Conference Cafe (Lubbock), 438
Conjunto, 286
The Conspiracy Museum (Dallas), 100

Contemporary Arts Museum (Houston), 187–188
Continental Airlines Vacations, 45
Continental Club (Austin), 330
Cool Arrows (San Antonio), 286
Copper Canyon, 357
Corpus Christi, 218–224
Corpus Christi Hooks, 221
Corpus Christi Racetrack, 222
Cotton Belt Train Depot (Grapevine), 120
Cottonwood Campground, 398
Cowboy Cool (Dallas), 113
Cowboy Roundup USA (Amarillo), 420
Cowboys Golf Club (Dallas), 109
Cowboys Red River Dancehall (Dallas), 116
Cowtown Boots (El Paso), 350
Cowtown Cattlepen Maze (Fort Worth), 137
Cowtown Coliseum (Fort Worth), 137, 146
Cowtown Marathon (Fort Worth), 145
Crawdaddy's (El Paso), 354
Crawford, Joan, 450
Credit cards, 30–31
Creekwalk (Del Rio), 378
The Crew's Inn (Dallas), 117
Cricket's Grill and Draft House (Lubbock), 438
Cross-Eyed Moose (Fort Worth), 147
Cross of Our Lord Jesus Christ (Groom), 427
Cru (Dallas), 116–117
Cuisine, Texan, 448–450
Cultural District (Fort Worth), 121
    accommodations, 130–131
    restaurants, 134–136
    sights and attractions, 139–144
Customs regulations, 29–30

Da Camera of Houston, 197
Dallas, 32, 70–117
    accommodations, 1, 82–90
        chains, 85
        family-friendly, 87
    arriving in, 70–72
    The Arts District, 101–104
    average temperatures and precipitation, 32
    babysitters, 81

Deep Ellum
    accommodations, 82–84
    nightlife, 114–115
    restaurants, 90–92
    shopping, 112
doctors and dentists, 81
downtown, 75
    accommodations, 82–84
    restaurants, 90–92
    sights and attractions, 99–104
drugstores, 81
gay and lesbian scene, 117
Greenville Avenue and East Dallas, 78
    accommodations, 87–89
    restaurants, 92–93
    shopping, 112
highway names, 82
hospitals, 81
Island, 81
layout of, 75
maps, 81
neighborhoods in brief, 75–78
newspapers and magazines, 81
nightlife, 114–117
North Dallas, 78
    accommodations, 87–89
organized tours, 108
outdoor activities, 108–109
Park Cities, 78
picnic places, 99
police, 81
post office, 81
restaurants, 1, 90–98
safety, 81
shopping, 111–114
sights and attractions, 99–108
spectator sports, 110
taxes, 81
transit information, 81
transportation, 78, 80
Uptown and Oak Lawn, 75, 78
    accommodations, 84–87
    restaurants, 93–98
    shopping, 112
visitor information, 74
weather information, 81
what's new in, 1
Dallas Alley, 116
Dallas Aquarium at Fair, 105
The Dallas Arboretum & Botanical Garden, 19, 104
Dallas Area Rapid Transit (DART), 78, 80
Dallas Arts District, 75
Dallas Children's Theater, 108, 114

Dallas Cowboy Cheerleaders, 110
Dallas Cowboys, 110
Dallas Desperados, 110–111
Dallas Farmers' Market, 113
Dallas/Fort Worth International Airport (DFW), 70–71
    accommodations near, 89–90
Dallas–Fort Worth Metroplex, 24, 70–150
Dallas Mavericks (Dallas), 110
The Dallas Museum of Art, 1, 101–102
Dallas Opera, 114
Dallas Stars, 111
Dallas Surrey Services, 108
Dallas Theater Center, 114
The Dallas World Aquarium, 107
Dallas Zoo, 107
Danceline (Austin), 329
DART Light Rail system (Dallas), 108
David's Pub (Dallas), 116
Davis Mountains State Park, 358, 359
Davy Crockett National Forest, 203
Davy Crockett's Tall Tales Ride (San Antonio), 279
Daylight saving time, 61
Dealey Plaza (Dallas), 75, 101
Debit cards, 31
Deep Ellum (Dallas), 75
    accommodations, 75
    restaurants, 90–92
Dell, Michael, 450
Del Rio, 377–381
    tickets to sporting events and performances, 115
Delta Vacations, 45
DeLuna (South Padre Island), 245
Depot Entertainment District (Lubbock), 438
Desert Sports, 391
    Big Bend National Park, 394
Devil's Rope Museum (McLean), 427
DFW Gun Club & Training Center (Dallas), 110
Dickens on the Strand (Galveston), 35, 211
Disabilities, travelers with, 38–39
Discover Houston Tours, 193
Discrimination, 38
Dog Canyon Campground, 404
Dolphin tours
    Corpus Christi, 222
    Port Aransas, 231

Rockport, 227–228
South Padre Island, 241
The Dome (Dallas), 117
Dome Bar (El Paso), 354
Don Harrington Discovery Center (Amarillo), 417
The Door (Dallas), 115
Double Wide (Dallas), 115
Downtown Aquarium (Houston), 184
Downtown Fort Worth Rail, 146
Dragonfly (Dallas), 117
Drinking laws, 56
The Driskill (Colbn), 321
Driving rules, 50
Dude ranching, 47–48
Dune sledding, Monahans Sandhills State Park, 370–371
Dyeing o' the River Green and Pub Crawl (San Antonio), 33

East Beach (Galveston), 209
East End Historic District (Galveston), 207
East Texas, 200–205
Eatzi's (Dallas), 99
Eclectic (Austin), 327
Eco-tourism, 40–41
Ego's (Austin), 331
EJ's (Houston), 200
Elderhostel, 40
Electricity, 56–57
Elephant Mountain Wildlife Management Area, 365–366
Elephant Room (Austin), 331
11th Street Cowboy Bar (Bandera), 291
Elisabet Ney Museum (Strongbn), 322
El Mercado (San Antonio), 283
Elm Grove Golf Course (Lubbock), 434
El Paso, 5, 338–356
    accommodations, 350–352
    getting around, 342–343
    for kids, 347
    newspapers and magazines, 344
    nightlife, 353–354
    organized tours, 347–348
    outdoor activities, 348–349
    restaurants, 352–353
    safety, 344
    shopping, 349–350
    side trip to Ciudad Juárez, 354–356
    sights and attractions, 344–348

spectator sports, 349
traveling to, 342
visitor information, 343
El Paso Chile Company, 18, 350
El Paso Diablos, 349
El Paso–Juárez Trolley Company, 345, 347–348, 355
El Paso Mission Trail, 21, 344–345
El Paso Museum of Art, 345–346
El Paso Museum of History, 346
El Paso Opera, 353
El Paso Playhouse, 353–354
El Paso Pro-Musica, 353
El Paso Symphony Orchestra, 353
El Paso Zoo, 346
Embassies and consulates, 57
Emerald Springs Golf and Conference Center (El Paso), 348
Emergencies, 57
Emma Long Metropolitan Park (Austin), 325
Emo's (Austin), 331
Enchanted Rock State Natural Area, 333
Engine Room (Houston), 198
Ensemble Theatre (Houston), 197
Entry requirements, 28–29
Ernest Tubb's Record Shop (Fort Worth), 147, 150
Escapade 2001 (Dallas), 116
Escorted tours, 46
Evans Gallery (Alpine), 365
E. V. Spence, Lake, 374
Exchange Avenue (Fort Worth), 148
Eyeopener Tours (Houston), 192

Fairchild, Morgan, 450
Fair Oaks (Dallas), 109
Fair Park (Dallas), 104–105
Families with children
    Austin
        hotels, 308
        restaurants, 315
        sights and attractions, 323–324
    Dallas
        accommodations, 87
        restaurants, 95
        sights and attractions, 107–108
    El Paso sights and attractions, 347
    Fort Worth
        restaurants, 133
        sights and attractions, 144

Houston
accommodations, 172
restaurants, 181
sights and attractions, 192
information and resources, 40
San Antonio
accommodations, 262
restaurants, 271
sights and attractions,
279
Far Flung Outdoor Center,
391, 395
Farmers markets
Austin, 328
Dallas, 113
San Antonio, 283
Fate Bell Cave Dwelling Tour
(Seminole Canyon State
Park), 384
Fawcett, Farrah, 450
FedEx Kinko's Classic
(Austin), 326
Festivals and special events,
32–35
Fiesta San Antonio, 33
Fiestas Navideñas (San Anto-
nio), 35
Fiestas Patrias (Houston), 34
Finesilver Gallery (San
Antonio), 282
Fire Station No. 1/150 Years of
Fort Worth Exhibit, 139
Fishing, 48
Amarillo, 419
Amistad National Recreation
Area, 382
Brazosport, 216
Corpus Christi, 222
East Texas national forests, 203
Goose Island State Park, 227
Lake Nasworthy, 374
Matagorda Island, 218
Padre Island National
Seashore, 236
Port Aransas, 231
Rockport, 227
San Angelo, 374
South Padre Island, 241
Fitzgerald's (Houston), 198
Floore's Country Store (San
Antonio), 18, 285
Flying Saucer Draught Empo-
rium (Fort Worth), 149
Flying Wheels Travel, 38–39
Foley's (Houston), 195
Football
Austin, 326
Dallas, 110
El Paso, 349
Houston, 194

Forest Park (Fort Worth), 145
Fort Clark Springs (Del Rio),
378–379
Fort Concho National Historic
Landmark (San Angelo), 372
Fort Davis, 358–360
Fort Davis National Historic
Site, 358–359
Fort Sam Houston (San
Antonio), 250
Fort Worth, 119–150
accommodations, 123–131
babysitters, 122
Cultural District, 121
accommodations,
130–131
restaurants, 134–136
sights and attractions,
139–144
doctors and dentists, 122–123
downtown, 121
accommodations,
126–128
restaurants, 132–134
sights and attractions,
138–144
drugstores, 123
hospitals, 123
layout of, 121
Medical District, 121
neighborhoods, 121
organized tours, 144–145
outdoor activities, 145
restaurants, 131–136
safety, 123
shopping, 146–148
sights and attractions, 136–144
spectator sports, 145–146
Stockyards National Historic
District, 17, 20, 121
accommodations,
124–126
restaurants, 131–132
shopping, 146
sights and attractions,
137–138, 144
taxes, 123
transit info, 123
transportation, 122
visitor information, 121
weather information, 123
what's new in, 1–2
Fort Worth Botanic & Japanese
Gardens, 19, 141
Fort Worth Brahmas, 146
Fort Worth Herd, 138
Fort Worth Museum of Science
and History, 21, 141
Fort Worth Stock Show &
Rodeo, 137

Fort Worth Water Gardens, 139
Fort Worth Zoo, 2, 141
Four Seasons Resort and Club
(Dallas), 109
Four-wheeling, 48
Padre Island National
Seashore, 236–237
Franklin Mountains State Park,
348, 349
Fredericksburg, 18, 332–334
French Legation Museum
(Austin), 323
Fretz Park (Dallas), 109
Friedrich Wilderness Park (San
Antonio), 280
Frijole Ranch (Guadalupe
Mountains National
Park), 402
Frisco Rough Riders (Dallas),
110
Frito pie, 449
Frommers.com, 43
Frontiers of Flight Museum
(Dallas), 71
Fulton, 225
Fulton Mansion (Rockport), 228

Galería Ortiz (San Antonio),
282
Galeria San Ysidro (El Paso),
349–350
The Galleria (Dallas), 113–114
Galleria (Houston), 196
Galveston, 3, 206–213
Garcia Art Glass (San Antonio),
282
Gardens. See also Botanical
gardens
Bayou Bend (Houston), 191
Fort Worth Water
Gardens, 139
Lady Bird Johnson Wildflower
Center (Austin), 320
Moody Gardens (Galveston),
210–211
San Antonio, 278–279
Gasoline, 57
Gateway (Dallas), 108
Gay and lesbian travelers, 39
Austin, 332
Dallas, 117
Houston, 199–200
San Antonio, 287–288
Gay.com Travel, 39
Gay Men's Health Crisis, 29
George, Phyllis, 450
George Bush Intercontinental
Airport (Houston), 152–153
accommodations near, 174

George Ranch Historical Park (Houston), 191
Ghostbar (Dallas), 1, 117
Ghost Tours of Galveston, 210
Gilley's Dallas (Dallas), 18, 116
The Ginger Man (Dallas), 117
Glassworks (San Antonio), 282
Glenn Springs (Big Bend National Park), 390
The Globe of the Great Southwest (Odessa), 368
Golden Access Passport, 38
Golden Age Passport, 40
Golden Light Cafe (Amarillo), 424
Golf, 48
    Amarillo, 419
    Austin, 325, 326
    Canyon, 426
    Dallas, 109, 111
    El Paso, 348–349
    Fort Worth, 145, 146
    Houston, 193, 194
    Lubbock, 434
    Midland-Odessa, 369
    San Angelo, 374
    San Antonio, 280, 281
Goose Island State Park, 227
GORPtravel, 46–47
Government Springs Campsite (Big Bend National Park), 393
Governors Landing Campground, 383
Governor's Mansion (Austin), 321
Granada Theater (Dallas), 115
Gran Fiesta de Fort Worth, 34
The Grape Escape (Fort Worth), 149
Grapefest (Fort Worth), 34
Grapevine, 120
Grapevine Hills Trail, 393
Grapevine Opry, 120
Grapevine Vintage Railroad, 140
Grasslands Nature Trail, 237
Gray Line/Coach USA (Dallas), 108
Gray Line Tours, 46
Greater Houston Convention and Visitors Bureau (GHCVB), 154
Great Texas Mosquito Festival (Fort Worth), 34
Greenville Bar & Grill (Dallas), 115
Greyhound racing, Corpus Christi, 221
Groom, 427

Grotto (Fort Worth), 149
Gruene, 336
Gruene Hall, 337
GSM (Global System for Mobiles) wireless network, 44
Guadalupe Arts Building (Austin), 327
Guadalupe Cultural Arts Center (San Antonio), 284
Guadalupe Mountains National Park, 5, 25, 398–404
Guadalupe Peak Trail, 403
Guadalupe River State Park (San Antonio), 280–281
Guest ranches, Bandera, 290–291
Guinness World's Record Museum (San Antonio), 279
Gulf Coast, 25, 206–245
Gypsy Tea Room (Dallas), 115

Haby's Alsatian Bakery (Boerne), 289
Half Price Books Records & Magazines (Dallas), 113
Hall of State (Dallas), 105
Hall of the White Giant Tour (Carlsbad Caverns National Park), 409
Halloween (Austin), 34–35
Harbor Lights Celebration (Corpus Christi), 35
Hardin, John Wesley, 346
Hard Rock Cafe (Houston), 198
Harrington Regional Medical Center Park (Amarillo), 419
Harry Ransom Humanities Research Center (Austin), 322
Harwin Drive (Houston), 196
Health concerns, 37–38
Health insurance, 36
HemisFair Park (San Antonio), 278
Heritage Society at Sam Houston Park (Houston), 185
Hermann Park (Houston), 188
    golf course, 193
Highland Gallery (Marfa), 365
Highland Park Village (Dallas), 114
Highland Range Scenic Lookout, 374
Highland Village (Houston), 195
Hiking, 48
    Amarillo, 419–420
    Austin, 325
    Big Bend National Park, 392–393

Big Thicket National Preserve., 200
Davis Mountains State Park, 359
East Texas national forests, 203
El Paso, 349
Guadalupe Mountains National Park, 402
Houston, 193
Lake Nasworthy, 374
Lubbock, 434
Padre Island National Seashore, 237
Palo Duro Canyon State Park, 427
San Angelo, 374
San Angelo State Park, 373
San Antonio, 280
Seminole Canyon State Park, 384
Hill Country State Natural Area, 290
Hippie Hollow (Austin), 325
Historic Accommodations of Texas, 28, 253, 299
Historic Route 66 District (Amarillo), 420
History, 439–443
HIV-positive visitors, 29
Hobby Airport (Houston), 153
Hobby Center for the Performing Arts (Houston), 196
Hockey
    Amarillo, 420
    Austin, 326
    Dallas, 111
    Fort Worth, 146
    Lubbock, 435
Hogan Park Golf Course (Midland), 369
Holidays, 57–58
Holly, Buddy, Statue (Lubbock), 432
Horseback riding
    Amarillo, 420
    Bandera, 290
    Big Bend National Park, 393
    Fort Worth, 145
    Guadalupe Mountains National Park, 403
    Palo Duro Canyon State Park, 427
    Port Aransas, 231
Horse racing, El Paso, 349
Hotels, 51–54
    best, 8–12
    surfing for, 42
Hot Springs (Big Bend National Park), 390

Hot Springs Trail, 392
Houston, 24–25, 32, 151–200
  accommodations, 163–174
  arriving in, 152–153
  doctors and dentists, 163
  downtown, 155
    accommodations,
      164–166
    restaurants, 174–176
    shopping, 195
    sights and attractions,
      184–185
  drugstores, 163
  East End, 155, 160
    accommodations,
      166–167
    restaurants, 176–178
    shopping, 195
    sights and attractions,
      185–187
  gay and lesbian nightlife,
    199–200
  Internet access, 163
  for kids, 192
  Kirby District and Greenway
    Plaza, 160
    accommodations, 170
    restaurants, 180–183
    shopping, 195
    sights and attractions,
      191
  layout of, 154–155
  maps, 163
  Midtown, 155
    restaurants, 174–176
  Montrose and the Heights, 160
    accommodations,
      168–169
    restaurants, 178–180
    shopping, 195
  Museum District, 160
    sights and attractions,
      187–190
  neighborhoods, 155, 160–161
  nightlife, 196–200
  North Houston, 161
  organized tours, 192–193
  outdoor activities, 193–194
  restaurants, 174–184
    family-friendly, 181
    fast food, 177
  shopping, 194–196
  sights and attractions,
    184–193
  South Main
    accommodations,
      167–168
    sights and attractions,
      187–190
  spectator sports, 194
  transit information, 163
  transportation, 161–162
  Uptown, 160–161
    accommodations,
      170–173
    restaurants, 183–184
    shopping, 196
  visitor information, 154
  weather information, 163
  what's new in, 2–3
Houston, Sam, 441, 442
Houston Astros, 194
Houston Ballet, 197
Houston Grand Opera, 197
Houston Livestock Show and
  Rodeo, 33, 194
Houston Museum of Natural
  Science, 188
Houston Rockets, 194
Houston Ship Channel, 185–186
Houston Symphony, 197
Houston Texans, 194
Houston Zoological
  Gardens, 188
Hueco Tanks State Historic Site
  (near El Paso), 348
Hughes, Howard, 450
Hunting, 48

Immigration and customs
  clearance, 44
Indian Meadow Nature Trail,
  402
In-line skating
  Dallas, 108–109
  Fort Worth, 145
Insights Science Museum
  (El Paso), 347
Institute of Texan Cultures
  (San Antonio), 278
Insurance, 35–36
  auto, 50
Intermodal Transportation Cen-
  ter (ITC; Fort Worth), 72
International Association for
  Medical Assistance to
  Travelers (IAMAT), 37
International Festival
  (Houston), 33
International Gay and Lesbian
  Travel Association (IGLTA), 39
International Society of Travel
  Medicine, 37
International Youth Travel Card
  (IYTC), 40
Internet access, 43, 58
InTouch USA, 44
Itineraries, suggested, 63–69
Ivey's Emporium (Alpine), 365

J&J Blues Bar (Fort Worth), 150
Jasper, 202
Jefferson, 203–205
Jessie Jane's (Lubbock), 438
Jogging
  Dallas, 108–109
  Fort Worth, 145
  Houston, 193
John F. Kennedy Memorial
  (Dallas), 99
John Neely Bryan Cabin
  (Dallas), 99
Johnson, Lyndon B.
  Boyhood Home (Johnson
    City), 334–335
  State and National Historical
    Parks at LBJ Ranch (near
    Stonewall), 334
Johnson City, 334
John S. Stiff Memorial Park
  (Amarillo), 419
Jones Hall (Houston), 196
Josephine Theater (San
  Antonio), 285
J. R.'s Bar and Grill (Dallas), 117
Juárez City Market (Mexico), 356
Juárez Museum of Art (Mexico),
  355
Jubilee Theatre (Fort Worth), 148
Jump-Start Performance Com-
  pany (San Antonio), 285
Juneteenth Festival, 33
J. Wilde's (San Angelo), 375

Katy Mills (Houston), 194
Kayaking
  Corpus Christi, 222
  Port Aransas, 232
  Rockport, 227
Keeton Park Golf Course
  (Dallas), 109
Kemah Boardwalk (Houston),
  186
Kentucky Club (Ciudad Juárez,
  Mexico), 356
Kimbell Art Museum (Fort
  Worth), 16, 142
King's Palace Guided Tour
  (Carlsbad Caverns National
  Park), 409
Kingston Tycoon Flats (San
  Antonio), 287
Kiowa Gallery (Alpine), 365
Kitchen Dog Theater Company
  (Dallas), 114
Kowbell Rodeo (Fort Worth), 146
Kwahadi Kiva Indian Museum
  (Amarillo), 417

La Carafe (Houston), 199
La Diosa Cellars (near Lubbock), 433
Lady Bird Johnson Wildflower Center (Austin), 19, 320–321
Laguna Madre Nature Trail, 240
La Harmonia Store (Big Bend National Park), 390
Lajitas Stables (Big Bend National Park), 393
Lake Amistad Marina, 382
Lake Meredith National Recreation Area, 418–420
La Misíon de Nuestra Señora Guadalupe (Ciudad Juárez), 354, 355
Landa Park (New Braunfels), 336
The Landing (San Antonio), 286–287
Landmark Inn State Historic Site (Castroville), 289
Language, 443–444
Las Posadas (San Antonio), 35
La Villita National Historic District (San Antonio), 274
La Zona Rosa (Austin), 331
LBJ Library and Museum (Austin), 320
Leaning Tower of Texas, 427
Leddy's Ranch at Sundance (Fort Worth), 147
Left Hand Tunnel (Carlsbad Caverns National Park), 409
Legal aid, 58
Legend Jewelers (San Angelo), 375
Legends of the Game Baseball Museum (Arlington), 110, 118
Leon Springs Dancehall (San Antonio), 285
Lesbian/Gay Rights Lobby of Texas, 39
The Lighthouse (Palo Duro Canyon State Park), 427
Lighting Ceremony and River Walk Holiday Parade (San Antonio), 35
Little's Boots (San Antonio), 283
Livestock Exchange Building (Fort Worth), 137
Livestock shows. See Rodeos and livestock shows
Lizard Lounge (Dallas), 116
Llano Estacado Winery (near Lubbock), 433
Log Cabin Village (Fort Worth), 142

Lone Star Ballet (Amarillo), 424
Lone Star Flight Museum (Galveston), 210–211
Longwood Golf Club (Houston), 193
Lost and found, 58
Lost-luggage insurance, 36
Louie's Backyard (South Padre Island), 245
Louis Tussaud's Palace of Wax & Ripley's Believe It or Not (Arlington), 118
Love Field (Dallas), 71
Lower Cave Tour (Carlsbad Caverns National Park), 409
Lubbock, 6, 429–438
    accommodations, 435–436
    getting around, 429–430
    nightlife, 437
    outdoor activities, 433–434
    restaurants, 436–437
    shopping, 435
    sights and attractions, 430–433
    spectator sports, 435
    traveling to, 429
    visitor information, 430
Lubbock Cotton Kings, 435
Lubbock Lake Landmark, 432
Lubbock Symphony Orchestra, 437
Lucchese Gallery (San Antonio), 283
Luqa and Petrus Lounge (Dallas), 117
Lyndon B. Johnson Country, 334–335
Lyndon B. Johnson State and National Historical Parks at LBJ Ranch (near Stonewall), 334

Mackenzie Park (Lubbock), 433–434
Mackenzie Park Disk Golf Course, The, (Lubbock), 434
McDonald Observatory (near Fort Davis), 17, 359
McGonigel's Mucky Duck (Houston), 199
McKelligon Canyon Theatre (El Paso), 353
McKittrick Canyon, 19, 398–404
McKittrick Canyon Trail, 402–403
McLean, 427

McMurtry, Larry, 451
Macy's (Houston), 195
Magik Theatre (San Antonio), 285
Magoffin Home State Historic Site (El Paso), 346–347
Mail, 58–59
Main Plaza (San Antonio), 3
Majestic Theater (Dallas), 114
Majestic Theatre (San Antonio), 284
Malick, Terrence, 450
Maps, 50
Marathon Baxter Gallery (Alpine), 365
Mardi Gras (Galveston), 32, 211
Marfa, 361–364
Marfa and Presidio County Museum, 362
Marfa Book Co., 364
Marfa Ghost Lights, 363
Marfa Lights Festival, 34, 363
Marfreless (Houston), 199
Marion Koogler McNay Art Museum (San Antonio), 4, 17, 275–276
Market Square (San Antonio), 274
Marsical Mine (Big Bend National Park), 391
Martin, Steve, 451
Martin Road Park (Amarillo), 419
MasterCard Colonial Golf Tournament (Fort Worth), 146
MasterCard traveler's checks, 31
Matagorda Bay, 218
Matagorda Island, 218
Maverick (Fort Worth), 17, 147
Mayfair Club (Amarillo), 424
Meadowbrook Golf Course (Lubbock), 434
Meadowbrooks Golf Course (Fort Worth), 145
Meadows Museum of Art (Dallas), 16, 106
Meat Loaf, 451
Medical insurance, 36
Medical requirements for entry, 29
Memorial Park (Houston), 193
Memorial Park Golf Course (Houston), 193
Menger Bar (San Antonio), 287
Menil Collection (Houston), 16, 190–191
Mesquite Championship Rodeo (near Dallas), 111

MEXIC-ARTE Museum (Austin), 321–322
Mexico, 52–53
Midland-Odessa, 366–371
Midland RockHounds, 369
Midnight Rodeo (Amarillo), 424
Miss Hattie's Bordello Museum (San Angelo), 376
Mission Socorro (El Paso), 345
Mission Ysleta (El Paso), 345
Miss Texas USA Pageant (Lubbock), 34
M. L. Leddy's (Fort Worth), 17, 146–147
Modern Art Museum of Fort Worth, 16, 142–143
Monahans Sandhills State Park, 370–371
Money matters, 30–31
Moody Gardens (Galveston), 210
Moody Mansion (Galveston), 210
Morton H. Meyerson Symphony Center (Dallas), 114
MossRehab, 39
Movies, recommended, 55
Moyers, Bill, 451
Mule Ears Spring Trail, 393
Museo Americano Smithsonian (San Antonio), 3–4, 277–278
Museum of Fine Arts, Houston (MFAH), 16, 188–189
Museum of Health & Medical Science (Houston), 189–190
Museum of Natural Science (Brazosport), 214
Museum of Nature and Science (Dallas), 105–106
Museum of Science and History (Corpus Christi), 221
Museum of Texas Handmade Furniture (New Braunfels), 336
Museum of Texas Tech University (Lubbock), 430–431
Museum of the American Railroad (Dallas), 105
Museum of the Big Bend (Alpine), 365
Museum of the Southwest (Midland), 368–369
Museums of Port Isabel, 240
Music, 55
   Texan, 446–448
Mustang Island State Park, 19, 231
Mystique Tours (Caddo Lake), 205

Nanette Richardson Fine Art (San Antonio), 282
Nasher Sculpture Center (Dallas), 15–16, 102–103, 117
Nasworthy, Lake, 374
National Border Patrol Museum (El Paso), 347
National Cowboys of Color Museum & Hall of Fame (Fort Worth), 138
National Cowgirl Museum and Hall of Fame (Fort Worth), 21, 143
National Museum of Funeral History (Houston), 191–192
National Museum of the Pacific War (Fredericksburg), 333
National Ranching Heritage Center (Lubbock), 431–432
Native Americans, 338
   Amistad National Recreation Area, 382–383
   history of, 439
   Kwahadi Kiva Indian Museum (Amarillo), 417
   petroglyphs, 373, 390
   pictographs, 276, 348, 374, 382–384, 390, 392
Natural Entrance Route (Carlsbad Caverns National Park), 408–409
Neiman Marcus (Dallas), 17, 112
Neo-Tropical Bird Sanctuary (Quintana Beach), 216
New Braunfels, 21, 335–336
New Braunfels Museum of Art & Music (Gruene), 336
Newspapers and magazines, 59
Nikita (Dallas), 116
Nokia Live Center (Dallas), 116
North Dallas, 78
Northern Prairie Wildlife Research Center, 47
NorthPark Center (Dallas), 17, 113
North Star Mall (San Antonio), 283
Now, Voyager, 39
Nueva Vista Golf Club (Midland), 369

Ocean Star (Galveston), 210
Odessa Jackalopes, 369
Odessa Meteor Crater and Museum, 369
O'Hair, Madalyn Murray, 451

O. H. Ivie, Lake, 374
Oilcan Harry's (Austin), 332
Old Chicken Farm Art Center (San Angelo), 375
Old City Park (Dallas), 21, 106–108
Old Lumber Yard (Johnson City), 335
The Old Monk (Dallas), 117
Old Red Courthouse (Dallas), 100
Old Route 66, 426–427
Olivia Cruises & Resorts, 39
The Orange Show (Houston), 186–187
Orbison, Roy, 451
Oslo (Austin), 330
Our Lady of Guadalupe Mission (Ciudad Juárez), 354
Outfitters and operators, 47

Package deals, 45
Padre Island National Seashore, 233–237
Paint Brush Alley (San Angelo), 5, 372
Painted Dunes Desert Golf Course (El Paso), 348
Palo Duro Canyon State Park, 19–20, 420, 424, 425, 427, 428, 434
The Panhandle Plains, 28, 412–438
Panhandle-Plains Historical Museum (Canyon), 17, 425–426
Panther Cave, 383
Panther Junction Visitor Center, 389
Panther Path, 392
Parida Cave, 383
Paris Hatters (San Antonio), 17–18, 283
The Park Shops (Houston), 195
Parque Chamizal (El Paso), 344
Paseo del Río (The River Walk; San Antonio), 274–275
Passports, 28–29, 59
Pawnee Bill's Wild West Show (Fort Worth), 146, 150
Pearl's Dancehall & Saloon (Fort Worth), 149–150
Pecan Valley Golf Course (Fort Worth), 145
Pecan Valley golf course (San Antonio), 280
Pecos River, 383
Pegasus (San Antonio), 287

Performing Arts Center (PAC; Austin), 329
The Permian Basin Petroleum Museum (Midland), 369
Peters Brothers Hats (Fort Worth), 147
Pete's Dueling Piano Bar (Dallas), 117
Petroglyphs, 373, 390
Petrol, 57
Pets, traveling with, 41–42
Petticoat Junction (San Antonio), 288
Pheasant Ridge Winery (near Lubbock), 433
Pictographs, 276, 348, 374, 382–384, 390, 392
Pictographs of Painted Rocks, 374
Pier 21 Theater (Galveston), 210
Pine Canyon Trail, 393
The Pinery (Guadalupe Mountains National Park), 401
Pinery Trail, 402
Pine Springs Campground, 404
Piney Woods, 200
Pinto Ranch (Houston), 196
Pioneer Days (Fort Worth), 34
Pioneer Museum Complex (Fredericksburg), 333
Pioneer West Historical Museum (Shamrock), 426
Placita Santa Fe (El Paso), 350
Planetarium (Brazosport), 214
Planet Earth Adventures, 47
Plano Balloon Festival (Dallas), 108
Plaza de los Lagartos (El Paso), 345
Plaza Wax Museum (San Antonio), 279
Police, 59
Ponder Boot Company (Fort Worth), 17, 147
Poor David's Pub, 115–116
Port Aransas, 230–233
Port Isabel Historical Museum, 240
Port Isabel Lighthouse State Historic Site, 240
Pratt Lodge (Guadalupe Mountains National Park), 401
Prescription medications, 37–38
The Presidential Museum (Odessa), 368, 369
Presidio Chapel San Elceario (El Paso), 345
Presidio County Courthouse (Marfa), 362

Quarry golf course (San Antonio), 280
Quarter Horse Hall of Fame & Museum (Amarillo), 416
Quicksand Golf Course (San Angelo), 374
Quintana Beach, 216
Quintana Beach County Park, 216, 217

Race relations in East Texas, 202
Ragwear (Dallas), 113
Railroads. See Trains and railways
The Rainbow Cattle Co. (Austin), 332
Rangers Stadium in Arlington, 110, 118
Rather, Dan, 451
Rawls Golf Course (Lubbock), 434
Red Cat Jazz Café (Houston), 198
Red-Eyed Fly (Austin), 331
Regions in brief, 24–25, 28
Republic of Texas, 441
Restaurants, best, 12–15
Retro Cowboy (Fort Worth), 147
Return of the Chili Queens (San Antonio), 33
Reunion Tower (Dallas), 101
Rich's (Houston), 200
Ridgelea and Vine Wineroom (Fort Worth), 150
Ridglea Theater (Fort Worth), 150
Rienzi (Houston), 191
Rio Grande, warning against crossing, 389
Rio Grande Village, 390
Rio Grande Village Campground, 397
Rio Grande Village Nature Trail, 392
Rio Grande Village Trailer Park, 397
Rio San Antonio River Cruise, 279–280
Ripley's Believe It or Not (Arlington), 118
Ripley's Believe It Or Not (San Antonio), 279
Ripley's Haunted Adventure (San Antonio), 279

Rivercenter Mall (San Antonio), 283
River cruises. See Boat tours and cruises
River Oaks Shopping Center (Houston), 195
River running, Big Bend National Park, 394
Riverside Golf Course (San Angelo), 374
The River Walk (Paseo del Río; San Antonio), 274–275
River Walk (San Angelo), 372
River Walk Mud Festival (San Antonio), 32
Road conditions, 50–51
RoadPost, 44
Rock art (pictographs), 276, 348, 374, 382–384, 390, 392
Rocketbuster Boots (El Paso), 350
Rock Island Rail Trail (Amarillo), 6, 419–420
Rockport, 225–230
Rockport Center for the Arts, 228
Rockwood Golf Course (Fort Worth), 145
Rodeo Exchange (Fort Worth), 150
Rodeos and livestock shows
    Amarillo, 420
    Dallas, 111
    El Paso, 349
    Fort Worth, 15, 32, 137, 143, 146, 150
    Houston, 33, 194
    San Angelo, 374
    San Antonio, 32, 281
Rogers, Ginger, 451
Rosa's Cantina (El Paso), 354
Rose Marine Theater (Fort Worth), 148
Ross Maxwell Scenic Drive, 388, 389
Ross Rogers Golf Course (Amarillo), 419
Rothko Chapel (Houston), 190
Round Rock Express (Austin), 325–326
Round-Up Saloon (Dallas), 117
Route 66 Historic District (Amarillo), 416
Route 66 Motor Speedway (near Amarillo), 420
Route 66 Roadhouse (Amarillo), 424
Run-Tex (Austin), 328
RV rentals, 49–50

RVs and RV parks, 47
Amarillo, 422
Big Bend National Park, 397–398
Carlsbad Caverns, 411
Corpus Christi, 223–224
El Paso, 352
Guadalupe Mountains National Park, 404
San Angelo State Park, 373
South Padre Island, 243

Sabine National Forest, 203
Safety, 38
Sailing, Corpus Christi, 222
The Saint (San Antonio), 288
St. Stanislaus (Bandera), 290
Salute! (San Antonio), 287
Samba Room (Dallas), 117
Sambuca (Dallas), 115
Sambuca Jazz Café (Houston), 198
Sam Houston National Forest, 203
San Angel Folk Art (San Antonio), 282
San Angelo, 5, 371–377
San Angelo Colts, 374
San Angelo Museum of Fine Arts, 372–373
San Angelo Nature Center, 374
San Angelo State Park, 373, 374
San Angelo Symphony, 376
San Antonio, 25, 32, 246–291
accommodations, 253–265
arriving in, 247–248
downtown, 249
restaurants, 266–268
sights and attractions, 273–275, 277–278
drugstores, 252
gay scene, 287–288
getting around, 251–252
Hill Country side trips from, 288–291
hospitals, 252
for kids, 279
King William Historic District, 249, 274
restaurants, 268–269
layout of, 248–249
neighborhoods, 249–250
nightlife, 283–288
organized tours, 279–280
outdoor activities, 280–281
parking, 251
restaurants, 266–273

safety, 252–253
shopping, 281–283
sights and attractions, 273–280
spectator sports, 281
taxes, 253
visitor information, 248
what's new in, 3–4
San Antonio Botanical Gardens, 278–279
San Antonio Children's Museum, 279
San Antonio IMAX Theater Rivercenter, 279
San Antonio Missions National Historical Park, 4, 20, 276
San Antonio Museum of Art, 16, 275
San Antonio Spurs, 281
San Antonio Stock Show and Rodeo, 281
San Antonio Symphony, 284–285
San Antonio Theater Coalition, 285
San Felipe Springs (Del Rio), 378
San Fernando Cathedral (San Antonio), 278
San Francisco de la Espada (San Antonio), 276
San Jacinto Festival and Texas History Day (West Columbia), 33–34
San Jacinto Monument & Museum (Houston), 20, 185
San José mission (San Antonio), 276
San Juan Capistrano (San Antonio), 276
San Pedro Campground, 383
San Pedro Playhouse (San Antonio), 285
Santa Elena Canyon, 389
Santa Elena Canyon Trail, 393
Sardines Ristorante Italiano (Fort Worth), 150
Sauer-Beckmann Living History Farm, 334
Saxon Pub (Austin), 331
Scenic Drive Park (El Paso), 347
Schlitterbahn Beach Water park, 241
Schlitterbahn (Gruene), 336
Schlitterbahn Galveston Water Park, 3, 211
Scholz Garten (Austin), 332
The Schultze House Cottage Garden (San Antonio), 278

Science Spectrum Museum (Lubbock), 433
Scott Gertner's Skybar (Houston), 198–199
Sea Center Texas (Brazosport), 215
Sea kayaking
Corpus Christi, 222
Port Aransas, 232
Rockport, 227
Seasons, 31
Sea turtles, 235, 242
SeaWorld San Antonio, 277
Seminole Canyon State Park & Historic Site, 383–384
Senior travelers, 39–40
Shadow Hills Golf Course (Lubbock), 434
Shamrock, 426
Shell Houston Open (Houston), 194
Shopping, best, 17–18
Shops at La Cantera (San Antonio), 281–283
Sid Richardson Collection of Western Art (Fort Worth), 139
Si! El Paso Tours, 348
The Silver Dollar (San Antonio), 287–288
Sí Texas Tours, 46
Six Flags AstroWorld (Houston), 3
Six Flags Fiesta Texas (San Antonio), 22, 277
Six Flags Hurricane Harbor (Arlington), 118–119
Six Flags Over Texas (Arlington), 119
Six Flags SplashTown (Houston), 192
The Sixth Floor Museum at Dealey Plaza (Dallas), 20, 100–101
6th Street (Austin), 322, 330
Slaughter Canyon Cave Tour, 410
Sleepy Hollow Country Club (Dallas), 109
Slick Willie's (Houston), 198
Smith, Jaclyn, 451
Smith, Liz, 451
Soccer, Dallas, 111
Social (Dallas), 117
Society Church (Fredericksburg), 333
Society for the Performing Arts (SPA; Houston), 196–197
Sons of Hermann Hall (Dallas), 115

Sophienburg Museum (New Braunfels), 336
South by Southwest (Austin), 33
Southeast Regional Park (Amarillo), 419
South Padre Island, 237–245
South Padre Island Kite Festival, 35
South Plains Mall (Lubbock), 435
South Texas Art Museum (Corpus Christi), 221
Southwestern Exposition and Livestock Show & Rodeo (Fort Worth), 15, 32, 137, 146
Southwestern International PRCA Rodeo (El Paso), 349
Space Center Houston, 22, 187
Spacek, Sissy, 451
Spanish Governor's Palace (San Antonio), 278
Speakeasy (Austin), 331
Special events and festivals, 32–35
Special-interest trips, 46–48
Spider Cave (Carlsbad Caverns National Park), 410
Stagecoach Ballroom (Fort Worth), 149
Stampede (El Paso), 354
Stanley Korshak (Dallas), 112–113
StarKeeper Gallery (San Angelo), 375
State Capitol (Austin), 21, 319–320
State Fair of Texas (Dallas), 34
State Theater Company (Austin), 330
STA Travel, 40
Stewart Beach (Galveston), 209
Stillwell Store and RV Park (Big Bend National Park), 398
Stock Show and Rodeo (San Antonio), 32
The Stockyards (Fort Worth), 21
The Stockyards Championship Rodeo (Fort Worth), 150
Stockyards Hotel (Fort Worth), 137
Stockyards Museum (Fort Worth), 137–138
Stockyards National Historic District (Fort Worth), 17, 20, 121
    accommodations, 124–126
    restaurants, 131–132
    shopping, 146
    sights and attractions, 137–138, 144

Stockyards Station (Fort Worth), 137, 147
Stockyards Wedding Chapel (Fort Worth), 147
Strand District (Galveston), 207–208
The Strip (San Antonio), 285
Stubb's (Austin), 331–332
Student travelers, 40
The Studios at Las Colinas (Dallas), 108
Style, Texan, 444–446
Sue Ellen's (Dallas), 117
Sundance Square (Fort Worth), 121, 138, 148
Sunday Houses (Fredericksburg), 333
Sunland Park Mall (El Paso), 350
Sunland Park Racetrack and Casino (El Paso), 349
Sunset Country Club (Odessa), 369
Sunset Mall (San Angelo), 375
Super Bull (Amarillo), 32
Surfing
    Padre Island National Seashore, 237
    Port Aransas, 232
Swimming
    Amistad National Recreation Area, 382
    Austin, 325
    Lubbock, 434
    Padre Island National Seashore, 237
    South Padre Island, 241
Swiss Avenue Historic District (Dallas), 107
Sycamore Creek Golf Course (Fort Worth), 145

Taco Land (San Antonio), 286
Tarantula Steam Train (Grapevine), 15, 120
Tauck World Discovery, 47
Taxes, 59–60
Tejano Conjunto Festival (San Antonio), 33, 286
Telegraph and telex services, 60
Telephone, 60
Temperatures, 32
Tenison Golf Course (Dallas), 109
Tennis
    Dallas, 109
    Fort Worth, 145

Houston, 194
San Antonio, 281
Tesoros (Austin), 4, 327
Texas, Battleship (Houston), 185
Texas Aviation Hall of Fame (Galveston), 210–211
Texas Café and Bar (Lubbock), 438
Texas Civil War Museum (Fort Worth), 2
Texas Cowboy Hall of Fame (Fort Worth), 138
Texas Gulf Coast, 25, 206–245
Texas Hill Country Wine and Food Festival (Austin), 33
Texas International Fishing Tournament (TIFT; South Padre Island), 241
Texas Jazz Festival (Corpus Christi), 34
Texas Maritime Museum (Rockport), 228
Texas Memorial Museum (Austin), 322–323
Texas Motor Speedway (near Fort Worth), 145
Texas Rangers (Dallas), 110
Texas Seaport Museum (Galveston), 210
Texas Ski Ranch (New Braunfels), 337
Texas Stadium (Irving), 110
Texas State Aquarium (Corpus Christi), 220–221
Texas State Railroad State Park, 204
Texas Tech Red Raiders (Lubbock), 435
Texas Tech University Theatre (Lubbock), 438
Texas Twisters (Dallas), 117
Texas Union Ballroom (Austin), 331
Texas Wine Tours, 46
Tex-Mex cooking, 449
Tex's (San Antonio), 287
Theatre Under The Stars (Houston), 197
Thistle Hill House Museum (Fort Worth), 144
Thompson Memorial Park (Amarillo), 419
Tienda Guadalupe Folk Art & Gifts (San Antonio), 282
Time zones, 60
Tipping, 61
T-Mobile Hotspot, 43

Toilets, 61
Top Rail Ballroom (Dallas), 116
Torian Log Cabin (Grapevine), 120
Tour 18 Dallas, 109
Tour 18 Houston, 48, 193
Tourist information, 28
Tournament Players Course at the Woodlands (Houston), 193
Tower of the Americas (San Antonio), 278
TPC at the Four Seasons Resort and Club (Dallas), 109, 111
Trader's Village (Arlington), 119
Trail of Fame (Fort Worth), 137
Trains and railways, 45
 Grapevine Vintage Railroad, 15, 140
 Museum of the American Railroad (Dallas), 105
 Texas State Railroad State Park, 204
 Zilker Zephyr Miniature Train (Austin), 324
Trammell & Margaret Crow Collection of Asian Art (Dallas), 103–104
Trammell Crow Center (Dallas), 104
Transportation, 48–51
Travel blogs and travelogues, 42
Travel CUTS, 40
Traveler's Aid Society International, 57
Traveler's checks, 31
Travelex Insurance Services, 36
Travel Guard International, 36
Travel insurance, 35–36
Travel Insured International, 36
Treasures of the Gulf Museum (Port Isabel), 240
Trevino, Lee, 451
Trinity Park (Fort Worth), 145
Trinity Railway Express (TRE), 72
Trinity River Trails (Fort Worth), 145
Trip-cancellation insurance, 35–36
Trolley tours, El Paso-Juárez Trolley Company, 345, 347–348, 355
Tubing, 15, 277, 280, 290, 336
Tuff Canyon Trail, 392
Twin Buttes Reservoir, 374

Uncertain, 205
Union Station (Dallas), 72
University of Texas at El Paso, Dinner Theatre, 354
University of Texas at El Paso (UTEP), the Miners, 349
University of Texas Longhorns (Austin), 325, 326
University Park (Dallas), 78
University Park Village (Fort Worth), 147–148
USIT, 40
USS Lexington Museum on the Bay (Corpus Christi), 20, 221

Valero Texas Open (San Antonio), 281
Val Verde Winery (Del Rio), 379
Vegetarian travel, 41
Vereins Kirche (Fredericksburg), 333
Verizon Wireless Amphitheater (San Antonio), 285
Verizon Wireless Theater (Houston), 198
Vidor, 202
Village (Houston), 195
Village Station (Dallas), 117
Visas, 29, 61–62
Visa traveler's checks, 31
Visitor information, 28
Visit USA, 49
Viva! El Paso, 353

Wahoo Saloon (South Padre Island), 245
Walking Arts District Strolls (Dallas), 108
Walking Tours of the Stockyards (Fort Worth), 144
WalkTex (Austin), 328
Wanna-Wanna (South Padre Island), 245
Waterloo Records and Video (Austin), 328
Watersports, 48
 Gruene, 336
 San Antonio, 280–281
WaterWorld (Houston), 3
Wayport, 43
Websites
 best, 22–23
 travel-planning and booking, 42–43
West End Historic District (Dallas), 75

West End MarketPlace (Dallas), 112
Western gear, Fort Worth, 146–147
Western Mercantile (Fort Worth), 146
Western Playland Amusement Park (El Paso), 347
Western Union, 58
Western Warehouse (Dallas), 113
Western wear and gear, 444–446
 Amarillo, 420
 Austin, 328
 Bandera, 290
 Dallas, 113
 El Paso, 350
 Houston, 196
 San Antonio, 283
Western Wear Exchange (Fort Worth), 147
Westgate Shopping Mall (Amarillo), 420
Westin La Cantera golf courses (San Antonio), 280
West Texas, 25, 338–384
West Texas Walk of Fame (Lubbock), 432
West Village (Dallas), 78
White Elephant (Fort Worth), 137
White Elephant Saloon (Fort Worth), 148–149
Whitehead Memorial Museum (Del Rio), 379
Whittington's (Johnson City), 335
Whole Foods Market (Austin), 327
Whole Foods Market (Dallas), 99
Whooping cranes, 226
 tours
  Corpus Christi, 222
  Rockport, 227–228
Wi-Fi access, 43
Wild About Music (Austin), 327
Wild Basin Wilderness Preserve, 325
Wild Bill's (Dallas), 113
Wildcat Bluff Nature Center (Amarillo), 419
Wildlife viewing, 47. See also Bird-watching
 Amistad National Recreation Area, 382
 Aransas National Wildlife Refuge (Rockport), 225–227
 Big Bend National Park, 391–392
 Brazosport, 216
 Carlsbad Caverns National Park, 410

Davis Mountains State
Park, 359
Elephant Mountain Wildlife
Management Area,
365–366
Guadalupe Mountains
National Park, 403–404
Padre Island National
Seashore, 236
San Angelo State Park, 373
Wild West (Lubbock), 438
William P. Hobby Airport
(Houston), 153
Williams Ranch House
(Guadalupe Mountains
National Park), 401
Windmill Nature Trail, 384
Window View Trail, 392
Windsurfing
Corpus Christi, 222
Padre Island National
Seashore, 237
South Padre Island, 241

Wines and wineries
Del Rio, 379
Grapevine, 120
Lubbock, 433
Wings over Houston
Airshow, 34
Witte Museum (San
Antonio), 276
Wolfman Jack, 378
Women & Their Work
(Austin), 327
Women's Museum
(Dallas), 105
Wonderland Amusement Park
(Amarillo), 417
World Birding Center, 41
World Championship Ranch
Rodeo (Amarillo), 420
Wortham Center (Houston),
196
Wreck Room (Fort Worth), 150
Wyler Aerial Tramway
(El Paso), 348

Y ard Dog Folk Art
(Austin), 327

Z achary Scott Theatre Center
(Austin), 330
Z. Boaz Golf Course (Fort
Worth), 145
Zen Bar (San Antonio), 287
Zilker Botanical Garden
(Austin), 323
Zilker Park (Austin), 323, 325
Zilker Park Tree Lighting
(Austin), 35
Zilker Zephyr Miniature Train
(Austin), 324
Zin Valle Vineyards (El Paso), 346
Zoos
Amarillo, 417
Dallas, 107
El Paso, 346
Fort Worth, 2, 141

FROMMER'S® COMPLETE TRAVEL GUIDES

Alaska
Amalfi Coast
American Southwest
Amsterdam
Argentina & Chile
Arizona
Atlanta
Australia
Austria
Bahamas
Barcelona
Beijing
Belgium, Holland & Luxembourg
Belize
Bermuda
Boston
Brazil
British Columbia & the Canadian
  Rockies
Brussels & Bruges
Budapest & the Best of Hungary
Buenos Aires
Calgary
California
Canada
Cancún, Cozumel & the Yucatán
Cape Cod, Nantucket & Martha's
  Vineyard
Caribbean
Caribbean Ports of Call
Carolinas & Georgia
Chicago
China
Colorado
Costa Rica
Croatia
Cuba
Denmark
Denver, Boulder & Colorado Springs
Edinburgh & Glasgow
England
Europe
Europe by Rail
Florence, Tuscany & Umbria

Florida
France
Germany
Greece
Greek Islands
Hawaii
Hong Kong
Honolulu, Waikiki & Oahu
India
Ireland
Israel
Italy
Jamaica
Japan
Kauai
Las Vegas
London
Los Angeles
Los Cabos & Baja
Madrid
Maine Coast
Maryland & Delaware
Maui
Mexico
Montana & Wyoming
Montréal & Québec City
Moscow & St. Petersburg
Munich & the Bavarian Alps
Nashville & Memphis
New England
Newfoundland & Labrador
New Mexico
New Orleans
New York City
New York State
New Zealand
Northern Italy
Norway
Nova Scotia, New Brunswick &
  Prince Edward Island
Oregon
Paris
Peru
Philadelphia & the Amish Country

Portugal
Prague & the Best of the Czech
  Republic
Provence & the Riviera
Puerto Rico
Rome
San Antonio & Austin
San Diego
San Francisco
Santa Fe, Taos & Albuquerque
Scandinavia
Scotland
Seattle
Seville, Granada & the Best of
  Andalusia
Shanghai
Sicily
Singapore & Malaysia
South Africa
South America
South Florida
South Pacific
Southeast Asia
Spain
Sweden
Switzerland
Tahiti & French Polynesia
Texas
Thailand
Tokyo
Toronto
Turkey
USA
Utah
Vancouver & Victoria
Vermont, New Hampshire & Maine
Vienna & the Danube Valley
Vietnam
Virgin Islands
Virginia
Walt Disney World® & Orlando
Washington, D.C.
Washington State

FROMMER'S® DAY BY DAY GUIDES

Amsterdam
Chicago
Florence & Tuscany

London
New York City
Paris

Rome
San Francisco
Venice

PAULINE FROMMER'S GUIDES! SEE MORE. SPEND LESS.

Hawaii

Italy

New York City

FROMMER'S® PORTABLE GUIDES

Acapulco, Ixtapa & Zihuatanejo
Amsterdam
Aruba
Australia's Great Barrier Reef
Bahamas
Big Island of Hawaii
Boston
California Wine Country
Cancún
Cayman Islands
Charleston
Chicago
Dominican Republic

Dublin
Florence
Las Vegas
Las Vegas for Non-Gamblers
London
Maui
Nantucket & Martha's Vineyard
New Orleans
New York City
Paris
Portland
Puerto Rico
Puerto Vallarta, Manzanillo &
  Guadalajara

Rio de Janeiro
San Diego
San Francisco
Savannah
St. Martin, Sint Maarten, Anguila &
  St. Bart's
Turks & Caicos
Vancouver
Venice
Virgin Islands
Washington, D.C.
Whistler

FROMMER'S® CRUISE GUIDES

Alaska Cruises & Ports of Call | Cruises & Ports of Call | European Cruises & Ports of Call

FROMMER'S® NATIONAL PARK GUIDES

Algonquin Provincial Park
Banff & Jasper
Grand Canyon

National Parks of the American West
Rocky Mountain
Yellowstone & Grand Teton

Yosemite and Sequoia & Kings
  Canyon
Zion & Bryce Canyon

FROMMER'S® MEMORABLE WALKS

London
New York

Paris
Rome

San Francisco

FROMMER'S® WITH KIDS GUIDES

Chicago
Hawaii
Las Vegas
London

National Parks
New York City
San Francisco

Toronto
Walt Disney World® & Orlando
Washington, D.C.

SUZY GERSHMAN'S BORN TO SHOP GUIDES

France
Hong Kong, Shanghai & Beijing
Italy

London
New York

Paris
San Francisco

FROMMER'S® IRREVERENT GUIDES

Amsterdam
Boston
Chicago
Las Vegas

London
Los Angeles
Manhattan
Paris

Rome
San Francisco
Walt Disney World®
Washington, D.C.

FROMMER'S® BEST-LOVED DRIVING TOURS

Austria
Britain
California
France

Germany
Ireland
Italy
New England

Northern Italy
Scotland
Spain
Tuscany & Umbria

THE UNOFFICIAL GUIDES®

Adventure Travel in Alaska
Beyond Disney
California with Kids
Central Italy
Chicago
Cruises
Disneyland®
England
Florida
Florida with Kids

Hawaii
Ireland
Las Vegas
London
Maui
Mexico's Best Beach Resorts
Mini Mickey
New Orleans
New York City

Paris
San Francisco
South Florida including Miami &
  the Keys
Walt Disney World®
Walt Disney World® for
  Grown-ups
Walt Disney World® with Kids
Washington, D.C.

SPECIAL-INTEREST TITLES

Athens Past & Present
Best Places to Raise Your Family
Cities Ranked & Rated
500 Places to Take Your Kids Before They Grow Up
Frommer's Best Day Trips from London
Frommer's Best RV & Tent Campgrounds
  in the U.S.A.

Frommer's Exploring America by RV
Frommer's NYC Free & Dirt Cheap
Frommer's Road Atlas Europe
Frommer's Road Atlas Ireland
Great Escapes From NYC Without Wheels
Retirement Places Rated

FROMMER'S® PHRASEFINDER DICTIONARY GUIDES

French | Italian | Spanish

THE NEW TRAVELOCITY GUARANTEE

EVERYTHING YOU BOOK WILL BE RIGHT, OR WE'LL WORK WITH OUR TRAVEL PARTNERS TO MAKE IT RIGHT, RIGHT AWAY.

To drive home the point,
we're going to use the word "right" in every single sentence.

Let's get right to it. Right to the meat! Only Travelocity guarantees everything about your booking will be right, or we'll work with our travel partners to make it right, right away. Right on!

Here's a picture taken smack dab right in the middle of Antigua, where the guarantee also covers you.

The guarantee covers all but one of the items pictured to the right.

Now, you may be thinking, "Yeah, right, I'm so sure." That's OK; you have the right to remain skeptical. That is until we mention help is always right around the corner. Call us right off the bat, knowing that our customer service reps are there for you 24/7. Righting wrongs. Left and right.

For example, what if the ocean view you booked actually looks out at a downright ugly parking lot? You'd be right to call – we're there for you. And no one in their right mind would be pleased to learn the rental car place has closed and left them stranded. Call Travelocity and we'll help get you back on the right track.

Now if you're guessing there are some things we can't control, like the weather, well you're right. But we can help you with most things – to get all the details in righting,* visit **travelocity.com/guarantee**.

*Sorry, spelling things right is one of the few things not covered under the guarantee.

I'd give my right arm for a guarantee like this, although I'm glad I don't have to.

travelocity
You'll never roam alone.

IF YOU BOOK IT, IT SHOULD BE THERE.

Only Travelocity guarantees it will be, or we'll work with our travel partners to make it right, right away. So if you're missing a balcony or anything else you booked, just call us 24/7. **1-888-TRAVELOCITY.**

travelocity

You'll never roam alone.